CHILTON BOOK COMPANY

REPAIR MANUAL

VOLVO 1970-89

S0-ARG-701

All U.S. and Canadian models of 1800E, 1800ES • 142S, 142E • 144S, 144E • 145S, 145E • 164, 164E • 242DL, 242GL, 242GT • 244DL, 244GL • 245DL • 262C, 262GL • 264DL, 264GL • 265DL, 265GL • 740GL, 740GLE, 740 Turbo • 760GLE • 780 • DL, GL, GT, GLE, GLT • Coupe, Diesel, Turbo

Sr. Vice President	Ronald A. Hoxter
Publisher and Editor-In-Chief	Kerry A. Freeman, S.A.E.
Managing Editors	Peter M. Conti, Jr. □ W. Calvin Settle, Jr., S.A.E.
Assistant Managing Editor	Nick D'Andrea
Senior Editors	Richard J. Rivele, S.A.E. □ Ron Webb
Director of Manufacturing	Mike D'Imperio
Manager of Manufacturing	John F. Butler
Editor	Jim Taylor

CHILTON BOOK COMPANY

ONE OF THE DIVERSIFIED PUBLISHING COMPANIES,
A PART OF CAPITAL CITIES/ABC, INC.

CONTENTS

SAFETY NOTICE

Proper service and repair procedures are vital to the safe, reliable operation of all motor vehicles, as well as the personal safety of those performing repairs. This book outlines procedures for servicing and repairing vehicles using safe, effective methods. The procedures contain many NOTES, CAUTIONS and WARNINGS which should be followed along with standard safety procedures to eliminate the possibility of personal injury or improper service which could damage the vehicle or compromise its safety.

It is important to note that repair procedures and techniques, tools and parts for servicing motor vehicles, as well as the skill and experience of the individual performing the work vary widely. It is not possible to anticipate all of the conceivable ways or conditions under which vehicles may be serviced, or to provide cautions as to all of the possible hazards that may result. Standard and accepted safety precautions and equipment should be used during cutting, grinding, chiseling, prying, or any other process that can cause material removal or projectiles.

Some procedures require the use of tools specially designed for a specific purpose. Before substituting another tool or procedure, you must be completely satisfied that neither your personal safety, nor the performance of the vehicle will be endangered.

Although the information in this guide is based on industry sources and is as complete as possible at the time of publication, the possibility exists that the manufacturer made later changes which could not be included here. While striving for total accuracy, Chilton Book Company cannot assume responsibility for any errors, changes, or omissions that may occur in the compilation of this data.

PART NUMBERS

Part numbers listed in this reference are not recommendations by Chilton for any product by brand name. They are references that can be used with interchange manuals and aftermarket supplier catalogs to locate each brand supplier's discrete part number.

SPECIAL TOOLS

Special tools are recommended by the vehicle manufacturer to perform their specific job. Use has been kept to a minimum, but where absolutely necessary, they are referred to in the text by the part number of the tool manufacturer. These tools can be purchased, under the appropriate part number, from your Volvo dealer or an equivalent tool can be purchased locally from a tool supplier or parts outlet. Before substituting any tool for the one recommended, read the SAFETY NOTICE at the top of this page.

ACKNOWLEDGMENTS

Chilton Book Company expresses its appreciation to AB Volvo for the technical information and illustrations contained within this manual and to Fred Loney, Clarks Summit Volvo, Clarks Summit, Pa.; Roy Tiger, Costas Auto Repair, Narberth, Pa. for their generous assistance.

Chilton's Repair Manual: Volvo 1970–89
ISBN 0-8019-7944-7 pbk.
Library of Congress Catalog Card No. 88-43188

General Information and Maintenance

HOW TO USE THIS BOOK

Chilton's Repair and Tune-Up and Tune-Up Guide for the Volvo is intended to teach you more about the inner workings of your automobile and save you money in its upkeep. The first two chapters will be the most used, since they contain maintenance and tune-up information and procedures. The following seven chapters concern themselves with the systems of the car. Operating systems from engine through brakes are covered to the extent that we feel the average do-it-yourselfer should get involved. Complicated repair procedures, such as internal transmission repairs, will not be covered. The knowledge, skills, and special tools required for such repairs are not generally available to the average car owner. We will tell you how to change your own brake pads and shoes, replace points, plugs,and filters and perform many more jobs that will save you money, give you personal satisfaction, and help you avoid problems. Chapter 10 is devoted to body and trim items. It will help you with items on doors, latches,windows (manual and power), antennas, locks and seats.

Before loosening any bolts, please read through the entire section and the specific procedure. This will give you the overall view of what will be required as far as tools, supplies, and skill level. There is nothing more frustrating than having to walk to the bus stop on Monday morning because you were short one part during your Sunday afternoon repair. So read ahead and plan ahead.

Most sections begin with a brief discussion of the system and what it involves. Adjustments and/or maintenance are then discussed, followed by removal and installation procedures, and then repair or overhaul procedures where they are feasible. When repair is considered to be out of your league, we tell you how to remove the part and then how to install the new or re-built replacement. In this way you at least save the labor costs. Backyard repair of such components as the alternator is just not practical.

It's necessary to mention the difference between maintenance and repair. Maintenance includes routine inspections, adjustments, and replacement of parts which show signs of wear. Maintenance compensates for wear or deterioration. Repair implies that something has broken or is not working. Need for repair is often caused by lack of maintenance. Example: Draining and refilling the automatic transmission fluid is maintenance recommended by the manufacturer at specific mileage intervals. Failure to do this will ruin the transmission, requiring very expensive repairs. While no maintenance program can prevent items from breaking or wearing out, a general rule can be stated: MAINTENANCE IS CHEAPER THAN REPAIR.

Some basic mechanic's rules should be learned. One, whenever the left side of the car is mentioned, it means the driver's side of the car. Conversely, the right side of the car means the passenger's side of the car. Second, most screws and bolts are removed by turning counterclockwise and tightened by turning clockwise. Safety is the most important rule. Constantly be aware of the dangers involved in working on an automobile and take the proper precautions.Think ahead, work slowly, and anticipate problems before they occur. Use jackstands when working under a raised vehicle. Don't smoke or allow an exposed flame to come near the battery or any parts of the fuel system.If you are using a kerosene heater during the winter, always turn it off or put it well away from the car when charging the battery or performing any item that could release liquid gasoline or gasoline vapors. Use the proper tool and use it correctly. Bruised knuckles and skinned fingers aren't a mechanic's standard equipment. Always take your time and have patience; once you have some experience and gain confidence, working on your car will become an enjoyable hobby.

TOOLS AND EQUIPMENT

Naturally, without the proper tools and equipment it is impossible to properly service your vehicle. It would be impossible to catalog each tool that you would need to perform each or any operation in this book. It would also be unwise for the amateur to rush out and buy an expensive set of tools on the theory that he may need one or more of them at sometime.

NOTE: *Beginning in 1978, most Volvos use metric nuts and bolts. Up to 1978, Volvo used either SAE fasteners only or a mixture of SAE and metric fasteners.*

The best approach is to proceed slowly, gathering together a good quality set of those tools that are used most frequently. Don't be misled by the low cost of bargain tools. It is far better to spend a little more for better quality. Forged wrenches, 6- or 12-point sockets and fine tooth ratchets are by far preferable to their less expensive counterparts. As any good mechanic can tell you, there are few worse experiences than trying to work on a car or truck with bad tools. Your monetary savings will be far outweighed by frustration and mangled knuckles.

Begin accumulating those tools that are used most frequently; those associated with routine maintenance and tune-up.

In addition to the normal assortment of screwdrivers and pliers you should have the following tools for routine maintenance jobs.

1. SAE or metric wrenches, sockets and combination open/box end wrenches in sizes from ⅛ in. (3mm) to ¾ in. (19mm). See the "NOTE" at the beginning of this section to find out if your car uses SAE or metric wrenches. Although your Volvo may only need one style of wrenches, you'll find that having a set of each (metric and SAE) can be very helpful in other situations.

2. Deep-well spark plug socket ($^{13}/_{16}$ in.) is used on both metric and SAE fasteners cars.

3. An assortment of socket drive extensions. You'll probably need at least a 3 in., a 6 in. and a 9 in. extension. One break in this department is that the metric sockets available in the U.S. will all fit the ratchet handles and extension you may already have (¼, ⅜, and ½ in. drives). Another time-saving tool to have is a universal joint for your socket set: this tool can be invaluable when working in cramped spaces, such as around the manifold, etc.

4. Jackstands for supporting the vehicle. You need a minimum of two; four are handy. Never go under a car which is supported only by a jack. Many have been killed or injured by thinking it was safe. If you must elevate both ends of the car, use four jackstands; they are readily available and inexpensive.

5. Oil filter wrench and drain pan.

6. Oil filler spout for pouring oil.

7. Grease gun for chassis lubrication.

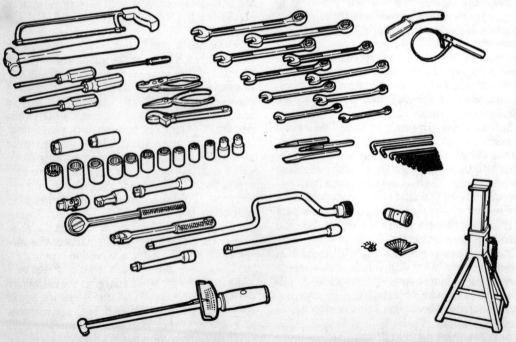

Basic assortment of tools needed to perform maintenance work on your Volvo

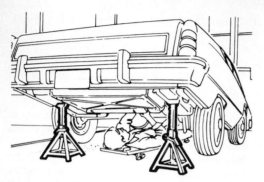

Always use jack stands when working under your car

8. Hydrometer for checking the battery.

9. Coolant tester for checking the freezing and boiling points of the engine coolant.

10. Many rags for wiping up the inevitable mess. A bag of cat litter is useful for absorbing spilled fluids under the car.

In addition to the above items there are several others that are not absolutely necessary, but handy to have around. These include a roll of masking tape and a marker for labeling hoses, ports, and wires, a roll of electrical tape, a transmission funnel and the usual supply of lubricants, antifreeze and fluids, although these can be purchased as needed. This is a basic list for routine maintenance, but only your personal needs and desire can accurately determine your list of tools.

The second list of tools is for tune-ups. While the tools involved here are slightly more sophisticated, they need not be outrageously expensive. There are several inexpensive tach/dwell meters on the market that are every bit as good for the average mechanic as a $100.00 professional model. Just be sure that it goes to at least 1,200-1,500 rpm on the tach scale and that it works on 4, 6 and 8 cylinder engines. A basic list of tune-up equipment could include the following.

1. Tach-dwell meter.

2. Spark plug wrench.

3. Timing light (Most are easy to use, connecting to the battery and one spark plug wire.)

4. Wire spark plug gauge and adjusting tools.

5. Set of blade type feeler guages.

In addition to these basic tools, there are several other tools and gauges you may find useful. These include:

1. A compression gauge. The screw-in type is slower to use, but eliminates the possibility of a faulty reading due to escaping pressure. For ease of reading the guage, get one with a long flexible hose.

2. A manifold vacuum gauge.

3. A test light; very helpful in answering the question "Is there electricity at this point?" To find out how much electricity is there (voltage), you'll need a volt-meter.

4. An induction meter. This is used for determining whether or not there is current in a wire. These are handy for use if a wire is broken somewhere in a wiring harness.

As a final note, you will probably find a torque wrench necessary for all but the most basic work. The beam type models are perfectly adequate, although the newer click type are more precise. Make sure you get one that matches your socket set: ½ in. or ⅜ in. drive.

Special Tools

NOTE: *Special tools are occasionally necessary to perform a specific job or are recommended to make a job easier. Their use has been kept to a minimum. When a special tool is indicated, it will be referred to by manufacturer's part number, and, where possible, an illustration of the tool will be provided so that an equivalent tool may be used.*

A list of tool suppliers and their addresss follows:

Your local Volvo dealer. Most Volvo special tools are available through normal ordering channels.

Volvo Cars of North America
Rockleigh Industrial Park
Rockleigh, New Jersey
07647

Robert Bosch Corp.
2800 S. 25th St.
Broadview, Illinois
60153

Snap-on Tools Corp.
Kenosha, Wisconsin
53141

CP/Matco Tools
4403 Allen Rd.
Stow, Ohio
44224

SERVICING YOUR CAR SAFELY

It is virtually impossible to anticipate all of the hazards involved with automotive maintenance and service, but care and common sense will prevent most accidents.

The rules of safety for mechanics range from "don't smoke around gasoline" to "use the proper tool for the job." The trick to avoiding injuries is to develop safe work habits and take every possible precaution.

Dos

• •Do keep a fire extinguisher and first aid kit within easy reach. Know how to use them before you need them.

• Do wear safety glasses or goggles when cutting, drilling, grinding or prying, even if you have 20-20 vision. If you wear glasses for the sake of vision, they should be made of hardened glass that can serve also as safety glasses, or wear safety goggles over your regular glasses.

• Do shield your eyes whenever you work around the battery. Batteries contain sulphuric acid. In case of contact with the eyes or skin, flush the area with water or a mixture of water and baking soda and get medical attention immediately.

• Do work neatly. A few minutes spent clearing a workbench or setting up a small table for tools is well worth the effort. Make yourself put tools back on the table when not in use; doing so means you won't have to grope around on the floor for that wrench you need right now. Protect your car while working on it with fender covers. If you don't wish to buy a fender cover, an old blanket makes a usable substitute.

• Do use safety stands for any undercar service. Jacks are for raising vehicles; safety stands are for making sure the vehicle stays raised until you want it to come down. Whenever the car is raised, block the wheels remaining on the ground and set the parking brake.

• Do use adequate ventilation when working with any chemicals or hazardous materials. Like carbon monoxide, the absestos dust resulting from brake lining wear can be poisonous in sufficient quantities.

• Do disconnect the negative battery cable when working on the electrical system. The secondary ignition system can contain up to 40,000 volts.

• Do follow manufacturer's directions whenever working with potentially hazardous materials. Both brake fluid and antifreeze are poisonous if taken internally. Housepets and small animals are attracted to the odor and taste of engine coolant (antifreeze). It is a highly poisonous mixture of chemicals; special care must be taken to protect open containers and spillage. If a housepet drinks any amount of coolant, it is a "drop everything" emergency--seek immediate veterinary care.

• Do properly maintain your tools. Loose hammerheads, mushroomed punches and chisels, frayed or poorly grounded electrical cords, excessively worn screwdrivers, spread wrenches (open end), cracked sockets, slipping ratchets, or faulty droplight sockets can cause

accidents. Working on your own car is not supposed to be a painful experience.

• Do use the proper size and type of tool for the job being done.

• Do, when possible, pull on a wrench handle rather than push on it, and adjust your stance to prevent a fall.

•Do use socket, open-end or box-end wrenches where possible. They are made to a precise measurement and will fit the hardware exactly. If you must use an adjustable wrench, be sure that the jaws are tightly closed on the nut or bolt and pulled so that the face is on the side of the fixed jaw.

• Do select a wrench or socket that fits the nut or bolt. The wrench or socket should sit straight, not cocked.

• Do strike squarely with a hammer; avoid glancing blows.

• Do set the parking brake and block the drive wheels if the work requires the engine running.

Don'ts

• Don't run an engine in a garage or anywhere else without proper ventilation--EVER! Carbon monoxide is poisonous; it takes a long time to leave the human body and you can build up a deadly supply of it in your system by simply breathing in a little every day. You may not realize you are slowly poisoning yourself. Always use power vents, windows, fans or open the garage doors.

Carbon monoxide is odorless and colorless. Your senses cannot detect its presence. Early symptoms of monoxide poisoning include headache, irritability, improper vision (blurred or hard to focus) and/or drowsiness. When you notice any of these symptoms in yourself or your helpers, stop working immediately and get to fresh, outside air. Ventilate the work area thoroughly before returning to the car.

• Don't work around moving parts while wearing a necktie or other loose clothing. Short sleeves are much safer than long, loose sleeves; hard-toed shoes with neoprene soles protect your feet and give a better grip on slippery surface. Jewelry (watches, fancy belt buckles, beads or body adornment of any kind) is not safe working around a car. Long hair should be hidden under a hat or cap.

• Don't use pockets for toolboxes. A fall or bump can drive a screwdriver deep into your body. Even a wiping cloth hanging from the back pocket can wrap around a spinning shaft or fan.

• Don't smoke when working around gasoline, cleaning solvent or other flammable material.Assume that all liquids and sprays are flammable unless specifically labled otherwise.

• Don't disconnect either terminal from the battery while the engine is running. Modern cars contain many solid-state components and "black-box" computers. You will not get a second chance with solid-state failures; you will get to buy some very expensive replacement parts.

• Don't smoke when working around the battery. When the battery is being charged, it gives off explosive hydrogen gas.

• Don't use gasoline, kerosene or solvents to wash your hands; there are excellent soaps available. Gasoline contains lead, and lead can enter the body through a cut, accumulating in the body until you are very ill. Gasoline also removes all the natural oils from the skin so that bone-dry hands will suck up oil and grease.

• Don't service the air conditioning system unless you are equipped with the necessary tools and training. The refrigerant, R-12, is extremely cold when compressed, and when released into the air will instantly freeze any surface it contacts, including your eyes. Although the refrigerant is normally non-toxic, R-12 becomes a deadly poisonous gas in the presence of an open flame. One good whiff of the vapors from burning refrigerant can be fatal.

SERIAL NUMBER IDENTIFICATION

In all correspondence with your Volvo dealer or when ordering spare parts, the vehicle type designation, chassis number, and, if applicable, the engine, transmission, and rear axle (final drive) numbers should be quoted for proper identification.

Vehicle Type Designation and Chassis Number

The vehicle model type (1800, 140, 240, 260, 740, 760 & 780) and chassis number appear at several locations on every Volvo. For the purpose of this book, the models sold in the early 1980s without number designation (ex: DL, GLT, Coupe) are considered members of the

200 Series of vehicles. The type designation and chassis number is stamped on the front door pillar on the right side of the car. Additionally, the numbers are stamped on a plate which is mounted under the hood on the right shock tower.

For example, the vehicle type designation and chassis number may appear: VC 24445 L 1275965. The VC is the manufacturer's code. Of the 24445, the first three digits, 244, indicate the model type (family is 240, model has 4 doors), while the last two digits indicate engine type and if the engine is fuel injected or uses a carburetor. The letter code indicates model year (in this case, "L" equals 1978), and the number following the letter code indicates location of the manufacturing plant that made this particular car. The final one to six digits compose the vehicle's chassis number.

On models 1981 and newer, the U.S. standard 17 digit Vehicle Identification Number (VIN) is used. This number is most easily found on a plate mounted on the left side of the dashboard and visible through the windshield from the outside of the car. Again, it may also be found on the plate mounted on the right shock tower.

It should be noted that although both styles of vehicle number (through 1980 and 1981 on) contain a letter code for model year, the codes are different before and after the the 80-81 change. For example, prior to 1981, the letter H denoted a 1977 model. In the longer, 17 digit VIN, H denotes a 1987 model. 1989 models are denoted by K; the letter I is not used.

Engine Identification

Volvo identifies its engines by a type or family, using a combination of letters and numbers. Examples of a type number are B20B, B21F, or D24T. These family designations will be used throughout this book. Each engine within a particular family is further identified by its engine number. These engine numbers are coded to show emission type, transmission

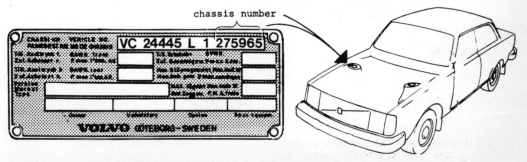

Sample Vehicle Identification Number for cars built before 1981

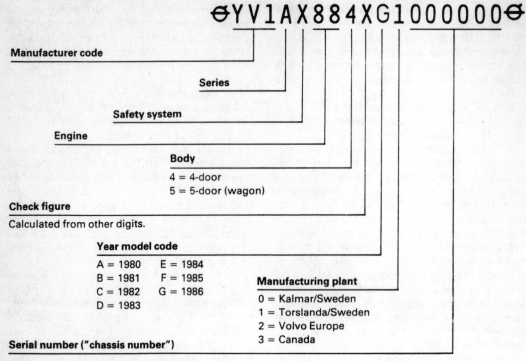

⊖YV1AX884XG1000000⊖

Manufacturer code

Series

Safety system

Engine

Body
4 = 4-door
5 = 5-door (wagon)

Check figure
Calculated from other digits.

Year model code

A = 1980	E = 1984
B = 1981	F = 1985
C = 1982	G = 1986
D = 1983	

Manufacturing plant
0 = Kalmar/Sweden
1 = Torslanda/Sweden
2 = Volvo Europe
3 = Canada

Serial number ("chassis number")

Sample Vehicle Identification Number for cars built 1981 and later years

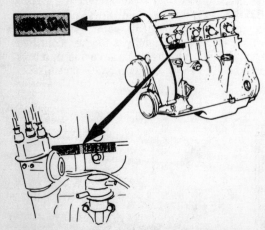

B20, B30 overhead valve engine serial number location

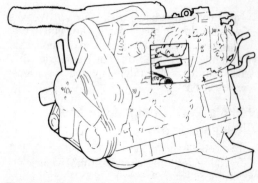

Diesel engine serial number location

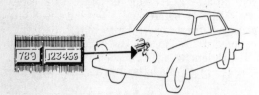

B21 and B23 series engine serial number location. The last three digits of the serial number are printed on a label on the timing belt cover

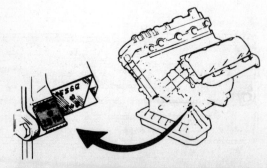

B28F V-6 engine serial number location. B27F similar

Engine Identification Chart

Year	Model	Engine Code Within Vehicle Number	Engine Series Identification	No. of Cylinders	Engine Displacement cu. in. (cc/liter)
1970	142		B20B	4	122 (1990/2.0)
	144		B20B	4	122 (1990/2.0)
	145		B20B	4	122 (1990/2.0)
	164		B30A	6	183 (2978/3.0)
	1800E		B20E	4	122 (1990/2.0)
1971	142		B20B/B20F*	4	122 (1990/2.0)
	144		B20B	4	122 (1990/2.0)
	145		B20B	4	127 (1990/2.0)
	164		B30A	6	183 (2978/3.0)
	1800E		B20E	4	122 (1990/2.0)
1972	142		B20B/B20F*	4	122 (1990/2.0)
	144		B20B/B20F*	4	122 (1990/2.0)
	145		B20B/B20F*	4	122 (1990/2.0)
	164		B30A	6	183 (2978/3.0)
	164 E		B30F	6	183 (2978/3.0)
	1800 E		B20E	4	122 (1990/2.0)
	1800 ES		B20E	4	122 (1990/2.0)
1973	142		B20F	4	122 (1990/2.0)
	144		B20F	4	122 (1990/2.0)
	145		B20F	4	122 (1990/2.0)
	164		B30F	6	183 (2978/3.0)
	1800 ES		B20E	4	122 (1990/2.0)
1974	142		B20F	4	122 (1990/2.0)
	144		B20F	4	122 (1990/2.0)
	145		B20F	4	122 (1990/2.0)
	164		B30F	6	183 (2978/3.0)
1975	164		B30F	6	183 (2978/3.0)
	242		B20F	4	122 (1990/2.0)
	244		B20F	4	122 (1990/2.0)
	245		B20F	4	122 (1990/2.0)
1976	242	45	B21F	4	130 (2127/2.2)
	244	45	B21F	4	130 (2127/2.2)
	245	45	B21F	4	130 (2127/2.2)
	262	65	B27F	6	162 (2660/2.7)
	264	65	B27F	6	162 (2660/2.7)
	265	65	B27F	6	162 (2660/2.7)
1977	240 DL	45	B21F	4	130 (2127/2.2)
	GL	45	B21F	4	130 (2127/2.2)
	GLE	45	B21F	4	130 (2127/2.2)
	260 GL	65	B27F	6	162 (2660/2.7)
	GLE	65	B27F	6	162 (2660/2.7)

ENGINE DESIGNATION STAMPED ON SIDE OF BLOCK

Year	Model	Engine Code Within Vehicle Number	Engine Series Identification	No. of Cylinders	Engine Displacement cu. in. (cc/liter)
1978	240 DL	45	B21F	4	130 (2127/2.2)
	GL	45	B21F	4	130 (2127/2.2)
	GLE	45	B21F	4	130 (2127/2.2)
	260 GLE	65	B27F	6	162 (2660/2.7)
	Coupe	65	B27F	6	162 (2660/2.7)
1979	240 DL	45	B21F	4	130 (2127/2.2)
	GL	45	B21F	4	130 (2127/2.2)
	GT	45	B21F	4	130 (2127/2.2)
	260 GLE	65	B27F	6	162 (2660/2.7)
	Coupe	65	B27F	6	162 (2660/2.7)
1980	DL	45	B21F	4	130 (2127/2.2)
	GL	45	B21F	4	130 (2127/2.2)
	GT	45	B21F	4	130 (2127/2.2)
	GLE	69	B28F	6	174 (2849/2.9)
	Coupe	69	B28F	6	174 (2849/2.9)
	Diesel	77	D24	6	145 (2383/2.4)
1981	DL	45	B21F	4	130 (2127/2.2)
	DL	41 (optional)	B21F-mpg	6	130 (2127/2.2)
	GL	45	B21F	4	130 (2127/2.2)
	Diesel	77	D24	6	145 (2383/2.4)
	GLT	47	B21F-Turbo	4	130 (2127/2.2)
	GLE	69	B28F	6	174 (2849/2.9)
	Coupe	69	B28F	6	174 (2849/2.9)
1982	240 DL	45	B21F	4	130 (2127/2.2)
	DL ①	41	B21A	4	130 (2127/2.2)
	GL	45	B21F	4	130 (2127/2.2)
	GL	77	D24	6	145 (2383/2.4)
	GL ①	84	B23E	4	140 (2320/2.3)
	GLT	47	B21F-Turbo	4	130 (2127/2.2)
	GLT	45	B21F	4	130 (2127/2.2)
	GLT ①	84	B23E	4	140 (2320/2.3)
	260 GLE	69	B28F	6	174 (2849/2.9)
1983	240 DL	88	B23F	4	140 (2320/2.3)
	DL	47	B21F-Turbo	4	130 (2127/2.2)
	DL	77	D24	6	145 (2383/2.4)
	DL ①	41	B21A	4	130 (2127/2.2)
	GL	88	B23F	4	140 (2320/2.3)
	GL	77	D24	6	145 (2383/2.4)
	GL ①	84	B23E	4	140 (2320/2.3)
	GLT ①	84	B23E	4	140 (2320/2.3)
	Turbo	47	B21F-Turbo	4	130 (2127/2.2)

Year	Model	Engine Code Within Vehicle Number	Engine Series Identification	No. of Cylinders	Engine Displacement cu. in. (cc/liter)
1983	760 GLE	69	B28F	6	174 (2849/2.9)
	GLE	76	D24-Turbo	6	145 (2383/2.4)
	Turbo	87	B23F-Turbo	4	140 (2320/2.3)
1984	240 Diesel	77	D24	6	145 (2383/2.4)
	DL	88	B23F	4	140 (2320/2.3)
	DL ①	44	B21A	4	130 (2127/2.2)
	GL	88	B23F	4	140 (2320/2.3)
	GLE ①	88	B23F	4	140 (2320/2.3)
	Turbo	47	B21F-Turbo	4	130 (2127/2.2)
	760 GLE	69	B28F	6	174 (2849/2.9)
	GLE	76	D24-Turbo	6	145 (2383/2.4)
	Turbo	87	B23F-Turbo	4	140 (2320/2.3)
1985	240 Diesel	77	D24	6	145 (2383/2.4)
	DL	88	B230F	4	140 (2320/2.3)
	GL	88	B230F	4	140 (2320/2.3)
	Turbo	47	B21F-Turbo	4	130 (2127/2.2)
	740 GLE	88	B230F	4	140 (2320/2.3)
	TD ②	76	D24-Turbo	6	145 (2383/2.4)
	Turbo	87	B230F-Turbo	4	140 (2320/2.3)
	760 GLE	69	B28F	6	174 (2849/2.9)
	GLE TD	76	D24-Turbo	6	145 (2383/2.4)
	Turbo	87	B230F-Turbo	4	140 (2320/2.3)
1986	240 DL	88	B230F	4	140 (2320/2.3)
	GL	88	B230F	4	140 (2320/2.3)
	740 GL	88	B230F	4	140 (2320/2.3)
	GLE	88	B230F	4	140 (2320/2.3)
	GLE TD	76	D24-Turbo	6	145 (2383/2.4)
	Turbo	87	B230F-Turbo	4	140 (2320/2.3)
	760 GLE	69	B28F	6	174 (2849/2.9)
	Turbo	87	B230F-Turbo	4	140 (2320/2.3)
1987	240 DL	88	B230F	4	140 (2320/2.3)
	GL	88	B230F	4	140 (2320/2.3)
	740 GL	88	B230F	4	140 (2320/2.3)
	GLE	88	B230F	4	140 (2320/2.3)
	Turbo	87	B230F-Turbo	4	140 (2320/2.3)
	760 GLE	69	B280F	6	174 (2849/2.9)
	Turbo	87	B230F-Turbo	4	140 (2320/2.3)
	780	69	B280F	6	174 (2849/2.9)
1988–89	240 DL	88	B230F	4	140 (2320/2.3)
	GL	88	B230F	4	140 (2320/2.3)
	740 GL	88	B230F	4	140 (2320/2.3)

Year	Model	Engine Code Within Vehicle Number	Engine Series Identification	No. of Cylinders	Engine Displacement cu. in. (cc/liter)
1988–89	GLE	88	B230F	4	140 (2320/2.3)
	740 GLE 16-valve	89	B234F	5	140 (2320/2.3)
	Turbo	87	B230F-Turbo	4	140 (2320/2.3)
	760 GLE	69	B280F	6	174 (2849/2.9)
	Turbo	87	B230F-Turbo	4	140 (2320/2.3)
	780	69	B280F	6	174 (2849/2.9)

* optional motor
① Canada only
② Station Wagon

match (manual or automatic), and other detailed information. While you can work from this manual knowing only the engine type, replacement parts must be ordered using the exact engine number.

Start by looking at the vehicle number and selecting the engine type codes from the proper positions. Refer to the chart below to identify the engine family. Write the family designation down so that it's available any time you need it.

The engine number, part number and serial number are located on the left side of the engine on all models. On the B20, B30 engines, the number is located on the left side front of the engine. On the B21 and B23 series engines, the last three digits of the engine number are printed on a label on the timing belt cover. On the B230 series engines, the serial number is a six-digit number located on the camshaft drive cover and is also stamped on the cylinder block, behind the distributor.

On the B27, B28 engines, the number is located low on the block. The B280 engines have the number stamped on the cylinder block. The early type is located between the cylinder banks toward the rear, and the later type is located on the front right side, between the intake manifold and the water pump.

On the D24 series diesel engines, the engine number is stamped on the block underneath the vacuum pump.

Transmission and Rear Axle Identification

The transmission type designation, serial number and part number are stamped on a metal plate which is riveted to the underside of the case on manual transmissions or the left side on automatic transmissions.

The final drive ratio, part number, and serial number for the rear axle are stamped on a met-

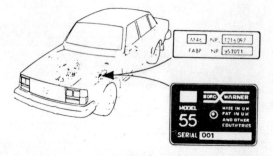

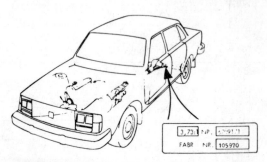

Location of transmission and rear axle identification plates

al plate which is riveted to the left-hand side of the differential case. Again, when these numbers are located, they should be written down for future reference.

ROUTINE MAINTENANCE

Volvo was one of the first car manufacturers with enough confidence in their product to install an odometer which can register 999,999.9 miles. While not every Volvo is destined to join the million mile club, the average car's life will be greatly increased if the owner is vigilant in performing regularly scheduled maintenance procedures.

Obviously, if the only time you peek under the hood is when something doesn't seem to be working right, you are flirting with disaster. Sooner or later something is bound to go thump on a rain-swept night, leaving you stranded along a road so remote that even the goblins are bussed in.

Consult the maintenance interval chart at the end of this section or use the one in your owner's manual and perform the following procedures in conjunction with the time or mileage intervals given. Remember that the intervals shown are maximums and should not be exceeded. Various items may need more frequent service or maintenance depending on where and how your Volvo is driven.

Air cleaner—142, 144, 145, 164 carbureted engines

Air Cleaner

Service the air cleaner according to the maintenance interval chart in this section. When operating the vehicle in extremely dusty areas, in areas of high industrial pollution, or in mostly low-speed city driving, the element should be changed more frequently than the given interval. Inspect the air filter at every tune-up. A clogged air cleaner will restrict air passage into the combustion chambers of the engine. This means that a less than normal amount of air will be mixed with the fuel, which will richen the air/fuel mixture and cause poor engine performance and excessive fuel comsumption.

Air cleaner—142, 144, 145 fuel injected engines through 1973

REMOVAL AND INSTALLATION

142, 144, 145, and 164 Carbureted Models

The element is removed from the air cleaner by disconnecting the hose clamp from the air preheating unit and unsnapping the clips holding the air cleaner housing halves together. The old element is then lifted out and new one is lowered in with the word **UP** on the element facing up. When securing the air cleaner housing halves together, take care not to damage the thermostat body for the intake air.

164 Fuel Injected Models

On fuel-injected 164 series Volvos, the clips securing the cover to the air cleaner must be undone and the old element removed. When refitting the cover to the air cleaner, make sure that the arrow points coincide.

142, 144, and 145 Fuel Injected Models (Through 1973)

On these models, the air cleaner is a one piece disposable unit. Since the elements cannot be removed from the air cleaner, the entire unit must be replaced.

Air cleaner—164 fuel injected models

To remove the air cleaner, turn the front wheels fully to the right, loosen and move the expansion tank for the cooling system to one side, disconnect the inlet duct hose and unfasten the attaching bolts which hold the air cleaner. Install the new air cleaner, reinstall and tighten the bolts, and reinstall the air inlet hose. Reposition and secure the coolant expansion tank.

142, 144, and 145 Fuel Injected Models (1974)

On these models the air cleaner is located beneath the air-fuel control unit for the fuel injection system. To remove the air cleaner element you must remove the air-fuel control unit: this is not a job for an inexperienced or fledgling mechanic.

To remove the air cleaner element, loosen the clamp and remove the rubber bellows from the top of the air-fuel control unit. Then disconnect the electrical connection at the air-fuel control unit and unlatch the retainers. Lift out the upper part of the air cleaner with the air-fuel control unit and replace the air cleaner element. Carefully re-assemble the air cleaner/air-fuel control unit, remembering to secure the clips, reattach the electrical connector and re-install the rubber bellows.

1800E and 1800ES

On all 1800E and 1800ES models, the radiator grille must first be removed to gain access to the air cleaner. Remove the grille clips by inserting pliers between the ribs of the grille and lifting up on the front end of the clips. Push each clip into its hole and remove the grille. Unscrew the wing nut on the air cleaner cover and remove the element.

242, 244, and 245 Models (1975 only)

The air filter is replaced in the same manner as on the 1974 fuel injected 142, 144 and 145 models. See above for procedures.

242, 244, and 245 Models (1976 and later)

The air cleaner is located to the left of the radiator. The element can be removed by unsnapping the clips retaining the air cleaner cover and separating the cover halves. Make sure the cover is properly seated and sealed when re-assembling.

262, 264 and 265 Models

The air filter is housed in the large, flat canister on top of the engine. To remove the filter elements, disconnect the air hose from the top of the air cleaner, disconnect the rubber bellows between the air cleaner and the air-fuel control unit, remove the three attaching bolts and remove the air cleaner. Remove the filter element by unsnapping the clips and separating the air cleaner halves. Install a new element and reassemble, making sure that all the pieces fit properly and all hardware is re-installed.

GL, GT, and DL (1980 and Later Models)

The air cleaner element on these models is located to the left of the radiator. Unsnap the clips and separate the air cleaner housing halves to replace the element.

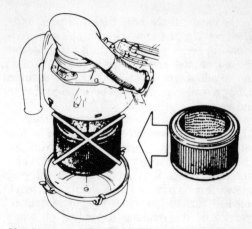

Air cleaner—142, 144, 145 fuel injected models 1974

Air cleaner—1800E, 1800ES

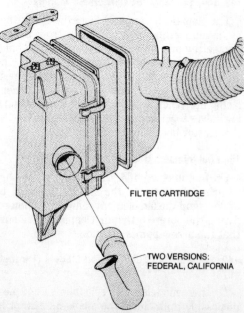

FILTER CARTRIDGE

TWO VERSIONS: FEDERAL, CALIFORNIA

Air cleaner—242, 244, 245 models 1976 and later, 1980 and later GL, GT, DL similar

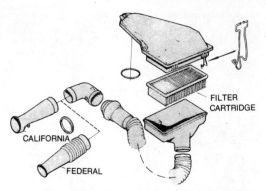

Air cleaner—262, 264, 265 models, 1980 and later GLE, Coupe, 760GLE similar

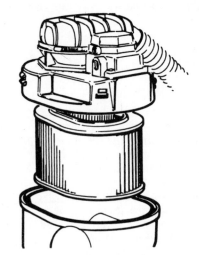

Air cleaner—GLT and Turbo models

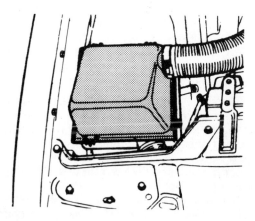

Air cleaner—diesel

GLE, Coupe and 760 GLE (1980 and Later Models)

Air cleaner element removal and installation is the same as on 262, 264, and 265 models. See above for procedures.

GLT and Turbo

The air cleaner is located to the right of the radiator. Unsnap the clips and separate the air cleaner housing halves to service the element.

Diesel

The air cleaner is located on the right fender well. Remove the rubber bellows hose from the air cleaner and unsnap the clips holding the air cleaner halves together to remove the element.

It should be noted that diesel and turbocharged engines are very sensitive to proper airflow; you may wish to check or replace the air filter element more frequently than the manufacturer recommends.

Fuel Filter
REPLACEMENT
Carbureted Engines

CAUTION: *Never smoke when working around gasoline! Avoid all sources of sparks or ignition. Gasoline vapors are EXTREMELY volatile!*

On all carbureted Volvos, the fuel filter is removed and cleaned every six months or 6,000 miles. The filter is located integral with the fuel pump in the driver's side of the engine. To remove the filter on B20B engines, loosen the retaining screws and lift off the cover. To remove the filter on B30A engines, unscrew the plug and filter assembly on the side of the fuel pump. The filter can be cleaned in a low-volatility, petroleum-based solvent such as kerosene, but replacement is better. After replacing the clean element, install the cover and retaining screw on B20B engines, and after installing the plug and filter assembly on B30A engines, run the engine at fast idle and check for fuel leaks. Replace the gasket if any fuel seepage is evident.

Mechanical Fuel Injection

CAUTION: *Never smoke when working around gasoline! Avoid all sources of sparks or ignition. Gasoline vapors are EXTREMELY volatile!*

On these models the fuel filter is located under the hood on the left side of the firewall. It is a large cylinder with threaded couplings on both ends.

These models are equipped with an injection system (mechanical) which maintains constant pressure within the lines, even when the engine is not running. When changing the fuel filter, have a container handy to catch the fuel which will squirt out or wrap a rag around the fittigs before loosening them. Do not smoke while changing the filter and do not attempt to

Fuel filter location—B20B engine

Fuel filter—vehicles equipped with electronic fuel injection

Fuel filter plug location— B30A

Fuel Filter—vehicles equipped with mechanical (constant injection system) fuel injection

change the filter when the engine is warm. The filter is removed by carefully unfastening the lines and removing the filter from its attaching bracket. When installing a new filter, make sure that arrow on the filter points in the direction of fuel flow.

Electronic Fuel Injection

CAUTION: *Never smoke when working around gasoline! Avoid all sources of sparks or ignition. Gasoline vapors are EXTREMELY volatile!*

ALL MODELS THROUGH 1981

The filter is located beneath the car, next to the fuel tank. Prior to removal of the filter, clean the fuel lines and the surrounding area to prevent dirt from entering the fuel systems during the change. Remove the fuel lines from the filter one at a time and pinch each shut to prevent fuel from spilling out. Discard the old filter and replace it with a new one. When installing the new filter, make sure that the arrow on the filter points in the direction of flow. After installation, run the engine at fast idle and check for leaks.

NOTE: *On some 6-cylinder models, the fuel filter is located with the fuel pump in a swingdown holder: remove the single attaching screw at the rear of the holder and allow it to hang down before attempting to remove the fuel filter.*

1982-89 MODELS

These fuel filters are found inside a metal bracket under the left rear of the car. Before changing the fuel filter, loosen or remove the gas cap; this will equalize pressure within the system. Remove the bolts holding the bracket to the car and carefully lower the assembly. Disconnect the fuel lines at the filter.

NOTE: *Have a container ready when loosening connections. The fuel in the system (not the tank) will drain out.*

Remove the clamp which holds the filter and transfer the clamp to the new filter, paying attention to the direction of flow as shown by the arrow on the new filter. Fuel flows FROM the tank TO the engine. Install the new filter with its clamp onto the bracket and connect the fuel lines. Make sure the copper seals are correctly

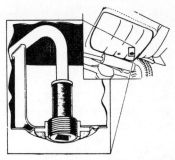

Fuel tank pick-up screen—all models through 1975, some 1976

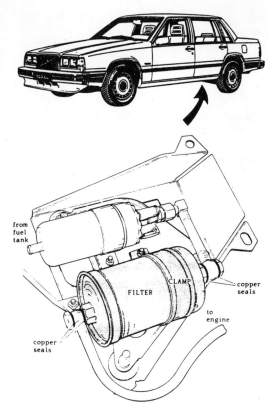

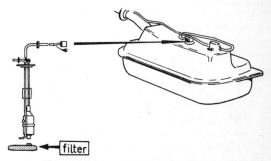

Fuel tank fuel filter—some 1976 models, all 1977 and later models (except diesel)

Location of gasoline fuel filter: 82-89 200 series and 83-89 700 series

installed and that all connections are tight. Re-install or tighten the gas cap.

FUEL TANK PICK-UP SCREEN/FILTER SERVICE

CAUTION: *Never smoke when working around gasoline! Avoid all sources of sparks or ignition. Gasoline vapors are EXTREMELY volatile!*

All models through 1975 are equipped with a fuel pick-up screen which is accessible after removing the countersunk plug in the bottom of the fuel tank with a drain plug wrench. For 1970-72 models, Volvo does not recommend regularly scheduled screen service. On 1973 and later models the screen should be removed and cleaned every 12,000 miles. Even though Volvo does not recommend cleaning the pick-up screen on 1970-72 models, it would be wise to remove and clean the screen periodically to insure sufficient fuel flow.

CAUTION: *It is advisable that the tank be as near to empty as possible, to avoid spillage of highly flammable gasoline. Have a container of sufficient size on hand.*

Pull the filter off the pick-up tube and soak it in solvent. When replacing the filter on the

tube, make sure that it is centered on the tube so as not to restrict the fuel flow.

Beginning in 1976, some models are equipped with an in-tank pump which has a fuel filter attached to its bottom. This filter is accessible by removing the fuel tank pump cap and withdrawing the pump and filter. The filter should be replaced every 60,000 miles. All 1977 and later models except the diesel are equipped with this type of filter.

NOTE:Some 1976 models are equipped with the fuel tank pick-up screen.

Diesel Engine

The diesel engine uses a canister type fuel filter which should be replaced every 15,000 miles under normal driving conditions, and more often under hard driving or severe climate conditions. The filter is located on the left side rear of the engine. For diesel cars built after 1983, Volvo recommends replacing the fuel filter at 30,000 mile intervals.

To replace the fuel filter:

1. Position an oil filter band wrench as high as possible on the fuel filter and loosen the filter.

2. Unscrew and remove the filter, being careful not to allow the fuel in the filter to spill out.

3. Apply diesel oil to the rubber gasket on the new filter and install the filter.

4. Tighten the filter by hand until the rubber gasket makes a tight fit, then tighten the filter ¼ turn more by hand.

NOTE: *Do not use the band wrench or any other tool to tighten the fuel filter.*

5. Start the engine and check for fuel leaks around the filter gasket. If the rubber gasket is not seated properly, air will be sucked into the system and adversely affect engine operation.

BLEEDING THE FUEL SYSTEM

Bleeding the fuel system is not required. After the filter or other fuel system parts have been replaced, simply crank the engine until it starts and accelerate a few times until the engine runs smoothly. This is also true if the car has simply run out of fuel; no bleeding is required.

DRAINING THE DIESEL FILTER

Diesel fuel tends to collect water, especially if the vehicle is routinely driven with a low or nearly empty fuel tank. Since oil − in this case diesel fuel − floats on water, the canister type filter will allow the accumulated water to sink to the bottom of the filter. It is important to drain the canister at regular intervals. Volvo recommends the water be drained every 7,500 miles. It is such a simple procedure that is well worth doing every time you change the engine oil and filter.

1. Position a collection pan under the drain screw (2) at the bottom of the filter.

2. Loosen the bleeder screw (1) several turns.

3. Loosen the drain screw (2) and allow the

Diesel engine fuel filter: "1" is vent screw, "2" is drain plug

filter to drain until only clean fuel flows out, then tighten the drain screw.

4. Tighten the bleeder screw.

Battery

Loose, dirty, or corroded battery terminals are a frequent cause of "no-start"conditions. Every 3 months or so, remove the battery terminals and clean them, giving them a light coating of petroleum jelly when you are finished. This will help to retard corrosion.

Check the battery cables for signs of wear or chafing and replace any cable or terminal that looks marginal. Battery terminals can be easily cleaned; inexpensive cleaning tools are an excellent investment that will pay for themselves many times over. They can usually be purchased from any well-equipped auto store or parts department. The accumulated white powder and corrosion can be cleaned from the top of the battery with an old toothbrush and a solution of baking soda and water.

Unless you have a "maintenance-free" battery, check the electrolyte (fluid) level frequently. Be sure that the vent holes in each cell cap are not blocked by grease or dirt. The vent holes allow hydrogen gas, formed by the chemical reaction in the battery, to escape safely.

Check the battery electrolyte level at least once a month, more often in hot weather or during periods of extended operation. The level should be maintained between the upper and lower levels marked on the battery case, or to the split ring within the well in each cell. If the electrolyte level is low, distilled water should be added until the proper level is reached. Tap water is to be avoided if possible; the minerals it contains can shorten battery life by reacting with the metal plates inside the battery. Each cell is completely separate from the others, so each cell must be filled individually. It's a good idea to add the distilled water with a squeeze bulb to avoid having electrolyte (sulphuric acid) splash out.

NOTE: *Cars that are regularly driven at highway speeds over moderate to long distances may require battery service more frequently. Constant charging of the battery will cause some water to evaporate.*

At least once a year check the specific gravity of the battery electrolyte. It should be between 1.22 and 1.28 at room temperature. A reading of 1.00 or slightly above indicates nothing but water within the battery. The electrical. process has stopped and its time for a new battery. You cannot successfully add acid to a used battery. If water is added in freezing weather, the vehicle should be driven several miles to allow the water to mix with the electrolyte and prevent freezing.

If the battery becomes corroded, or if electrolyte should splash out during additions of water, a mixture of baking soda and water will neutralize the acid. This should be washed off with cold water after making sure that the cell caps are tight. Battery fluid is particularly nasty to painted surfaces; work carefully to avoid spillage on fenders and other painted bodywork.

If a charging is required while the battery is in the car, disconnect the battery cables, negative (ground) cable first. If you have removed the battery from the vehicle for charging, make sure the battery is not sitting on bare earth or concrete while being charged. A block of wood or a small stack of newspapers will prevent the battery from losing internal heat while charging.

When replacing a battery, it is important that the replacement have an output rating equal to or when greater than original equipment. See Chapter 3 for details on battery.

CAUTION: *If you get battery acid in your eyes or on your skin, rinse it off immediately with lots of water. Go to a doctor if it gets in your eyes.*

The gases formed inside the battery cells are highly explosive. Never check the level of the electrolyte in the presence of flame or when smoking.

Never charge a battery in an unventilated area. Never smoke around a battery being charged.

Belts

Accessory drive-belt tension is checked every 6,000 to 7,500 miles. Loose belts can cause poor engine cooling and diminish alternator or power steering pump output. A belt that is too tight places a severe strain on the water pump, alternator, and power steering pump bearings. A belt will loosen with age and wear. A belt loose enough to slip on its pulleys will make a loud, squealing noise. The noise is usually heard under acceleration or during a sharp turn.

To check drive belt tension, push lightly on the belt midway between the pullies. Correct deflection of the belt is 3/16–5/16 in. or about 5-10 mm. Longer or shorter belts may have slightly more or less deflection. Remember that too tight is as damaging as too loose. Any belt that is glazed, frayed, or stretched so that it cannot be tightened sufficiently must be replaced.

Incorrect belt tension is corrected by moving the driven accessory (alternator, power steering pump,etc.) away from or toward the driving pulley. Loosen the mounting and adjusting

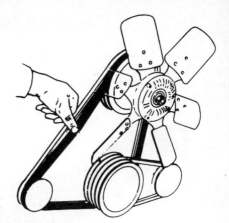

Checking belt tension

bolts on the accessory and move it to loosen or tighten the belt. Once the belt tension is correct, retighten the mounting bolts and recheck the tension. Never position a metal pry bar on the rear end of the alternator housing or against the power steering pump reservoir; they can be deformed easily.

If a belt must be replaced, the driven unit must be loosened and moved to its extreme loosest position, generally by moving it toward the center of the motor. After removing the old belt, check the pulleys for dirt or built-up material which could affect belt contact. Carefully install the new belt, remembering that it is new and unused--it may appear to be just a little too small to fit over the pulley flanges. Fit the belt over the largest pulley (usually the crankshaft pulley at the bottom center of the motor) first, then work on the smaller one(s). Gentle pressure in the direction of rotation is helpful. Some belts run around a third or idler pulley, which acts as an additional pivot in the belt's path. It may be possible to loosen the idler pulley as well as the main component, making your job much easier. Depending on which belt(s) you are changing, it may be necessary to loosen or remove other interfering belts to get at the one(s) you want.

When buying replacement belts, remember that the fit is critical according to the length of the belt ("diameter"), the width of the belt, the depth of the belt and the angle or profile of the V shape. The belt shape should exactly match the shape of the pulley; belts that are not an exact match can cause noise, slippage and premature failure.

After the new belt is installed, draw tension on it by moving the driven unit away from the motor and tighten its mounting bolts. This is sometimes a three or four-handed job; you may find an assistant helpful. Make sure that all the bolts you loosened get retightened and that any other loosened belts also have the correct ten-

HOW TO SPOT WORN V-BELTS

V-Belts are vital to efficient engine operation—they drive the fan, water pump and other accessories. They require little maintenance (occasional tightening) but they will not last forever. Slipping or failure of the V-belt will lead to overheating. If your V-belt looks like any of these, it should be replaced.

Cracking or weathering

This belt has deep cracks, which cause it to flex. Too much flexing leads to heat build-up and premature failure. These cracks can be caused by using the belt on a pulley that is too small. Notched belts are available for small diameter pulleys.

Softening (grease and oil)

Oil and grease on a belt can cause the belt's rubber compounds to soften and separate from the reinforcing cords that hold the belt together. The belt will first slip, then finally fail altogether.

Glazing

Glazing is caused by a belt that is slipping. A slipping belt can cause a run-down battery, erratic power steering, overheating or poor accessory performance. The more the belt slips, the more glazing will be built up on the surface of the belt. The more the belt is glazed, the more it will slip. If the glazing is light, tighten the belt.

Worn cover

The cover of this belt is worn off and is peeling away. The reinforcing cords will begin to wear and the belt will shortly break. When the belt cover wears in spots or has a rough jagged appearance, check the pulley grooves for roughness.

Separation

This belt is on the verge of breaking and leaving you stranded. The layers of the belt are separating and the reinforcing cords are exposed. It's just a matter of time before it breaks completely.

sion. A new belt can be expected to stretch a bit after installation so be prepared to re-adjust your new belt, if needed, within the first hundred miles of use.

Hoses

Hoses should be inspected at least once a month for cracks, swelling and softness. When inspecting hoses, be sure to check the bottom radiator hose, as this one can be easily overlooked. Since the hoses are generally the weakest link in the cooling system, always inspect them before going on a long trip and at the onset of cold or hot weather. The hoses to and from the radiator are the most visible, but there are also other water hoses under the hood, notably the heater hoses running to the firewall. Check these hoses at the same time you check the radiator hoses.

HOSE REPLACEMENT

Replacing hoses requires draining the cooling system. This potentially messy job involves working under the car and handling antifreeze, a slippery, smelly, stain-making chemical. Have a large drain pan or bucket available along with healthy supply of rags. Be prepared to deal with fluid spills immediately. See the previous list of Do's and Don'ts for other hints.

1. Drain the cooling system. This is always done with the motor cold. Attempting to drain hot coolant is very foolish; you can be badly scalded.

a. Remove the radiator cap.

b. Position the drain pan under the point where the lower radiator hose hooks to the radiator. Loosen the clamp on the hose and slide it back so it's out of the way.

c. Gently break the grip of the hose on its fitting by twisting or prying with a suitable tool. Do not exert too much force or you will damage the radiator fitting. As the hose loosens, you can expect a gush of fluid to come out--be ready.

d. Remove the hose end from the radiator and direct the hose into the drain pan. You now have fluid running from both the hose and the radiator. When the system stops draining, proceed with replacement of the damaged hose.

CAUTION: *When draining the coolant, keep in mind that cats and dogs are attracted by the ethylene glycol antifreeze, and are quite likely to drink any that is left in an uncovered container or in puddles on the ground. This will prove fatal in sufficient quantity. Always drain the coolant into a sealable container. Coolant should be reused unless it is contaminated or several years old.*

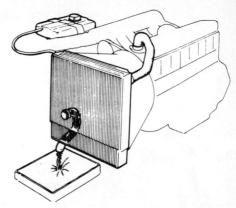

Drain cooling system by removing lower radiator hose

2. Loosen the hose clamps on the damaged hose with a screwdriver and slide the clamps either off the hose altogether or in toward center.

3. Break the grip of the hose at both ends by prying it free with a suitable tool or by twisting it with your hand.

4. Remove the hose.

5. Install a new hose. A small amount of soapy water on the inside of the hose end will ease installation.

NOTE: *Radiator hoses should be routed with no kinks and, when installed, should be in the same position as the original. If other than specified hose is used, make sure it does not rub against either the engine or the frame while the engine is running, as this may wear a hole in the hose. Contact points may be insulated with a piece of sponge or foam; plastic wire ties are particularly handy for this job.*

6. Slide the hose clamps back into position and retighten. When tightening the clamps, tighten them enough to seal in the coolant but not so much that the clamp cuts into the hose or causes it internal damage. If a clamp shows signs of any damage (bent, too loose, hard to tighten, etc.) now is the time to replace it. A good rule of thumb is that a new hose is always worth new clamps.

7. Reinstall the lower radiator hose and secure its clamp.

8. Fill the system with coolant. Volvo strongly recommends the coolant mixture be a 50-50 mix of antifreeze and water. This mixture gives best combination of anti-freeze and anti-boil characteristics for year-round driving.

9. Replace and tighten the radiator cap. Start the engine and check visually for leaks. Allow the engine to warm up fully and continue to check your work for signs of leakage. A very small leak may not be noticed until the system develops internal pressure. Leaks at hose ends are generally clamp related and can be cured by snugging the clamp. Larger leaks may require

HOW TO SPOT BAD HOSES

Both the upper and lower radiator hoses are called upon to perform difficult jobs in an inhospitable environment. They are subject to nearly 18 psi at under hood temperatures often over 280°F., and must circulate nearly 7500 gallons of coolant an hour—3 good reasons to have good hoses.

Swollen hose

A good test for any hose is to feel it for soft or spongy spots. Frequently these will appear as swollen areas of the hose. The most likely cause is oil soaking. This hose could burst at any time, when hot or under pressure.

Cracked hose

Cracked hoses can usually be seen but feel the hoses to be sure they have not hardened; a prime cause of cracking. This hose has cracked down to the reinforcing cords and could split at any of the cracks.

Frayed hose end (due to weak clamp)

Weakened clamps frequently are the cause of hose and cooling system failure. The connection between the pipe and hose has deteriorated enough to allow coolant to escape when the engine is hot.

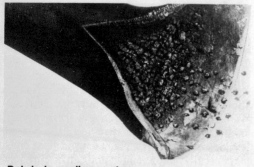

Debris in cooling system

Debris, rust and scale in the cooling system can cause the inside of a hose to weaken. This can usually be felt on the outside of the hose as soft or thinner areas.

removing the hose again--to do this you MUST WAIT UNTIL THE ENGINE HAS COOLED DOWN, GENERALLY A PERIOD OF HOURS. NEVER UNCAP A HOT RADIATOR. After all leaks are cured, check the coolant level in the radiator (with the engine cold) and top up as necessary.

Air Conditioning

SAFETY PRECAUTIONS

There are two particular hazards associated with air conditioning systems and they both relate to the refrigerant gas.The refrigerant (generic designation: R-12, trade name: Freon®, a registered trademark of the DuPont Co.) is an extremely cold substance. When exposed to air, it will instantly freeze any surface it comes in contact with, including your eyes. The other hazard invloves fire. Although normally non-toxic, refrigerant gas becomes highly poisonous in the presence of an open flame. One good whiff of the vapor formed by burning refrigerant can be fatal. Keep all forms of fire (including cigarettes) well clear of the air-conditioning system.

Further, it is being established that the chemicals in R-12 (dichlorodifluoromethane) contribute to the damage occuring in the upper atmosphere. The time may soon come when sophisticated recovery equipment will be necessary to prevent the release of this gas when working on an air condiditoning system. Any repair work should be left to a professional. Do not, under any circumstances, attempt to loosen or tighten any fittings or perform any work other than that outlined here.

SYSTEM INSPECTION

A lot of A/C problems can be avoided by simply running the air conditioner at least once a week, regardless of the season. Let the system run for at least 5 minutes a week (even in the winter), and you'll keep the internal parts lubricated as well as preventing the hoses from hardening.

Refrigerant leaks show up as oily areas on the components because the compressor oil is transported around the entire system with the refrigerant. Look for oily spots on all the hoses and lines, and especially on the hose and tubing connections. If there are oily deposits, the system may have a leak. A small area of oil on the front of the compressor is normal and no cause for alarm.

The compressor drive belt should be checked frequently for tension and condition. Refer to the section in this chapter on "Belts".

Periodically inspect the front of the condenser for bent fins or foreign material (dirt, bugs, leaves, etc.). If any cooling fins are bent, straighten them carefully with needle nosed pliers. You can remove any debris with a stiff bristle brush or hose.

REFRIGERANT LEVEL CHECK

The first order of business when checking the refrigerant level is to find the sight glass. It is located in the head of the receiver/drier. Once

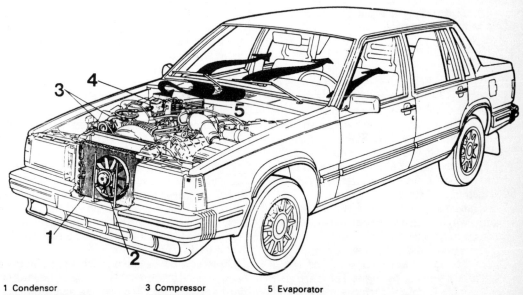

1 Condensor
2 Electric cooling fan
3 Compressor
4 Receiver/drier
5 Evaporator

Air conditioning components

you've found it, wipe it clean and proceed as follows:

1. With the engine and the air conditioning system running, look for the flow of refrigerant in the sight glass. If the air conditioner is working properly, you'll be able to see a continuous flow of clear refrigerant through the sight glass, with perhaps an occasional bubble at very high temperatures.

2. Cycle the air conditioner on and off to make sure what you are seeing is clear refrigerant. Since the refrigerant is clear, it is possible to mistake a completely discharged system for one that is fully charged. Turn the system off and watch the sight glass. If there is refrigerant in the system, you'll see bubbles during the off cycle. If you observe no bubbles when the system is running, and the air flowing from the unit in the car is cold, everything is OK.

3. If you observe bubbles in the sight glass while the system is operating, the system may be low on refrigerant. It should be noted that some late model cars are equipped with an automatic temperature switch which will turn the system off even though the dash controls are still on. If you are seeing bubbles in the sight glass, open the car doors for a few minutes. The system should switch back on and the bubbles will disappear. The system switching on and off is accompanied by a loud click as the compressor engages and disengages.

4. Oil streaks in the sight glass are an indication of trouble. Most of the time, if you see oil in the sight glass, it will appear as a series of streaks, although occasionally it may be a solid stream of oil. In either case, it means that part of the charge has been lost. This is almost always accompanied by a reduction in cold air output within the car.

DISCHARGING AND RECHARGING THE SYSTEM

If anything indicates a low charge or loss of refrigerant, the system must be discharged (emptied) and refilled to the proper level. It is not acceptable to simply add refrigerant to a partially discharged system. Since you have no way of knowing how much remains in the system, you cannot accurately monitor the amount you add. Too much refrigerant can cause instant and expensive failures.

Most modern systems have a built-in low pressure switch, which will shut the system off if it senses insufficient refrigerant. No system can guard against too much refrigerant.

Before attempting any charge-related work, you will need a set of A/C gauges. These are generally available from good parts suppliers and automotive tool suppliers. Generally described, this tool is a set of two gauges and three hoses.

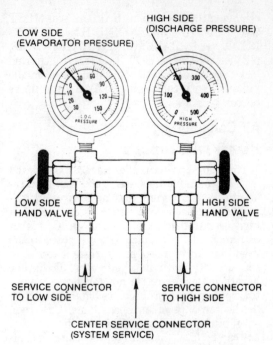

Typical manifold gauge set for air conditioning

By connecting the proper hoses to the car's system, the gauges can be used to "see" the air conditioning system at work. The gauge set is also used to discharge and recharge the system. Additionally, if a component must be removed from the system, a vacuum pump will be needed to evacuate (draw vacuum) within the system to eliminate any moisture which has entered during repairs. These pumps can be purchased outright; many find it easier to rent one from a supplier on an as-needed basis. Small cans of refrigerant will be needed; make sure you purchase enough meet the capacity of the system. Since the refrigerant is measured by weight (generally in ounces), you'll need a small scale to weigh the refrigerant can(s) as the system is recharged.

CAUTION: *Wear protective goggles and gloves before proceeding with repairs!*

Connecting and disconnecting the gauges should always be done with the engine off to prevent injury from moving parts. To hook up the gauges, first make sure that the valves on the gauges are turned to the closed (off) position. The hose from the low-pressure gauge will attach to the low pressure side of the A/C system. On early systems with a York compressor, this fitting is found on the compressor and is labled **SUCTION**.

On later model systems with either Delco or Sankyo compressors, this fitting is located on the receiver/drier. Remove the screw-on dust cap from the fitting and attach the hose finger tight.

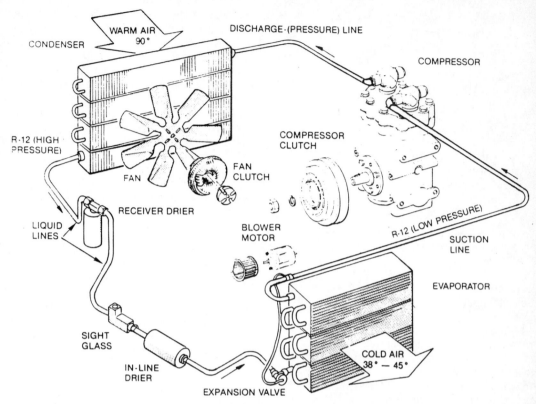

Typical air conditioning system

Now locate the high pressure fitting. On the York compressors, it is labled **DISCH** (for discharge). On other compressors, it may or may not be labled DISCH. Again, remove the dust cap and install the hose from the high-pressure gauge finger tight.

1. Place the center hose of the gauge set into a container.

2. Slowly open the valve on the low-pressure gauge to allow refrigerant to flow into the container. You should just hear a light hissing, indicating a slow discharge from the system. If you empty the system too quickly you will drain the lubricating oil as well. This oil is critical to the system's well being and replacing it is not within the scope of this book.If no discharge occurs, first check for proper hose hook-up. If all checks of your hook-up are OK, you may be attempting to discharge an already empty system.

3. Close the gauge valve when the gauge indicates zero pressure in the system. There should be very little, if any, oil in your drainage container. You have now discharged the system.

If you wish to thoroughly evacuate the system, follow the lettered steps below. To recharge the system without evacuation, proceed with step 2.

1. Confirm that high and low pressure hoses are correctly attached and secure on their fittings. Confirm that gauge valves are closed. Connect the center gauge hose to the vacuum pump.

a. Start the vacuum pump,then open both gauge valves slowly and at the same time.

b. Run the pump until the low pressure gauge shows 28 in. of vacuum. Note the time that 28 in. is reached; if the temperature is above 85°F (29°C), run the pump another 30 minutes. If the temperature is below 85°F (29°C), run the pump another 50 minutes. The target value of 28 in. of vacuum is valid at or close to sea level. For every 1000 feet of altitude in your area, reduce the expected reading by 1 in. of vacuum. Example: At 2000 feet above sea level, you would expect a reading of 26 in. of vacuum.

c. When the pump has been run for the proper period of time, and the proper gauge readings have been maintained, close both gauge valves and shut off the pump. Disconnect the hose from the vacuum pump. The air conditioning system has now been evacuated and sealed. A system which is not leaking should hold this vacuum with the pump off.

2. Confirm that the high and low pressure

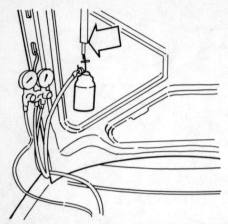

Keep the refrigerant can upright during charging. Arrow shows a spring scale for measuring weight of container

hoses are correctly connected and secure on their fittings. Confirm that the gauge valves are closed.

3. Attach the center hose to the R-12 refrigerant source, usually a 16-ounce can. Make sure the control valve for the can is closed before connecting.

4. Hang or position the can so that it stays upright during the remaining procedures. DO NOT turn the can upside down or on its side during charging. Severe damage to the system can occur.

5. Open both gauge valves and refrigerant container valve. Connect a new container when the first one is emptied.

6. Close the high pressure gauge valve when the whistling sound has stopped.

NOTE: *This valve MUST NOT be opened again during the charging operation!*

7. Open the vehicle front doors, start the engine, and set the blower fan on top speed with the air conditioning controls ON and set for maximum cooling. Run the engine at 2000 rpm and continue filling the system. Use the scale to determine total weight delivered into the system. DO NOT exceed the specified charge weight.

REFRIGERANT QUANTITIES
- 164: 28 ounces
- 240: 42 ounces
- 260: 51 ounces
- 740, 780: 42 ounces
- 760: Through 1977 – 42 ounces
  1988 – 39 ounces

8. Stop filling when the specified weight has been delivered into the system. Turn off the control valve on the R-12 container and turn off the low pressure gauge valve. Use a small thermometer to check the output of cold air at the center grille vents.

9. Shut off the engine. Disconnect all hoses from the car's fittings. Reinstall the protective dust caps on the service fittings.

NOTE: *Unscrew the hose connectors rapidly to avoid refrigerant loss from the system.*

CAUTION: *Do not disconnect the gauge line(s) at the gauge set while the hoses are hooked to the car. This would result in rapid refrigerant loss from the system causing possible personal injury.*

Windshield Wipers

Intense heat and ultra-violet rays from the sun, snow, ice and frost, road oils, acid rain, and industrial pollution all combine quickly to deteriorate the rubber wiper refills. One pass on a frosty windshield can reduce a new set of refills to an unusable condition. The refills should be replaced about twice a year or whenever they begin to streak or chatter on wet glass.

Blade life can be prolonged by frequent cleanings of the glass with a rag and a commercial glass cleaner. The use of a ammonia based cleaner will ease the removal of built-up road oils and grease from the glass. Ammonia based cleaners are harmful to painted surfaces. Be careful when applying them and don't fill the washer jug with an ammonia based solvent; when used it will run onto the painted bodywork.

WIPER REFILL REPLACEMENTS

If the wipers are not cleaning the windshield properly, only the refill has to be replaced. The blade and arm usually require replacement only in the event of damage. It is not necessary (except on new Tridon® refills) to remove the arm or the blade to replace the refill (rubber part), though you may have to position the arm higher on the glass. You can do this by turning the ignition switch on and operating the wipers. When they are positioned where they are accessible, turn the ignition switch off.

There are several types of refills and your vehicle could have any kind, since aftermarket blades and arms may not use exactly the same type refill as the original equipment.

Most Anco® styles use a release button that is pushed down to allow the refill to slide out of the yoke jaws. The new refill slides in and locks in place. Some Anco® refills are removed by noting where the metal backing strips or the refill is wider. Insert a small screwdriver blade between the frame and metal backing strip. Press down to release the refill from the retaining tab.

The Trico® style is unlocked at one end by squeezing 2 metal tabs, and the refill is slid out of the frame jaws. When the new refill is in-

Troubleshooting Basic Air Conditioning Problems

Problem	Cause	Solution
There's little or no air coming from the vents (and you're sure it's on)	• The A/C fuse is blown • Broken or loose wires or connections • The on/off switch is defective	• Check and/or replace fuse • Check and/or repair connections • Replace switch
The air coming from the vents is not cool enough	• Windows and air vent wings open • The compressor belt is slipping • Heater is on • Condenser is clogged with debris • Refrigerant has escaped through a leak in the system • Receiver/drier is plugged	• Close windows and vent wings • Tighten or replace compressor belt • Shut heater off • Clean the condenser • Check system • Service system
The air has an odor	• Vacuum system is disrupted • Odor producing substances on the evaporator case • Condensation has collected in the bottom of the evaporator housing	• Have the system checked/repaired • Clean the evaporator case • Clean the evaporator housing drains
System is noisy or vibrating	• Compressor belt or mountings loose • Air in the system	• Tighten or replace belt; tighten mounting bolts • Have the system serviced

Sight glass condition
  Constant bubbles, foam or oil streaks
  Clear sight glass, but no cold air
  Clear sight glass, but air is cold
  Clouded with milky fluid
	
	• Undercharged system
	
	• No refrigerant at all
	• System is OK
	• Receiver drier is leaking dessicant
		
		• Charge the system
		
		• Check and charge the system
		
		• Have system checked

Large difference in temperature of lines	• System undercharged	• Charge and leak test the system
Compressor noise	• Broken valves • Overcharged • Incorrect oil level • Piston slap • Broken rings • Drive belt pulley bolts are loose	• Replace the valve plate • Discharge, evacuate and install the correct charge • Isolate the compressor and check the oil level. Correct as necessary. • Replace the compressor • Replace the compressor • Tighten with the correct torque specification
Excessive vibration	• Incorrect belt tension • Clutch loose • Overcharged • Pulley is misaligned	• Adjust the belt tension • Tighten the clutch • Discharge, evacuate and install the correct charge • Align the pulley
Condensation dripping in the passenger compartment	• Drain hose plugged or improperly positioned • Insulation removed or improperly installed	• Clean the drain hose and check for proper installation • Replace the insulation on the expansion valve and hoses
Frozen evaporator coil	• Faulty thermostat • Thermostat capillary tube improperly installed • Thermostat not adjusted properly	• Replace the thermostat • Install the capillary tube correctly • Adjust the thermostat
Low side low—high side low	• System refrigerant is low • Expansion valve is restricted	• Evacuate, leak test and charge the system • Replace the expansion valve
Low side high—high side low	• Internal leak in the compressor—worn	• Remove the compressor cylinder head and inspect the compressor. Replace the valve plate assembly if necessary. If the compressor pistons, rings or

Troubleshooting Basic Air Conditioning Problems (cont.)

Problem	Cause	Solution
Low side high—high side low (cont.)		cylinders are excessively worn or scored replace the compressor
	• Cylinder head gasket is leaking	• Install a replacement cylinder head gasket
	• Expansion valve is defective	• Replace the expansion valve
	• Drive belt slipping	• Adjust the belt tension
Low side high—high side high	• Condenser fins obstructed	• Clean the condenser fins
	• Air in the system	• Evacuate, leak test and charge the system
	• Expansion valve is defective	• Replace the expansion valve
	• Loose or worn fan belts	• Adjust or replace the belts as necessary
Low side low—high side high	• Expansion valve is defective	• Replace the expansion valve
	• Restriction in the refrigerant hose	• Check the hose for kinks—replace if necessary
	• Restriction in the receiver/drier	• Replace the receiver/drier
	• Restriction in the condenser	• Replace the condenser
Low side and high side normal (inadequate cooling)	• Air in the system	• Evacuate, leak test and charge the system
	• Moisture in the system	• Evacuate, leak test and charge the system

stalled, the tabs will click into place, locking the refill.

The polycarbonate type is held in place by a locking lever that is pushed downward (out of the groove in the arm) to free the refill. When the new refill is installed, it will lock in place automatically.

The Tridon® refill has a plastic backing strip with a notch about an inch from the end. Hold the blade (frame) on a hard surface so that the frame is tightly bowed. Grip the tip of the backing strip and pull up while twisting counterclockwise. The backing strip will snap out of the retaining tab. Do this for the remaining tabs until the refill is free of the arm. The length of these refills is molded into the end and they should be replaced with identical types.

No matter which type of refill you use, be sure that all of the frame claws engage the refill. Before operating the wipers, be sure that no part of the metal frame is contacting the windshield.

Tires

Common sense and good driving habits will afford maximum tire life. Fast starts and stops, and hard cornering are hard on tires and will shorten their useful life span. If you start at normal speeds, allow yourself sufficient time to stop, and take corners at a reasonable speed, the life of your tires will increase greatly. Also make sure that you don't overload your vehicle or run with incorrect pressure in the tires. Both of these practices increase tread wear.

Inspect your tires frequently. Be especially careful to watch for bubbles in the tread or side wall, deep cuts, or underinflation. Remove any tires with bubbles. If the cuts are so deep that they penetrate to the cords, discard the tire. Any cut in the sidewall of a radial tire renders it unsafe. Also look for uneven tread wear patterns that indicate that the front end is out of alignment or that the tires are out of balance.

TIRE ROTATION

NOTE: *Mark the wheel position or direction of rotation on radial tires or studded snow tires before removal.*

So that the tires wear more uniformly, it is recommended that the tires be rotated every 6,000 miles. This can be done when all four tires are of the same size and load rating capacity. Any abnormal wear should be investigated and the cause corrected.

Radical tires should not be cross-switched; they'll last longer if their direction of rotation is not changed. They will wear very rapidly if reversed. Studded snow tires will lose their studs if their direction of rotation is reversed.

CAUTION: *Avoid overtightening the lug nuts or the brake disc or drum may become permanently distorted. Alloy wheels can be cracked by overtightening. Generally, nut torque should not exceed 60 ft.lbs. Always tighten the nuts in a criss-cross pattern.*

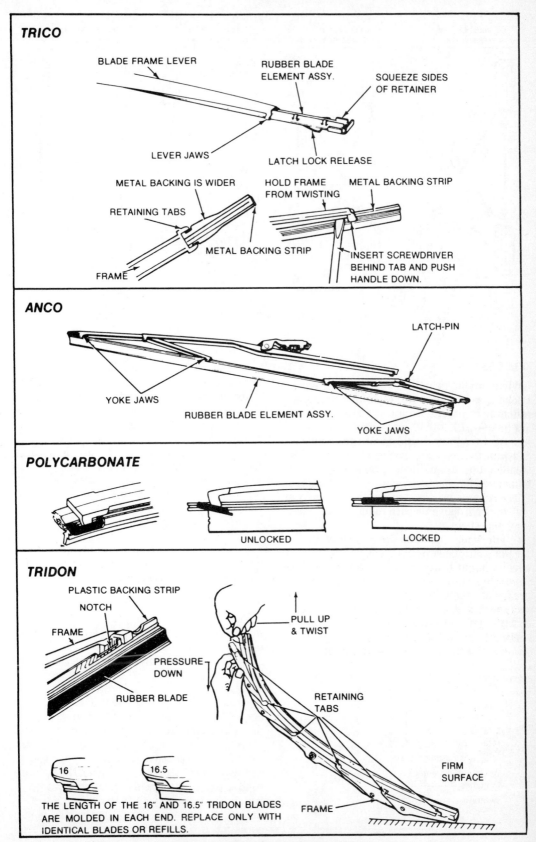

Typical windshield wiper blade removal

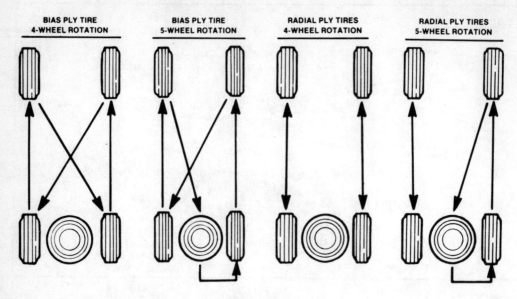

| BIAS PLY TIRE
4-WHEEL ROTATION | BIAS PLY TIRE
5-WHEEL ROTATION | RADIAL PLY TIRES
4-WHEEL ROTATION | RADIAL PLY TIRES
5-WHEEL ROTATION |

Tire rotation

TIRE DESIGN

When buying new tires, you should keep the following points in mind, especially if you are switching to larger tires or a different profile series (50, 60, 70, 78):

1. All four tires should be of the same construction type. Radial, bias, or bias-belted tires should not be mixed. Radial tires are highly recommended for their excellent handling and fuel mileage characteristics. Most new vehicles from 1980 on were delivered with radial tires as standard equipment.

2. The wheels must be the correct width for the tire. Tire dealers have charts of tire and wheel compatibility. A mismatch can cause sloppy handling and rapid tread wear. The tread width should match the rim width (inside bead to inside bead) within an inch. For radial tires the rim width should be 80% or less of the tire (not tread) width. The chart below gives an example of a tire size designation number.

3. The height (mounted diameter) of the new tires can change speedometer accuracy, engine speed per given road speed, fuel mileage, acceleration, and ground clearance. Tire manufacturers furnish full measurement specifications to their dealers.

4. The spare tire should be usable, at least for low speed operation, with the new tires. In the early 1980's, most manufacturers began using a space-saving spare tire mounted on a special wheel. This wheel and tire is for emergency use only. Never try to mount a regular tire on a special spare wheel.

5. There shouldn't be any body interference when the car is loaded, on bumps or in turning through maximum range.

TIRE INFLATION

The importance of proper tire inflation cannot be overemphasized. A tire employs air under pressure as part of its structure. It is designed around the supporting strength of air at a specified pressure. For this reason, improper inflation drastically reduces the tire's ability to perform as it was intended. Tire pressures should be checked regularly with a reliable pressure gauge. Too often the gauge on the end of the air hose at your corner garage is not accurate enough because it suffers too much abuse.

Always check tire pressure when the tires are cold, as pressure increases with temperature. If you must move the vehicle to check the tire inflation, do not drive more than a mile before checking. A cold tire is one that has not been driven for a period of about three hours.

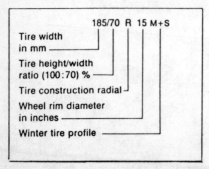

185/70 R 15 M+S

Tire width in mm

Tire height/width ratio (100:70) %

Tire construction radial

Wheel rim diameter in inches

Winter tire profile

Tire designation numbers and their meaning

CAUTION: *Never exceed the maximum tire pressure embossed on the tire. This maximum pressure is rarely the correct pressure for everyday driving. Consult your owners' manual for the proper tire pressures for your vehicle.*

CARE OF SPECIAL WHEELS

If you have invested money in magnesium, aluminum alloy or sport wheels, special precautions should be taken to make sure your investment is not wasted and that your special wheels look good for the lifetime of the car.

Tire Size Comparison Chart

"Letter" sizes			Inch Sizes	Metric-inch Sizes		
"60 Series"	"70 Series"	"78 Series"	1965–77	"60 Series"	"70 Series"	"80 Series"
			5.50-12, 5.60-12	165/60-12	165/70-12	155-12
		Y78-12	6.00-12			
		W78-13	5.20-13	165/60-13	145/70-13	135-13
		Y78-13	5.60-13	175/60-13	155/70-13	145-13
			6.15-13	185/60-13	165/70-13	155-13, P155/80-13
A60-13	A70-13	A78-13	6.40-13	195/60-13	175/70-13	165-13
B60-13	B70-13	B78-13	6.70-13	205/60-13	185/70-13	175-13
			6.90-13			
C60-13	C70-13	C78-13	7.00-13	215/60-13	195/70-13	185-13
D60-13	D70-13	D78-13	7.25-13			
E60-13	E70-13	E78-13	7.75-13			195-13
			5.20-14	165/60-14	145/70-14	135-14
			5.60-14	175/60-14	155/70-14	145-14
			5.90-14			
A60-14	A70-14	A78-14	6.15-14	185/60-14	165/70-14	155-14
	B70-14	B78-14	6.45-14	195/60-14	175/70-14	165-14
	C70-14	C78-14	6.95-14	205/60-14	185/70-14	175-14
D60-14	D70-14	D78-14				
E60-14	E70-14	E78-14	7.35-14	215/60-14	195/70-14	185-14
F60-14	F70-14	F78-14, F83-14	7.75-14	225/60-14	200/70-14	195-14
G60-14	G70-14	G77-14, G78-14	8.25-14	235/60-14	205/70-14	205-14
H60-14	H70-14	H78-14	8.55-14	245/60-14	215/70-14	215-14
J60-14	J70-14	J78-14	8.85-14	255/60-14	225/70-14	225-14
L60-14	L70-14		9.15-14	265/60-14	235/70-14	
	A70-15	A78-15	5.60-15	185/60-15	165/70-15	155-15
B60-15	B70-15	B78-15	6.35-15	195/60-15	175/70-15	165-15
C60-15	C70-15	C78-15	6.85-15	205/60-15	185/70-15	175-15
	D70-15	D78-15				
E60-15	E70-15	E78-15	7.35-15	215/60-15	195/70-15	185-15
F60-15	F70-15	F78-15	7.75-15	225/60-15	205/70-15	195-15
G60-15	G70-15	G78-15	8.15-15/8.25-15	235/60-15	215/70-15	205-15
H60-15	H70-15	H78-15	8.45-15/8.55-15	245/60-15	225/70-15	215-15
J60-15	J70-15	J78-15	8.85-15/8.90-15	255/60-15	235/70-15	225-15
	K70-15		9.00-15	265/60-15	245/70-15	230-15
L60-15	L70-15	L78-15, L84-15	9.15-15			235-15
	M70-15	M78-15				255-15
		N78-15				

Note: Every size tire is not listed and many size comparisons are approximate, based on load ratings. Wider tires than those supplied new with the vehicle, should always be checked for clearance.

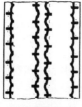

Underinflated

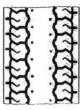

Overinflated

Unbalance

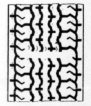

Wear indicator exposed. Tire is worn, replace.

Examples of tire wear

Special wheels are easily scratched and/or damaged. Occasionally check the rims for cracking, impact damage or air leaks. If any of these ae found, replace the wheel. In order to prevent this type of damage, and the costly replacement of a special wheel, observe the following precautions:

• Use extra care not to damage the wheels during removal, installation, balancing, etc. After removal of the wheels from the car, place them on a mat or other protective surface.

• While driving, watch for sharp obstacles.

• When washing, use a mild detergent and water. Avoid cleansers with abrasives or the use of hard brushes. There are many cleaners and polishes for special wheels. Use them.

• If possible, remove your special wheels from the car during the winter months. Salt and sand used for snow removal can severly damage the finish.

• Make sure that the recommended lug nut torque is never exceeded or the wheel may

Troubleshooting Basic Wheel Problems

Problem	Cause	Solution
The car's front end vibrates at high speed	• The wheels are out of balance • Wheels are out of alignment	• Have wheels balanced • Have wheel alignment checked/adjusted
Car pulls to either side	• Wheels are out of alignment • Unequal tire pressure • Different size tires or wheels	• Have wheel alignment checked/adjusted • Check/adjust tire pressure • Change tires or wheels to same size
The car's wheel(s) wobbles	• Loose wheel lug nuts • Wheels out of balance • Damaged wheel • Wheels are out of alignment • Worn or damaged ball joint • Excessive play in the steering linkage (usually due to worn parts) • Defective shock absorber	• Tighten wheel lug nuts • Have tires balanced • Raise car and spin the wheel. If the wheel is bent, it should be replaced • Have wheel alignment checked/adjusted • Check ball joints • Check steering linkage • Check shock absorbers
Tires wear unevenly or prematurely	• Incorrect wheel size • Wheels are out of balance • Wheels are out of alignment	• Check if wheel and tire size are compatible • Have wheels balanced • Have wheel alignment checked/adjusted

Troubleshooting Basic Tire Problems

Problem	Cause	Solution
The car's front end vibrates at high speeds and the steering wheel shakes	• Wheels out of balance • Front end needs aligning	• Have wheels balanced • Have front end alignment checked
The car pulls to one side while cruising	• Unequal tire pressure (car will usually pull to the low side) • Mismatched tires • Front end needs aligning	• Check/adjust tire pressure • Be sure tires are of the same type and size • Have front end alignment checked
Abnormal, excessive or uneven tire wear See "How to Read Tire Wear"	• Infrequent tire rotation • Improper tire pressure • Sudden stops/starts or high speed on curves	• Rotate tires more frequently to equalize wear • Check/adjust pressure • Correct driving habits
Tire squeals	• Improper tire pressure • Front end needs aligning	• Check/adjust tire pressure • Have front end alignment checked

crack. Never use snow chains on special wheels; severe scratching will occur.

FLUIDS AND LUBRICANTS

Fuel and Engine Oil Recommendations

IMPORTANCE OF GASOLINE OCTANE RATING

Octane rating is based on the quantity of anti-knock compounds added to the gasoline and determines the speed at which the gas will burn; the lower the octane, the faster it burns. The higher the numerical octane rating, the slower the fuel will burn and the greater the percentage of compounds in the fuel to prevent sparking (knock), detonation, and pre-ignition. As the temperature of the engine increases, the air-fuel mixture shows a tendency to ignite before the spark plug is fired and the exhaust valve is opened. This is especially critical in high compression engines (any engine with a compression ratio greater than 9.0:1), where the use of low-octane gas will cause combustion to occur before the piston has completed its compression stroke, thereby forcing the piston down while it is still traveling up. Fuel of the proper octane rating for the compression ratio of your car will slow the combustion process sufficiently to allow the spark plug time to ignite the mixture completely and allow time for the exhaust valve to open. Spark ping, detonation, and pre-ignition may result in damage to the top of the pistons and burned exhaust valves.

Gasoline Engines

All gasoline engine Volvos produced before the 1975 model year are designed to run on leaded (regular) gasoline. Many 1970-72 models with high compression ratios (9.3:1 to 10.5:1) require high octane fuel (97-100 RON). In recent years it has become almost impossible to find gasoline with an octane rating this high, although some oil companies were making available a "Super Regular" fuel which approaches these premium levels. In these days of low-compression, fuel efficient motors, pre-1975 cars may require a special lead-bearing additive which may be mixed with pump grade unleaded fuel.

1975 and later cars equipped with catalytic converters must use lead-free fuel or the catalyst will be rendered ineffective. These models carry an "Unleaded Gasoline Only" sticker in conspicuous view near the fuel filler cap. Other 1975 and later Volvos are designed to run on regular or low-lead fuel.

On most models, the octane rating needed to prevent engine knock is printed on a sticker inside the fuel filler cap lid. If no sticker is evident, consult your owners manual. The most common octane requirement for Volvos is 91 RON, and this fuel is readily available.

Diesel Engine

The early Volvo diesel engine is designed to run on Diesel Fuel No. 2. From 1984 through 1986, Volvo diesels can run on either No.1 or No.2 fuel. Since diesel fuel is generally available along major truck routes, supply is not a problem, though it is wise to check in advance.

Several diesel station guides are available from fuel companies and are normally sold at diesel fuel stations. Some U.S. states and Canadian provinces require purchasers of diesel fuel to obtain a special permits. Check with your Volvo dealer or fuel supplier for regulations in your area. Volvo recommends that you buy diesel fuel from major suppliers to insure a uniform high quality of fuel. For proper operation, diesel fuel systems must not contaminated by using inferior quality fuel. Special winter blends are available and should be used when temperatures fall below 14^0F(-10^0C). These fuels reduce the potential of wax deposit formation in the system and the resulting fuel flow restrictions. Most diesel fuel stations automatically switch to these blends when the cold weather approaches, but just to be sure, ask the attendant before filling up.

Warning: *There is a heaven-and-earth difference between the refinement levels of diesel fuel and home heating oil. As some diesel owners have found out the hard way, substituting home heating oil for diesel fuel will clog the fuel system with impurities and ash, resulting in a major fuel system cleaning and overhaul.*

OIL AND LUBRICANT RECOMMENDATIONS

Oils and lubricants are classified and graded according to standards established by the Society of Automobile Engineers (SAE), American Petroleum Institute (API) and the National Lubricating Grease Institute (NLGI). Engine oils are classified by the SAE and API designations found on the top of the oil can. The SAE grade number indicates the viscosity of engine oil. SAE 10W-40, for example, is a good all-temperature motor oil suitable for use in winter. The API classifications system defines oil performance in terms of usage. For gasoline engine Volvos, only oils designated **SE** or **SF** should be used. These oils provide sufficient additives to give maximum engine protection over a wide range of operating conditions.

Oils of the SE or SF variety performs a multitude of functions in addition to their basic task of lubricating. Through a balanced formula of metallic detergents and polymeric disperants, the oil prevents high-temperature and low-temperature deposits and also keeps sludge and dirt particles in suspension. Acids, particularly sulphuric acid, as well as other by-products of combustion, are neutralized by the oil. These acids, if permitted to concentrate, may cause corrosion and rapid wear of the internal parts of the engine.

Volvo diesels must use SE/CC or SF/CC motor oils. After 1984, Volvo diesels require oil designated CD. Note that the letters CD or CF appear in addition to all the other designations on the can. A sample designation might read: SAE 15W/40 SF/CD. This indicates that the oil provides protection from rust, corrosion and high temperature deposits in diesel engines used in moderate to severe service. Use the accompanying oil temperature range charts to select the correct SAE weight motor oil for the climate in which you will be driving.

OIL LEVEL CHECK

Always check the engine oil with the engine warm. Check the engine oil at least once a week.

With the vehicle on a level surface, allow the engine to sit at least three to five minutes after it has been shut off before checking the oil level; this will give the oil that has been circulating through the engine a chance to drip back down into the oil pan. Locate the engine dipstick: it is usually located on the left side of the engine. On the V6 engines (B28 and 280 family) the dipstick is on the right side of the motor, just forward of the right side shock tower.

Remove the dipstick and clean the oil off the end with a rag. Insert the dipstick again, wait a few seconds and pull it out. The oil level should be within the cross-hatched section of the dipstick. Oil level should never drop below or rise above the cross-hatched marks. If the oil level is below or near the bottom of the cross-hatched marks, add oil of the same type and viscosity, a little at a time, until the oil level is brought back within normal operating range.

Oil Recommendations

140, 1800 SERIES, 164

Temperature	Oil Viscosity
Above +10°F (−12°C)	SAE 20W-40 SAE 20W-50
Below +10°F (−12°C)	SAE 10W-30
Consistently below 0°F	SAE 5W-20 ①

240, 260 SERIES, ALL GASOLINE ENGINE 1980 AND LATER MODELS

Temperature	Oil Viscosity
All year round	SAE 10W-40 SAE 10W-30
Above +14°F (−10°C)	SAE 20W-50
Consistently below 0°F	SAE 5W-20 ①

① Should not be used at temperature continuously above 32°F (0°C)

DIESEL ENGINE

Temperature	Oil Viscosity
Above 86°F (+30°C)	SAE 20W-50 SAE 30W
Between 86°F (+30°C) and 14°F (−10°C)	SAE 10W-30 SAE 15W-50 SAE 20W-20
Below 14°F (−10°C)	SAE 10W-40 SAE 10W ①

① Should not be used under high engine revs or heavy engine load

CHANGING OIL AND FILTER

Change the engine oil and filter according to the maintenance intervals chart in this chapter. WARNING: *Used motor oil may cause skin cancer if repeatedly left in contact with the skin for prolonged periods. Although this is*

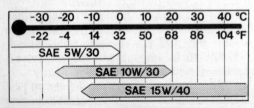

Diesel engines, 1984 and later: Recommended oil viscosity

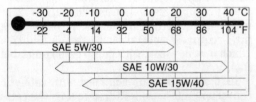

Gasoline engines, 1984 and later: Recommended oil viscosity

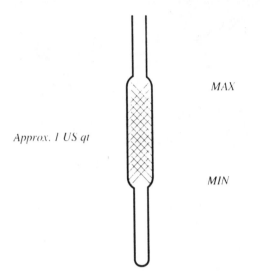

MAX

Approx. 1 US qt

MIN

Engine oil should always be within crosshatched area

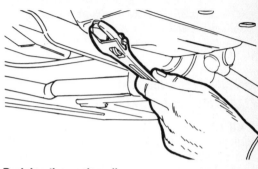

Draining the engine oil

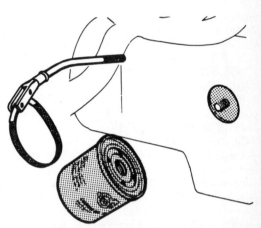

Remove the oil filter with a strap wrench

unlikely unless you handle oil on a daily basis, it is wise to thoroughly wash your hands with soap and water immediately after handling used motor oil.

After the engine has reached operating temperature, shut it off, place a drip pan under the sump (oil pan), and remove the drain plug. Allow the engine to drain thoroughly before replacing the drain plug. Make certain the drain plug is in place and tightened before continuing. Place the drip pan beneath the oil filter. To remove the filter, turn it counterclockwise with a strap wrench.

Wipe the contact surface of the new filter clean of all dirt and coat the rubber gasket with clean engine oil. Also wipe clean the adaptor on the block. To install, hand-turn the new filter clockwise until the gasket just contacts the cylinder block. Do not use a strap wrench to install. Then hand-turn the filter ½ additional turn.

NOTE: *Volvo recommends replacing the oil filter at every oil change.*

Unscrew the filler cap on the valve cover and fill the crankcase to the proper level on the dipstick with the recommended grade of oil. Replace the cap, start the engine, and operate at fast idle. Check the oil filter contact area and the drain plug for leaks and attend to any leaks as necessary.

NOTE: *Certain operating conditions may warrant more frequent changes. If the vehicle is used for short trips, water condensation and low-temperature deposits may make it necessary to change the oil sooner. If the vehicle is used mostly in stop-and-go city traffic, corrosive acids and high-temperature depos-*

Filter on the B27 and B28 engines is removed and installed from beneath the vehicle. When installing a new filter, tighten it in the direction shown by hand

its may necessitate shorter oil changing intervals. The shorter intervals are also true for industrial or rural areas where high concentration of dust contaminate the oil.

Cars used for carrying heavy loads, pulling trailers, or in mountainous areas may also need more frequent oil and filter changes.

NOTE: *Please dispose of used motor oil properly. Do not throw it in the trash or pour it on the ground. Take it to your dealer or local service station for recycling.*

Manual Transmission

FLUID RECOMMENDATION

All 140 series Volvos (without overdrive) equipped with the M40 gearbox use SAE 80 gear oil, or if none is available, SAE 30 engine oil. All 140 series Volvos with overdrive and all 1800 series Volvos equipped with the M410 gearbox use SAE 30 or SAE 20W-40 engine oil. Model 164 Volvos, without overdrive, and equipped with the M400 gearbox use SAE 90 gear oil or SAE 40 engine oil.

1975 240 series Volvos equipped with the M40 transmission use SAE 80W/90 or SAE 80/90 gear oil, while all 1975 240 series Volvos equipped with the M41 overdrive transmission use SAE 30 or SAE 20W-40 oil.

On a number of 1976 240 series and 260 series models equipped with the M45 transmission and the M46 overdrive transmission, the transmissions are filled with SAE 80W/90 or SAE 80/90 gear oil, while all other M45 and M46 transmissions (used on 1976-88 models) are filled with Type F or Type G automatic transmission fluid. You are reading that correctly; Automatic trans fluid in a manual (stick shift) transmission. An easy way to tell if the transmission uses gear oil or ATF is: on ATF filled transmissions, the figure eight shaped flat casting located at the filler plug is stamped "ATF-OIL" in white. Do not attempt to use gear oil in these transmissions, or vice versa. The M47 5-speed transmission introduced in 1987 also uses Type F or G fluid.

LEVEL CHECK

At 6,000 to 7,500 mile intervals, the fluid level should be checked. After making sure that the vehicle is standing on level ground, unscrew the filler plug and check to see that the fluid level is even with the bottom of the filler plug hole or just flowing out of it. Top up as necessary with the gear oil recommended in the "Lubrication" section, below.

NOTE: *On vehicles with overdrive units, the overdrive gears are lubricated by the transmission oil: no separate filler plug is used.*

DRAIN AND REFILL

After the transmission has reached operating temperature (driven 5-7 miles), the oil may be changed. Place a drip pan beneath the vehicle and remove the drain plug and the filler plug. On vehicles equipped with overdrive, remove the six bolts and cover, allowing the unit to

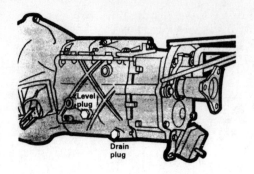

Manual 5-speed transmission

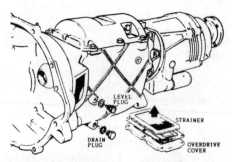

Manual 4-speed transmission with overdrive

Drain and fill locations, manual transmissions

drain also. At this time, the prefilter and fine filter must be removed and cleaned in solvent. To remove the fine filter, Volvo special tool no. 2836 or similar must be used to unscrew the filter housing. After blowing the filters dry with compressed air, install the fine filter in its socket with a new seal. Torque the plug for the filter housing with special tool no. 2836 or similar to 16 ft. lbs. Install the prefilter and the cover with a new gasket making sure that the magnet is in place. On overdrive units from 1983, the strainer is external; it will come off with the cover and can be easily cleaned.

Overdrive filter assembly

Replace the drain plug in the transmission and fill up to the filler plug with the proper oil. See "Lubrication" section in this chapter for oil recommendations.

WARNING: *Allow the oil time to seep into the overdrive unit on vehicles so equipped before driving the car.*

Automatic Transmission

FLUID RECOMMENDATION

Until 1983, all Volvo automatic transmissions used type F automatic transmission fluid. 1979-83 models can also use type G automatic transmission fluid.

From 1983 on, transmisssions designated AW 70, AW 71 and ZF 4 HP 22 use fluid identified as Dexron®II. Only the BW 55 transmission continued to use Type F or G fluid.

LEVEL CHECK

The fluid level of the automatic transmission should be checked every 6,000 to 7,500 miles. Position the vehicle on level ground, place the selector lever in Park, and let the engine idle. Remove the dipstick from the filler tube on the right side of the engine, and wipe it clean with a chamois or similar lint-free cloth. Reinsert the dipstick, pull it straight out, and take the reading. Any transmission that has been driven for 5-7 miles is a warm transmission and its proper level is the upper range of marks on the dipstick. The proper level for a cold transmission is the lower range of marks. When necessary, top up with the proper automatic transmission fluid. The difference between the minimum and maximum marks is only one pint, so add the fluid slowly. Overfilling the transmission may cause it to overheat.

On many later model automatic transmission cars, the transmission dipstick is calibrated on

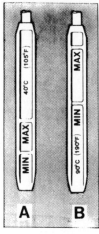

Fluid temperature ranges on dipstick

both sides: one for cold ATF fluid — below 105°F (41°C) and one for warm fluid — above 190°F (88°C). The fluid temperature will be in the warm range after 20 to 30 minutes of driving. Be sure to read the appropriate side when checking the fluid level.

DRAIN AND REFILL

Up to 1983, the oil in the automatic transmission need only be changed when the unit is torn down for repairs or rebuilding. In normal use, only topping up the fluid is required as needed. Internal repairs or rebuilding is best referred to a Volvo agency.

During the model year 1983, Volvo began to equip all automatic transmissions with an oil drain plug in the bottom of the pan. The drain and refill interval was established at 20,000 miles for all cars from 1983 to the present. Again, adverse operating conditions may dictate more frequent changes. Fresh transmission oil is very cheap insurance in a very expensive unit. To drain the transmission:

1. With the engine off and the rear wheels blocked, safely elevate the front of the car and support with jackstands.

2. Position a drain pan under the transmission drain plug and carefully remove the plug. CAUTION: *The oil can be scalding hot if vehicle was recently driven.*

3. After the oil has drained, reinstall the drain plug and tighten.

4. Disconnect and remove the dipstick tube from the pan. Remove the bolts holding the pan to the transmission body and remove the pan.

5. Clean the oil pan, strainer, particle magnet and other removed parts.

6. Reinstall strainer and magnets, making certain that each part is in its proper place.

7. Place a new gasket on the oil pan and lightly coat it with fresh ATF. Reinstall the oil

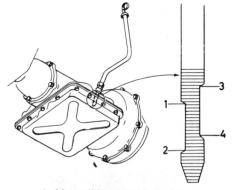

1. Max. oil level, cold gearbox
2. Min. oil level, cold gearbox
3. Max. oil level, warm gearbox
4. Min. oil level, warm gearbox

Checking automatic transmission fluid level

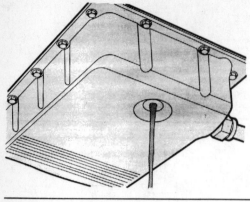

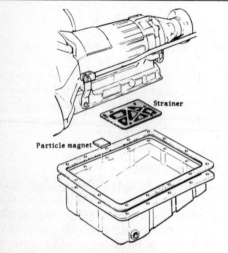

Strainer

Particle magnet

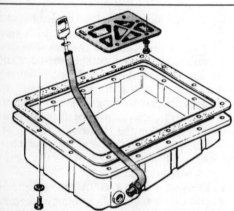

**Service components in automatic transmission.
Type AW70/AW71 shown; others similar**

match the pan shape; torque these bolts to 4 ft. lbs.

8. Reinstall the dipstick tube, making certain that it is properly threaded before tightening. Correct torque is 60-65 ft. lbs.

9. Using a funnel, deliver the correct amount of automatic transmission fluid through the dipstick tube under the hood.

10. Remove all items from under the car, return it to the ground, and start the engine. Allow it to warm up fully and check for leakage at the drain plug, gasket, and dipstick tube. Attend to leaks as necessary.

Rear Axle

FLUID RECOMMENDATION

All Volvo rear axles use API GL-5 SAE 90W gear oil. For climates where the temperature is constantly below 15°F (−10°C), API GL-5 SAE 80W oil can be used. On cars with limited slip differentials, use oils with the proper additives to protect these units.

LEVEL CHECK

Check the rear axle fluid level at least twice a year. The vehicle must be level and, if raised on jackstands, both ends of the car must be raised the same amount. To check the oil level, remove the filler plug in the back of the differential case. Gear oil should be even with or just flowing out of the filler hole. If not, add gear oil according to the specifications given under "Lubricants", below. On cars equipped with limited slip differentials, use only gear oils with the appropriate additives.

DRAIN AND REFILL

The oil in the rear axle is changed after the first 1,200-1,500 miles, and thereafter only if the unit is rebuilt. When changing the oil after the break-in period, remove the filler plug and the drain plug, allowing the warm oil to drain into a container. Clean the plug of all metal

pan to the transmission body and install the bolts. make sure the gasket is properly placed on the pan before installing. When tightening the pan bolts, DO NOT OVERTIGHTEN. Torque only to 3.5 ft. lbs; overtightening will deform the pan, crush the gasket, and cause oil leaks. If the transmission pan uses retaining clips, make sure they are properly positioned to

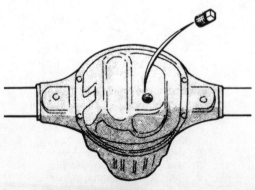

Rear axle filler plug location

filings and foreign impurities. Install the drain plug and fill the axle to the bottom of the filler hole with API GL-5 SAE 90 gear oil.

Cooling System

FLUID RECOMMENDATION AND LEVEL CHECK

Check the coolant level at fuel stops on all models. The level should appear between the maximum and minimum marks of the translucent expansion tank. Do not remove the expansion tank filler cap except to top up the system, as air might become trapped in the system and reduce cooling efficiency. Top up the system with a mixture of 50% anti-freeze and 50% water; use this mixture all year round. If the engine is warm when you top up the cooling system, remove the filler cap slowly in order to allow any excess pressure to escape.

CAUTION: *Always check or add fluid at the expansion tank. NEVER remove the radiator cap on a hot motor. You can be badly scalded by steam and hot liquid.*

DRAINING AND REFILLING

Perform this operation with the engine cold.
1. Jack up the front of the car and support it on jack stands.
2. Remove the gravel shield, if equipped. Remove the expansion tank cap and set the heater controls to **Hot**.

CAUTION: *When draining the coolant, keep in mind that cats and dogs are attracted by the ethylene glycol antifreeze, and are quite likely to drink any that is left in an uncovered container or in puddles on the ground. This will prove fatal in sufficient quantity. Always drain the coolant into a sealable container. Coolant should be reused unless it is contaminated or several years old.*

Cylinder block drain petcock location—B27F engine. Second drain is on other side of engine

3. Open the petcock on the right side of the engine block on all but the V6 engine and the diesel. The V6 engine petcocks are located on both sides of the block. The diesel engine does not have an accessible block drain and must be drained at the radiator. If the coolant is to be reused, collect it in a clean pan.
4. On all models, while the block is draining, disconnect the lower radiator hose and allow the coolant to drain into another pan. On models with an expansion tank, either use a syphon or unfasten the tank and hold it up so that all of the coolant in it flows into the radiator.
5. Close the petcock(s), re-connect the lower radiator hose and add coolant to the expansion tank until coolant is level with the MAX mark on the tank.
6. Run the engine to normal operating temperature and check for leaks. Check the coolant level and refill if necessary. Refer also to previous sections on "Hose Replacement" and "Do's and Don'ts" for other hints.

FLUSHING AND CLEANING THE SYSTEM

Proceed with draining the system as outlined above. When the system has drained, reconnect hoses and secure as necessary. Move the temperature control for the heater to its hottest position; this allows the heater core to be flushed as well. Using a garden hose, fill the radiator and allow the water to run out the engine drain cocks. Continue until the water runs clear. Be sure to clean the expansion tank as well.

If the system is badly contaminated with rust or scale, you can use a commercial flushing solution to clean it out. Follow the manufacturer's instructions. Some causes of rust are air in the system, failure to change the coolant regularly, use of excessively hard or soft water, and/or failure to use the correct mix of antifreeze and water.

After the system has been flushed, continue with the refill procedures outlined above. Check the condition of the radiator cap and its gasket, replacing the cap if anything looks improper.

NOTE: *Volvo specifies that the cooling system on diesel engines must be bled after refilling the cooling system. This eliminates trapped air from the system and insures proper operation.*

To do this, disconnect the upper hose running to the cold start device on the right side of the engine. Place a drain pan under the hose and hold the hose approximately at the same height as the top of the expansion tank. Fill the cooling system through the expansion tank, then start the engine and run at fast idle.

Run the engine for five minutes and contin-

ue to fill the cooling system during this time. Reconnect the hose to the cold start device. Continue to fill the cooling system until the correct level is reached, then reinstall the cap on the expansion tank.

Brake Master Cylinder

FLUID LEVEL

The level of brake fluid in the master cylinder should be checked weekly. The master cylinder is located on the left side of the engine compartment in front of the firewall. The level may be checked without removing the cap by simply observing whether or not the fluid is up to the maximum mark on the translucent reservoir. Top up as necessary with DOT 4 quality fluid. Take care not to drop any foreign matter or dirt into the reservoir. Make sure that the vent hole in the reservoir cap is not blocked. Always wipe off the cap and reservoir area before opening

the reservoir; this will help assure that no dirt gets into the fluid.

WARNING: *Do not allow brake fluid to come in contact with any painted surfaces of the car. If this occurs, immediately rinse the area with clear water.*

Clutch Master Cylinder

FLUID LEVEL

260 series, and 1980 and later models with the V6 engine and manual transmissions are equipped with a hydraulic clutch release system rather than the cable clutch release used on other Volvos. You can check the fluid level without removing the master cylinder cap by looking through the translucent sides of the reservoir. If fluid is not even with the **MAX** line, add DOT 4 brake fluid through the capped opening.

WARNING: *Do not allow brake fluid to come in contact with any painted surfaces of the car. If this occurs, immediately rinse the area with clear water.*

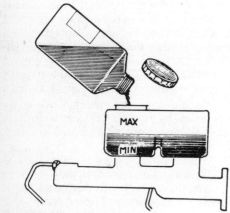

Check brake fluid level

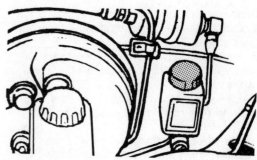

Check clutch fluid level—260 series and 1980 and later vehicles with V6 engine and manual transmission.

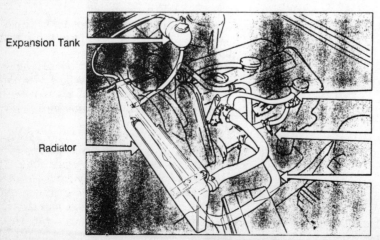

Expansion Tank

Radiator

Upper hose to cold start device

Draincock

Lower radiator hose

Diesel cooling system

Manual Steering Gear

LUBRICANT CHECK

142, 144, 145, and 1800 Models

These models use a worm and roller type steering gear box. The oil level should be checked at least twice a year. Oil level should be to the bottom of the filler plug in the gear box. Top up if necessary using oil specified in the "Lubricants" section in this chapter.

242, 244, 254 AND 1980 AND LATER MODELS

These models are equipped with a rack and pinion manual steering system which is permanently filled with lubricant. Two different types of rack and pinion systems are used, one manufactured by Cam and one by ZF. The ZF system is packed with grease while the Cam system is filled with 20W-50 motor oil.

On both types, check the rubber bellows boots for rips and degeneration. If a ripped boot is noticed, replace it as soon as possible. See Chapter 8 "Suspension and Steering" for more information.

Steering gear filler plug location—worm and roller type steering box

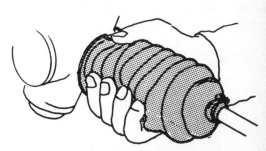

On vehicles with rack and pinion steering, check the bellows boots for cracks and rips

Power Steering Pump

FLUID LEVEL

142, 144, 145, 164 Models

Check the power steering reservoir fluid level at least twice a year. With the engine shut off the fluid level should appear approximately ¼ in. above the level mark inside the reservoir. Top up as necessary with Type A automatic transmission fluid or Dexron®II. Top up the system only with engine off to prevent air from being sucked into the system.

If necessary, bleed the air out of the system according to the instructions given in Chapter 8, "Suspension and Steering".

200 and 700 Series Models

Check the power steering reservoir fluid level at least twice a year. On the 240 series (242, 244 and 245 models) through 1976, check the oil level with the engine running. Level should be at the level mark on the inside of the reservoir. The oil level will rise when the engine is stopped.

On all other models, the fluid level is checked with the engine running and the fluid hot (after driving). The fluid level should be between the MAX and MIN marks which are located either on the side of the translucent plastic reservoir or on the dipstick attached to the filler cap. Add automatic transmission fluid, Type A, F, or G as necessary. If necessary, bleed the air out of the system according to the instructions given in Chapter 8, "Suspension and Steering".

Power steering reservoir—arrow indicates level line

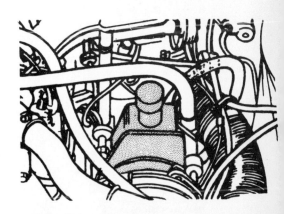

Power steering fluid reservoir—cap has dipstick attached. Some models have see-through reservoir

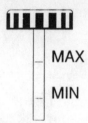

MAX

MIN

Power steering reservoir cap with dipstick. Check level with engine idling

It should be noted that the power steering fluid is never drained and replaced as a maintenance procedure. If you are constantly adding fluid, the system is leaking somewhere and requires prompt attention.

Carburetor Oil

On carbureted 1970-72 series, 164 series and Canadian models, the oil level in the center spindle of the carburetors must be checked every six months or 6,000 miles. Unscrew the black knob on top of each carburetor and remove each damping plunger. The oil level should be maintained at about ¼ in. from the edge of the spindle. Top up as necessary with automatic transmission fluid Type A, or Dexron®II.

Chassis greasing

Aside from the yearly greasing of all the joints for the throttle linkage, parking brake, and pedal linkages, no regular greasing of front-end components or universal joints is required. Use regular chassis lube on the above-mentioned joints once a year or if binding is noticed.

The upper and lower control arm ball joints as well as the tie rod and steering rod ball joints are lined with plastic (Teflon®) and do not require lubrication. However, every 12,000 miles, check the rubber seals of these ball joints for cracking or damage. Replace any damaged seal with a new one, making sure to pack the new seal with multipurpose chassis grease.

Distributor Lubrication
BREAKER POINT IGNITIONS

Every six months or 6,000 miles, the distributor shaft, cam lobes, and advance mechanism are lubricated. To lubricate the distributor shaft, fill the oil cup on the side of the distributor with light engine oil. The cam lobes are lightly smeared with Bosch Ft 1 v 4 or similar silicone cam lobe grease. The advance mechanism is lubricated by pouring two or three drops of SAE 10W engine oil on the wick of the distributor shaft.

ELECTRONIC IGNITIONS

Since there is no rubbing block, cam, or breaker points in the electronic ignition system, the only lubrication required is to remove the distributor cap and rotor and soak the felt wick in the distributor shaft center with one or two drops of motor oil.

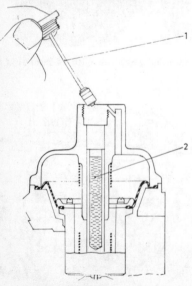

1. Damper piston
2. Oil (ATF fluid type "A")

Check the damper oil level on carbureted models

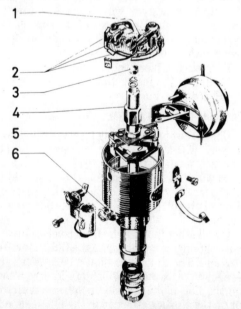

1. Grease contact lip
2. Grease
3. Lubricate
4. Grease very lightly
5. Grease
6. Fill with oil

Breaker point distributor lubrication

NOTE: *If you cannot remove the distributor cap because it seems to be catching on something, rotate the engine to a different position by hand, then remove the cap.*

When oiling the felt wick, be very careful not to splash any oil on the impulse sender or any other electronic ignition components inside the distributor.

Body Lubrication

In order to avoid rattles and unnecessary wear, lubricate the body parts as shown on the diagram every 6,000-7,000 miles or twice a year.

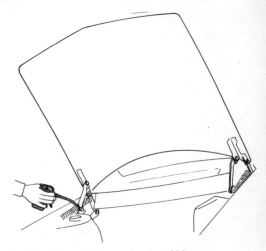

Lubrication point—engine hood hinges

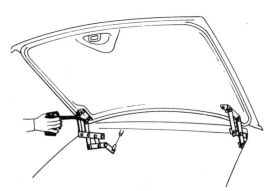

Lubrication point—trunk hinges

Lubrication point—door stop

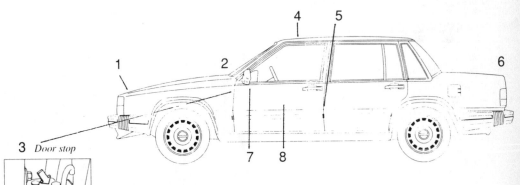

3 *Door stop*

No.	Lubricating point	Lubricant
1	Hood lock and latch	Paraffin wax
2	Hood hinges	Oil
3	Door stop	Oil
4	Sunroof wind deflector	Oil
5	Door lock catch plate	Paraffin wax
6	Trunk lid lock	Lock oil
7	Window regulator	Oil, grease
	Locking device	Silicone
	(on inside of door)	grease
8	Front seat slide rail and latch	Oil

Lubricate these points at least twice per year

Wheel Bearings
ADJUSTMENT AND PACKING

The rear wheel bearings are not adjustable and are lubricated by the rear axle oil. The front wheel bearings are replaced and adjusted as explained below. Note that you will need either Volvo special tools or their equivalent to perform the service.

1. Remove the hub cap, and loosen the lug nuts a few turns.

2. Firmly apply the parking brake and block the rear wheels. Jack up the front of the car and place jackstands beneath the jacking points. Remove the front wheels.

3. Remove the front caliper as outlined in Chapter 9 under, Front Caliper Removal and Installation.

CAUTION: *Brake pads and shoes contain asbestos, which has been determined to a cancer causing agent. Never clean the brake surfaces with compressed air! Avoid inhaling and dust from brake surfaces! When cleaning brakes, use commercially available brake cleaning fluids.*

4. Pry off the grease cap from the hub. Remove the cotter pin and castle nut. Use a hub puller to pull off the hub. On the 760 GLE remove the brake disc. If the inner bearing remains lodged on the stub axle, remove it with a puller.

5. Using a drift, remove the inner and outer bearing rings.

6. Thoroughly clean the hub, brake disc, and grease cap.

7. Press in the new inner and outer bearing rings with a drift or bearing installation tool.

8. Press grease onto both bearings with a bearing packer. If one is not available, pack the bearings with as much wheel bearing grease as possible by hand. Also coat the outside of the bearings and the outer rings pressed into the

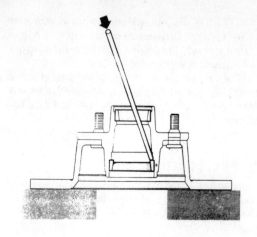

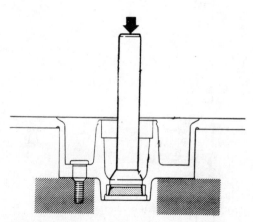

Above: Removing inner bearing race with a drift. Below: Removing outer race with a bearing removal tool

Removing front hub

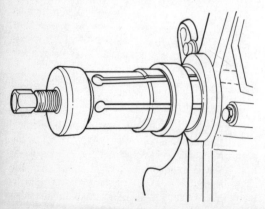

Removing inner bearing with puller; Volvo special tool shown

hub. Fill the recess in the hub with grease up to the smallest diameter on the outer ring for the outer bearing. Place the inner bearing in position in the hub and press its seal in with a drift.

The felt ring should be thoroughly coated with light engine oil.

9. Place the hub onto the stub axle. Install the outer bearing, washer, and castle nut.

10. Adjust the front wheel bearings by tightening the castle nut to 45 ft. lbs. to seat the bearings. Then, back off the nut ⅓ of a turn counterclockwise. Torque the nut to 12 in. lbs. If the nut slot does not align with the hole in the stub axle, tighten the nut until the cotter pin may be installed. Make sure that the wheel spins freely without any side play.

11. Fill the grease cap halfway with wheel bearing grease, and install it on the hub.

12. Install the front caliper.

13. Install the wheels. Remove the jackstand and lower the car. Tighten the lug nuts to 60-70 ft. lbs. and install the hub cap.

TRAILER TOWING

Trailer and Tongue Weight Limits

Trailer weight is the first and most important factor in determining whether or not your vehicle is suitable for towing the trailer you have in mind. The horsepower-to-weight ratio should be calculated. The basic standard is a ratio of 35:1. That is, 35 pounds of GVW for every horsepower.

To calculate this ratio, multiply your engine's rated horsepower by 35, then subtract the weight of the vehicle, including passengers and luggage. The resulting figure is the ideal maximum trailer weight that you can tow. One point to consider: a numerically higher axle ratio can offset what appears to be a low trailer weight. If the weight of the trailer that you have in mind is somewhat higher than the weight you just calculated, you might consider changing your rear axle ratio to compensate.

For vehicles produced up to the end of 1982, Volvo recommends a maximum trailer weight of 2000 lbs (908 kgs) with a tongue weight of 200 lbs (90 kgs). In 1983, the limits were generally raised to a maximum of a 3300 lb. trailer (1500 kgs.) and an absolute maximum tongue weight of 200 lbs.(90 kgs.). The 780 family is the only exception to this rule, having a maximum recommended trailer weight of 1985 lbs.(900 kgs.) with a tongue weight of 110 lbs (50 kgs.). A general rule is that the tongue weight of the trailer should never exceed ten percent of the total weight of the trailer.

Cars with overdrive transmissions must not use the overdrive when towing. Volvo recommends the installation of a transmission oil cooler when towing heavy trailers; this will allow the transmission to operate closer to its normal temperature range. When towing, remember that the engine and transmission are subjected to heavier than normal load; engine temperature should be watched closely for overheating and fluids should be checked regularly.

Hitch Weight

There are three kinds of hitches: bumper mounted, frame mounted, and load equalizing.

Bumper mounted hitches are those which attach solely to the vehicle's bumper. Many states prohibit towing with this type of hitch when it attaches to the vehicle's stock bumper, since it subjects the bumper to stresses for which it was not designed. Aftermarket rear step bumpers, designed for trailer towing, are acceptable for use with bumper mounted hitches.

Frame mounted hitches can be of the type which bolts to two or more points on the frame, plus the bumper, or just to several points on the frame. Frame mounted hitches can also be of the tongue type, for Class I towing, or of the receiver type, for classes II and III.

Load equalizing hitches are usually used for large trailers. Most equalizing hitches are welded in place and use equalizing bars and chains to level the vehicle after the trailer is hooked up.

The bolt-on hitches are the most common, since they are relatively easy to install.

Check the gross weight rating of your trailer. Tongue weight is usually figured as 10% of gross trailer weight. Therefore, a trailer with a maximum gross weight of 2,000 lb. will have a maximum tongue weight of 200 lb. Class I trailers fall into this category. Class II trailers are those with a gross weight rating of 2,000-3,500 lb., while Class III trailers fall into the 3,500-6,000 lb. category. Class IV trailers are those over 6,000 lb. and are for use with fifth wheel trucks, only.

When you've determined the hitch that you'll need, follow the manufacturer's installation instructions exactly, especially when it comes to fastener torques. The hitch will subjected to a lot of stress and good hitches come with hardened bolts. Never substitute an inferior bolt for a hardened bolt.

Wiring

Wiring the car for towing is fairly easy. There are a number of good wiring kits available and these should be used, rather than trying to design your own. All trailers will need brake lights and turn signals as well as tail lights and side marker lights. Most states require extra marker lights for overwide trailers. Also, most states have recently required back-up lights for trailers, and most trailer manufacturers have been building trailers with back-up lights for several years.

Additionally, some Class I, most Class II and just about all Class III trailers will have electric brakes.

Add to this number an accessories wire, to operate trailer internal equipment or to charge the trailer's battery, and you can have as many as seven wires in the harness.

Determine the equipment on your trailer and buy the wiring kit necessary. The kit will contain all the wires needed, plus a plug adapter set which included the female plug, mounted on the bumper or hitch, and the male plug, wired into, or plugged into the trailer harness.

When installing the kit, follow the manufacturer's instructions. The color coding of the wires is standard throughout the industry.

One point to note: some domestic vehicles, and most imported vehicles, have separate turn signals. On most domestic vehicles, the brake lights and rear turn signals operate with the same bulb. For those vehicles with separate turn signals, you can purchase an isolation unit so that the brake lights won't blink whenever the turn signals are operated, or, you can go to your local electronics supply house and buy four diodes to wire in series with the brake and turn signal bulbs. Diodes will isolate the brake and turn signals. The choice is yours. The isolation units are simple and quick to install, but far more expensive than the diodes. The diodes, however, require more work to install properly, since they require the cutting of each bulb's wire and soldering in place of the diode.

One, final point, the best kits are those with a spring loaded cover on the vehicle mounted socket. This cover prevent dirt and moisture from corroding the terminals. Never let the vehicle socket hang loosely; always mount it securely to the bumper or hitch.

Cooling
ENGINE

One of the most common, if not THE most common, problems associated with trailer towing is engine overheating.

With factory installed trailer towing packages, a heavy duty cooling system is usually included. Heavy duty cooling systems are available as optional equipment on most Volvo vehicles, with or without a trailer package. If you have one of these extra-capacity systems, you shouldn't have any overheating problems.

If you have a standard cooling system, without an expansion tank, you'll definitely need to get an aftermarket expansion tank kit, preferably one with at least a 2 quart capacity. These kits are easily installed on the radiator's over-

flow hose, and come with a pressure cap designed for expansion tanks.

Another helpful accessory is a Flex Fan. These fan are large diameter units are designed to provide more airflow at low speeds, with blades that have deeply cupped surfaces. The blades then flex, or flatten out, at high speed, when less cooling air is needed. These fans are far lighter in weight than stock fans, requiring less horsepower to drive them. Also, they are far quieter than stock fans.

If you do decide to replace your stock fan with a flex fan, note that if your Volvo has a fan clutch, a spacer between the flex fan and water pump hub will be needed.

Aftermarket engine oil coolers are helpful for prolonging engine oil life and reducing overall engine temperatures. Both of these factors increase engine life.

While not absolutely necessary in towing Class I and some Class II trailers, they are recommeded for heavier Class II and all Class III towing.

Engine oil cooler systems consist of an adapter, screwed on in place of the oil filter, a remote filter mounting and a multi-tube, finned heat exchanger, which is mounted in front of the radiator or air conditioning condenser.

TRANSMISSION

An automatic transmission is usually recommended for trailer towing. Modern automatics have proven reliable and, of course, easy to operate, in trailer towing.

The increased load of a trailer, however, causes an increase in the temperature of the automatic transmission fluid. Heat is the worst enemy of an automatic transmission. As the temperature of the fluid increases, the life of the fluid decreases.

It is essential, therefore, that you install an automatic transmission cooler.

The cooler, which consists of a multi-tube, finned heat exchanger, is usually installed in front of the radiator or air conditioning compressor, and hooked inline with the transmission cooler tank inlet line. Follow the cooler manufacturer's installation instructions.

Select a cooler of at least adequate capacity, based upon the combined gross weights of the Volvo and trailer.

Cooler manufacturers recommend that you use an aftermarket cooler in addition to, and not instead of, the present cooling tank in your Volvo radiator. If you do want to use it in place of the radiator cooling tank, get a cooler at least two sizes larger than normally necessary.

One note: the transmission cooler can, sometimes, cause slow or harsh shifting in the transmission during cold weather, until the fluid has a chance to come up to normal operating temperature. Some coolers can be purchased with or retrofitted with a temperature bypass valve which will allow fluid flow through the cooler only when the fluid has reached operating temperature, or above.

PUSHING and TOWING

Pushing is not recommended for your Volvo as possible mismatching of bumper heights, especially over undulating road surfaces, may result in rear-end body damage.

Any Volvo may be towed, however, by attaching a tow line to the towing loop located beneath the car on the front axle member. The 140,240,260 series and 164 model and all later Volvos may also be towed from the rear by the towing loop under the spare wheel housing or under the rear bumper. Note that the front tow loop may be hidden behind a swing down panel in the front spoiler (below the bumper) on some models. The panel is easily opened with a small screwdriver. Never attach a tow line to the bumper.

CAUTION: *When towing the car on a rope or chain, the steering must be unlocked. Remember that the power assists for steering and brakes are inoperative when the engine is off. The brake and steering systems will still operate, but will require 3-4 times the normal effort.*

If the car is equipped with an automatic transmission, special precautions must be taken. The car must be towed with the selector lever in the neutral (N) position. If the fluid level is correct in the transmission, the car may be towed a maximum distance of 20 miles at maximum towing speed of 20 mph. If the transmission is faulty, or if it is necessary to tow the car for a distance greater than 20 miles, the driveshaft must be disconnected, or the car must be towed with the rear wheels raised. Failure to observe these precautions may result in damage to the automatic transmission.

If your Volvo fails to start and is equipped with a manual transmission, it may be started by towing. The towing vehicle should start out smoothly and be driven at an even speed. Switch the ignition "on" and depress the clutch. On carbureted models, pull out the choke fully if the engine is cold. Do not pump the accelerator pedal. Place the transmission in third gear and, as the towing car picks up speed, gradually release the clutch. Once the engine fires, depress the clutch pedal and feather the gas, so as not to collide with the friend who is towing you.

Cars with automatic transmission MAY NOT be started by towing. If the battery is dead, the car may be started with the use of jumper cables. See the following section on Jump Starting. Never use a high-speed battery charger as a starting aid on fuel-injected models, as serious damage to the electronic components may result. If the high-speed charger is used to recharge the battery, the engine must be turned off and the battery completely disconnected from the car's electrical system.

Tow Trucks

If it becomes necessary to tow your Volvo with a tow truck, carefully observe the placement of hooks, slings and chains. Through 1987, Volvos can be towed using conventionsl slings and J-hooks. From 1988 on, it is recom-

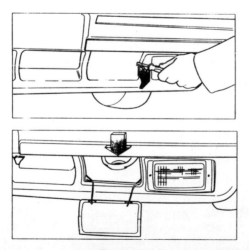
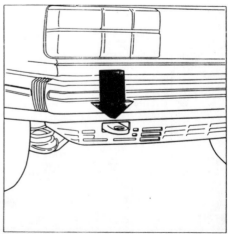

Towing hooks are located at the front and rear of the car

JUMP STARTING A DEAD BATTERY

The chemical reaction in a battery produces explosive hydrogen gas. This is the safe way to jump start a dead battery, reducing the chances of an accidental spark that could cause an explosion.

Jump Starting Precautions

1. Be sure both batteries are of the same voltage.
2. Be sure both batteries are of the same polarity (have the same grounded terminal).
3. Be sure the vehicles are not touching.
4. Be sure the vent cap holes are not obstructed.
5. Do not smoke or allow sparks around the battery.
6. In cold weather, check for frozen electrolyte in the battery. Do not jump start a frozen battery.
7. Do not allow electrolyte on your skin or clothing.
8. Be sure the electrolyte is not frozen.
CAUTION: *Make certain that the ignition key, in the vehicle with the dead battery, is in the OFF position. Connecting cables to vehicles with on-board computers will result in computer destruction if the key is not in the OFF position.*

Jump Starting Procedure

1. Determine voltages of the two batteries; they must be the same.
2. Bring the starting vehicle close (they must not touch) so that the batteries can be reached easily.
3. Turn off all accessories and both engines. Put both cars in Neutral or Park and set the handbrake.
4. Cover the cell caps with a rag—do not cover terminals.
5. If the terminals on the run-down battery are heavily corroded, clean them.
6. Identify the positive and negative posts on both batteries and connect the cables in the order shown.
7. Start the engine of the starting vehicle and run it at fast idle. Try to start the car with the dead battery. Crank it for no more than 10 seconds at a time and let it cool off for 20 seconds in between tries.
8. If it doesn't start in 3 tries, there is something else wrong.
9. Disconnect the cables in the reverse order.
10. Replace the cell covers and dispose of the rags.

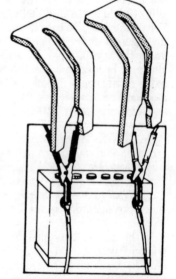

Side terminal batteries occasionally pose a problem when connecting jumper cables. There frequently isn't enough room to clamp the cables without touching sheet metal. Side terminal adaptors are available to alleviate this problem and should be removed after use.

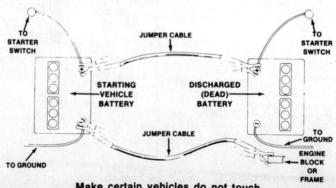

TO STARTER SWITCH   JUMPER CABLE   TO STARTER SWITCH

STARTING VEHICLE BATTERY   DISCHARGED (DEAD) BATTERY

JUMPER CABLE

TO GROUND

TO GROUND

ENGINE BLOCK OR FRAME

Make certain vehicles do not touch

This hook-up for negative ground cars only

Maintenance Intervals
In thousand of miles

Procedure	1970–74 Models	1975–83 Models	84–86 Models	87–89 Models
Engine				
Air filter change	24	30	30	30
Battery	6	7.5	7.5	7.5
Idle speed	12	15	30	30
Carb. oil level	6	7.5	—	—
Contact point adj.	6	7.5	—	—
Coolant replacement	12	30	30	30
Distributor lub., ck cap & rotor	6	15	30	30
Belt adj.	6	7.5	15	30
EGR valve replacement	24 ①	30	—	—
EGR system check	12 ①	15	—	—
Oxygen sen. replacement	—	15 ②	30 ⑧ ⑨	—
PCV system check & clean	12	15	20 ⑥	30
Evap canister replace	24	45	—	—
Ignition timing check	6	15	30	30
Fuel filter clean (carb)	6	—	—	—
Fuel filter replace (FI)	12	30 ③	30	30
Fuel tank pick-up screen cleaning	12	15	—	—
Spark plugs replace	12	15	30	30
Spark plugs cleaning	6	—	—	—
Oil change and filter replace	6	7.5 ⑤	7.5	7.5
Valve lash adj.	12	15	30 ⑦	60
Fuel filter draining (Diesel)	—	7.5	7.5	10
Fuel filter replacement (Diesel)	—	15	30	30
Body lubrication	6	7.5	7.5	7.5
Chassis				
Ball joints, steering rods check	12	7.5	7.5	7.5
Brake inspection	6	7.5	7.5	7.5
Driveshaft, U-joint check	6	7.5	7.5	7.5
Tire wear, align if nec.	6	7.5	7.5	15
Power steering fluid check	6	7.5	7.5	7.5
Rear axle fluid level-check	6	7.5	7.5	7.5
Manual trans. fluid-check	6	7.5	7.5	7.5
Auto. trans. fluid-check	6	7.5	7.5	7.5
Transmission oil change-auto	24	30 ④	22.5	22.5

① Not all models are equipped with an EGR valve
② 1980–83 models—30,000 miles
③ Electronic fuel injection—15,000 miles
④ Manual transmission only. No change needed on 1979–89 models
⑤ Turbo—3,750 miles
⑥ Clean flame guard
⑦ 84 & 85 diesel—15,000 miles.
⑧ Except B21A motor
⑨ For 85: 760 GLE only

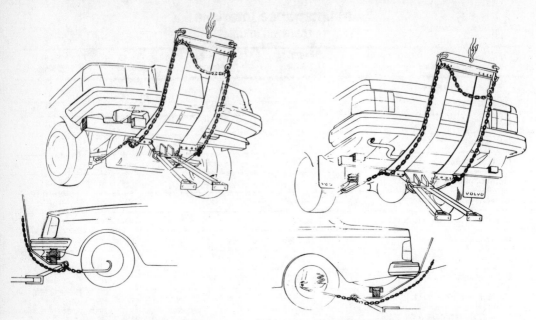

Towing with sling hoist. Note placement of wooden spacers between vehicle and sling

mended that the car ONLY be towed by wheel-lift equipment or transported on a flatbed. Hooking slings under the 1988 and 1989 cars can cause severe damage to the radiator and to the air conditioning lines at the front and to the bumper and spoiler at the rear.

JACKING

When raising the car with a floor jack, position the jack under the crossemember at the front of the car and under the differential case of the rear axle at the rear. When jacking at the

front of the car, do not position the jack under the gravel shield or the engine oil pan or you will damage these components.

NEVER crawl under a car supported only by a floor jack: use support stands. Do not position the support stands under lower control arms or other slanted surfaces as they might slip and allow the car to fall. The support stands can be placed beneath the rear axle tubes at the rear of the car, and beneath the reinforced areas of the rocker panels or front frame members. The car's weight should push vertically (downward) on the stands; the stands should be on a level and solid base.

CAUTION: *Never use the tire changing jack to support the car when working under it.*

Capacities

Year	Model	Engine Displacement Cu in. (cc)	Engine Crankcase (qt) With Filter	Engine Crankcase (qt) Without Filter	Transmission (pts) Manual 4 spd *	Transmission (pts) Automatic	Drive Axle (pt)	Gasoline Tank (gal)	Cooling System (qt)
1970	142, 144, 145	122 (1990)	4.0	3.4	1.6 (3.4)	13.1	2.7	15.3	9.0
	164	183 (2978)	6.3	5.5	1.3 (3.0)	17.3	3.4	15.3	13.0
	1800	122 (1990)	4.0	3.4	m3.3 (3.4)	—	2.7	12.0	9.0

Capacities (cont.)

Year	Model	Engine Displacement Cu in. (cc)	Engine Crankcase (qt) With Filter	Engine Crankcase (qt) Without Filter	Transmission (pts) Manual 4 spd *	Transmission (pts) Automatic	Drive Axle (pt)	Gasoline Tank (gal)	Cooling System (qt)
1971	142, 144, 145	122 (1990)	4.0	3.4	1.6 (3.4)	13.1	2.7	15.3	10.5
	164	183 (2978)	6.3	5.5	1.3 (3.0)	17.3	3.4	15.3	13.0
	1800	122 (1990)	4.0	3.4	(3.4)	13.3	2.7	12.0	9.0
1972	142, 144, 145	122 (1990)	4.0	3.4	1.6 (3.4)	13.5	2.7	15.3	10.5
	164	183 (2978)	6.3	5.5	1.3 (3.0)	17.7	3.4	15.3	13.0
	1800	122 (1990)	4.0	3.4	(3.4)	13.5	2.7	12.0	9.0
1973	142, 144, 145	122 (1990)	4.0	3.4	1.6 (3.4)	13.5	2.7	15.3	10.5
	164	183 (2978)	6.3	5.5	1.3 (3.0)	17.7	3.4	15.3	13.0
	1800	122 (1990)	4.0	3.4	(3.4)	13.5	2.7	12.0	9.0
1974	142, 144, 145	122 (1990)	4.0	3.4	1.6 (3.4)	13.5	2.7	15.8	10.0
	164	183 (2978)	6.3	5.5	(3.1)	18.0	3.4	15.8	13.0
1975	242, 244, 245	122 (1990)	4.0	3.4	1.6 (3.4)	13.5	2.7	15.8	10.0
	164	183 (2978)	6.3	5.5	(3.1)	18.0	3.4	15.8	11.0
1976–77	242, 244, 245	130 (2127)	4.0	3.5	1.6 (4.8)	13.8	3.4	15.8	10.0 ①
	262, 264, 265	162 (2660)	7.4	6.8	1.6 (4.8)	13.8	3.4	15.8	12.0
1978	242, 244, 245	130 (2127)	4.0	3.5	1.6 (3.8)	14.0	3.4	15.8	10.0
	262, 264, 265	162 (2660)	6.8	6.3	1.6 (4.8)	14.0	3.4	15.8	11.5
1979	242, 244, 245	130 (2127)	4.0	3.5	3.8	14.0 ②	3.4	15.8	10.0
	262, 264, 265	162 (2660)	6.8	6.3	4.8	14.0 ②	3.4	15.8	11.5
1980–83	DL, GL, GT ④	130 (2127)	4.0 ⑤	3.5 ⑤	4.8	14.6 ③	3.4	15.8	10.0
	GLE, Coupe	174 (2849)	6.8	6.3	4.8	14.6 ③	3.4	15.8	11.5
	DL, GL Diesel	145 (2383)	7.4	6.6	4.8	14.6 ③	3.4	15.8	10.0 ①
	DL, GL	140 (2320)	3.5	4.0	4.8	14.6 ③	3.4	15.8	10.0
	GLT Wagon, DL Turbo	130 (2127)	4.0 ⑤	3.5 ⑤	4.8	14.6 ③	3.4	15.8	10.0
	760 GLE	174 (2849)	6.8	6.3	4.8	14.6 ③	3.4	15.8 ⑥	10.5
	760 GLE Turbo Diesel	145 (2383)	7.0	6.2	4.8	14.6 ③	3.4	15.8 ⑥	11.5 ⑦

* Figures in parentheses are for overdrive transmissions
① 9.8 qts w/auto trans
② With extra capacity fluid pan: 14.6
③ AW70 and AW71 (1982 and later 4-speed) 15.6 pts.
④ Includes station wagons
⑤ Cars w/turbo: if oil cooler is drained, add 0.7 qt.
⑥ With increased capacity tank 21.6 gal.
⑦ With auto. trans. 10.5 qt.

Capacities

Year	Model	Engine Displacement Cu in. (cc)	Engine Crankcase (qt)		Transmission (pts)			Drive Axle (pts.)	Fuel Tank (gal.)	Cooling System (qts.)
			With Filter	Without Filter	4-Spd	5-Spd	Auto.			
1984	240 Diesel	145 (2383) D24	7.4	6.6	4.8	—	15.6	④	15.8	10.0
	DL	140 (2320) B23F	4.0	3.5	4.8	—	15.6	④	15.8	10.0
	DL	130 (2127) B21A ①	4.0	3.5	4.8	—	15.6	④	15.8	10.0
	GL	140 (2320) B23F	4.0	3.5	4.8	—	15.6	④	15.8	10.0
	GLE	140 (2320) B23F ①	4.0	3.5	4.8	—	15.6	④	15.8	10.0
	Turbo	130 (2127) B21F-Turbo	4.0	3.5	4.8	—	15.6	④	15.8	10.0
	760 GLE	174 (2849) B28F	6.9	6.3	4.8	—	15.6	④	15.8	10.5
	GLE	145 (2383) D24-Turbo	6.3	5.2	4.8	—	15.6	④	15.8	11.5
	Turbo	140 (2320) B23F-Turbo	4.1	3.6	4.8	—	15.6	④	15.8	10.0
1985	740 GLE	140 (2320) B230F	4.1	3.6	4.8	—	15.6	④	15.8	10.0
	TD ②	145 (2383) D24-Turbo	6.3	5.2	4.8	—	15.6	④	15.8	11.5
	Turbo	140 (2320) B230F-Turbo	4.1 ③	3.6 ③	4.8	—	15.6	④	15.8	10.0
	760 GLE	174 (2849) B28F	6.9	6.3	4.8	—	15.6	④	15.8	10.5
	GLE TD	145 (2383) D24-Turbo	6.3	5.2	4.8	—	15.6	④	15.8	11.5
	Turbo	140 (2320) B230F-Turbo	4.1 ③	3.6 ③	4.8	—	15.6	④	15.8	10.0
1986	240 DL	140 (2320) B230F	4.0	3.5	4.8	—	15.6	④	15.8	10.0
	GL	140 (2320) B230F	4.0	3.5	4.8	—	15.6	④	15.8	10.0
	740 GL	140 (2320) B230F	4.1	3.6	4.8	—	15.6	④	15.8	10.0
	GLE	140 (2320) B230F	4.1	3.6	4.8	—	15.6	④	15.8	10.0
	GLE TD	145 (2383) D24-Turbo	6.3	5.2	4.8	—	15.6	④	15.8	11.5
	Turbo	140 (2320) B230F-Turbo	4.1 ③	3.6 ③	4.8	—	15.6	④	15.8	10.0
	760 GLE	174 (2849) B28F	6.9	6.3	4.8	—	15.6	④	15.8	10.5
	Turbo	140 (2320) B230F-Turbo	4.1 ③	3.6 ③	4.8	—	15.6	④	15.8	10.0

Capacities (cont.)

Year	Model	Engine Displacement Cu in. (cc)	Engine Crankcase (qt)		Transmission (pts)			Drive Axle (pts.)	Fuel Tank (gal.)	Cooling System (qts.)
			With Filter	Without Filter	4-Spd	5-Spd	Auto.			
1987	240 DL	140 (2320) B230F	4.0	3.5	—	2.8	15.6	④	15.8	10.0
	GL	140 (2320) B230F	4.0	3.5	—	2.8	15.6	④	15.8	10.0
	740 GL	140 (2320) B230F	4.1	3.6	4.8	—	15.6	④	15.8	10.0
	GLE	140 (2320) B230F	4.1	3.6	4.8	—	15.6	④	15.8	10.0
	Turbo	140 (2320) B230F-Turbo	4.1 ③	3.6 ③	4.8	—	15.6	④	15.8	10.0
	760 GLE	174 (2849) B280F	6.3	5.8	4.8	—	15.8	④	15.8	10.5
	Turbo	140 (2320) B230F-Turbo	4.1 ③	3.6 ③	4.8	—	15.8	④	15.8	10.0
	780	174 (2849) B280F	6.3	5.8	4.8	—	15.8	④	15.8	10.5
1988–89	240 DL	140 (2320) B230F	4.0	3.5	—	3.2	15.8		15.8	10.0
	GL	140 (2320) B230F	4.0	3.5	—	3.2	15.8		15.8	10.0
	740 GL	140 (2320) B230F	4.1	3.6	—	3.2	15.8		15.8	10.0
	GLE	140 (2320) B230F	4.1	3.6	—	3.2	15.8		15.8	10.0
	Turbo	140 (2320) B230F-Turbo	4.1 ③	3.6 ③	—	4.8	15.8		15.8	10.0
	760 GLE	174 (2849) B280F	6.3	5.8	—	—	15.8		21.1	10.5
	Turbo	140 (2320) B230F-Turbo	4.1 ③	3.6 ③	—	—	15.8		21.1	10.0
	780	174 (2849) B280F	6.3	5.8	—	—	15.8		21.1	10.5

① Canada only
② Station Wagon
③ Models w/turbo: add 0.6 qt. If oil cooler has been drained
④ 1030 axle: 2.8 pts.
   1031 axle: 3.4 pts.

Engine Performance and Tune-Up

TUNE-UP PROCEDURES

The procedures listed here are intended as specific procedures. If there is something wrong with your engine (i.e., a misfire, stumbling idle, etc.) turn to the troubleshooting chart. The chart gives step by step tests which can isolate your engine's problem quickly.

NOTE: *1970-74 Volvos are equipped with breaker point ignition systems. 1975 and later Volvos have electronic ignition systems.*

Neither tune-up nor troubleshooting can be considered independently, since each has a direct bearing on the other. An engine tune-up is a service designed to restore the maximum power, performance, economy and reliability in an engine and, at the same time, assure the owner of efficiency and trouble-free performance. Engine tune-up becomes increasingly important each year, to insure that pollutant levels are in compliance with federal emissions standards.

It is advisable to follow a definite and thorough tune-up procedure. Tune-up consists of three separate steps: Analysis, the process of determining whether normal wear is responsible for performance loss, and whether the parts require replacement or service; Parts Replacement, the removal of worn or failed mechanical parts, and Service/Adjustment, during which parts may be cleaned, reset, or tightened and factory specifications are maintained or adjusted.

The extent of an engine tune-up is usually determined by the length of time since the previous service, although the type of driving and the general mechanical condition of the engine must be considered. Specific maintenance should also be performed at regular intervals, depending on operating conditions.

Troubleshooting is a logical sequence of procedures designed to lead you to the particular cause of trouble. The troubleshooting section of this manual is general in nature, yet specific enough to locate the problem. Service usually comprises two areas, diagnosis and repair. While the apparent cause of trouble, in many cases, is worn or damaged parts, performance problems are less obvious. The first job is to locate the problem and cause. Once the problem has been isolated, refer to the appropriate section for repair, removal or adjustment procedures.

It is advisable to read the entire chapter before beginning a tune-up, although those who are more familiar with tune-up procedures any wish to go directly to the instructions.

Spark Plugs

A typical spark plug consists of a metal shell surrounding a ceramic insulator. A metal electrode extends downward through the center of the insulator and protrudes a small distance at the bottom. Located at the end of the plug and attached to the side of the outer metal shell is the side electrode. The side electrode bends in at a 90 degree angle so that its tip is even with, and parallel to, the tip of the center electrode. The distance between these two electrodes (measured in thousandths of an inch or in millimeters) is called the spark plug gap. The spark plug in no way produces a spark but merely provides a gap across which the current can arc. The coil produces anywhere from 20,000 to 40,000 volts. This electric charge passes to the distributor which then sends the charge through each spark plug wire to the plug itself. The current passes along the center electrode and jumps the gap to the side electrode, and in so doing, ignites the air/fuel mixture in the combustion chamber.

Spark plug life and efficiency depend upon the condition of the engine and the temperature to which the plug is exposed. Combustion

Troubleshooting Engine Performance

Problem	Cause	Solution
Hard starting (engine cranks normally)	• Binding linkage, choke valve or choke piston	• Repair as necessary
	• Restricted choke vacuum diaphragm	• Clean passages
	• Improper fuel level	• Adjust float level
	• Dirty, worn or faulty needle valve and seat	• Repair as necessary
	• Float sticking	• Repair as necessary
	• Faulty fuel pump	• Replace fuel pump
	• Incorrect choke cover adjustment	• Adjust choke cover
	• Inadequate choke unloader adjustment	• Adjust choke unloader
	• Faulty ignition coil	• Test and replace as necessary
	• Improper spark plug gap	• Adjust gap
	• Incorrect ignition timing	• Adjust timing
	• Incorrect valve timing	• Check valve timing; repair as necessary
Rough idle or stalling	• Incorrect curb or fast idle speed	• Adjust curb or fast idle speed
	• Incorrect ignition timing	• Adjust timing to specification
	• Improper feedback system operation	• Refer to Chapter 4
	• Improper fast idle cam adjustment	• Adjust fast idle cam
	• Faulty EGR valve operation	• Test EGR system and replace as necessary
	• Faulty PCV valve air flow	• Test PCV valve and replace as necessary
	• Choke binding	• Locate and eliminate binding condition
	• Faulty TAC vacuum motor or valve	• Repair as necessary
	• Air leak into manifold vacuum	• Inspect manifold vacuum connections and repair as necessary
	• Improper fuel level	• Adjust fuel level
	• Faulty distributor rotor or cap	• Replace rotor or cap
	• Improperly seated valves	• Test cylinder compression, repair as necessary
	• Incorrect ignition wiring	• Inspect wiring and correct as necessary
	• Faulty ignition coil	• Test coil and replace as necessary
	• Restricted air vent or idle passages	• Clean passages
	• Restricted air cleaner	• Clean or replace air cleaner filler element
	• Faulty choke vacuum diaphragm	• Repair as necessary
Faulty low-speed operation	• Restricted idle transfer slots	• Clean transfer slots
	• Restricted idle air vents and passages	• Clean air vents and passages
	• Restricted air cleaner	• Clean or replace air cleaner filter element
	• Improper fuel level	• Adjust fuel level
	• Faulty spark plugs	• Clean or replace spark plugs
	• Dirty, corroded, or loose ignition secondary circuit wire connections	• Clean or tighten secondary circuit wire connections
	• Improper feedback system operation	• Refer to Chapter 4
	• Faulty ignition coil high voltage wire	• Replace ignition coil high voltage wire
	• Faulty distributor cap	• Replace cap
Faulty acceleration	• Improper accelerator pump stroke	• Adjust accelerator pump stroke
	• Incorrect ignition timing	• Adjust timing
	• Inoperative pump discharge check ball or needle	• Clean or replace as necessary
	• Worn or damaged pump diaphragm or piston	• Replace diaphragm or piston

Troubleshooting Engine Performance (cont.)

Problem	Cause	Solution
Faulty acceleration (cont.)	• Leaking carburetor main body cover gasket	• Replace gasket
	• Engine cold and choke set too lean	• Adjust choke cover
	• Improper metering rod adjustment (BBD Model carburetor)	• Adjust metering rod
	• Faulty spark plug(s)	• Clean or replace spark plug(s)
	• Improperly seated valves	• Test cylinder compression, repair as necessary
	• Faulty ignition coil	• Test coil and replace as necessary
	• Improper feedback system operation	• Refer to Chapter 4
Faulty high speed operation	• Incorrect ignition timing	• Adjust timing
	• Faulty distributor centrifugal advance mechanism	• Check centrifugal advance mechanism and repair as necessary
	• Faulty distributor vacuum advance mechanism	• Check vacuum advance mechanism and repair as necessary
	• Low fuel pump volume	• Replace fuel pump
	• Wrong spark plug air gap or wrong plug	• Adjust air gap or install correct plug
	• Faulty choke operation	• Adjust choke cover
	• Partially restricted exhaust manifold, exhaust pipe, catalytic converter, muffler, or tailpipe	• Eliminate restriction
	• Restricted vacuum passages	• Clean passages
	• Improper size or restricted main jet	• Clean or replace as necessary
	• Restricted air cleaner	• Clean or replace filter element as necessary
	• Faulty distributor rotor or cap	• Replace rotor or cap
	• Faulty ignition coil	• Test coil and replace as necessary
	• Improperly seated valve(s)	• Test cylinder compression, repair as necessary
	• Faulty valve spring(s)	• Inspect and test valve spring tension, replace as necessary
	• Incorrect valve timing	• Check valve timing and repair as necessary
	• Intake manifold restricted	• Remove restriction or replace manifold
	• Worn distributor shaft	• Replace shaft
	• Improper feedback system operation	• Refer to Chapter 4
Misfire at all speeds	• Faulty spark plug(s)	• Clean or replace spark plug(s)
	• Faulty spark plug wire(s)	• Replace as necessary
	• Faulty distributor cap or rotor	• Replace cap or rotor
	• Faulty ignition coil	• Test coil and replace as necessary
	• Primary ignition circuit shorted or open intermittently	• Troubleshoot primary circuit and repair as necessary
	• Improperly seated valve(s)	• Test cylinder compression, repair as necessary
	• Faulty hydraulic tappet(s)	• Clean or replace tappet(s)
	• Improper feedback system operation	• Refer to Chapter 4
	• Faulty valve spring(s)	• Inspect and test valve spring tension, repair as necessary
	• Worn camshaft lobes	• Replace camshaft
	• Air leak into manifold	• Check manifold vacuum and repair as necessary
	• Improper carburetor adjustment	• Adjust carburetor
	• Fuel pump volume or pressure low	• Replace fuel pump
	• Blown cylinder head gasket	• Replace gasket
	• Intake or exhaust manifold passage(s) restricted	• Pass chain through passage(s) and repair as necessary
	• Incorrect trigger wheel installed in distributor	• Install correct trigger wheel

Troubleshooting Engine Performance (cont.)

Problem	Cause	Solution
Power not up to normal	• Incorrect ignition timing	• Adjust timing
	• Faulty distributor rotor	• Replace rotor
	• Trigger wheel loose on shaft	• Reposition or replace trigger wheel
	• Incorrect spark plug gap	• Adjust gap
	• Faulty fuel pump	• Replace fuel pump
	• Incorrect valve timing	• Check valve timing and repair as necessary
	• Faulty ignition coil	• Test coil and replace as necessary
	• Faulty ignition wires	• Test wires and replace as necessary
	• Improperly seated valves	• Test cylinder compression and repair as necessary
	• Blown cylinder head gasket	• Replace gasket
	• Leaking piston rings	• Test compression and repair as necessary
	• Worn distributor shaft	• Replace shaft
	• Improper feedback system operation	• Refer to Chapter 4
Intake backfire	• Improper ignition timing	• Adjust timing
	• Faulty accelerator pump discharge	• Repair as necessary
	• Defective EGR CTO valve	• Replace EGR CTO valve
	• Defective TAC vacuum motor or valve	• Repair as necessary
	• Lean air/fuel mixture	• Check float level or manifold vacuum for air leak. Remove sediment from bowl
Exhaust backfire	• Air leak into manifold vacuum	• Check manifold vacuum and repair as necessary
	• Faulty air injection diverter valve	• Test diverter valve and replace as necessary
	• Exhaust leak	• Locate and eliminate leak
Ping or spark knock	• Incorrect ignition timing	• Adjust timing
	• Distributor centrifugal or vacuum advance malfunction	• Inspect advance mechanism and repair as necessary
	• Excessive combustion chamber deposits	• Remove with combustion chamber cleaner
	• Air leak into manifold vacuum	• Check manifold vacuum and repair as necessary
	• Excessively high compression	• Test compression and repair as necessary
	• Fuel octane rating excessively low	• Try alternate fuel source
	• Sharp edges in combustion chamber	• Grind smooth
	• EGR valve not functioning properly	• Test EGR system and replace as necessary
Surging (at cruising to top speeds)	• Low carburetor fuel level	• Adjust fuel level
	• Low fuel pump pressure or volume	• Replace fuel pump
	• Metering rod(s) not adjusted properly (BBD Model Carburetor)	• Adjust metering rod
	• Improper PCV valve air flow	• Test PCV valve and replace as necessary
	• Air leak into manifold vacuum	• Check manifold vacuum and repair as necessary
	• Incorrect spark advance	• Test and replace as necessary
	• Restricted main jet(s)	• Clean main jet(s)
	• Undersize main jet(s)	• Replace main jet(s)
	• Restricted air vents	• Clean air vents
	• Restricted fuel filter	• Replace fuel filter
	• Restricted air cleaner	• Clean or replace air cleaner filter element
	• EGR valve not functioning properly	• Test EGR system and replace as necessary
	• Improper feedback system operation	• Refer to Chapter 4

Tune-Up Specifications

When analyzing compression test results, look for uniformity among cylinders, rather than specific pressures.

Year	Engine Type	Spark Plugs Type	Gap (in.)	Distributor Point Dwell (deg)	Point Gap (in.)	Ignition Timing (deg) MT	AT	Intake Valve Opens (deg)	Fuel Pump Pressure (psi)	Idle Speed (rpm) MT	AT	Valve Clearance (in.) In	Ex
1970–72	B 20 B	Bosch W200T35 ③	0.030	59–65	②	10B	10B	TDC	1.56–3.55	800	700	0.020–0.022	0.020–0.022
1970–71	B 20 E	Bosch W225T35 ④	0.030	59–65	0.016–0.020	10B	10B	5.5B	28	900	800	0.016–0.018	0.016–0.018
1972–73	B 20 F	⑤	0.030	59–65	0.014 min.	10B	10B	5.5B	28	900	800	0.016–0.018	0.016–0.018
1970–72	B 30 A	Bosch W200T35	0.030	37–43	0.010 min.	10B	10B	TDC	2.1–3.5	800	700	0.020–0.022	0.020–0.022
1972–73	B 30 F	Bosch W200T35	0.030	37–43	0.010 min.	10B	10B	TDC	28	900	800	0.020–0.022	0.020–0.022
1974	B 20 F	Bosch W200T35	0.030	59–65	0.014 min.	10B ①	10B ①	5.5B	71	900	800	0.016–0.018	0.016–0.018
	B 30 F	Bosch W200T35	0.030	37–43	0.010 min.	10B ①	10B ①	TDC	28	900	800	0.020–0.022	0.020–0.022
1975	B 20 F	Bosch W200T35	0.030	Electronic		10B ①	10B ①	5.5B	71	900	800	0.016–0.018	0.016–0.018
	B 30 F	Bosch W200T35	0.030	Electronic		10B ①	10B ①	TDC	28	900	800	0.020–0.022	0.020–0.022
1976	B 21 F	Bosch W175T30	0.030	Electronic		15B ①	15B ①	15B	64–75	900	800	0.014–0.016	0.014–0.016
	B 27 F	Bosch WA200T30 Champ BN9Y	0.026	Electronic		10B ①	10B ①	⑥	64–75	900	900	0.004–0.006	0.010–0.012

Year	Engine	Spark Plug (Bosch)	Gap	Points (Dwell / Gap)	Ign. Timing	Ign. Timing		Compression 64–75	Idle Speed	Idle Speed	Valve Clearance	Valve Clearance
1977	B 21 F	WA175T30	0.030	Electronic	12B ⑧	12B ⑧	—	64–75	900	900	0.014–0.016	0.014–0.016
	B 27 F	WA200T30	0.026	Electronic	10B ⑧	10B ⑧	—	64–75	900	900	0.004–0.006	0.010–0.012
1978	B 21 F	WA175T30	0.030	Electronic	12B ⑧	12B ⑧	—	64–75	900	900	0.014–0.016	0.014–0.016
	B 27 F	WA200T30	0.030	Electronic	10B ⑧	10B ⑧	—	64–75	900	900	0.004–0.006	0.010–0.012
1979	B 21 F	W6DC	0.030	Electronic	10B ⑦⑧	10B ⑦⑧	—	64–75	900	900	0.014–0.016	0.014–0.016
	B 27 F	WA200T30	0.030	Electronic	10B ⑧	10B ⑧	—	64–75	900	900	0.004–0.006	0.010–0.012
1980–'83	B 21 F ⑨	WR7DS	0.030	Electronic	8B ⑧⑩⑪	8B ⑧⑩⑪	—	64–75	950	950	0.014–0.016	0.014–0.016
	B 21 FT (turbo)	WR7DS	0.030	Electronic	12B ⑪⑫	12B ⑪⑫	—	64–75	900	900	0.014–0.016	0.014–0.016
	B 21 A	W7DC	0.030	62 / 0.016–0.018	12B ⑪⑬⑭	12B ⑪⑬⑭	—	64–75	900	900	0.014–0.016	0.014–0.016
	B 23 E	W6DC	0.030	Electronic	10B ⑪⑬	10B ⑪⑬	—	64–75	900	900	0.014–0.016	0.014–0.016
	B 23 F ⑮	WR7DS	0.030	Electronic	12B ⑪⑬	12B ⑪⑬	—	64–75	750	750	0.014–0.016	0.014–0.016
	B 28 F	WR7DS	0.030	Electronic	10B ⑧⑪⑱	10B ⑧⑪⑱	—	64–75	950	950	0.008–0.010	0.012–0.014

B—Before Top Dead Center
① @ 700 rpm
② 1972: 0.014 in.
  1970–71: 0.016–0.020 in.
③ Severe service: W225T35
④ Severe service: W240T1
⑤ 1972: Bosch W225T35
  1973: Bosch W200T35
⑥ Left side: 9B
  Right side: 7B
⑦ Calif: 8B
⑧ 1980–82: @ 700–800 rpm
⑨ Includes Calif. and L-Jetronic models
⑩ 1982 and later: 12°
⑪ Vacuum advance disconnected, A/C turned off
⑫ @ 900 rpm
⑬ @ 750 rpm
⑭ 1982 and later: 7°
⑮ LH-Jetronic injection w/constant idle speed
  and knock sensor
⑯ 1983: 0.026 in.
⑰ 1983: 0.016 in.
⑱ 1983: @ 800 rpm

Diesel Engine Tune-Up Specifications

Year	Model	Engine Displacement cu. in. (cc)	Valve Clearance ① Intake (in.)	Exhaust (in.)	Intake Valve Opens (deg.)	Injection Pump Setting ⑧ (deg.)	Injection Nozzle Pressure (psi) New Used	Idle Speed (rpm)	Cranking Compression Pressure (psi) ⑤
1982	240 GL	145 (2383) D24	0.006–0.010	0.014–0.018	NA	0.0265–0.0295 ②	1845–1700 ③	720–880 ④	340–455
1983	240 DL	145 (2383) D24	0.006–0.010	0.014–0.018	NA	0.0265–0.0295 ②	1845–1700 ③	720–880 ④	340–
	GL	145 (2383) D24	0.006–0.010	0.014–0.018	NA	0.0265–0.0295 ②	1845–1700 ③	720–880 ④	340–455
	760 GLE	145 (2383) D24-Turbo ⑥	0.006–0.010	0.014–0.018	NA	0.0283–0.0315	2318–2062 ⑦	750	313–455
1984	240 Diesel	145 (2383) D24	0.006–0.010	0.014–0.018	NA	0.0265–0.0295 ②	1845–1700 ③	720–880 ④	340–455
	760 GLE	145 (2383) D24-Turbo	0.006–0.010	0.014–0.010	NA	0.0283–0.0315	2318–2062 ⑦	750	313–455
1985	240 Diesel	145 (2383) D24	0.006–0.010	0.014–0.018	NA	0.0265–0.0295 ②	1845–1700 ③	720–880 ④	340–455
	740 TD (S)	145 (2383) D24-Turbo ⑥	0.006–0.010	0.014–0.018	NA	0.0283–0.0315	2318–2062 ⑦	830	313–455
1986	760 GLE TD	145 (2383) D24-Turbo ⑥	0.006–0.010	0.014–0.018	NA	0.0283–0.0315	2318–2062 ⑦	830	313–455
	740 GLE TD	145 (2383) D24-Turbo ⑥	0.006–0.010	0.014–0.018	NA	0.0283–0.0315	2318–2062 ⑦	830	313–455

NOTE: When setting injection timing, distributor plunger stroke must be at Top Dead Center

① Cold
② See text. Acceptable range when checking 0.0287–0.0315 in.
③ Acceptable range. When servicing set to 1775–1920 psi
④ Maximum safe speed: 5100–5200 rpm (high idle)
⑤ Maximum difference between cylinders 115 lbs. psi
⑥ Turbo-Diesel
⑦ Acceptable range. When servicing set to 2205–2318 psi.
⑧ Plunger stroke

Gasoline Engine Tune-Up Specifications

| Year | Model | Engine Displacement cu. in. (cc) | Spark Plugs | | Ignition Timing ③ (deg.) | | Compression Pressure (psi) | Fuel Pump (psi) | Idle Speed (rpm) | | Valve Clearance | |
			Type	Gap (in.)	MT	AT			MT	AT	In.	Ex.
1984	240 DL	140 (2320) B23F	WR7DS	0.030	12B ④	12B ④	NA	64–75	750	750	0.014–0.016	0.014–0.016
	DL	130 (2127) B21A ①	W7DC	0.030	12B ④	12B ④	NA	64–75	900	900	0.014–0.016	0.014–0.016
	GL	140 (2320) B23F	WR7DS	0.030	12B ④	12B ④	NA	64–75	750	750	0.014–0.016	0.014–0.016
	GLE	140 (2320) B23F ①	WR7DS	0.030	12B ④	12B ④	NA	64–75	750	750	0.014–0.016	0.014–0.016
	Turbo	130 (2127) B21F-Turbo	WR7DS	0.030	12B ⑤	12B ⑤	NA	64–75	900	900	0.014–0.016	0.014–0.016
	760 GLE	174 (2849) B28F	WR6DS	0.026	23B ⑦	23B ⑦	NA	64–75	750	750	0.004–0.006	0.010–0.012
	Turbo	140 (2320) B23F-Turbo	WR7DC	0.026	12B ④	12B ④	NA	64–75	750	750	0.014–0.016	0.014–0.016
1985	240 DL	140 (2320) B230F	WR7DC	0.030	12B ④	12B ④	NA	36	750	750	0.014–0.016	0.014–0.016
	GL	140 (2320) B230F	WR7DC	0.030	12B ④	12B ④	NA	36	750	750	0.014–0.016	0.014–0.016
	Turbo	130 (2127) B21F-Turbo	WR7DS	0.030	12B ④	12B ④	NA	64–75	900	900	0.014–0.016	0.014–0.016
	740 GLE	140 (2320) B230F	WR7DC	0.030	12B ④	12B ④	NA	36	750	750	0.014–0.016	0.014–0.016
	Turbo	140 (2320) B230F-Turbo	WR7DC	0.026	12B ④	12B ④	NA	43	750	750	0.014–0.016	0.014–0.016
	760 GLE	174 (2849) B28F	HR6DC	0.026	23B ⑦	23B ⑦	NA	64–75	750	750	0.004–0.006	0.010–0.012
	Turbo	140 (2320) B230F-Turbo	WR7DC	0.026	12B ④	12B ④	NA	43	750	750	0.014–0.016	0.014–0.016
1986	240 DL	140 (2320) B230F	WR7DC	0.030	12B ④	12B ④	NA	36	750	750	0.014–0.016	0.014–0.016
	GL	140 (2320) B230F	WR7DC	0.030	12B ④	12B ④	NA	36	750	750	0.014–0.016	0.014–0.016
	740 GL	140 (2320) B230F	WR7DC	0.030	12B ④	12B ④	NA	36	750	750	0.014–0.016	0.014–0.016
	GLE	140 (2320) B230F	WR7DC	0.030	12B ④	12B ④	NA	36	750	750	0.014–0.016	0.014–0.016
	Turbo	140 (2320) B230F-Turbo	WR7DC	0.026	12B ④	12B ④	NA	43	750	750	0.014–0.016	0.014–0.016
	760 GLE	174 (2849) B28F	HR6DC	0.026	23B ⑦	23B ⑦	NA	64–75	750	750	0.004–0.006	0.010–0.012
	Turbo	140 (2320) B230F-Turbo	WR7DC	0.026	12B ④	12B ④	NA	43	750	750	0.014–0.016	0.014–0.016
1987	240 DL	140 (2320) B230F	WR7DC	0.030	12B ④	12B ④	NA	36	750	750	0.014–0.016	0.014–0.016
	GL	140 (2320) B230F	WR7DC	0.030	12B ④	12B ④	NA	36	750	750	0.014–0.016	0.014–0.016
	740 GL	140 (2320) B230F	WR7DC	0.030	12B ④	12B ④	NA	36	750	750	0.014–0.016	0.014–0.016

Gasoline Engine Tune-Up Specifications (cont.)

| Year | Model | Engine Displacement cu. in. (cc) | Spark Plugs | | Ignition Timing ③ (deg.) | | Compression Pressure (psi) | Fuel Pump (psi) | Idle Speed (rpm) | | Valve Clearance | |
			Type	Gap (in.)	MT	AT			MT	AT	In.	Ex.
1987	GLE	140 (2320) B230F	WR7DC	0.030	12B ④	12B ④	NA	36	750	750	0.014–0.016	0.014–0.016
	Turbo	140 (2320) B230F-Turbo	WR7DC	0.026	12B ④	12B ④	NA	43	750	750	0.014–0.016	0.014–0.016
	760 GLE	174 (2849) B280F	HR6DC	0.026	16B ④	16B ④	NA	35	750	750	0.004–0.006	0.010–0.012
	Turbo	140 (2320) B230F-Turbo	WR7DC	0.026	12B ④	12B ④	NA	43	750	750	0.014–0.016	0.014–0.016
	780 780	174 (2849) B280F	HR6DC	0.026	16B ④	16B ④	NA	35	750	750	0.004–0.006	0.010–0.012
1988	240 DL	140 (2320) B230F	WR7DC	0.030	12B ④	12B ④	NA	36	750	750	0.014–0.016	0.014–0.016
	GL	140 (2320) B230F	WR7DC	0.030	12B ④	12B ④	NA	36	750	750	0.014–0.016	0.014–0.016
	740 GL	140 (2320) B230F	WR7DC	0.030	12B ④	12B ④	NA	36	750	750	0.014–0.016	0.014–0.016
	GLE	140 (2320) B230F	WR7DC	0.030	12B ④	12B ④	NA	36	750	750	0.014–0.016	0.014–0.016
	Turbo	140 (2320) B230F-Turbo	WR7DC	0.026	12B ④	12B ④	NA	43	750	750	0.014–0.016	0.014–0.016
	760 GLE	174 (2849) B280F	HR6DC	0.026	16B ④	16B ④	NA	35	750	750	0.004–0.006	0.010–0.012
	Turbo	140 (2320) B230F-Turbo	WR7DC	0.026	12B ④	12B ④	NA	43	750	750	0.014–0.016	0.014–0.016
	780 780	174 (2849) B280F	HR6DC	0.026	16B ④	16B ④	NA	35	750	750	0.004–0.006	0.010–0.012
1989	ALL	SEE UNDERHOOD SPECIFICATIONS STICKER										

NOTE: Some models are equipped with the Constant Idle Speed system (CIS) and cannot be adjusted.
① Canada only
② Station Wagon
③ Vacuum advance disconnected, A/C turned off
④ @ 750 rpm
⑤ @ 900 rpm
⑥ @ 800 rpm
⑦ @ 2500 rpm

chamber temperatures are affected by many factors such as compression ratio of the engine, air/fuel mixtures, exhaust emission equipment and the type of driving you do. Spark plugs are designed and classified by number according to the heat range at which they will operate most efficiently.

SPARK PLUG HEAT RANGE

While spark plug heat range has always seemed to be somewhat of a mystical subject for many people, in reality the subject is quite simple. Basically, it boils down to this; the amount of heat the plug absorbs is determined by the length of the lower insulator. The longer the insulator (or the farther it extends into the engine), the hotter the plug will operate. A shorter insulator operates cooler.

A plug that absorbs little heat and remains too cool will quickly accumulate deposits of oil and carbon since it is not hot enough to burn them off. This leads to plug fouling and consequently to misfiring. A plug that absorbs too much heat will have no deposits, but, due to the excessive heat, the electrodes will burn away quickly and in some instances, preignition

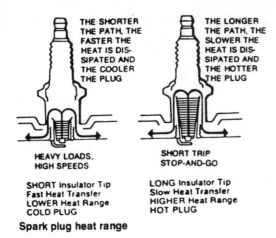

THE SHORTER THE PATH, THE FASTER THE HEAT IS DISSIPATED AND THE COOLER THE PLUG

THE LONGER THE PATH, THE SLOWER THE HEAT IS DISSIPATED AND THE HOTTER THE PLUG

HEAVY LOADS, HIGH SPEEDS

SHORT TRIP STOP-AND-GO

SHORT Insulator Tip
Fast Heat Transfer
LOWER Heat Range
COLD PLUG

LONG Insulator Tip
Slow Heat Transfer
HIGHER Heat Range
HOT PLUG

Spark plug heat range

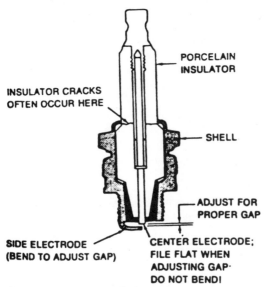

PORCELAIN INSULATOR

INSULATOR CRACKS OFTEN OCCUR HERE

SHELL

SIDE ELECTRODE (BEND TO ADJUST GAP)

ADJUST FOR PROPER GAP

CENTER ELECTRODE; FILE FLAT WHEN ADJUSTING GAP. DO NOT BEND!

Cross section of a spark plug

("ping") may result. Preignition takes place when plug tips get so hot that they glow sufficiently to ignite the fuel/air mixture before the actual spark occurs.

This early ignition will usually cause a pinging during low speed operation or under heavy loads such as accelerating up a hill. In severe cases, the heat may become high enough to start the fuel/air mixture burning throughout the cylinder, rather than just in front of the plug as is normal. The burning mass is compressed and a premature explosion results, forcing the piston back down in the cylinder while it is still trying to go up. Obviously, this is not a healthy situation for the piston--quite frequently pistons are severely damaged. For this reason, severe or continuous preignition (pinging) should never be ignored.

The general rule of thumb for choosing the correct spark plug heat range is that if most of your driving is long distance or high speed trav-

el, use a colder plug; if most of your driving is stop and go, or low speed travel, use a hotter plug. Factory-installed plugs are, of course, a compromise, since the factory has no way of knowing what sort of driving you do. It should be noted that most people never have occasion to change their plugs from the factory-recommended heat range. If you wish to use an alternate plug, consult the emissions label under the hood of cars from 1978 to the present; it will give you the recommended standard plug and the recommended alternate (generally colder) plug description.

REMOVAL AND INSTALLATION

Every six months or 6,000 miles, the spark plugs should be removed for inspection on older cars. At this time they should be cleaned and regapped. At 12 month or 12,000 mile intervals on 1973-74 models and at 15,000 mile intervals on 1975 and later models, the plugs should be replaced. Although Volvo recommends replacing the plugs at 30,000 miles on 1984 and later vehicles, it should be noted that this is a maximum interval. For some owners, 30,000 miles represents more than three years of driving. A prudent owner will remove and check or replace the plugs more frequently. Even if they are not heavily worn, a new set will improve performance.

NOTE: *Remove and install spark plugs only when the engine is cold; this is particularly important on engines with aluminum heads.*

Remove each spark plug wire by grasping its rubber boot at the end and twisting slightly to free the wire from the plug. Using a spark plug socket, turn the plugs counterclockwise to remove them. Do not allow any foreign matter to enter the cylinders through the spark plugs holes.

The gap must be checked with a wire gauge before installing the plug in the engine. With the ground electrode positioned parallel to the center electrode, the specified wire gauge must pass through the opening with a slight drag. If the air gap between the two electrodes is not correct, the ground electrode must be bent to bring it to specifications.

After the plugs are gapped correctly, they may be inserted into their holes and hand-tightened. Be careful not to crossthread the plugs. After each plug is hand threaded several turns, it may be tightened with the wrench: DO NOT OVERTIGHTEN SPARK PLUGS. Correct torque is 15-18 ft. lbs except B28 and B280 engines which require only 9 ft. lbs. Overtightening a $2.00 spark plug can cost you three hundred times as much if you damage the cylinder head. Install each spark plug wire on

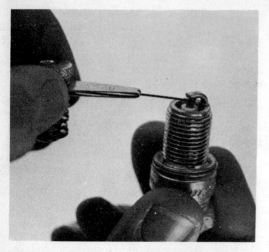

Measure spark plug gap with a wire gauge

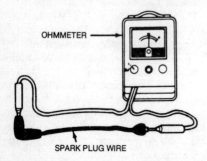

Check spark plug cable resistance with an ohmmeter. Remember, the longer the wire, the more the resistance will be

its respective plug, making sure that each spark plug end is making good metal-to-metal contact in its wire socket.

SPARK PLUG ANALYSIS

Refer to the four-color "Tune-Up Tips" section in the center of this book to diagnose your spark plugs' firing characteristics.

CHECKING AND REPLACING SPARK PLUG WIRES

Visually inspect the spark plug cables for burns, cuts, or breaks in the insulation. Check the spark plug boots and the nipples on the distributor cap and coil. Replace any damaged wiring. If no physical damage is obvious, the wires can be checked with an ohmmeter for excessive resistance. Remove the distributor cap and leave the wires connected to the cap. Connect one lead of the ohmmeter to the corresponding electrode inside the cap and the other lead to the spark plug terminal (remove it from the spark plug for the test). Replace any wire which

shows over 50,000 ohms. Generally speaking, resistance should not run over 35,000 ohms and 50,000 ohms should be considered the outer limits of acceptability.

Test the coil wire by connecting the ohmmeter between the center contact in the cap and either of the primary terminals at the coil. If the total resistance of the coil and cable is more than 25,000 ohms, remove the cable from the coil and check the resistance of the cable alone. If the resistance is higher than 15,000 ohms, replace the cable. It should be remembered that wire resistance is a function of length, and that the longer the cable, the greater the resistance. Thus, if the cables on your car are longer than the factory originals, resistance will be higher and quite possibly outside of these limits.

When installing a new set of spark plug cables, replace the cables one at a time so there will be no mixup. Start by replacing the longest cable first. Install the boot firmly over the spark plug. Route the wire exactly the same as the original. Insert the nipple firmly into the tower on the distributor cap. Repeat the process for each cable.

Firing Orders

NOTE: *To avoid confusion when replacing wires, remove and tag them one at a time.*

FIRING ORDER

1 - 3 - 4 - 2

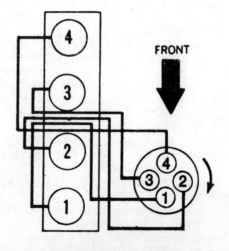

B21F, B23 and B230 series

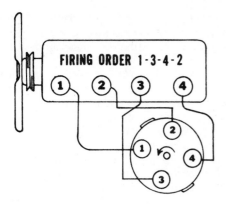

B20 engine

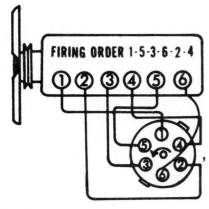

B30 engine

FIRING ORDER
1-6-3-5-2-4

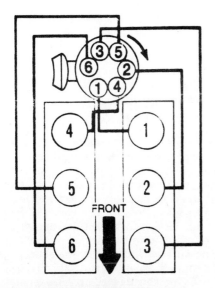

B27, B28 and BZ80 series engines

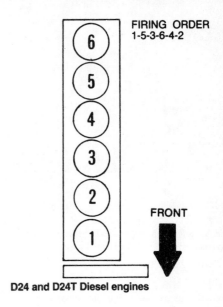

FIRING ORDER
1-5-3-6-4-2

FRONT

D24 and D24T Diesel engines

Breaker Points and Condenser

REPLACEMENT

1970-74 Models and Canadian B21A engine

Volvo recommends that the breaker points be inspected and adjusted every six months or 6,000 miles. If, upon inspection, the points prove to be faulty, they must be replaced with the condenser as unit.

CAUTION: *Make sure the ignition is off.*

Remove the distributor cap and rotor from the top of the distributor, taking note of their placement. On fuel-injected six cylinder models, remove the breaker point protective cover. Place a screwdriver against the breaker points and examine the condition of the contacts. Replace the points if the contacts are blackened, pitted, or worn excessively, if the breaker arm has lost its tension, or if the fiber rubbing block on the breaker has become worn or loose. Contact points that have become slightly burned (light gray) may be cleaned with a point file.

To replace the points and condenser, disconnect the electrical leads for both at the primary connection. Remove the lockscrew for the contact breakers and lift them straight up. Loosen the condenser bracket retaining screw and slide out the condenser. While the points are out, lubricate the breaker cam with a very light coating of silicone-based grease. Clean the distributor base plate with alcohol to free it of any oil film that might impede completion of the ground circuit. Also clean the contact point surfaces with the solvent. Install the new points and new condenser and tighten their retaining screws. Connect the electrical leads for both at the primary connection. Make sure that the point contacts are aligned horizontally and ver-

Circle indicates recess for adjusting the contact points on breaker point distributors

tically. If the points are not aligned properly, bend the stationary arm as necessary.

The breaker points must be correctly gapped before proceeding any further. Turn the engine until the rubbing block on the point assembly is resting on the high point of the distributor cam. Loosen the holddown screw lightly and insert a feeler gauge of the proper thickness between the point contacts. Fine adjustment is made by inserting a screwdrive into the adjusting recess and turning the screwdriver until the proper size feeler gauge passes between the point contacts with a slight drag. Without disturbing the setting, tighten the breaker point retaining screw.

If a dwell meter is available, proceed to "Dwell Angle Adjustment". A dwell meter is considered a more accurate means of measuring point gap. If the meter is not available, except on fuel-injected six cylinder models, proceed to replace the rotor on top of the distributor shaft, making sure that the tab inside the rotor aligns with the slot on the distributor. Before replacing the rotor on fuel-injected six cylinder models, install the breaker point protective cover. Place the distributor cap on top of the distributor, make sure it is properly seated, and snap the cap clasps into the slots on the cap. Make sure that all the spark plug wires fit snugly into the cap. Proceed to "Ignition Timing Adjustment".

DWELL ANGLE

NOTE: *It is not possible to set the dwell on electronic ignition systems, although it is possible to measure it.*

Adjustment

1970-74 Models and Canadian B21A

The dwell angle is the number of degrees of distributor cam rotation through which the

breaker points remain fully closed (conducting electricity). Increasing the point gap decreases dwell, while decreasing the point gap increases dwell.

Using a dwell meter, connect the red lead (positive) of the meter to the distributor primary wire connection on the positive (+) side of the coil, and the black lead (negative) wire of the meter to a good ground on the engine (e.g. thermostat housing nut).

The dwell angle may be checked either with the distributor cap and rotor installed and the engine running, or with the cap and rotor removed and the engine cranking at starter speed. The meter gives a constant reading with the engine running. With the engine cranking, the reading will fluctuate between zero degrees dwell and the maximum figure for that angle. While cranking, the maximum figure is the correct one for that setting. Never attempt to change dwell angle while the ignition is on. Touching the point contacts or primary wire connection with a metal screwdriver may result in a 12 volt shock.

To change the dwell angle, loosen the point retaining screw slightly and make the approximate correction. Tighten the retaining screw and test the dwell with the engine cranking. If the dwell appears to be correct, install the breaker point protective cover, if so equipped, the rotor and distributor cap, and test the dwell with the engine running. Take the engine through its entire rpm range and observe the dwell meter. The dwell should remain within specifications at all times. Great fluctuation of dwell at different engine speeds indicates worn distributor parts.

Following the dwell angle adjustment, the ignition timing must be checked. A 1° increase in dwell results in the ignition timing being retarded 2° and vice versa.

Electronic Ignition
1975 AND LATER MODELS

There are two major differences from the point type systems: First, the points and condenser are replaced by an induction type impulse sender. Second, an electronic module has been added to amplify the electrical impulses between the distributor and coil. The impulse sender is located inside the distributor where the points used to be. Instead of opening and closing an electrical circuit, the sender opens and closes a magnetic circuit. This induces impulses in a magnetic pick-up. The sender consists of a stator, pick-up, rotor, and permanent

1. Distributor cap
2. Distributor arm
3. Contact breaker
4. Lock screw for breaker contacts
5. Lubricating felt
6. Vacuum regulator
7. Distributor housing
8. Cap clamp
9. Rubber seal
10. Fibre washer
11. Steel washer
12. Lock pin
13. Spring ring
14. Flange
15. Lubricator

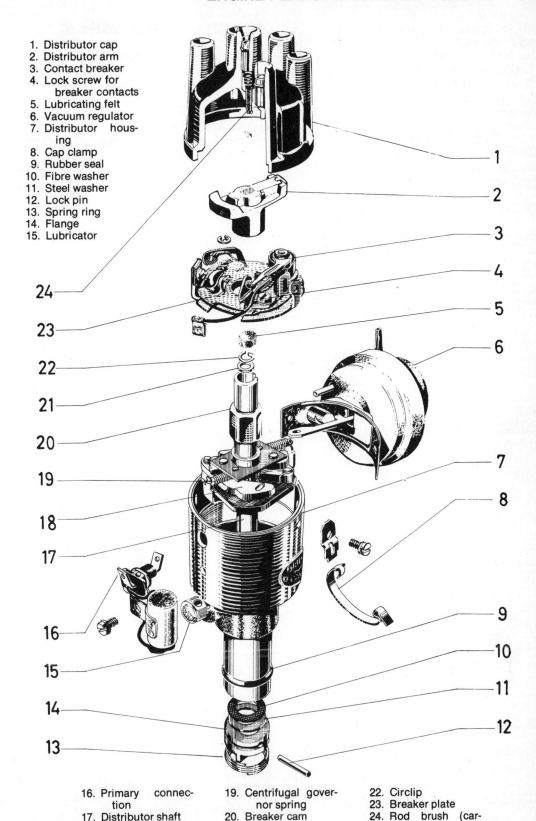

16. Primary connection	19. Centrifugal governor spring	22. Circlip
17. Distributor shaft	20. Breaker cam	23. Breaker plate
18. Centrifugal weight	21. Washer	24. Rod brush (carbon)

Breaker point distributor—six cylinder shown

magnet. The stator and armature each have the same number of teeth as there are cylinders. The permanent magnet creates a magnetic field which goes through the stator. The circuit is closed when the teeth are opposite each other. This means that the rotor opens and closes the magnetic field while rotating. This generates current pulses in the magnetic pick-up.

The electronic module is a solid state design which is fully transistorized. It amplifies the impulses from the sender and controls the dwell angle.

REPLACING THE IMPULSE SENDER

1. Unsnap the lock clasps.
2. Remove the cap, rotor and dust cover.
3. Remove the vacuum advance unit and the cap holddown clips.
4. Remove the screw securing the contact and pull the contact straight out.
5. Remove the impulse sender plate screws.
6. Remove the snap ring and shims and pull the rotor straight off along with the small lock pin.

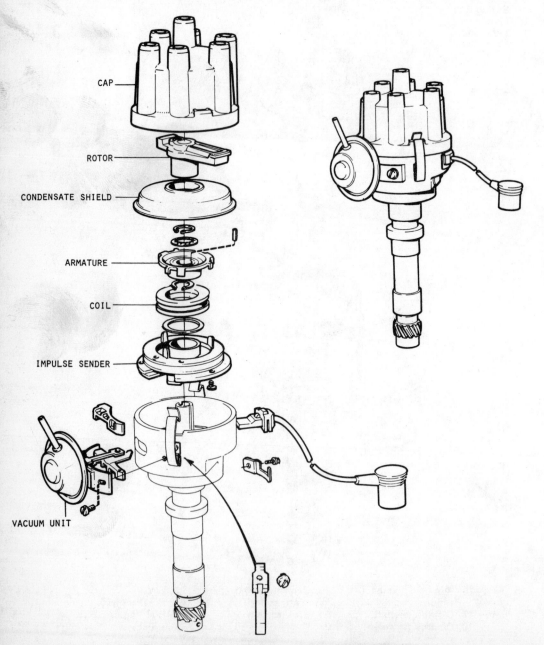

Electronic ignition distributor—six cylinder engine

7. Remove the snap ring holding the sender and lift off the sender and plate.

8. Install the new sender, making sure that the snap ring is properly seated.

9. Continue reassembling in reverse order, noting that the screws for the vacuum unit and the holddown clips are different lengths. When attaching the new sender to the plate, the connector pins should be directly opposite and above the attachment ear on the plate. When installation is complete, rotate the shaft several times to make sure there is no noise or binding.

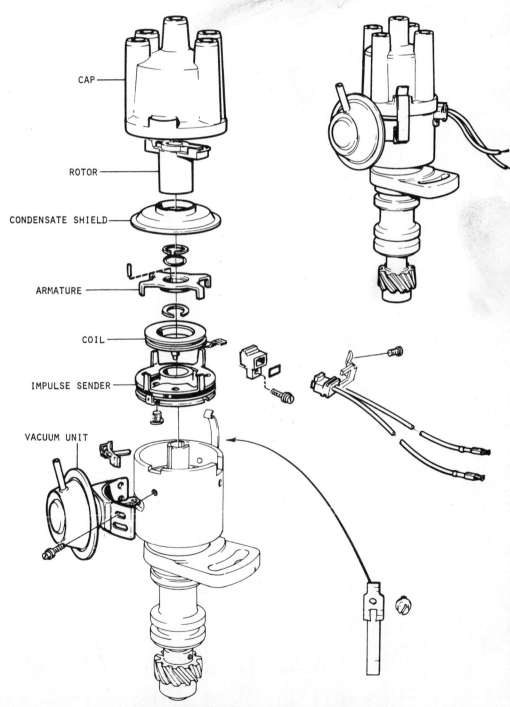

CAP

ROTOR

CONDENSATE SHIELD

ARMATURE

COIL

IMPULSE SENDER

VACUUM UNIT

Electronic ignition distributor—four cylinder engine

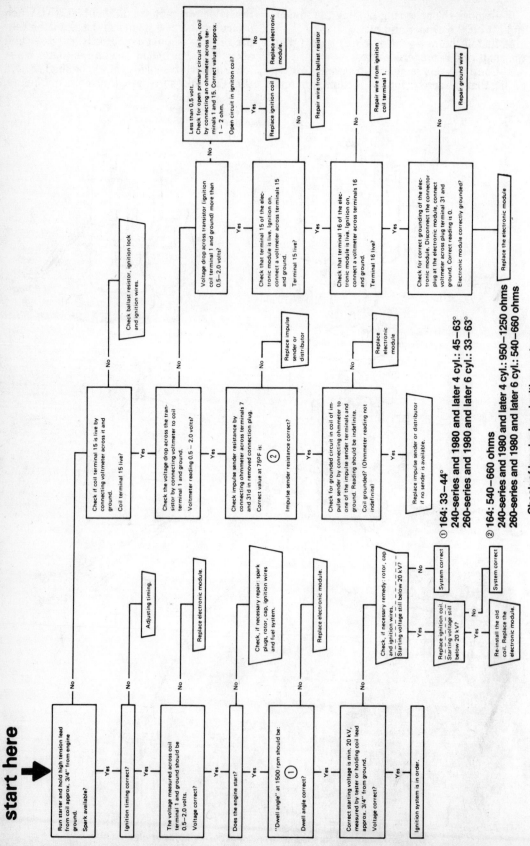

Check of breakerless ignition system

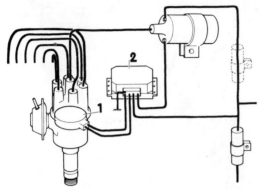

Electronic ignition system: "1" impulse sender, "2" electronic module

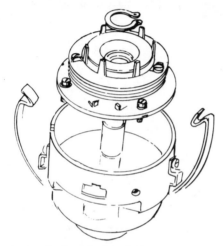

Replacing the impulse sender

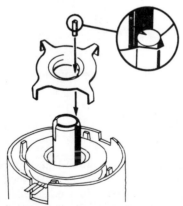

When installing the trigger wheel, the split pin must fit in the notch on the distributor shaft

Ignition Timing Adjustment
GASOLINE ENGINES

Volvo recommends that the ignition timing be checked every 6,000 miles (1970-74), 15,000 miles (1975-1983), and 30,000 miles (1984-89).

The timing adjustment should always follow a breaker point gap and/or dwell angle adjustment (1970-74 models only), and be made with the engine at operating temperature.

Clean the crankshaft damper and pointer on the water pump housing with a solvent-soaked rag so that the marks can be seen. Connect a timing light according to the manufacturer's instructions. Reinforce the marks on the crankshaft damper and on the pointer with chalk or luminescent (day-glo) paint to highlight the correct timing position. Disconnect and plug the distributor vacuum line (all models) and also disconnect the hose between the air cleaner and the inlet duct at the duct (electronic fuel injected only). Disconnect and plug the vacuum hose at the EGR valve (1973-74 models only). Disconnect and plug the hose from the AIR pump on 1976-77 models so equipped.

Attach a tachometer to the engine and set the idle speed to specifications. With the engine running, aim the timing light at the pointer and the marks on the damper. If the marks do not coincide, stop the engine, loosen the distributor

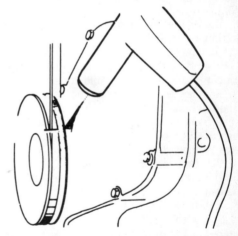

Aim a timing light at the pointer and the marks on the damper

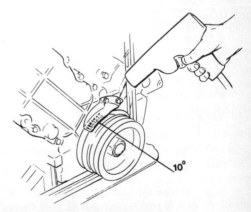

B27F, B28F engine timing marks

pinch bolt, and start the engine again. While observing the timing light flashes on the markers, grasp the distributor vacuum regulator and rotate the distributor until the marks do coincide. Stop the engine and tighten the distributor pinch bolt, taking care not to disturb the setting.

CAUTION: *Do not grasp the distributor cap or wires! You may receive a nasty, high-voltage shock.*

Reconnect all disconnected hoses and remove the timing light and tachometer leads from the engine.

DIESEL ENGINES

WARNING: *The use of the correct special tools or their equivalent is REQUIRED for this procedure.*

1. Remove the rear timing gear cover and disconnect the cold-start device. Loosen the forward screw on the cold-start device control lever, press the lever back toward the stop.

NOTE: *Do not loosen the screw closest to the timing belt.*

2. Rotate the engine to align the mark on the injection gear with the mark on the pump bracket. The "0" mark on the flywheel should be centered at the timing mark window and with No. 1 cylinder at top dead center.

3. Remove the plug from the rear of the pump and install the Volvo dial indicator adapter No. 5194 or equivalent, with a measuring range of 0-0.1 in. (0-3mm). Set the indicator gauge at approximately 0.08 in. (2mm).

4. Rotate the engine slowly counterclockwise until the lowest reading on the dial indicator is observed, then re-set the dial indicator to zero.

5. Rotate the engine slowly in the clockwise direction until the "0" mark on the flywheel is centered at the timing mark window. The dial indicator should read within the specified range.

NOTE: *When the engine is turned past the timing mark, turn the engine back a ¼ of a turn. Rotate the engine in the clockwise direction until the "0" mark on the flywheel is centered in the timing mark window.*

6. If the dial indicator setting is outside the specified range, loosen the pump bolts and turn the pump until the dial indicator shows the correct setting. Then re-tighten the pump bolts.

7. Crank the engine over by hand two revolutions and re-check the injection pump timing. If it is still out of specifications readjust as necessary.

8. Remove the dial indicator and adapter, re-install the rear plug and rear timing gear cover, then reconnect the cold start device.

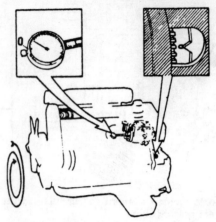

D24 and D24T injection pump timing check

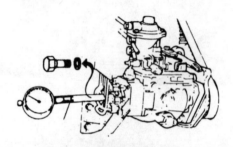

Installing the dial indicator

Setting the injection pump

Valve Lash
ADJUSTMENT

The recommended maintenance interval for valve clearance adjustment is 12 months or 12,000 miles on 1970-74 models and 15,000 miles on 1975-76 models. 1984-86 gasoline engines require valve adjustment at 30,000 miles (diesels, 15,000 miles) and 1987-89 gasoline engines require inspection and adjustment at 60,000 miles. The clearance may be checked with the engine hot or cold.

Remove the valve cover and crank the engine until number one cylinder is at Top Dead Center (TDC). TDC is the point at which both intake and exhaust valves are fully closed and the piston is on its compression stroke. To find

TDC, crank the engine, preferably with a remote starter switch, until the pushrods for both valves on the subject cylinder stop rising (both valves closed). Stop cranking the engine. At this point, it will be easier to find TDC by turning the engine over manually. To accomplish this, remove all of the spark plugs so the compression and resistance to cranking are diminished, and remove the distributor cap so the position of the rotor may be observed. To crank the engine manually, position a socket or closed-end wrench--with a long handle for greater leverage--on the crankshaft damper bolt and turn the crankshaft in the required direction.

WARNING: *Do not attempt to crank the engine by grasping the viscous-drive fan as damage to the fan may result.*

At TDC, the piston for the subject cylinder should be at its highest point of travel. Make a visual check or insert a screwdriver through the spark plug hole to make sure that the piston is no longer traveling upward. As an additional check, the distributor rotor should be pointed to the spark plug wire for the subject cylinder at TDC.

Number one cylinder is at TDC when the 0 degree mark on the crankshaft damper aligns with the pointer on the water pump housing. On four-cylinder models, with number one cylinder at TDC, valves (counting from the front) 1,2,3, and 5 may be adjusted. On six-cylinder models, with number one cylinder at TDC, valves 1,2,3,6,7, and 10 may be adjusted.

B20 and B30 Engines

Insert a feeler gauge of the specified thickness between the rocker arm and the valve stem. Adjustment is accomplished by loosening the locknut and turning the adjusting screw

Adjusting the valve clearance—B20, B30 engines

and then, without disturbing the adjustment, retightening the locknut.

The remainder of the valves may be adjusted in the following manner. On four-cylinder models, with no. 4 cylinder at TDC, valves (counting form the front) 4,6,7, and 8 may be adjusted. On six-cylinder models, with no. 6 cylinder at TDC, valves 4,5,8,9,11, and 12 may be adjusted.

B21,B23, B230 and B234 Engines

NOTE: *The B234 16-valve engine has self adjusting valves and hydraulic tappets. They cannot be adjusted during routine maintenance.*

Valve clearance is checked every 15,000 miles. If it is necessary to adjust valve clearance, you will need three special tools: first, a valve tappet depressor tool used to push down the tappet sufficiently to remove the adjusting disc (Volvo tool #999 5022); second, specially shaped pliers to actually remove and install the valve adjusting disc (Volvo tool #999 5026); and third, a set of varying-thickness valve adjusting discs(sometimes called shims) to make the necessary corrections. We've included pictures of these special tools so that you might be able to find a suitable substitute.

WARNING: *The use of the correct special tools or their equivalent is REQUIRED for this procedure.*

The procedure for checking, and, if necessary, adjusting the valves is as follows:

1. Remove the valve cover. Scribe and number chalkmarks on the distributor body indicating each of the four spark plug wire leads in the cap. Remove the distributor cap.

2. Crank over the engine with a remote starter switch or with a wrench on the crankshaft pulley center bolt (22mm hex) until the engine is in the firing position for no. 1 cylinder. At this point, the 0 degree or TDC mark on the crankshaft pulley is aligned with the timing pointer, the rotor is pointing at the no. 1 spark plug wire cap position, and the cam shaft lobes for no. 1 cylinder are pointing at the 10 o'clock and 2 o'clock positions.

At this point, the clearance between the rocker arm and valve depressor (tappet) may be checked for the intake and exhaust valves of cylinder no. 1, using a feeler gauge. When checking clearance, the wear limit is 0.010-0.018 in. (0.25–0.45mm) for a cold engine, and 0.012-0.020 in. (0.30–0.50mm) for a hot one — above 176°F (80°C).

3. Repeat step 2 for cylinders 3,4, and 2 (in that order). Each time, rotate the crankshaft pulley 180° so that the rotor is pointing to the spark plug wire cap position for the cylinder, and the cam lobes are pointing at the 10 and 12 o'clock positions for the valves of that cylinder.

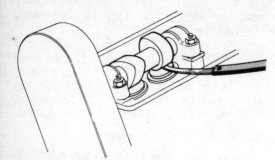

Measuring valve clearance—B21 and B23 engines. Note the position of the camshaft lobes for no. 1 cylinder: they are in the correct position for checking the clearance

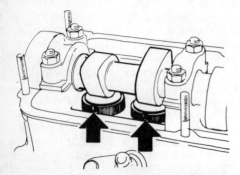

To adjust valve clearances, first rotate the valve depressors (tappets) until their notches are at right angles to the engine center line—B21 and B23 engines

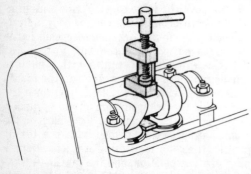

Adjusting valve clearances, B21 and B23 series engines—attach valve depressor tool to the camshaft and screw down

4. If any of the valve clearance measurements are outside the wear limit, you will have to remove the old valve adjusting disc and install a new one to bring the clearance within specifications. First, rotate the valve depressors (tappets) until their notches are at a right angle to the engine center line. Attach valve depressor tool 999 5022 to the camshaft and screw down the tool spindle until the depressor (tappet) groove is just above the edge of its bore and still accessible with the special pliers (tool no. 999 5026).

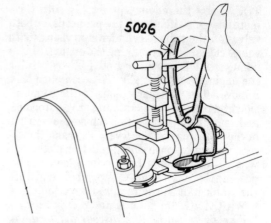

Remove the adjusting disc with special pliers

5. Remove the valve adjusting disc and measure with a micrometer. Once you've gone to all this trouble, the valve clearance should be set to these tolerances: 0.014-0.016 in. (0.35–0.40mm) for a cold engine, and 0.016-0.018 in. (0.40–0.45mm) for a hot one. So, if the measured clearance had been 0.019 in. (0.48mm) and the desired clearance 0.016 in. (0.40mm), for a net difference of 0.003 in. (0.08mm), then the new valve adjusting disc should be 0.003 in. (0.08mm) thicker than the old one to take up the clearance.

Valve adjusting discs are available from Volvo in sizes from 0.35mm to 0.45mm (in 0.05mm increments). Always oil the new disc and install it with the marks facing down.

6. Remove the valve tappet depressor tool. Rotate the engine a few times and recheck clearance. Install the valve cover with a new gasket. Volvo does not recommend the use of any sealer on its gaskets.

B27, B28 and B280 Engines

Valve clearance is checked every 15,000 miles. No special tools are required.

1. In order to gain access to the valve covers, disconnect or remove the following:

    a. Air conditioning compressor from bracket (do not disconnect refrigerant hoses)

    b. EGR valve and hoses

    c. Air conditioning compressor bracket

    d. Fuel injection control pressure regulator

    e. Air pump

    f. Vacuum pump

    g. Hoses and wires from solenoid valve (Calif. only)

2. Using a 36mm hex socket on the crankshaft pulley bolt, rotate the crankshaft to the no.1 cylinder TDC position. At this point the "O" mark on the timing plate aligns with the crankshaft pulley notch, the distributor rotor is

pointing to the no.1 cylinder spark plug wire cap position, and both valves for no. 1 cylinder have clearance. Be careful, these engines have two notches: one for No. 1 cylinder TDC and one for No. 6 cylinder TDC.

At this position, adjust the intake valves of cylinders no. 1, 2, and 4, and the exhaust valves of cylinders no. 1, 3 and 6. Insert a feeler gauge between the rocker arm and valve stem. Loosen the locknut and turn the adjusting screw in the required direction. Tighten the locknut and re-check clearance. Clearances are given in the Tune-Up chart in this chapter.

3. Rotate the crankshaft pulley one full 360° turn to adjust the remaining valves. At this point, the "O" mark will again align with the pulley notch, the rotor is pointing 180° opposite to its former position, and the no. 1 cylinder rockers contact the ramps of the camshaft. At this position (see illustration), adjust the intake valves of cylinders no. 3, 5 and 6, and the exhaust valves of cylinders no. 2, 4, and 5.

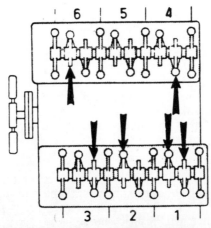

Adjusting the valve clearances—B27, B28 engines

On B27, B28, with no. 1 cylinder at TDC compression stroke, adjust these valves (arrows)

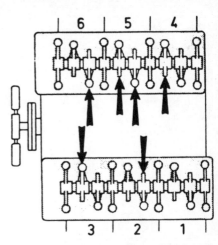

On B27, B28, turn the engine crankshaft 360° and adjust remaining valves (arrows)

4. Install the valve covers with new gaskets. Connect all disconnected equipment, taking care that all lines and hoses are attached to the correct ports and not pinched or kinked. Check also that the compressor bolts are secure and that the belt is properly adjusted for tension.

D24 and D24T engines

WARNING: *The use of the correct special tools or their equivalent is REQUIRED for this procedure.*

Always check valve clearances with the cylinder at TDC; turn the engine ¼ turn past TDC to set valves.

1. Remove the valve cover.

2. Use a 17mm socket on the crankshaft pulley. Turn the pulley until the engine is ready to fire on the No. 1 cylinder. The flywheel timing mark should be at zero.

NOTE: *The piston should be at ¼ turn past top dead center when setting the valve clearance.*

3. Line up the valve depressors.

4. Turn them so that the notches point slightly upward.

NOTE: *Use tool No. 5196 or equivalent to depress the valve depressors. This tool is available from your Volvo dealer.*

5. The depressor grooves must be above the face so that the disc can be gripped with pliers. These pliers are available from your Volvo dealer under part No. 5195.

6. Remove the disc.

7. Calculate the disc thickness, using a micrometer. The discs are available in thicknesses of 0.33–0.43mm with increments of 0.05mm.

8. Cold engine: 0.02mm − intake
              0.04mm − exhaust.
Warm engine: 0.025mm − intake
              0.045mm − exhaust.

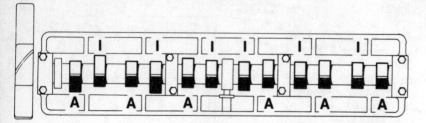

Diesel engine intake and exhaust valve layout

I = intake valve
A = exhaust valve

Diesel engine—adjusting the valves. The camshaft lobes must be positioned as shown with the piston on TDC before checking the valve lash

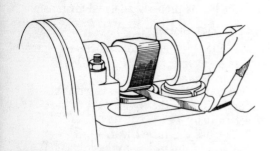

Diesel engine—checking the valve lash with a flat bladed feeler gauge

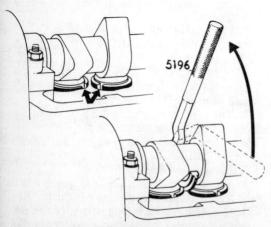

When actually adjusting the valves, turn the engine ¼ turn past TDC, align the notches in the valve depressors as shown and using the special tool, depress the valves

NOTE: *Always use new discs when performing this procedure.*

9. Oil the new disc and install it with the marked side down.

10. Check the remaining valve clearances.

11. Use the following sequence 1, 5, 3, 6, 2, 4.

12. Recheck the valve clearance for all cylinders.

13. Rotate the engine several times, and recheck the clearance.

14. Install the valve cover with a new gasket.

Carburetor

IDLE SPEED AND MIXTURE ADJUSTMENTS

Zenith-Stromberg 175 CD 2SE

1. Check the oil level in the damper cylinders. Top up as necessary as outlined in chapter one.

2. Run the engine until it has reached full operating temperature. A good way to check this is to feel the upper radiator hose. When the engine reaches operating temperature, the thermostat opens and fills the upper radiator hose with 180° coolant.

3. Adjust the idling speed of the engine to the specifications on the tune-up chart by turning the throttle stopscrews. Turn the screws on both carburetors equally. Check to make sure that both carburetors have the same air valve lift by visually comparing the distance between the carburetor hosing bridge and the air valve.

4. Adjust the idle mixture of the engine with the idle trimming screws until the highest engine speed is attained. The basic setting is two turns counterclockwise from lock. Again, turn the screws on both carburetors equally.

5. Adjust the idling speed of the engine to specifications with the throttle stopscrews.

SU HIF 6

1. Check the oil level in the damper cylinders. Top up as necessary as outlined in chapter one.

2. Remove the air cleaner.

3. Adjust the fuel jets to their basic setting by lifting the air valve and turning the adjust-

1. Lever for throttle control
2. Clamp for choke wire
3. Suction chamber
4. Hydraulic damper
5. Vent drilling from floatchamber
6. Drilling for air supply under diaphragm
7. Drilling for air supply to temp. compensator and idle trimming screw
8. Cold start device
9. Cam disc for fast idle
10. Connection for choke control
11. Fast idle stop screw
12. Throttle stop screw

Stromberg 175 CD 2SE carburetor—left side

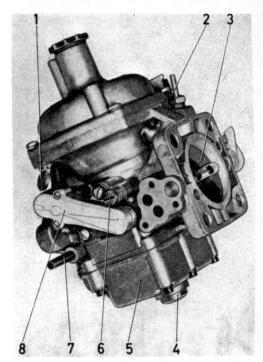

1. Sealed plug
2. Connection for vacuum hose to distributor
3. Primary throttle
4. Floatchamber plug
5. Floatchamber
6. Idle trimming screw
7. Connection for fuel hose
8. Temperature compensator

Stromberg 175 CD 2SE carburetor—right side

ment screw until the upper edge of the fuel jet is level with the bridge. The jet is then lowered two and one-half turns clockwise. This basic jet setting is correct for a carburetor temperature of approximately 70°F. Turning the adjusting screw a quarter turn in either direction compensates for a temperature differences. Turn the adjusting screw less than the two and one-half turns for temperatures above 70°F, and more than two and one-half turns for lower temperatures.

4. Run the engine until it has reached full operating temperature. The upper radiator hose should be very warm at this point.

5. Adjust the idling speed of the engine to the specifications on the tune-up chart by turning the throttle stopscrews. Turn the screws on both carburetors equally. Check to make sure that both carburetors have the same air valve

lift by visually comparing the distance between the carburetor housing bridge and the air valve.

6. Remove the plastic caps over the mixture adjusting screws. Turn both adjusting screws equally until maximum rpm is achieved. Turn both adjusting screws equally in the opposite direction until the engine just starts to falter. Remember that, in this case, the proper setting is not when maximum rpm is reached but when the engine just starts to falter. As a further check, unscrew the adjusting screws ¼–½ of a turn. The speed should then drop a further 20-40 rpm. Turn back the screws equally to the point where the engine just starts to falter and install the plastic caps over the screws.

7. Adjust the idling speed of the engine to specifications with the throttle stopsrews.

BALANCING DUAL CARBURETORS

Balancing dual carburetors is covered above under idle speed and mixture adjustments. To balance the carburetors, make sure both carburetors have the same air valve lift by visually comparing the distance between the carburetor

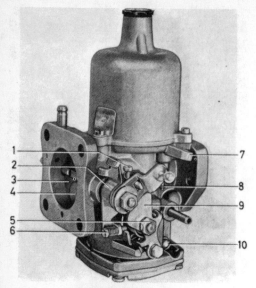

1. Throttle stop screw
2. Return spring
3. Throttle
4. Overrev valve
5. Cold-start device
6. Fast-idle stop screw
7. Attachment for choke control
8. Lift pin
9. Cam disc for fast idle
10. Screw head for float shaft

SU HIF 6 carburetor—front, left side

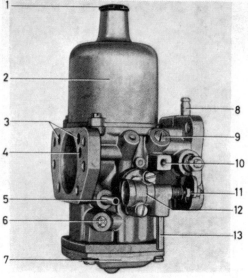

1. Hydraulic damper
2. Suction chamber
3. Drilling for air supply under air valve
4. Vent hole from floatchamber
5. Connection for fuel line
6. Jet adjusting screw
7. Floatchamber cover
8. Connection (positive) for hose to venting filter
9. Plug for outlet for speed compensator (air condition)
10. Boss for guard
11. Hot start valve adjusting screw
12. Hot start valve
13. Outlet from floatchamber (connection for hose to venting filter)

SU HIF 6 carburetor—front, right side

housing bridge and the air valve. A more accurate synchronization is not necessary.

Bosch Electronic fuel Injection

Adjustment (L-Jetronic 1975 and earlier)

IDLE SPEED AND MIXTURE

NOTE: *For 1981 and later models see CIS (constant idle speed) system.*

The idle mixture adjustment or CO value may be set only with the use of a CO meter. This adjustment is made by attaching a CO meter to the exhaust pipe of a vehicle with a warm (176°F) engine, and turning the adjusting screw of the Bosch control unit (beneath the passenger seat) until the correct CO value is obtained. The correct value is 1-1.5 percent for cars with manual transmissions and 0.5-1.0 percent for cars with automatic transmissions. Because this operation requires highly technical skills and expensive equipment, it is best referred to a Volvo or Bosch agency. In simple words, don't mess with the control unit.

The idle speed adjustment may, on the other hand, be set with a tachometer and an average amount of expertise. The check should be made with the engine idling at temperature (176°F). On 140 and 1800 series Volvos, remove the air cleaner-to-inlet duct hose. Check to see that the auxiliary air regulator is closed properly by removing the inlet duct-to-regulator hose and covering the opening with your hand. If the idle speed differs greatly, the engine is not fully warm or the regulator is faulty. Fit the hose again and adjust the idle speed to specifications with the idle adjusting screw. The idle adjusting screw is located on the inlet duct below the air cleaner hose opening on four-cylinder models, and inline in the auxiliary air pipe on six-cylinder models (see illustrations). On 140 and 1800 series Volvos, install the air cleaner hose.

Bosch Continuous Fuel Injection Adjustment (Mechanical)

IDLE SPEED AND MIXTURE

NOTE: *For 1981 and later models see CIS (constant idle speed) system.*

1974 140 series models, and all 240 and 260 series and 1980 models are equipped with the continuous fuel injection system. With this system, the injectors are open all the time, and the amount of fuel injected is directly proportional to the amount of air drawn into the intake.

1974-75 B20 F

WARNING: *The use of the correct special tools or their equivalent is REQUIRED for this procedure.*

The idle mixture adjustment or CO value may be set only with the use of a CO meter. Also, a special tapered setscrew tool is needed to turn the mixture adjusting screw. The adjustment is made with the engine idling at curb idle speed and at operating temperature — 176°F (80°C) with the CO meter attached to the exhaust pipe. 1975 models with air injection require disconnecting and plugging the air pump output hose to prevent an erroneous CO reading. With the special setscrew tool inserted into the small hose between the fuel distributor and

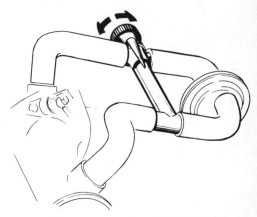

Idle speed adjusting screw—1975 B20F with mechanical fuel injection

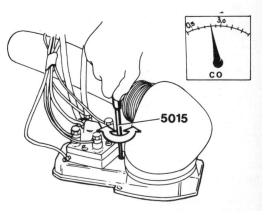

Idle mixture adjustment—1975 B20F with mechanical fuel injection

Idle speed adjusting screw—B20E, B20F with electronic fuel injection

Idle speed adjusting screw location—B30F

the bellows for the air sensor plate, engage the adjusting screw and adjust to a 1.5% CO value.

The idle speed ajdustment is a simple matter of rotating the idle adjusting screw located in-line in the auxiliary air pipe. With the engine idling at operating temperature — 176°F (80°C), and the transmission in neutral, adjust to 800 rpm on cars with automatic transmission, and 900 rpm on cars with manual transmission.

B21F

Special Tools Required: CO meter and CO idle mixture adjusting allen wrench (Volvo tool #999 5015).

1. Disconnect and plug the air injection pump output hose and the EGR vacuum hose.

2. With the engine warmed to operating temperature — 176°F (80°C) — check that the idle speed is 900 rpm (manual trans) or 800 rpm (automatic) with the car idling in neutral. Adjust as necessary by rotating the air adjusting screw (knob) located beneath the intake air box.

3. With the engine at specified idle speed, check that the CO value is 2.0% (1.0% 1977-80).

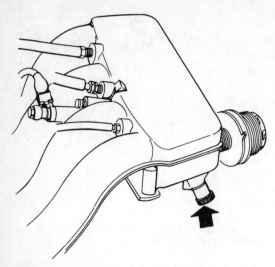

Mechanical (K-Jetronic) injection idle speed adjustment

Turbo

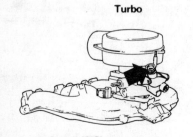

Constant Idle Speed (CIS) components

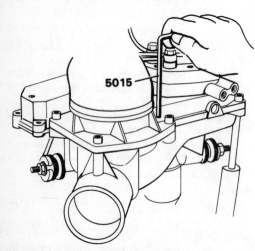

5015

B21F idle mixture (CO) adjustment

Adjust as necessary by inserting special tool #5015 into adjustment hole located between the air intake bellows and the fuel distributor. Recheck the idle speed.

CAUTION: *Do not race the engine with the tool inserted.*

4. Stop the engine.

B27F, B28F

Special Tools Required: CO meter with two position switch capable of isolating left or right cylinder banks, CO meter plumbing and fittings to screw into exhaust pipe gas pickup points and CO idle mixture adjusting allen wrench (Volvo tool #999 5102).

1. Remove the air cleaner and housing. Disconnect the air pump output hose (large hose on rear of pump) and plug it with a large diameter screwdriver shaft. Disconnect and plug the vacuum hose at the EGR valve.

2. Set the idle balance screws (#1 and #2) to their basic setting by screwing them in clockwise until they bottom out, and then backing them off counterclockwise 4 full turns each.

3. Start the engine and allow it to reach operating temperature (176°F). Using the idle air adjusting screw (#3), set the idle speed to 900 rpm.

4. Using the CO meter, check that the carbon monoxide level is 1.4-2.0% (1.0% 1977-80) at 900 rpm. If necessary, adjust CO level by inserting the special allen wrench (Volvo tool #5102) into the adjustment hose between the fuel distributor and throttle valve, and turning it clockwise to increase CO and counterclockwise to reduce CO. Before inserting the tool, remove the copper washer and plug covering the hose. Also, between adjustments, remove the tool and plug the hose to prevent a lean mixture and erroneous reading. Do not race the engine with tool inserted.

NOTE: *On oxygen sensor equipped models, perform CO adjustments with sensor disconnected. When sensor is connected after adjustment, CO should drop below 1%.*

5. The final step is to check the CO balance between the right and left cylinder banks. Both must have equal CO value; (see step 4). Air adjusting screw #3 controls the total amount of

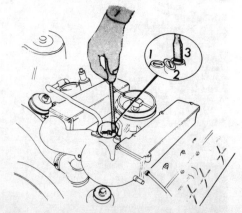

B27F, B28F idle balance ("1" and "2") and air adjusting screw ("3")

air bypassing the throttle at idle, whereas screws number 1 and 2 divide this air to the two cylinder banks. Screw #1 is for the right (passenger) side cylinders, and screw #2 is for the left side. If you decrease the airflow past screw #2, it will increase the airflow past screw #1, and vice versa.

More air means a leaner mixture, and less air a richer mixture. After balancing the CO value of each cylinder bank, recheck the total CO value at 900 rpm. Stop the engine.

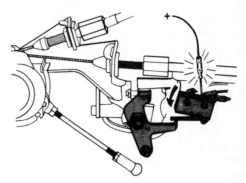

Adjusting throttle micro switch, B21F with Continuous Fuel Injection (mechanical). Adjust the idle speed if test light lights up at idle speed

BOSCH CONSTANT IDLE SPEED SYSTEM (CIS)

Adjustments, 1981 and Later Models

This system, introduced in 1981, controls the engine idle speed by regulating air flow around (bypassing) the throttle valve in the intake manifold. It is used on engines with both mechanical and LH-Jetronic electronic fuel injection system.

Basic Setting and Idle Speed Adjustment, CIS System

1981 B21F

1. Run the engine to normal operating temperature. Disconnect the throttle control rod at the lever. Make sure the cable and pulley run smoothly and do not bind in any position.

2. Remove the Emission Control Unit (ECU) cover panel. De-activate the ECU by disconnecting the white-red wire form terminal 12 of the blue connector plug at the ECU. Reinstall the connector plug.

NOTE: *The same wire ends at the ignition coil but cannot be disconnected there.*

3. Connect a tachometer to the engine according to the manufacturer's instructions. Connect a test light across the battery positive terminal and the terminal on the throttle microswitch with the yellow wire connected. Start the engine. The test light must NOT light up. If it does, adjust the micro switch position by slackening the switch retaining screws. Move the switch down until the light goes out, then retighten the screws.

NOTE: *This adjustment is temporary; final adjustment will follow later on.*

4. Idle speed should be 850-900 rpm. If outside these limits, adjust idle speed by proceeding to step 5. If idle speed is within these limits, continue to step 6.

5. If the idle speed is outside the stated limits, use the throttle position adjustment screw to adjust the speed to 850-900 rpm. The test light must NOT light up; if it does, readjust the micro switch position. Reconnect the white-red wire in terminal 12 of the blue connector plug at the ECU to reactivate the ECU. The idle

speed should have changed to 900 rpm (850-950 rpm is permitted). Stop the engine.

6. Reconnect the throttle control rod at the lever, making sure the cable pulley is completely retracted. If the control rod length must be adjusted, disconnect the throttle cable and automatic transmission kickdown cable (if equipped). Loosen the locknuts on either end of the rod and adjust the rod as necessary by turning the nut on the end of the cable.

Automatic transmission kickdown cable length should be checked at closed and open throttle with the engine OFF. Open throttle cable measurement should be checked with the throttle pedal in the car depressed, NOT by actuating the linkage by hand. The cable should be pulled out 50mm, or, about 2 in.

7. Adjust the micro switch by moving the switch UP, with the engine not running and the throttle closed. Adjust the switch UP until the test light lights up. Set the switch position by moving the switch DOWN 2.0-5.5mm or 0.08-0.10 in. Test light must NOT light or the adjustment will have to be performed again.

8. Remove the test light, reinstall the ECU panel.

1981 B21FMPG, 1982-83 B21F, B23E

The procedures for these engine models are the same as those for the 1981 B21F above, EXCEPT that the ECU from 1982 on has two extra terminals, 7 and 10, to de-activate the ECU, ground terminal 10 with the connector in place by inserting a copper wire along the terminal wire. Also, the idle speed should be 700 rpm with the ECU de-activated, and 750 rpm (700-800 rpm permitted) with the ECU activated. On step 2, DO NOT reinstall the connector plug.

1981-85 B21F TURBO

1. Follow steps 1 and 2 of the 1981 B21F procedure EXCEPT do not reinstall the connector

plug. Note the procedure above for de-activating 1982 and later ECUs.

2. Connect the test light across the battery positive terminal and the orange wire terminal on the throttle microswitch. The test light must NOT light up while adjusting the idle speed. (The electric circuit through the micro switch is open.) If the test light illuminates, adjust the micro switch position by loosening the switch retaining screws and moving the switch down until the test light goes out. Tighten the screws. This is a temporary adjustment; the final adjustment will follow later on.

3. Run the engine to normal operating temperature if not already done. Connect a tachometer to the engine and check idle speed; idle speed should be 850 rpm. If idle speed is outside these limits, follow the procedure below.

4. Using the throttle position adjustment screw, adjust throttle position until the idle speed reaches 850 rpm. The test light must NOT light up. If necessary, adjust the micro switch position DOWN.

5. Activate the ECU by reconnecting the white-red wire in terminal 12 of the blue connector on 1981 models, and by disconnecting the ground wire that was inserted at terminal 10 of the blue connector on 1982 and later models.

6. After activating the ECU, the idle speed should change to 900 rpm on (850-950 permit-

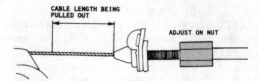

CABLE LENGTH BEING PULLED OUT

ADJUST ON NUT

B21F Turbo automatic transmission kickdown cable adjustment

ted) on 1981 models, and to 900 rpm (880-920 rpm permitted) on 1982 and later models. Stop the engine and install the ECU panel.

7. Reconnect and adjust the throttle control rod and cable, and the automatic transmission kickdown cable (if equipped) by following step 6 of the 1981 B21F procedure.

8. Adjust the B21F Turbo throttle switch by inserting a 0.3mm feeler gauge between the throttle adjustment screw and the throttle control lever. Move the switch UP until the test light lights up. Set the switch by moving it DOWN until the test light just goes out. Disconnect all test instruments, install the ECU panel.

1982 B21F-LH JETRONIC, 1983-89 B23F AND B230F WITH LH-JETRONIC

1. Seat the throttle butterfly valve by loosening the stop nut on the adjuster one or two turns. Set the adjuster screw by screwing it in until it just touches the lever, then screw it in an additional ¼ turn. Tighten the locknut.

2. Disconnect the CIS connector in the firewall. This is the connector that is directly behind the engine.

3. Connect a test light across the battery positive terminal and the orange wire terminal in the connector. Start the engine. The test light SHOULD LIGHT up at idle speed. If it does not, readjust the adjuster screw for the throttle butterfly valve position.

4. Open the throttle slightly (by hand) at the throttle control lever, with the engine running. The test light should go out. If it does not, run through the procedure again and try a new throttle switch.

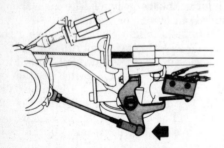

Disconnect the throttle control rod at this location on B21 engines

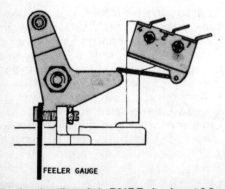

FEELER GAUGE

Adjusting throttle switch, B21F Turbo. Insert 0.3 mm feeler gauge between the throttle adjustment screw and the throttle control lever

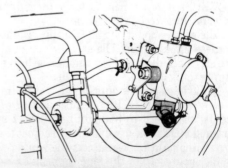

LH-Jetronic idle adjustment location

1981-1983 B23F

1. Disconnect the throttle rod at the cable pulley. Check the cable assembly, making sure the cable and pulley run smoothly and do not bind in any position. check the throttle; make sure the throttle shaft and plate do not bind during operation.

2. Screw in the idle speed adjustment screw all the way until it just seats.

NOTE: *This screw is used to adjust the idle speed on engines without the CIS system.*

3. Remove the access panel to the ECU module. (The ECU is located on the passenger's side kick panel on all models except the 760 GLE, on which the ECU is mounted on the driver's side kick panel).

4. On 1981 models, disconnect the white-red wire at terminal 12 of the blue connector plug at the ECU. On 1982 and later models, ground terminal 10 with the connector in place. This can be done by inserting a copper wire along the number 10 terminal wire.

5. Connect a test light across the positive battery terminal and the orange wire terminal on the throttle microswitch. On 1981 models, the test light should light up while adjusting the microswitch, indicating current is flowing through the switch.

On 1982 and later models, the test light should NOT light up while adjusting the switch, indicating the electric circuit through the microswitch is interrupted.

6. Connect a tachometer to the engine, and run the engine up to normal operating temperature.

7. Adjust the idle speed by adjusting the throttle position adjustment screw. DO NOT adjust the idle speed screw (it should still be screwed in on its seat).

8. Activate the ECU by reconnecting the white-red wire in the blue connector at the ECU. With the ECU activated, the idle speed should change to 900 rpm on 1981 and 1982 models (850-950 permitted on 1981, 880-920 permitted on 1982) and 750 rpm on 1983. Shut off the engine and install the ECU panel.

9. Reconnect the throttle control rod at the cable pulley. Disconnect the throttle cable and automatic transmission kickdown cable. The cable pulley should be completely retracted. Adjust the control rod length as necessary. Attach and adjust the throttle cable.

10. Check automatic transmission kickdown cable length at closed and open throttle with the engine off. Open throttle measurement should be checked with the throttle pedal in the car depressed, NOT by actuating the linkage by hand. Cable movement should be 50mm or about 2 in. Cable length with closed throttle should be 1mm; with open throttle, 51mm.

11. To adjust the throttle micro switch, insert 0.12 in. (3mm) feeler gauge between the throttle position adjustment screw and the throttle stop. On 1981 models, adjust the switch by turning the adjustment screw until the test light comes on.

1982-86 B28F ENGINE

1. Disconnect the throttle rod at the cable pulley. Check the cable assembly, making sure the cable and pulley run smoothly and do not bind in any position. Check the throttle, make sure the throttle shaft and plate do not bind during operation.

2. Screw in the idle speed adjustment screw all the way until it just seats.

NOTE: *This screw is used to adjust the idle speed on engines without the CIS system.*

3. Remove the access panel to the ECU module. (The ECU is located on the passenger's side kick panel on all models except the 760 GLE, on which the ECU is mounted on the driver's side kick panel).

4. On 1982-86 models, ground terminal 10 with the connector in place. This can be done by inserting a copper wire along the number 10 terminal wire.

5. Connect a test light across the positive battery terminal and the orange wire terminal on the throttle micro switch. The test light should NOT light up while adjusting the switch, indicating the electric circuit through the micro switch is interrupted.

6. Connect a tachometer to the engine, and run the engine up to normal operating temperature.

7. Adjust the idle speed by adjusting the throttle position adjustment screw. DO NOT adjust the idle speed screw (it should still be screwed in on its seat).

8. Activate the ECU. With the ECU activated, the idle speed should change to 900 rpm

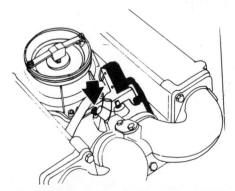

On 1981 and later B28F engines, make sure the idle speed adjustment screw is bottomed on its seat; this screw is used to adjust the idle speed on non-CIS equipped engines

1982 models (880-920 rpm permitted) and 750 rpm on 1983-86. Shut off the engine and install the ECU panel.

9. Reconnect the throttle control rod at the cable pulley. Disconnect the throttle cable and automatic transmission kickdown cable. The cable pulley should be completely retracted. Adjust the control rod length as necessary. Attach and adjust the throttle cable.

10. Check automatic transmission kickdown cable length at closed and open throttle with the engine off. Open throttle measurement should be checked with the throttle pedal in the car depressed, NOT by actuating the linkage by hand. Cable movement should be 50mm or about 2 in. Cable length with closed throttle should be 1mm; with open throttle, 50mm.

11. To adjust the throttle micro switch, insert 0.12 in. (3mm) feeler gauge between the throttle position adjustment screw and the throttle stop. Turn the adjustment screw until the test light lights up.

FULL THROTTLE ENRICHMENT SWITCH

NOTE: *The B28F V6 is equipped with two micro switches actuated by throttle control. This second micro switch closes a Lambda-Sond (the oxygen sensor) circuit at full throttle to provide richer air/fuel mixture at maximum acceleration. Vehicles sold in high-altitude areas have this switch disconnected.*

1. To adjust the switch, loosen the micro switch retaining screws. Turn the switch sideways. The test light should come on, then go out 2.5mm ($\frac{3}{32}$ in.) before the pulley touches the full throttle stop. Tighten the retaining screws.

2. To check full throttle enrichment switch operations, disconnect the green wire at the micro switch. Connect a test light between the micro switch terminal and the positive battery terminal.

3. Turn the pulley slowly to the full throttle stop. The test light should light up 1-4mm ($\frac{1}{32}$-$\frac{5}{32}$ in.) before the pulley touches the stop. Adjust the switch as necessary, following the switch adjustment procedure above.

1987-89 B280F ENGINE

1. Ground the CIS test point. The CIS test point is the red/white wire in the two wire connector which is located in the engine compartment across from the air conditioning compressor.

2. The green/white wire is the test point location for the oxygen sensor test.

3. Grounding the red/white wire will set the air valve in the wide open position.

4. Adjust the basic idle speed to 700 rpm.

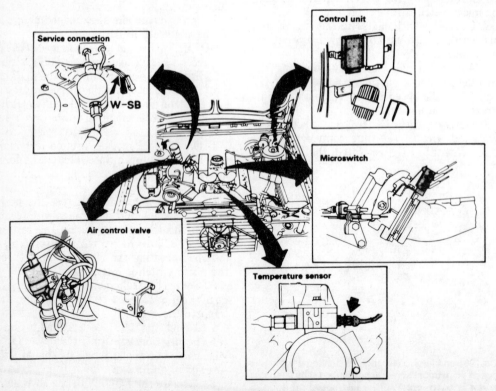

CIS component location, 760GLE with B28F engine

Disconnect the ground wire from the CIS test point. The idle speed should increase to 750 rpm.

DIESEL ENGINE TUNE-UP PROCEDURES

Due to the relative simplicity of the diesel engine compared to the gasoline engine, tune-up procedures consist of adjusting the valves, setting the maximum and minimum engine speeds and adjusting the throttle linkage (every 15,000 miles), and taking a compression test (every 75,000 miles).

Valve adjustment procedures are discussed under the heading "Valve Lash Adjustment" elsewhere in this chapter.

SETTING THE IDLE SPEED

WARNING: *The use of the correct special tools or their equivalent is REQUIRED for this procedure.*

To correctly set the idle speed you will need either the Volvo Monotester and adapter 9950 or a suitable photoelectric tachometer. A gasoline engine tachometer by itself cannot be used on a diesel engine because the diesel does not have an electric ignition system.

1. Connect a suitable tachometer to the engine and run the engine to normal operating temperature.

2. Idle speed should be 720-880 rpm.

3. If not, adjust the idle speed by loosening the locknut and turning the idle speed screw on the fuel injection pump.

4. Tighten the locknut and apply a dab of paint or thread sealer to the adjusting screw to prevent it from vibrating loose.

5. After adjusting idle speed and maximum engine speed, adjust the engine throttle linkage.

Diesel engine—maximum speed stop. Turn the pulley to bring the engine to maximum speed. Do not prolong engine revs at maximum speed

SETTING THE MAXIMUM ENGINE SPEED

The diesel engine is governed by the fuel injection pump so that engine rpms will not exceed 5,100-5,300 rpm. Because of the extremely high compression ratio (23.5:1) and the great stored energy diesel oil contains, the diesel engine cannot be run at the high rpm levels of modern gasoline engines, as it would place a tremendous strain on the pistons, wrist pins, connecting rods and bearings of the engine.

To adjust the maximum idle speed you will need a special tachometer which will work on the diesel engine.

1. Connect the tachometer and run the engine to normal operating temperature.

2. Run the engine to maximum speed by turning the cable pulley counterclockwise.

CAUTION: *Do not race the engine longer than absolutely necessary.*

3. Maximum speed should be between 5100-5300 rpm.

4. If not, loosen the locknut and adjust using the maximum speed screw.

5. Tighten the locknut and apply a dab of paint or thread sealer to the adjusting screw to prevent it from vibrating loose.

CAUTION: *Do not attempt to squeeze more power out of your diesel by extending the maximum speed.*

6. After adjusting the maximum speed, adjust the engine throttle linkage.

THROTTLE LINKAGE ADJUSTMENT

If the engine is cold, the cold start device must be disengaged before the linkage can be adjusted. To disengage the cold start device, loosen screw (1) in the illustration, push the lever forward and turn the sleeve 90°

Diesel engine—idle speed stop

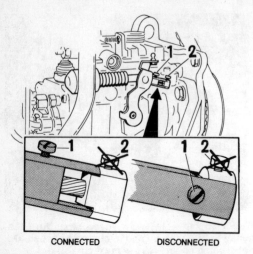

CONNECTED   DISCONNECTED

Diesel engine throttle linkage adjustment—disconnecting the cold start device

WARNING: *Do not touch screw (2) in the illustration, or the cold start device will have to be reset on the test bench.*

To adjust the linkage:

1. Disconnect the link rod lever on the injection pump by unsnapping the plastic clamp on the ball joint of the link rod and pulling the lever off the socket on the accelerator arm.

2. Turn the plastic cable adjuster until the cable is stretched out but does not cause the pulley to move from its idle stop.

3. Have an assistant press the accelerator pedal to the floor and check to see that the pulley notch touches the maximum speed stop.

For manual transmission models, proceed to step 7.

4. To adjust the kickdown cable on models with automatic transmission, have an assistant press the accelerator pedal to the floor and measure how much inner cable is exposed on the kickdown cable. It should be exposed approximately 2.05 in. (52mm) between the end positions.

5. Return the accelerator pedal to idle posi-

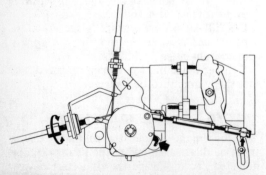

Adjusting throttle linkage. Disconnect the link rod lever and adjust the cable at its plastic adjuster

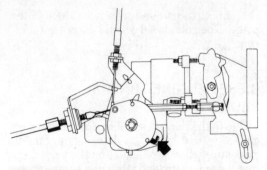

Depress the accelerator pedal and make sure the pulley notch touches the maximum speed stop

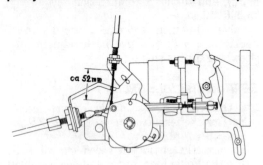

ca 52mm

Adjusting the kickdown cable—automatic transmission models

tion. The kickdown cable should be stretched and the distance between the kickdown cable clip and the cable sheath should be 0.01-0.04 in. (0.25-1.00mm).

6. If either of these measurements are not correct, adjust them at the threaded end of the cable sheath.

7. On all models, connect the link rod to the injection pump accelerator arm.

8. Have an assistant floor the accelerator pedal and adjust the link rod length so that the injection pump accelerator arm touches the maximum speed adjusting screw.

9. Return the accelerator pedal to the idle position and check to see that the accelerator arm touches the idle speed adjusting screw. If not, loosen and move the link rod ball joint in its oblong slot on the accelerator arm until the arm touches the idle speed adjusting screw. Tighten the ball joint.

10. Repeat steps 8 and 9 until the linkage is correctly adjusted.

NOTE: *A maximum clearance of 0.012 in. (0.3mm) is permitted between the pulley and the maximum speed stop.*

11. Reconnect the cold start device, if disconnected.

DIESEL ENGINE COMPRESSION TEST

WARNING: *The use of the correct special tools or their equivalent is REQUIRED for this procedure.*

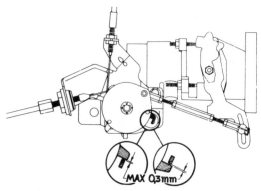

A maximum clearance of 0.012 in. (0.3 mm) is permitted between the pulley and the maximum speed stop

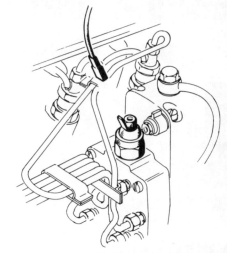

Diesel engine compression test—disconnect the wire at the stop valve on the fuel injection pump

Special Volvo adapter (tool 5191) and a compression gauge which reads to at least 600 psi must be used to test the compression on the Volvo diesel.

1. Disconnect the wire at the stop valve on the fuel pump so that the pump will not spray fuel while the compression is being tested.

2. Unbolt and remove the vacuum pump and its plunger from the engine.

3. Clean all of the fuel delivery pipes and connections, then unbolt and remove the fuel delivery pipes from the fuel injection pump and the injectors. Plug all connections to prevent dirt from entering the fuel system.

4. Using a 17mm socket, remove the injectors. Remove the disc-like heat shields under the injectors otherwise they will blow out and be lost during the compression test.

5. Beginning with cylinder No. 1, fit the heat shield in place, screw in the adapter (Volvo tool 5191) and seal and torque to 50 ft. lbs.

6. Connect compression tester to the adapter.

7. Turn the engine over with the starter motor and read the compression pressure:

New engine: 485 psi

Min. acceptable pressure: 400 psi

Maximum allowable difference between any two cylinders is 70 psi.

8. After reading the compression pressure for all six cylinders, install the injectors with their heat shields and torque them to 50 ft. lbs. Install the heat shields as shown in the illustration.

9. Install the fuel delivery lines and torque their attachments to 18 ft. lbs.

10. Re-connect the wire to the stop valve on the fuel injection pump and install the vacuum pump and its plunger. Check that the O-ring on the pump is in good condition.

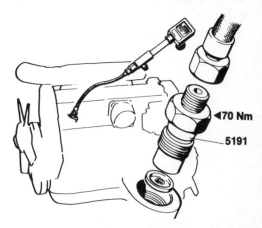

Diesel engine compression test—install heat shield and adaptor, then install compression gauge

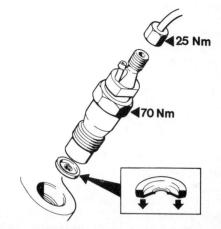

Reinstall injectors, making sure you install the heat shield in the position shown

Engine and Engine Overhaul

3

ENGINE ELECTRICAL

Understanding the Engine Electrical System

The engine electrical system can be broken down into three separate and distinct systems:

1. The starting system.
2. The charging system.
3. The ignition system.

BATTERY AND STARTING SYSTEM

Basic Operating Principles

The battery is the first link in the chain of mechanisms which work together to provide cranking of the automobile engine. In most modern cars, the battery is a lead/acid electrochemical device consisting of six 2v subsections connected in series so the unit is capable of producing approximately 12v of electrical pressure. Each subsection, or cell, consists of a series of positive and negative plates held a short distance apart in a solution of sulfuric acid and water. The two types of plates are of dissimilar metals. This causes a chemical reaction to be set up, and it is this reaction which produces current flow from the battery when its positive and negative terminals are connected to an electrical appliance such as a lamp or motor. The continued transfer of electrons would eventually convert the sulfuric acid in the electrolyte to water, and make the two plates identical in chemical composition. As electrical energy is removed from the battery, its voltage output tends to drop. Thus, measuring battery voltage and battery electrolyte composition are two ways of checking the ability of the unit to supply power. During the starting of the engine, electrical energy is removed from the battery. However, if the charging circuit is in good condition and the operating conditions are normal, the power removed from the battery will be replaced by the generator (or alternator) which will force electrons back through the battery, reversing the normal flow, and restoring the battery to its original chemical state.

The battery and starting motor are linked by very heavy electrical cables designed to minimize resistance to the flow of current. Generally, the major power supply cable that leaves the battery goes directly to the starter, while other electrical system needs are supplied by a smaller cable. During starter operation, power flows from the battery to the starter and is grounded through the car's frame and the battery's negative ground strap.

The starting motor is a specially designed, direct current electric motor capable of producing a very great amount of power for its size. One thing that allows the motor to produce a great deal of power is its tremendous rotating speed. It drives the engine through a tiny pinion gear (attached to the starter's armature), which drives the very large flywheel ring gear at a greatly reduced speed. Another factor allowing it to produce so much power is that only intermittent operation is required of it. This, little allowance for air circulation is required, and the windings can be built into a very small space.

The starter solenoid is a magnetic device which employs the small current supplied by the starting switch circuit of the ignition switch. This magnetic action moves a plunger which mechanically engages the starter and electrically closes the heavy switch which connects it to the battery. The starting switch circuit consists of the starting switch contained within the ignition switch, a transmission neutral safety switch or clutch pedal switch, and the wiring necessary to connect these in series with the starter solenoid or relay.

A pinion, which is a small gear, is mounted to a one-way drive clutch. This clutch is splined to the starter armature shaft. When the ignition switch is moved to the **start** position, the solenoid plunger slides the pinion toward the fly-wheel ring gear via a collar and spring. If the teeth on the pinion and flywheel match proper-ly, the pinion will engage the flywheel immedi-ately. If the gear teeth butt one another, the spring will be compressed and will force the gears to mesh as soon as the starter turns far enough to allow them to do so. As the solenoid plunger reaches the end of its travel, it closes the contacts that connect the battery and start-er and then the engine is cranked.

As soon as the engine starts, the flywheel ring gear begins turning fast enough to drive the pinion at an extremely high rate of speed. At this point, the one-way clutch begins allow-ing the pinion to spin faster than the starter shaft so that the starter will not operate at ex-cessive speed. When the ignition switch is re-leased from the starter position, the solenoid is de-energized, and a spring contained within the solenoid assembly pulls the gear out of mesh and interrupts the current flow to the starter.

Some starter employ a separate relay, mount-ed away from the starter, to switch the motor and solenoid current on and off. The relay thus replaces the solenoid electrical switch, buy does not eliminate the need for a solenoid mounted on the starter used to mechanically engage the starter drive gears. The relay is used to reduce the amount of current the starting switch must carry.

THE CHARGING SYSTEM

Basic Operating Principles

The automobile charging system provides electrical power for operation of the vehicle's ig-nition and starting systems and all the electri-cal accessories. The battery services as an elec-trical surge or storage tank, storing (in chemi-cal form) the energy originally produced by the engine driven generator. The system also pro-vides a means of regulating generator output to protect the battery from being overcharged and to avoid excessive voltage to the accessories.

The storage battery is a chemical device in-corporating parallel lead plates in a tank con-taining a sulfuric acid/water solution. Adjacent plates are slightly dissimilar, and the chemical reaction of the two dissimilar plates produces electrical energy when the battery is connected to a load such as the starter motor. The chemi-cal reaction is reversible, so that when the gen-erator is producing a voltage (electrical pres-sure) greater than that produced by the bat-tery, electricity is forced into the battery, and the battery is returned to its fully charged state.

Newer automobiles use alternating current generators or alternators, because they are more efficient, can be rotated at higher speeds,

and have fewer brush problems. In an alterna-tor, the field rotates while all the current pro-duced passes only through the stator winding. The brushes bear against continuous slip rings rather than a commutator. This causes the cur-rent produced to periodically reverse the direc-tion of its flow. Diodes (electrical one-way switches) block the flow of current from travel-ing in the wrong direction. A series of diodes is wired together to permit the alternating flow of the stator to be converted to a pulsating, but unidirectional flow at the alternator output. The alternator's field is wired in series with the voltage regulator.

The regulator consists of several circuits. Each circuit has a core, or magnetic coil of wire, which operates a switch. Each switch is con-nected to ground through one or more resis-tors. The coil of wire responds directly to sys-tem voltage. When the voltage reaches the re-quired level, the magnetic field created by the winding of wire closes the switch and inserts a resistance into the generator field circuit, thus reducing the output. The contacts of the switch cycle open and close many times each second to precisely control voltage.

While alternators are self-limiting as far as maximum current is concerned, DC generators employ a current regulating circuit which re-sponds directly to the total amount of current flowing through the generator circuit rather than to the output voltage. The current regula-tor is similar to the voltage regulator except that all system current must flow through the energizing coil on its way to the various accessories.

All Volvos are equipped with a 12 volt, nega-tive ground electrical system which consists of a battery, alternator and voltage regulator, start-er motor, ignition system (gasoline engines) or glow plugs (diesel engine), lighting system, ac-cessories, and signaling and instrumentation components. See Chapter 6, Chassis Electrical, for repair procedures on non-engine related electrical components.

Troubleshooting the Electronic Ignition System

An electronic ignition troubleshooting chart is included in Chapter 2 along with a brief ex-planation of the Volvo electronic ignition sys-tem.

Troubleshooting procedures for breaker point ignition systems are found in this chapter.

IGNITION COIL

All spark-ignition systems (gasoline engines) use a coil as the first component in the ignition system. The coil is simply a step-up transformer, which takes the 12 to 14 volts of the engine's electrical system and increases it to very high voltage. This change is necessary so that the electrical charge can form a sufficently hot spark when it jumps to ground through the spark plug electrode gap.

CAUTION: *Electronic ignition systems operate at very high voltages, often in excess of 30,000 volts. Such high voltages are a danger to life and special precautions must be taken on vehicles equipped with electronic ignition.*

Even the older, breaker point ignition systems can deliver a nasty shock to a careless worker.

The coil is easily found by tracing the center wire in the distributor cap to its opposite end. The coil is generally retained by a bracket, held to the car by one or two bolts. Depending on its position and ease of access, the coil may not need to be removed for testing.

To properly test a coil, you must have an ohmmeter. Generally, this tool is found as a volt/ohmmeter (VOM) and is very useful in automotive diagnosis. The resistance values for the primary side of the coil and ballast resistor (if so equipped) will be very low; make sure your VOM is set on the 0–10 ohm scale. When testing the secondary side of the coil, resistance will be much higher and the scale is usually set on 0–10,000 ohms.

Testing the Coil and Ballast Resistor

Perform this work with the engine off and the key out of the ignition so that there is NO possibility of the ignition being on. Carefully remove the wire to the distributor from the top of the coil. Label and disconnect the other wires attached to the coil, taking care not to lose any of the very small nuts and washers.

Clean off the coil and look for the numbers stamped near the terminals. Terminal number

Checking coil secondary windings, using terminal 1 and HT port

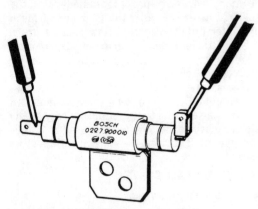

Checking resistance of the coil ballast

1 is ground (or negative), number 15 is PRIMARY voltage (12 volts) and the terminal labeled HT is SECONDARY or high tension voltage. The HT terminal is the center tower, from which runs the wire to the distributor. Inspect the tower for any signs of cracking. If cracks are found, replace the coil. Check carefully, most coil cracks are hairline thin and hard to see.

To measure the primary side of the coil, connect the leads of the meter to terminals 1 and 15. To read the secondary side, connect to terminals 1 and HT.

The values given in the chart below are based on a coil temperature of 68°F (20°C).

Distributor (Gasoline Engines Only)

The distributor performs two functions within the ignition system. Its breaker points or impulse sender (electronic ignition) time the collapse of the magnetic field of the ignition coil in relation to engine speed and convert primary voltage (12 volt) to secondary (high) voltage.

Checking coil primary windings, using terminals 1 and 15

The rotor and cap then distribute the high voltage spark to the correct spark plug.

The distributor incorporates both centrifugal and vacuum ignition timing mechanisms. Centrifugal advance is controlled by two weights located beneath the breaker plate. As engine speed increases, centrifugal force moves the weights out from the distributor shaft and advances the ignition by changing the position of the cam in relation to the shaft. This advanced positioning of the cam will then open the breaker points sooner and ignite the air/fuel mixture quickly enough in relation to piston speed. Centrifugal advance is necessary because as engine speed increases, the time period available to ignite the mixture decreases. (For example, at idle speed the ignition setting is, perhaps 10° BTDC. This is adequate for the spark plug to ignite the mixture at idle, but not at 2,500 rpm. The weights, governed by springs, move out at a predetermined rate to advance the timing to match engine speed).

Centrifugal advance is not sufficient to provide the proper advance under all conditions, and so we also have vacuum advance. Under light load conditions, such as very gradual acceleration and low speed cruising, the throttle opening is not sufficient to draw enough air/fuel mixture into the cylinder. Vacuum advance is used to provide the extra spark advance needed to ignite the smaller mixture. The round can on the side of the distributor is the vacuum advance unit. The rubber hose supplies vacuum from the intake manifold to draw on the diaphragm in the unit which is connected by a link to the breaker plate in the distributor.

Under part-throttle operation, the vacuum advance moves the breaker plate or impulse sender as necessary to provide the correct advance for efficient operation.

REMOVAL AND INSTALLATION

1. Unsnap the distributor cap clasps and remove the cap.

2. Crank the engine until No. 1 cylinder is at Top Dead Center (TDC). At this point, the rotor should point to the spark plug wire socket for No. 1 cylinder, and the 0° timing mark on the crankshaft damper should be aligned with the pointer. For ease of assembly, scribe a chalkmark on the distributor housing to note the position of the rotor.

3. Disconnect the primary lead from the coil at its terminal on the distributor housing. On electronic fuel injected models, disconnect the plug for the triggering contacts. On 1975 and later models with electronic ignition, remove the retaining screw for the primary voltage wire connector and pull it from the distributor housing.

4. Label and remove the vacuum hose(s) from the vacuum advance regulator. Take care not to damage the connection during removal.

5. On B20 and B30 engines, loosen the distributor attaching screw and holddown clamp enough to slide the distributor up and out of position. On B21, B23, B27 and B28 engines, remove the distributor attaching screw and lift out the distributor.

6. Perform the needed tests, repairs or adjustments on the distributor. If the engine has not been disturbed (the crankshaft was not

Ignition Specifications

Ignition Type and Engine Family	Coil Resistance			Ballast Resistance
	Primary		Secondary	
Breaker Point Ignition	Ohms		Ohms × 1000 (or K Ω)	Ohms
B20A, B17–B23A through 1978	2.85 ± 0.15		9.5 ± 2.5	—
B20A, B17–B23A 1979 & later	1.9 ± 0.1		9.5 ± 1.5	1.3 ± 0.1
Breakerless ignition B20F–B19, E, ET B21E, ET, F, FT B23E	1.9 ± 0.1		9.5 ± 1.5	0.9 ± 0.1
B27A, E, F B28A, E, F	0.5 ± 0.1		9.5 ± 1.5	1.0 ± 0.1
Computerized IGN Systems	Essex Coil	Bosch Coil	Essex Coil	Bosch Coil	
1981 B21F-MPG 1982 B21 F-CI 1982 B21 F-LH 1983–84 B23F 1985-on B230F	1.2 ± 0.1	1.2 ± 0.1	10.6 ± 1.0	8.5 ± 0.8	—

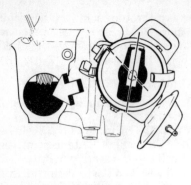

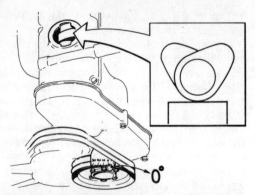

On the B21F engine, the engine can be set up for distributor installation by removing the oil filler cap, turning the crankshaft by hand until the camshaft lobes for no. 1 cylinder are as shown, then aligning the 0° mark with the notch in the pulley. This is an alternate method to removing the spark plug

Installing the distributor. On the B21, B23 and B27, B28 engines, back the rotor clockwise to compensate for bevelled gears. B21 engine shown

moved since the distributor was taken out), install the distributor with the rotor pointing to the No. 1 cylinder spark plug wire socket, which should be in line with the chalkmark you make prior to removal. If the engine was disturbed, proceed to step 7.

On the B20 and B30 engines, the distributor has an offset driving collar which can only be inserted one way. On the B21, B23, B27 and B28 engines, the distributor drive has bevelled gear teeth which will cause the rotor to turn counterclockwise as the distributor is installed. For this reason, it is necessary to back off the rotor clockwise (about 60° on the B21, B23, and 40° on the B27, B28) to compensate for this. When the distributor is engaged, the rotor must align with the mark made prior to removal.

7. If the engine was disturbed after the distributor was removed, remove the spark plug for No. 1 cylinder and put your finger over the plug hole while you turn the engine over by hand. When you start to feel air pressure push against your finger, it means the cylinder is

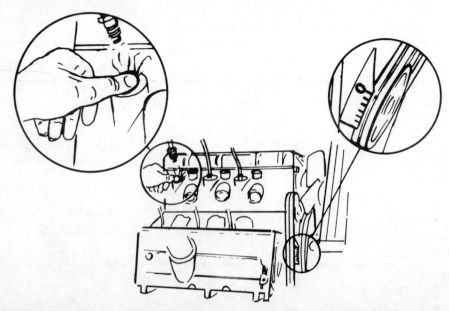

Setting engine for distributor installation if the crankshaft was turned. Air pressure pushes against your finger, then align timing marks. See text. B27F engine shown

coming up on its compression stroke. With the engine on this compression stroke, turn the crankshaft around until the TDC mark on the harmonic balancer aligns with the timing pointer on the front of the engine. Install the distributor as explained in paragraph 2 of step 6.

8. Connect the primary lead to its terminal on the distributor housing. On electronic fuel injected models, connect the plug for the triggering contacts. On 1975 and later models equipped with electronic ignition, push the primary voltage wire connector into its slot in the distributor housing and tighten the retaining screw.

9. Connect the vacuum hose(s) to the connection(s) on the vacuum regulator, (if so equipped)

10. If the distributor was disassembled, or if the contact point setting was disturbed on models so equipped, proceed to set the point gap and/or dwell angle.

11. Install the distributor cap and secure the clasps. Start the engine and set the ignition timing. See Chapter 2. Tighten the distributor attaching screw.

DIESEL ENGINE

Checking the Glow Plugs

1. With the engine cold, connect a test light between the glow plug terminal and ground.
2. Have an assistant sit in the car and turn on the ignition key to ON (not START) and observe the glow plug light on the dash board:

a. If the glow plug light does not light and the test light does not light, it indicates a failure at the control unit.

b. If the glow plug light does light but the test light does not, it indicates a failure at the glow plug relay.

c. If the glow plug light does not light but the test light does, it indicates a failure at the temperature sender or at the control unit.

3. Turn the ignition key to its 0 (off) position and remove the flat bar connector between the glow plug terminals. Connect a test light be-

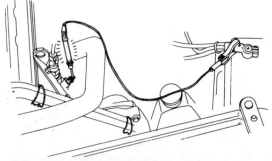

Checking the glow plugs—diesel

tween the positive battery terminal and each glow plug terminal. If the test light does not light, it indicates a faulty glow plug.

Alternator
PRECAUTIONS

Several precautions must be observed when performing work on alternator equipment.

1. If the battery is removed for any reason, make sure that it is reconnected with the correct polarity. Reversing the battery connections may result in damage to the one-way rectifiers.

2. Never operate the alternator with the main circuit broken. Make sure that the battery, alternator, and regulator leads are not disconnected while the engine is running.

3. Never attempt to polarize an alternator.

4. When charging a battery that is installed in the vehicle, disconnect the negative battery cable.

5. When utilizing a booster battery as a starting aid, always connect it in parallel; negative to negative, and positive to positive.

6. When arc (electric) welding is to be performed on any part of the vehicle, disconnect the negative battery cable, disconnect the alternator leads, and unplug the voltage regulator.

7. Never unplug any ECU, computer or "black box" while the engine is running or the ignition is ON. Severe and expensive damage may result within the solid state equipment.

REMOVAL AND INSTALLATION

NOTE: *On some models, it will be necessary to remove the air pump and place it to one side to gain access to the alternator.*

1. Disconnect the negative battery cable.
2. Disconect the electrical leads to the alternator.
3. Remove the adjusting arm-to-alternator bolt and adjusting arm-to-engine bolt.
4. Remove the alternator-to-engine mounting bolt.
5. Remove the fan belt and lift the alternator forward and out.
6. Reverse the above procedure to install, taking care to properly tension the fan (drive) belt as outlined in the Routine Maintenance section of Chapter 1.

Voltage Regulator
REMOVAL AND INSTALLATION

1. Disconnect the negative battery cable.
2. Disconnect the leads or plug socket from the old regulator taking note of their (its) location.
3. Remove the holddown screws from the old regulator and install the new one.

4. Connect the leads or plug socket and re-connect the negative battery cable.

VOLTAGE ADJUSTMENT

Motorola (S.E.V. Marchal) Regulator

If the Motorola A.C. Regulator is found to be defective, it must be replaced. No adjustments can be made on this unit.

The following test may be performed on the Motorola regulator to see if it is functioning properly. Am ammeter, tachometer, and volt-meter are required. Note that the ammeter cir-cuit commonly found on a volt/ohmmeter (VOM) is for very small amperages and is NOT sufficient for this test. An ammeter reading to at least 75 amperes is required.

1. Connect the test equipment to the alter-nator and regulator as shown in the illustration.

2. Run the engine at 2500 rpm (5000 alter-nator rpm) for 15 seconds. With no load on the alternator, (all electrical equipment turned off) and the regulator ambient temperature at 77°F (25°C), the reading on the voltmeter should be 13.1–14.4 volts. For regulator ambient temper-atures other than 77°F (25°C), consult the volt-age-temperature diagram for cold regulator.

3. Load the alternator with 10–15 amps (high beam headlights) while the engine is run-ning at 2500 RPM. The voltmeter reading should again be 13.1–14.4 V. Replace the regu-lator if it does not fall within these limits.

4. For a more accurate indication of the reg-ulator's performance, drive the vehicle for about 45 minutes at a minimum speed of 30

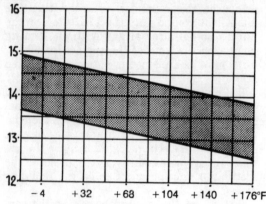

Volts

Voltage-temperature diagram for cold regulator

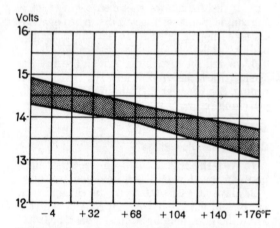

Volts

Voltage-temperature diagram for warm regulator

mph. The regulator will be at the correct work-ing temperature immediately after this drive.

5. With the engine running at 2500 rpm and the regulator ambient temperature at 77°F (25°C), the voltmeter reading should be 13.85–14.25 V. For regulator ambient temperatures other than 77°F (25°C), consult the voltage-temperature diagram for warm regulator.

Bosch Regulator (35, 55, 70 amp)

The Bosch regulator is fully adjustable. To determine which adjustments are necessary — if any — perform the following test. An amme-ter, 12 V. test lamp, tachometer, and voltmeter are required for this test.

NOTE: *Where the numerical values differ for the 35 amp voltage regulator and the 55 amp unit, the figures for the 55 amp regula-tor will be given in parentheses.*

1. Connect the alternator and regulator shown in the illustration.

NOTE: *The first reading must be taken with-in 30 seconds of beginning of test.*

2. While running the engine at 2000 rpm,

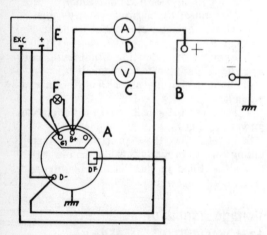

A. Alternator
B. Battery
C. Voltmeter
D. Ammeter, 0-50 amps
E. Voltage regulator
F. 12v test light

Wiring diagram for testing Motorola regulator

load the alternator with 28–30 amps. (44–46 for 55 amp alternator).

3. Rapidly lower the engine to idle speed or 500 rpm and then return it to 2000 rpm. With a load of 28–30 amp (44–46 for 55 amp alternator), the voltmeter reading should be 14.0–15.0 V. (13.9–14.8 V. for 55 amp alternator). The regulator should be regulated on the left (lower) contact.

4. Reduce the alternator load to 3–8 amps. The voltmeter reading should not decrease more than 0.3v. (0.4 for 55 amp alternator) The regulator should be regulated on the right (upper) contact.

5. Adjustment is made by bending the stop bracket for the bimetal spring. Bending the stop bracket down lowers the regulating voltage; bending it up raises the voltage. If the voltmeter reading for the low amp alternator load decreased more than 0.3v. (0.4 for 55 amp alternator) compared to the reading for the high amp alternator load, adjust the regulator by bending the holder for the left (lower) contact and simultaneously adjust the gap between the right (upper) contact and the movable contact.

The gap should be adjusted to 0.010–0.015 in. (0.25–0.40mm). If the holder is bent toward the right (upper) contact, the regulating voltage under high amp alternator load will be lowered.

To avoid faulty adjustments due to residual magnetism in the regulator core, it may be necessary to rapidly lower the engine rpm to idle after each adjustment, and then raise it to 2000 rpm to take a new reading.

NOTE: *Warm regulators may be cooled to ambient temperature by directing a stream of compressed air on them. Final readings should be made with the regulator at ambient temperature.*

From 1983 onwards, the Bosch alternators use an integrated voltage regulator. This device is mounted directly on the back of the alternator. Due to its solid state construction, no internal testing or adjustment is possible.

The function of this type of regulator can be simply tested with a voltmeter in the following fashion:

1. Connect voltmeter between terminals **B +** and **D** – on the alternator. DO NOT disconnect any other wires on these terminals when testing.

2. Have an assistant start the engine and accelerate it to 3000 rpm and apply the specifed electrical load. For an alternator rated at 55amps, apply a 47 amp load. For a 70 amp alternator, apply 60 amps and for a 90 amp alternator apply a 77 amp load. This load tests the alternator at 85% of its rated output.

3. If the regulator is cold – 77°F (25°C) – and the reading is taken within one minute of

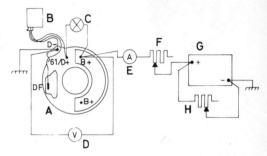

A. Alternator	E. Ammeter 0–50 amps
B. Voltage lamp 12 volts	F. Regulator resistance
C. Control lamp 12 volts,	G. Battery
2 watts	H. Load resistance
D. Voltmeter 0–20 volts	

Wiring diagram for testing Bosch regulator

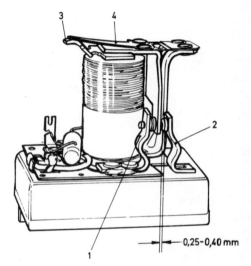

1. Regulator contact for lower control range (lower contact)	3. Spring tensioner
2. Regulator contact for upper control range (upper contact)	4. Spring upper section: Steel spring Lower section: Bimetal spring

Bosch voltage regulator adjustments

start-up, the correct voltage should be 14.4–14.8v for 1983 and 1984 models. 1985 and later models should show 14.1–14.9 volts.

4. Under hot regulator conditions (car has been driven at least 15 minutes) the test voltages should now be between 0 and 0.3v lower than the cold test above.

5. Any readings outside these limits (either over or under) require the replacement of the regulator. This is done with the engine off by unplugging the connector (if there is one) and removing the two mounting bolts which hold the regulator.

WARNING: *When removing the regulator, a set of alternator brushes will come out with it.*

Alternator and Regulator Specifications

Year	Vehicle Model	Alternator			Regulator	
		Part No. and Manufacturer	Output (amps.)	Min. Brush Length (in.)	Part No. and Manufacturer	Volts @ Alternator rpm (cold)
1970	140	S.E.V. Motorola 14V 26641	35	0.20	S.E.V. Motorola 14V 33525	13.1–14.4 @ 4000
1970–71	140, 1800	Bosch K1 14V 35A20	35	0.31	Bosch AD 14V	14.0–15.0 @ 4000
1970–75 1972–74	164 140, 1800	S.E.V. Motorola 14V 34833	55	0.20	S.E.V. Motorola 14V 33544	13.1–14.4 @ 4000
1971 1971–72	1800 140	S.E.V. Motorola 14V 71270202	35	0.20	S.E.V. Motorola 14V 33525	13.1–14.4 @ 4000
1972–73	1800	Bosch K1 14V 55A20	55	0.53	Bosch AD 14V	13.9–14.8 @ 4000
1975–83	240, DL, GL, GT, 760 GLE	Bosch 14V 55A20	55 [3]	0.20	Bosch	13.5–14.1 @ 4000 [1]
1976–82	260, GLE, Coupe	S.E.V. Marchal A14/55A 7160410	55 [2]	0.20	S.E.V. Marchal 72710502	13.5–14.1 @ 4000 [1]
1983	DL, GL, 760 GLE, GLT, DL, Turbo	Bosch N114V 70A20	70	0.20	Bosch 0197311008	14.4–14.8 @ 6000 [1]
1983	760 GLE	Bosch N114V 90A20	90	0.20	Bosch [4] 0192052027	14.1–14.8 @ 3000 [1]

Year	Model	Alternator	Amps		Regulator	Output
1984	240 Diesel 4 DL [5]	Bosch K114V 55A20	55	0.20	Bosch 0120489066 [6]	14.4–14.8 @ 3000
	240 DL (US) GL, GLE Turbo / 760 GLE Gas & Diesel	Bosch N114V 70A20	70	0.20	Bosch 0120469568	14.4–14.8 @ 3000
1985–89	DL & GL	Bosch N114V 70A20	70	0.20	Bosch 0120469568	14.4–14.8 @ 3000
	85-Turbo	Bosch N114V 31/80A	80	0.20	Bosch 0120429787	14.1–14.8 @ 6000
85–89	740, 760, 780	Bosch K114V 55A20	55	0.20	Bosch 0120489066	14.4–14.8 @ 3000
		Bosch N114V 70A20	70	0.20	Bosch 0120469568	14.4–14.8 @ 3000
		Bosch N114V 31/80A	80	0.20	Bosch 0120 429 787	14.1–14.8 @ 6000
		Bosch N114V 90A20	90	0.20	Bosch 0192052027	14.1–14.8 @ 6000
		Bosch N114V 31/100A	100	0.20	Bosch 13634977 [7]	14.1–14.9 @ 6000

[1] After driving 10 minutes
[2] 1979–82: 70
[3] 1982 B21F Turbo rated output 770W; max. current 55A
[4] Early type; late type Bosch 1197311008
[5] Canada only
[6] Diesel: 0120489070
[7] '88 760: 13635107

Bosch   N1 14V   70A 20

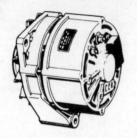

Bosch   N1 14V   90A 20

Bosch   K1 14V   55A 20

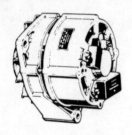

Bosch   N1 14V   70A 20

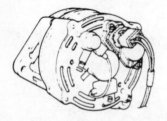

Bosch   N1 14V   70A 20

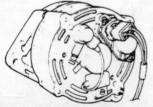

Examples of alternators with internal regulators. Amperage ratings appear on a plate on the alternator case

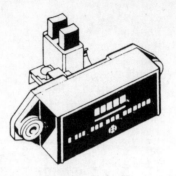

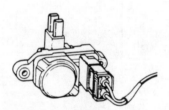

Examples of integrated voltage regulators found on 1983 and later Volvos

Don't lose any small parts. Reinstall carefully, paying attention to proper brush placement and seating within the alternator.

Battery

REMOVAL AND INSTALLATION

1. Remove the positive and negative cables from their terminals on the top of the battery. If the cables remain stuck to the terminals after loosening the cable clamps, use a puller to free them. Do not try to pry the cables off the terminals; damage to the battery case and/or the terminals may result.

2. Remove the battery holddown bar and lift out the battery. Keep the battery upright to avoid spilling acidic electrolyte.

3. Clean the battery case and support shelf with a brush and rinse with clean, lukewarm water. Remove any deposits from the terminals and cable ends with a wire brush or battery terminal tool.

4. Replace the battery on its support shelf and install the holddown bar.

5. Install the cables in their proper terminals and tighten the clamps. Coat the exposed metal of the cables and terminals with petroleum jelly to prevent corrosion.

Starter
REMOVAL AND INSTALLATION

1. Disconnect the negative battery cable at the battery.

2. Disconnect the leads from the starter motor. On later model cars, it may be necessary to loosen or remove other components to gain access to the starter bolts.

3. Remove the bolts retaining the starter motor brace to the cylinder block (B21 through 1977 only) and the bolts retaining the starter motor to the flywheel housing and lift it off.

4. To reinstall, position the starter motor to the flywheel housing. Apply locking compound to the bolt threads and install the retaining bolts finger-tight. Torque the bolts to approximately 25 ft. lbs.

5. Connect the starter motor leads and the negative battery cable.

DRIVE REPLACEMENT

In order to remove the starter pinion drive, it is necessary to disassemble the starter. The procedure for disassembling the starter is as follows:

1. Remove the starter from the car as outlined in Starter Removal and Installation.

2. Unscrew the two screws and remove the small cover from the front end of the starter shaft.

3. Unsnap the lockwasher and remove the adjusting washer from the front end of the shaft.

4. Unscrew the two screws retaining the commutator bearing shield and the shield.

5. Lift up the brushes and retainer and remove the brush bridge from the rotor shaft. The negative brushes are removed with the bridge while the positive brushes remain in the field winding. Do not remove the steel washer and the fiber washer at this time.

6. Unscrew the nut retaining the field terminal connection to the control solenoid.

7. Unscrew the two solenoid-to-starter housing retaining screws and remove the solenoid.

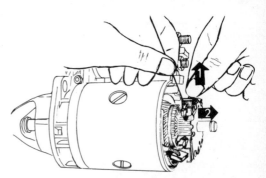

Lift up the brushes and remove the brush bridge

Troubleshooting Basic Charging System Problems

Problem	Cause	Solution
Noisy alternator	• Loose mountings • Loose drive pulley • Worn bearings • Brush noise • Internal circuits shorted (High pitched whine)	• Tighten mounting bolts • Tighten pulley • Replace alternator • Replace alternator • Replace alternator
Squeal when starting engine or accelerating	• Glazed or loose belt	• Replace or adjust belt
Indicator light remains on or ammeter indicates discharge (engine running)	• Broken fan belt • Broken or disconnected wires • Internal alternator problems • Defective voltage regulator	• Install belt • Repair or connect wiring • Replace alternator • Replace voltage regulator
Car light bulbs continually burn out—battery needs water continually	• Alternator/regulator overcharging	• Replace voltage regulator/alternator
Car lights flare on acceleration	• Battery low • Internal alternator/regulator problems	• Charge or replace battery • Replace alternator/regulator
Low voltage output (alternator light flickers continually or ammeter needle wanders)	• Loose or worn belt • Dirty or corroded connections • Internal alternator/regulator problems	• Replace or adjust belt • Clean or replace connections • Replace alternator or regulator

8. Remove the drive end shield and rotor from the stator.

9. Remove the rubber and metal sealing washer from the housing.

10. Unscrew the nut and remove the screw on which the engaging arm pivots.

11. Remove the rotor, with the pinion and engaging arm attached, from the drive end shield.

12. Push back the stop washer and remove the snapring from the rotor shaft.

13. Remove the stop washer and pull off the starter pinion.

NOTE: *While the starter is disassembled, a few quick checks may be performed. Check the rotor shaft, commutator, and windings. If the rotor shaft is bent or worn, it must be replaced. Maximum rotor shaft radial throw is 0.003 in. (0.08mm). If the commutator is*

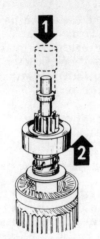

Use a socket to push back the stop collar and remove the snap-ring to remove the starter drive

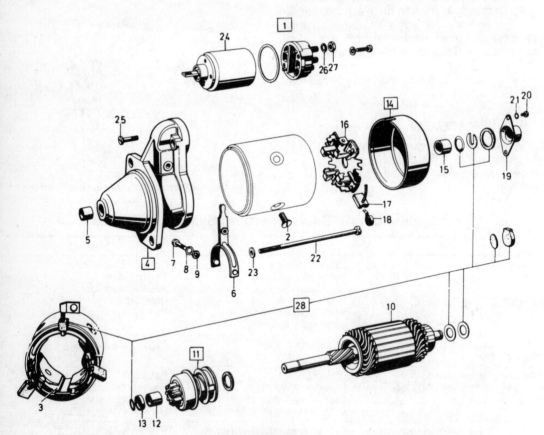

1. Solenoid	11. Starter drive	19–21. Cap
2. Screw	12. Bushing	22. Through bolt
3. Field housing	13. Stop collar	23. Washer
4. Drive housing	14. Brush cover	24. Solenoid housing
5. Bushing	15. Bushing	25. Screw
6. Engagement lever	16. Brush holder	28. Washers and pads
7–9. Screw, washer and nut	17. Brush	
10. Armature	18. Brush tension spring	

Exploded view of starter motor. Typical of all models through 1984

Battery and Starter Specifications

All cars use 12 volt, negative ground electrical systems

Year	Model	Battery Amp Hour Capacity	Starter							
			Lock Test			No Load Test			Brush Spring Tension (lbs.)	Min. Brush Length (in.)
			Amps	Volts	Torque (ft. lbs.)	Amps	Volts	RPM		
All	140 Series, 164, 180	60	300–350	6	—	40–50	12	6900–8100	2.53–2.86	0.60
All ③	240 Series, 260 Series, GL, GT, DL, GLT, Turbo, 740 GLE, Coupe, 760 GLE, 780	60 ①	400–490	7	—	30–50	11.5	5800–7800	3.10–3.50	0.52
All ③	D24, D24T Diesel	88 ②	700–880	7	—	65–95	11.5	6500–8500	5.10–5.50	0.35
'84	760 GLE	450 ④	480–560	7.4	—	max 70	11.5	7500	4.0–4.8	0.41
'85	740 GL, GLE Turbo, All 760	450 ④	480–560	7.4	—	max 70	11.5	7500	4.0–4.6	0.51
	D24T	450	700–880	4.5	—	max 95	11.5	7500	5.0–6.0	0.51
'86	760 GLE, Turbo	450 ④	700–880	4.5	—	max 95	11.5	7500	5.0–6.0	0.51
'88	740, 760, 240	450 ④	650 ⑥	6.0	—	max 60	12.0	7000	2.5–3.8	0.43
'89	240	450 ④	625–800	4.5	—	max 75	11.5	2900	3.5–4.8	0.31
'89	740, 760 Turbo, 780	500 ⑤	Bosch 700–800 Hitachi max 880	4.5 / 3.0	—	max 95 / max 140	11.5 / 11.0	6500 / 3900	5–6 / 6.0–7.8	0.33 / 0.35

① 260 series, GLE, Coupe—70 amp hour battery
② 90 amp hour High Output
③ Except below.
④ 90 minutes
⑤ 90 min; exc 780, 110 min.
⑥ Hitachi starter

scored or worn unevenly, it should be turned by a machine shop. Minimum commutator diameter is 1.3 in. (33mm). Check the end shield, which houses the brushes, for excessive wear. Maximum bearing clearance is 0.005 in. (0.13mm).

14. Lubricate the starter.

15. Press the starter pinion onto the rotor shaft. Install the stop washer and secure it with a new snapring.

16. Position the engaging arm on the pinion. Install the rotor into the drive end frame.

17. Install the screw and nut for the engaging arm pivot.

18. Install the rubber and metal sealing washers into the drive end housing.

19. Install the stator onto the rotor and drive end shield.

20. Position the solenoid so that the eyelet on the end of the solenoid plunger fits onto the en-

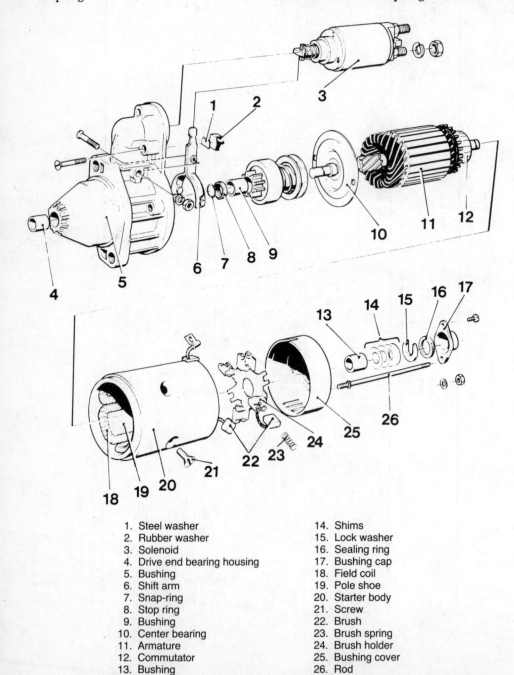

1. Steel washer	14. Shims
2. Rubber washer	15. Lock washer
3. Solenoid	16. Sealing ring
4. Drive end bearing housing	17. Bushing cap
5. Bushing	18. Field coil
6. Shift arm	19. Pole shoe
7. Snap-ring	20. Starter body
8. Stop ring	21. Screw
9. Bushing	22. Brush
10. Center bearing	23. Brush spring
11. Armature	24. Brush holder
12. Commutator	25. Bushing cover
13. Bushing	26. Rod

Exploded view of starter motor, D24 and D24T

gaging arm (shift lever). Tighten the solenoid retaining screws.

21. Place the metal and fiber washers on the rotor shaft.

22. Install the brush bridge on the rotor shaft and replace the brushes.

23. Fit the commutator bearing shield into position and install the retaining screws.

24. Install the adjusting washers and snap a new lockwasher into position on the end of the shaft. Make sure that the rotor axial clearance does not exceed 0.12 in. (0.03mm). If necessary, adjust the clearance with washers, maintaining a minimum clearance of 0.012 in. (0.05mm).

25. Replace the small cover over the front end of the shaft and install the two retaining screws.

26. Install the starter in the car as outlined in Starter Removal and Installation.

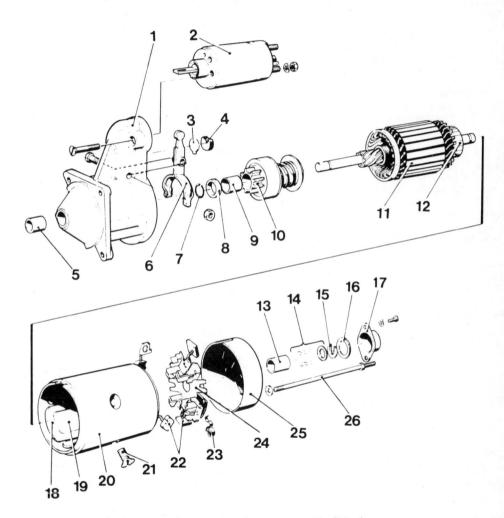

1. Drive end bearing housing
2. Solenoid
3. Steel washer
4. Rubber washer
5. Bushing
6. Shift arm
7. Snap-ring
8. Stop ring
9. Spacer bushing
10. Drive
11. Armature
12. Commutator
13. Bushing
14. Shims
15. Lock washer
16. Sealing ring
17. Bushing cap
18. Field coil
19. Pole shoe
20. Starter body
21. Pole screw
22. Carbon brush
23. Brush spring
24. Brush holder
25. Bushing cover
26. Rod

Exploded view of starter motor, B28F and B280F

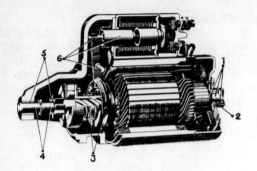

1. Place a thin layer of grease on the insulation washers, the shaft end, the adjusting washers and lock washer.
2. Place the bushing in oil for one hour before installing.
3. Apply plenty of grease in the rotor thread and the engaging lever groove.
4. Lightly grease the armature shaft.
5. Place the bushings in oil for one hour before installing.
6. Lightly grease the lever joints and the iron core of the solenoid.

Proper lubrication of the starter when reassembling

SOLENOID REPLACEMENT

If the starter will not crank, before replacing the solenoid check the battery for sufficient charge. If the no-crank condition persists when the battery is known to be good, connect a jumper wire between the positive terminal of the battery and the contact screw for the solenoid lead. If the solenoid engages the starter pinion, the starter switch or leads are at fault. If the starter still does not crank, replace the solenoid. To remove the solenoid:

1. Remove the starter from the car as outlined in Starter Removal and Installation.
2. Unscrew the two solenoid-to-starter housing retaining screws and remove the solenoid.
3. As a final test, wipe the solenoid clean and press in the armature. Test its operation by connecting it to a battery. If the solenoid still does not function, replace it with a new unit.
4. Position the new solenoid so that the eyelet on the end of the plunger fits into the engaging arm. Tighten the retaining screws.
5. Replace the starter in the car as outlined in Starter Removal and Installation.

ENGINE MECHANICAL

Four basic gasoline engine families and the diesel/turbo diesel are covered in this book:

Troubleshooting Basic Starting System Problems

Problem	Cause	Solution
Starter motor rotates engine slowly	• Battery charge low or battery defective	• Charge or replace battery
	• Defective circuit between battery and starter motor	• Clean and tighten, or replace cables
	• Low load current	• Bench-test starter motor. Inspect for worn brushes and weak brush springs.
	• High load current	• Bench-test starter motor. Check engine for friction, drag or coolant in cylinders. Check ring gear-to-pinion gear clearance.
Starter motor will not rotate engine	• Battery charge low or battery defective	• Charge or replace battery
	• Faulty solenoid	• Check solenoid ground. Repair or replace as necessary.
	• Damage drive pinion gear or ring gear	• Replace damaged gear(s)
	• Starter motor engagement weak	• Bench-test starter motor
	• Starter motor rotates slowly with high load current	• Inspect drive yoke pull-down and point gap, check for worn end bushings, check ring gear clearance
	• Engine seized	• Repair engine
Starter motor drive will not engage (solenoid known to be good)	• Defective contact point assembly	• Repair or replace contact point assembly
	• Inadequate contact point assembly ground	• Repair connection at ground screw
	• Defective hold-in coil	• Replace field winding assembly

Troubleshooting Basic Starting System Problems (cont.)

Problem	Cause	Solution
Starter motor drive will not disengage (cont.)	• Starter motor loose on flywheel housing • Worn drive end busing • Damaged ring gear teeth • Drive yoke return spring broken or missing	• Tighten mounting bolts • Replace bushing • Replace ring gear or driveplate • Replace spring
Starter motor drive disengages prematurely	• Weak drive assembly thrust spring • Hold-in coil defective	• Replace drive mechanism • Replace field winding assembly
Low load current	• Worn brushes • Weak brush springs	• Replace brushes • Replace springs

the B20, the B30, the B21/B23/B230/B234 and the B27/B28/B280. The 4-cylinder, 1999 cc B20 and the 6-cylinder, 2980 cc B30 are both based on the same inline, overhead valve design. The B21 (2127 cc) is an overhead camshaft engine with a cast iron block and an aluminum, cross flow head (intake and exhaust manifolds are on separate sides of the head). The B23 (2320 cc), which is very similar to the B21 series, but has a bigger bore and a new block design. The B230 series, introduced in 1985, is a further refinement of the B23. Lighter pistons and pins, low-friction rings and assorted other modifications to increase economy and reduce vibration.

The B27 and its 1980 version, the B28, are 90° V6 engines with aluminum alloy blocks and heads. Both engines are basically the same. The B28's cylinder displacement (2849 cc) is larger than the B27's (2664 cc). Many parts on the B28 have been redesigned and, therefore, cannot be exchanged with B27 parts. Each cylinder head of the B27/B28 is equipped with a single overhead camshaft which is chain driven from the crankshaft. The block is fitted with cast iron cylinder liners. The B280 features improved oil cooling, cam-driven distributor, and redesigned manifolds with swirl chamber intakes.

The B234 engine was introduced in the late 1988 740 GLE. This 16 valve twin camshaft engine is the B230 with a different head and valve layout. Its sophisticated design allows it to deliver more power more smoothly. It incorporates two balance shafts on the side of the block to damp out harsh engine vibration. These shafts are belt driven, as are the two camshafts.

The inline 6-cylinder diesel engine, the D24, used by Volvo is built by Volkswagen and is fundamentally the same as the Audi 5000 except, of course, for the extra cylinder tacked on at the end. The cylinder block is cast iron while the head is aluminum alloy. The overhead camshaft is driven by a belt at the front of the engine and in turn drives the fuel injection pump via a belt at the back of the engine. The D24T is a turbocharged variant of the D24 and shares most of the design features.

Engine Overhaul Tips

Most engine overhaul procedures are fairly standard. In addition to specific parts replacement procedures and complete specifications for your individual engine, this chapter also is a guide to accepted rebuilding procedures. Examples of standard rebuilding practice are shown and should be used along with specific details concerning your particular engine.

Competent and accurate machine shop services will ensure maximum performance, reliability and engine life.

In most instances it is more profitable for the do-it-yourself mechanic to remove, clean and inspect the component, buy the necessary parts and deliver these to a shop for actual machine work.

On the other hand, much of the rebuilding work (crankshaft, block, bearings, piston rods, and other components) is well within the scope of the do-it-yourself mechanic.

TOOLS

The tools required for an engine overhaul or parts replacement will depend on the depth of your involvement. With a few exceptions, they will be the tools found in a mechanic's tool kit (see Chapter 1). More in-depth work will require any or all of the following:

• a dial indicator (reading in thousandths) mounted on a universal base
• micrometers and telescope gauges
• jaw and screw-type pullers
• scraper
• valve spring compressor
• ring groove cleaner

- piston ring expander and compressor
- ridge reamer
- cylinder hone or glaze breaker
- Plastigage®
- engine stand

Occasionally, the use of special tools is called for. See the information on Special Tools and Safety Notice in the front of this book before substituting another tool.

The use of most of these tools is illustrated in this chapter. Many can be rented for a one-time use from a local parts jobber or tool supply house specializing in automotive work.

INSPECTION TECHNIQUES

Procedures and specifications are given in this chapter for inspecting, cleaning and assessing the wear limits of most major components. Other procedures such as Magnaflux® and Zyglo® can be used to locate material flaws and stress cracks. Magnaflux® is a magnetic process applicable only to ferrous materials. The Zyglo® process coats the material with a fluorescent dye penetrant and can be used on any material. Checks for suspected surface cracks can be more readily made using spot check dye. The dye is sprayed onto the suspected area, wiped off and the area sprayed with a developer. Cracks will show up brightly.

OVERHAUL TIPS

Aluminum has become extremely popular for use in engines, due to its low weight. Observe the following precautions when handling aluminum parts:

- Never hot tank aluminum parts (the caustic hot tank solution will eat the aluminum.
- Remove all aluminum parts (identification tag, etc.) from engine parts prior to the tanking.
- Always coat threads lightly with engine oil or anti-seize compounds before installation, to prevent seizure.
- Never overtorque bolts or spark plugs especially in aluminum threads.

Stripped threads in any component can be repaired using any of several commercial repair kits (Heli-Coil®, Microdot®, Keenserts®, etc.).

When assembling the engine, any parts that will be under frictional contact must be prelubed to provide lubrication at initial start-up. Any product specifically formulated for this purpose can be used, but engine oil is NOT recommended as a prelube.

When semi-permanent (locked, but remov-

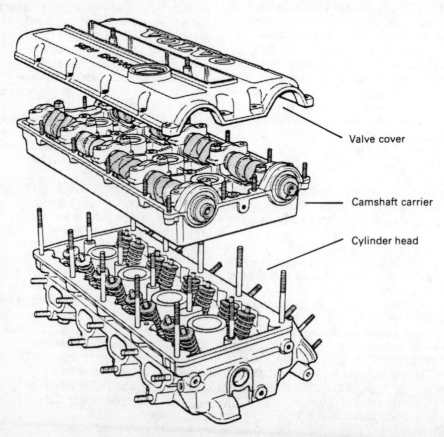

Head, camshaft and valve layout of B234 motor

- Valve cover
- Camshaft carrier
- Cylinder head

able) installation of bolts or nuts is desired, threads should be cleaned and coated with Loctite® or other similar, commercial non-hardening sealant.

REPAIRING DAMAGED THREADS

Several methods of repairing damaged threads are available. Heli-Coil® (shown here), Keenserts® and Microdot® are among the most widely used. All involve basically the same principle – drilling out stripped threads, tapping the hole and installing a prewound insert – making welding, plugging and oversize fasteners unnecessary.

Two types of thread repair inserts are usually supplied: a standard type for most Inch Coarse, Inch Fine, Metric Course and Metric Fine thread sizes and a spark plug type to fit most spark plug port sizes. Consult the individual manufacturer's catalog to determine exact applications. Typical thread repair kits will contain a selection of prewound threaded inserts, a tap (corresponding to the outside diameter threads of the insert) and an installation tool. Spark plug inserts usually differ because they require a tap equipped with pilot threads and a combined reamer/tap section. Most manufacturers also supply blister-packed thread repair inserts separately in addition to a master kit containing a variety of taps and inserts plus installation tools.

Before effecting a repair to a threaded hole, remove any snapped, broken or damaged bolts or studs. Penetrating oil can be used to free frozen threads. The offending item can be removed with locking pliers or with a screw or stud extractor. After the hole is clear, the thread can be repaired, as shown in the series of accompanying illustrations.

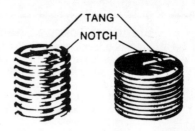

Standard thread repair insert (left) and spark plug thread insert (right)

Drill out the damaged threads with specified drill. Drill completely through the hole or to the bottom of a blind hole

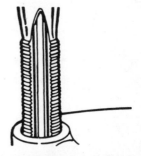

With the tap supplied, tap the hole to receive the thread insert. Keep the tap well oiled and back it out frequently to avoid clogging the threads

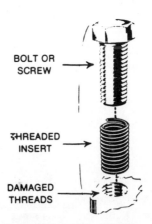

Damaged bolt holes can be repaired with thread repair inserts

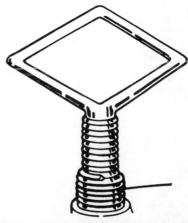

Screw the threaded insert onto the installation tool until the tang engages the slot. Screw the insert into the tapped hole until it is ¼–½ turn below the top surface, After installation break off the tang with a hammer and punch

Standard Torque Specifications and Fastener Markings

In the absence of specific torques, the following chart can be used as a guide to the maximum safe torque of a particular size/grade of fastener.

- There is no torque difference for fine or coarse threads.
- Torque values are based on clean, dry threads. Reduce the value by 10% if threads are oiled prior to assembly.
- The torque required for aluminum components or fasteners is considerably less.

U.S. Bolts

SAE Grade Number	1 or 2			5			6 or 7		
Number of lines always 2 less than the grade number.									
Bolt Size (Inches)—(Thread)	**Maximum Torque**			**Maximum Torque**			**Maximum Torque**		
	Ft./Lbs.	Kgm	Nm	Ft./Lbs.	Kgm	Nm	Ft./Lbs.	Kgm	Nm
¼ — 20	5	0.7	6.8	8	1.1	10.8	10	1.4	13.5
— 28	6	0.8	8.1	10	1.4	13.6			
5/16 — 18	11	1.5	14.9	17	2.3	23.0	19	2.6	25.8
— 24	13	1.8	17.6	19	2.6	25.7			
3/8 — 16	18	2.5	24.4	31	4.3	42.0	34	4.7	46.0
— 24	20	2.75	27.1	35	4.8	47.5			
7/16 — 14	28	3.8	37.0	49	6.8	66.4	55	7.6	74.5
— 20	30	4.2	40.7	55	7.6	74.5			
½ — 13	39	5.4	52.8	75	10.4	101.7	85	11.75	115.2
— 20	41	5.7	55.6	85	11.7	115.2			
9/16 — 12	51	7.0	69.2	110	15.2	149.1	120	16.6	162.7
— 18	55	7.6	74.5	120	16.6	162.7			
5/8 — 11	83	11.5	112.5	150	20.7	203.3	167	23.0	226.5
— 18	95	13.1	128.8	170	23.5	230.5			
¾ — 10	105	14.5	142.3	270	37.3	366.0	280	38.7	379.6
— 16	115	15.9	155.9	295	40.8	400.0			
7/8 — 9	160	22.1	216.9	395	54.6	535.5	440	60.9	596.5
— 14	175	24.2	237.2	435	60.1	589.7			
1 — 8	236	32.5	318.6	590	81.6	799.9	660	91.3	894.8
— 14	250	34.6	338.9	660	91.3	849.8			

Metric Bolts

Relative Strength Marking	4.6, 4.8			8.8		
Bolt Markings						
Bolt Size Thread Size x Pitch (mm)	**Maximum Torque**			**Maximum Torque**		
	Ft./Lbs.	Kgm	Nm	Ft./Lbs.	Kgm	Nm
6 x 1.0	2–3	.2–.4	3–4	3–6	.4–.8	5–8
8 x 1.25	6–8	.8–1	8–12	9–14	1.2–1.9	13–19
10 x 1.25	12–17	1.5–2.3	16–23	20–29	2.7–4.0	27–39
12 x 1.25	21–32	2.9–4.4	29–43	35–53	4.8–7.3	47–72
14 x 1.5	35–52	4.8–7.1	48–70	57–85	7.8–11.7	77–110
16 x 1.5	51–77	7.0–10.6	67–100	90–120	12.4–16.5	130–160
18 x 1.5	74–110	10.2–15.1	100–150	130–170	17.9–23.4	180–230
20 x 1.5	110–140	15.1–19.3	150–190	190–240	26.2–46.9	160–320
22 x 1.5	150–190	22.0–26.2	200–260	250–320	34.5–44.1	340–430
24 x 1.5	190–240	26.2–46.9	260–320	310–410	42.7–56.5	420–550

Checking Engine Compression

A noticeable lack of engine power, excessive oil consumption and/or poor fuel mileage measured over an extended period are all indicators of internal engine war. Worn piston rings, scored or worn cylinder bores, blown head gaskets, sticking or burnt valves and worn valve seats are all possible culprits here. A check of each cylinder's compression will help you locate the problems.

As mentioned in the Tools and Equipment section of Chapter 1, a screw-in type compression gauge is more accurate that the type you simply hold against the spark plug hole, although it takes slightly longer to use. It's worth it to obtain a more accurate reading. Follow the procedures below.

Gasoline Engines

1. Warm up the engine to normal operating temperature.
2. Remove all the spark plugs.
3. Disconnect the high tension lead from the ignition coil.
4. On fully open the throttle either by operating the carburetor throttle linkage by hand or by having an assistant floor the accelerator pedal.
5. Screw the compression gauge into the no.1 spark plug hole until the fitting is snug.
  WARNING: *Be careful not to crossthread the plug hole. On aluminum cylinder heads use extra care, as the threads in these heads are easily ruined.*
6. Ask an assistant to depress the accelerator pedal fully on both carbureted and fuel injected vehicles. Then, while you read the compression gauge, ask the assistant to crank the engine two or three times in short bursts using the ignition switch.
7. Read the compression gauge at the end of each series of cranks, and record the highest of these readings. Repeat this procedure for each of the engine's cylinders. Compare the highest reading of each cylinder to the compression pressure specification in the Tune-Up Specifications chart in Chapter 2. The specs in this chart are maximum values.

A cylinder's compression pressure is usually acceptable if it is not less than 80% of maximum. The difference between any two cylinders should be no more than 12–14 pounds.

8. If a cylinder is unusually low, pour a tablespoon of clean engine oil into the cylinder through the spark plug hole and repeat the compression test. If the compression comes up after adding the oil, it appears that the cylinder's piston rings or bore are damaged or worn. If the pressure remains low, the valves may not be seating properly (a valve job is needed), or the head gasket may be blown near that cylinder. If compression in any two adjacent cylinders is low, and if the addition of oil doesn't help the compression, there is leakage past the head gasket. Oil and coolant water in the combustion chamber can result from this problem. There may be evidence of water droplets on the engine dipstick when a head gasket has blown.

Diesel Engines

Checking cylinder compression on diesel engines is basically the same procedure as on gasoline engines except for the following:

1. A special compression gauge adaptor suitable for diesel engines (because these engines have much greater compression pressures) must be used.
2. Remove the injector tubes and remove the injectors from each cylinder.
  WARNING:
  Don't forget to remove the washer underneath each injector. Otherwise, it may get lost when the engine is cranked.
3. When fitting the compression gauge adaptor to the cylinder head, make sure the bleeder of the gauge (if equipped) is closed.
4. When reinstalling the injector assemblies, install new washers underneath each injector.

Engine
REMOVAL AND INSTALLATION
B20, B30

All Volvo engines and transmissions are removed as a unit. In most cases, a good chain hoist will suffice. Do not attempt to lift the engine with the chain wrapped around either the oil filter or the distributor. Lifting eyes may be fabricated from heavy gauge steel or angle iron.

1. Scribe the outline of the hinges on the hood and remove the hood.
  CAUTION: *When draining the coolant, keep in mind that cats and dogs are attracted by the ethylene glycol antifreeze, and are quite likely to drink any that is left in an uncovered container or in puddles on the ground. This will prove fatal in sufficient quantity. Always drain the coolant into a sealable container. Coolant should be reused unless it is contaminated or several years old.*
2. Drain the oil from the crankcase. Open the drain plug on the right hand side of the engine block, disconnect the lower radiator hose at the radiator, and drain the cooling system. On Volvos with automatic transmission, disconnect and plug the transmission cooler lines.
  CAUTION: *The EPA warns that prolonged*

Troubleshooting Engine Mechanical Problems

Problem	Cause	Solution
External oil leaks	• Fuel pump gasket broken or improperly seated	• Replace gasket
	• Cylinder head cover RTV sealant broken or improperly seated	• Replace sealant; inspect cylinder head cover sealant flange and cylinder head sealant surface for distortion and cracks
	• Oil filler cap leaking or missing	• Replace cap
	• Oil filter gasket broken or improperly seated	• Replace oil filter
	• Oil pan side gasket broken, improperly seated or opening in RTV sealant	• Replace gasket or repair opening in sealant; inspect oil pan gasket flange for distortion
	• Oil pan front oil seal broken or improperly seated	• Replace seal; inspect timing case cover and oil pan seal flange for distortion
	• Oil pan rear oil seal broken or improperly seated	• Replace seal; inspect oil pan rear oil seal flange; inspect rear main bearing cap for cracks, plugged oil return channels, or distortion in seal groove
	• Timing case cover oil seal broken or improperly seated	• Replace seal
	• Excess oil pressure because of restricted PCV valve	• Replace PCV valve
	• Oil pan drain plug loose or has stripped threads	• Repair as necessary and tighten
	• Rear oil gallery plug loose	• Use appropriate sealant on gallery plug and tighten
	• Rear camshaft plug loose or improperly seated	• Seat camshaft plug or replace and seal, as necessary
	• Distributor base gasket damaged	• Replace gasket
Excessive oil consumption	• Oil level too high	• Drain oil to specified level
	• Oil with wrong viscosity being used	• Replace with specified oil
	• PCV valve stuck closed	• Replace PCV valve
	• Valve stem oil deflectors (or seals) are damaged, missing, or incorrect type	• Replace valve stem oil deflectors
	• Valve stems or valve guides worn	• Measure stem-to-guide clearance and repair as necessary
	• Poorly fitted or missing valve cover baffles	• Replace valve cover
	• Piston rings broken or missing	• Replace broken or missing rings
	• Scuffed piston	• Replace piston
	• Incorrect piston ring gap	• Measure ring gap, repair as necessary
	• Piston rings sticking or excessively loose in grooves	• Measure ring side clearance, repair as necessary
	• Compression rings installed upside down	• Repair as necessary
	• Cylinder walls worn, scored, or glazed	• Repair as necessary
	• Piston ring gaps not properly staggered	• Repair as necessary
	• Excessive main or connecting rod bearing clearance	• Measure bearing clearance, repair as necessary
No oil pressure	• Low oil level	• Add oil to correct level
	• Oil pressure gauge, warning lamp or sending unit inaccurate	• Replace oil pressure gauge or warning lamp
	• Oil pump malfunction	• Replace oil pump
	• Oil pressure relief valve sticking	• Remove and inspect oil pressure relief valve assembly
	• Oil passages on pressure side of pump obstructed	• Inspect oil passages for obstruction

Troubleshooting Engine Mechanical Problems (cont.)

Problem	Cause	Solution
No oil pressure (cont.)	• Oil pickup screen or tube obstructed	• Inspect oil pickup for obstruction
	• Loose oil inlet tube	• Tighten or seal inlet tube
Low oil pressure	• Low oil level	• Add oil to correct level
	• Inaccurate gauge, warning lamp or sending unit	• Replace oil pressure gauge or warning lamp
	• Oil excessively thin because of dilution, poor quality, or improper grade	• Drain and refill crankcase with recommended oil
	• Excessive oil temperature	• Correct cause of overheating engine
	• Oil pressure relief spring weak or sticking	• Remove and inspect oil pressure relief valve assembly
	• Oil inlet tube and screen assembly has restriction or air leak	• Remove and inspect oil inlet tube and screen assembly. (Fill inlet tube with lacquer thinner to locate leaks.)
	• Excessive oil pump clearance	• Measure clearances
	• Excessive main, rod, or camshaft bearing clearance	• Measure bearing clearances, repair as necessary
High oil pressure	• Improper oil viscosity	• Drain and refill crankcase with correct viscosity oil
	• Oil pressure gauge or sending unit inaccurate	• Replace oil pressure gauge
	• Oil pressure relief valve sticking closed	• Remove and inspect oil pressure relief valve assembly
Main bearing noise	• Insufficient oil supply	• Inspect for low oil level and low oil pressure
	• Main bearing clearance excessive	• Measure main bearing clearance, repair as necessary
	• Bearing insert missing	• Replace missing insert
	• Crankshaft end play excessive	• Measure end play, repair as necessary
	• Improperly tightened main bearing cap bolts	• Tighten bolts with specified torque
	• Loose flywheel or drive plate	• Tighten flywheel or drive plate attaching bolts
	• Loose or damaged vibration damper	• Repair as necessary
Connecting rod bearing noise	• Insufficient oil supply	• Inspect for low oil level and low oil pressure
	• Carbon build-up on piston	• Remove carbon from piston crown
	• Bearing clearance excessive or bearing missing	• Measure clearance, repair as necessary
	• Crankshaft connecting rod journal out-of-round	• Measure journal dimensions, repair or replace as necessary
	• Misaligned connecting rod or cap	• Repair as necessary
	• Connecting rod bolts tightened improperly	• Tighten bolts with specified torque
Piston noise	• Piston-to-cylinder wall clearance excessive (scuffed piston)	• Measure clearance and examine piston
	• Cylinder walls excessively tapered or out-of-round	• Measure cylinder wall dimensions, rebore cylinder
	• Piston ring broken	• Replace all rings on piston
	• Loose or seized piston pin	• Measure piston-to-pin clearance, repair as necessary
	• Connecting rods misaligned	• Measure rod alignment, straighten or replace
	• Piston ring side clearance excessively loose or tight	• Measure ring side clearance, repair as necessary
	• Carbon build-up on piston is excessive	• Remove carbon from piston

Troubleshooting Engine Mechanical Problems (cont.)

Problem	Cause	Solution
Valve actuating component noise	• Insufficient oil supply	• Check for: (a) Low oil level (b) Low oil pressure (c) Plugged push rods (d) Wrong hydraulic tappets (e) Restricted oil gallery (f) Excessive tappet to bore clearance
	• Push rods worn or bent	• Replace worn or bent push rods
	• Rocker arms or pivots worn	• Replace worn rocker arms or pivots
	• Foreign objects or chips in hydraulic tappets	• Clean tappets
	• Excessive tappet leak-down	• Replace valve tappet
	• Tappet face worn	• Replace tappet; inspect corresponding cam lobe for wear
	• Broken or cocked valve springs	• Properly seat cocked springs; replace broken springs
	• Stem-to-guide clearance excessive	• Measure stem-to-guide clearance, repair as required
	• Valve bent	• Replace valve
	• Loose rocker arms	• Tighten bolts with specified torque
	• Valve seat runout excessive	• Regrind valve seat/valves
	• Missing valve lock	• Install valve lock
	• Push rod rubbing or contacting cylinder head	• Remove cylinder head and remove obstruction in head
	• Excessive engine oil (four-cylinder engine)	• Correct oil level

Troubleshooting the Cooling System

Problem	Cause	Solution
High temperature gauge indication—overheating	• Coolant level low	• Replenish coolant
	• Fan belt loose	• Adjust fan belt tension
	• Radiator hose(s) collapsed	• Replace hose(s)
	• Radiator airflow blocked	• Remove restriction (bug screen, fog lamps, etc.)
	• Faulty radiator cap	• Replace radiator cap
	• Ignition timing incorrect	• Adjust ignition timing
	• Idle speed low	• Adjust idle speed
	• Air trapped in cooling system	• Purge air
	• Heavy traffic driving	• Operate at fast idle in neutral intermittently to cool engine
	• Incorrect cooling system component(s) installed	• Install proper component(s)
	• Faulty thermostat	• Replace thermostat
	• Water pump shaft broken or impeller loose	• Replace water pump
	• Radiator tubes clogged	• Flush radiator
	• Cooling system clogged	• Flush system
	• Casting flash in cooling passages	• Repair or replace as necessary. Flash may be visible by removing cooling system components or removing core plugs.
	• Brakes dragging	• Repair brakes
	• Excessive engine friction	• Repair engine
	• Antifreeze concentration over 68%	• Lower antifreeze concentration percentage
	• Missing air seals	• Replace air seals
	• Faulty gauge or sending unit	• Repair or replace faulty component
	• Loss of coolant flow caused by leakage or foaming	• Repair or replace leaking component, replace coolant
	• Viscous fan drive failed	• Replace unit

Troubleshooting the Cooling System (cont.)

Problem	Cause	Solution
Low temperature indication—undercooling	• Thermostat stuck open • Faulty gauge or sending unit	• Replace thermostat • Repair or replace faulty component
Coolant loss—boilover	• Overfilled cooling system • Quick shutdown after hard (hot) run • Air in system resulting in occasional "burping" of coolant • Insufficient antifreeze allowing coolant boiling point to be too low • Antifreeze deteriorated because of age or contamination • Leaks due to loose hose clamps, loose nuts, bolts, drain plugs, faulty hoses, or defective radiator • Faulty head gasket • Cracked head, manifold, or block • Faulty radiator cap	• Reduce coolant level to proper specification • Allow engine to run at fast idle prior to shutdown • Purge system • Add antifreeze to raise boiling point • Replace coolant • Pressure test system to locate source of leak(s) then repair as necessary • Replace head gasket • Replace as necessary • Replace cap
Coolant entry into crankcase or cylinder(s)	• Faulty head gasket • Crack in head, manifold or block	• Replace head gasket • Replace as necessary
Coolant recovery system inoperative	• Coolant level low • Leak in system • Pressure cap not tight or seal missing, or leaking • Pressure cap defective • Overflow tube clogged or leaking • Recovery bottle vent restricted	• Replenish coolant to FULL mark • Pressure test to isolate leak and repair as necessary • Repair as necessary • Replace cap • Repair as necessary • Remove restriction
Noise	• Fan contacting shroud • Loose water pump impeller • Glazed fan belt • Loose fan belt • Rough surface on drive pulley • Water pump bearing worn • Belt alignment	• Reposition shroud and inspect engine mounts • Replace pump • Apply silicone or replace belt • Adjust fan belt tension • Replace pulley • Remove belt to isolate. Replace pump. • Check pulley alignment. Repair as necessary.
No coolant flow through heater core	• Restricted return inlet in water pump • Heater hose collapsed or restricted • Restricted heater core • Restricted outlet in thermostat housing • Intake manifold bypass hole in cylinder head restricted • Faulty heater control valve • Intake manifold coolant passage restricted	• Remove restriction • Remove restriction or replace hose • Remove restriction or replace core • Remove flash or restriction • Remove restriction • Replace valve • Remove restriction or replace intake manifold

NOTE: *Immediately after shutdown, the engine enters a condition known as heat soak. This is caused by the cooling system being inoperative while engine temperature is still high. If coolant temperature rises above boiling point, expansion and pressure may push some coolant out of the radiator overflow tube. If this does not occur frequently it is considered normal.*

Troubleshooting the Serpentine Drive Belt

Problem	Cause	Solution
Tension sheeting fabric failure (woven fabric on outside circumference of belt has cracked or separated from body of belt)	• Grooved or backside idler pulley diameters are less than minimum recommended • Tension sheeting contacting (rubbing) stationary object • Excessive heat causing woven fabric to age • Tension sheeting splice has fractured	• Replace pulley(s) not conforming to specification • Correct rubbing condition • Replace belt • Replace belt
Noise (objectional squeal, squeak, or rumble is heard or felt while drive belt is in operation)	• Belt slippage • Bearing noise • Belt misalignment • Belt-to-pulley mismatch • Driven component inducing vibration • System resonant frequency inducing vibration	• Adjust belt • Locate and repair • Align belt/pulley(s) • Install correct belt • Locate defective driven component and repair • Vary belt tension within specifications. Replace belt.
Rib chunking (one or more ribs has separated from belt body)	• Foreign objects imbedded in pulley grooves • Installation damage • Drive loads in excess of design specifications • Insufficient internal belt adhesion	• Remove foreign objects from pulley grooves • Replace belt • Adjust belt tension • Replace belt
Rib or belt wear (belt ribs contact bottom of pulley grooves)	• Pulley(s) misaligned • Mismatch of belt and pulley groove widths • Abrasive environment • Rusted pulley(s) • Sharp or jagged pulley groove tips • Rubber deteriorated	• Align pulley(s) • Replace belt • Replace belt • Clean rust from pulley(s) • Replace pulley • Replace belt
Longitudinal belt cracking (cracks between two ribs)	• Belt has mistracked from pulley groove • Pulley groove tip has worn away rubber-to-tensile member	• Replace belt • Replace belt
Belt slips	• Belt slipping because of insufficient tension • Belt or pulley subjected to substance (belt dressing, oil, ethylene glycol) that has reduced friction • Driven component bearing failure • Belt glazed and hardened from heat and excessive slippage	• Adjust tension • Replace belt and clean pulleys • Replace faulty component bearing • Replace belt
"Groove jumping" (belt does not maintain correct position on pulley, or turns over and/or runs off pulleys)	• Insufficient belt tension • Pulley(s) not within design tolerance • Foreign object(s) in grooves • Excessive belt speed • Pulley misalignment • Belt-to-pulley profile mismatched • Belt cordline is distorted	• Adjust belt tension • Replace pulley(s) • Remove foreign objects from grooves • Avoid excessive engine acceleration • Align pulley(s) • Install correct belt • Replace belt
Belt broken (Note: identify and correct problem before replacement belt is installed)	• Excessive tension • Tensile members damaged during belt installation • Belt turnover • Severe pulley misalignment • Bracket, pulley, or bearing failure	• Replace belt and adjust tension to specification • Replace belt • Replace belt • Align pulley(s) • Replace defective component and belt

Troubleshooting the Serpentine Drive Belt (cont.)

Problem	Cause	Solution
Cord edge failure (tensile member exposed at edges of belt or separated from belt body)	• Excessive tension • Drive pulley misalignment • Belt contacting stationary object • Pulley irregularities • Improper pulley construction • Insufficient adhesion between tensile member and rubber matrix	• Adjust belt tension • Align pulley • Correct as necessary • Replace pulley • Replace pulley • Replace belt and adjust tension to specifications
Sporadic rib cracking (multiple cracks in belt ribs at random intervals)	• Ribbed pulley(s) diameter less than minimum specification • Backside bend flat pulley(s) diameter less than minimum • Excessive heat condition causing rubber to harden • Excessive belt thickness • Belt overcured • Excessive tension	• Replace pulley(s) • Replace pulley(s) • Correct heat condition as necessary • Replace belt • Replace belt • Adjust belt tension

contact with used engine oil may cause a number of skin disorders, including cancer! You should make every effort to minimize your exposure to used engine oil. Protective gloves should be worn when changing the oil. Wash your hands and any other exposed skin areas as soon as possible after exposure to used engine oil. Soap and water, or waterless hand cleaner should be used.

3. Remove the expansion tank, radiator cover plate, upper radiator hose, radiator, and fan shroud, if so equipped.

4. Remove the negative lead from the battery.

5. Remove and label the electric cables for the starter, the coil high tension wire, the distributor lead, alternator wires, water and oil temperature sensors, and the lead for the oil pressure sensor, if so equipped.

6. Remove and label the vacuum hoses for the distributor advance, and the power brake booster, if so equipped. Remove the positive crankcase ventilation (PCV) hoses, and the oil pressure gauge hose at the pipe connection, if so equipped.

7a. On electric fuel injected models, remove the air cleaner and intake hoses; pressure sensor hose from the inlet duct; the plug contacts for the temperature sensor, cold start valve, throttle valve switch, fuel injectors, and distributor impulse unit. Label all lines and hoses.

In addition, remove the ground wire from the inlet duct, the throttle cable bracket from the inlet duct, the throttle cable from the throttle valve switch, the cold start valve fuel hose from the distribution pipe, the fuel return line from the pressure regulator, and the fuel inlet line from the distribution pipe. Remove the injectors by turning the lockrings counterclockwise

and lifting them out of their bayonet fittings. The injectors should then be fitted with protective covers and plugs to prevent dirt from entering.

7b. On continuous (air-flow controlled) fuel injected models, disconnect the rubber hose to the control pressure regulator, the plastic hose from the pressure regulator to the fuel distributor, the hose at the cold start injector, the fuel filter hose, and the fuel return hose at the fuel distributor. Remove the pipe connecting the air cleaner and the intake manifold. Label all lines and hoses.

Disconnect the electrical leads from the cold start injector, control pressure regulator, auxiliary air valve, coolant temperature sensor and the thermal time switch (engine side). Disconnect the ground wire for the control pressure regulator. Disconnect and plug the 4 fuel hoses at the injectors. Disconnect the throttle cable from the throttle and intake manifold. Disconnect the brake booster vacuum hose. Remove the thermal time switch.

7c. On carbureted models, remove the air cleaner, air intake hoses, and preheating plate. Also disconnect and plug the inlet hose to the fuel pump, disconnect the choke linkage, and remove the throttle control shaft from the pedal shaft, intermediate shaft, and bracket.

8. Disconnect the heater pipes from all models. Remove the exhaust pipe flange nuts and disconnect the exhaust pipe from the manifold. Remove the EGR valve pipe from the manifold. On models equipped with power steering, remove the steering pump bolts and place the pump and reservoir to one side.

9. On Volvos with manual transmission, place the gearshift in neutral and remove the shifter lever. On Volvos with automatic trans-

General Engine Specifications

Year	Engine Designation	Engine Displacement Cu in. (cc)	Fuel Delivery	Horsepower @ rpm (gross)	Torque @ rpm (ft. lbs.) (gross)	Bore x Stroke (in.)	Com-pression Ratio	Oil Pressure @ rpm (psi)
1970	B 20 B	122 (1990)	2 sidedraft Zenith-Stromberg 175 CD 2SE	118 @ 5800	123 @ 3500	3.500 x 3.150	9.3:1	36–85 @ 2000
1971–72	B 20 B	122 (1990)	2 sidedraft SU HIF 6	118 @ 5800	123 @ 3500	3.5004 x 3.150	9.3:1	36–85 @ 2000
1970–71	B 20 E	122 (1990)	Bosch electronic fuel injection	130 @ 6000	130 @ 3500	3.5008 x 3.150	10.5:1	36–85 @ 2000
1972	B 20 F	122 (1990)	Bosch electronic fuel injection	125 @ 3500	123 @ 3500	3.5008 x 3.150	8.7:1	36–85 @ 2000
1970–72	B 30 A	183 (2978)	2 sidedraft Zenith-Stormberg 175 CD 2SE	145 @ 5500	163 @ 3000	3.5000 x 3.150	9.3:1	36–85 @ 2000
1972	B 30 F	183 (2978)	Bosch electronic fuel injection	160 @ 5800	167 @ 2500	3.5010 x 3.150	8.7:1	36–85 @ 2000
1973–74	B 30 F	183 (2978)	Bosch electronic fuel injection	138 @ 5500	155 @ 3500	3.501 x 3.150	8.7:1	36–85 @ 2000
1975	B 30 F	183 (2978)	Bosch electronic fuel injection	130 @ 5250 ③	150 @ 4000 ④	3.501 x 3.150	8.7:1	36–85 @ 2000
1976–78	B 27 F	162 (2660)	Bosch continuous injection	125 @ 5500 ⑦	150 @ 2750 ⑧	3.4646 x 2.8740	8.2:1	58 @ 3000
1973	B 20 F	122 (1990)	Bosch electronic fuel injection	112 @ 6000	115 @ 3500	3.5008 x 3.150	8.7:1	36–85 @ 2000
1974	B 20 F	122 (1990)	Bosch continuous injection	109 @ 6000	115 @ 3500	3.5008 x 3.150	8.7:1	36–85 @ 2000
1975	B 20 F	122 (1990)	Bosch continuous injection	98 @ 6000 ①	110 @ 3500 ②	3.5008 x 3.150	8.7:1	36–85 @ 2000
1976–78	B 21 F	130 (2127)	Bosch continuous injection	102 @ 5200 ⑤	114 @ 2500 ⑥	3.623 x 3.150	8.5:1	35–85 @ 2000
1979–82	B 21 F	130 (2127)	Bosch continuous fuel injection	107 @ 5250	117 @ 2500 ⑨	3.623 x 3.150	9.3:1	35–85 @ 2000

① 94 @ 6000 w/catalytic converter
② 105 @ 3500 w/catalytic converter
③ 125 @ 5250 w/catalytic converter
④ 145 @ 4000 w/catalytic converter
⑤ 99 @ 5200 in Calif.
⑥ 114 @ 2500 in Calif.
⑦ 121 @ 5500 in Calif.
⑧ 148 @ 2750 in Calif.
⑨ 114 in Calif.

General Engine Specifications (cont.)

Year	Model	Engine Displacement cu. in. (cc)	Fuel System Type	Net Horsepower @ rpm	Net Torque @ rpm (ft. lbs.)	Bore x Stroke (in.)	Com- pression Ratio	Oil Pressure @ rpm
1982	240 DL	130 (2127) B21F	CIS	98 @ 5000	112 @ 3000	3.62 x 3.15	9.3:1	35–85 @ 2000
	DL ③	130 (2127) B21F	LH	105 @ 5400	119 @ 3000	3.62 x 3.15	9.3:1	35–85 @ 2000
	DL ①	130 (2127) B21A	1-bbl Zenith	100 @ 5250	122 @ 2500	3.62 x 3.15	9.3:1	35–85 @ 2000
	GL	130 (2127) B21F	CIS	98 @ 5000	112 @ 3000	3.62 x 3.15	9.3:1	35–85 @ 2000
	GL	145 (2383) D24	DFI	76 @ 4800	98 @ 2800	3.01 x 3.40	23.0:1	28 @ 2000
	GL ①	140 (2320) B23E	CIS	127 @ 5500	133 @ 4500	3.78 x 3.15	10.0:1	35–85 @ 2000
	GLT	130 (2127) B21F-Turbo	CIS	127 @ 5400	150 @ 3750	3.62 x 3.15	7.5:1	35–85 @ 2000
	GLT	130 (2127) B21F	CIS	98 @ 5000	112 @ 3000	3.62 x 3.15	9.3:1	35–85 @ 2000
	GLT ①	140 (2320) B23E	CIS	127 @ 5500	133 @ 4500	3.78 x 3.15	10.0:1	35–85 @ 2000
	260 GLE	174 (2849) B28F	CIS	130 @ 5500	153 @ 2750	3.58 x 2.86	8.8:1	60 @ 3000
1983	240 DL	140 (2320) B23F	LH	107 @ 5400	127 @ 3500	3.78 x 3.15	10.3:1	35–85 @ 2000
	DL	130 (2127) B21F-Turbo	CIS	127 @ 5400	150 @ 3750	3.62 x 3.15	7.5:1	35–85 @ 2000
	DL	145 (2383) D24	DFI	78 @ 4800	102 @ 3000	3.01 x 3.40	23.5:1	28 @ 2000
	DL ①	130 (2127) B21A	1-bbl Zenith	100 @ 5250	122 @ 2500	3.62 x 3.15	9.3:1	35–85 @ 2000
	GL	140 (2320) B23F	LH	107 @ 5400	127 @ 3500	3.78 x 3.15	10.3:1	35–85 @ 2000
	GL	145 (2383) D24	DFI	78 @ 4800	102 @ 3000	3.01 x 3.40	23.5:1	28 @ 2000
	GL ①	140 (2320) B23E	CIS	115 @ 5000	133 @ 3000	3.62 x 3.15	10.3:1	35–85 @ 2000
	GLT ①	140 (2320) B23E	CIS	115 @ 5000	133 @ 3000	3.62 x 3.15	10.3:1	35–85 @ 2000
	Turbo	130 (2127) B21F-Turbo	CIS	127 @ 5400	150 @ 3750	3.62 x 3.15	7.5:1	35–85 @ 2000
	760 GLE	174 (2849) B28F	CIS	134 @ 5500	159 @ 2700	3.58 x 2.86	8.8:1	60 @ 3000
	GLE	145 (2383) D24-Turbo	DFI	106 @ 4800	140 @ 2400	3.01 x 3.40	23.0:1	28 @ 2000
	Turbo	140 (2320) B23F-Turbo	LH	157 @ 5300	184 @ 2900	3.78 x 3.15	8.7:1	35–85 @ 2000
1984	240 Diesel	145 (2383) D24	DFI	78 @ 4800	102 @ 3000	3.01 x 3.40	23.5:1	28 @ 2000
	DL	140 (2320) B23F ④	LH	113 @ 5400	136 @ 2750	3.78 x 3.15	9.5:1	35–85 @ 2000

General Engine Specifications (cont.)

Year	Model	Engine Displacement cu. in. (cc)	Fuel System Type	Net Horsepower @ rpm	Net Torque @ rpm (ft. lbs.)	Bore x Stroke (in.)	Compression Ratio	Oil Pressure @ rpm
1986	DL	140 (2320) B23F ⑤	LH	114 @ 5400	133 @ 3500	3.78 x 3.15	10.3:1	35–85 @ 2000
	DL ①	130 (2127) B21A	1-bbl Zenith	100 @ 5250	122 @ 2500	3.62 x 3.15	9.3:1	35–85 @ 2000
	GL	140 (2320) B23F ④	LH	113 @ 5400	136 @ 2750	3.78 x 3.15	9.5:1	35–85 @ 2000
	GL	140 (2320) B23F ⑤	LH	114 @ 5400	133 @ 3500	3.78 x 3.15	10.3:1	35–85 @ 2000
	GLE ①	140 (2320) B23F ④	LH	113 @ 5400	136 @ 2750	3.78 x 3.15	9.5:1	35–85 @ 2000
	GLE ①	140 (2320) B23F ⑤	LH	114 @ 5400	133 @ 3500	3.78 x 3.15	10.3:1	35–85 @ 2000
	Turbo	130 (2127) B21F-Turbo	CIS	131 @ 5400	155 @ 3750	3.62 x 3.15	7.5:1	35–85 @ 2000
	760 GLE	174 (2849) B28F	CIS	134 @ 5500	159 @ 2700	3.58 x 2.86	8.8:1	60 @ 3000
	GLE	145 (2383) D24-Turbo	DFI	106 @ 4800	140 @ 2400	3.01 x 3.40	23.0:1	28 @ 2000
	Turbo	140 (2320) B23F-Turbo	LH	157 @ 5300	184 @ 2900	3.78 x 3.15	8.7:1	35–85 @ 2000
1985	240 Diesel	145 (2383) D24	DFI	80 @ 4800	103 @ 2800	3.01 x 3.40	23.0:1	28 @ 2000
	DL	140 (2320) B230F	LH	114 @ 5400	136 @ 2750	3.78 x 3.15	9.8:1	35–85 @ 2000
	GL	140 (2320) B230F	LH	114 @ 5400	136 @ 2750	3.78 x 3.15	9.8:1	35–85 @ 2000
	Turbo	130 (2127) B21F-Turbo	CIS	162 @ 5100	181 @ 3900	3.62 x 3.15	7.5:1	35–85 @ 2000
	740 GLE	140 (2320) B230F	LH	114 @ 5400	136 @ 2750	3.78 x 3.15	9.8:1	35–85 @ 2000
	TD	145 (2383) D24-Turbo	DFI	106 @ 4800	140 @ 2400	3.01 x 3.40	23.0:1	28 @ 2000
	Turbo	140 (2320) B230F-Turbo	LH	160 @ 5300	187 @ 2900	3.78 x 3.15	8.7:1	35–85 @ 2000
	760 GLE	174 (2849) B28F	CIS	134 @ 5500	159 @ 2700	3.58 x 2.86	8.8:1	60 @ 3000
	GLE TD	145 (2383) D24-Turbo	DFI	106 @ 4800	140 @ 2400	3.01 x 3.40	23.0:1	28 @ 2000
	Turbo	140 (2320) B230F-Turbo	LH	160 @ 5300	187 @ 2900	3.78 x 3.15	8.7:1	35–85 @ 2000
1986	240 DL	140 (2320) B230F	LH	114 @ 5400	136 @ 2750	3.78 x 3.15	9.8:1	35–85 @ 2000
	GL	140 (2320) B230F	LH	114 @ 5400	136 @ 2750	3.78 x 3.15	9.8:1	35–85 @ 2000
	740 GL	140 (2320) B230F	LH	114 @ 5400	136 @ 2750	3.78 x 3.15	9.8:1	35–85 @ 2000
	GLE	140 (2320) B230F	LH	114 @ 5400	136 @ 2750	3.78 x 3.15	9.8:1	35–85 @ 2000

General Engine Specifications (cont.)

Year	Model	Engine Displacement cu. in. (cc)	Fuel System Type	Net Horsepower @ rpm	Net Torque @ rpm (ft. lbs.)	Bore x Stroke (in.)	Com-pression Ratio	Oil Pressure @ rpm
	GLE TD	145 (2383) D24-Turbo	DFI	106 @ 4800	140 @ 2400	3.01 x 3.40	23.0:1	28 @ 2000
	Turbo	140 (2320) B230F-Turbo	LH	160 @ 5300	187 @ 2900	3.78 x 3.15	8.7:1	35–85 @ 2000
	760 GLE	174 (2849) B28F	CIS	136 @ 5500	159 @ 2700	3.58 x 2.86	8.8:1	60 @ 3000
	Turbo	140 (2320) B230F-Turbo	LH	160 @ 5300	187 @ 2900	3.78 x 3.15	8.7:1	35–85 @ 2000
1987	240 DL	140 (2320) B230F	LH	114 @ 5400	136 @ 2750	3.78 x 3.15	9.8:1	35–85 @ 2000
	GL	140 (2320) B230F	LH	114 @ 5400	136 @ 2750	3.78 x 3.15	9.8:1	35–85 @ 2000
	740 GL	140 (2320) B230F	LH	114 @ 5400	136 @ 2750	3.78 x 3.15	9.8:1	35–85 @ 2000
	GLE	140 (2320) B230F	LH	114 @ 5400	136 @ 2750	3.78 x 3.15	9.8:1	35–85 @ 2000
	Turbo	140 (2320) B230F-Turbo	LH	160 @ 5300	187 @ 2900	3.78 x 3.15	8.7:1	35–85 @ 2000
	760 GLE	174 (2849) B280F	LH	146 @ 5100	173 @ 3750	3.58 x 2.86	9.5:1	57 @ 3000
	Turbo	140 (2320) B230F-Turbo	LH	160 @ 5300	187 @ 2900	3.78 x 3.15	8.7:1	35–85 @ 2000
	780	174 (2849) B280F	LH	146 @ 5100	173 @ 3750	3.58 x 2.86	9.5:1	57 @ 3000
1988–89	240 DL	140 (2320) B230F	LH	114 @ 5400	136 @ 2750	3.78 x 3.15	9.8:1	35–85 @ 2000
	GL	140 (2320) B230F	LH	114 @ 5400	136 @ 2750	3.78 x 3.15	9.8:1	35–85 @ 2000
	740 GL	140 (2320) B230F	LH	114 @ 5400	136 @ 2750	3.78 x 3.15	9.8:1	35–85 @ 2000
	GLE	140 (2320) B230F	LH	114 @ 5400	136 @ 2750	3.78 x 3.15	9.8:1	35–85 @ 2000
	740 GLE 16v.	140 (2320) B234F	LH	153 @ 5700	150 @ 4450	3.78 x 3.15	10.0:1	35–85 @ 2000
	Turbo	140 (2320) B230F-Turbo	LH	160 @ 5300	187 @ 2900	3.78 x 3.15	8.7:1	35–85 @ 2000
	760 GLE	174 (2849) B280F	LH	146 @ 5100	173 @ 3750	3.58 x 2.86	9.5:1	57 @ 3000
	Turbo	140 (2320) B230F-Turbo	LH	160 @ 5300	187 @ 2900	3.78 x 3.15	8.7:1	35–85 @ 2000
	780	174 (2849) B280F	LH	146 @ 5100	173 @ 3750	3.58 x 2.86	9.5:1	57 @ 3000

CIS—Continuous Injection System
DFI—Diesel Fuel Injection
LH—LH-Jetronic Injection
① Canada only
② Station Wagon
③ California only
④ With manual transmission
⑤ With automatic transmission

Valve Specifications

Year	Engine and displacement Cu. in. (cc)	Seat Angle (deg)	Face Angle (deg)	Seat Width (in.)	Spring Test Pressure (lbs. @ in.)	Spring Installed Height (in.)	Stem to Guide Clearance (in.)		Stem Diameter (in.)	
							Intake	Exhaust	Intake	Exhaust
1970–72	B 20 B 109 (1780)	44.5	45	0.055	181.5 @ 1.18	1.81	0.0010–0.0022	0.0026–0.0037	0.3419–0.3425	0.3403–0.3409
1970–71	B 20 E 122 (1990)	44.5	45	0.08	181.5 @ 1.18	1.81	0.0012–0.0026	0.0024–0.0038	0.3132–0.0138	0.3120–0.3126
1972–75	B 20 F 122 (1990)									
1970–72	B 30 A 183 (2978)	44.5	45	0.08	145.0 @ 1.20	1.77	0.0012–0.0026	0.0024–0.0038	0.3132–0.3138	0.3120–0.3126
1972–75	B 30 F 183 (2978)	44.5	45	0.08	181.5 @ 1.18	1.81	0.0012–0.0026	0.0024–0.0038	0.3132–0.3138	0.3120–0.3126
1976–83	B 21 130 (2127)	44.75	45.5	0.08	170 @ 1.06	1.77	0.0012–0.0024	0.0024–0.0035	0.3132–0.3135	0.3126–0.3128
1983	B 23 140 (2320)	45	44.5	③	165 @ 1.06	1.77	0.0012–0.0024	0.0024–0.0035	0.3132–0.3138	0.3124–0.3128
1976–79	B 27 F 162 (2660)	29.5 Int 30 Exh	29.5 Int 20 Exh	①	124.3 @ 1.27	1.86	②	②	0.3136–0.3142 to 0.3140–0.3146	0.3128–0.3134 to 0.3136–0.3142
1980–83	B 28 F 173 (2849)	29.5 Int 30 Exh	29.5 Int 30 Exh	①	143 @ 1.181	1.854	②	②	0.3136–0.3142 to 0.3140–0.3146	0.3128–0.3134 to 0.3136–0.3142
1980–81	D 24, D 24 T Diesel	45	④	⑤	⑥	⑦	⑧	⑧	0.314	0.313

NOTE: Exhaust valves for the turbocharged engines are stellite coated and must not be machined. They may be ground against the valve seat.
① 0.067–0.083 Intake; 0.079–0.094 Exhaust   ③ 0.051–0.075 intake; 0.066–0.091 exhaust
② Tapered; valve guide ID is 0.3150–0.3158   ④ 44.5° intake; 45° exhaust
⑤ 0.08 intake; 0.094 exhaust
⑥ Two springs per valve; inner spring 49 lbs. @ 0.72 in.; outer spring 100 lbs. @ 0.878 in.
⑦ Inner 1.335 in.; outer 1.583 in.
⑧ Clearance measured with new valve guide and with valve stem edge to edge with valve guide upper end. Max. clearance 0.051 in.; new clearance 0.012 in.

Valve Specifications

Year	Engine Displacement cu. in. (cc)	Seat Angle (deg.)	Face Angle (deg.)	Spring Test Pressure (lbs. @ in.)	Spring Installed Height (in.)	Stem-to-Guide Clearance (in.)		Stem Diameter (in.)	
						Intake	Exhaust	Intake	Exhaust
1982	130 (2127) B21F	44.75	45.5	170 @ 1.06	1.77	0.0012–0.0024	0.0024–0.0035	0.3132–0.3135	0.3128–0.3126
	130 (2127) B21A①	44.75	45.5	170 @ 1.06	1.77	0.0012–0.0024	0.0024–0.0035	0.3132–0.3135	0.3128–0.3126
	130 (2127) B21F-Turbo	44.75	45.5	170 @ 1.06	1.77	0.0012–0.0024	0.0024–0.0035	0.3132–0.3135	0.3128–0.3126
	140 (2320) B23E①	45	44.5	165 @ 1.06	1.77	0.0012–0.0024	0.0024–0.0035	0.3132–0.3138	0.3128–0.3124
	145 (2383) D24	45	⑤	⑥	⑦	⑧	⑧	0.3140	0.3130
	174 (2849) B28F	②	②	143 @ 1.18	1.85	③	③	④	④
1983	130 (2127) B21A①	44.75	45.5	170 @ 1.06	1.77	0.0012–0.0024	0.0024–0.0035	0.3132–0.3135	0.3128–0.3126
	130 (2127) B21F-Turbo	44.75	45.5	170 @ 1.06	1.77	0.0012–0.0024	0.0024–0.0035	0.3132–0.3135	0.3128–0.3126
	140 (2320) B23F	45	44.5	165 @ 1.06	1.77	0.0012–0.0024	0.0024–0.0035	0.3132–0.3138	0.3128–0.3124
	140 (2320) B23E①	45	44.5	165 @ 1.06	1.77	0.0012–0.0024	0.0024–0.0035	0.3132–0.3138	0.3128–0.3124
	140 (2320) B23F-Turbo	45	44.5	165 @ 1.06	1.77	0.0012–0.0024	0.0024–0.0035	0.3132–0.3138	0.3128–0.3124
	145 (2383) D24	45	⑤	⑥	⑦	⑧	⑧	0.3140	0.3130
	145 (2383) D24-Turbo	45	⑤	⑥	⑦	⑧	⑧	0.3140	0.3130
	174 (2849) B28F	②	②	143 @ 1.18	1.85	③	③	④	④

Valve Specifications (cont.)

Year	Engine Displacement cu. in. (cc)	Seat Angle (deg.)	Face Angle (deg.)	Spring Test Pressure (lbs. @ in.)	Spring Installed Height (in.)	Stem-to-Guide Clearance (in.)		Stem Diameter (in.)	
						Intake	Exhaust	Intake	Exhaust
1984	130 (2127) B21A①	44.75	45.5	170 @ 1.06	1.77	0.0012–0.0024	0.0024–0.0035	0.3132–0.3135	0.3128–0.3126
	130 (2127) B21F-Turbo	44.75	45.5	170 @ 1.06	1.77	0.0012–0.0024	0.0024–0.0035	0.3132–0.3135	0.3128–0.3726
	140 (2320) B23F	45	44.5	165 @ 1.06	1.77	0.0012–0.0024	0.0024–0.0035	0.3132–0.3138	0.3128–0.3124
	140 (2320) B23F-Turbo	45	44.5	165 @ 1.06	1.77	0.0012–0.0024	0.0024–0.0035	0.3132–0.3138	0.3128–0.3124
	145 (2383) D24	45	⑤	⑥	⑦	⑧	⑧	0.3140	0.3130
	145 (2383) D24-Turbo	45	⑤	⑥	⑦	⑧	⑧	0.3140	0.3130
	174 (2849) B28F	②	②	143 @ 1.18	1.85	③	③	④	④
1985	130 (2127) B21F-Turbo	44.75	45.5	170 @ 1.06	1.77	0.0012–0.0024	0.0024–0.0035	0.3132–0.3135	0.3128–0.3126
	140 (2320) B230F	45	44.5	170 @ 1.06	1.79	0.0012–0.0024	0.0024–0.0036	0.3132–0.3138	0.3128–0.3134
	140 (2320) B230F-Turbo	45	44.5	170 @ 1.06	1.79	0.0012–0.0024	0.0024–0.0036	0.3132–0.3138	0.3128–0.3134
	145 (2383) D24	45	⑤	⑥	⑦	⑧	⑧	0.3140	0.3130
	145 (2383) D24-Turbo	45	⑤	⑥	⑦	⑧	⑧	0.3140	0.3130
	174 (2849) B28F	②	②	143 @ 1.18	1.85	③	③	④	④

Year	Engine cu in (cc)/ID								
1986	140 (2320) B230F	45	44.5	158 @ 1.08	1.79	0.0012–0.0024	0.0024–0.0036	0.3132–0.3138	0.3128–0.3134
	140 (2320) B230F-Turbo	45	44.5	158 @ 1.08	1.79	0.0012–0.0024	0.0024–0.0036	0.3132–0.3138	0.3128–0.3134
	145 (2383) D24-Turbo	45	⑤	⑥	⑦	⑧	⑧	0.3140	0.3130
	174 (2849) B28F	②	②	143 @ 1.18	1.85	③	③	④	④
1987	140 (2320) B230F	45	44.5	158 @ 1.08	1.79	0.0012–0.0024	0.0024–0.0036	0.3132–0.3138	0.3128–0.3134
	140 (2320) B230F-Turbo	45	44.5	158 @ 1.08	1.79	0.0012–0.0024	0.0024–0.0036	0.3132–0.3138	0.3128–0.3134
	174 (2849) B280F	45	44.5	143 @ 1.18	1.85	③	③	④	④
1988–89	140 (2320) B230F	45	44.5	158 @ 1.08	1.79	0.0012–0.0024	0.0024–0.0036	0.3132–0.3138	0.3128–0.3134
	140 (2320) B230F-Turbo	45	44.5	158 @ 1.08	1.79	0.0012–0.0024	0.0024–0.0036	0.3132–0.3138	0.3128–0.3134
	174 (2849) B280F	45	44.5	143 @ 1.18	1.85	③	③	④	④
	140 (2320) B234F	45	44.5	144 @ 1.04	1.46	0.0012–0.0024	0.0016–0.0028	0.3132–0.3138	0.3128–0.3134

NOTE: Exhaust valves for turbo engines (including turbo diesel) are stellite coated and must not be machined. They may be ground against the valve seat.

① Canada only
② Intake: 29.5 degrees
   Exhaust: 30 degrees
③ Tapered valve guide ID: 0.3150–0.3158
④ Tapered valve stem;
   Intake: Base = 0.3135–0.3141 Top = 3139–0.3145
   Exhaust: Base = 0.3127–0.3133 Top = 3136–0.3141
⑤ Intake: 44.5 degrees
   Exhaust: 45 degrees
⑥ Two springs per valve; inner spring 49 lbs. @ 0.72 in.; outer spring 100 lbs. @ 0.878 in.
⑦ Inner 1.335 in.; outer 1.583 in.
⑧ Clearance measured w/new valve guide and w/valve stem edge to edge to edge w/valve guide upper end. Max. clearance 0.051 in.; new clearance 0.012 in.

Crankshaft and Connecting Rod Specifications
All measurements are given in inches

Year	Engine Displacement Cu. in. (cc)	Crankshaft				Connecting Rod		
		Main Brg Journal Dia	Main Brg Oil Clearance	Shaft End-Play	Thrust on No.	Journal Diameter	Oil Clearance	Side Clearance
1970–71	B 20 122 (1990)	2.4981–2.4986	0.0011–0.0031	0.0018–0.0054	5	2.1299–2.1304	0.0012–0.0028	0.006–0.014
1972–73	B 20 122 (1990)	2.4981–2.4986	0.0011–0.0033	0.0018–0.0054	5	2.1299–2.1304	0.0012–0.0028	0.006–0.014
1974–75	B 20 122 (1990)	2.4981–2.4986	0.0011–0.0033	0.0018–0.0054	5	2.1255–2.1260	0.0012–0.0028	0.006–0.014
1970–71	B 30 183 (2978)	2.4981–2.4986	0.0011–0.0031	0.0018–0.0054	7	2.1299–2.1304	0.0012–0.0028	0.006–0.014
1972–73	B 30 183 (2978)	2.4981–2.4986	0.0011–0.0033	0.0018–0.0054	7	2.1299–2.1304	0.0012–0.0028	0.006–0.014
1974–75	B 30 183 (2978)	2.4981–2.4986	0.0011–0.0033	0.0018–0.0054	7	2.1255–2.1260	0.0012–0.0028	0.006–0.014
1976–83	B 21 130 (2127)	2.4981–2.4986	0.0011–0.0033	0.0015–0.0058	5	2.1255–2.1260	0.0009–0.0028	0.006–0.014
1983	B 23 140 (2320)	2.4981–2.4986	0.0011–0.0033	0.0015–0.0058	5	2.1255–2.1260	0.0009–0.0028	0.006–0.014
1976–83	B 27 162 (2660) B 28 173 (2849)	2.7576–2.7583	0.0015–0.0035	0.0028–0.0106	4	2.0578–2.0585	0.0012–0.0031	0.008–0.015
1980–83	D 24 145 (2383) Diesel	2.2833–2.2825	0.0006–0.0029	0.0028–0.0071	4	1.8802–1.8810	0.0047 ①	0.0158
1983	D 24 T 145 (2383) Turbo Diesel	2.2816–2.2824	0.0006–0.0029	0.0027–0.0071		1.8802–1.8810	0.0047 ①	0.0157

① New clearance 0.0005–0.0024 in.

Torque Specifications
All readings in ft. lbs.

Year	Engine Displacement cu. in. (cc)	Cylinder Head Bolts	Main Bearing Bolts	Rod Bearing Bolts	Crankshaft Pulley Bolts	Flywheel Bolts	Manifold		Spark Plugs
							Intake	Exhaust	
1984	130 (2127) B21A ①	⑧	85–91	43–48	107–128	47–54	15	15	15–18
	130 (2127) B21F-Turbo	⑧	85–91	43–48	107–128	47–54	15	15	15–18
	140 (2320) B21F	⑧	85–91	43–48	107–128	47–54	15	15	15–18
	140 (2320) B23F-Turbo	⑧	85–91	43–48	107–128	47–54	15	15	15–18
	145 (2383) D24	⑤	48	33	332 ⑥	55	18	18	⑦
	145 (2383) D24-Turbo	⑤	48	33	332 ⑥	55	18	18	⑦
	174 (2849) B28F	③	④	33–37	177–206	33–37	7–11	7–11	8–11
1985	130 (2127) B21F-Turbo	⑧	85–91	43–48	107–128	47–54	15	15	15–18
	140 (2320) B230F	⑧	80	14 ⑨	43 ⑩	47–54	12	12	18
	140 (2320) B230F-Turbo	⑧	80	14 ⑨	43 ⑩	47–54	12	12	18

Torque Specifications (cont.)

All readings in ft. lbs.

Year	Engine Displacement cu. in. (cc)	Cylinder Head Bolts	Main Bearing Bolts	Rod Bearing Bolts	Crankshaft Pulley Bolts	Flywheel Bolts	Manifold		Spark Plugs
							Intake	Exhaust	
	145 (2383) D24	⑤	48	33	332 ⑥	55	18	18	⑦
	145 (2383) D24-Turbo	⑤	48	33	332 ⑥	55	18	18	⑦
	174 (2849) B28F	③	④	33–37	177–206	33–37	7–11	7–11	8–11
1986	140 (2320) B230F	⑧	80	14 ⑨	43 ⑩	47–54	12	12	18
	140 (2320) B230F-Turbo	⑧	80	14 ⑨	43 ⑩	47–54	12	12	18
	145 (2383) D24-Turbo	⑤	48	33	332 ⑥	55	18	18	⑦
	174 (2849) B28F	③	④	33–37	177–206	33–37	7–11	7–11	8–11
1987	140 (2320) B230F	⑧	80	14 ⑨	43 ⑩	47–54	12	12	18
	140 (2320) B230F-Turbo	⑧	80	14 ⑨	43 ⑩	47–54	12	12	18
	174 (2849) B280F	⑪	④	33–37	177–206	33–37	7–11	7–11	8–11
1988–89	140 (2320) B230F	⑧	80	14 ⑨	43 ⑩	47–54	12	12	18
	140 (2320) B230F-Turbo	⑧	80	14 ⑨	43 ⑩	47–54	12	12	18
	174 (2849) B280F	⑪	④	33–37	177–206	33–37	7–11	7–11	8–11
	140 (2320) B234	⑫	80	14 ⑨	43 ⑩	47–54	12	12	14–20

① Canada only

② Torque head bolts in two stages; first, tighten in sequence to 43 ft. lbs., then to 76–83 ft. lbs.

③ Torque head bolts in sequence to 7 ft. lbs., then 22 ft. lbs., then 44 ft. lbs. Wait 10–15 minutes and slacken the bolts ½ turn. Then torque to 11–14 ft. lbs. and then protractor torque to 116–120° (⅓ of a turn). Finally run to operating temperature, shut off and allow to cool for 30 min. Following the sequence, slacken, torque to 11–14 ft. lbs., and protractor torque to 113–117° each bolt.

④ Torque main bearing nuts to 22 ft. lbs., in sequence. Then slacken 1st nut ½ turn, tighten to 22–26 ft. lbs., and protractor torque to 73–77°. Repeat for remaining nuts following the sequence.

⑤ Torquing these bolts is a six-step procedure:
  A. Torque to 30 ft. lbs.
  B. Torque to 44 ft. lbs.
  C. Torque to 55 ft. lbs.
  D. Tighten 180°, in one movement, without stopping.
  E. Run engine until oil temperature is minimum 50°C–120°F.
  F. Tighten 90°, in one movement, without stopping. After driving 600–1,000 miles, retorque bolts w/engine cold. DO NOT slacken first.

⑥ Using regular torque wrench. If Volvo tool 5188 is used, torque to 255 ft. lbs.

⑦ Injector: 50 ft. lbs.

⑧ Torque head bolts in three stages; first, tighten in sequence to 15 ft. lbs., then to 44 ft. lbs. Protractor (angle) tighten 90° more in one movement.

⑨ Angle—tighten 90°

⑩ Angle—tighten 60°

⑪ Torque all head bolts in sequence to 44 ft. lbs. (60Nm), then loosen bolt #1 and retorque it to 15 ft. lbs. (20Nm), then tighten it to 106°; repeat for all bolts following number sequence. Loosen and tighten one bolt at a time. Run engine to operating temperature. Then let cool for 2 hours. Finally, tighten each bolt in sequence an additional 45°.

⑫ Torque all head bolts in sequence to 15 ft. lbs. Then repeat sequence tightening to 30 ft. lbs. Repeat sequence, protractor (angle) tightening through an *additional* 115° in one movement.

Crankshaft and Connecting Rod Specifications
All measurements are given in inches

Year	Engine Displacement Cu. in. (cc)	Crankshaft				Connecting Rod		
		Main Brg Journal Dia	Main Brg Oil Clearance	Shaft End-Play	Thrust on No.	Journal Diameter	Oil Clearance	Side Clearance
1984	130 (2127) B21A ①	2.4981–2.4986	0.0011–0.0033	0.0015–0.0058	5	2.1255–2.1260	0.0009–0.0028	0.006–0.014
	130 (2127) B23F	2.4981–2.4986	0.0011–0.0033	0.0015–0.0058	5	2.1255–2.1260	0.0009–0.0028	0.006–0.014
	140 (2320) B23F-Turbo	2.4981–2.4986	0.0011–0.0033	0.0015–0.0058	5	2.1255–2.1260	0.0009–0.0028	0.006–0.014
	140 (2320) B23F-Turbo	2.4981–2.4986	0.0011–0.0033	0.0015–0.0058	5	2.1255–2.1260	0.0009–0.0028	0.006–0.014
	145 (2383) D24	2.2833–2.2825	0.0006–0.0030	0.0028–0.0071	4	1.8802–1.8810	0.0047 ②	0.0158
	145 (2383) D24-Turbo	2.2833–2.2825	0.0006–0.0030	0.0028–0.0071	4	1.8802–1.8810	0.0047 ②	0.0158
	174 (2849) B28F	2.7583	0.0035	0.0106	4	2.0585	0.0031	0.015
1985	130 (2127) B21F-Turbo	2.4981–2.4986	0.0011–0.0033	0.0015–0.0058	5	2.1255–2.1260	0.0009–0.0028	0.006–0.014
	140 (2320) B230F	2.4981–2.4986	0.0011–0.0033	0.0015–0.0058	5	2.1255–2.1260	0.0009–0.0028	0.006–0.014
	140 (2320) B230F-Turbo	2.4981–2.4986	0.0011–0.0033	0.0015–0.0058	5	2.1255–2.1260	0.0009–0.0028	0.006–0.014
	145 (2383) D24	2.2833–2.2825	0.0006–0.0030	0.0028–0.0071	4	1.8802–1.8810	0.0047 ②	0.0158
	145 (2383) D24-Turbo	2.2833–2.2825	0.0006–0.0030	0.0028–0.0071	4	1.8802–1.8810	0.0047 ②	0.0158
	174 (2849) B28F	2.7583	0.0035	0.0106	4	2.0585	0.0031	0.015
1986	140 (2320) B230F	2.4981–2.4986	0.0011–0.0033	0.0015–0.0058	5	2.1255–2.1260	0.0009–0.0028	0.006–0.014
	140 (2320) B230F-Turbo	2.4981–2.4986	0.0011–0.0033	0.0015–0.0058	5	2.1255–2.1260	0.0009–0.0028	0.006–0.014
	145 (2383) D24-Turbo	2.2833–2.2825	0.0006–0.0030	0.0028–0.0071	4	1.8802–1.8810	0.0047 ②	0.0158
	174 (2849) B28F	2.7583	0.0035	0.0106	4	2.0585	0.0031	0.015
1987–88	140 (2320) B230F	2.4981–2.4986	0.0011–0.0033	0.0015–0.0058	5	2.1255–2.1260	0.0009–0.0028	0.006–0.014
	140 (2320) B230F-Turbo	2.4981–2.4986	0.0011–0.0033	0.0015–0.0058	5	2.1255–2.1260	0.0009–0.0028	0.006–0.014
	174 (2849) B280F	2.7583	0.0035	0.0106	4	2.0585	0.0031	0.015
	140 (2320) B234F	2.4981–2.4986	0.0011–0.0033	0.0015–0.0058	5	2.047	0.0009–0.0028	0.006–0.018

① Canada only
② New clearance: 0.0005–0.0024 in.

Torque Specifications (cont.)

All readings in ft. lbs.

Year	Engine	Cyl. Head Bolts	Rod Bearing Bolts	Main Bearing Bolts	Crankshaft Pulley Bolt	Flywheel-To-Crankshaft Bolts	Manifold Bolts		Spark Plug	Camshaft Nut	Oil Pan
							Intake	Exhaust			
1970–73	All	65 ①	38–42	87–94	50–58	36–40	13–16	13–16	25–29	94–108	6–8
1974–75	All	65 ①	51–57	87–94	69–76 ②	47–51	13–16	13–16	25–29	94–108	6–8
1976–83	B 21 F	76–83 ③	43–48	85–91	107–128	47–54	15	15	25–29	32–38	8
1981–83	B 21 A B 21 FT B 23	⑫	43–48	85–91	107–128	47–54	15	15	15–18	32–38	8
1976–83	B 27 F, B 28 F	④	33–37	⑤	118–132 ⑥	33–37	7–11	7–11	13–15	51–59	7–11
1980–83	D 24, D 24 T Diesel	65 ⑦⑪	33	48	330 ⑧	55	18	18	⑨	⑩	N/A

① Torque head bolts in three stages; first, torque in sequence to 29 ft. lbs., then to 58 ft. lbs., and finally after driving the car for 10 minutes, torque to the final figure of 65 ft. lbs.
② Double pulley—80–101 ft. lbs.
③ Torque head bolts in two stages; first, tighten in sequence to 43 ft. lbs., then to 76–83 ft. lbs.
④ Torque head bolts in sequence to 7 ft. lbs., then 22 ft. lbs., then 44 ft. lbs. Wait 10–15 minutes and slacken the bolts ½ turn. Then torque to 11–14 ft. lbs. and then protractor torque to 116–120° (⅓ of a turn). Finally run to operating temperature, shut off and allow to cool for 30 min. Following the sequence, slacken, torque to 11–14 ft. lbs., and protractor torque to 113–117° each bolt.
⑤ Torque main bearing nuts to 22 ft. lbs. in sequence. Then slacken 1st nut ½ turn, tighten to 22–26 ft. lbs., and protractor torque to 73–77°. Repeat for remaining nuts following the sequence.
⑥ 1978–83: 175–200
⑦ Torque head bolts in two stages; first to 30 ft. lbs., then to 65 ft. lbs. After driving 1,000 miles, torque to 62 ft. lbs. (engine warm).
⑧ Using regular torque wrench. If Volvo wrench 5188 is used with torque wrench, tighten to 255 ft. lbs.
⑨ Fuel injector: 50 ft. lbs.
⑩ Front camshaft bolt: 33 ft. lbs.
     Rear camshaft bolt: 73 ft. lbs.
⑪ From late 1980 new type cylinder head bolts are used on the diesels. They are longer and 1 mm wider. Torquing these bolts is a six-step procedure:
     a. Torque to 30 ft. lbs.
     b. Torque to 44 ft. lbs.
     c. Torque to 55 ft. lbs.
     d. Tighten 180°, in one movement, without stopping.
     e. Run engine until oil temperature is minimum 50°C–120°F, Tighten 90°, in one movement.
     f. After driving 600–1,000 miles, retorque bolts w/engine cold.
⑫ Torque head bolts in three stages; first, tighten in sequence to 15 ft. lbs., then to 44 ft. lbs. Protractor torque 90°, in one movement, without stopping.

Piston and Ring Specifications

All measurements in inches

Year	Engine Displacement Cu. In. (cc)	Piston Clearance	Ring Gap			Ring Side Clearance		
			Top Compression	Bottom Compression	Oil Control	Top Compression	Bottom Compression	Oil Control
1970	B 20 B 122 (1990)	0.0008–0.0016	0.016–0.022	0.016–0.022	0.016–0.022	0.0017–0.0028	0.0017–0.0028	0.0017–0.0028
	B 30 A 183 (2978)	0.0008–0.0016	0.016–0.022	0.016–0.022	0.016–0.022	0.0017–0.0028	0.0017–0.0028	0.0017–0.0028
1971	B 20 B 122 (1990)	0.0014–0.0022	0.016–0.022	0.016–0.022	0.016–0.022	0.0017–0.0028	0.0017–0.0028	0.0017–0.0028
1971	B 20 E 122 (1990)	0.0016–0.0024	0.016–0.022	0.016–0.022	0.016–0.022	0.0017–0.0028	0.0017–0.0028	0.0017–0.0028
	B 30 A 183 (2978)	0.0016–0.0024	0.016–0.022	0.016–0.022	0.016–0.022	0.0017–0.0028	0.0017–0.0028	0.0017–0.0028
1972	B 20 B 122 (1990)	0.0014–0.0020	0.016–0.022	0.016–0.022	0.016–0.022	0.0016–0.0028	0.0016–0.0028	0.0016–0.0028
1972–75	B 20 F 122 (1990)	0.0016–0.0024 ①	0.016–0.022	0.016–0.022	0.016–0.022	0.0016–0.0028	0.0016–0.0028	0.0016–0.0028
1972	B 30 A 183 (2978)	0.0016–0.0024	0.016–0.022	0.016–0.022	0.016–0.022	0.0016–0.0028	0.0016–0.0228	0.0016–0.0028
1972–75	B 30 F 183 (2978)	0.0016–0.0024 ①	0.016–0.022	0.016–0.022	0.016–0.022	0.0016–0.0032	0.0016–0.0028	0.0016–0.0028

Year	Engine							
1976–83	B 21 130 (2127)	0.0004– 0.0012 [3][6]	0.0138– 0.0217 [4]	0.0138– 0.0217 [4]	0.010– 0.016 [4]	0.0016– 0.0028	0.0016– 0.0028	0.0016– 0.0028 [5]
1983	B 23 140 (2320)	0.0020– 0.0028 [7]	0.014– 0.026	0.014– 0.022	0.010– 0.024	0.0015– 0.0028	0.0015– 0.0028	0.0012– 0.0024
1976–83	B 27 F 162 (2660), B 28 F 173 (2849)	0.0008– 0.0016 [2]	0.016– 0.022	0.016– 0.022	0.015– 0.055	0.0018– 0.0029	0.0010– 0.0021	0.0004– 0.0092
1980–83	D 24 Diesel 145 (2383)	0.0012– 0.0020 [8]	0.012– 0.020 [9]	0.012– 0.020 [9]	0.010– 0.016 [9]	0.0024– 0.0035 [10]	0.0020– 0.0032 [10]	0.0012– 0.0024 [11]
1983	D 24 T Diesel 145 (2383)	0.0012– 0.0020	0.012– 0.020	0.012– 0.020	0.010– 0.019	0.0043– 0.0055	0.0028– 0.0039	0.0012– 0.0028

[1] 1974–75 piston clearance—0.0004–0.0012 in.
[2] Mahle pistons. Demolin pistons: 0.00315–0.00394 in.
[3] 0.0004–0.0016 in. 1983
[4] 1983 0.014–0.026 in. top compression; 0.014–0.022 in. bottom compression; 0.010–0.024 in. oil control
[5] 0.0012–0.0024 in. 1983
[6] 0.0008–0.0016 in. 1983 Turbo
[7] Pistons with two different heights have been fitted to B23E engines. Piston clearance on version 1 (3.1654 in. piston height) is as shown above; clearance on version 2 pistons (3.0079 in. piston height) is 0.0004–0.0016 in.
[8] Clearance when new; max. wear compared with normal diameter 0.0016 in.
[9] Gap when new; maximum is 0.040 in.
[10] Clearance when new; maximum 0.0079 in.
[11] Clearance when new; maximum 0.0059 in.

Piston and Ring Specifications
All measurements in inches

Year	Engine Displacement cu. in. (cc)	Piston Clearance	Ring Gap			Ring Side Clearance		
			Top Compression	Bottom Compression	Oil Control	Top Compression	Bottom Compression	Oil Control
1983	130 (2127) B21A①	0.0004–0.0016	0.0140–0.0260	0.0140–0.0220	0.010–0.024	0.0016–0.0026	0.0016–0.0028	0.0012–0.0024
	130 (2127) B21F-Turbo	0.0008–0.0016	0.0140–0.0260	0.0140–0.0220	0.010–0.024	0.0016–0.0028	0.0016–0.0028	0.0012–0.0024
	140 (2320) B23F	0.0020–0.0028 ②	0.0014–0.0026	0.0014–0.0022	0.010–0.024	0.0015–0.0028	0.0015–0.0028	0.0012–0.0024
	140 (2320) B23E①	0.0020–0.0028 ②	0.0014–0.0026	0.0014–0.0022	0.010–0.024	0.0015–0.0028	0.0015–0.0028	0.0012–0.0024
	140 (2320) B23F-Turbo	0.0020–0.0028 ②	0.0014–0.0026	0.0014–0.0022	0.010–0.024	0.0015–0.0028	0.0015–0.0028	0.0012–0.0024
	145 (2383) D24	0.0012–0.0020	0.0012–0.0020	0.0012–0.0020	0.010–0.019	0.0043–0.0055	0.0028–0.0039	0.0012–0.0028
	145 (2383) D24-Turbo	0.0012–0.0020	0.0012–0.0020	0.0012–0.0020	0.010–0.019	0.0043–0.0055	0.0028–0.0039	0.0012–0.0028
	174 (2849) B28F	0.0007–0.0015	0.0157–0.0236	0.0157–0.0236	0.0157–0.0570	0.0017–0.0029	0.0009–0.0212	0.0003–0.0091
1984	130 (2127) B21A①	0.0004–0.0016	0.0140–0.0260	0.0140–0.0220	0.010–0.024	0.0016–0.0028	0.0016–0.0028	0.0012–0.0024
	130 (2127) B21F-Turbo	0.0008–0.0016	0.0140–0.0260	0.0140–0.0220	0.010–0.024	0.0016–0.0028	0.0016–0.0028	0.0012–0.0024
	140 (2320) B23F	0.0020–0.0028 ②	0.0014–0.0026	0.0014–0.0022	0.010–0.024	0.0015–0.0028	0.0015–0.0028	0.0012–0.0024

Year	Engine	1	2	3	4	5	6	7
	140 (2320) B23F-Turbo	0.0020–0.0028 ②	0.0014–0.0026	0.0014–0.0022	0.010–0.024	0.0015–0.0028	0.0015–0.0028	0.0012–0.0024
	145 (2383) D24	0.0012–0.0020	0.0012–0.0020	0.0012–0.0020	0.010–0.019	0.0043–0.0055	0.0028–0.0039	0.0012–0.0028
	145 (2383) D24-Turbo	0.0012–0.0020	0.0012–0.0020	0.0012–0.0020	0.010–0.019	0.0043–0.0055	0.0028–0.0039	0.0012–0.0028
	174 (2849) B28F	0.0007–0.0015	0.0157–0.0236	0.0157–0.0236	0.0157–0.0570	0.0017–0.0029	0.0009–0.0212	0.0003–0.0091
1985	130 (2127) B21F-Turbo	0.0008–0.0016	0.0140–0.0260	0.0140–0.0220	0.010–0.024	0.0016–0.0028	0.0016–0.0028	0.0012–0.0024
	140 (2320) B230F	0.0004–0.0012	0.0118–0.0217	0.0118–0.0217	0.0118–0.0236	0.0024–0.0036	0.0016–0.0028	0.0012–0.0026
	140 (2320) B230F-Turbo	0.0004–0.0012	0.0118–0.0217	0.0118–0.0217	0.0118–0.0236	0.0024–0.0036	0.0016–0.0028	0.0012–0.0026
	145 (2383) D24	0.0012–0.0020	0.0012–0.0020	0.0012–0.0020	0.010–0.019	0.0043–0.0055	0.0028–0.0039	0.0012–0.0028
	145 (2383) D24-Turbo	0.0012–0.0020	0.0012–0.0020	0.0012–0.0020	0.010–0.019	0.0043–0.0055	0.0028–0.0039	0.0012–0.0028
	174 (2849) B28F	0.0007–0.0015	0.0157–0.0236	0.0157–0.0236	0.0157–0.0570	0.0017–0.0029	0.0009–0.0212	0.0003–0.0091
1986	140 (2320) B230F	0.0004–0.0012	0.0118–0.0217	0.0118–0.0217	0.0118–0.0236	0.0024–0.0036	0.0016–0.0028	0.0012–0.0026
	140 (2320) B230F-Turbo	0.0004–0.0012	0.0118–0.0217	0.0118–0.0217	0.0118–0.0236	0.0024–0.0036	0.0016–0.0028	0.0012–0.0026
	145 (2383) D24-Turbo	0.0012–0.0020	0.0012–0.0020	0.0012–0.0020	0.010–0.019	0.0043–0.0055	0.0028–0.0039	0.0012–0.0028
	174 (2849) B28F	0.0007–0.0015	0.0157–0.0236	0.0157–0.0236	0.0157–0.0570	0.0017–0.0029	0.0009–0.0212	0.0003–0.0091
1987	140 (2320) B230F	0.0004–0.0012	0.0118–0.0217	0.0118–0.0217	0.0118–0.0236	0.0024–0.0036	0.0016–0.0028	0.0012–0.0026
	140 (2320) B230F-Turbo	0.0004–0.0012	0.0118–0.0217	0.0118–0.0217	0.0118–0.0236	0.0024–0.0036	0.0016–0.0028	0.0012–0.0026

Piston and Ring Specifications (cont.)
All measurements in inches

Year	Engine Displacement cu. in. (cc)	Piston Clearance	Ring Gap			Ring Side Clearance		
			Top Compression	Bottom Compression	Oil Control	Top Compression	Bottom Compression	Oil Control
1987								
	174 (2849) B280F	0.0007–0.0015	0.0157–0.0236	0.0157–0.0236	0.0157–0.0570	0.0017–0.0029	0.0009–0.0212	0.0003–0.0091
1988–89								
	140 (2320) B230F	0.0004–0.0012	0.0118–0.0217	0.0118–0.0217	0.0118–0.0236	0.0024–0.0036	0.0016–0.0028	0.0012–0.0026
	140 (2320) B230F-Turbo	0.0004–0.0012	0.0018–0.0217	0.0118–0.0217	0.0118–0.0236	0.0024–0.0036	0.0016–0.0028	0.0012–0.0026
	174 (2849) B280F	0.0007–0.0015	0.0157–0.0236	0.0157–0.0236	0.0157–0.0570	0.0017–0.0029	0.0009–0.0212	0.0003–0.0091
	140 (2320) B234F	0.0004–0.0012	0.012–0.022	0.012–0.022	0.012–0.024	0.0024–0.0036	0.0016–0.0028	0.0012–0.0026

① Canada only
② Pistons with two different heights have been fitted to B23E engines. Piston clearance on version 1 (3.1654 in piston height) listed above; clearance on version 2 pistons (3.0079 in.) is 0.004–0.0016 in.

mission, place the selector in PARK , disconnect the control rod from the selector lever, and the ground cable from the start inhibitor switch.

10. Disconnect the wires for the backup lights and overdrive, if so equipped. Remove the speedometer drive cable from the transmission. Remove the clamp for the exhaust manifold and the clamp for the automatic transmission filler tube, if so equipped.

11. Jack up the vehicle and place two jackstands under the front jack attachments and two more in front of the rear jack attachments.

12. Place a hydraulic jack under the transmission. On manual transmission cars, remove the return spring from the throw-out fork, and disconnect the clutch cable.

13. Separate the transmission (or overdrive) from the front universal joint by unbolting the flange. Unbolt the rear crossmember.

14. Disconnect the negative ground cable from the engine.

15. Remove the rear crossmember and rear engine mounts. Remove the lower nuts from the front engine mounts.

16. Install the lifting eyes and lifting crossbar. The lifting eyes are attached by ⅜ in. × 1¾ in. × 1 in. bolts. The engine is removed by raising its front and lowering its back while pulling forward until it clears the front crossmember, then leveling it and raising the complete unit. Lift out the engine and set it on an engine stand or rack.

To reinstall the engine:

17. Install the lifting apparatus on the engine. Make sure that the jackstands are located beneath the front jack attachments and in from of the rear jack attachments. Place the hydraulic jack beneath the transmission tunnel.

18. Carefully lower the engine into the engine compartment. Place the hydraulic jack under

the transmission and guide the unit into place. Be careful not to damage the oil filter, or oil pressure sending unit against the exhaust pipe. Be careful not to damage the distributor against the steering column.

19. Tighten the nuts for the front engine mounts.

20. Connect the wires for the back-up lights, start inhibitor switch (automatic transmission), and overdrive, it so equipped.

21. Install the brackets for the exhaust manifold and the automatic transmission filler tube. Install the rear engine mounts and rear crossmember, then tighten the nuts.

22. Remove the hydraulic jack from the transmission and the lifting apparatus from the engine. Connect the negative ground cable to the engine.

23. Connect the front universal joint to the transmission (or overdrive) flange. Connect the speedometer drive cable.

24. On manual transmission cars, connect the clutch cable and install the return spring. Adjust clutch free-play. See Chapter 7. On automatic transmission cars, connect the control rod to the selector lever, and the ground cable to the start inhibitor switch.

25. Connect the exhaust pipe to the exhaust manifold with new gaskets and tighten the nuts. Connect the EGR valve pipe.

26. Remove the jackstands from the jack attachments and lower the vehicle.

27. Connect the heater hoses. On models with power steering, install the pump and reservoir to the engine block and adjust the drive belt tension.

28a. On continuous (air-flow controlled) fuel injected models, install the thermal time switch and connect the hose for the brake booster. Install the throttle cable and connect the 4 fuel hoses to the injectors. Connect the control pressure regulator ground wire and the cold start

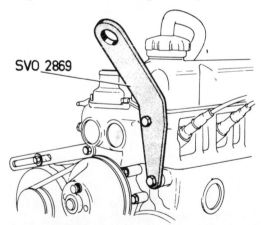

SVO 2869

Front lifting eye installed on B20 engine. Volvo special tool shown

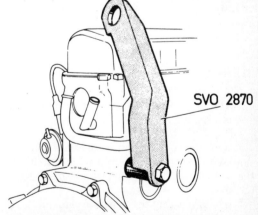

SVO 2870

Rear lifting eye installed on B20 engine. Volvo special tool shown injector, control pressure regulator, auxiliary air valve, temperature sensor, and thermal time switch leads.

Connect the fuel hoses to the control pressure regulator and fuel distributor. Connect the hoses to the fuel filter, cold start injector, and the fuel return hose to the fuel distributor. Install the pipe between the air filter and the intake manifold.

28b. On electronic fuel injected models, place the injectors in their bayonet fittings with new rubber seals, and turn them clockwise to install. In addition, connect the fuel inlet line and the cold start valve hose to the distribution pipe and return line from the pressure regulator. Install the ground wire and the throttle cable bracket to the inlet duct, and connect the throttle cable.

Connect the plug contact for the temperature sensor, cold start valve, throttle valve switch, fuel injectors, and distributor impulse. Install the pressure sensor vacuum hose, air cleaner, and intake hoses.

29. On all models, connect the positive crankcase ventilation hoses, and the distributor vacuum advance hose. Connect the vacuum hose for the power brake booster, and the oil pressure gauge hose at the pipe connection, if so equipped.

30. Install the electric cables for the starter, the coil high tension wire, the distributor lead, alternator wires, water and oil temperature sensors, and the lead for the oil pressure sensor, if so equipped.

31. Connect the positive lead to the battery.

32. Install the radiator and fan shroud, if so equipped, and the radiator cover plate. Install the expansion tank, the upper and lower radiator hoses, and, on automatic transmission cars, the transmission cooler lines. Make sure that the cooler lines clear the engine mounts and brake tubes by a generous ¾ in.

33. Fill the crankcase and cooling system.

34. Install the hood. Install the gearshift lever.

35. Start the engine and check for leaks.

B21 and B23/B230 Series Engines

NOTE: *All wires and hoses should be labled at the time of removal. The amount of time saved during re-assembly makes the extra effort well worthwhile.*

1. On cars equipped with manual transmission, remove the four retaining clips and lift up the shifter boot. Then, remove the snapring for the shifter.

2. Disconnecting the negative cable first, remove the battery.

3. Disconnect the windshield washer hose, engine compartment light wire and remove the hood.

4. Remove the overflow tank cap. Drain the cooling system by disconnecting the lower radiator hose and opening the engine drain cock (beneath the exhaust manifold).

CAUTION: *When draining the coolant, keep in mind that cats and dogs are attracted by the ethylene glycol antifreeze, and are quite likely to drink any that is left in an uncovered container or in puddles on the ground. This will prove fatal in sufficient quantity. Always drain the coolant into a sealable container. Coolant should be reused unless it is contaminated or several years old.*

5. Remove the upper and lower radiator hoses. Disconnect the overflow hoses at the radiator. Disconnect PCV hose at the cylinder head.

6. On cars equipped with automatic transmission, disconnect the oil cooler lines at the radiator.

7. Remove the radiator and fan shroud.

8. Remove the air cleaner assembly and hose.

9. Disconnect the hoses at the air pump. Remove the air pump and drive belt.

10. Disconnect the vacuum pump hoses and remove the vacuum pump. Disconnect the power brake booster vacuum hose.

11. Remove the power steering pump, drive belt and bracket. Position to one side.

12. On cars equipped with air conditioning, remove the crankshaft pulley (5mm Allen wrench), and compressor drive belt. Then install the pulley again for reference. Remove the air conditioning wire connector and the compressor from its bracket and position to one side. Remove the bracket. Note that you are simply unbolting and moving various air conditioning components; it IS NOT necessary to discharge the system.

13. Disconnect the vacuum hoses from the engine. Disconnect the carbon canister hoses.

14. Disconnect the distributor wire connector, high tension lead, starter cables, and the clutch cable clamp.

15. Disconnect the wiring harness at the voltage regulator. Disconnect the throttle cable at the pulley; and the wire for the compressor at the intake manifold solenoid.

16. Remove the gas cap. Disconnect the fuel lines at the filter and return pipe.

17. At the firewall, disconnect the electrical connectors for the ballast resistor, and relays. Disconnect the heater hoses.

18. Disconnect the micro-switch connectors at the intake manifold, and all remaining harness connectors to the engine.

19. Drain the crankcase.

CAUTION: *The EPA warns that prolonged*

contact with used engine oil may cause a number of skin disorders, including cancer! You should make every effort to minimize your exposure to used engine oil. Protective gloves should be worn when changing the oil. Wash your hands and any other exposed skin areas as soon as possible after exposure to used engine oil. Soap and water, or waterless hand cleaner should be used.

20. Remove the exhaust manifold flange retaining nuts. Loosen the exhaust pipe clamp bolts and remove the bracket for the front exhaust pipe mount.

21. On cars equipped with automatic transmission, place the gear selector lever in **Park** and disconnect the gear shift control rod from the transmission.

23. On manual transmission cars, disconnect the clutch cable. Then loosen the setscrew, drive out the pivot pin, and remove the shifter from the control rod.

24. Disconnect the speedometer and the driveshaft from the transmission.

25. On overdrive equipped models, disconnect the control wire from the shifter.

26. Jack up the front of the car and place jack stands beneath the reinforced box member areas to the rear of each front jacking attachment. Then, using a floor jack and a wooden block, support the weight of the engine beneath the transmission.

27. Remove the bolts for the rear transmission mount. Remove the transmission support crossmember.

28. Lift out the engine and support on suitable rack or stand. To reinstall:

29. After lifting the motor into position within the car, reinstall the rear transmission mount and secure the bolts. Lower or adjust the jack as necessary to position the motor on the front mounts.

30. Attach the speedometer cable and driveshaft to the transmission. If equipped with overdrive, reconnect the control wire from the shifter.

31. On manual transmission cars, attach the shifter to the control rod. Install the pivot pin, tighten the set-screw, and hook up the clutch cable.

32. On cars with automatic transmission, reconnect the gear shift control rod.

33. Install and tighten the front motor mount bolts.

34. Install the bracket for the front exhaust pipe mount. Install and tighten the exhaust manifold flange retaining nuts. Tighten the exhaust pipe clamp bolts.

35. Beginning with the larger, easily identified harnesses, reconnect electrical circuits at the firewall and the engine. Check the firewall

Remove the front motor mount bolts from beneath the car—B21, B23, B27, B28 engines similar

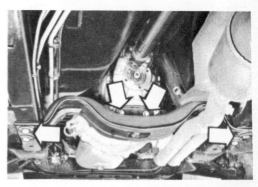

Remove rear transmission mount—B21 and B23

area for ballast resistor, and relays. Check also for correct hook ups at the voltage regulator, distributor and starter. Smaller harnesses and single wires also run to the micro-switch at the intake manifold and the AC solenoid on the intake manifold.

36. Connect and secure the heater hoses.

37. Re-attach the fuel lines at the filter and return pipe; reinstall the gas cap.

38. Connect the throttle cable at the pulley. Install the clutch cable clamp if so equipped.

39. Connect all engine vacuum hoses and connect the charcoal cannister.

40. On cars equipped with air conditioning, reinstall the compressor bracket and the compressor. Reconnect the compressor wiring. Once again, remove the crankshaft pulley, install the AC belt and reinstall the pulley in its correct location. Adjust the AC belt to the correct tension.

41. Reinstall the power steering pump, bracket and belt. Adjust the belt to the proper tension.

42. Attach the vacuum pump and its hoses. Connect the power brake booster vacuum hose.

43. Reattach the air pump, connect the hoses and install the belt. Set the belt to the correct tension.

44. Install the air cleaner assembly and hoses.

45. Reinstall the radiator and fan shroud. On cars with automatic transmission, connect the transmission cooler lines to the radiator.

46. Connect the upper and lower radiator hoses, attach the overflow line and install the overflow tank cap. If not already done, close the draincocks on the engine block.

47. Refill oil and coolant to the proper levels. Connect the PCV hose to the cylinder head.

48. Reinstall the hood. Connect the wire for the underhood light and the windshield washer hoses.

49. Install and reconnect the battery.

50. On manual transmission cars, reinstall the shifter and its snap ring. Secure the shifter boot and its four retaining clips.

51. Double check all installation items, paying particular attention to loose hoses or hanging wires, untightened nuts, poor routing of hoses and wires (too tight or rubbing) and tools left in the engine area.

52. Start the engine, allow it to run at idle and check for leaks. Make needed adjustments to throttle cable, clutch, and idle speed as necessary. Check ALL fluid levels and top off as needed.

B234

1. Disconnect the battery, negative cable first.

2. Disconnect the ground connection at the top of the side frame rail.

3. Release the bolted joint at the exhaust manifold front bracket.

4. Attach the sling or lifting equipment to the rear of the motor and support the motor from above. Release any wiring harnesses from their clips and place the wiring out of the way of the lifting gear.

5. Remove the splashguard under the engine, drain the engine oil and remove the air intake duct.

CAUTION: *The EPA warns that prolonged contact with used engine oil may cause a number of skin disorders, including cancer! You should make every effort to minimize your exposure to used engine oil. Protective gloves should be worn when changing the oil. Wash your hands and any other exposed skin areas as soon as possible after exposure to used engine oil. Soap and water, or waterless hand cleaner should be used.*

6. Undo the wiring clips on the front crossmember and right frame rail. Release the battery from the clips and work the wiring free of the roll bar.

7. If the vehicle is equipped with air conditioning, remove the compressor from its mount and position it out of the way. Do not disconnect any lines or hoses on the compressor.

8. Remove the bottom nut on the left engine mount.

9. On manual transmission cars, remove the clutch slave cylinder and position out of the way. Be careful of the rubber boot; it retains the piston within the cylinder.

10. Separate the front and rear universal joints. Unbolt the center support bearing and withdraw the driveshaft towards the rear of the car.

11. Cut the rear cable tie holding the transmission wiring and separate the connectors.

12. For cars with manual transmission, the gear lever is removed by removing the locking bolt, removing the pivot pin between the lever and the selector rod and removing the circlip from the lever sleeve. Push the shift lever up and remove the bushings.

For cars with automatic transmissions, the selector lever is disconnected by removing the clips from the joints between the lever and the selector rod. Withdraw the arm from the mounting.

13. Release the bolted joint at the front of the catalytic converter and release the oxygen sensor wire from the rear clip.

14. Remove the front exhaust pipe by removing the bolts at its joint to the exhaust manifold.

15. If equipped with automatic transmission, disconnect the oil lines at the transmission and plug the lines.

16. Remove the transmission crossmember. As soon as it is removed, position a floor jack below the transmission to support it.

NOTE: *The following steps are in the upper engine area. It may be helpful to temporarily remove the hoist equipment for access. The hoist will need to be reinstalled later in the removal.*

17. Remove the upper heat shield from the exhaust manifold. Remove the air hose from the lower heat shield.

18. Remove the top nut from the right motor mount.

19. Open the draincock on the right side of the engine block and drain the coolant into a container.

CAUTION: *When draining the coolant, keep in mind that cats and dogs are attracted by the ethylene glycol antifreeze, and are quite likely to drink any that is left in an uncovered container or in puddles on the ground. This will prove fatal in sufficient quantity. Always drain the coolant into a sealable container. Coolant should be reused unless it is contaminated or several years old.*

20. Label and remove the wiring from the distributor cap. Remove the cap and rotor and disconnect the braided engine ground wire.

21. Disconnect the wire to terminal 1 on the coil. Separate the wiring connectors on the right shock tower and release the cable clips on the firewall. Free the wiring from the clips.

22. Disconnect the heater hoses on the left firewall.

23. Release the fuel line connection at the left firewall and attend to any fuel spillage immediately. Plug the fuel lines.

24. Disconnect the wiring connector on the left side of the firewall and free the wires from the clips.

25. Disconnect the air mass meter, its wiring and the hoses connected to the air intake.

26. Release the throttle cable from the pulley.

27. Remove the vacuum hose to the brake booster from the intake manifold. Remove the evaporation hose from the intake manifold and the return line from the fuel distributor.

28. At the left shock tower, release the engine wiring harness from its clips and disconnect the wiring connectors. Remove the power steering reservoir from its clips.

29. Disconnect the coolant hoses at the thermostat housing and at the water pump.

30. Remove the drive belts.

31. Remove the radiator fan, the fan shroud and the drive pulley.

32. Remove the power steering pump from its mount. Place the pump on paper or rags atop the left shock tower. Do not disconnect any hoses from the pump.

33. If the lifting equipment was removed earlier, reconnect it.

34. Check the surroundings of the engine and transmission unit. With the exception of the jack and the motor mounts, there should be nothing connecting the engine/trans assembly to the body of the car. Take slight tension on the hoist and check that the engine is balanced. Reposition the lift points if the engine is not balanced.

35. Lift out the engine and the gearbox, being very careful of the radiator and surrounding components. Support the engine on appropriate stands.

36. When reinstalling, check the position and security of the hoist equipment. Lift the engine and gearbox into place in the body of the car.

37. Guide the engine mounts into place and support the transmission on the floor jack.

38. Replace the transmission crossmember and make sure the wiring for the oxygen sensor runs above the crossmember. Remove the floor jack when the crossmember is secure. The engine hoisting equipment may also be removed.

39. Use a new gasket and attach the exhaust pipe to the manifold. Attach the wire to the oxygen sensor.

40. Reconnect the shifting mechanism to the transmission.

41. Reconnect the transmission wiring and secure the harness with new wire ties.

42. Install the drive shaft. Tighten the front and rear universal joints and attach the center support bearing.

43. On manual transmission car connect the clutch slave cylinder. On automatic transmissions, connect the oil cooler lines.

44. Install the lower nut for the left motor mount. On cars with air conditioning, remount the comproessor on its brackets.

45. Track the wiring between the anti-roll bar and the front crossmember. Install the cable clips on the crossmember and rightside frame rail. Install the splash guard under the car. Reconnect the wiring to the ground connection on the right frame rail.

46. Install the nut on the top of the right engine mount. Install the upper heat shield on the manifold and the air tube to the lower heat shield.

47. Reconnect the coolant hoses. The bottom hose connects to the water pump and the upper hose to the thermostat housing.

WARNING: *Note the marking on the upper hose. The hose must run at least one inch away from the alternator belt.*

48. Remount the power steering pump. Install its belt (and the air conditioning belt if so equipped) and adjust to the correct tension.

49. Install the fan, pulley and shroud. Secure the wiring below the fan with new wire ties. Install the drive belt and adjust to the correct tension.

50. Reconnect the rear wiring harnesses on the firewall. Plug all connectors carefully and secure harnesses within the clips. Don't forget the wire to terminal 1 on the coil.

51. Reinstall the distributor rotor, cap and wires. Connect the braided engine ground cable.

52. Reconnect the wiring at the left shock tower. Make sure the wiring is secure in its clips. Install the power steering reservoir.

53. At the intake manifold, connect the vacuum line to the brake booster, the evaporation line and the return line for the fuel distributor.

54. At the left side of the firewall, attach the heater hoses and connect the fuel line.

55. Reattach the throttle cable to the pulley.

56. Install the air mass meter with its hoses and connections.

57. Fill the engine with proper coolant, set the heater to its hottest setting and check the system for leaks.

58. Install the engine oil.

59. Reconnect the battery leads (positive first) and the protective cap on the terminals.

60. Double check all installation items, paying particular attention to loose hoses or hanging wires, untightened nuts, poor routing of hoses and wires (too tight or rubbing) and tools left in the engine area.

61. Start the engine and check for leaks. This engine may be somewhat noisy when started; the noise will disappear as the tappets fill with oil.

B27F, B28F and B280F

NOTE: *All wires and hoses should be labeled at the time of removal. The amount of time saved during re-assembly makes the extra effort well worthwhile.*

1. On cars equipped with manual transmission, remove the shifter assembly. From underneath, loosen the setscrew and drive out pivot pin. Pull up the boot, remove the reverse pawl bracket and snap ring for the shifter, and lift out the shifter.

B27F, B28F engine—from under the car loosen the lock screw (1) and press out the lock pin (2). Inside the car uncover rubber dust cover, remove bracket for reversing pawl (3), remove the snap ring (4) and remove the gear lever

2. Disconnecting the negative cable first, remove the battery.

3. Disconnect the windshield washer hose and engine compartment light wire. Scribe the

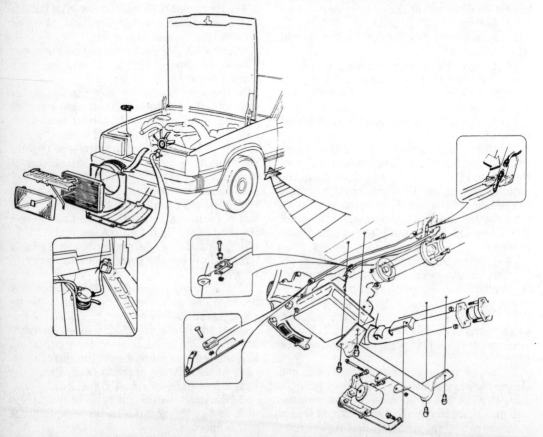

Preparation to remove engine. 760 shown, others similar

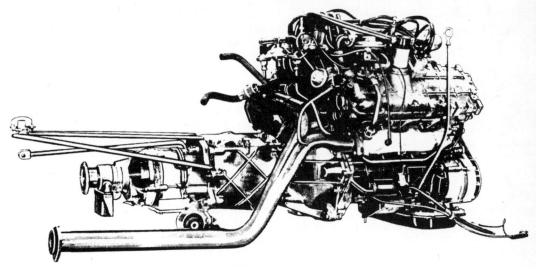

B28/B280 engine and transmission assembly

outline of the hood hinges on the hood and re-move the hood.

4. Remove the air cleaner assembly. On B28, remove the intake air preheating assembly.

5. Remove the splash guard under the engine.

6. Drain the cooling system by disconnecting the lower radiator hose and opening the drain cocks on both sides of the cylinder block.

CAUTION: *When draining the coolant, keep in mind that cats and dogs are attracted by the ethylene glycol antifreeze, and are quite likely to drink any that is left in an uncovered container or in puddles on the ground. This will prove fatal in sufficient quantity. Always drain the coolant into a sealable container. Coolant should be reused unless it is contaminated or several years old.*

7. Remove the overflow tank cap. Remove the upper and lower radiator hoses, and disconnect the overflow hoses at the radiator.

8. On cars equipped with automatic transmission, disconnect the transmission cooler lines at the radiator.

9. Remove the radiator, fan shroud and grille.

10. Disconnect heater hoses, power brake hose at the intake manifold and the vacuum pump hose at the pump. Remove the vacuum pump and O-ring in the valve cover. Remove the gas cap.

CAUTION: *The fuel system retains high pressure. Observe no smoking/no open flame rules. Discharge pressure slowly. Be prepared to contain spillage.*

11. At the firewall, disconnect the fuel lines at the filter and the return pipe. Disconnect the relay connectors and all other wire connectors. Disconnect the distributor wires.

12. Disconnect the evaporative control carbon canister hoses and the vacuum hose at the EGR valve.

13. Disconnect the voltage regulator wire connector.

14. Disconnect the throttle cable (and kickdown cable on automatic transmission cars), the vacuum amplifier hose at the T-pipe, and the hose at the wax thermostat.

15. Disconnect the air pump hose at the backfire valve, the solenoid valve wire, and the micro-switch wire.

16. Remove the exhaust manifold flange retaining nuts (both sides). On the B28, disconnect the exhaust downpipe above the catalytic converter and remove it after disconnecting the oxygen sensor.

17. On cars equipped with air conditioning, remove the compressor and drive belt, and place it to one side. Note that you are simply unbolting and moving various AC components; it IS NOT necessary to discharge the system. Do not disconnect the refigerant hoses.

18. Drain the crankcase.

CAUTION: *The EPA warns that prolonged contact with used engine oil may cause a number of skin disorders, including cancer! You should make every effort to minimize your exposure to used engine oil. Protective gloves should be worn when changing the oil. Wash your hands and any other exposed skin areas as soon as possible after exposure to used engine oil. Soap and water, or waterless hand cleaner should be used.*

19. Remove the power steering pump, drive belt, and bracket. Position to one side.

20. From underneath, remove the retaining nuts for the front motor mounts.

21a. On B27 California models equipped with

Disconnect the front engine mounts: three nuts on left side, one on right (arrows)

a catalytic converter, remove the front exhaust pipe.

21b. On B27 49 states models, remove the front exhaust pipe hangers and clamps and allow the system to hang.

21c. On the B28 and B280, disconnect the exhaust system clamp from the transmission and allow exhaust to hang.

22. On cars equipped with automatic transmission, place the shift lever in **Park**. Disconnect the shift control lever at the transmission.

23. On manual transmission cars, disconnect the clutch slave cylinder from the bell housing. Leave the cylinder connected to its hoses and secure the cylinder out of the way.

24. Disconnect the speedometer cable and driveshaft at the transmission.

25. Jack up the front of the car and place jack stands beneath the reinforced box member area to the rear of each front jacking attachment. Using a floor jack and a thick, wide wooden block, support the weight of the engine beneath the oil pan.

26. Remove the bolts for the rear transmission mount. Remove the transmission support crossmember.

27. Lift out the engine and transmission.

28. Support the engine on a suitable rack or stand. To reinstall the engine:

29. Lower the engine and transmission into the car. Support the weight of the engine with the floor jack and a thick, wide piece of wood under the oil pan.

30. Replace the transmission crossmember; install and tighten the bolts.

31. At the transmission, connect the speedometer cable and driveshaft.

32. On manual transmission cars, reattach and secure the clutch slave cylinder. On automatic transmissions, reconnect the shift control lever.

33. Install and secure exhaust system pieces as necessary. Check for proper placement of all brackets, mounts and clamps. Check for interference between exhaust pipes and bodywork.

34. Install the front motor mount retaining nuts.

35. Install the power steering pump, bracket, and drive belt. Adjust the belt to the proper tension.

36. If equipped with air conditioning, reinstall the compressor and drive belt. Adjust the belt to the proper tension.

37. Reconnect the exhaust manifold flange retaining nuts on both sides of the motor and and secure. On B28/B280, reconnect the oxygen sensor.

38. Re-attach the air pump hose to the backfire valve, connect the solenoid valve wire, and the wire to the micro-switch.

39. Reconnect the hose to the wax thermostat, the vacuum amplifier hose and the throttle cable. On automatic transmission cars, reconnect the kick-down cable.

40. Attach the wiring to the voltage regulator and replace the hoses to the carbon canister. Install the vacuum hose to the EGR valve.

41. At the firewall, connect the wiring to all relays and components, beginning with the larger harnesses first. Reinstall the distributor wiring.

42. Connect and secure all fuel lines at the filter and the return pipe. These are high pressure lines; make sure the fittings are tight and will not leak. Reinstall the gas cap.

43. Reinstall the vacuum pump and O-ring, and the pump hose. Connect the heater hoses; connect the power brake hose to the intake manifold.

44. Install the radiator, fan shroud and grille. On cars with automatic transmission, reconnect the transmission cooler lines to the radiator.

45. Install the upper and lower radiator hoses, the overflow hoses and replace the overflow tank cap. If not already done, close the drain cocks on both sides of the engine.

46. Attach the under-engine splash guard. Reinstall the air cleaner assembly, and, on B28/B280, the intake air preheating assembly.

47. Remount the hood and attach the washer lines and under hood light wire.

48. Add oil and coolant to specified levels.

49. Reinstall the battery. Secure the battery holddown clamp and the wiring terminals.

50. On cars with manual transmissions, reinstall the shifter with particular attention to the snapring and the setscrew which locks the pivot pin.

51. Double check all installation items, paying particular attention to loose hoses or hanging

wires, untightened nuts, poor routing of hoses and wires (too tight or rubbing) and tools left in the engine area.

52. Start the engine, allow it to run at idle and check for leaks. Make needed adjustments to throttle cable, clutch, and idle speed as necessary. Check ALL fluid levels and top off as needed.

D24 & D24T Engines

NOTE: *Cleanliness is extremely important when working on diesel fuel systems. Wipe off all line joints before disconnecting and plug open lines immediately. If drained fuel is to be re-used, collect in clean container and cap immediately.*

All wires and hoses should be labled at the time of removal. The amount of time saved during re-assembly makes the extra effort well worthwhile.

1. Matchmark and remove the hood.
2. Disconnect the negative battery terminal.
3. Drain the radiator coolant.

CAUTION: *When draining the coolant, keep in mind that cats and dogs are attracted by the ethylene glycol antifreeze, and are quite likely to drink any that is left in an uncovered container or in puddles on the ground. This will prove fatal in sufficient quantity. Always drain the coolant into a sealable container. Coolant should be reused unless it is contaminated or several years old.*

4. Remove the four clips and pull up the rubber boot on the shift lever.
5. Disconnect the back-up light and overdrive connector if so equipped.
6. Remove the bracket for the reverse inhibitor.
7. Release the lock ring on the shift lever.
8. Move the lock ring, rubber ring, and plastic journal up on the lever.

NOTE: *On cars with automatic transmissions place the shift lever in P before disconnecting.*

9. Disconnect the top and bottom radiator hoses.
10. Disconnect the lower hose at the cold start device, and drain the coolant into a suitable container.
11. On vehicles with automatic transmissions, remove the cooling lines from the radiator.
12. Disconnect the expansion tank hose.
13. Unbolt and remove the grille, the radiator and the fan shroud.
14. Disconnect the electrical connections at the firewall.
15. Remove the heater hoses at the control valve.

16. Disconnect the hose from the vacuum pump.
17. Disconnect the accelerator cable from the pulley and bracket. On automatic cars, disconnect the kickdown cable.
18. Disconnect the vacuum line to the brake booster.
19. Disconnect the fuel supply line at the filter and the return line at the injection pump.

NOTE: *Thoroughly clean all connections prior to disconnecting them.*

20. Plug all fuel lines to prevent dirt from entering them.
21. Disconnect the wires at the main terminal.
22. Disconnect the glow plug relay.
23. Remove the relay retaining screws and hang the relay and the wire bundle on the engine.
24. Remove the power steering pump and brackets, and use a piece of wire to tie it out of the way. It is not necessary to disconnect the hoses from the pump, but DO NOT allow the pump to hang by its hoses.

If so equipped, detach the air conditioner compressor from its mounts and tie it out of the way. DO NOT disconnect any hoses to the compressor and DO NOT allow the compressor to hang by its hoses.

25. Remove the starter wires and the battery ground strap.
26. Remove the fan, spacer, pulley and drive belts.
27. Remove the air cleaner and all necessary hoses.
28. Disconnect the alternator wires.
29. Disconnect the exhaust pipe at the front exhaust manifold.
30. Drain the engine oil.

CAUTION: *The EPA warns that prolonged contact with used engine oil may cause a number of skin disorders, including cancer!*

Disconnect the glow plug relay's thin black wire and hang relay and wire bundle on the engine—Diesel

You should make every effort to minimize your exposure to used engine oil. Protective gloves should be worn when changing the oil. Wash your hands and any other exposed skin areas as soon as possible after exposure to used engine oil. Soap and water, or waterless hand cleaner should be used.

31. Disconnect the exhaust pipe at the rear exhaust manifold.

32. On D24T models, remove the inlet hose from the turbo pipe, and the snapring from the turbo intake pipe. Remove the compressor intake pipe and plug the hole immediately with a clean rag.

Disconnect the oil return pipe bolts, and move the return pipe aside. Plug the hoses. Remove the oil delivery pipe from the turbo unit, and plug the hoses. Remove the compressor and exhaust pipes from the turbo unit, and remove the turbocharger.

33. Disconnect the clutch cable, return spring, vibration damper, and rubber buffer.

34. Pull out the clutch cable from the clutch lever and housing.

35. Disconnect the speedometer from the transmission.

NOTE: *On cars with automatic transmissions disconnect the gear shift control rod from the transmission.*

36. Disconnect the shift lever and push it up into the car.

37. Remove the driveshaft from the transmission.

38. Support the transmission with a jack and remove the rear crossmember.

39. Remove the engine mounts.

a. Left side: Remove the nuts from the front axle member.

b. Right side: Remove the lower nut from the rubber pad.

40. Gently put tension on your engine removal hoist.

41. Remove the left engine mount assembly.

42. Tilt the engine and remove it using the proper lifting device.

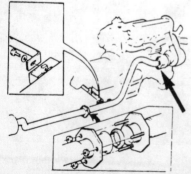

Disconnecting exhaust pipe and bracket, D24T

43. Support the engine on a suitable rack or stand. To reinstall the engine:

44. After positioning the engine in the car, attach the left engine mount to the block, gently lower the engine to its final position and secure both the left and right side engine mount nuts.

45. With the transmission resting on the jack, install the rear transmission crossmember.

46. Reconnect the driveshaft to the transmission. On automatic transmissions, reconnect the gear shift control rod to the transmission. On manual shift cars, reconnect the clutch cable to the lever and housing, remembering to install the return spring, vibration damper and buffer. Reconnect the speedometer cable.

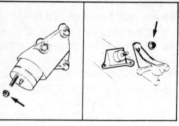

Removing the retaining nuts from the left and right engine mounts, D24 and D24T

47. On D24T models, reinstall the turbocharger unit, using new gaskets. Install the compressor and exhaust pipes. Remove the plugs from the lines and attach the oil delivery and oil return lines to the turbo unit.

Remove the plugs and install the compressor intake pipe and air inlet hose.

48. Connect the exhaust pipes to the front and rear exhaust manifolds.

49. Connect the wiring to the alternator.

50. Replace the air cleaner assembly and its hoses and ductwork.

51. Install the fan, spacer, pulley and drive belts. Adjust the belts as necessary.

52. Connect the wiring to the starter and the battery ground strap.

53. Remount the power steering pump and brackets and, if equipped, the air conditioner compressor. Install the belts and adjust to the proper tension. Check the hoses for proper routing; make sure there is no possibility of the hoses rubbing on anything nearby.

54. Reinstall the glow plug relay at the firewall and connect its wiring. Attach the wiring at the main terminal.

55. Remove the plugs from the fuel delivery and return lines and connect them to the proper ports. Maintain extreme cleanliness throughout this operation.

56. Reconnect to vacuum line to the brake booster.

57. Attach the throttle cable to the pulley and

bracket. Reattach the kickdown cable on cars with automatic transmissions.

58. Reconnect the hose to the vacuum pump. Attach and secure the heater hoses at the control valve.

59. Reconnect the electrical harnesses and wires at the firewall. Begin with the larger harnesses first.

60. Reinstall the radiator, fan shroud and grille. Connect the expansion tank hose. If equipped with automatic transmission, reconnect the oil cooler lines at the radiator.

61. Attach and secure the upper and lower radiator hoses and the lower hose to the cold start device.

62. Reinstall the shift lever assembly and reverse inhibitor. Connect the wiring for the reverse lights and, if equipped, the overdrive. Replace the shifter boot and secure with the four clips.

63. Reconnect the negative battery cable. Install the hood and connect the underhood light and the washer lines.

64. Install oil and coolant to specified levels.

65. Double check all installation items, paying particular attention to loose hoses or hanging wires, untightened nuts, poor routing of hoses and wires (too tight or rubbing) and tools left in the engine area.

66. Start the engine, allow it to run at idle and check for leaks. Make needed adjustments to throttle cable, clutch, and idle speed as necessary. Check ALL fluid levels and top off as needed.

Rocker Arm Cover (Valve Cover)

REMOVAL AND INSTALLATION

1. Disconnect and reposition as necessary any vacuum or PCV hoses that obstruct the valve cover(s).

2. Label and remove any wires (spark plug wiring, etc.) that may obstruct the valve cover(s).

3. Unbolt and remove the valve cover(s). If the cover is to be off for a period of hours or days, cover the exposed rockers with a rag to prevent dirt accumulation.

NOTE: *Do not pry the cover off if it seems stuck. Instead, gently tap around each cover with a rubber mallet until the old gasket breaks loose. A bent valve cover is extremely hard to straighten and will provide endless oil leaks for you to pursue.*

4. To install, always use a new valve cover gasket. Install the valve cover(s) and tighten cover bolts to 3 ft. lbs. Do not overtighten the bolts; you may distort the cover and cause oil leaks.

NOTE: *On B234 engines, silicone sealant must be applied at the front and rear camshaft bearing caps before the gasket is installed.*

5. Connect and reposition all vacuum and PCV hoses, and reconnect any electrical wires that were removed.

Rocker Shaft and Arm Assmebly

REMOVAL AND INSTALLATION

B20, B30

1. Remove the retaining screws and the valve cover and gasket.

2. Remove the rocker shaft-to-cylinder head bolts and lift out the shaft and rocker arms as a unit.

3. Lift out the pushrods, keeping them in order (an upside down shoebox with numbered holes makes an excellent holder) and check them for straightness by rolling them on a flat surface. Replace any bent pushrods.

4. Inspect the rocker shaft arms. If the shaft and rockers are coated with baked-on sludge, oil may not be reaching them. Clean out the oil feed holes in the rocker shaft with 0.020 in. (0.5mm) wire (piano wire).

If the clearance between the rocker arms and shaft exceeds 0.004 in. (0.1mm), the rocker arm needs to be rebushed. The rocker arm bushings are press fitted, and are removed with a drift. When pressing a new bushing, make sure that the oil hole in the bushing aligns with the hole in the arm.

5. Position the pushrods on their respective lifters. Install the rocker shaft and arm assembly on the head, and install the retaining bolts. Use a three step tightening procedure. Working from front to rear, tighten all the retaining bolts to 10 ft. lbs. Following the same pattern, tighten all the bolts to 15 ft. lbs, then make a final pass tightening all the bolts to 20 ft. lbs.

6. Check to see that valve lash has remained within specifications. Adjust valve lash, if necessary, as outlined in Chapter 1.

7. Install the valve cover with a new gasket, and tighten the valve cover retaining screws. Do not overtighten the valve cover bolts.

B27F, B28F and B280F

1. Disconnect the negative battery cable.

2. Disconnect the ignition system connector located on the right shock tower.

3. Using a 5mm Allen wrench, disconnect the control pressure regulator and lay the regulator on the intake manifold.

4. Remove the oil filler cap and hoses.

5. Remove the vacuum pump (left rear of engine); on B27, remove air pump if so equipped. Remove the air inlet duct running to the top center of the motor.

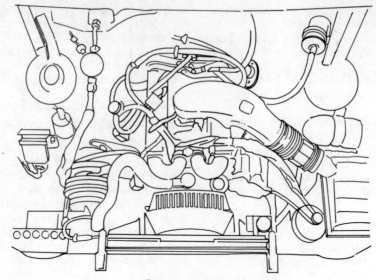

1. Battery negative cable
2. Connector, ignition system
3. Control pressure regulator
4. Oil filler cap and hoses
5. Vacuum pump
6. Air inlet duct

Location of items to be removed for access to valve covers on B27, B28 and B280 engines

6. On air conditioned models, remove the AC compressor. On B27s, remove the rear bracket. DO NOT loosen or remove any hoses at the compressor; simply remove the entire unit and use wire to tie it out of the way. Do not allow the compressor to hang by its hoses.

7. Loosen the valve cover bolts and remove the valve covers.

8. The rocker arm bolts double as cylinder head bolts. When loosening, follow the cylinder head bolt tightening sequence diagram. If removing both rocker shafts, mark them left and right.

NOTE: *Do not jar or strike the head while rockers and bolts are out, as the cylinder liner O-rings may break. If this happens, the en-*

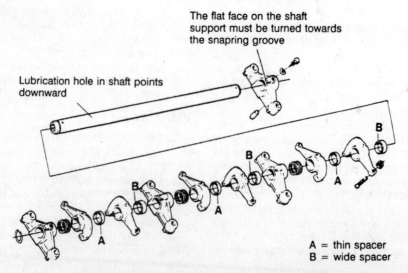

The flat face on the shaft support must be turned towards the snapring groove

Lubrication hole in shaft points downward

B
B
B
A
A
A

A = thin spacer
B = wide spacer

Rocker arm shaft assembly, B28 and B280 engines

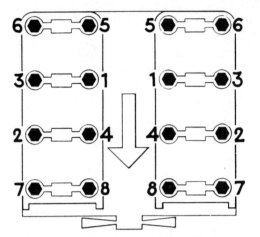

Loosening and tightening order for cylinder head and rocker assembly bolts, B27, B28 and B280 engines. Arrow points to front of car

gine requires a full tear-down to clean coolant out of crankcase and install new seals.

9. To install, place the rocker shaft in position on the proper side of the engine. Install the bolts finger tight, then use a three step tightening procedure. Tighten the bolts in the order shown in the illustration.

- First tightening: 7 ft. lbs.
- Second tightening: 22 ft. lbs.
- Third tightening: 44 ft. lbs.

10. Reinstall valve covers with new gaskets. Refer to step 6 above and replace all components in reverse order, remembering to adjust belts as necessary. When reinstalling the vacuum pump, use a new gasket and make sure the pump contacts the top side of the camshaft.

Thermostat

To operate at peak efficiency, an engine must maintain its internal temperatures within certain upper and lower limits. The cooling system circulates fluid around the combustion cylinders and conducts this heated fluid to the radiator, where the heat is exchanged into the airflow created by the fan and the motion of the car.

While most people realize that an engine running too hot (overheated) is a sign of trouble, few know that an engine can run too cool as well. If the proper internal temperatures are not achieved, fuel is not burned efficiently, and the lubricating oil does not reach its best working temperature. While a too cold condition is rarely disabling, it can cause a variety of problems which can be mistaken for tune-up or electrical causes.

The thermostat controls the flow of coolant within the system. It reacts to the heat of the coolant and allows more fluid (or less) to circu-

late. Depending on the amount of fluid being circulated, more or less heat is drawn away from the inside of the engine. While we are beyond the days of having to install different thermostats for summer and winter driving, it is wise to check the function of the thermostat periodically. Special use of the car such as trailer towing or carrying heavy loads may require the installation of a thermostat with different temperature characteristics.

REMOVAL AND INSTALLATION

1. Disconnect the lower radiator hose and drain the cooling system.

CAUTION: *When draining the coolant, keep in mind that cats and dogs are attracted by the ethylene glycol antifreeze, and are quite likely to drink any that is left in an uncovered container or in puddles on the ground. This*

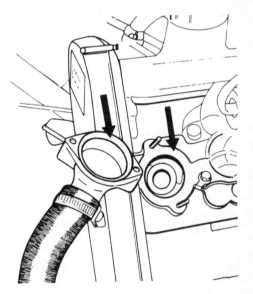

Thermostat location, B23 and B230 engines. Arrows show areas to be scraped clean of old gasket material

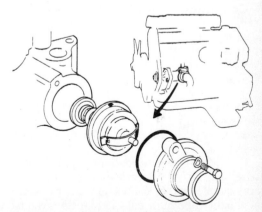

Thermostat location, D24 and D24T

will prove fatal in sufficient quantity. Always drain the coolant into a sealable container. Coolant should be reused unless it is contaminated or several years old.

2. Remove the two bolts securing the thermostat housing to the cylinder head on gasoline engines and to the block on the diesel. Carefully lift the housing free. Before removing the thermostat, look at it carefully to know which end is up. It is possible--and very embarassing--to install one upside down. Pay attention!

3. Remove all old gasket material from the mating surfaces and remove the thermostat. Do not use metal blades to scrape these surfaces; you may gouge the metal and cause a leak. Use a wooden or plastic scraper.

4. Test the operation of the thermostat by immersing it in a container of heated water. Replace any thermostat that does not open at the correct temperature. Most thermostats will begin to open at approximately 190°F.

5. Place the thermostat, with a new gasket, in position. Fit the thermostat housing and hand-tighten the bolts. Tighten the bolts ¼ turn past finger tight; overtightening can crack the brittle housing.

6. Connect the lower radiator hose and replace the coolant. On gasoline engined cars, leave the radiator cap off, start the engine and allow it to reach normal operating temperture. Inside the car place the heater temperature selector to full hot and turn on the blower. This allows the coolant to circulate fully throughout the system and purge any air bubbles which may be trapped. After a few minutes (during which you may observe air bubbles in the radiator neck) shut the engine off, top up the coolant and secure the radiator cap.

Cars with diesel engines require a different bleeding procedure. Please refer to Cooling System in Chapter 1.

Intake and Exhaust Manifolds

On early carbureted Volvos, the intake and exhaust manifolds are cast integrally. A preheating chamber is located within the combination manifold. The chamber's function is to transfer the heat from the exhaust ports to the fuel-air mixture in the intake manifold for improved cold weather operation. As the manufacturer moved to fuel injection for the US cars in the early 1970s, the few remaining carbureted cars used separate intake and exhaust manifolds.

On all fuel injected and diesel Volvos, the intake manifold (inlet duct) and exhaust manifold are separate units. The inlet duct is constructed of a light aluminum alloy, while the exhaust manifold is cast iron.

Combination Manifold (Carbureted Engines)
REMOVAL AND INSTALLATION

1. Remove the exhaust manifold preheating plate. Remove the nuts and disconnect the exhaust pipe from the exhaust manifold.

2. Remove the air cleaner. Disconnect the throttle, choke, and downshift linkage, if so equipped. Label and disconnect the positive crankcase ventilation hoses, and the vacuum hoses for the distributor advance, and power brake, if so equipped.

3. Remove the nuts and slide the combination manifold off the studs. Remove and discard the old manifold gasket.

4. To install, reverse the above procedure. Remember to use a new manifold gasket and exhaust pipe flange gasket in assembly. Most manifold gaskets have definite inside and outside faces; make sure it is correctly positioned. Torque the manifold retaining nuts to 13–16 ft. lbs.

Intake Manifold (Inlet Duct)
REMOVAL AND INSTALLATION
B20E, B20F, B30F

1. On B30F engines, remove the air cleaner. On B20E and B20F engines, remove the inlet duct-to-air cleaner hose at the inlet duct.

2. Disconnect the battery, negative cable first.

3. Disconnect the throttle and downshift linkage. Remove and label the hoses from the manifold to the PCV valve, distributor advance, and power brake booster.

4. Disconnect the contact for the throttle valve switch, and remove the ground cable for the inlet duct. On CI engines, remove fuel injectors.

5. Remove the bolts for the inlet duct stay. Remove the inlet duct-to-cylinder head retaining nuts and slide the inlet duct off the studs.

6. Discard the old gasket. To install, reverse the above procedure. Use a new inlet duct gasket.

B21F, B21FT, B23F, and B230F

1. Disconnect the pipe between the EGR valve and the manifold.

2. Disconnect and remove the cold start injector and remove the crankcase ventilation hose.

NOTE: *It is not necessary to physically remove the cold start injector from the manifold if its fuel line and electrical connector are removed.*

3. Remove the rubber pipes and electrical connection and remove the auxiliary air valve.

4. Remove the brace between the engine block and intake manifold. On B21FT engines, disconnect the turbocharger inlet hose (between the turbo unit and the intake manifold) and plug the hose with a clean rag.

5. Label and disconnect the distributor vacuum hose at the intake manifold.

6. Loosen the clamp and slide off the large rubber hose at the bottom of the intake manifold.

7. Remove the eight 13mm nuts and remove the intake manifold and gasket. Reinstall with new gaskets. Remember to remove the plug from the turbo inlet hose if so equipped. Installation is the reverse of removal. Torque the manifold-to-cylinder head nuts to 15 ft. lbs. Double check all hose and wiring connections for proper placement and routing.

B234F

1. Remove the air mass meter and the air intake hose.

2. Detach the throttle pulley from the intake manifold and remove the link rod from the throttle lever.

3. Separate the throttle housing from the intake manifold and cut the cable tie holding the wiring to the vacuum hose connections.

4. Disconnect the lines and hoses from the manifold, including the brake booster vacuum hose, the evaporation line, the oil trap, the fuel pressure regulator line and the air control valve line. If the car is equipped with a vacuum tank, disconnect its line at the manifold.

5. Disconnect the fuel return line at the distribution pipe. Disconnect the wiring to the injectors and remove the distribution pipe and injectors. Immediately protect these components from the entry of any dirt.

6. Unbolt and remove the intake manifold from the engine.

7. If installing a new manifold, it is necessary to transfer the various hose nipples and plugs to the new part. Install the manifold with a new gasket. Starting with the center bolts and working outward, tighten the bolts to 15 ft. lbs.

8. Reconnect the hoses to their proper ports.

9. Position the injector wiring between cylinders 2 and 3 and reinstall the fuel distributor rail and the injectors. Tighten the pipe and the ground wires to the block. Connect the fuel pressure regulator line to the intake manifold.

10. Install the throttle pulley and connect the link rod.

11. Install the throttle housing with a new gasket. Check the operation of the throttle stops and switches.

12. Install the air mass meter and air inlet hose.

B27, B28, B280

NOTE: *Instructions below are for B280 family of engines. B27 and B28 are similar, but older engines may not contain all components noted below.*

All wires and hoses should be labled at the time of removal. The amount of time saved during re-assembly makes the extra effort well worthwhile.

1. Disconnect the negative battery cable. Loosen gas cap, allow pressure within tank to equalize and retighten cap.

2. Remove the air intake duct. Remove the oil filler cap and hoses.

3. Disconnect the fuel lines from the filter and the fuel return pipe.

CAUTION: *The fuel system is under pressure. Release pressure slowly and contain spillage. Observe no smoking/no open flame precautions*

4. Remove the air control valve from the inlet manifold.

5. Remove the spark plug wires from the spark plugs, the ignition coil and the wire holder; position the wires out of the way.

6. Remove the injectors from the cylinder head. Plug the injector holes with paper or a rag.

7. Loosen clips and remove distributor cap. This prevents damage to the cap when removing the manifold.

8. Label and remove the vacuum hoses from the charcoal canister and the power brake booster. Also disconnect the vacuum hose at the right rear corner of the manifold and the hose to the T-connector. For ease of reinstallation, disconnect all of these hoses only at the manifold end.

9. Loosen the retaining bolts and remove the front (double horseshoe) section of the intake manifold. Plug the large holes in the manifold with crumpled paper.

10. Remove cables from the throttle control

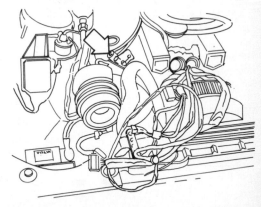

Location of control pressure regulator, B280 engines

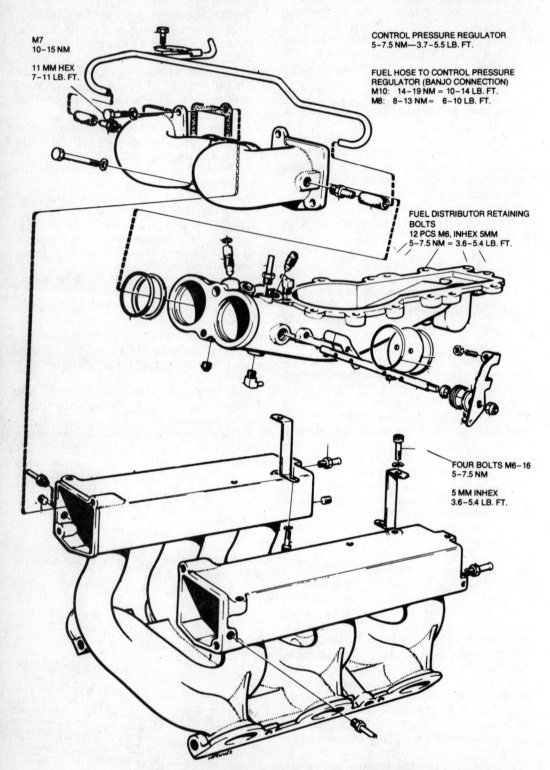

M7
10–15 NM

11 MM HEX
7–11 LB. FT.

CONTROL PRESSURE REGULATOR
5–7.5 NM—3.7–5.5 LB. FT.

FUEL HOSE TO CONTROL PRESSURE
REGULATOR (BANJO CONNECTION)
M10: 14–19 NM = 10–14 LB. FT.
M8:   8–13 NM = 6–10 LB. FT.

FUEL DISTRIBUTOR RETAINING
BOLTS
12 PCS M6, INHEX 5MM
5–7.5 NM = 3.6–5.4 LB. FT.

FOUR BOLTS M6–16
5–7.5 NM

5 MM INHEX
3.6–5.4 LB. FT.

Intake manifold (inlet duct) B27F engine. B28F similar

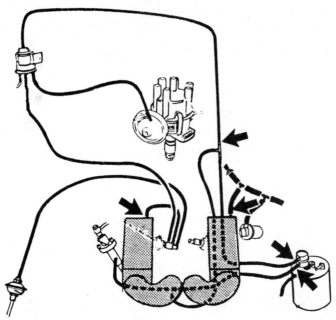

Vacuum hose routing at B280F intake manifold. Arrows show points to be disconnected when removing manifold

pulley. There will always be a throttle cable; there may be a kickdown cable (automatic transmission) and possibly a cruise control cable.

11. Label, disconnect, and move to one side the wiring harness(es).

12. Using a 5mm Allen wrench, loosen and remove the control pressure regulator. Lay the regulator on top of the engine.

13. Remove the four bolts holding the intake manifold. Remove the manifold carefully. Plug the intake ports in the engine immediately.

14. To reinstall: Remove the plugs from the intake ports on the engine. Using NEW O-rings (seals), install the manifold in place, install the four bolts and torque to between 7 and 11 ft. lbs. Do not overtighten these bolts

15. Reattach the distributor cap.

16. Install the injectors.

17. Connect and fasten the spark plug wires.

18. Replace the control pressure regulator and air control valve.

19. Connect and fasten wiring harness(es).

20. Connect cables to the throttle pulley.

21. Using NEW gaskets and O-rings, install the front section of the manifold. Do not over tighten bolts. Don't forget to remove the plugs in the ends of the manifold.

22. Connect all vacuum hoses. Refer to illustration for help.

23. Reconnect the lines to the fuel filter and the fuel return. Reconnect the air intake tube and replace the oil filler cap and hoses.

24. Connect the battery cable. Start the engine and check your work. It may be necessry to adjust the throttle cable and/or idle speed.

Diesel D24, D24T

1. Remove the air cleaner to intake manifold bellows.

2. Remove the preheat hose and panels. Remove the hose and wire from the safety valve, located on the front end of the manifold. Remove the hose to the fuel limiter; this hose is located on the rear of the manifold.

3. On the D24T engine, disconnect the turbocharger inlet hose (between the turbo unit and the intake manifold) and plug the hole immediatly. The hose can be pushed up into the manifold.

4. Using a 6mm Allen wrench, remove the ten attaching bolts and remove the intake manifold.

5. Installation is the reverse of removal. When installing gasket, make sure the green side faces the cylinder head and apply a light coat of lubricant to keep the gasket in place during installation.

Check the O-rings for the safety valve and compressor (turbo) tube and replace the rings if needed. Torque the manifold bolts to 18 ft. lbs.

NOTE: *When installing the bellows to the intake manifold, make sure the PCV hose is positioned so that it will not make contact with the hood when the hood is closed.*

Exhaust Manifold

REMOVAL AND INSTALLTION

NOTE: *Exhaust manifold removal and installation for most carbureted engines is contained in the Combination Manifold, Removal and Installation section, above.*

B20, B30 (Electric Fuel Injection Engines)

NOTE: *This procedure is for exhaust manifold gasket removal and installation only.*

1. Disconnect the negative battery cable.
2. Remove the air cleaner.
3. Label and remove the throttle control, all hoses and electrical cables from the intake manifold.
4. Remove the battery. Disconnect the EGR valve from the upper pipe, then remove the lower pipe with the EGR valve.
5. Remove the nuts and lift off the intake manifold.
6. Remove the clamp holding the exhaust pipes to the gearbox.
7. Pull out the exhaust manifold from the cylinder head and remove the manifold gasket.
8. Clean the contact surfaces on the manifold and the cylinder head.
9. Fit a new gasket on the cylinder head studs.
10. Fit the exhaust manifold in position and install the retaining nuts. Torque the nuts to 13–16 ft. lbs.
11. Remaining installation is the reverse of removal. Use a new gasket when reinstalling the intake manifold. Remember to tighten the exhaust clamp at the transmission.

B20 (Continuous Fuel Injection Engines)

NOTE: *This procedure is for exhaust manifold gasket removal and installation only.*

1. Disconnect the negative battery cable.
2. On automatic transmission models, remove the ATF filler pipe retaining screw and turn the pipe out of the way.
3. Remove the retainer above the control pressure regulator.
4. Remove the connection pipe between the air flow sensor and the intake manifold.
5. Loosen the upper bolts for the intake manifold bracket, then remove the lower bolt.
6. Remove the exhaust pipe clamp at the transmission, then remove the exhaust manifold flange nuts.
7. Remove the manifold nuts and bolts.
8. Lift out the manifold to expose the gasket. Then remove the gasket and clean the mating surfaces on the manifold and cylinder head. Install the new gasket and position the manifold on its studs; install the nuts and tighten to 6.5 ft. lbs. Remaining installation is the reverse of

the removal process. Remember to secure the exhaust hardware at the transmission and to tighten the retaining screw on the automatic transmission filler pipe.

B21F, B21T, B23F

NOTE: On models equipped with air pumps, the pump may have to be removed to gain access to the manifold.

1. Remove the EGR valve pipe from the rear of the exhaust manifold or from the turbo on the B21FT engine.
2. Jack up the car and support it on stands.
3. Remove the nuts and disconnect the exhaust pipe at the manifold flange.
4. Remove the eight nuts and remove the exhaust manifold.
When installing new gaskets, the gasket side marked UT should face out. Install the manifold and fit the lifting eye on the top stud for cylinder number 3.

Washers stamped with the marks UT or OUT should face out or away from the engine. Tighten the manifold nuts to 10–20 ft. lbs., and the manifold to exhaust pipe nuts to 22–30 ft. lbs.

B234F

1. Disconnect the front exhaust pipe from the manifold. Disconnect the catalytic converter from the front muffler.
2. Remove the heat shields (top and bottom) from the manifold and remove the air preheat hose.
3. Disconnect the front exhaust pipe from the bracket on the bell housing.
4. Unbolt the exhaust manifold and remove it from the car.
5. Install the manifold with a new gasket and tighten the bolts to 15 ft. lbs.
6. Install the front exhaust pipe with a new gasket; tighten the joint to the manifold to 20 ft. lbs. Reattach the catalytic converter to the front muffler.
7. Install the heat shields and the preheat hose.

B27F and B28F

Depending on the type of optional equipment your particular vehicle has, the exhaust manifolds may be removed from underneath the car.

1. Jack up the vehicle and properly support it with jacks stands.
2. Unbolt the crossover pipe from the left and right side of the exhaust manifolds, (if so equipped).
NOTE: *If your car has the Y-type exhaust pipe, disconnect this pipe at the left and right manifolds.*

3. Remove any other necessary hardware and the manifold retaining nuts.

4. Remove the left and right side manifolds.

5. When reinstalling, always use new gaskets. Gaskets must be installed with the reinforced metal edge facing the cylinder head. Tighten the manifold bolts to 7–11 ft. lbs. Remember to reconnect and secure the exhaust pipes under the car.

Diesel D24

1. Disconnect the negative battery terminal.

2. Remove the air cleaner and all necessary hoses.

3. Remove the exhaust pipes from the manifold.

4. Loosen and remove the manifold retaining nuts. (Access to the upper nuts will be difficult; they are located under the intake manifold flanges.)

5. Remove the manifold in two pieces.

6. When reinstalling, always use new gaskets and new nuts. Torque the retaining nuts to 18 ft. lbs.

D24T (Turbocharged Diesel)

NOTE: *This procedure requires removal of the turbocharger. While no special tools are required, the turbocharger must be handled carefully and kept completely free of dirt and fluid contamination.*

1. Disconnect the negative battery cable, the inlet hose to the turbocharger, the air filter and the pre-heat hose.

2. Disconnect the hoses to the compressor inlet and the safety valve. Plug the ends of these hoses.

3. Loosen and remove the exhaust pipe from the turbocharger and disconnect the exhaust system from the transmission crossmember.

4. Detach oil delivery and return lines from the turbocharger and plug the line ends.

5. Remove the pre-heating panels.

6. Push or slide the compressor tube into the intake manifold. Loosen and remove the twelve manifold retaining nuts and gently pull the manifold away from the engine. Remove the gaskets from the cylinder head.

7. Detach the turbocharger from the branch pipe and carefully remove the manifold and turbocharger from the car.

8. The turbocharger may be separated from the manifold on the workbench; plug all ports on the turbocharger with rags and keep the unit as clean as possible. Do not drop or jar the turbo unit.

9. The exhaust manifold may be separated into three (older cars, two) sections. If the same manifold unit is to be reinstalled on the engine, DO NOT separate the sections.

Two piece and three piece exhaust manifolds found on turbocharged diesel engines

If the sections must be separated, do so by tapping with a plastic mallet. After needed repairs have ben performed, re-assemble by removing all traces of soot and lubricating the contact faces. Place the flanges on a level surface and tap the pieces together. Don't forget to install the spacers.

Since the bolt holes must fit over the studs on the head, correct separation must be maintained between the holes. When re-assembling the manifold, maintain 3.54 in (90mm) between the center of the bolt holes.

Check spacing with trial fittings onto the head; adjust the manifold sections as necessary to get the proper fit.

10. Using a light coat of sealer and new nuts, attach the turbocharger to the exhaust manifold. Torque the nuts to 43 ft. lbs. Remember to remove plugs from the ports in the turbocharger.

11. Place new exhaust gaskets on the cylinder head. The raised section of the gasket should face out or towards the exhaust manifold.

12. Install the manifold with the turbocharger attached. Use new nuts and torque to 18 ft. lbs.

13. Pull or slide the compressor tube down from the intake manifold. Check the seals and O-rings for condition and replace if necessary. Attach the tube to the turbocharger.

14. Remove the plugs and connect the oil delivery and oil return lines to the tubocharger. Use new gaskets.

15. Install the pre-heating panels. Using new

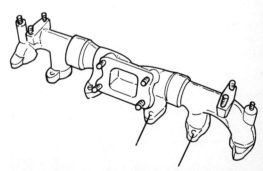

Maintain correct hole spacing when reassembling turbo-diesel manifolds. 90 mm = 3.54 inches

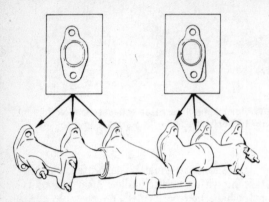

Correct placement of exhaust manifold gaskets, D24T

gaskets, connect the exhaust pipe to the turbocharger. Volvo recommends the use of an anti-rusting compond on the threads. Re-attach the exhaust fittings and brackets at the transmission and crossmember.

16. Reconnect the hose from the safety valve to the turbo inlet. Attach the PCV hose and attach the air filter unit. reinstall the air inlet hose and the pre-heat hose.

17. Reconnect the negative battery cable. Double check all installation items, paying particular attention to loose hoses or hanging wires, untightened nuts, poor routing of hoses and wires (too tight or rubbing) and tools left in the engine area.

Turbocharger
REMOVAL AND INSTALLATION
B21FT and B23FT

NOTE: *Due to the complexity and close tolerances involved with the turbocharger unit, we recommend that any service other than removal and installation be performed by an experienced turbo technician. It should also be mentioned that the turbocharger unit has other controls mounted on it. These devices control various pressures developed by the turbocharger. DO NOT attempt to alter or adjust the linkages or settings; severe and immediate damage to the motor may occur if the turbo air flow is altered.*

1. Disconnect the negative battery cable.
2. Disconnect the expansion tank and its retainer.
3. Remove preheater hose to the air clenaer. Remove the pipe and rubber bellows between the air/fuel control unit and the turbocharger unit. Pull out the crankcase ventilation hose from the pipe.

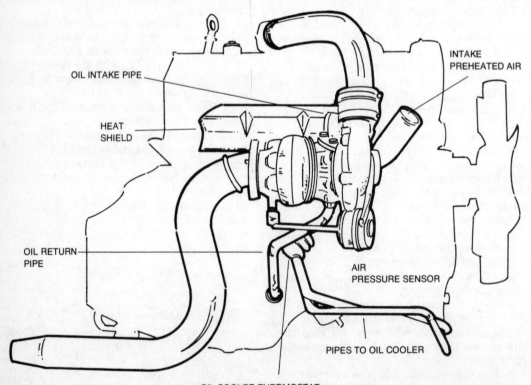

Turbocharger system component location

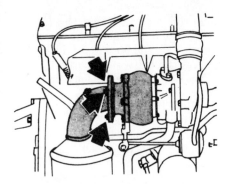

Disconnect the turbocharger unit from the exhaust system

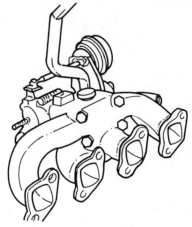

Bolt tightening sequence for turbocharger-to-manifold bolts on B21FT and B23FT engines

4. Remove the pipe and pipe connector between the turbocharger unit and the intake. Cover the turbocharger intake and outlet ports to keep dirt out of the system.

5. Disconnect the exhaust pipe and secure it out of the way.

6. Disconnect the spark plug wires at the plugs.

7. Remove the upper head shield. Remove the brace between the turbocharger unit and the manifold.

8. Remove the lower heat shield by removing the one retaining screw underneath the manifold.

9. Remove the oil pipe clamp, the retaining screws on the turbo unit and the pipe connection screw in the cylinder block under the manifold. DO NOT allow any dirt to enter the oilways.

10. Remove the manifold retaining screws and washers. Let one nut remain in place to keep the manifold in position.

11. Remove the oil delivery pipe. Cover the opening on the turbo unit.

12. Disconnect the air/fuel control unit by loosening the clamps. Move the unit with the lower section of the air cleaner up to the right side wheel housing. Place a cover over the wheel housing as protection.

13. Remove the air filter.

14. Remove the remaining nut and washer on the manifold. Lift the assembly forward and up. Remove the manifold gaskets. Disconnect the return oil pipe O-ring from the cylinder block.

15. Disconnect the turbocharger unit from the manifold.

16. When reinstalling, be sure to use a new gasket for the exhaust manifold and a new O-ring to the return oil pipe. Keep everything clean during assembly, and use extreme care in keeping dirt out of the various turbo inlet and outlet pipes and hoses. Remember to remove the plugs from various ports and lines before reassembly.

17. Assemble the turbocharger to the exhaust manifold. Tighten the four bolts in the sequence shown. Use a three step tightening procedure:

Step 1: 0.7 ft. lbs.

Step 2: 30 ft. lbs.

Step 3: Tighten the bolts an additional 120°.

18. Install the turbo and manifold assembly onto the engine. The designation UT or the word OUT on the new gaskets should face away from the engine.

19. Lightly grease a new O-ring and install it on the oil return pipe. Lift the pipe into position by guiding it through the hole in the cylinder block. Make sure the O-ring seats properly.

20. Install one washer and nut to hold the manifold and turbocharger in place.

21. Install the air/fuel control unit and the air filter.

22. Fill the turbocharger oil inlet port with oil. This will pre-lube the compressor when the engine is first started.

23. Install the oil delivery pipe and make connection finger tight. Make sure no dirt enters the pipe or clings to fittings.

24. Install manifold washers and nuts. Don't forget to install the lifting eye (hook). Torque the manifold retaining bolts to 18 ft. lbs. Using new seals, connect the oil delivery pipe to the turbocharger. Install the pipe-clamp for the oil delivery pipe and tighten connection(s) for this pipe.

25. Install the upper and lower heat shields, install the brace between the manifold and the turbocharger, and reconnect the spark plug wiring.

26. Connect the exhaust pipe.

27. Reattach the pipe and rubber bellows between the air/fuel control unit and the turbocharger. Reconnect the PCV hose and the pre-

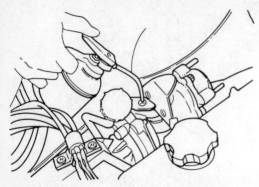

On gasoline engines, fill the turbocharger oil inlet port with oil when reassembling

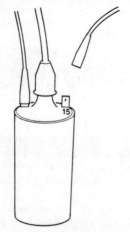

Disconnect terminal 15 on the coil to prelube the turbocharger by cranking the engine

heat hose to the air cleaner. Install the intake pipe between the turbocharger and the intake manifold. Double check all hoses for proper positioning and tightened clamps.

28. Replace the expansion tank and its retainer. Connect the negative battery cable.

29. IMPORTANT: Disconnect the wire (usually brown) at terminal number 15 of the ignition coil. Use the ignition key to run the starter for about 30 seconds; the engine will turn but will not start. This circulates the oil within the turbocharger, insuring proper lubrication when the engine is started.

With the ignition key off, reconnect the wire to terminal 15 on the coil.

30. Start the engine and allow it to idle for at least 30 seconds before increasing engine speed.

D24T

1. Remove the negative battery cable.
2. Remove the inlet hose from the turbo pipe.
3. Remove the complete air cleaner assembly, and the preheater hoses.

4. Remove the snapring from the turbocharger intake pipe, and remove the compressor intake pipe. Plug the hose immediately.

5. Disconnect the bolts securing the oil return pipe to the turbo unit. Move the pipe aside, and plug the holes immediately.

6. Remove the oil delivery pipe from the turbocharger and plug the holes.

7. Press or slide the compressor pipe into the intake manifold. Remove the exhaust pipe from the turbocharger.

8. Jack up the car, and place stands safely underneath. Remove the exhaust pipe from the transmission support bracket and disassemble the joint. Remove the exhaust pipe.

9. Remove the turbocharger securing nuts, and lower the front end of the turbo unit. Remove the turbocharger and then remove the compressor pipe.

10. If the turbocharger is replaced complete, transfer the necessary parts to the new unit. Always use new gaskets.

11. During installation, make sure all hoses are connected without the addition of any dirt into the system. This is crucial to the life of the turbocharger and the engine.

Mount the turbocharger onto the manifold. Use new nuts (no gasket is required) and tighten the nuts to 44 ft. lbs. Slide the compressor intake pipe down onto the turbocharger.

12. Remember to remove all plugs and line covers. Attach the oil delivery pipe, the oil return pipe (with a new seal) and the exhaust pipe with a new gasket.

13. Under the car, attach the exhaust pipes and secure the brackets at the transmission.

14. Install the turbocharger intake pipe. Apply oil to the inside of the tube and to the O-ring; install it on the outer groove of the turbocharger.

15. Reconnect the hose for the safety valve.

16. Reinstall the air cleaner with the intake and pre-heat hoses. Connect the negative battery cable.

Air Conditioning Compressor

Removing the air conditioning compressor is generally a straightforward task. It may be necessary to remove the compressor for unit repair or for access to other parts of the motor. Removing the compressor from the car requires discharging and recharging the system. It is possible to remove the compressor from its mounts and reposition it out of the way WITHOUT discharging the system or removing the refrigerant hoses.

PLEASE RE-READ THE AIR CONDITIONING SECTION IN CHAPTER 1 SO THAT THE SYSTEM MAY BE DIS-

CHARGED PROPERLY. ALWAYS WEAR EYE PROTECTION AND GLOVES WHEN DISCHARGING THE SYSTEM. OBSERVE NO SMOKING/NO OPEN FLAME RULES.

The first three steps of removal are always the same, regardless of type of compressor or system:

1. Disconnect the negative battery cable.
2. Discharge the system safely, in accordance with the instructions in Chapter 1.
3. Remove or reposition any components blocking access to the compressor belt and bolts. Depending on your vehicle, it may be necessary to remove the air intake duct, the power steering pump (Don't disconnect the hoses--just move the pump!) and/or an assortment of vacuum hoses and wires. Where possible, relocate hoses and wires without disconnecting either end. On earlier cars it may be necessary to gently tie the upper radiator hose out of the way; this can be done without draining the coolant system.
4. Carefully loosen and disconnect the refrigerant lines from the compressor. Immediately cap the lines and compressor ports with tape to prevent entry of dirt and moisture.
5. Loosen the compressor bolts; move it to loosen the belt and then remove the belt.

On the B21, B23 and B230 family of engine, the belt cannot be removed in this fashion. On these engines it is necessary to remove the six bolts holding the crankshaft pulley together. As the pulley comes apart, note the number and placement of the shims between the pulley halves. These shims determine the belt adjustment; it is important that the same number be put back in the same location during re-assembly.

6. Disconnect the wiring to the compressor.
7. Remove the compressor mounting bolts and remove the compressor. Most compressors are heavier than they appear; support the compressor securely when removing. Keep the compressor in an upright position on the workbench--do not allow oil to run out!
8. During re-assembly, torque the refrigerant lines to 20 ft. lbs. and make certain that any small washers or O-rings are in place and properly seated. Remember to remove plugs and tape form lines and ports before installing.
9. On B21, B23 and B230 engines, the shims within the crank pulley determine belt adjustment. Add or subtract shims as necessary to get the correct belt tension.

On all other models, install the belt and draw the correct tension by moving the compressor to the proper position and tightening the mounting bolts.

10. Attach and secure any components, wires or hoses moved to gain access.

B21, B23 and B230: Remove the compressor belt by separating the crankshaft pulley

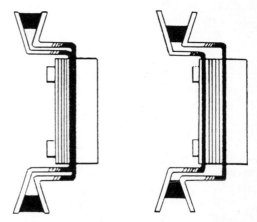

Cross section of crankshaft pulley and compressor belt, B21, B23 and B230 engines. Shim placement affects belt tension

11. Double check all installation items, paying particular attention to loose hoses or hanging wires, untightened nuts, poor routing of hoses and wires (too tight or rubbing) and tools left in the engine area.
12. Refer to Air Conditioning section in Chapter 1 for detailed instructions on recharging the air conditioning system.

Radiator

REMOVAL AND INSTALLATION

1. Perform this work only on a cold engine. Remove the radiator and expansion tank caps, disconnect the lower radiator hose at the radiator, and drain the cooling system.

CAUTION: *When draining the coolant, keep in mind that cats and dogs are attracted by the ethylene glycol antifreeze, and are quite likely to drink any that is left in an uncovered container or in puddles on the ground. This will prove fatal in sufficient quantity. Always drain the coolant into a sealable container. Coolant should be reused unless it is contaminated or several years old.*

2. Remove the expansion tank and hose, and drain the coolant. Remove the upper radiator hose. On cars with automatic transmissions, disconnect the transmission oil cooler lines at the radiator. Plug the lines immediately. Catch the spillage from the radiator in a separate pan.

3. On later cars equipped with electric fans, carefully disconnect the wiring to the temperature sensor at the bottom of the radiator. Remove the retaining bolts for the radiator and fan shroud and lift out the radiator.

To install:

4. Place the radiator and fan shroud in position and install the retaining bolts. Note that the placement of the radiator is important to its proper operation. The radiator must lie flush with the front bodywork, otherwise some air will go around the radiator instead of through it.

Either adjust the position of the front panel or use plastic foam to seal the gaps between the radiator and the front panel.

5. On automatic transmission cars, connect the oil cooler lines.

6. Install the lower and upper radiator hoses.

7. Install the expansion tank with its hose. Make sure that the overflow hose is clear of the fan and is free of any sharp bends.

8. Fill the cooling system with a 50 percent antifreeze, 50 percent water solution. Replace the caps.

9. Start the engine and check for leaks. After the engine has reached operating temperature, make sure the coolant level in the expansion tank is between the maximum and minimum marks. Check and top up the automatic transmission fluid level.

Air Conditioning Condenser

REMOVAL AND INSTALLATION

The air conditioning condenser operates under the pressures generated within the air conditioning system. Its removal requires discharging the system and recharging after reinstallation.

The condenser is a frequent source of leaks within AC systems. Because of its position at the very front of the car, it is prone to impact damage from stones and road hazards as well as cracks and loosened hoses from vibration.

PLEASE RE-READ THE AIR CONDITIONING SECTION IN CHAPTER 1 SO THAT THE SYSTEM MAY BE DISCHARGED PROPERLY. ALWAYS WEAR EYE PROTECTION AND GLOVES WHEN

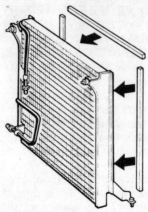

Don't forget to transfer the air seals when installing new condenser

DISCHARGING THE SYSTEM. OBSERVE NO SMOKING/NO OPEN FLAME RULES.

1. Remove the negative battery cable. Carefully remove the grille from the front of the car.

2. Remove the support brace in front of the condenser. Disconnect the hood release cable.

3. Loosen and remove the bolts holding the upper radiator support. Remove the air guide panel from the upper radiator support, remove the screws which hold the condenser to the upper support, and remove the upper radiator support itself.

4. Under the front bumper, remove the three screws holding the plastic air guide and remove the guide. If the car is equipped with a electric fan, unbolt it as a unit and set it aside.

5. Discharge the refrigerant from the system in accordance with the instructions in Chapter 1.

6. Using TWO wrenches of the proper size, disconnect the pipes at the joints nearest to the condenser. Use one wrench to hold one line and the other wrench to turn the opposite fitting. Failure to do this may result in kinked or bro-

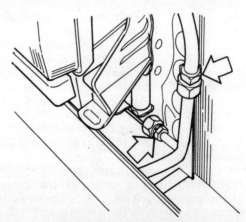

Use two wrenches on air conditioner line joints. When reasembling, do not overtighten

ken lines. Plug the lines immediately to prevent dirt from entering the system.

7. Remove the nuts at the bottom of the condenser and remove the condenser from the car. Use a small jar to collect the oil which will run out of the condenser. The same amount of oil should be added back into the system when the unit is reinstalled.

8. When reinstalling, transfer the foam and rubber seals to the new condenser if one is being used. Add compressor oil into condenser to equal amount which drained out.

9. Position condenser in car and insure that there is a tight fit between the foam seals and the surrounding body work. This directs the airflow through the unit instead of around it.

10. Using the two wrench method, reconnect the pipes at the joints. Use new O-rings lightly coated with compressor oil. Tighten the joints to a maximum of 13 ft. lbs. Replace the bolts at the bottom of the condenser.

11. Reinstall the upper radiator support, the condenser support brace and the upper and lower air guide panels. If the car is equipped with an electric fan, reinstall it.

12. Connect the hood release cable and replace the grille. Hook up the negative battery cable.

13. Double check all installation items, paying particular attention to loose hoses or hanging wires, untightened nuts, poor routing of hoses and wires (too tight or rubbing) and tools left in the engine area.

14. Recharge the air conditioning system as described in Chapter 1.

Water Pump

REMOVAL AND INSTALLATION

B20, B30

1. Disconnect the negative battery cable. Drain the cooling system and remove the radiator as previously described.

CAUTION: *When draining the coolant, keep in mind that cats and dogs are attracted by the ethylene glycol antifreeze, and are quite likely to drink any that is left in an uncovered container or in puddles on the ground. This will prove fatal in sufficient quantity. Always drain the coolant into a sealable container. Coolant should be reused unless it is contaminated or several years old.*

2. Loosen the fan belt by slackening the alternator adjusting bolt. Remove the fan belt; remove the fan.

3. Remove the housing bolts from the water pump. Carefully remove the aluminum housing from the engine along with all the old gasket material. Remove the sealing rings.

To install:

4. Position the water pump assembly to the block, using a new housing gasket and water resistant sealer. Make sure that the sealing rings on the upper side of the pump are seated fully. Press the pump upward against the cylinder head extension to seat the seals. Hand-tighten the housing bolts until snug. Do not tighten the bolts more than ½ turn further to avoid cracking the housing or breaking the bolts.

6. Install the fan and adjust the (drive) belt tension.

7. Install the radiator as previously described. Fill the cooling system.

8. Attach the negative battery cable. Start the engine and check for leaks.

B21, B23 and B230

1. Disconnect the negative battery cable. Remove the overflow tank cap. Drain the cooling system by opening the cylinder block drain cock (beneath the exhaust manifold) and disconnecting the lower radiator hose.

CAUTION: *When draining the coolant, keep in mind that cats and dogs are attracted by the ethylene glycol antifreeze, and are quite likely to drink any that is left in an uncovered container or in puddles on the ground. This will prove fatal in sufficient quantity. Always drain the coolant into a sealable container. Coolant should be reused unless it is contaminated or several years old.*

2. Remove the fan and fan shroud.

3. Remove the alternator and air pump drive belts. Remove the water pump pulley.

4. Remove the timing belt cover.

5. Remove the lower radiator hose.

6. Remove the retaining bolts for the coolant pipe (beneath exhaust manifold) and pull the pipe towards the rear of the car.

7. Remove the retaining bolts and lift off the water pump.

8. Clean the gasket contact surfaces thoroughly. When reassembling, the use of new gaskets and O-rings is required.

9. When reinstalling pump, make certain that it seats firmly in position and that all gaskets and seals are properly located.

10. After the pump is securely mounted, replace and secure the lower pipe and bracket, the radiator hoses and the timing belt cover.

11. Attach the water pump pulley and all the drive belts. Adjust the belts to the proper tension.

12. Install the fan and fan shroud. Close the drain cock on the side of the engine and replace the expansion tank cap. Fill the cooling system with a 50-50 mixture of antifreeze and water.

13. Reconnect the negative battery cable.

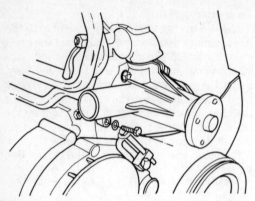

New water pump in position on B21, B23 and B230 engines

Start the engine and check for leaks. After the engine has reached normal operating temperature, check the expansion tank for the proper coolant level; add fluid if necessary.

B234

1. Set the heater control for maximum heat, remove the cap on the expansion tank and open the draincock on the right side of the engine block.

CAUTION: *When draining the coolant, keep in mind that cats and dogs are attracted by the ethylene glycol antifreeze, and are quite likely to drink any that is left in an uncovered container or in puddles on the ground. This will prove fatal in sufficient quantity. Always drain the coolant into a sealable container. Coolant should be reused unless it is contaminated or several years old.*

2. Disconnect the bottom radiator hose from the pump. Close the draincock when the system is empty.

3. Remove the alternator drive belt, the radiator fan and pulley.

4. Remove the retaining bolts and nuts and remove the water pump from the engine.

5. Clean the joint faces and mating surfaces.

6. During reassembly, use new gaskets and seals. Place the O-ring on the return tube and the gasket on the block. Make sure the ring is seated in the groove. Fit the pump into position and install the two nuts just tight enough to hold the pump against the block.

7. Press the pump vertically against the cylinder head and install the remaining bolts and washers. Reconnect the return pipe.

8. Install the bottom radiator hose, the radiator fan and pulley and the alternator drive belt.

9. Fill the system with coolant, cap the expansion tank and run the engine to normal operating temperature to check for leaks.

B27F, B28F

1. Disconnect the negative battery cable. Remove the front and main sections of the intake manifold. See the section on intake manifold removal and installation elsewhere in this chapter.

2. Remove the overflow tank cap and drain the cooling system by opening the drain cock on the side of the block and disconnecting the lower radiator hose.

CAUTION: *When draining the coolant, keep in mind that cats and dogs are attracted by the ethylene glycol antifreeze, and are quite likely to drink any that is left in an uncovered container or in puddles on the ground. This will prove fatal in sufficient quantity. Always drain the coolant into a sealable container. Coolant should be reused unless it is contaminated or several years old.*

3. Disconnect both radiator hoses. On automatic transmission cars, disconnect the transmission cooler lines at the radiator. Remove the radiator and fan shroud.

4. Remove the fan.

5. Remove the hoses from the water pump to each cylinder head.

6. Remove the fan belts. Remove the water pump pulley.

7. Loosen the hose clamps at the rear of the water pump.

8. Carefully remove and transfer the thermal time sender and temperature sensor to the new pump.

9. Remove the water pump from the block (three bolts).

10. Transfer the thermostat cover, thermostat, and rear pump cover to the new pump. Clean all mating surfaces and remove any trace of old gasket material. Check all coolant hoses and replace them if stiff or cracked.

11. Using new gaskets, install the water pump onto the block. Do not overtighten the bolts. Correct torque is 11–15 ft. lbs.

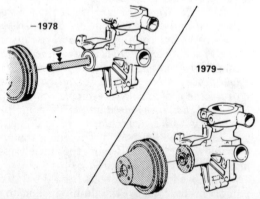

B27 and B28: Different styles of water pump pulleys

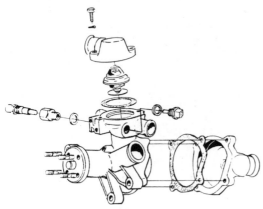

Water pump assembly, B28F

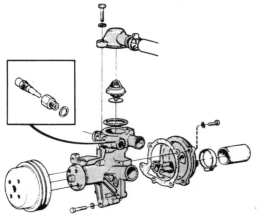

Water pump assembly, B280. Removal of intake manifold is not required

12. Connect and secure all hoses to the water pump.

13. Position the drive belts and install the pulley and cooling fan. Adjust all belts to the correct tension. Reconnect wiring to the electrical components on the water pump.

14. Reinstall the intake manifold. See Intake Manifold, Removal and Installation elsewhere in this chapter.

15. Install the radiator and fan shroud. Connect the radiator hoses to the radiator. On cars with automatic transmissions, reconnect the oil cooler lines to the radiator. If the car has electric fans, remember to connect the wiring to the temperature sensor in the radiator.

16. Put the cap on the expansion tank and close the drain cock in the side of the engine. Reconnect the negative battery cable.

17. Double check all installation items, paying particular attention to loose hoses or hanging wires, untightened nuts, poor routing of hoses and wires (too tight or rubbing) and tools left in the engine area.

18. Refill the cooling system with a 50-50 mixture of antifreeze and water.

19. Start the engine and check for leaks. Allow the engine to reach normal operating temperature and check the coolant level; add fluid if needed. Inspect and top-up the fluid level in the automatic transmission if so equipped.

B280

The B280 engine, introduced in 1987, is a variant of the B28. The steps to replace the water pump are essentially the same as the B28, but the intake manifold DOES NOT need to be removed. The spark plug wires and various small hoses and brackets need removal for access, but the steps above (B28) will guide you through. Simply omit the steps for removal and installation of the intake manifold.

Diesel D24, D24T

WARNING: *The use of the correct special tools or their equivalent is REQUIRED for this procedure. This procedure requires the removal of the timing belt. If the special tools needed are not available, do not attempt to remove the water pump.*

1. Disconnect the negative battery cable. Drain the coolant system by disconnecting the lower radiator hose at the radiator and disconnect the lower hose of the cold start device.

CAUTION: *When draining the coolant, keep in mind that cats and dogs are attracted by the ethylene glycol antifreeze, and are quite likely to drink any that is left in an uncovered container or in puddles on the ground. This will prove fatal in sufficient quantity. Always drain the coolant into a sealable container. Coolant should be reused unless it is contaminated or several years old.*

2. Remove the radiator. Remove the cooling fan with its spacer and pulley.

3. Remove the fan belt(s) and the power steering drive belt.

4. Remove the timing gear cover. When this cover is removed, the timing belt will be exposed. Do not allow fluids, dirt or oil to contact the belt. It must be kept clean and dry or premature wear and breakage may result.

5. Remove the large center bolt in the center of the vibration damper (pulley) and the crankshaft. Do not allow the pulley to turn while removing the nut. Volvo has two special tools available to accomplish this.

6. When the nut is removed, turn the pulley (and therefore, the engine) about ¼ turn counter clockwise. This transfers the slack in the timing belt to the opposite side, making it easier to remove.

7. Using a 6mm Allen wrench, remove the four small bolts holding the crank damper and

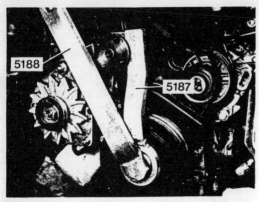

Using Volvo special tools to remove crankshaft nut on D24 and D24T engines

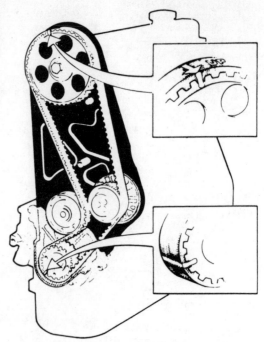

Carefully mark the timing belt and gears before removing the belt. Exact reinstallation is critical to avoid motor damage

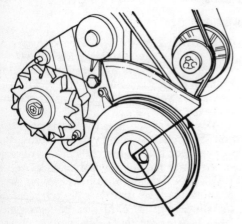

Turn the engine ¼ turn counterclockwise to transfer the slack in the timing belt

remove the damper. Note that the crankshaft gear may stick to the damper. When the damper is off, remove the lower timing gear cover.

8. Loosen and remove the three bolts holding the bracket for the alternator and cooling fan. Place the assembly to one side and secure it out of the way.

9. Mark the position of the timing belt relative to the timing gears. Mark the belt, camshaft gear and crankshaft gear. Identify the outside and topside of the belt. It is critical that the belt be reinstalled in exactly the same position as it was found.

10. Loosen the water pump mounting bolts and and the timing belt. Some coolant may leak out when the bolts are loosened. Remove the timing belt.

11. Remove the cover panel and bolts holding the water pump. Move the panel to one side and remove the pump. Be careful not to crack the panel.

12. Dry off spilt coolant from the block, gears, etc. Clean the contact surfaces on the block.

Make sure no sealing material remains on the surface.

To install:

13. Lightly grease the new O-ring and place it on the pump. Do not use any other sealer. Carefully move the cover plate aside and install the new pump on the engine. Attach the pump retaining bolts; leave them loose at this stage.

14. Replace the cover plate retaining bolts and remount the bracket for the cooling fan and alternator.

15. Install the timing belt. Align the marks on the upper and lower gears with the marks on the belt. It is critical that the belt be refitted exactly as it was removed.

16. Draw tension on the belt by moving the water pump by hand. Tighten the water pump mounting bolts.

17. Install the lower timing gear cover and the vibration damper. Note that the damper can only be fitted one way--the pin on the crank gear must fit into the damper. Torque the four bolts to 15 ft. lbs. Install the large center nut, using the special tools as before. Torque the center nut to 255 ft. lbs.

18. Turn the engine clockwise ¼ turn. Use a belt tension gauge to check the timing belt tension. Adjust the tension by moving the water pump as necessary. If using Volvo tool 5197, the correct tension is 12.5 units.

19. Reinstall the front timing gear cover. In-

stall the fan with its spacer and pulley. Tighten the fan bolts to 7 ft. lbs.

20. Install the belts for the fan and power steering pump. Adjust the belts to the proper tension.

21. Reinstall the radiator. Connect the hoses to the radiator and the hose to the cold start device. Refill the coolant system with a 50-50 mixture of antifreeze and water.

22. Reconnect the negative battery cable. Start the engine and check for leaks.

23. Disconnect the upper hose to the cold start device. Place a collecting pan or jug beneath the hose and hold the hose level with the top edge of the expansion tank. Allow the engine to come to normal operating temperature

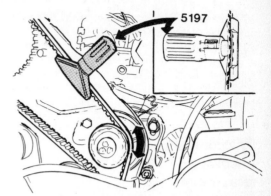

D24 and D24T: Use belt tension gauge and move water pump as necessary to adjust timing belt. Volvo special tool shown

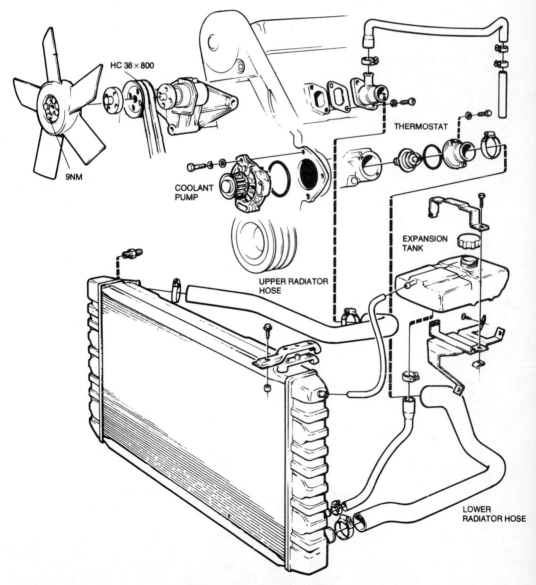

Diesel engine cooling system

with the cap off the expansion tank. Add coolant as necessary as the engine warms up.

24. When the coolant level is stable and no air is coming from the disconnected hose, shut the engine off. Reconnect the upper hose to the cold start device, top up the coolant in the expansion tank and put the cap back on the tank.

Cylinder Head
REMOVAL AND INSTALLATION
B20B and B30A

WARNING: *To prevent warpage of the head, removal should be attempted only on a cold engine.*

All wires and hoses should be labled at the time of removal. The amount of time saved during re-assembly makes the extra effort well worthwhile.

1. Drain the cooling system by opening the drain plug on the right hand side of the engine and disconnecting the lower radiator hose at the radiator.

CAUTION: *When draining the coolant, keep in mind that cats and dogs are attracted by the ethylene glycol antifreeze, and are quite likely to drink any that is left in an uncovered container or in puddles on the ground. This will prove fatal in sufficient quantity. Always drain the coolant into a sealable container. Coolant should be reused unless it is contaminated or several years old.*

2. Disconnect the choke control cables at the carburetors. Remove the positive crankcase ventilation hoses from the air cleaner and intake manifold. Remove the vacuum hoses for the distributor advance and the power brake booster, if so equipped.

3. Remove the throttle control shaft from the pedal shaft, link rods, and bracket. (Disconnect the downshift linkage on cars with automatic transmissions).

4. Remove the air cleaner, inlet hose, and heat control valve hose from the engine.

5. Remove the upper radiator hose. Remove the heater hose clamp from the head.

6. Remove and plug the fuel line at the carburetors.

7. Label the spark plug wires and disconnect them from the plugs. Disconnect the coolant temperature sensor.

8. Remove the exhaust manifold preheating plate. Remove the nuts and disconnect the exhaust pipe from the exhaust manifold.

9. Unbolt the alternator adjusting arm from the head.

10. Remove the valve cover. Remove the rocker shaft and arm assembly as a unit and draw out the pushrods, keeping them in order.

11. Loosen the head bolts gradually, in the same order as their tightening sequence. Remove the head bolts, noting their locations, and lift off the head.

Do not attempt to pry off the head. The head may be tapped lightly with a rubber mallet to break the gasket seal. If any residual water in the cooling passages of the head falls into the combustion chambers during removal, remove it immediately and coat the cylinder walls with oil.

12. Remove the integrally cast intake and exhaust (combination) manifold from the cylinder head.

13. Remove the old head gasket, flange gasket, and rubber sealing rings for the water pump.

14. Inspect the condition of the valves in the combustion chambers, and the intake and exhaust ports in the head. Small deposits may be removed with rotating brushes. If large deposits are present, however, proceed to Cylinder Head Reconditioning in the Engine Rebuilding section of this chapter. Make sure that no foreign matter has fallen into the cylinders or onto the tops of the pistons. Thoroughly clean the mating surfaces of the cylinder head and block, removing any traces of the old head gasket. Check the mating surfaces for warpage.

There is an oil feed hole for the rocker arm assembly on the tappet side, in the middle of the head. Make sure it is clean. A clogged oil feed hole may be opened with a length of thin gauge metal wire and some kerosene to dissolve the deposits. Clean the top of the cylinder head and the oil return holes to remove any gum or foreign matter. Clean and oil the head bolts.

15. Install the combination intake and exhaust manifold on the head with new gaskets.

16. Install new sealing rings for the water pump.

17. Use a pair of guide studs for proper alignment of the cylinder head, head gasket, and block. Guide studs can be easily made by cutting the heads off a pair of spare head bolts. The tops of the bolts are then filed to a tapered edge and slotted so that they may be installed and removed with a screwdriver. The guide studs should be installed in the cylinder block; one in the front right hand head bolt hole, and the other in the rear left hand head bolt hole.

18. Fit a new head gasket on the cylinder block with the lettering **TOP** (wide edge) facing up. Slide the gasket down over the two guide studs.

19. Carefully lower the cylinder head over the guide studs onto the block. Install, but do not tighten, two heads bolts at opposite ends to secure the gasket, and remove the guide studs. Install the remaining head bolts finger-tight.

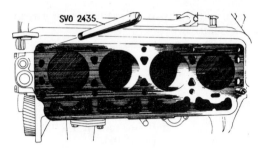

Guide stud installation—B20, B30 engines

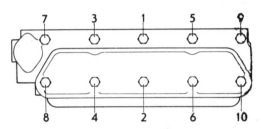

Cylinder head tightening sequence—B20 engine

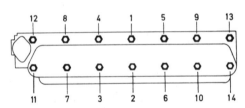

Cylinder head tightening sequence—B30 engine

Torque the head bolts in proper sequence first to 29 ft. lbs., and then to 58 ft. lbs.

20. Roll the pushrods on a level surface to inspect them for straightness. Replace any bent pushrods. Install the pushrods in their original positions and install the rocker shaft and arm assembly. Torque the bolts to approxiamtely 20 ft. lbs.

21. Adjust the valve clearance to a *preliminary* setting of 0.018–0.020 in. (0.45–0.50mm) for the B30A, and 0.022–0.024 in. (0.55–0.60mm) for the B20B. Use the procedure outlined under Valve Lash Adjustment in Chapter 2. Install the valve cover with a new gasket.

22. Install the alternator adjusting arm and adjust the drive (fan) belt tension.

23. Install the following: exhaust manifold preheating plate, exhaust pipe and flange nuts (with new gaskets), spark plugs wires, coolant temperature sensor, heater hose clamp, upper and lower radiator hoses, fuel line, air cleaner, inlet hose, heat control valve hose, choke and throttle linkage (down shift linkage on cars with automatic transmissions), vacuum hoses for the distributor and power brake (if so equipped), and the positive crankcase ventilation hoses.

24. Close the drain plug and fill the cooling system with a 50 percent antifreeze, 50 percent water solution.

25. Run the engine until it reaches operating temperature. Stop the engine.

26. Remove the valve cover and torque the head bolts in proper sequence to the final figure of 65 ft. lbs. Adjust the valve clearance to the final setting of 0.020–0.022 in. (0.50–0.55mm). Install the valve cover.

B20E, 1972–73 B20F, and B30F

The procedure for removal and installation of the cylinder head for the fuel injected engines differs from the carbureted engines only in the type of fuel system equipment that must be moved to gain access to the head.

WARNING: *To prevent warpage of the head, removal should only be attempted on a cold engine.*

All wires and hoses should be labled at the time of removal. The amount of time saved during re-assembly makes the extra effort well worthwhile.

1. Drain the cooling system by opening the drain plug on the right hand side of the engine and disconnecting the lower radiator hose at the radiator.

CAUTION: *When draining the coolant, keep in mind that cats and dogs are attracted by the ethylene glycol antifreeze, and are quite likely to drink any that is left in an uncovered container or in puddles on the ground. This will prove fatal in sufficient quantity. Always drain the coolant into a sealable container. Coolant should be reused unless it is contaminated or several years old.*

2. Disconnect the negative battery cable from the engine.

3. On the B30F engine, remove the air cleaner.

4. Remove the following hoses from the inlet duct: pressure sensor, power brake (if so equipped), distributor advance, and crankcase ventilation (PCV).

5. Remove the electrical contacts for the throttle valve switch, cold start valve, thermal timer, temperature sensor, and injectors.

6. Remove the ground cable from the inlet duct and remove the cable harness.

7. Disconnect the sensor for the coolant temperature gauge. Remove the spark plug wires from the plugs.

8. On the B20E and B20F engines, remove the inlet hose.

9. Disconnect the throttle control cable from the throttle valve and inlet duct.

10. Remove the upper radiator hose.

11. Remove the heater control valve hose and the clamp for the heater pipe.

12. Unbolt the alternator adjusting arm from the head.

13. Remove the bolts for the inlet duct (intake manifold) stay. Remove the inlet duct-to-cylinder head retaining nuts and disconnect the inlet duct.

14. If any cleaning or machine work is to be performed on the cylinder head, remove the fuel injectors beforehand. Turn the lockrings on the injectors counterclockwise and lift out the injectors and distributing pipe as a unit. Remove the injector holders from the head.

> CAUTION: *The fuel system is under pressure. Release pressure slowly and contain spillage. Observe no smoking/no open flame precautions*

15. Remove the exhaust manifold-to-exhaust pipe flange nuts and disconnect the pipe.

16. Refer to steps 10 and 11 under Cylinder Head Removal and Installation for the B20B and B30A.

17. Remove the exhaust manifold from the head.

18. Refer to steps 13 and 14 under Cylinder Head Removal and Installation for the B20B and B30A.

19. Install the exhaust manifold on the head with a new gasket.

20. Refer to steps 16–20 under Cylinder Head Removal and Installation for the B20B and B30A engines.

21. Adjust the valve clearance to a *preliminary* setting of 0.018–0.020 in. (0.45–0.50mm) for the B20E and B20F, and 0.022–0.024 in. (0.55–0.60mm) for the B30F. Use the procedure outlined under Valve Lash Adjustment in Chapter 2. Install the valve cover with a new gasket.

22. If the injectors were removed, install the holders with new sealing rings. Install the injectors and distributing pipe as a unit.

23. Install the alternator adjusting arm and adjust the drive (fan) belt tension.

24. Install the inlet duct with a new gasket. Install the inlet duct retaining nuts and the bolts for the inlet duct stay. On B20 engines, install the inlet hose.

25. Install the following: upper and lower radiator hoses, heater hose, heater hose clamp, exhaust pipe flange nuts, fuel line, throttle linkage, temperature gauge sensor, ground cable to inlet duct, cable harness, electrical contacts for the throttle valve switch, cold start valve, thermal timer, temperature sensor and injectors, pressure sensor hose, power brake hose, distributor advance line, crankcase ventilation hoses, and the battery cable.

26. On the B30F engine, install the air cleaner.

27. Close the drain plug and fill the cooling system with a 50 percent antifreeze, 50 percent water solution.

28. Start the engine and run it until it reaches normal operating temperature, then shut it off.

29. Remove the valve cover and torque the head bolts in proper sequence to the final figure of 65 ft. lbs. Adjust the valve clearance to the final setting of 0.016–0.018 in. (0.40–0.45mm) for the B20E and B20F, and 0.020–0.022 in. (0.50–0.55mm) for the B30F.

1974–75 B20F

> WARNING: *To prevent head warpage, removal should be performed only on a cold engine.*
>
> *All wires and hoses should be labled at the time of removal. The amount of time saved during re-assembly makes the extra effort well worthwhile.*

1. Drain the cooling system by removing the plug on the right side of the engine and disconnecting the lower radiator hose.

> CAUTION: *When draining the coolant, keep in mind that cats and dogs are attracted by the ethylene glycol antifreeze, and are quite likely to drink any that is left in an uncovered container or in puddles on the ground. This will prove fatal in sufficient quantity. Always drain the coolant into a sealable container. Coolant should be reused unless it is contaminated or several years old.*

2. Remove the negative lead from the battery.

3. Disconnect hoses to brake vacuum booster and crankcase ventilation.

4. Remove the cold start injector hose and the fuel return hoses on both sides of the T-connection (at the control pressure regulator).

5. Remove the outlet fuel hose at the fuel filter and remove fuel filter with its clamp from the firewall.

6. Disconnect the fuel hose from the fuel distributor at the control pressure regulator.

7. Disconnect electrical wires at cold start injector, auxiliary air valve, control pressure regulator and temperature sensor.

8. Remove the air cleaner connecting pipe.

9. Disconnect the throttle cable at the intake manifold.

10. Disconnect the hose for heater and the upper radiator hose.

11. Remove the alternator adjustment bracket.

12. Remove the straps from the injector hoses. Remove the injectors and hoses from the cylinder head, by turning the lockrings counterclockwise.

13. Remove the bracket for the intake manifold, and remove the manifold.

14. Remove the exhaust manifold from exhaust pipe and cylinder head.

15. Remove the spark plugs and spark plug wires.

16. Remove the valve cover, rocker arm shaft and the pushrods.

17. Remove the cylinder head bolts and lift off the head. Take off the cylinder head gasket, the flange gasket and the rubber rings for the water pump.

18. Follow steps 14, 16, 17, 18, 19 and 20 under Cylinder Head Removal and Installation for the B20B.

19. Install pushrods and rocker arm shaft. Adjust the valves to a *preliminary* clearance of 0.018–0.020 in. (0.45–0.50mm).

20. Continue reassembly in the opposite order of disassembly. Torque the manifold nuts to 18 ft. lbs. Use care in refitting the fuel injection lines and maintain their cleanliness.

When all hoses are attached and secure, refill the cooling system with a 50-50 mixture of antifreeze and water.

21. Double check all installation items, paying particular attention to loose hoses or hanging wires, untightened nuts, poor routing of hoses and wires (too tight or rubbing) and tools left in the engine area.

22. Start the engine and allow it to reach normal operating temperature. Remove the valve cover and tighten the head bolts--in the correct order--to 65 ft. lbs. Adjust the valves to their final setting of 0.016–0.018 in. (0.40–0.45mm). Replace the valve cover.

B21 and B23 Series Engines

1. Disconnect the battery.

2. Remove the overflow tank cap and drain the coolant. Disconnect the upper radiator hose.

CAUTION: *When draining the coolant, keep in mind that cats and dogs are attracted by the ethylene glycol antifreeze, and are quite likely to drink any that is left in an uncovered container or in puddles on the ground. This will prove fatal in sufficient quantity. Always drain the coolant into a sealable container. Coolant should be reused unless it is contaminated or several years old.*

3. Remove the distributor cap and wires.

4. Remove the PCV hoses.

5. Remove the EGR valve and vacuum pump.

6. Remove the air pump, and air injection manifold. Plug all open hoses, lines and ports.

7. Remove the exhaust manifold and header pipe bracket.

8. Remove the intake manifold. Disconnect the manifold brace and the hose clamp to the bellows for the fuel injection air/flow unit. Dis-

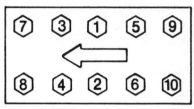

Cylinder head bolt tightening sequence—B21 and B23 engines

connect the throttle cable, and all vacuum hoses and electrical connectors to the fuel injection unit.

NOTE: *All wires and hoses should be labled at the time of removal. The amount of time saved during re-assembly makes the extra effort well worthwhile.*

9. Remove the fuel injectors.

10. Remove the valve cover.

11. Loosen the fan shroud and remove the fan. Remove the shroud. Remove the upper belts and pulleys.

12. Remove the timing belt cover. Remove the timing belt as described later in this section.

13. Remove the camshaft (if so desired) as outlined later in this chapter.

14. Remove the cylinder head (10mm Allen head bolts). Loosen the bolts in order opposite to the tightening sequence. (10–9–8...etc).

To install:

15. Use a new gasket and lightly oil the head bolts. Carefully place the head on the block and tighten the bolts in the prescribed order to 44 ft. lbs. When all bolts are at 44 ft. lbs., repeat the pattern and tighten to 81 ft. lbs.

16. If the camshaft was removed, reinstall it.

17. Replace the timing belt. Follow the procedures listed under Timing Beltinstallation and Removal later in this chapter.

18. Attach the upper belts and pulleys. Reinstall the fan and shroud.

19. Reinstall the valve cover.

20. Reinstall the fuel injectors.

21. Using new gaskets, attach the intake manifold. Secure its brace and attach the bellows for the air/flow unit. Reconnect the throttle cable.

22. Connect all vacuum lines and the electrical connectors to the fuel injectors.

23. Install the exhaust manifold and header pipe bracket.

24. Remembering to remove all of the plugs, reconnect the lines to the turbocharger if so equipped. If equipped with an air pump, reinstall it along with the air injecton manifold.

25. Install the EGR valve and lines and connect the PCV hoses. Replace the distributor cap and wires.

26. Connect the hoses to the radiator. Fill the

system with a 50-50 mix of antifreeze and water.

27. Reconnect the battery. Double check all installation items, paying particular attention to loose hoses or hanging wires, untightened nuts, poor routing of hoses and wires (too tight or rubbing) and tools left in the engine area.

28. Start the motor and check for leaks. As the engine warms up, observe the coolant level and top off as needed.

29. When the engine has reached normal operating temperature, shut it off and allow it to cool for at least 30 minutes. Carefully remove the valve cover. Be careful; the engine parts will be hot.

30. Observe the correct tightening sequence and loosen each bolt enough to relieve any pretension. Tighten each bolt to 81 ft. lbs. before loosening the next.

31. Perform any needed valve lash adjustments and replace the valve cover.

B230F

1. Disconnect battery negative cable.

2. Drain the coolant from the motor. Open the drain cock on the right side of the engine and connect a short piece of hose to prevent spillage.

CAUTION: *When draining the coolant, keep in mind that cats and dogs are attracted by the ethylene glycol antifreeze, and are quite likely to drink any that is left in an uncovered container or in puddles on the ground. This will prove fatal in sufficient quantity. Always drain the coolant into a sealable container. Coolant should be reused unless it is contaminated or several years old.*

3. Remove the valve cover. Remove the retaining nuts for the exhaust manifold. Gently pull the manifold off the studs just enough to allow clearance.

4. Remove the intake manifold. Follow the detailed instructions under Intake Manifold Removal and Installation earlier in this chapter.

5. Remove the fan, the fan shroud, and the clamp for the pre-heat hose, located under the fan shroud.

6. Remove the drive belts (loosen the adjustors as necessary) and remove the pulley for the water pump.

7. Remove the upper timing gear cover.

8. Remove the spark plugs. Remove the spark plug wires and distributor cap.

9. Use the center bolt of the crankshaft to turn the engine. Slowly rotate the engine until the mark on the camshaft pulley is opposite the mark on the inner timing gear cover. The crankshaft mark should align with the **0** on the lower timing gear cover.

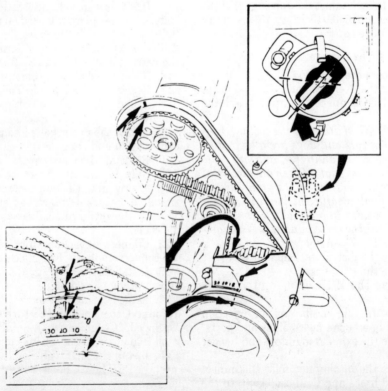

On B230F, align crankshaft and camshaft marks before removing timing belt

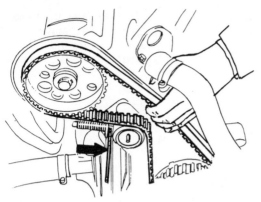

B230F, placement of 3mm drill bit to hold belt tensioner spring

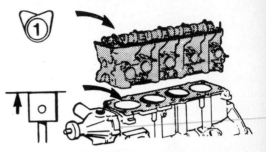

Insure correct placement of camshaft and no. 1 piston before reinstalling head on B230 engines

If the distributor is located on the side of the engine (not in the cylinder head), check that the rotor is aligned with the mark (notch) in the case of the distributor.

10. Remove the nut and washer for the timing belt tensioner. Pull on the timing belt to compress the tensioner spring. Use a 3mm drill bit to lock the tensioner spring. Remove the belt and the tensioner.

WARNING: *Once the timing belt has been removed, do not allow either the crankshaft or the camshaft to turn while the head is on the car. The pistons may hit the valves causing severe damage.*

11. Remove the camshaft gear and spacer. Do not allow the cam to turn during removal.

12. Remove the stud bolt for the timing belt tensioner.

13. Consult the head bolt diagram. Loosen the head bolts in REVERSE order to that shown in the diagram. (Begin with 10, then 9, 8, etc.) Remove the cylinder head.

The head is made of aluminum alloy; when placing it on the workbench, support it on wooden blocks so that the gasket face is not scratched or gouged.

To reinstall the head:

14. Check the position of the crankshaft. Number one piston should be at TDC. Check the position of the camshaft. The lobes for cylinder number one should point at equally large angles. (Both valves are closed.)

15. Position the new head gasket and and the cylinder head. Make sure that the O-ring for the water pump is correctly placed in its groove. Remember that from this point, the camshaft and crankshaft must not be rotated or valve and piston damage may result.

16. Inspect the cylinder head bolts. Replace them if the center section shows any sign of stretching or other wear. If there is any doubt, replace them.

17. Apply a light coat of oil to the bolts and in-

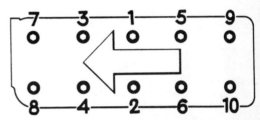

Head bolt tightening sequence for B230F. When removing, loosen bolts in reverse order.

stall them in the head. Using the sequence shown in the diagram, use a three stage tightening procedure:

First stage: Tighten all bolts to 14 ft. lbs.
Second stage: Tighten all bolts to 43 ft. lbs.
Third stage: Tighten all bolts exactly 90°.

18. Install the camshaft gear and spacer. Do not allow the cam to turn during installation.

19. Install the stud bolt for the belt tensioner, then install the tensioner wirh its washer and nut.

20. Double check that all marks on cam and crank pulleys align as described in step 9, above.

21. Place the timing belt around the crankshaft gear and intermediate shaft gear. Gently stretch the belt and place it over the camshaft

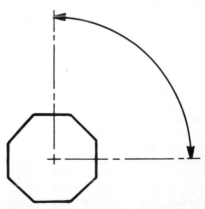

Protractor (angle) torquing, 90° shown. DO NOT exceed specified degrees

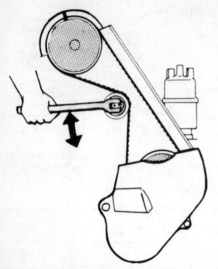

B230F; adjust timing belt by loosening tensioner bolt about one full turn and retightening. Internal spring will tension the belt

gear and belt tensioner. Don't use sharp or pointed tools to pry on the belt.

22. Remove the drill bit from the tensioner. Double check that the camshaft and crankshaft pulleys are still in their exact, proper postions.

23. Rotate the engine one full rotation until it returns to top dead center and the marks align as before. Loosen the timing belt tensioner nut about one turn; the spring will set the correct tension on the timing belt. Retighten the nut.

24. Adjust the valve lash if not done during head repairs or overhaul.

25. Install the valve cover with a new gasket.

26. Reinstall the intake and exhaust manifolds. Refer to the detailed instructions in the appropriate sections earlier in this chapter.

27. Replace the spark plugs, the distributor cap and the spark plug wires.

28. Reinstall the upper timing gear cover. Attach the water pump pulley and the drive belts.

29. Attach the fan and fan shroud. Reconnect the clamp and pre-heater hose. Adjust the drive belts.

30. If not already done, close the drain cock on the side of the engine. Refill the cooling system with a 50-50 mixture of antifreeze and water.

31. Double check all installation items, paying particular attention to loose hoses or hanging wires, untightened nuts, poor routing of hoses and wires (too tight or rubbing) and tools left in the engine area.

32. Reconnect the battery cable. Start the engine and check for leaks. After the engine has come to normal operating temperature, check the coolant level and top off as needed.

33. While the head bolts DO NOT need to be retorqued, the timing belt should be readjusted

after 500–600 miles of driving. Remove the rubber plug in the timing gear cover, rotate the engine (turn the crankshaft pulley nut) to the TDC position on cylinder number one, and loosen the belt tensioner nut. The spring will correctly tension the belt; tighten the nut and replace the rubber plug.

B234F

WARNING: *The use of the correct special tools or their equivalent is REQUIRED for this procedure.*

1. Disconnect the negative battery cable.

2. Remove the heat shield over the exhaust manifold.

3. Remove the cap from the expansion tank and open the draincock on the right side of the motor. Collect the drained coolant in a suitable container.

CAUTION: *When draining the coolant, keep in mind that cats and dogs are attracted by the ethylene glycol antifreeze, and are quite likely to drink any that is left in an uncovered container or in puddles on the ground. This will prove fatal in sufficient quantity. Always drain the coolant into a sealable container. Coolant should be reused unless it is contaminated or several years old.*

4. Unbolt the exhaust pipe from the bracket, remove the manifold nuts and remove the manifold from the head.

5. On the left side of the motor, remove the support under the intake manifold. and remove the bottom bolt in the cylinder block.

6. Remove the manifold intact and tie it or support it safely.

7. Disconnect the temperature sensor connectors, the heating hose under cylinders 3 and 4 and the upper radiator hose at the thermostat.

8. Remove the upper and lower timing belt covers.

9. Align the camshaft and crankshaft marks. Turn the engine to TDC on cylinder 1 and make sure the pulley marks and the crank marks align.

10. Remove the protective cap over the timing belt tensioner locknut. Loosen the lock nut, compress the tensioner (so as to release tension on the belts) and retighten the locknut, holding the tensioner in place.

11. Remove the timing belt from the camshafts. Do not crease or fold the belt.

WARNING: *The camshafts and the crankshaft MUST NOT be moved when the belt is removed.*

12. Remove the timing belt idler pulleys.

13. Remove the camshaft drive pulleys. Use a counterhold wrench to prevent the cam from turning.

14. Remove the plate or panel behind the pulleys. Remove the cover plate for the ignition wires. Label and disconnect the ignition wiring from the spark plugs and the distributor cap; remove the coil wire from the distributor cap.

15. Remove the valve cover and gasket. Clean the surfaces of any gasket remains.

16. Remove the distributor housing from the camshaft carrier. Remove the ignition wire clip next to the left bolt.

17. Plug the spark plug holes with crumpled paper. Remove the center bearing cap for each camshaft. Remove the third nut in the center. Mark the cam bearing caps for proper reinstallation.

18. Install a camshaft press tool, such as Volvo 5021 or similar on the exhaust side cam in place of the removed bearing cap. When it is securely in place, remove the remaining bearing caps and nuts. Remove the tool and remove the exhaust camshaft.

19. Remove the intake camshaft in identical fashion.

WARNING: *Label or identify each cam and its bearing caps. All removed components should be kept in neat order.*

20. Using a magnet or a small suction cup, remove the tappets. Store them upside down (to prevent oil drainage) and keep them in order. They are not interchangable!

21. Remove the remaining four nuts in the center of the cam carrier and detach the carrier from the head. If it is stuck, tap it very gently with a plastic mallet. Remove the O-rings around the spark plug holes.

22. Wipe the remaining oil off the cylinder head and remove the bolts in the order shown. When all the bolts are removed, the cylinder head may be lifted free of the car.

WARNING: *The head is aluminum. Support it on clean wood blocks or similar to avoid scoring the face.*

23. Clean the camshaft carrier and the head assembly of all gasket material and sealer.

Carefully scrape the joint surfaces with a plastic scraper. Do NOT use metal tools to scrape or clean. Wash the surfaces with a degreasing compound and blow the surfaces completely dry.

Inspect the head bolts for any sign of stretching or elongation in the midsection. If this is observed or suspected, discard the bolt. Bolts may not be used more than five times.

24. Install the new headgasket and a new O-ring for the water pump. Carefully place the cylinder head into position; do not damage the gasket.

25. Clean the head bolts and apply a light coat of oil. Install them and tighten (in the order shown) in three steps: All to 15 ft. lbs., then all to 30 ft. lbs. Third step is to tighten each bolt through 115° of arc in one continuous motion. The use of Volvo tool 5098 (protractor fitting) is strongly recommended for this task.

26. Install the exhaust manifold with a new gasket. Attach the front exhaust pipe to its bracket and install the heat shields.

27. On the left side of the motor, connect the temperature sensors, the heating hose under cylinders 3 and 4 and the upper coolant hose to the thermostat.

28. Fill the cooling system and check carefully for leaks, particularly around the head to block joint.

29. Install the intake manifold with a new gasket. Tighten the bottom bolts a few turns and place the manifold in position. Tighten all the bolts from the center outwards.

30. Reattach the support under the intake manifold and the cable clip. Double check all connections on and around the intake manifold.

31. Apply Volvo liquid sealing compound to the camshaft carrier. Use a small paint roller and coat the surfaces which match to the head and the bearing cap joint faces.

31. Install the cam carrier on the head and secure it with four of the five center nuts tightened to 15 ft. lbs. Do not install the middle nut.

Head bolt removal sequence, B234F

Head bolt tightening sequence, B234F. Tool 5098 is a protractor used for the last stage in tightening

32. Oil all matching surfaces on the cam carrier, bearing caps and tappets.

33. Insert the tappets; they MUST be inserted in their original order and place.

34. Install the exhaust side camshaft by placing it in the carrier with the pulley guide pin facing up. Using the rear bearing cap as a guide, press the cam into place with the press tool. Install the bearing caps in the original order.

35. Install the bearing cap nuts and tighten them in stages to 15 ft. lbs. Remove the press tool and install the center bearing cap; tighten it in stages to 15 ft. lbs.

36. Install the intake camshaft in the carrier with the pulley guide pin facing upwards.

37. Turn the distributor shaft to align the driver with the markings on the distributor housing. Install new O-rings on the housing and rotor shaft.

38. Using the rear bearing cap as a guide, press the cam into place with the press tool. Install the bearing caps in the original order.

39. Install the bearing cap nuts and tighten them in stages to 15 ft. lbs. Remove the press tool and install the center bearing cap; tighten it in stages to 15 ft. lbs.

40. Install the center nut in the cam carrier and tighten it to 15 ft. lbs.

41. Double check the tightness of all the camshaft carrier nuts and the bearing cap nuts. All should be 15 ft. lbs.; do not overtighten.

42. Reinstall the distributor, connect the coil wire and install the ignition wire clip at the left bolt. Remove the paper plugs from the spark plug holes.

43. Use a silicone sealer and apply to the front and rear camshaft bearing caps. Install new gaskets for the valve cover and the spark plug wells. Install the spark plug gasket with the arrow pointing towards the front of the car and the word **UP** facing up.

Make sure the valve cover gasket is correctly positioned and install the valve cover.

44. Reconnect the ground wire at the distributor.

45. Install the ignition wires and the cover plate.

46. Using a compression seal driver (Volvo tool 5025 or similar), install the oil seals for the front of each camshaft. Camshafts MUST NOT be allowed to turn during this operation.

47. Install the upper backing plate over the ends of the camshafts and adjust the plate so that the cams are centered in the holes.

48. Replace the idler pulleys and tighten their mounts to 18.5 ft. lbs.

49. Install the camshaft drive pulleys, using a counterhold to prevent the cams from turning.

50. Making sure that the camshaft pulleys are properly aligned with the marks on the backing

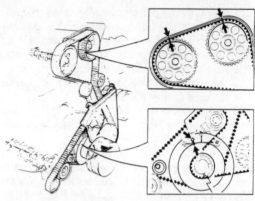

Make certain that all the marks align and the engine is on TDC, cylinder no. 1

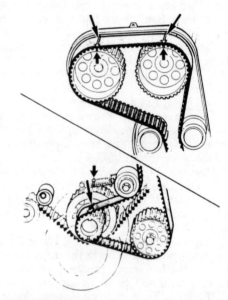

B234F: The marks on the timing belt must align with the pulley marks. Install the belt on the right side pulley first

plate, position the timing belt so that the double mark on the belt coincides exactly with the top mark on the belt guide plate (at the top of the crankshaft).

Place the belt onto the cam pulleys and make sure the single marks on the belt line up exactly with the marks on the pulleys. Fit the belt over the idler pulleys; right side idler first, then the left.

51. Double check that the engine is on TDC for cylinder 1 and that all the belt markings line up as they should.

52. Loosen the tensioner locknut. Rotate the crankshaft clockwise one full turn until the belt markings again coincide with the pulley markings.

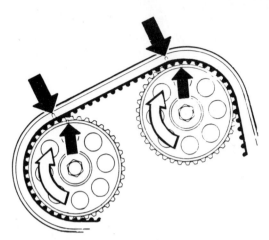

Correct position of B234 cam pulleys before tightening the idler pulley

WARNING: *The engine must not be rotated counterclockwise while the tensioner is loose.*

53. Turn the crankshaft smoothly clockwise until the pulley marks are 1½ teeth beyond the marks on the backing plate.

54. Tighten the tensioner locknut. Install the lower timing belt cover.

55. Install the radiator fan and pulley, the alternator drive belt and the negative battery cable.

56. Double check all installation items, paying particular attention to loose hoses or hanging wires, untightened nuts, poor routing of hoses and wires (too tight or rubbing) and tools left in the engine area.

57. Start the engine and allow it to run until the thermostat opens. Use extreme caution--the moving timing belt is exposed!

NOTE: *This engine may be somewhat noisy when started. The noise will subside as oil reaches the tappets. Do not exceed 2500 rpm while the tappets are noisy.*

58. Shut the engine off, rotate the crankshaft to bring the engine to TDC on cylinder 1 and use Volvo tool 998 8500 to check the belt tension. Correct deflection is 5.5 ± 0.2 units when measured between the exhaust camshaft pulley and the idler. If the tension is not correct repeat steps 51–54, above.

59. Install the upper timing belt cover. Start the engine and final check all functions.

B28F and B280F

WARNING: *The use of the correct special tools or their equivalent is REQUIRED for this procedure.*

All wires and hoses should be labeled at the time of removal. The amount of time saved during re-assembly makes the extra effort well worthwhile.

1. Disconnect the battery. Drain the coolant. CAUTION: *When draining the coolant, keep in mind that cats and dogs are attracted by the ethylene glycol antifreeze, and are quite likely to drink any that is left in an uncovered container or in puddles on the ground. This will prove fatal in sufficient quantity. Always drain the coolant into a sealable container. Coolant should be reused unless it is contaminated or several years old.*

2. Remove the air cleaner assembly and all attaching hoses. On B28F and B280F, remove the intake air pre-heating hose and heat stove from the left side exhaust manifold, if that cylinder head is being removed.

3. Disconnect the throttle cable. On automatic transmission equipped cars, disconnect the kick-down cable.

4. Disconnect the EGR vacuum hose and remove the pipe between the EGR valve and manifold.

5. Remove the oil filler cap, and cover the hole with a rag. Disconnect the PCV pipe from the intake manifold.

6. Remove the front section of the intake manifold. CAUTION: *The fuel system is under pressure. Release pressure slowly and contain spillage. Observe no smoking/no open flame precautions*

7. Disconnect the electrical connector and fuel line at the cold start injector. Disconnect the vacuum hose, both fuel lines, and the electrical connector from the control pressure regulator.

8. Disconnect the hose, pipe, and electrical connector from the auxiliary air valve and remove the auxiliary air valve.

9. Disconnect the electrical connector from the fuel distributor. Remove the wire looms from the intake manifolds and disconnect the spark plug wires.

10. Disconnect the fuel injectors from their holders.

11. Disconnect the distributor vacuum hose, charcoal cannister hose, and diverter valve hose from the intake manifold. Also disconnect the power brake hose and heater hose at the intake manifold.

12. Disconnect the throttle control link from its pulley.

13. On cars equipped with an EGR vacuum amplifier, disconnect the wires from the throttle micro switch and solenoid valve.

14. At the firewall, disconnect the fuel lines from the fuel filter and return line.

15. Remove the two attaching screws and lift out the fuel distributor and throttle housing assembly.

16. On cars not equipped with an EGR vacu-

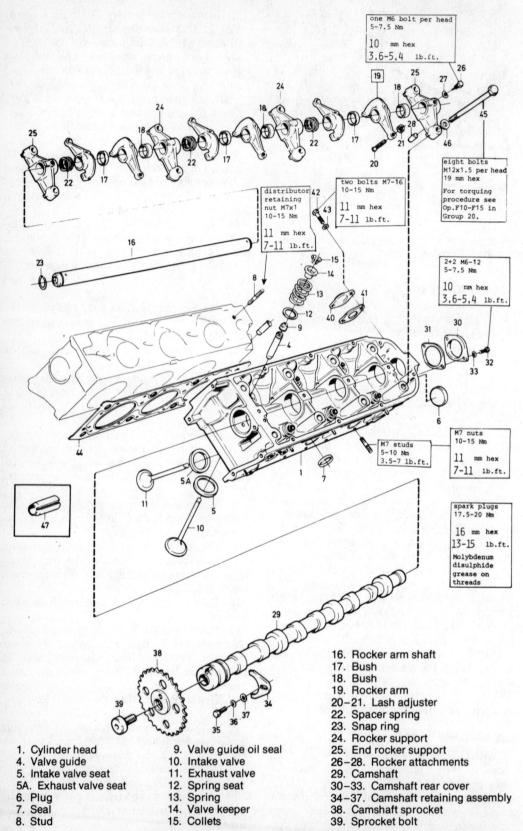

one M6 bolt per head
5-7.5 Nm

| 10 | mm hex |
| 3.6-5.4 | lb.ft. |

eight bolts
M12x1.5 per head
19 mm hex

For torquing
procedure see
Op.F10-F15 in
Group 20.

two bolts M7-16
10-15 Nm

| 11 | mm hex |
| 7-11 | lb.ft. |

distributor
retaining
nut M7x1
10-15 Nm

| 11 | mm hex |
| 7-11 | lb.ft. |

2+2 M6-12
5-7.5 Nm

| 10 | mm hex |
| 3.6-5.4 | lb.ft. |

M7 studs
5-10 Nm
3.5-7 lb.ft.

M7 nuts
10-15 Nm

| 11 | mm hex |
| 7-11 | lb.ft. |

spark plugs
17.5-20 Nm

| 16 | mm hex |
| 13-15 | lb.ft. |

Molybdenum
disulphide
grease on
threads

16. Rocker arm shaft
17. Bush
18. Bush
19. Rocker arm
20-21. Lash adjuster
22. Spacer spring
23. Snap ring
24. Rocker support
25. End rocker support
26-28. Rocker attachments
29. Camshaft
30-33. Camshaft rear cover
34-37. Camshaft retaining assembly
38. Camshaft sprocket
39. Sprocket bolt

1. Cylinder head
4. Valve guide
5. Intake valve seat
5A. Exhaust valve seat
6. Plug
7. Seal
8. Stud

9. Valve guide oil seal
10. Intake valve
11. Exhaust valve
12. Spring seat
13. Spring
14. Valve keeper
15. Collets

B27F head assemblies—B28F engine similar

um amplifier, disconnect the EGR valve hose from underneath the throttle housing.

17. Remove the cold start injector, rubber ring and pipe.

18. Remove the four retaining bolts and lift off the intake manifold. Remove the rubber rings.

19. Remove the splash guard beneath the engine.

20. If removing the left cylinder head, remove the air pump from its bracket.

21. Remove the vacuum pump and O-ring in the valve cover. Remove the vacuum hoses from the wax thermostat.

22. If removing the right cylinder head, disconnect the upper radiator hose.

23. On air conditioned models, remove the AC compressor. Use wire to tie it out of the way. Do not disconnect the refrigerant lines.

24. Disconnect the distributor leads and remove the distributor. Remove the EGR valve, bracket and pipe. At the firewall, disconnect the electrical connnectors at the relays.

25. On air conditioned models, remove the rear compressor bracket.

26. Disconnect the coolant hose(s) from the water pump to the cylinder head(s). If removing the left cylinder head, disconnect the lower radiator hose at the water pump. Disconnect the coolant temperature sensor.

27. Disconnect the air injection system supply hose from the applicable cylinder head. Separate the air manifold at the rear of the engine. If removing the left cylinder head, remove the backfire valve and air hose.

28. Remove the valve cover(s).

29. On the left cylinder head, remove the Allen head screw and four upper bolts to the timing gear cover. On the right cylinder head, remove the four upper bolts to the timing gear cover and the front cover plate.

30. From beneath the car, remove the exhaust pipe clamps for both header pipes on the B27F. On B28 and B280, carefully remove the oxygen sensor. Then remove the downpipe/crossover pipe above catalystic converter and at the manifolds.

31. If removing the right cylinder head, remove the retainer bracket bolt and pull the dipstick tube out of the crankcase.

32. Remove the cover plate at the rear of the cylinder head.

33. Rotate the camshaft sprocket (for the applicable cylinder head) into position so that the large sprocket hole aligns with the rocker arm shaft. With the camshaft in this position, loosen the cylinder head bolts in sequence (same sequence as tightening), and remove the rocker arm and shaft assembly. If both heads are to be removed, label the left and right rocker assem-

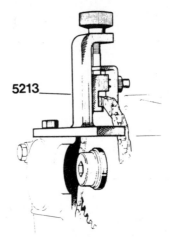

5213

Volvo special tool for retaining timing sprocket and chain on B280 engines. B27 and B28 similar

blies so they are returned to the matching head; they are not interchangable.

34. Loosen the camshaft locking bolt (directly in back of sprocket) and slide the locking plate to one side.

35. It is necessary to hold the cam chain stretched during camshaft removal. Otherwise, the chain tensioner will automatically take up the slack, making it impossible to reinstall the sprocket on the cam.

To accomplish this, a special sprocket retainer tool (Volvo #5104) is installed over the sprocket with two bolts in the top of the timing chain cover. A bolt is then screwed into the sprocket to hold it in place. For the B28F and B280F, use special tool 5213. Fasten the tool to the timing gear cover and draw tension on the chain by turning the upper knob.

36. Remove the camshaft sprocket center bolts and push the camshaft to the rear, so it clears the sprocket.

37. Remove the cylinder head.

NOTE: *Do not remove the cylinder head by pulling straight up. Instead, lever the head off by inserting two spare head bolts into the front and rear inboard cylinder head bolt holes, and pulling toward the applicable wheel housing.*

Otherwise, the cylinder liners may be pulled up, breaking the lower seals and leaking coolant into the crankcase. If any do pull up, new liner seals must be used, and the crankcase completely drained.

38. Remove the head gasket. Clean the contact surfaces with a plastic scraper and lacquer thinner.

39. If the head is going to be off for any length of time, install liner holder (Volvo special tool #5093) or two strips of thick stock sheet steel with holes for the head bolts, so that the liners

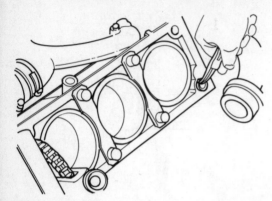

B28 and B280 engines must have cylinder liners held in place when heads are removed. (Volvo special tool shown.) Note guide sleeve being raised from block

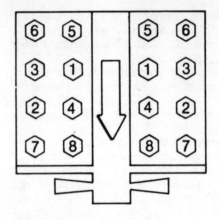

Cylinder head bolt tightening sequence, B27, B28

stay pressed down against their seals. Install the holders widthwise between the middle four head bolt holes.

40. When reinstalling, remember that the timing chain must be kept taut at all times. Install the guide sleeves (dowels) at the outboard corners of the block (if they were not removed, pull them up with a pair of narrow tipped pliers) and prop them up with a ⅛ in. (3mm) drill shank inserted in the block hole. This will prevent the dowels from collapsing into the block when the head is installed.

41. Remove the liner holders which are clamped across the cylinders.

42. The right and left head gaskets are different. Remove any plugs and/or paper from the passages before placing the head gasket on the block.

43. Position the cylinder head on the block, making sure the guide dowels engage the holes in the head.

43. Slide the camshaft forward to engage the sprocket and install the center bolt. Make sure the head does not move. Double check that the cam is not caught in the locking fork and that the stud on the sprocket fits correctly into the groove in the camshaft. Remove the timing chain retainer tool.

44. Remove the drill bits below the guide dowels. Install the rocker arm assembly. Remember to install the rocker assemblies on the correct head if both heads were removed. The circlips (snaprings) on the end of the rocker shaft should face forward on the left side head and rearward on the right head.

45. The bolts threads should be clean and lightly oiled. Install the bolts finger tight.

46. Tighten the bolts in the correct sequence and in three stages:
First stage: all to 7 ft.lbs
Second stage: all to 22 ft.lbs.
Third stage: all to 44 ft.lbs.

Note the time of day this tightening takes place.

47. Position the camshaft locking fork and tighten its bolt.

48. Tighten the camshaft center bolt. Use a 10mm hex key and tighten to 52-66 ft. lbs. Use a small bar or other tool inserted through the sprocket to keep it from turning.

49. Install the four upper bolts in the timing gear case. Depending on which head was installed, either install the screw plug in the left side or the cover and washer on the rightside. Using a new gasket, install the cover(s) at the rear of the cylinder head(s).

50. If both heads were removed, install the other head by repeating steps 40 through 49.

51. No less than 30 minutes after performing step 46 (longer is better), loosen the head bolts in the same order in which they were tightened.

When all are loose, tighten in the correct sequence to 13 ft. lbs.

The final setting is gained by tightening each bolt in the correct sequence through 115° of rotation.

52. With the head(s) properly tightened, check the valve lash and adjust adjust as necessary, following procedures outlined previously.

53. After adjusting the valves, turn the engine to its TDC/compression position. This aligns the crankshaft marks at zero and provides clearance at both valves for cylinder number 1.

54. Install new gaskets and install the valve covers. Install only four bolts and do not tighten them excessively--the covers will be removed later on.

55. If the right cylinder head was removed, reinstall the dipstick tube and the dipstick. Secure the mounting bolt for the tube bracket.

56. Under the car, connect the exhaust system to the manifolds and connect the crossover pipe at the catalytic converter. Carefully reinstall the oxygen sensor.

57. If the left cylinder head was removed, install the backfire valve and connect the air hose. Install the air manifold at the rear of the engine.

58. Connect the coolant temperature sensor wiring. Install the coolant hoses to heads. Use new clamps to insure a good seal.

58. Install the rear compressor bracket if equipped with air conditioning.

59. Install the distributor making sure the rotor points toward the mark on the distributor body when installed. Place the distributor cap in position but DO NOT attach the clips or the spark plug wires. Damage may result when the intake manifold is installed.

60. Attach the EGR valve, bracket and pipe.

61. Connect the wiring to the relays at the firewall.

62. On air conditioned models, reinstall the compressor on its mounts. Install the belt and adjust it to the proper tension.

63. If the vacuum pump was removed, reinstall it, making sure the arm contacts the cam correctly. Use a new gasket and connect the hose properly.

64. Install the air pump if the left head was removed.

65. Use new rubber rings and install the intake manifold. Tighten the retaining bolts to 10 ft. lbs.

66. Install the cold start injector with its line and seal.

67. Attach the fuel distributor and throttle housing assembly. Connect the EGR hose under the throttle housing.

68. Connect the fuel lines to the fuel filter and return lines.

69. Clamp down the distributor cap and install the spark plug wires.

70. If the car is equipped with a vacuum amplifier for the EGR system, connect the wiring to the throttle micro-switch and the solenoid valve.

71. Install the throttle cable to its pulley and , if automatic, the kick-down cable.

72. Connect the various vacuum hoses, observing the labels made during disassembly.

73. Connect the heater hose(s) at the intake manifold.

74. Reinstall the fuel injectors. Connect the wiring to the injectors and route the wiring properly along the intake manifold. Install the spark plug wires.

75. Install the auxilary air valve and connect it to its wire and hose.

76. Connect the hose, both fuel lines and the wiring to the control pressure regulator.

77. Remove any plugs in the system and install the front sections of the intake manifold.

78. Install the oil filler cap, the air cleaner as-sembly, the pre-heat hoses and fittings if removed and the PCV pipe and valve.

79. Confirm that the draincocks in both the cylinder block and the radiator are closed and refill the engine with coolant.

80. Double check all installation items, paying particular attention to loose hoses or hanging wires, untightened nuts, poor routing of hoses and wires (too tight or rubbing) and tools left in the engine area.

81. Connect the negative battery cable.

82. Set the dashboard temperature control to maximum heat. Start the engine and allow it to warm up to normal operating temperature. During this time, closely examine the work area for signs of leakage. Since the valve cover(s) are not tightly retained, there may be some seepage. Don't tighten them yet.

83. Shut the engine off and allow it to cool for 30 to 45 minutes. Remove the valve covers. It may be necessary to remove the vacuum pump from the left hand cover.

84. The final setting of the head bolts is accomplished by:

a. Observe the loosening sequence chart. Loosen the first bolt only, then tighten it to 10 ft. lbs., then angle-tighten it through 115° of motion.

b. Repeat this procedure with the second bolt, the third and so on until all the bolts have been reset individually.

WARNING: *DO NOT loosen all the bolts at once. Deal with each bolt individually and follow the correct sequence. If all the bolts are loosened, the head will lift and the gasket will need to be replaced.*

85. Install the valve cover(s) with all the bolts. Tighten the bolts to 10 ft. lbs. Install the vacuum pump with a new gasket if it was removed. Make sure the pump shaft meshes on top of the cam shaft.

86. Restart the engine. Check the ignition timing and idle speed and adjust if necessary. Install the splash shields.

Diesel D24 and D24T

NOTE: *Special tools are needed to perform this operation. If you do not have the tools, do not attempt to remove the head.*

1. Disconnect the negative battery cable.

2. Remove the splash guard and disconnect the exhaust pipe at the manifold and its transmission bracket. On the D24T model, disconnect all hoses to the turbocharger, and plug any open ports and hoses.

3. Remove the expansion tank after draining the radiator. Disconnect the lower hose at the cold start device on the fuel injection pump and point the end of the hose down to drain the block.

CAUTION: *When draining the coolant, keep in mind that cats and dogs are attracted by the ethylene glycol antifreeze, and are quite likely to drink any that is left in an uncovered container or in puddles on the ground. This will prove fatal in sufficient quantity. Always drain the coolant into a sealable container. Coolant should be reused unless it is contaminated or several years old.*

4. Disconnect all remaining coolant hoses from the engine. Remove the vacuum pump and its plunger from the left side of the cylinder head.

5. Clean and remove the fuel delivery pipes. Plug all openings to prevent dirt contamination.

6. Disconnect the wire for the temperature gauge, the glow plug wires, the wire bundle for the rear glow plugs, the return hose from the rear injector, and the wire for the temperature gauge sender at the rear of the head.

7. Remove the valve cover and remove the front and rear timing belt cover.

8. Set the engine on No. 1 cylinder TDC compression stroke. Both camshaft lobes for cylinder no. 1 should point up at equally large angles and the flywheel timing pointer should be aligned with the 0 mark on the flywheel.

9. Remove the timing gear belt from the front camshaft gear by loosening the retaining bolts for the coolant pump and belt idler pulley.

10. Using a wrench to hold the gear (special tool 5199), remove the front gear center bolt. Do not allow the camshaft to turn at all. Remove the gear by tapping it off the camshaft.

11. Remove the injection pump drive belt by loosening the retaining bolts for the injection pump bracket to release belt tension. Tighten one bolt to hold the pump in the upper position after the belt is removed.

12. Remove the camshaft rear gear center bolt and gear while holding the gear with a wrench (special tool 5199). Access to the center bolt will be easier if special tool 5201 is used. Make sure the camshaft does not rotate.

13. Remove the cylinder head bolts and remove the cylinder head. Position the head on wooden blocks so that the valves do not hold the weight of the head.

14. Use a steel ruler to check for head warpage. Lengthwise warpage cannot exceed 0.008 in. (0.2mm) and crosswise warpage cannot exceed 0.002 in. Warpage in excess of these tolerances requires replacing the head; it cannot be resurfaced.

To install:

15. Remove the rear glow plug so that it does not strike the injection pump bracket when installing.

16. Install special dowel pins (to center the

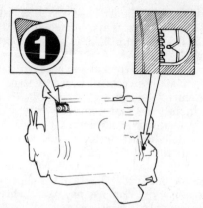

Diesel engine—set the engine on no. 1 cylinder TDC compression stroke: both camshaft lobes for no. 1 cylinder should point up at equally large angles (insert) and the O mark on the flywheel should align with the pointer

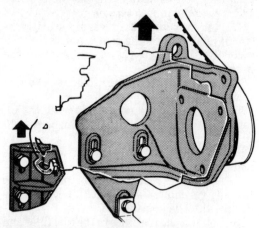

Diesel engine—remove the injection pump drive belt by loosening retaining bolts for the injection pump bracket

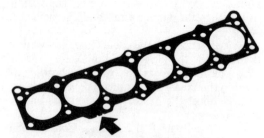

Head gasket thickness is indicated by 1, 2 or 3 notches in the gasket

head on the block) in the front and rear head bolt holes on the injection pump side of the engine (special tool 5189).

17. Install the new head gasket. There are three different thicknesses for gaskets, indicated by 1, 2 or 3 notches in the gasket. Use a gas-

ket with the same number of notches as were on the gasket just removed. Any time pistons, connecting rods or crankshaft are repaired or disassembled, piston projection above the block deck must be measured and an appropriate gasket selected.

- Piston Projection: 0.026–0.031 in. (0.66–0.78mm); 1 Notch; Gasket thickness; 0.055 in. (1.4mm)
- Piston Projection: 0.032–0.035 in. (0.81–0.89mm); 2 Notches; Gasket thickness; 0.059 in. (1.5mm)
- Piston Projection: 0.036–0.040 in. (0.91–1.00mm); 3 Notches; Gasket thickness; 0.063 in. (1.6mm)

18. Set the engine to No. 1 cylinder TDC, if not already set.

19. Set the camshaft in position on the head so that both camshaft lobes on No. 1 cylinder point up at equally large angles (both valves closed). Lock the camshaft in this position by installing special tool 5190 in the slot in the rear of the camshaft.

20. Install the cylinder head. Install several of the head bolts, remove the dowel pins and install all of the head bolts. The threads and washers on the bolts should be oiled before installation. Tighten the bolts in two stages in the sequence shown: first all to 30 ft. lbs., then all to 65 ft. lbs.

NOTE: *From late 1980, new cylinder head bolts are used on the D24 Diesel. They are longer and 1mm wider. Torquing these bolts is a 6 step procedure:*

a. Torque to 30 ft. lbs.

b. Torque to 44 ft. lbs.

c. Torque to 55 ft. lbs.

d. Tighten 180°, in one movement, without stopping.

e. Run engine until oil temperature is minimum 120°F.

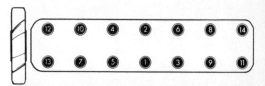

Diesel head bolt tightening sequence. When removing, start at 14 and work back to 1

f. Tighten 90°, in one movement, without stopping.

21. Install the bolts for the front belt shield.

22. Complete steps 11, 13, 17 through 21 under Timing Belt Removal and Installation; below.

23. Remaining installation procedes in the reverse order of removal. After driving 600–1200 miles retorque the head with the engine warm to 62 ft. lbs. Do not loosen the head bolts before retorqing.

CLEANING AND INSPECTION

1. Clean all components parts with a suitable parts cleaner.

2. Remove the carbon deposits in the combustion chambers using a liquid carbon dissolving solvent. Clean the cylinder head face with a soft plastic scraper and paint remover or a liquid gasket striper.

3. Check the cylinder head(s), valve seats and valve guides for damage or cracks. You may wish to take the head to professional machine shop for chemical or dye crack checking. Cracks can occur internally where they cannot be seen with the naked eye.

CHECKING FOR HEAD WARPAGE

Lay the cylinder head down with the combustion chamber facing up. Place a straightedge across the gasket surface of the head, both diagonally and straight across the center. Using a flat feeler gauge, determine the clearance at the center of the straightedge. If the warpage ex-

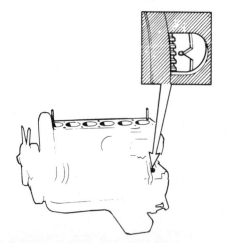

Set the engine on no. 1 cylinder TDC

Cleaning the cylinder head gasket surface

Checking the cylinder head for warpage

ceeds 0.002 in. (0.05mm) in a span of 4 in. (100mm), the cylinder head must be replaced.

NOTE: *If the cylinder head exceeds specification it must be replaced. It cannot be machined.*

Valves and Springs

NOTE: *Please refer to Chapter 2 Tune-Up for valve adjustment procedures.*

REMOVAL AND INSTALLATION

NOTE: *On all engines, the cylinder head(s) must be removed to service the valves.*

B20 and B30

Remove the valve springs by first compressing them with a standard valve spring compressor and removing the valve collets. (A small magnet can be very helpful for this.) Release the compressor slowly and remove the spring washer and valve.

Check that the parts are in good condition

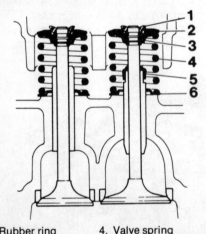

1. Rubber ring
2. Upper spring seat
3. Retainer
4. Valve spring
5. Valve seal (intake valve)
6. Lower spring seat

Typical valve spring components—B21F shown

and clean them. Test the spring pressures and compare them with the specifications given in the valve specification chart in this chapter. Place the valve in position, fit the valve guide seal, valve spring, upper washer and the valve collets.

NOTE: *Valves must be installed in the same combustion chamber they were removed from.*

B21, B23, B230 and B234

The camshaft must be removed to gain access to the valve spring. Please refer to Camshaft Removal and Installation for detailed instructions.

Remove the valve depressors and the rubber rings. Depress the valve springs with a C-clamp type depressor and remove the valve collets, the upper valve seat, the spring, the lower valve seat and the valve. Remove the valve stem seals from the intake valve guides. On B234 engines, remove the lower spring collars.

On B230 and B234 engines, remove the tappets (valve depressors) and keep them in order. During reassembly, they should be returned to the same location; they are not interchangable.

To assemble, install new valve seals (intake valves only) and install the valve and spring assemblies in the reverse order of removal.

B27, B28 and B280

To gain access to the valves, the camshaft(s) must be removed from the head(s). Please refer to Camshaft Removal and Installation for detailed instructions.

To remove the valves, depress the valve spring with a valve spring compressor and remove the collets with a small magnet or similar tool. Release the tension on the spring compressor and remove the valve spring, its parts and the valve. Remove the valve guide seals.

To assemble, install new valve guide seals, being careful not to rip them when installing. After lapping the valves, assemble the valve spring parts in the reverse order of removal.

Diesel

The camshaft must be removed. Please refer to Camshaft Removal and Installation for detailed instructions.

Remove the valve depressors and using a suitable spring compressor, compress the springs and remove the spring retainer collets. Release the compressor and remove the spring and valve assembly. Assemble in the reverse order. Be sure to fit new valve seals.

VALVE INSPECTION

Minor pits or grooves may be removed from the valve face. However, discard any valves that are severely damaged. If the face runout cannot

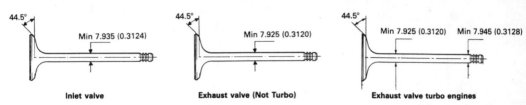

Inlet valve   Exhaust valve (Not Turbo)   Exhaust valve turbo engines

Check valve stem diameter when head is disassembled. B230 valves shown, measurement in millimeters and (inches). Note slight taper on turbo exhaust valve

be corrected by refinishing or if the stem clearance exceeds specifications, the valve must be replaced. Discard any worn or damaged valve train parts.

REFACING THE VALVES

CAUTION: *The valves in the B21F, B21FT, B230F, B230FT, B234F and ALL Diesel engines are stellite coated. This process provides extra heat insulation to the valve. These valves cannot be reground; grinding the face will destroy the coating. They may however be lapped-in (with paste) against valve seat.*

Using a valve grinder, resurface the valves according to specifications given earlier in this chapter.

NOTE: *Valve face angle is not always identical to valve seat angle.*

A minimum margin of $\frac{1}{32}$ in (0.8mm). should remain after grinding the valve. The valve stem top should also be squared and resurfaced by placing the stem in the V-block of the grinder, and turning it while pressing lightly against the grinding wheel.

LAPPING THE VALVES

Invert the cylinder head, lightly lubricate the valve stems, and install the valves in the head as numbered. Coat valve seats with fine valve grinding compound, moisten the suction cup on the lapping tool and attach the cup to a valve head.

Rotate the tool, changing position and lifting the tool often to prevent grooving. Lap the valve until a smooth, polished seat is evident. Remove the valve and tool, and rinse away all traces of grinding compound.

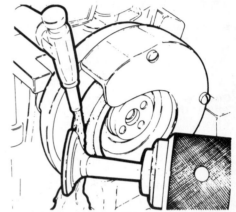

Valve grinding by machine

Lapping the valves

CHECKING THE VALVE SPRINGS

Check the valve spring for proper pressure at the specified spring lengths using a valve spring pressure tool. Weak valve springs cause poor

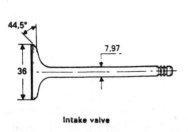

Intake valve

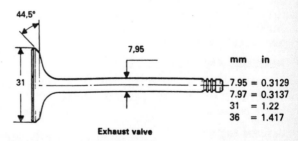

Exhaust valve

	mm	in
	7.95	= 0.3129
	7.97	= 0.3137
	31	= 1.22
	36	= 1.417

Valve dimensions for diesel engines (D24 and D24T). Measurements are in millimeters with inch conversion at right

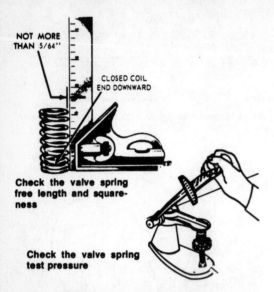

Check the valve spring free length and square-ness

Check the valve spring test pressure

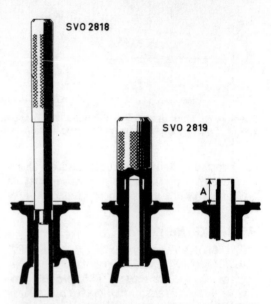

Valve guides: removing (left) with tool SVO 2818, installing (center) with tool SVE 2819 and final height of guide above cylinder head—B20, B30 engines

performance; therefore, if the pressure of any spring is lower than the service limit replace the spring.

Springs should be ± 5 lbs of all other springs. Check each valve spring for squareness. Stand the spring on a flat surface next to a carpenter's square. Measure the height of the spring; rotate the spring slowly and observe the space between the top coil of the spring and the square. If the spring is out of square more than $\frac{5}{64}$ in. (2mm) or the height varies (by comparsion) by more than $\frac{1}{16}$ in. (1.5mm), replace the spring.

Valve Guides and Seats

The valve guides are so named because they guide the stem of the valve during its motion. By properly locating the stem of the valve, the head and face of the valve are kept in proper relationship to the head. Occasionally, the valve guides will wear, causing poor valve sealing and poor engine performance. If this problem is suspected, check the sideways play of the valve within the guide.

If the play is minimal, it may not be necessary to replace the guides. A competant machine shop can knurl the guides. This process raises a spiral ridge on the inside of the guide, thereby eliminating the wobble and properly locating the valve. This is not a cure-all; it can only be done to correct minimal wear. Severe wear requires replacement of the valve guides.

REMOVAL AND INSTALLATION

WARNING: *The use of the correct special tools or their equivalent is REQUIRED for this procedure.*

Gasoline Engines

The valve guides on the B20 and B30 engines can be pressed out with Volvo special tool num-

ber 2818 and a press. New guides are installed with special tool number 2819 and a press. Substitution tools can be used for either of these operations, however, when installing the new guides, distance **A** in the illustration must equal 0.689 in. (17.5mm) for all B20 and B30 engines except the B20E and the B20F. For the B20E and B20F, distance **A** should equal 0.705 in. (18mm).

The valve guides on the B21 and the B27/B28/B280 are also pressed out with tool number 2818. When removing the valve guides on the B27/B28/B280 engines, place the cylinder head on the press so that the guide (not the head) is vertical. This allows the guide to be pressed straight out and not at an angle to the press.

To fit new valve guides on the B21 and B23 engine, heat the head to approximately 140° F. in water and, using special tool number 5027 for the intake valves and tool number 5028 for the exhaust valves, press the valve guides in until the tool abuts the cylinder head.

The B230 head requires heating to 212°; the installation tools are the same. If these tools are not available, press in the guides until the guide's height above the cylinder head surface, at the base of the guide, is 0.6061–0.6139 in. (15.4–15.6mm) for intake valve guides and 0.7051–0.7129 in. (17.9–18.1mm) for exhaust valve guides. When replacing the guides on the B230 engine, make sure the new guides have the same number of grooves at the end as the old guide. The number of grooves is an indication of the size of the guide.

Observe number of notches in end of valve guides

B234 heads do not require heating but do require the guides to be installed under a minimum pressure of 2025 lbs. The pressing operation is conducted in three steps with three different drifts of exact size. The final installation step leaves the top of the guide projecting above the head by 0.60 in. (15mm). The height is set by the installation tool.

After installing new guides, they must be reamed with a hand tool and the valves and seats must be ground (lapped).

On the B27/28 engines, the valve guides come in two oversizes. For oversize number 1, the valve guide hole must be reamed out to 0.5195–0.5207 in. (13.20–13.23mm). For oversize number 2, the hole must be reamed out to 0.5315–0.5326 in. (13.50–13.52mm). The grip in the cylinder head must be 0.0020–0.0037 in. (0.05–0.09mm).

After the holes have been reamed, press in the valve guides with special tool number 5108 (for intake valves) and number 5109 for exhaust. The correct pressing-in measurement for intake guides is 1.5551–1.5945 in. (39.5–40.5mm) and for exhaust guides 1.4370–1.4921 in. (36.5–37.9mm). After the guides are installed, ream them out to 0.3150–0.3158 in. (8.00–8.02mm) diameter.

The B28F and B280 heads require heating to about 300°F (149°C); it is generally outside the ability of the average home mechanic to safely deal with this level of heat. It is recommended that the head be taken to a machine shop for professional installation of new vlave guides.

The valve seats on all engines are removeable. Since the usual method of removing and installing valve seats includes either freezing or heating the valve seat or the cylinder head, this job should be performed by a competent machine shop or garage. The intake valve seats on the B28 engine are of a new design and should not be replaced with the old style seats.

Diesel

The valve guides are pressed out of the cold cylinder head toward the camshaft with an appropriate drift and press. To install a new guide, oil it lightly and press it into the cold cylinder head from the camshaft side. Press the guide in as far as it will go.

WARNING: *Once the guide shoulder is seat-*ed, do not use more than one ton of pressure or you may break the guide shoulder.

Once installed, the guide must be reamed out to the appropriate diameter.

The valve seats can be refaced but cannot be replaced. Reface the exhaust seats by hand only: do not use a machine.

Oil Pan

REMOVAL AND INSTALLATION

B20 (except 240 series)
B30

The oil pan may be removed from the engine while the engine is still in chassis.

1. Place supports on the frame side members. Insert a lifting hook into the plate bolted to the front of the engine. Using lifting apparatus, raise the engine until there is no weight on the front engine mounts. Remove the oil dipstick.

2. Jack up the vehicle and place jackstands under the front jacking points. Drain the crankcase oil.

CAUTION: *The EPA warns that prolonged contact with used engine oil may cause a number of skin disorders, including cancer! You should make every effort to minimize your exposure to used engine oil. Protective gloves should be worn when changing the oil. Wash your hands and any other exposed skin areas as soon as possible after exposure to used engine oil. Soap and water, or waterless hand cleaner should be used.*

3. Remove the lower nuts for the engine mounts. On 140 series models, remove the steering rods from the pitman arm and relay arm with a puller.

4. Place a hydraulic floor jack beneath the front axle member. Remove the rear bolts of the front axle member and replace them with two longer auxiliary bolts (UNC ½–13 × 114mm). Remove the front bolts for the front axle member and lower the hydraulic jack, allowing the axle member to hang on the auxiliary bolts.

5. Remove the plug for the oil temperature gauge, if so equipped, and the reinforcing bracket at the flywheel.

6. Unscrew the oil pan bolts and lower the pan. Remove the old gasket and clean the surfaces of the cylinder block and oil pan. Remove any sludge or foreign matter that has accumulated at the bottom of the pan.

7. Using a new gasket, position the pan to the cylinder block and install the oil pan bolts. Torque the bolts to 6–8 ft. lbs.

8. Install the plug for the oil temperature gauge, if so equipped. Position the reinforcing bracket to the cylinder block and flywheel casing and install the bolts fingertight. Snugly

tighten the bolts for the flywheel casing and then those for the cylinder block.

9. Raise the hydraulic jack, lifting the front axle member, and tighten the front bolts. Remove the auxilary bolts and install the original rear bolts of the front axle member.

10. Install the lower nuts for the front engine mounts. On 140 series models, connect the steering rods at the pitman arm and relay arm, and fit the nuts.

11. Remove the jackstands and hydraulic jack. Lower the vehicle. Remove the lifting apparatus.

12. Insert the dipstick. Fill the crankcase with the proper amount and grade of oil.

13. Start the engine and check for leaks.

1975 240 Series (B20)

On these models, the motor mounts are located high in the chassis, permitting more than 2 inches of clearance between the bottom of the oil pan and the steering linkage and suspension. Therefore, oil pan removal is a simple matter of unbolting the attaching bolts.

Always use a new gasket when installing the pan. A few dabs of oil-resistant sealer on the gasket at the front and rear mainseals will help prevent oil leaks. Tighten the attaching bolts to no more than 6–8 ft. lbs. of torque in a diagonal criss-cross pattern.

B21 (To May, 1979)

1. Attach lifting equipment or chain hoist to the lifting eye on the thermostat housing.

2. On air conditioned models, remove the compressor from its bracket to gain access to the motor mount.

3. Remove the retaining bolts for the left motor mount at the cylinder block.

4. Drain the crankcase.

CAUTION: *The EPA warns that prolonged contact with used engine oil may cause a number of skin disorders, including cancer! You should make every effort to minimize your exposure to used engine oil. Protective gloves should be worn when changing the oil. Wash your hands and any other exposed skin areas as soon as possible after exposure to used engine oil. Soap and water, or waterless hand cleaner should be used.*

5. Remove the splash guard.

6. Raise the engine slightly.

7. Remove the left motor mount from the chassis.

8. Remove the engine-to-clutch housing brace.

9. Remove the oil pan retaining bolts. Tap the pan loose, swivel and remove.

10. Remove the old gasket and clean the surfaces of the cylinder block and oil pan. Remove

any sludge or foreign matter that has accumulated at the bottom of the pan.

11. Using a new gasket, position the pan to the cylinder block and install the oil pan bolts. Torque the bolts to 6-8 ft. lbs.

12. Install the engine-to-clutch housing brace.

13. Reattach the left motor mount to the chassis and lower the motor to its normal position.

14. Attach the left motor mount to the cylinder block. When the engine is securely mounted, the lifting apparatus may be removed.

15. Fill the engine oil to the proper level.

16. Reinstall the air conditioning compressor if it was removed for access.

17. Start the engine and allow it to warm up to normal operating temperature. Check the pan area carefully for signs of leaks or seepage.

18. Install the lower splash shield.

B21 (May, 1979 and Later)
B23 and B230

NOTE: *Due to the deeper oil pan on these models, the front axle member must be disconnected and lowered to remove the pan.*

1. Raise the vehicle and support it on jack stands. Disconnect the negative battery cable.

2. Drain the engine oil, then replace and tighten the drain plug.

CAUTION: *The EPA warns that prolonged contact with used engine oil may cause a number of skin disorders, including cancer! You should make every effort to minimize your exposure to used engine oil. Protective gloves should be worn when changing the oil. Wash your hands and any other exposed skin areas as soon as possible after exposure to used engine oil. Soap and water, or waterless hand cleaner should be used.*

3. Remove the splash guard from underneath the engine. Disconnect the exhaust system at the flange in front of the muffler.

4. From underneath, remove the engine mount retaining nuts. On B23E and B230E

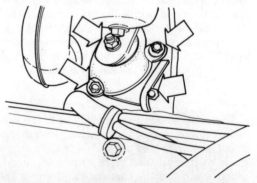

B21, B23, B230: Location of nuts for left side engine mount

models, it is also necessary to disconnect the bracket at the intake manifold.

5. Disconnect the steering shaft at the steering gear. On vehicles with manual transmissions, pull up the shield.

6. Lift the engine slightly using either a chain hoist or a crossbar lifter. Do not lift too high or other components will be damaged. It may be necessary to loosen the fan shroud to allow clearance during the lifting process.

7. On vehicles with power steering, disconnect the hose at the reservoir. Pinch or plug the line to prevent leakage and the entry of dirt.

Place a jack under the front axle member for support. Remove the retaining bolts from the front axle member and lower it on the jack.

8. Remove the left side engine mount.

9. Remove the support bracket across the rear of the engine.

10. Remove the oil pan retaining bolts. Loosen, turn and remove the oil pan. Clean the gasket surfaces. Install the new gasket on the oil pan and install the pan. Tighten the bolts to eight ft. lbs. To reassemble:

11. Attach the reinforcing bracket. If the car has power steering, reconnect the lines at the reservoir.

12. Raise the front axle on the jack and install and tighten the retaining bolts.

13. Reconnect the steering shaft at the steering gear. The flange will only fit in one position.

14. Install the left side engine mount. On E-series motors, reconnect the bracket at the intake manifold.

15 Lower the engine into position. Fit the mount onto the front axle member. Disconnect and remove the lifting equipment when the engine is in position.

16. Install the dipstick and tube. Install and tighten the nuts on the engine mounts.

17 Secure the fan shroud if it was loosened and install the splash guard under the engine. Attach the exhaust system at the muffler flange.

18. Return the car to the ground by safely removing the jackstands.

19. Fill engine oil to proper capacity. Double check all installation items, paying particular attention to loose hoses or hanging wires, untightened nuts, poor routing of hoses and wires (too tight or rubbing) and tools left in the engine area.

20. Start the engine and check carefully for leaks, particularly after the engine is warm.

B234

1. Safely elevate the car and support it on jackstands. Disconnect the negative battery cable and remove the engine oil dipstick.

2. Remove the air mass meter and air inlet hose. Loosen the fan shroud.

3. Remove the bolts at both ends of the crossmember.

4. Fit a chain hoist or lifting apparatus to the top of the engine and relieve the weight of the engine by lifting the at the front.

5. At the right motor mount, unbolt the bottom mounting plate from the crossmember. At the left motor mount, unbolt the upper mounting plate from the cylinder block.

6. Drain the engine oil and replace the drain bolt when the pan is empty. Use a new washer and tighten the bolt to 44 ft. lbs.

CAUTION: *The EPA warns that prolonged contact with used engine oil may cause a number of skin disorders, including cancer! You should make every effort to minimize your exposure to used engine oil. Protective gloves should be worn when changing the oil. Wash your hands and any other exposed skin areas as soon as possible after exposure to used engine oil. Soap and water, or waterless hand cleaner should be used.*

7. Remove the splashguard from under the engine, the bottom nut for the left motor mount and the wiring harness bracket from transmission cover.

8. At the steering shaft, remove the lower clamping bolt and loosen the upper bolt. Matchmark the position of the splined joint and slide the fitting up the steering shaft.

9. Remove the rubber bumpstop on the front crossmember and remove the reinforcing bracket between the engine and transmission.

10. Disassemble the bolted joint at the front of the catalytic converter.

11. Carefully elevate the engine with the hoist. Make very certain that no hoses or wires are strained and that clearance is maintained at the firewall.

Raise the motor only enough to perform the next steps of the procedure.

12. Remove the left motor mount.

13. Unbolt and remove the oil pan. It will need to be lifted and turned during removal.

14. Clean the gasket surfaces and install the new gasket (always!) so that the small tab on the gasket is on the same side as the starter. Lift the pan into place, install the retaining bolts and tighten them to 8 ft. lbs.

15. Install the reinforcing bracket between the engine and transmission. Attach it first to the transmission and then to the engine block. Tighten the bracket in stages so that all the bolts pull up evenly.

16. Install the bumpstop on the front crossmember. Lift the crossmember into position against the side rails, install the bolts and tighten only a few turns to hold it in place.

17. When all the bolts are installed, tighten the crossmember bolts to 70 ft. lbs. Install the left motor mount and secure the plate to the cylinder block. Don't forget to attach the cable clip on the upper bolt.

18. Paying close attention to the placement of the motor mounts, lower the engine into position. When the engine is correctly seated, the lifting equipment may be removed from the car.

19. At the right motor mount, tighten the plate onto the crossmember. Check the connection of the air preheat tube at the exhaust manifold.

20. Tighten the fan shroud. Adjust the position of the bottom bracket as needed.

21. Reconnect the wiring harness bracket at the transmission, the bolted joint at the front of the catalytic converter and install the splashguard under the engine.

22. Tighten the left motor mount.

23. Observing the markings made earlier, reassemble the steering shafts. Insert and tighten the bottom bolt to 15 ft. lbs. Tighten the upper bolt the same. Don't forget to install the small spring clips on the bolts.

24. Install the air mass meter and its hoses and connectors.

25. Fill the engine with the correct amount of oil and reinstall the dipstick.

26. Lower the car to the ground, reconnect the battery cable and start the engine. Check for leaks.

B27, B28 and B280

NOTE: *The following procedure is for the small steel oil pan at the front of the engine. This will not expose the crankshaft.*

1. Remove the splash guard.

2. Drain the crankcase and reinstall the drain plug.

CAUTION: *The EPA warns that prolonged contact with used engine oil may cause a number of skin disorders, including cancer! You should make every effort to minimize your exposure to used engine oil. Protective gloves should be worn when changing the oil. Wash your hands and any other exposed skin areas as soon as possible after exposure to used engine oil. Soap and water, or waterless hand cleaner should be used.*

3. Remove the oil pan retaining bolts. Swivel the pan past the stabilizer bar and remove the pan. Remove the old gasket and clean the surfaces of the cylinder block and oil pan. Remove any sludge or foreign matter that has accumulated at the bottom of the pan.

4. Using a new gasket, position the pan to the cylinder block and install the oil pan bolts. Torque the bolts to 6–8 ft. lbs. Fill the oil to the proper capacity and reinstall the splash shield.

Diesel

The oil pan cannot be removed without either lifting the engine or removing it from the car. The combination procedure for removing the oil pan and the oil pump is found in Oil Pump Removal and Installation later in this chapter.

Oil Pump

REMOVAL AND INSTALLATION

B20, B30

The oil pump may only be removed with the engine elevated in the car or removed from the car. Do not attempt this procedure if you cannot properly lift and support the engine.

1. Remove the oil pan as described previously.

2. Crank the engine to TDC at no. 1 cylinder. Remove the distributor.

3. Remove the oil pump retaining bolts.

4. Disconnect the oil pump from the delivery tube by unscrewing the connecting flange. Be careful not to discard the rubber sealing rings from the sealing flange.

5. Unscrew the connecting flange and remove the delivery tube from the block.

To install:

6. Fit the delivery tube with its sealing rings to the oil pump, and then to the block. If the tube does not seat properly in the block, it may be tapped lightly with a soft mallet. Tightly screw the connecting flanges together.

7. With no. 1 cylinder at TDC, install the oil pump drive and distributor. Make sure that the shaft goes down into its groove in the pump shaft. Tighten the oil pump retaining bolts.

8. Install the oil pan with a new gasket and fill the crankcase.

B21, B23 and B230

1. Remove the oil pan as described previously.

2. Remove the two oil pump retaining bolts, and pull the delivery tube from the block.

3. When installing, use new sealing rings at either end of the delivery tube.

B234

1. Remove the timing belt following the procedures outlined in Timing Belt Removal and Installlation.

2. Using a counterholding device such as Volvo tool 5039 or similar, remove the oil pump drive pulley.

3. Thoroughly clean the area around the oil pump. Place sheets of newspaper or a container on the splashguard to contain any spillage and remove the oil pump mounting bolts. Remove the pump from the engine.

4. Remove the seal from the groove in the

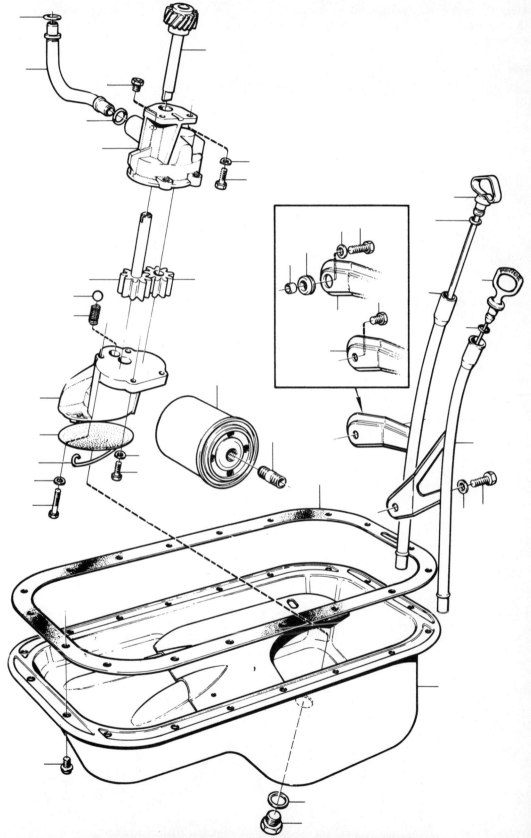

Lubrication system and oil pan—B21 and B23 engines. B230 similar

block. Clean the area with solvent, making certain there are no particles of dirt trapped in the pump area.

5. Install the new seal in the groove and install the new oil pump. Lubricate the pump with clean engine oil before installation. Tighten the mounting bolts to 7.5 ft. lbs.

6. Using the counterhold, install the drive pulley and tighten the center bolt to 15 ft. lbs. PLUS 60° of rotation.

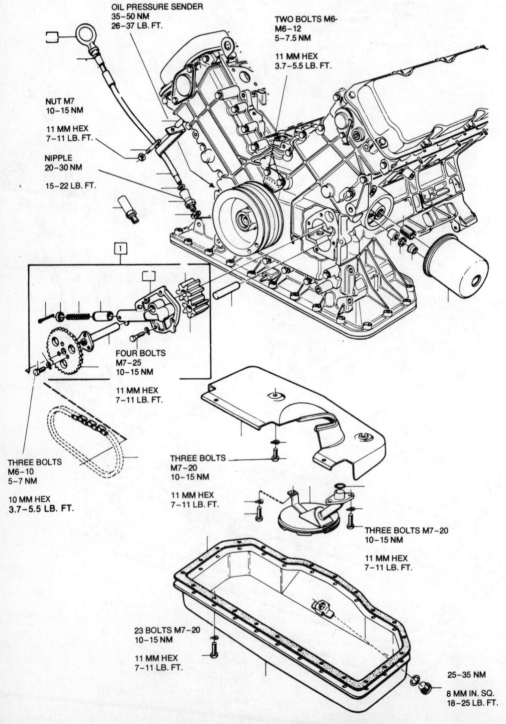

OIL PRESSURE SENDER
35-50 NM
26-37 LB. FT.

TWO BOLTS M6-
M6-12
5-7.5 NM

11 MM HEX
3.7-5.5 LB. FT.

NUT M7
10-15 NM

11 MM HEX
7-11 LB. FT.

NIPPLE
20-30 NM

15-22 LB. FT.

FOUR BOLTS
M7-25
10-15 NM

11 MM HEX
7-11 LB. FT.

THREE BOLTS
M6-10
5-7 NM

10 MM HEX
3.7-5.5 LB. FT.

THREE BOLTS
M7-20
10-15 NM

11 MM HEX
7-11 LB. FT.

THREE BOLTS M7-20
10-15 NM

11 MM HEX
7-11 LB. FT.

23 BOLTS M7-20
10-15 NM

11 MM HEX
7-11 LB. FT.

25-35 NM

8 MM IN. SQ.
18-25 LB. FT.

Lubrication system—B27F engine. B28F and B280F similar

7. Clean the area of any oil spillage; remove the paper or container from the splashguard.

8. Install the timing belt following the procedures outlined in Timing Belt Removal and Installation.

B27, B28 and B280

The oil pump body is cast integrally with the cylinder block. It is chain driven by a separate sprocket on the crankshaft and is located behind the timing chain cover. The pick-up screen and tube are serviced by removing the oil pan. To check the pump gears or remove the oil pump cover:

1. Disconnect the negative battery terminal. Drain the coolant by opening the drain cock on the left side of the engine. A radiator hose may also be disconnected to speed draining.

> CAUTION: *When draining the coolant, keep in mind that cats and dogs are attracted by the ethylene glycol antifreeze, and are quite likely to drink any that is left in an uncovered container or in puddles on the ground. This will prove fatal in sufficient quantity. Always drain the coolant into a sealable container. Coolant should be reused unless it is contaminated or several years old.*

2. After removing any electrical leads to the radiator, disconnect the oil cooler lines to the radiator on cars with automatic transmissions. Remove the fan shroud from the radiator, disconnect the hoses and remove the radiator. Remove the fan shroud.

3. Remove the splash shield under the engine. Loosen the alternator and power steering belts.

4. Remove the power steering pump from its bracket and secure it with wire out of the way. Do not disconnect any lines or hoses. After the pump is moved and secure, remove the bracket from the engine.

5. Detach and secure to one side the air conditioning compressor, if so equipped. Don't disconnect any lines or hoses.

6. Remove the fan, fan pulley and drive belts.

7. After removing the air intake duct and the vacuum pump, remove the left valve cover.

8. Using a 5mm Allen wrench, remove the fuel pressure regulator and lay it on the intake manifold. Disconnect the main ignition wire (near the right side shock tower) and remove the oil filler cap. Remove the right valve cover.

9. Turn the crankshaft to the overlap position on cylinder number one. This means the rocker arms for cylinder number one do NOT have clearance and the first mark on the crank pulley is aligned with the **O** mark on the pointer.

10. Using either Volvo special tool 5112 or an acceptable substitute, lock the flywheel in posi-

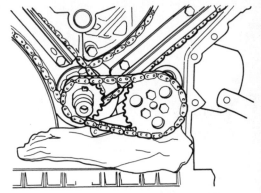

Chain driven oil pump, B28 and B280 engines

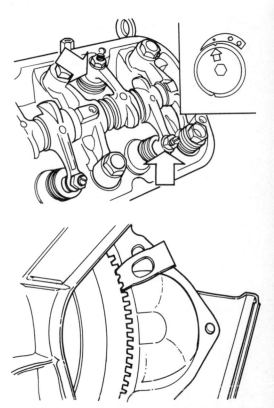

B28 and B280 engines: Upper; engine set to "overlap" position on cylinder no. 1. (There is no rocker clearance in this position.) Crankshaft pulley mark is set to 0 mark on timing pointer. Lower; locking device to hold flywheel in place. Volvo special tool shown

tion so that the engine cannot be moved out of position.

11. By using a 36mm socket, remove the crankshaft pulley. Take care that the small locking (Woodruff) key on the crankshaft does not fall into the lower part of the engine.

12. Move the wiring harness on the timing cover to one side and remove the timing cover. The timing chains, gears, sliders and tensioners

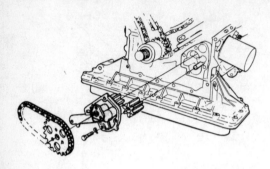

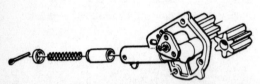

Exploded view of oil pump, B28 and B280 engines

will be exposed. Do not loosen or meddle with any components or you may cost yourself great time and expense.

13. Remove the oil pump sprocket and its chain. This is the outermost drive system and can be removed with no disturbance of the other chains. The oil pump itself may now be removed by loosening its retaining bolts and carefully lifting it away from the engine.

Clean all the parts before reinstallation. Clean the housing in the cylinder block. Install the pump and tighten its mounting bolts to 7–11 ft. lbs.

14. Using a plastic (not metal) scraper, clean the gasket surfaces on the timing cover, the valve covers, and the front of the engine block. Tap the center seal out of the timing cover and replace it with a new one.

15. Reinstall the oil pump drive pulley and its chain. Use a light coat of locking fluid on the pulley retaining bolts.

16. Install the timing gear cover with a new gasket. Apply a light coat of locking fluid to the four lower bolts; tighten all the bolts to 10–11 ft. lbs.

17. Install the crankshaft pulley. Tighten to 190–200 ft. lbs. Remove the locking device from the flywheel.

18. Apply new gaskets and reinstall both valve covers.

19. On the right side of the motor, replace the oil filler cap, the ignition lead and the fuel control pressure regulator.

20. Close the drain cock on the left side of the engine.

21. On the left side of the motor, reconnect the vacuum pump (with a new gasket) and the air inlet duct.

22. Reinstall the fan, pulley, and drivebelts. Replace the bracket and the power steering pump with its belt. Adjust all the belts to the correct tension.

23. Install the air conditioning compressor and set the belt tension.

24. Install the fan shroud and the radiator. Connect the oil cooler lines to the radiator (cars with automatic transmission), and connect all the hoses to the radiator. Reconnect any wiring to sensors on the radiator.

25. Install the splash guard under the car.

26. Double check all installation items, paying particular attention to loose hoses or hanging wires, untightened nuts, poor routing of hoses and wires (too tight or rubbing) and tools left in the engine area.

27. Reconnect the battery cable. Fill the cooling system with a 50-50 mixture of coolant and water. Start the engine and check for leaks. After the engine has fully warmed up, check the coolant level and top up as needed.

Diesel D24, D24T

WARNING: *The use of the correct special tools or their equivalent is REQUIRED for this procedure.*

This procedure covers removal of both the oil pump and the oil pan. While it is easier to do this with the engine out of the car, the repair can be performed with the engine lifted and supported while still in the vehicle.

1. Disconnect the negative battery cable. Drain the coolant system by disconnecting the lower radiator hose at the radiator and disconnect the lower hose of the cold start device.

CAUTION: *When draining the coolant, keep in mind that cats and dogs are attracted by the ethylene glycol antifreeze, and are quite*

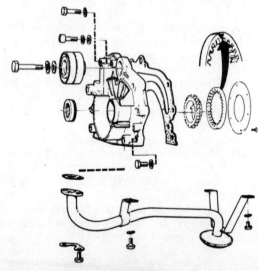

Diesel engine oil pump assembly

likely to drink any that is left in an uncovered container or in puddles on the ground. This will prove fatal in sufficient quantity. Always drain the coolant into a sealable container. Coolant should be reused unless it is contaminated or several years old.

2. Remove the radiator. Remove the cooling fan with its spacer and pulley.

3. Remove the fan belt(s) and the power steering drive belt.

4. Remove the timing gear cover. When this cover is removed, the timing belt will be exposed. Do not allow fluids, dirt or oil to contact the belt. It must be kept clean and dry or premature wear and breakage may result.

5. Remove the large center bolt in the center of the vibration damper (pulley) and the crankshaft. Do not allow the pulley to turn while removing the nut. Volvo has two special tools available to accomplish this.

6. When the nut is removed, turn the pulley (and therefore, the engine) about ¼ turn counter clockwise. This transfers the slack in the timing belt to the opposite side, making it easier to remove.

7. Using a 6mm Allen wrench, remove the four small bolts holding the crank damper and remove the damper. Note that the crankshaft gear may stick to the damper. When the damper is off, remove the lower timing gear cover.

8. Loosen and remove the three bolts holding the bracket for the alternator and cooling fan. Place the assembly to one side and secure it out of the way.

9. Mark the position of the timing belt relative to the timing gears. Mark the belt, camshaft gear and crankshaft gear. Identify the outside and topside of the belt. It is critical that the belt be reinstalled in exactly the same position as it was found.

10. Loosen the water pump mounting bolts and and the timing belt. Some coolant may leak out when the bolts are loosened. Remove the timing belt.

11. Remove the idler pulley. Use a pulley puller; do not pry on the idler.

12. Remove the seal from the oil pump. Remove all the retaining screws from cover, but do not remove the cover at this time.

13. Lift the dipstick about 2½ inches and remove the upper retaining bolt from the steering joint. Remove the wire from the oil level sender if so equipped.

14. Install the lifting equipment or chain hoist on the engine. When securely mounted, raise engine slightly.

Using Volvo special tools to remove crankshaft nut on D24 and D24T engines

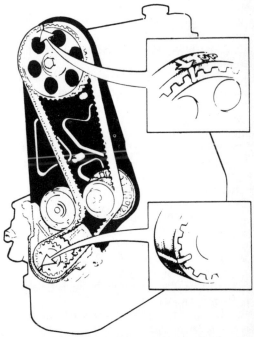

Turn the engine ¼ turn counterclockwise to transfer the slack in the timing belt

Carefully mark the timing belt and gears before removing the belt. Exact reinstallation is critical to avoid motor damage

15. Loosen the bolts holding the front axle crossmember at both sides.

16. Drain the engine oil. Replace the drain plug when draining is complete.

CAUTION: *The EPA warns that prolonged contact with used engine oil may cause a number of skin disorders, including cancer! You should make every effort to minimize your exposure to used engine oil. Protective gloves should be worn when changing the oil. Wash your hands and any other exposed skin areas as soon as possible after exposure to used engine oil. Soap and water, or waterless hand cleaner should be used.*

17. Remove the swaybar retaining bolts from the side members.

18. Loosen the wiring harness clamp on the right side of the engine, and loosen the clamp holding the battery cable (near the right engine mount).

19. Remove the retaining nuts for the engine mounts. Lower the sidemember and detach the steering column from the joint.

20. Disconnect the oil return line from the oil pan.

21. Remove the retaining bolts for the oil pan. Note that the bolts you remove are different sizes. It is important to record location of each bolt. Proper gasket sealing during reassembly depends on use of the correct bolt.

The rear and center bolts are reached through openings in the flywheel. Remove the four bolts from the flywheel casing. Remove the oil pan.

22. With the pan removed, disconnect the oil tube bolts at the oil pump. The tube may manipulated by loosening the bolts which hold it to the block.

23. Remove the bolts remaining in the oil pump and remove the pump. Take care not to damage the pump body.

24. Remove the gaskets for the oil pan and pump. Clean the mating surfaces.

25. When installing the new pump, always use a new gasket. Make sure the pump gear aligns with the crankshaft flange. Secure the pump with three bolts, the longest of which goes in the rightside hole.

26. Connect the oil pump tube. Use a new gasket and tighten to 7 ft. lbs. Tighten the tube retaining bolts on the block.

27. Install the oil pan with a new gasket. Hold the gasket in place with a light coating of grease. Remember to install the proper size bolt in the proper spot.

28. Using a new gasket, reconnect the oil return line to the pan.

29. Raise the front axle crossmember with a jack and position the steering shaft joint. Guide the engine mounts into position. Loosely attach

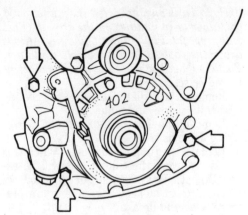

Location of pump retaining bolts, D24 and D24T

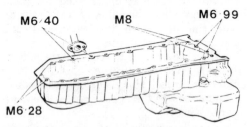

Diesel oil pans require correct placement of different sized retaining bolts. Remaining bolts are M6 × 18

the crossmember retaining nuts and attach the nuts to the engine mounts. The jack may be removed when the pieces are secured.

30. Reconnect the wiring harness clamp and the clamp for the battery lead.

31. Tighten the mounting bolts for the front crossmember to 60 ft. lbs. Double check engine mount nuts and relieve tension on the lifting equipment. Disconnect and remove the lifting equipment.

32. Reconnect and secure the steering shaft joint. Reconnect the wire to the oil level transmitter and push in the dipstick.

33. Replace the cover retaining bolts, the idler pulley, and the oil pump seal.

34. Remount the bracket for the cooling fan and alternator.

35. Install the timing belt. Align the marks on the upper and lower gears with the marks on the belt. It is critical that the belt be refitted exactly as it was removed.

36. Draw tension on the belt by moving the water pump by hand. Tighten the water pump mounting bolts.

37. Install the lower timing gear cover and the vibration damper. Note that the damper can only be fitted one way--the pin on the crank gear must fit into the damper. Torque the four bolts to 15 ft. lbs. Install the large center nut, using the special tools as before. Torque the center nut to 255 ft. lbs.

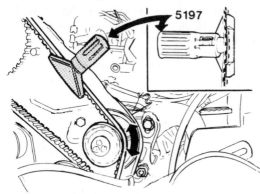

5197

D24 and D24T: Use belt tension gauge and move water pump as necessary to adjust timing belt. Volvo special tool shown

38. Turn the engine clockwise ¼ turn. Use a belt tension gauge to check the
timing belt tension. Adjust the tension by moving the water pump as necessary. If using Volvo tool 5197, the correct tension is 12.5 units.

39. Reinstall the front timing gear cover. Install the fan with its spacer and pulley. Tighten the fan bolts to 7 ft. lbs.

40. Install the belts for the fan and power steering pump. Adjust the belts to the proper tension.

41. Reinstall the radiator. Connect the hoses to the radiator and the hose to the cold start device. Refill the coolant system with a 50-50 mixture of antifreeze and water.

42. Double check all installation items, paying particular attention to loose hoses or hanging wires, untightened nuts, poor routing of hoses and wires (too tight or rubbing) and tools left in the engine area.

43. Reconnect the negative battery cable. Start the engine and check for leaks.

44. Disconnect the upper hose to the cold start device. Place a collecting pan or jug beneath the hose and hold the hose level with the top edge of the expansion tank. Allow the engine to come to normal operating temperature with the cap off the expansion tank. Add coolant as necessary as the engine warms up.

45. When the coolant level is stable and no air is coming from the disconnected hose, shut the engine off. Reconnect the upper hose to the cold start device, top up the coolant in the expansion tank and put the cap back on the tank.

Timing Gear Cover
REMOVAL AND INSTALLATION
B20

1. Loosen the fan (drive) belt. Remove the fan and water pump pulley. Disconnect the stabilizer attachment from the frame.

2. Remove the crankshaft pulley and bolt.

3. Remove the retaining bolts and the timing gear cover. Loosen a few oil pan bolts, being careful not to damage the pan gasket.

4. Remove the circlip, washer, and felt ring from the cover. Replace any gasket in questionable condition. Make sure that the oil drain hole is open and clean.

5. Place the cover in position and install the retaining bolts finger-tight.

6. Center the cover with a sleeve. Turn the sleeve while tightening and adjust the position of the cover so that the sleeve may be easily rotated without jamming.

7. Install a new felt ring, washer, and circlip. Push them into their positions with the engaging sleeve. Check to make sure that the circlip has seated in its groove.

8. Tighten the cover bolts. Install the pulleys and fan. Tension the accessory drive belts. Tighten the stabilizer attachment firmly to the frame.

Timing Gear Cover Oil Seal
REPLACEMENT
B20

1. Remove the fan belt. Loosen the stabilizer attachment at the frame.

2. Remove the crankshaft pulley and bolt.

3. Remove the circlip for the washer retaining the felt ring. Check to make sure that the cover is correctly installed by inserting a 0.004 in. (0.10mm) feeler gauge between the casing and the crankshaft hub. If the feeler gauge jams at any point, the cover must be centered.

4. Install a new felt ring. Place the washer in position and install the circlip in its groove.

5. Install the crankshaft pulley and fan. Ten-

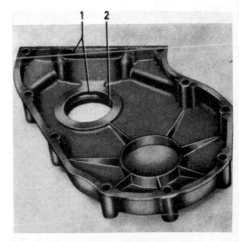

1. Drain holes   2. Sealing ring

Timing gear cover—B20 engine

sion the fan (drive) belt. Tighten the stabilizer attachment at the frame.

B30

1. Drain the cooling system by opening the engine drain plug and disconnecting the lower radiator hose. On automatic transmission cars, disconnect and plug the transmission oil cooler lines at the radiator. Remove the radiator, fan shroud, and grille.

CAUTION: *When draining the coolant, keep in mind that cats and dogs are attracted by the ethylene glycol antifreeze, and are quite likely to drink any that is left in an uncovered container or in puddles on the ground. This will prove fatal in sufficient quantity. Always drain the coolant into a sealable container. Coolant should be reused unless it is contaminated or several years old.*

2. Remove the fan (drive) belt. Remove the bolts for the pulley and crankshaft damper.

3. Remove the center bolt and pull off the hub by hand or, if necessary, with a puller.

4. Remove the oil seal. Lubricate the sealing lip on the new seal and install the seal with a drift. The seal may be installed in one of three positions, depending on the amount of wear on the hub. With a new hub, the seal will be in-stalled in its outer position (position 1). With a wear mark on the hub, install the seal in position 2. With two wear marks on the hub, install the seal in position 3. With three wear marks on the hub, you have either a very old engine or you have gone through more than a normal share of oil seals. It's time to think about re-placing the old hub with a new one.

5. Grease the sliding surfaces of the hub and install the hub. Note the center punch marks on the crankshaft end and hub. Install the cen-ter bolt and torque it to 50–57 ft. lbs.

6. Install the crankshaft damper and pulley.

7. Install and properly tension the fan (drive) belt. Install the radiator, fan shroud, and grille. Install the lower radiator hose, close the drain plug, and fill the cooling system. On cars with automatic transmissions, connect the trans-mission oil cooler lines at the radiator.

Timing Belt Cover
REMOVAL AND INSTALLATION
B21, B23 and B230

1. Loosen the fan shroud and remove the fan. Remove the shroud.

2. Loosen the alternator, air pump, power steering pump (if so equipped), and AC com-pressor (if so equipped) and remove their drive belts. Note that no hoses are to be disconnected; simply move the entire unit out of the way.

3. Remove the water pump pulley. This step is not necessary on B234 engines.

4. Remove the four retaining bolts and lift off the timing belt cover. On the B234, the tim-ing belt cover is in three sections; remove the upper section first and work to the lowest one.

5. Reverse the above procedure to install. Double check all installation items, paying par-

Remove the crankshaft hub by hand or with a puller to service timing gear oil seal—B30 engine

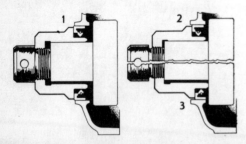

Center spindle position—B30 engine

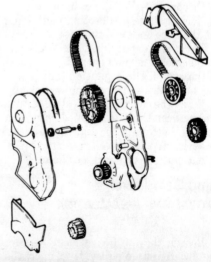

D24 Diesel timing belt cover and assembly

ticular attention to loose hoses or hanging wires, untightened nuts, poor routing of hoses and wires (too tight or rubbing) and tools left in the engine area.

Diesel D24, D24T

FRONT TIMING GEAR COVER

The front timing gear cover is removed by unsnapping the spring clips holding the cover and pulling the cover up and out. To install the cover, simply reverse the procedure.

REAR TIMING GEAR COVER

To remove the rear timing gear cover, remove the two bolts in the cover and lift the cover out. When installing, adjust the cover in the bolt slots so that it is not touching the drive belt or other moving parts.

Timing Chain Cover

REMOVAL AND INSTALLATION

B27F, B28F and B280F

1. Disconnect the negative battery terminal. Drain the coolant by opening the drain cock on the left side of the engine. A radiator hose may also be disconnected to speed draining.

> CAUTION: *When draining the coolant, keep in mind that cats and dogs are attracted by the ethylene glycol antifreeze, and are quite likely to drink any that is left in an uncovered container or in puddles on the ground. This will prove fatal in sufficient quantity. Always drain the coolant into a sealable container. Coolant should be reused unless it is contaminated or several years old.*

2. After removing any electrical leads to the radiator, disconnect the oil cooler lines to the radiator on cars with automatic transmissions. Remove the fan shroud from the radiator, disconnect the hoses and remove the radiator. Remove the fan shroud.

3. Remove the splash shield under the engine. Loosen the alternator and power steering belts.

4. Remove the power steering pump from its bracket and secure it with wire out of the way. Do not disconnect any lines or hoses. After the pump is moved and secure, remove the bracket from the engine.

5. Detach and secure to one side the air conditioning compressor, if so equipped. Don't disconnect any lines or hoses.

6. Remove the fan, fan pulley and drive belts.

7. After removing the air intake duct and the vacuum pump, remove the left valve cover.

8. Using a 5mm Allen wrench, remove the fuel pressure regulator and lay it on the intake manifold. Disconnect the main ignition wire

Timing chain cover retainer bolt locations—B27F, B28F

(near the right side shock tower) and remove the oil filler cap. Remove the right valve cover.

9. Turn the crankshaft to the overlap position on cylinder number one. This means the rocker arms for cylinder number one do NOT have clearance and the first mark on the crank pulley is aligned with the **O** mark on the pointer.

10. Using either Volvo special tool 5112 or an acceptable substitute, lock the flywheel in position so that the engine cannot be moved out of position.

11. By using a 36mm socket, remove the crankshaft pulley. Take care that the small locking (Woodruff) key on the crankshaft does not fall into the lower part of the engine.

12. Move the wiring harness on the timing cover to one side and remove the timing cover.

13. Using a plastic (not metal) scraper, clean the gasket surfaces on the timing cover, the valve covers, and the front of the engine block.

14. Tap the center seal out of the timing cover and replace it with a new one.

15. Install the timing gear cover with a new gasket. Apply a light coat of locking fluid to the four lower bolts; tighten all the bolts to 10–11 ft. lbs.

16. Install the crankshaft pulley. Tighten to 190–200 ft. lbs.

17. Remove the locking device from the flywheel.

18. Apply new gaskets and reinstall both valve covers.

19. On the right side of the motor, replace the oil filler cap, the ignition lead and the fuel control pressure regulator.

20. Close the drain cock on the left side of the engine.

21. On the left side of the motor, reconnect the vacuum pump (with a new gasket) and the air inlet duct.

22. Reinstall the fan, pulley, and drivebelts. Replace the bracket and the power steering

pump with its belt. Adjust all the belts to the correct tension.

23. Install the air conditioning compressor and set the belt tension.

24. Install the fan shroud and the radiator. Connect the oil cooler lines to the radiator (cars with automatic transmission), and connect all the hoses to the radiator. Reconnect any wiring to sensors on the radiator.

25. Install the splash guard under the car.

26. Double check all installation items, paying particular attention to loose hoses or hanging wires, untightened nuts, poor routing of hoses and wires (too tight or rubbing) and tools left in the engine area.

27. Reconnect the battery cable. Fill the cooling system with a 50–50 mixture of coolant and water. Start the engine and check for leaks. After the engine has fully warmed up, check the coolant level and top up as needed.

Timing Belt

REMOVAL AND INSTALLATION

B21, B23 and B230

1. Remove the timing belt cover as outlined previously.

2. To remove the tension from the belt, loosen the nut for the tensioner and press the idler roller back. The tension spring can be locked in this position by inserting the shank end of a 3mm drill bit through the pusher rod.

3. Remove the six retaining bolts and the crankshaft pulley.

4. Remove the belt, taking care not to bend it at any sharp angles. The belt should be replaced routinely at 45, 000 mile intervals, or anytime it becomes oil soaked or frayed.

5. If the crankshaft, idler shaft, or camshaft were disturbed while the belt was off, align each shaft with its corresponding index mark (to as-

B21, B23: position crankshaft so the notch aligns with the mark on the cover

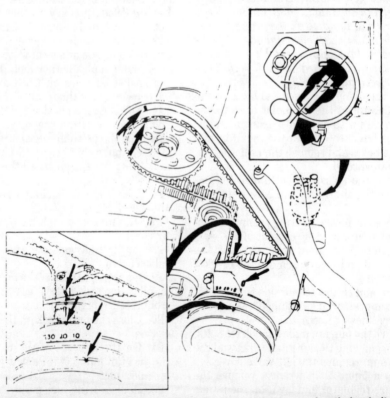

On B230F, align crankshaft and camshaft marks before removing timing belt

B21, B23: align dot on idler shaft with notch on timing belt rear cover

B21, B23: align notch on camshaft sprocket with notch on the valve cover

sure proper valve timing and ignition timing) as follows:

  a. Rotate the crankshaft so that the notch in the crankshaft gear belt guide aligns with the embossed mark on the front cover (12 o'clock position).

  b. Rotate the idler shaft so that the dot on the idler shaft drive sprocket aligns with the notch on the timing belt rear cover (four o'clock position).

  c. Rotate the camshaft so that the notch in the camshaft sprocket inner belt guide aligns with the notch in the forward edge of the valve cover (12 o'clock position).

6. Install the timing belt (don't use any sharp tools) over the sprockets, and then over the tensioner roller. Loosen the tensioner nut and let the spring tension automatically take up the slack. Tighten the tensioner nut to 37 ft. lbs.

7. Rotate the crankshaft one full revolution clockwise, and make sure the timing marks still align.

8. Reverse steps 1-3 to install.

B234

NOTE: *The B234 engine has two belts, one driving the camshafts and one driving the balance shafts. The camshaft belt may be removed separately; the balance shaft belt requires removal of the cam belt. During reassembly, the EXACT placement of the belts and pulleys must be observed.*

1. Remove the negative battery cable and the alternator belt.

2. Remove the radiator fan, its pulley and the fan shroud.

3. Remove the drive belts for the power steering belts and the air conditioning compressor.

4. Beginning with the top cover, remove the retaining bolts and remove the timing belt covers.

5. Turn the engine to TDC on cylinder 1. Make sure the marks on the cam pulleys align with the marks on the backing plate and that the marking on the belt guide plate (on the crankshaft) is opposite the TDC mark on the engine block.

6. Remove the protective cap over the timing belt tensioner locknut. Loosen the lock nut, compress the tensioner (so as to release tension on the belts) and retighten the locknut, holding the tensioner in place.

7. Remove the timing belt from the camshafts. Do not crease or fold the belt.

WARNING: *The camshafts and the crankshaft MUST NOT be moved when the belt is removed.*

8. Check the tensioner by spinning it (counterclockwise) and listening for any bearing noise within. Check also that the belt contact surface is clean and smooth. In the same fashion, check the timing belt idler pulleys. Make sure the are tightened to 18.5 ft. lbs.

If the balance shaft belt is to be removed:

  a. Remove the balance shaft belt idler pulley from the engine.

  b. Loosen the locknut on the tensioner and remove the belt. Slide the belt under the crankshaft pulley assembly. Check the tensioner and idler wheels carefully for any sign of contamination; check the ends of the shafts for any sign of oil leakage.

  c. Check the position of the balance shafts and the crankshaft after belt removal. The balance shaft markings on the pulleys should align with the markings on the backing plate and the crankshaft marking should still be aligned with the TDC mark on the engine block.

  d. When refitting the balance shaft belt, observe that the belt has colored dots on it. These marks assist in the critical placement of the belt. The yellow dot will align the right (lower) shaft, the blue dot will align on the crank and the other yellow dot will match to the upper (left) balance shaft.

e. Carefully work the belt in under the crankshaft pulley. Make sure the blue dot is opposite the bottom (TDC) marking on the belt guide plate at the bottom of the crankshaft. Fit the belt around the left (upper) balance shaft pulley, making sure the yellow mark is opposite the mark on the pulley. Install the belt around the right (lower) balance shaft pulley and again check that the mark on the belt aligns with the mark on the pulley.

f. Work the belt around the tensioner. Double check that all the markings are still aligned.

g. Set the belt tension by inserting an Allen key into the adjusting hole in the tensioner. Turn the crankshaft carefully through a few degrees on either side of TDC to check that the belt has properly engaged the pulleys. Return the crank to the TDC position and set the adjusting hole just below the 3 o'clock position when tightening the adjusting bolt. Use the Allen wrench (in the adjusting hole) as a counter hold and tighten the locking bolt to 29.5 ft. lbs.

h. Use Volvo tool 998 8500 to check the tension of the belt. Install the gauge over the position of the removed idler pulley. The tension must be 1-4 units on the scale or the belt must be readjusted.

9. Reinstall the camshaft belt by aligning the double line marking on the belt with the top marking on the belt guide plate at the top of the crankshaft. Stretch the belt around the crank pulley and place it over the tensioner and the right side idler.

Place the belt on the camshaft pulleys. The single line marks on the belt should align exactly with the pulley markings. Route the belt around the oil pump drive pulley and press the belt onto the left side idler.

10. Check that all the markings align and that the engine is still positioned at TDC for cylinder 1.

11. Loosen the tensioner locknut.

12. Turn the crankshaft clockwise. The cam pulleys should rotate one full turn until the marks again align with the marks on the backing plate.

WARNING: *The engine must not be rotated counterclockwise during this procedure.*

13. Smoothly rotate the crankshaft further clockwise until the cam pulley markings are 1½ teeth beyond the marks on the backing plate. Tighten the tensioner locknut.

14. Check the tension on the balance shaft belt; it should now be 3.8 units. If the tension is too low, adjust the tensioner clockwise. If the tension is too high, repeat step 8g above.

15. Check the belt guide for the balance shaft belt and make sure it is properly seated. Install the center timing belt cover (the one that covers the tensioner) the fan shroud, fan pulley and fan. Install all the drive belts and connect the battery cable.

16. Double check all installation items, paying particular attention to loose hoses or hanging wires, untightened nuts, poor routing of hoses and wires (too tight or rubbing) and tools left in the engine area.

17. Start the engine and allow it to run until the thermostat opens.

CAUTION: *The upper and lower timing belt covers are still removed. The belt and pulleys are exposed and moving at high speed.*

18. Shut the motor off and bring the motor to TDC on cylinder 1.

19. Check the tension of the camshaft belt. Position the gauge between the right (exhaust) cam pulley and the idler. Belt tension must be 5.5 ±0.2 units.

If the belt needs adjustment, remove the rubber cap over the tensioner locknut (cap is located on the timing belt cover) and loosen the locknut.

20. Insert a screwdriver between the tensioner wheel and the spring carrier pin to hold the tensioner. If the belt needs to be tightened, move the roller to adjust the tension to 6.0 units. If the belt is too tight, adjust to obtain a reading of 5.0 units on the gauge. Tighten the tensioner locknut.

21. Rotate the crankshaft so that the cam pulleys move through one full revolution and recheck the tension on the camshaft belt. It should now be 5.5 ±0.2 units. Install the plastic plug over the tensioner bolt.

22. Final check the tension on the balance shaft belt by fitting the gauge and turning the tensioner clockwise. Only small movements are needed. After any needed readjustments, rotate the crankshaft clockwise through one full revolution and recheck the balance shaft belt. The tension should now be on the final specification of 4.9 ±0.2 units.

23. Install the idler pulley for the balance shaft belt. Reinstall the upper and lower timing belt covers.

24. Start the engine and final check performance.

Diesel D24, D24T

When replacing both the front and rear camshaft belts at the recommended 75,000 mile interval, you must also replace the front idler pulley.

NOTE: *Due to the number of special tools*

needed to perform this operation, it is recommended that timing belt removal and installation be performed by a competent garage. However, if you have access to the required special tools, the procedure is given below.

1. Disconnect the negative battery cable. Drain the coolant and remove the splash guard from under the engine.

CAUTION: *When draining the coolant, keep in mind that cats and dogs are attracted by the ethylene glycol antifreeze, and are quite likely to drink any that is left in an uncovered container or in puddles on the ground. This will prove fatal in sufficient quantity. Always drain the coolant into a sealable container. Coolant should be reused unless it is contaminated or several years old.*

2. Disconnect the lower radiator hose and remove the expansion tank cap.

3. Remove the radiator, the cooling fan with spacer and pulley, the fan belt and the drive belt for power steering pump.

4. Remove the valve cover and the front and rear timing belt covers.

5. Set number 1 cylinder on top dead center of its compression stroke and align the flywheel timing mark at 0.

6. Using special wrench 5187 to hold the vibration damper, remove the damper center bolt with wrench 5188. It may be necessary to turn the engine slightly to permit wrench 5187 to rest on the cooling fan journal. After the center bolt is removed, use wrench 5187 to put number 1 cylinder on TDC again.

7. Remove the four bolts and remove the vibration damper. You may have to tap it to free it from the crankshaft gear.

8. Remove the lower timing belt shield, release the retaining bolts for the coolant pump and loosen and remove the belt.

9. Remove the idler pulley center bolt and remove the idler pulley using puller 5202. Tap a

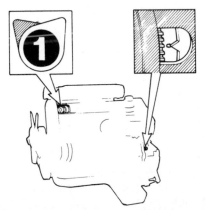

Diesel set no. 1 cylinder on TDC compresssion stroke

Diesel—remove the lower timing belt shield and loosen the coolant pump retaining bolts to release tension on belt

Lock camshaft with gauge 5190, then insert 0.008 in. (0.2 mm) feeler gauge under the left side of the gauge

new idler pulley into place and install its center bolt.

10. Use wrench 5199 to hold the rear gear and use wrench 5201 to remove its center bolt. Remove the rear camshaft gear and remove the cover gasket.

11. Install gauge 5190 in the groove on the camshaft rear end to lock the camshaft in position. Position a 0.008 in. (0.2mm) feeler blade under the left side of the gauge to compensate for clearances in the timing gears.

12. Remove the front camshaft gear bolt using tool 5199 to hold the gear in position. Do not allow the camshaft to turn. Tap the gear loose.

13. After checking to make sure that the flywheel mark is still at 0 and that the camshaft has not moved, install the new belt and the camshaft front gear. Make sure the belt fits securely on the gears.

Install the center bolt on the camshaft front gear finger tight. The camshaft gear must be able to rotate by itself. The camshaft must not be rotated.

14. Install the lower belt shield and vibration damper. The damper fits only one way. Tighten the damper attaching bolts to 15 ft. lbs.

15. Install the crankshaft center bolt after applying sealer to the threads and contact surfaces. Use wrench 5187 to hold the vibration damper. It can rest on the cooling fan journal. Use wrench 5188 to torque the center bolt to 255 ft. lbs.

NOTE: *This torque applies only if tool 5188 is used. If only a torque wrench is used, torque to 330 ft. lbs.*

16. Verify that No. 1 cylinder is still at TDC.

17. Using the cooling pump movement, adjust the belt tension. Install belt tension gauge 5197 on the belt. Set the gauge to 12.5. Adjust belt tension with the water pump until the mark on the plunger is flush with the gauge sleeve.

18. Press heavily on the belt with your hand and once again check the belt tension. Adjust if necessary.

19. Using wrench 5199 to hold the gear, tighten the front gear center bolt to 33 ft. lbs. Make sure the camshaft does not rotate.

Use wrench 5187 to hold vibration damper, then use wrench 5188 and torque wrench to tighten the center bolt

Install camshaft gear and new belt, then adjust belt tension at the coolant pump

20. Remove the feeler gauge and the lock gauge at the rear of the engine.

21. Set the injection pump timing as instructed in Chapter 5.

22. Reinstall the front and rear timing gear covers. Reinstall the valve cover.

23. Install the fan with its spacer and pulley. Tighten the fan bolts to 7 ft. lbs.

24. Install the belts for the fan and power steering pump. Adjust the belts to the proper tension.

25. Reinstall the radiator. Connect the hoses to the radiator and the hose to the cold start device. Refill the coolant system with a 50-50 mixture of antifreeze and water.

26. Double check all installation items, paying particular attention to loose hoses or hanging wires, untightened nuts, poor routing of hoses and wires (too tight or rubbing) and tools left in the engine area.

27. Reconnect the negative battery cable. Start the engine and check for leaks.

28. Disconnect the upper hose to the cold start device. Place a collecting pan or jug beneath the hose and hold the hose level with the top edge of the expansion tank. Allow the engine to come to normal operating temperature with the cap off the expansion tank. Add coolant as necessary as the engine warms up.

29. When the coolant level is stable and no air is coming from the disconnected hose, shut the engine off. Reconnect the upper hose to the cold start device, top up the coolant in the expansion tank and put the cap back on the tank.

Timing Chain

REMOVAL AND INSTALLATION

B27F, B28F, and B280F

1. Remove the timing chain cover as outlined previously.

2. Remove the oil pump sprocket and drive chain.

3. Loosen the tension in both camshaft timing chains by rotating each tensioner lock ¼ turn counterclockwise and pushing in the rubbing block piston.

4. Remove both chain tensioners. Remove the two curved and the two straight chain damper/runners.

5. Remove the camshaft sprocket retaining bolt (10mm Allen head) and the sprocket and chain assembly. Repeat for other side.

6. Install the chain tensioners and tighten to 5 ft. lbs. Install the curved chain damper/runners and tighten to 7–11 ft. lbs. Install the straight chain damper/runners and torque to 60 in. lbs.

7. Install the left side camshaft sprocket and chain first. Rotate the crankshaft (use crank-

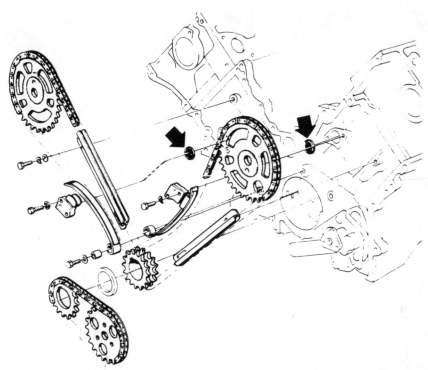

B28 and B280 timing chain arrangement. Arrows show oil screens which should be cleaned during timing chain replacement

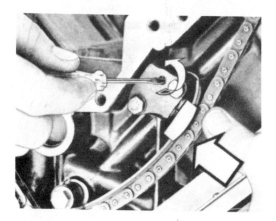

Slacken the tension in the camshaft timing chains—B27F, B28F

Rotate the crankshaft until no. 1 cylinder is at top dead center. At this point, crankshaft key is pointing directly toward left side camshaft, and left side camshaft key is pointing toward 12 o'clock position—installing left side timing chain

shaft nut, if necessary) until no. 1 cylinder is at TDC. (At this point, the crankshaft key is pointing directly to the left side camshaft and the left side camshaft key groove is pointing straight up.) Place the chain on the left side sprocket so that the camshaft sprocket notchmark is centered precisely between the two white lines on the chain.

Position the chain on the inner crankshaft sprocket, making sure that the other white line on the chain aligns with the crankshaft sprock-et notch. While holding the left side chain and sprockets in this position, install the sprocket and chain on the left side camshaft (chain stretched on tension side) so that the sprocket pin fits into the camshaft recess.

Tighten the sprocket center bolt to 51–59 ft. lbs. Use a screwdriver to keep cam from turning.

Installation of left side timing chain on crankshaft pulley

Install the right side camshaft timing chain

Installing left side camshaft sprocket with chain

Install the right side camshaft sprocket and timing chain

To install the right side timing chain, rotate the crankshaft until the crankshaft key points straight down, then align camshaft key groove until it is pointing in the position shown—B27F, B28F engines

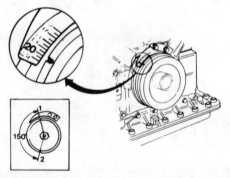

B28F static timing. Rotate the crankshaft until the engine is approximately 20° B.T.D.C. on cylinder no. 1. The pully has two marks: "1" is T.D.C. for cylinder no. 1; "2" is T.D.C. for cylinder no. 6. The marks are 150° apart.

8. To install the right side camshaft sprocket and chain, rotate the crankshaft clockwise until the crankshaft key points straight down. Align the camshaft key groove so that it is pointing in

the position shown; at this position, the no. 6 cylinder rocker arms will rock.

Place the chain on the right side sprocket so that the sprocket notchmark is centered precisely between the two white lines on the chain. Then, position the chain on the middle crankshaft sprocket, making sure that the other white line aligns with the crankshaft sprocket notch. Install the sprocket and chain on the camshaft so that the sprocket notch fits into the camshaft recess. Tighten the sprocket nut to 51–59 ft. lbs.

9. Rotate each of the chain tensioners ¼ turn clockwise. The chains are tensioned by rotating the crankshaft two full turns clockwise. Recheck to make sure the alignment marks coincide.

10. Install the oil pump sprocket and chain.

11. Install the timing chain cover and engine accessories as outlined previously.

Timing Gear and Camshaft
REMOVAL AND INSTALLATION
B20, B30

1. Disconnect the lower radiator hose, open the engine drain plug, and drain the cooling system. On cars with automatic transmissions, disconnect the plug the transmission oil cooler lines at the radiator. Remove the fan shroud and the radiator.

CAUTION: *When draining the coolant, keep in mind that cats and dogs are attracted by the ethylene glycol antifreeze, and are quite likely to drink any that is left in an uncovered container or in puddles on the ground. This will prove fatal in sufficient quantity. Always drain the coolant into a sealable container. Coolant should be reused unless it is contaminated or several years old.*

2. Remove the fan and the pulley on the water pump. Remove the crankshaft bolt and remove the pulley using a puller.

3. Remove the timing gear cover. Loosen a few oil pan bolts, being careful not to damage the pan gasket.

4. Measure the tooth flank clearance. Maximum permissible gear backlash is 0.005 in. (0.13mm). Check to make sure that the end-play of the camshaft does not exceed 0.002 in. (0.05mm). Camshaft end-play is determined by the shim behind the camshaft timing gear.

5. Try to align the marks on the timing gears dot to dot (or line to dot) prior to removing the gears. If this is not possible, note the correct relative position of the timing gear marks. Remove the hub from the crankshaft with a puller. Remove the crankshaft gear and the camshaft gear with a puller.

Remove the oil jet, blow it clean, and reposition it. Oil fed through this jet lubricates the timing gears.

6. If the camshaft is being replaced, it is necessary to remove the distributor (noting its position), the distributor/oil pump driveshaft, fuel pump, valve cover, rocker shaft and arm assem-

Remove the camshaft gear with a puller—B20 engine

Remove the crankshaft gear with a puller—B30 engine

1. Oil nozzle   2. Markings

Timing gear alignment—B20 engine shown, B30 engine similar

Angle "A"—B20, B30 engines. See camshaft removal text

Four cylinder camshaft press tool installed

bly, pushrods, cylinder head, valve lifters, and the thrust flange. The camshaft may then be pulled out the front.

7. Reverse the above procedure to install. Replace the camshaft if the lobes exhibit excessive or uneven wear. Install the crankshaft and camshaft timing gears, making sure that they align in the correct relative positions.

Do not push the camshaft backward, or the seal washer on the rear end may be forced out. Recheck the tooth flank clearance and the camshaft endplay.

8. Bring no.1 piston to Top Dead Center. Install the distributor/oil pump driveshaft so that the offset position of the distributor slot (angle A) is 35° for the B30A and B30F engines, and 5° for the B20B, B20E and B20F engines.

NOTE: *Make sure that the distributor/oil pump driveshaft seats fully in the slot at the top of the oil pump. If necessary, use a long screwdriver to turn the pump manually until the slot aligns.*

9. When installing the timing case cover, make sure that the drain holes are open. Center the cover with a sleeve. Install the distributor, making sure the rotor points to the no. 1 cylinder position.

10. Install the pulleys and fan. Install the fan (drive) belt and adjust the tension. Refit the radiator hose, close the drain plug, and fill the cooling system.

11. Adjust the ignition timing.

B21, B23 and B230 Engines

WARNING: *The use of the correct special tools or their equivalent is REQUIRED for this procedure.*

1. Remove the timing belt cover and timing belt as outlined in their appropriate sections.

2. Remove the valve cover.

3. Remove the camshaft center bearing cap. Install special camshaft press tool (Volvo #5021) over the center bearing journal to hold

the camshaft in place while removing the other bearing caps.

4. Remove the four remaining bearings caps.

5. Remove the seal from the forward edge of the camshaft.

6. Release camshaft press tool, and lift out the camshaft.

7. Reverse the above procedure to install. The camshaft press tool must be used during reasssembly.

B27F, B28F and B280F

1. Remove the cylinder head as outlined previously.

2. Remove the camshaft rear cover plate.

3. Remove the camshaft retaining fork at the front of the cylinder head.

4. Pull the camshaft out the rear of the head.

5. Reverse the above to install. Tighten the front retaining bolt to 7–11 ft. lbs. and the rear cover bolts to 3.7–5.5 ft. lbs.

Diesel D24, D24T

WARNING: *The use of the correct special tools or their equivalent is REQUIRED for this procedure.*

1. Remove the front and rear timing covers as outlined above. Remove the valve cover.

2. Set No. 1 cylinder on TDC compression stroke. Verify that the flywheel 0 mark is aligned with the pointer on the bell housing. Remove the expansion tank cap.

3. Remove the front camshaft gear belt by loosening the cooling pump retaining bolts to release belt tension. Tighten the two lower retaining bolts to avoid coolant loss. Work the belt off the camshaft gear.

4. Using special wrench 5199 or an equivalent tool, hold the camshaft front timing gear in place and remove the center bolt. Do not allow the camshaft to turn or you may bend several valves.

5. Release the belt shield from the front of the camshaft. If necessary, loosen the upper retaining bolts for the coolant pump. Pull the

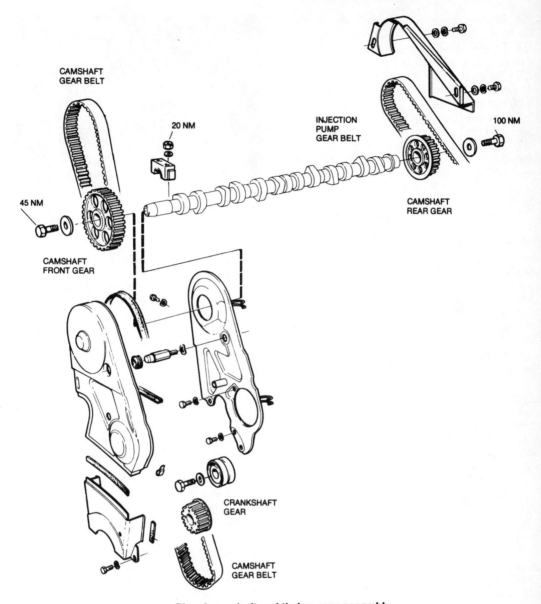

CAMSHAFT
GEAR BELT

20 NM

INJECTION
PUMP
GEAR BELT

100 NM

45 NM

CAMSHAFT
REAR GEAR

CAMSHAFT
FRONT GEAR

CRANKSHAFT
GEAR

CAMSHAFT
GEAR BELT

Diesel camshaft and timing gear assembly

shield out from the camshaft and hold it in this position by jamming a piece of wood between it and the engine.

6. Remove the rear timing belt by loosening the retaining bolts for the injection pump bracket to release belt tension. Slide the belt off the rear timing gear and tighten one of the injection pump mount bolts so that the pump remains in the upper position.

7. Remove the rear gear from the camshaft using wrench 5199 to hold the camshaft from turning. Using wrench 5201 or an appropriate substitute, remove the center bolt and the gear.

8. Remove the vacuum pump and its plunger.

9. Remove camshaft bearing caps 1 and 4.
10. Remove camshaft bearing caps 2 and 3. Lift out the camshaft and remove the seals.
11. Oil the bearing surfaces and install the camshaft in the head. Install gauge 5190 on the camshaft rear end to position the camshaft on the cylinder head. When the camshaft is correctly installed, both cam lobes on No. 1 cylinder should point up at equally large angles.
12. Install camshaft bearing caps 2 and 3. Take note to correctly install the caps, as their centers are staggered. The caps are marked: do not interchange them.
13. Tighten the bearing cap nuts alternately to avoid uneven loadings on the camshaft.

14. Remove gauge 5190. Install new oil seals but do not bottom them in their holders.

15. Install camshaft bearing caps 1 and 4. Fit bearing cap 4 against the thrust bearing.

16. Torque all cap nuts to 15 ft. lbs. Press the oil seals into final position. Use special tool 5200 and the center bolt to install the rear seal, and use tool 5200 and a hammer to tap the front seal into position.

17. Install gauge 5190 in the groove on the camshaft rear end to lock the camshaft in position. Position a 0.008 in. (0.2mm) feeler blade under the left side of the gauge to compensate for clearances in the timing gears.

18. After checking to make sure that the flywheel mark is still at 0 and that the camshaft has not moved, install the new belt and the camshaft front gear. Make sure the belt fits securely on the gears.

Install the center bolt on the camshaft front gear finger tight. The camshaft gear must be able to rotate by itself. The camshaft must not be rotated.

19. Install the lower belt shield and vibration damper. The damper fits only one way. Tighten the damper attaching bolts to 15 ft. lbs.

20. Install the crankshaft center bolt after applying sealer to the threads and contact surfaces. Use wrench 5187 to hold the vibration damper. It can rest on the cooling fan journal. Use wrench 5188 to torque the center bolt to 255 ft. lbs.

NOTE: *This torque applies only if tool 5188 is used. If only a torque wrench is used, torque to 330 ft. lbs.*

21. Verify that No. 1 cylinder is still at TDC.

22. Using the cooling pump movement, adjust the belt tension. Install belt tension gauge 5197 on the belt. Set the gauge to 12.5. Adjust belt tension with the water pump until the mark on the plunger is flush with the gauge sleeve.

23. Press heavily on the belt with your hand

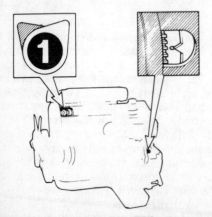

Diesel set no. 1 cylinder on TDC compresssion stroke

Lock camshaft with gauge 5190, then insert 0.008 in. (0.2 mm) feeler gauge under the left side of the gauge

and once again check the belt tension. Adjust if necessary.

24. Using wrench 5199 to hold the gear, tighten the front gear center bolt to 33 ft. lbs. Make sure the camshaft does not rotate.

25. Remove the feeler gauge and the lock gauge at the rear of the engine.

26. Set the injection pump timing as instructed in Chapter 5.

27. Reinstall the front and rear timing gear covers. Reinstall the valve cover.

B234

WARNING: *The use of the correct special tools or their equivalent is REQUIRED for this procedure.*

1. Disconnect the negative battery cable.

2. Remove the alternator drive belt, the radiator fan and its pulley.

3. Remove the upper and lower timing belt covers.

4. Align the camshaft and crankshaft marks. Turn the engine to TDC on cylinder 1 and make sure the pulley marks and the crank marks align align with their matching marks on either the backing plate (cam pulleys) or the belt guide plate (crankshaft).

5. Remove the protective cap over the timing belt tensioner locknut. Loosen the lock nut, compress the tensioner (so as to release tension on the belts) and retighten the locknut, holding the tensioner in place.

6. Remove the timing belt from the camshafts. Do not crease or fold the belt.

WARNING: *The camshafts and the crankshaft MUST NOT be moved when the belt is removed.*

7. Remove the timing belt idler pulleys.

8. Remove the camshaft drive pulleys. Use a counterhold wrench to prevent the cam from turning.

9. Remove the plate or panel behind the pulleys. Remove the cover plate for the ignition

wires. Label and disconnect the ignition wiring from the spark plugs and the distributor cap; remove the coil wire from the distributor cap.

10. Remove the valve cover and gasket. Clean the surfaces of any gasket remains.

11. Remove the distributor housing from the camshaft carrier. Remove the ignition wire clip next to the left bolt.

12. Plug the spark plug holes with crumpled paper. Remove the center bearing cap for each camshaft. Mark the cam bearing caps for proper reinstallation.

13. Install a camshaft press tool, such as Volvo 5021 or similar on the exhaust side cam in place of the removed bearing cap. When it is securely in place, remove the remaining bearing caps and nuts. Remove the tool and remove the exhaust camshaft.

14. Remove the intake camshaft in identical fashion.

WARNING: *Label or identify each cam and its bearing caps. All removed components should be kept in neat order.*

15. Using a magnet or a small suction cup, remove the tappets. Store them upside down (to prevent oil drainage) and keep them in order-- they are not interchangable!

16. Clean and inspect the camshaft carrier and tappet bores for any sign of wear or scoring.

17. Oil all matching surfaces on the cam carrier, bearing caps and tappets.

18. Insert the tappets; they MUST be inserted in their original order and place.

19. Install the exhaust side camshaft by placing it it in the carrier with the pulley guide pin facing up. Using the rear bearing cap as a guide, press the cam into place with the press tool. Install the bearing caps in the original order.

20. Install the bearing cap nuts and tighten them in stages to 15 ft. lbs. Remove the press tool and install the center bearing cap; tighten it in stages to 15 ft. lbs.

21. Install the intake camshaft in the carrier with the pulley guide pin facing upwards.

22. Turn the distributor shaft to align the driver with the markings on the distributor housing. Install new O-rings on the housing and rotor shaft.

23. Using the rear bearing cap as a guide, press the cam into place with the press tool. Install the bearing caps in the original order.

24. Install the bearing cap nuts and tighten them in stages to 15 ft. lbs.

25. Double check the tightness of all the camshaft bearing cap nuts. All should be 15 ft. lbs.; do not overtighten.

26. Reinstall the distributor, connect the coil wire and install the ignition wire clip at the left bolt. Remove the paper plugs from the spark plug holes.

27. Use a silicone sealer and apply to the front and rear camshaft bearing caps. Install new gaskets for the valve cover and the spark plug wells. Install the spark plug gasket with the arrow pointing towards the front of the car and the word **UP** facing up.

Make sure the valve cover gasket is correctly positioned and install the valve cover.

28. Reconnect the ground wire at the distributor.

29. Install the ignition wires and the cover plate.

30. Using a compression seal driver (Volvo tool 5025 or similar), install the oil seals for the front of each camshaft. Camshafts MUST NOT be allowed to turn during this operation.

31. Install the upper backing plate over the ends of the camshafts and adjust the plate so that the cams are centered in the holes.

32. Replace the idler pulleys and tighten their mounts to 18.5 ft. lbs.

33. Install the camshaft drive pulleys, using a counterhold to prevent the cams from turning.

34. Reinstall the camshaft belt by aligning the double line marking on the belt with the top marking on the belt guide plate at the top of the crankshaft. Stretch the belt around the crank pulley and place it over the tensioner and the right side idler.

Place the belt on the camshaft pulleys. The single line marks on the belt should align exactly with the pulley markings. Route the belt around the oil pump drive pulley and press the belt onto the left side idler.

35. Check that all the markings align and that the engine is still positioned at TDC for cylinder 1.

36. Loosen the tensioner locknut.

37. Turn the crankshaft clockwise. The cam pulleys should rotate one full turn until the marks again align with the marks on the backing plate.

WARNING: *The engine must not be rotated counterclockwise during this procedure.*

38. Smoothly rotate the crankshaft further clockwise until the cam pulley markings are 1½ teeth beyond the marks on the backing plate. Tighten the tensioner locknut.

39. Reinstall the fan pulley and fan. Install all the drive belts and connect the battery cable.

40. Double check all installation items, paying particular attention to loose hoses or hanging wires, untightened nuts, poor routing of hoses and wires (too tight or rubbing) and tools left in the engine area.

41. Start the engine and allow it to run until the thermostat opens.

CAUTION: *The upper and lower timing belt covers are still removed. The belt and pulleys are exposed and moving at high speed!*

NOTE: *This engine may be somewhat noisy when started. The noise will subside as oil reaches the tappets. Do not exceed 2500 rpm while the tappets are noisy.*

42. Shut the motor off and bring the motor to TDC on cylinder 1.

43. Check the tension of the camshaft belt. Position the gauge between the right (exhaust) cam pulley and the idler. Belt tension must be 5.5 ±0.2 units.

If the belt needs adjustment, remove the rubber cap over the tensioner locknut and loosen the locknut.

44. Insert a screwdriver between the tensioner wheel and the spring carrier pin to hold the tensioner. If the belt needs to be tightened, move the roller to adjust the tension to 6.0 units. If the belt is too tight, adjust to obtain a reading of 5.0 units on the gauge. Tighten the tensioner locknut and remove the screwdriver.

45. Rotate the crankshaft so that the cam pulleys move through one full revolution and recheck the tension on the camshaft belt. It should now be 5.5 ±0.2 units. Install the plastic plug over the tensioner bolt.

46. Reinstall the remaining belt covers. Start the engine and final check performance.

Intermediate Shaft

REMOVAL AND INSTALLATION

B21, B23 and B230

1. Remove the timing belt cover and the timing belt as explained previously.

2. Remove the hub on the crankshaft, the crankshaft sprocket and the belt guide.

3. Using Volvo tool 5034 to hold the intermediate shaft sprocket, remove the center bolt and pull the sprocket off by hand.

4. Remove the two clamps holding the wiring harness on the bottom of the front cover.

5. Remove the six front bolts on the oil pan.

6. Remove the timing belt guard plate and the front cover.

7. Remove the oil pump drive gear cover and lift out the oil pump drive gear.

8. Pull out the intermediate shaft, being careful not to damage the bearings within the block. When reinstalling, extreme care must be taken to install the shaft without damage to the internal bearing surfaces.

9. Reinstall the oil pump drive gear and its cover.

10. Replace the timing belt guard plate and its cover

11. Install the six front bolts on the oil pan and secure the wiring harness to the bottom of the front cover.

12. Attach the intermediate shaft gear using tool 5034. Install and tighten the center bolt.

Removing intermediate shaft sprocket

Removing intermediate shaft using slide hammer

13. Reinsall the belt guide, the crank gear and the hub on the crankshaft.

14. Install the timing belt and cover as explained in previous sections.

Balance Shafts

REMOVAL AND INSTALLATION

B234 Engine

WARNING: *The use of the correct special tools or their equivalent is REQUIRED for this procedure.*

LEFT SHAFT AND HOUSING.

1. Remove the timing and balance shaft belts as described under Timing Belt Removal and Installation.

2. Use a counterhold such as Volvo tool 5362 and remove the left side balance shaft pulley.

3. Remove the air mass meter and inlet hose.

4. Unfasten the bracket under the intake manifold and remove the bracket holding the alternator and power steering pump. These may be swung out of the way and tied with wire to the left shock tower.

5. Remove the bolts securing the balance shaft housing to the block. Using an extractor

such as Volvo tool 5376 or similar, carefully separate the housing from the block. The housing must be removed evenly from both its front and rear mounts.

6. Clean the joint faces on the cylinder block. Place new O-rings in the grooves around the oil passages on the housing. The rings can be held in place with a light coating of grease.

7. Install the balance shaft housing. Make absolutely sure the housing is evenly mounted on the front and rear mountings. Tighten the bolts alternately in a diagonal pattern. Tighten each bolt ½ turn at a time; tighten them to 15 ft. lbs.

When all the bolts are at 15 ft. lbs., loosen them individually and tighten each one to 7.5 ft. lbs. PLUS 90° of rotation.

WARNING: *Make certain that the shaft does not seize within the housing during installation.*

8. If the halves of the housing were split apart during the repair, tighten the joint bolts to 6 ft. lbs.

9. Install the drive pulley. Use a counterholding tool. Note that the pulley has a slot which will align with the guide on the shaft. The shallow side of the pulley faces inward (toward the engine). Tighten the center bolt for the pulley to 37 ft. lbs.

10. Reinstall the bracket for the alternator and power steering pump. Double check their connections and hoses. Attach the support under the intake manifold and don't forget the wire clamp on the bottom bolt.

11. Install the air mass meter and its intake hose.

12. Install the balance shaft belt and camshaft belt following the procedures outlined under Timing Belt Removal and Installation.

RIGHT SHAFT AND HOUSING

1. Remove the timing and balance shaft belts as described under Timing Belt Removal and Installation.

2. Use a counterhold such as Volvo tool 5362 and remove the left side balance shaft pulley.

3. Remove the balance shaft belt tensioner and remove the bolt running through the backing plate to the balance shaft housing.

4. Remove the air mass meter and its air inlet hose.

5. Remove the air preheat hose from the bottom heat shield at the exhaust manifold. Remove the nuts holding the right engine mount to the crossmember.

6. Connect a hoist or engine lift apparatus to the top of the engine. Lift the engine at the right side, being careful to maintain clearance between the brake master cylinder and the intake manifold.

7. Remove the complete motor mount from the block, including the pad and lower mounting plate.

8. Remove the bolts securing the balance shaft housing to the block. Using an extractor such as Volvo tool 5376 or similar, carefully separate the housing from the block. The housing must be removed evenly from both its front and rear mounts.

9. Clean the joint faces on the cylinder block. Place new O-rings in the grooves around the oil passages on the housing. The rings can be held in place with a light coating of grease.

10. Install the balance shaft housing. Make absolutely sure the housing is evenly mounted on the front and rear mountings. Tighten the bolts alternately in a diagonal pattern. Tighten each bolt ½ turn at a time; tighten them to 15 ft. lbs.

When all the bolts are at 15 ft. lbs., loosen them individually and tighten each one to 7.5 ft. lbs. PLUS 90° of rotation.

WARNING: *Make certain that the shaft does not seize within the housing during installation.*

11. If the halves of the housing were split apart during the repair, tighten the joint bolts to 6 ft. lbs.

12. Install the drive pulley. Use a counterholding tool. Note that the pulley has a slot which will align with the guide on the shaft. The shallow side of the pulley faces inward (toward the engine). Tighten the center bolt for the pulley to 37 ft. lbs.

13. Install the engine mount onto the block.

14. Using the studs on the crossmember as a guide, lower the engine into place on the front crossmember. When the engine is correctly seated, the lifting apparatus may be removed.

15. Reinstall the air mass meter and its air intake hose.

16. Reinstall the motor mount bolts and the air preheat tube at the lower part of the exhaust manifold.

17. Install the bolt through the backing plate and into the balance shaft housing. Reinstall the belt tensioner, tightening the bolt so that the pulley is movable when the belt is in position.

18. Reinstall the balance shaft and camshaft belts as described in Timing Belt Removal and Installation.

Pistons and Connecting rods
REMOVAL
B20, B30, B21, B23, B230 and B234 Engines

This procedure is more easily accomplished with the engine removed from the vehicle and placed on an engine stand.

1. Remove the cylinder head. Remove any ridge and/or carbon deposits from the upper end of the cylinder bores with a ridge reamer.

2. Remove the oil pan. Check connecting rods and pistons for identification numbers and, if necessary, number them.

3. Remove the connecting rod nuts and caps from the crankshaft. Push the rods away from the crankshaft and install the bearing shells, caps, and nuts on the rods to avoid possible interchange of parts.

4. Push the piston and rod assemblies up and out of the cylinders. Remove the rings. Use care not to let the ends of the rods bang against the cylinder walls.

B27F, B28F

NOTE: *Pistons and cylinder liners are sold as a unit.*

1. Remove the engine from the vehicle and remove the cylinder heads. Be sure to hold the liners in place with retainer straps.

2. Remove the 23 holding the front oil pan and remove the oil pan and gasket.

3. Remove the three bolts hoding the oil strainer. Remove the rubber ring from the suction pipe.

4. Remove the front baffle plate.

5. Remove the eight main bearing nuts and all of the lower crankcase bolts and remove the lower crankcase. Remove the rubber ring for the oil channel.

6. Install spacers on the main bearing studs and install the main bearing nuts to hold the main bearing caps in position.

7. Check the markings on the connecting rods and caps; make sure they agree with the markings in the illustration. If not, mark each rod and cap yourself.

8. Remove the nuts and bearing caps and press the connecting rods and pistons out of the cylinders.

Diesel D24, D24T

The best method for engine rebuilding is with the engine removed from the vehicle.

1. Remove the cylinder head and the oil pan.

2. Number the pistons for identification.

Number the connecting rods and their caps for identification.

3. Remove the connecting rod nuts, remove the caps, and push the pistons with connecting rods out of the top of the block.

PISTON AND CONNECTING ROD INSPECTION

1. Inspect the cylinder walls for scoring, roughness, or ridges formed by excessive wear. With an accurate cylinder gauge or inside micrometer, check for cylinder taper and out-of-round at the top, middle, and bottom of the bore. Check in directions parallel and at right angles to the center line of the engine.

Wear is indicated by the difference between the highest and lowest readings. The cylinder is in need of reboring when wear reaches 0.010 in. (0.25mm), or if scoring is evident. Hone or rebore the cylinder for fitting of smallest possible oversized piston and rings. Clearance between the piston and cylinder wall, with the rings removed, should be 0.0008–0.0016 in. (0.02–0.04mm) for the B20 and B30 engines and 0.0004–0.0012 in. (0.01–0.03mm) for the B21/B23/B230/B234 engines.

For the B27 engine equipped with Demolin pistons, clearance should be 0.00315–0.00394 in. (0.08–0.10mm). On the B27/B28/B280 engine equipped with Mahle pistons, clearance should be 0.0008–0.0016 in. (0.02–0.04mm).

2. Check the piston ring endgap by pressing each ring into the cylinder bore and squaring it in the bore with the piston. Insert a feeler gauge into the gap. Check the gap against the specifications given earlier in this chapter. The gap may be widened by filing the ring ends with a thin flat file.

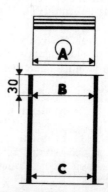

Measuring cylinder taper and wear—B27F, B28F. Measurement "B" is made 30 mm (1.20 in.) from block face. Make several measurements between "B" and "C" (bottom dead center). Measurement "A" is piston diameter

Cylinder number	1	4	2	5	3	6
Marking on connecting rod and cap	A	B	C	D	E	F
Crankshaft crank number, from rear	1		2		3	

Connecting rod marking identification—B27F, B28F engine

B21, B23: ring gap placement

Ring gap placement—B27F, B28F engines

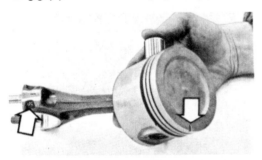

All models—the notch or arrow in the piston top faces the front of the engine. On B21, B23 engines the connecting rod marking faces the front of the engine

3. Clean the ring grooves on the sides of the pistons. With the rings installed in their respective grooves, measure the side clearance at several points around the piston, and check the reading against the specifications. Inspect the ring grooves for wear, especially the upper edge of the chromed top compression ring.

4. The wrist pins on the B20, B30, and B21/B23/B230/B234 engines are removed after the circlips are taken out of the wrist pin bores. The wrist pins should slide out.

The wrist pins on the B27/B28/B280 engine and the diesel must be pressed out using a hydraulic press. On the B27/B28/B280 engine, press the wrist pin in and out in the direction opposite to the arrow on the piston.

When installing, heat the connecting rod to 480°F (249°C). On the B27/B28/B280, once the wrist pin is removed the piston cannot be reused because of deformation. On the diesel engine, remove the circlips, then press out the pin. If the pin is tight, heat the piston to 140°F (60TC).

5. Check the connecting rods for straightness, and check the bushings for excessive wear. The wrist pin should slide through the bushing with light thumb pressure, but without noticeable looseness.

PISTON AND CONNECTING ROD POSITIONING

On all engines, the notch or arrow stamped on top of the piston must face the front of the engine. On B20 and B30 engines, the connecting rod crank end marking must face away from the camshaft side. On the B21/B23/B230/B234, the connecting rod marking must face the front of the engine.

On the B27/B28/B280, the shoulder on the crankshaft end of the connecting rod must point toward the front of the engine for connecting rods marked B, D, or F (for cylinders 4, 5 and 6). The shoulder on the crankshaft end of the connecting rod must face toward the rear end of the engine for connecting rods marked A, C, or E (for cylinder 1, 2 and 3).

For diesel engines, the cast marks on the connecting rod and cap must face toward the oil filter side of the engine.

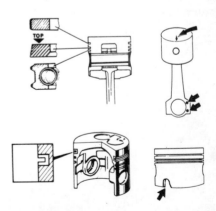

D24 and D24T piston markings. The arrow on the piston crown and marks on the connecting rod big-end denote the front of the engine (must be facing front). The lower compression ring is marked with the word "TOP" to indicate this side must face up.

Cylinder Liners and Seals

REMOVAL AND INSTALLATION

B27, B28 and B280 Series Engines

These models are equipped with wet cylinder liners which are inserted into the block and are sealed off from the coolant jacket by the head gasket and a bottom shim. The tightness of the heads on the block seals the liners. After the pistons have been removed, the liners may be removed from the block. Check the mating surfaces and make sure they are clean and free of defects.

When installing liners, it is very important to obtain the correct liner height above the block. The correct height is 0.0063–0.0091 in. (0.16–0.23mm) with 0.0091 in. (0.23mm) preferred. This height is adjustable by using shims at the bottom of the liner.

Install the new liner in cylinder number one and use the retainer bar finger tight to hold it in place. Measure the liner height at three different locations. Use the highest reading as a basis for calculating the proper shim height. Select a shim which is at or just under the calculated necessary thickness.

Install the same size shim on all liners and install the liners in the motor. The color marking should face upward and be visible when the liner is installed. The tongues on the inside of the shim should fit into the groove in the liner. (In the diagram **A** is the color marking, **B** shows the tongues and **C** indicates the liner groove). Again measure the liner projection above the deck for EACH liner and exchange shims as necessary.

LOWER CRANKCASE INSTALLATION

B27, B28 and B280

After the pistons and connecting rods have been installed, install the rubber ring for the oil channel and apply sealing compound to the block surfaces. Remove the main bearing nuts and the spacers and make certain that none of the studs have come loose.

Position the lower crankcase in place and install all nuts and bolts but do not tighten. Make sure that lower crankcase and the block are flush at the rear of the block to prevent warapage of the flywheel casing. Tighten the eight main bearing nuts to 22 ft. lbs. in the sequence shown in the illustration. Loosen nut no. 1 in the illustration then tighten it to 22–25 ft. lbs.

Install a protractor attachment to the torque wrench socket and set up a stationary pointer for reference. Tighten nut No.1 to 73–77° according to the protractor on the socket. Repeat this procedure with nuts 2, 3, 4, 5, 6, 7 and 8 in the illustration in that order. Tighten all of the attaching bolts in lower crankcase except the rear seal retainer bolts to 11–15 ft. lbs. Tighten the rear seal retainer bolts to 7–11 ft. lbs.

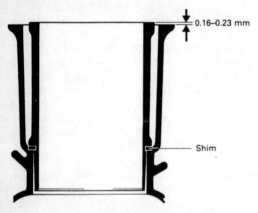

Relationship of cylinder liner, shim and block

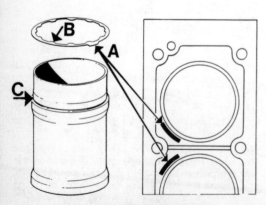

Correct placement of cylinder liner shim

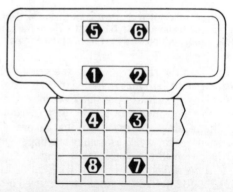

B27F, B28F and B280F lower crankcase main bearing torque sequence

Rear Main Oil Seal

REMOVAL AND INSTALLATION

All Models

1. Remove the transmission, clutch (if so equipped), and flywheel (match mark with crankshaft) from the engine. Remove the two pan bolts from the bottom of the sealing flange on all models except the diesel, and loosen two more on each side so that the pressure on the sealing flange is reduced.

2. On B20, B30, and B21 engines, remove the sealing flange retaining bolts and pull off the sealing flange and old gasket. Press out the sealing ring in the flange with a drift. On the B20 with felt ring type seal, remove the circlip and washer first.

3. For all other models, including the diesel, use a screwdriver to pry the rear seal out of the flange. Do not remove the flange from the engine and use caution not to damage surfaces on flange (holder) or crankshaft. For the B23/B230/B234 family, note the position of the seal in relation to the flange; the new seal must be reinstalled in the same position.

4. Make sure the sealing surfaces of the flange are clean. Also, make sure that the oil drain hole is not blocked by the oil pan gasket.

5. On the B20 with rubber seal, and all other engines, oil and install the oil seal in the flange. This job is correctly done with a seal driver of the proper diameter. Volvo has several special tools available for this purpose (tool numbers vary by engine application); similar tools are available from reliable retail suppliers. If buying tools, make sure the set includes the diameter you

need for the particular job at hand.

NOTE: *When installing the oil seal in the flange on the B30 engine, if you have access to Volvo tool 2817, the oil seal can be installed in three different positions according to crankshaft wear. On a new or unworn crankshaft, fit the seal in its outer position (the center bolt in the tool fully screwed in). On a worn crankshaft, fit the seal with the center bolt in the tool screwed out a couple of turns or completely.*

The seals for the B23/B230/B234 can also be sized by removing the appropriate spacer rings before installation; to do this, the use of Volvo tool 5276 is required.

On the B20 engine with felt seal, install and center the flange on the engine (Tool 2439) then check that the flange is flush against the under side of the block and fit a new felt ring, washer and circlip. Make sure the circlip is engaged in its groove. On the diesel, oil and install the rear seal in the

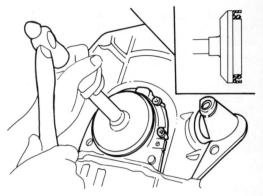

Installing rear crankshaft seal with Volvo special tools. D24T shown, others similar

flange, being careful not to damage the seal lip.

6. Using gentle force, tap the seal in until the installing tool abuts the crankshaft.

7. Install and tighten such oil pan bolts as were loosened for access.

8. Reinstall flywheel (or flexplate for automatic trans), observing proper placement onto crankshaft. Carefully observe placement of any shims, washers or locking hardware involved. Tighten the bolts in a diagonal pattern as follows:

- B21/B23/B230/B234 engines: 50 ft. lbs.
- B27/B28/B280 engines: 35 ft. lbs.
- D24/D24T engines: 55 ft. lbs.

9. Reinstall clutch assembly if so equipped.

10. Reinstall the transmission.

Crankshaft and Main Bearings

REMOVAL AND INSTALLATION

NOTE: *This procedure requires the removal of the engine from the vehicle and placement on an engine stand. It cannot be done with the motor in the car.*

1. Follow the procedures under piston and connecting rod removal in this section.

2. Remove the pressure plate and clutch disc or, if automatic transmission, the flexplate. Loosen the bolts diagonally, a few turns at a time, to prevent warping. It will be necessary to lock the flywheel (or flexplate) in position while loosening its retaining bolts. Matchmark the flywheel and crankshaft before disassembly so that the parts may be reconnected in the same relationship.

3. Remove the rear sealing flange and the front cover plate from the block.

4. Check the main bearing caps for identification numbers and, if necessary, number them.

5. Unbolt and remove the main bearing caps and lift the crankshaft out of the block. You are reminded that the crankshaft is a heavy component.

NOTE: *Do not interchange bearing shells and caps.*

6. Remove the bearings from the main caps and the block.

7. Installation is the reverse of the removal procedures taking note of the following:

a. Make sure that matched bearing pairs are installed together.

b. The holes in the bearing shells must coincide with the oilways in the engine block.

c. Check the bearing clearances with Plastigage.

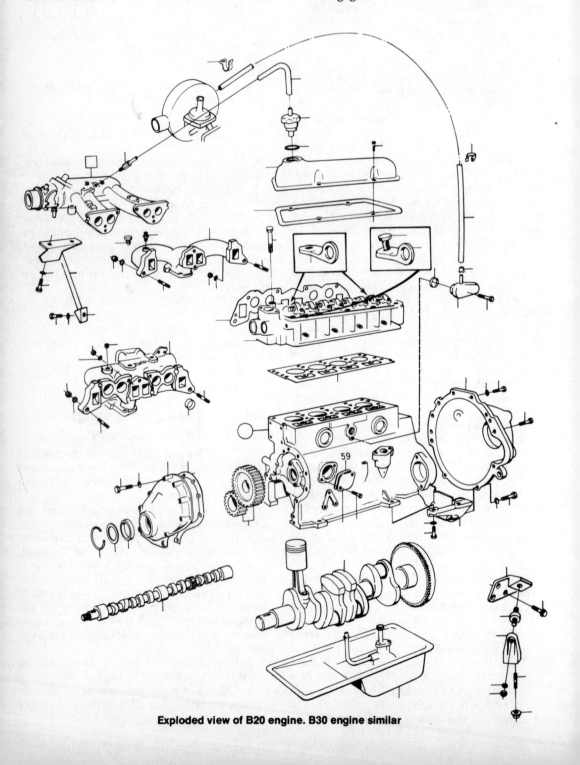

Exploded view of B20 engine. B30 engine similar

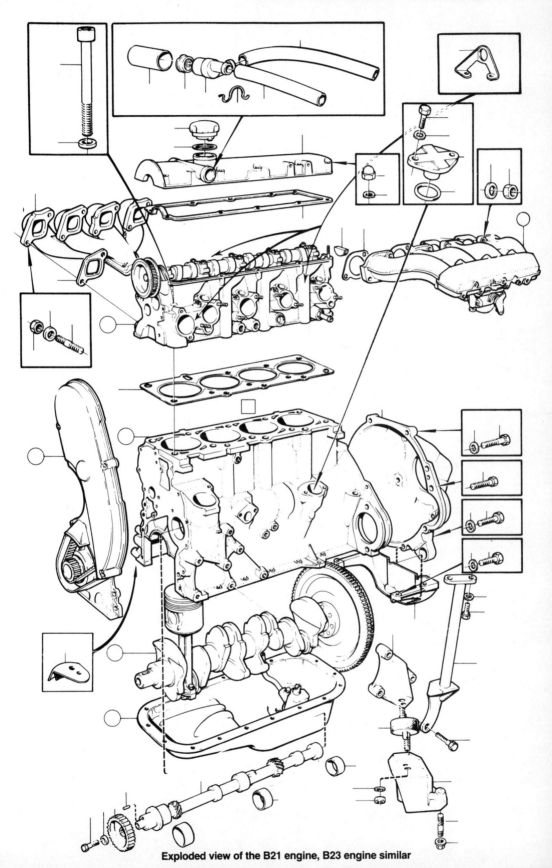

Exploded view of the B21 engine, B23 engine similar

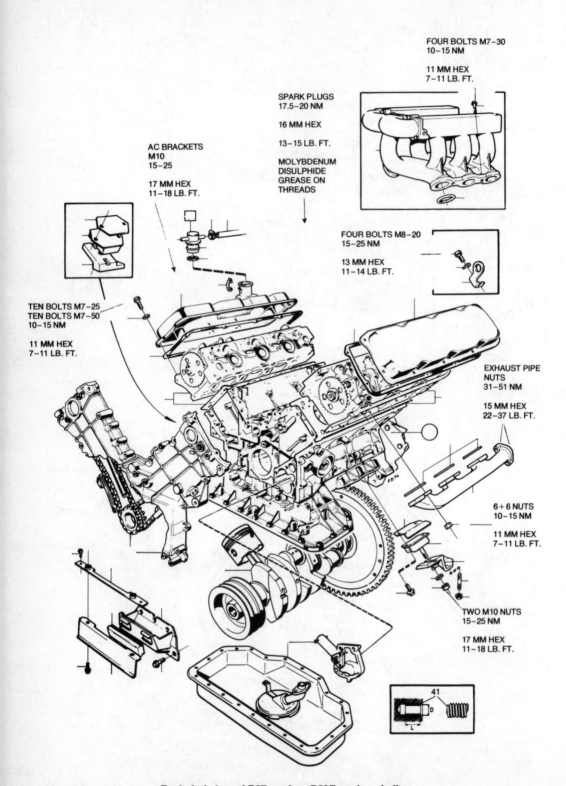

FOUR BOLTS M7–30
10–15 NM

11 MM HEX
7–11 LB. FT.

SPARK PLUGS
17.5–20 NM

16 MM HEX

13–15 LB. FT.

MOLYBDENUM
DISULPHIDE
GREASE ON
THREADS

AC BRACKETS
M10
15–25

17 MM HEX
11–18 LB. FT.

FOUR BOLTS M8–20
15–25 NM

13 MM HEX
11–14 LB. FT.

TEN BOLTS M7–25
TEN BOLTS M7–50
10–15 NM

11 MM HEX
7–11 LB. FT.

EXHAUST PIPE
NUTS
31–51 NM

15 MM HEX
22–37 LB. FT.

6+6 NUTS
10–15 NM

11 MM HEX
7–11 LB. FT.

TWO M10 NUTS
15–25 NM

17 MM HEX
11–18 LB. FT.

41

Exploded view of B27 engine. B28F engine similar

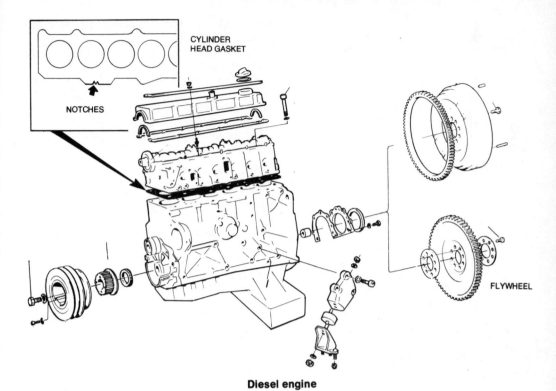

Diesel engine

d. Lubricate the bearing shells and bearing surfaces on the crankshaft.

e. Torque the main bearing caps to specification and check the crankshaft end play.

CRANKSHAFT CLEANING AND INSPECTION

1. Clean the oilways in the crankshaft with a piece of wire and blow them out with compressed air. Also check and clean the sealing surfaces on the crankshaft.

2. Measure out-of roundness and taper of crank pins (journals). Use a micrometer and take measurements at several different positions. Maximum out-of-round is 0.0003 in.

Checking crankshaft end play

(0.008mm) and the maximum taper is 0.0004 in.(0.01mm).

Crank pins can be ground to a smaller size. Regrinding should be perfomed by a competent machine shop.

3. If a warped crankshaft is suspected, it should be checked with a dial indicator. Support the crankshaft by the two outer main bearing journals on V-blocks. Rotate the crankshaft one turn and measure the out-of-true for the two center crankpins. Maximum warpage is 0.02mm (0.0008 in.).

CHECKING THE BEARING CLEARANCE

Invert the engine on its stand and remove the cap from the bearing to be checked. Using a clean dry rag, thoroughly clean all oil from crankshaft journal and bearing insert.

NOTE: *Plastigage® is soluble in oil; any oil on the journal or bearing could result in erroneous readings.*

Place a piece of Plastigage® along the full length of journal, reinstall cap, and torque to the specifications given in the chart earlier in this chapter.

Remove bearing cap, and determine bearing clearance by comparing the width of Plastigage® to the scale on Plastigage® envelope. Journal taper is determined by comparing width of the Plastigage® strip near its ends. Ro-

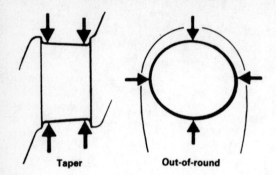

Taper   Out-of-round

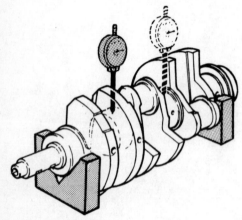

Checking crankshaft journals

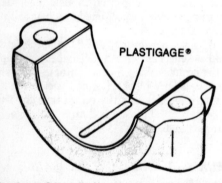

PLASTIGAGE®

Plastigage® installed on the lower bearing shell

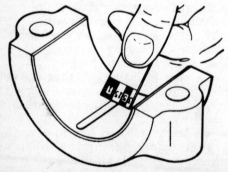

Measure Plastigage® to determine main bearing clearance

tate crankshaft 90° and retest, to determine journal eccentricity.

NOTE: *Do not rotate crankshaft with Plastigage® installed.*

If bearing insert and journal appear intact and are within tolerances, no further main bearing service is required. If bearing or journal appear defective, cause of failure should be determined and repaired before replacement and reassembly.

Flywheel and Ring Gear
REMOVAL AND INSTALLATION

The ring gear is contacted by the starter gear during engine start up. If any damage is found on the ring gear (broken or chipped teeth, cracks, etc.) the cause of the failure should be identified and repaired. The starter should be checked as a possible cause.

On vehicles with automatic transmission, the ring gear is an integral part of the flexplate and cannot be replaced. On vehicles with manual gearboxes, the ring gear on the flywheel can be removed and replaced. This replacement involves heating the ring to 450°F, and handling the heated ring. It is usually found to be easier to buy a complete flywheel and ring gear assembly than to attempt the replacement. If you posess the proper equipment for heating and handling the ring gear, the procedure is as follows:

1. Remove the transmission.
2. Remove the clutch plate and disc.
3. Remove the bolts attaching the flywheel to the crankshaft flange. Remove the flywheel.
4. Inspect the flywheel for cracks, and inspect the ring gear for burrs or worn teeth. Replace the flywheel or ring gear if any damage is apparent. Remove burrs with a mill file.
5. To replace a ring gear use the following steps.

    a. Use a 10mm drill and drill a hole between two cogs (teeth) on the ring gear, being careful not to drill into the flywheel.

    b. Mount the flywheel in a vise protected by soft jaws and split the ring gear at the hole with a chisel.

    c. Heat the new ring gear to approximately 450°F. When handling the heated ring, wear heavy gloves and use tongs.

    d. Position the ring gear with the bevelled side facing the flywheel.

    e. Use a brass drift and tap the ring gear until flush. Allow to air cool before installation; do not attempt to cool the metal with water, oil or other fluids.

6. Install the flywheel. Install the bolts and torque to specification.

EXHAUST SYSTEM

Removal and Installation

GENERAL

The exhaust system serves to conduct and silence the flow of hot gasses out of the engine. While it appears to be simple plumbing, the science of exhaust flow is quite complex. Pipe diameter, bend radius, manifold design and internal structure of components all play a part in the efficient extraction of exhaust gasses.

When performing repairs on the exhaust system, it is important to use replacement parts which are virtually identical to the originals. Failure to do so may result in impaired or restricted function and/or a host of body rattles caused by improperly mounted pipes hitting the undercarriage.

The exhaust system is generally mounted in such a way as to be insulated from the body of the car. Many rubber hangers, washers and bushings are used to reduce noise and vibration. Their placement should be accurately noted during removal so that they can be properly reinstalled. If any rubber component has lost its flexibility, it should be replaced.

Working on an exhaust system is a project of mixed emotions; being held together simply with nuts and bolts, and generally having easy access, one could lulled into thinking it a simple job. On any car more than a year old, those simple nuts and bolts have rusted solid from both heat and water. Joints have solidified and the entire system has become brittle. Chances are high that if one component has rusted through, its adjoining pieces are suspect.

Arm yourself in advance. Have a healthy supply of rust penetrant and rags on hand. In addition to the proper assortment of wrenches, you'll need good eye protection, gloves, a hammer, probably a cold chisel and possibly a small pry bar. On very old systems, it is sometimes easier to simply chisel the end off the bolt and replace it than to attempt to loosen the nut. New hardware and gaskets are always recommended during any exhaust repair.

Since exhaust systems vary by engine design, fuel system and country of sale, it would be impossible to describe each component and system. Several representative diagrams have been included, showing component placement and hook up. To remove the complete system, follow the general rules below:

CAUTION: *Only work on the exhaust system when ALL components are cool to the touch. Catalytic converters can develop surface temperatures of 300°. Always wear eye protection and gloves. Make sure the car is properly supported on jackstands.*

1. Work from the front joint to the rear. If the system hangs at the rear, it can create enough force to crack or damage the exhaust manifold. In general the manifold pipe connects to the exhaust pipe near the transmission case. Loosen and disconnect the bracket holding the exhaust to the transmission case, then disconnect the joint at the manifold pipe.

2. Working towards the rear of the car, disconnect the various hangers and mounts until the complete system is free of the car. Remove the system from under the car; it is easier to work on specific pipe joints with the system removed.

3. Perform necessary replacements or repairs. Carefully observe the placement of all seal and gaskets when disassembling. Safe and quiet operation depends on these seals being properly installed.

4. When reassembling any joint, the use of new gaskets, seals and hardware is highly recommended. Reassemble the entire system and place it under the car.

5. Lift the system to the underside of the car and connect one or two of the hangers, allowing the system to swing as necessary.

6. Again working from front to rear, secure the joint at the exhaust manifold and progress

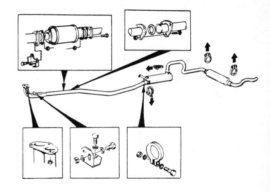

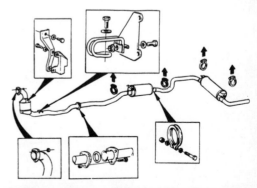

Exhaust systems on B21 and B23 engines. Upper: A, E and F models. Lower: ET and FT (turbocharged) models

towards the rear of the car, installing the hangers and clamps.

7. Constantly check for pipe to body interference; remember that the system is not rigidly mounted and must be free to move under the car. Minimum clearance to any body part should be ⅜ inch, with ½–¾ inch preferred where possible.

8. It may be necessary to adjust the length of the system for proper fit. Do this by loosening the clamp at one of the pipe joints at the muffler or resonator (pre-muffler) and telescoping the pipe in or out as needed. Don't forget to retighten the clamp when the proper length is achieved.

9. After the system is installed, lower the car from its elevated position. Start the engine and check for rattles and exhaust leaks. A quick check for system leaks is to protect your palm with a folded rag and place it over the end of the

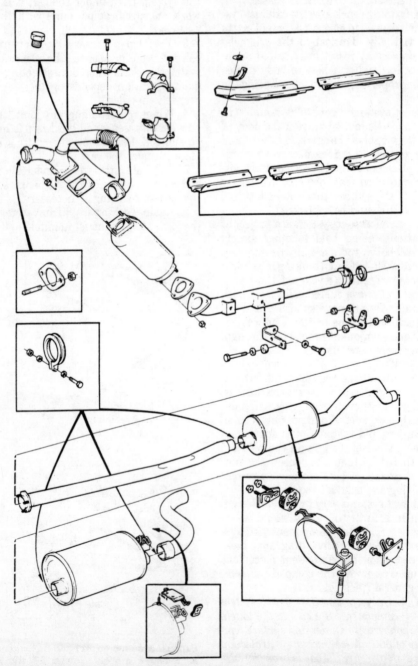

B28F exhaust system. Heat shields shown in upper right of illustration are not found on all models

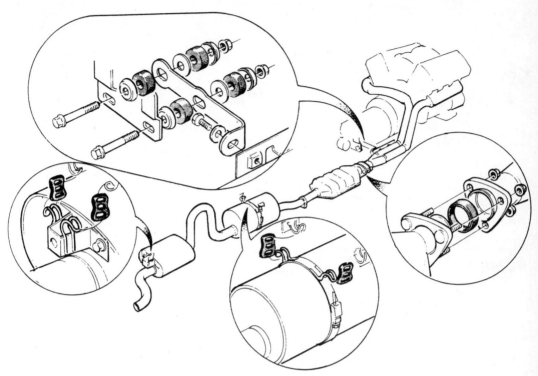

Exhaust system, B280F. Note the extensive use of rubber hangers and insulators

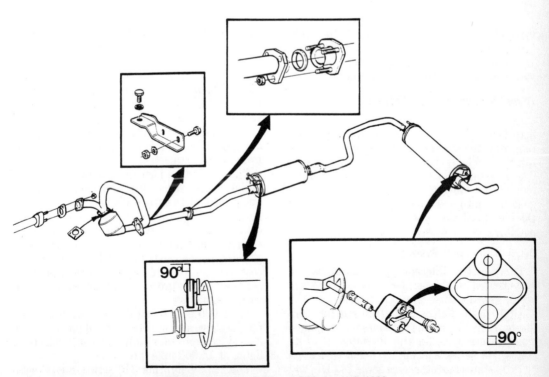

Exhaust system, B27 and B28 through 1983

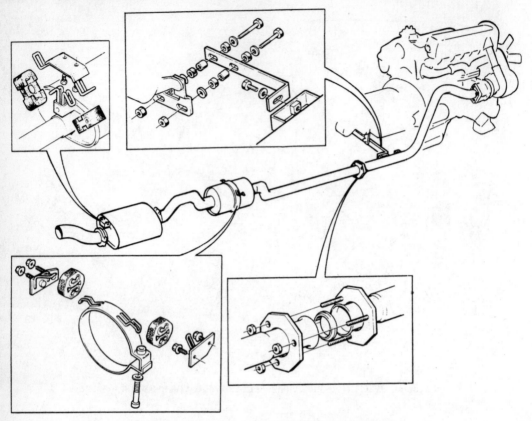

Exhaust system and muffler, D24T. D24 similar

exhaust pipe, blocking the flow. An air tight system will develop enough pressure to push your hand away very quickly. If there's a leak, you'll be able to hear a hissing under the car.

COMPONENT REPLACEMENT

As a rule, if any component is attached at both ends, it's easier to remove the entire system from the car and do the repair where you can see it. The rear muffler can be removed by disconnecting it at the pipe joint and then removing the hanger(s). Remember to use new gaskets and hardware when reassembling. Double check the muffler and eliminate any possible contact with the undercarriage.

Catalytic Converter System

There are two different types of catalytic converters used on Volvos: the oxidation type converter and the three way converter.

All 1975–76 Volvos manufactured for California, 1975 164 models with manual transmission and overdrive for the 49 states, 1977 49 states 240 series and all 1977 260 series, all 1978 49 states models except some 242 DL, 242 GT and 262 C models, and all 1979 49 states

240 models except the 242 GT are equipped with the oxidation type converter.

The converters are installed in these vehicles to further control emissions of carbon monoxide and hydrocarbons which have resisted the treatment of the air injection system. The converter is installed in the exhaust system ahead of the muffler. The converter uses platinum and palladium metals in a substrate or beaded form as the catalyst.

The catalyst and the oxygen supplied by the air pump then react with the exhaust gases producing harmless carbon dioxide and water vapor, as well as a minute amount of sulphur dioxide or sulphuric acid. The converter is designed to last 50,000 miles as long as leaded gasoline is not used. The lead in gasoline will coat the catalytic substrate or beads, preventing the reaction process and rendering the converter ineffective.

At 15,000 mile intervals, the retaining bolts for the converter must be checked for tightness. A service reminder light on the dashboard lights at 15,000 mile intervals.

The 1977 California 240 series, all 1978–80 260 California series, all 1979 49 states 260 series, all 1980 and later (except Diesel) models and the 1979 49 states 242 GT are equipped with three way catalytic converters.

The purpose of the three way catalytic converter is to neutralize carbon monoxide, hydrocarbons and oxides of nitrogen in the exhaust gases. The main difference between this catalytic converter and the oxidation converter is that the three way coverter is able to process large amounts of oxides of nitrogen (NOx), while the oxidation catalyst cannot.

As with the oxidation catalytic converter, the use of leaded fuel or fuel additives in the engine will render the three way catalyst ineffective.

Emission Controls

EMISSION CONTROLS

On gasoline engines, there are three sources of automotive pollutants: crankcase fumes, exhaust gasses, and gasoline evaporation. The pollutants formed from these substances fall into three categories: unburnt hydrocarbons (HC), carbon monoxide (CO), and oxides of nitrogen (NOx). The equipment used to limit these pollutants is called emission control equipment. This equipment ranges from the inherent internal design of the motor (combustion chamber, heads, valves, camshaft, etc) to external additive pieces such as temperature activated vacuum valves, solenoids, relays and computers. As the emission laws of the US and other nations become stiffer, emission control systems change year to year to maintain the required balance of vehicle performance and driveability as well as reduced emissions.

Due to varying state, federal, and provincial regulations, specific emission control equipment has been devised for each of the three pollutants. The U.S. emission equipment is divided into two categories: California and 49 State. In this section, the term: "California" applies only to cars originally built to be sold in California. California emissions equipment is generally not shared with equipment installed on cars built to be sold in the other 49 States. In 1986, Volvo began phasing out the California designation; in 1987, all cars sold were "50 state" certified, although some models built to be sold in Canada remained different from US versions.

Since diesel engines use a completely different principle of combustion (compression fired rather than spark fired), almost all of the emission control is designed into the construction of the engine. While diesel exhaust is more visible, it actually contains fewer atmospheric pollutants than a gasoline engine's exhaust. The great bulk of diesel exhaust is particulate carbon-soot-which quickly settles out of the air.

The only serviceable emission control on the diesel engine is the positive crankcase ventilation hose located between the valve cover and the intake manifold.

Positive Crankcase Ventilation (PCV) System

OPERATION

Blow-by gasses, combustion gasses that squeeze past the piston rings, tend to collect in the bottom of the engine and, if not vented, will build pressure inside the crankcase until they force their way out. These gasses usually exit through a gasket or an oil seal, creating an oil leak. On older cars, a simple breather pipe was used to vent the blow-by gasses into the atmosphere. This method cannot be used today because blow-by gasses are air pollutants.

On all of the Volvos covered in this book, a PCV system is used which routes the blow-by gasses into the air cleaner or intake manifold

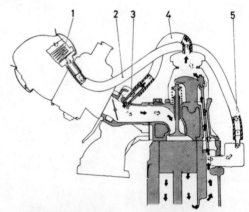

1. Air cleaner insert
2. Hose
3. Nipple
4. Hose
5. Flame guard

PCV system—B20B shown

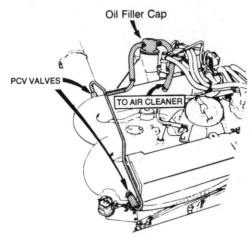

PCV system—B27F shown. B28F similar

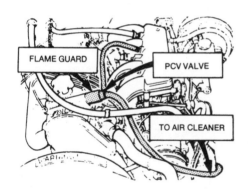

PCV system—B21F

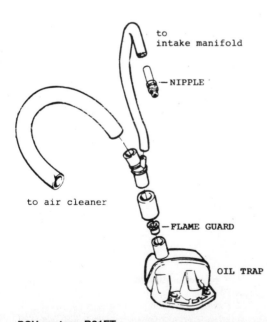

PCV system, B21FT

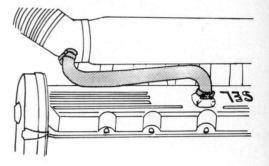

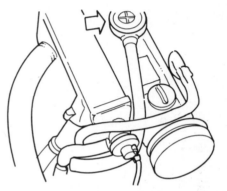

Diesel PCV systems. Upper, D24. Lower, D24 Turbo

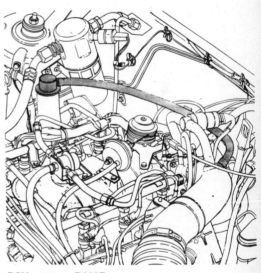

PCV system, B280F

where they are burned with the air/fuel mixture.

SERVICING THE PCV SYSTEM

Although the gasses build up at the bottom of the engine, the pressure is distributed throughout the inside of the engine. It is easiest to vent them at the top of the motor and conduct them back to the air intake system. For this reason,

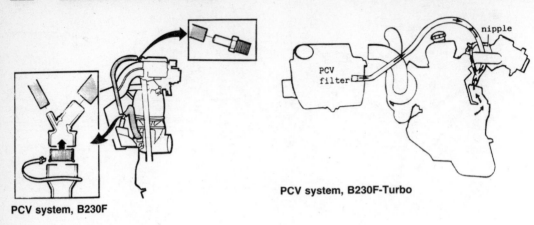

PCV system, B230F

PCV system, B230F-Turbo

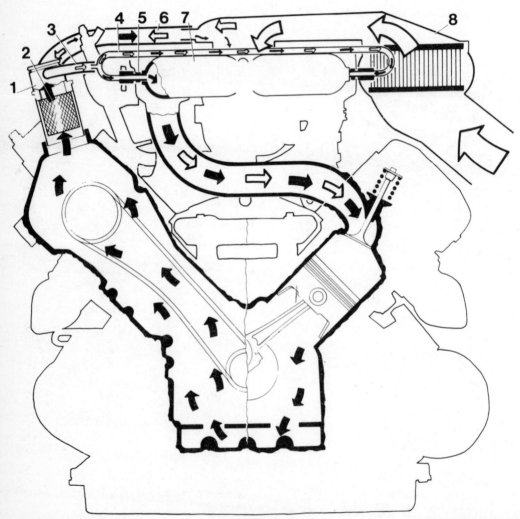

1. Oil trap
2. Flame guard
3. Hose, channeling crankcase fumes
   to the intake manifold
4. Distributor pipe
5. Nipple with orifice

6. Hose, channeling:
   —fresh air from the air cleaner to the
   crankcase (idle)
   —crankcase fumes to the air cleaner
   (cruising speeds)

7. Intake manifold.
8. Air cleaner.

Crankcase ventilation system—B27F, B28F and B280F engines

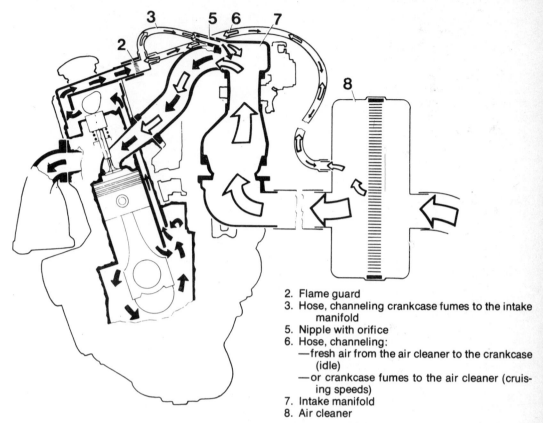

2. Flame guard
3. Hose, channeling crankcase fumes to the intake
   manifold
5. Nipple with orifice
6. Hose, channeling:
   —fresh air from the air cleaner to the crankcase
   (idle)
   —or crankcase fumes to the air cleaner (cruising speeds)
7. Intake manifold
8. Air cleaner

Crankcase ventilation system—B21, B23 and B230 engines

look for the hoses which run to the valve cover(s) on top of the motor. They are usually found close to the oil filler cap.

Carefully remove the hoses from their fittings one at a time. You are dealing with plastic and/or rubber hoses which have been subjected to engine heat and fumes; they may be brittle or stuck in place. Make sure all hoses and PCV valve nipples are clean and not damaged. Check hoses for blockage and make sure the flame protector, found on some cars after 1983, is not blocked. Replace any torn or disintegrating hoses with heat treated, preferably factory replacement, hose. The PCV nipple(s) in the intake manifold, the flame guard and the oil trap should be removed and cleaned every 12,000-15,000 miles on cars so equipped. The PCV nipple may need replacement at 60,000 miles.

Evaporative Control System (Charcoal Canister)

OPERATION

All post-1969 model Volvos are equipped with an evaporative control system to prevent fuel vapors in the fuel tank and (in carbureted mod-

els) the float chambers from escaping into the atmosphere. An expansion tank above the fuel tank provides for thermal expansion of fuel vapors in warm weather. Those vapors which do not condense and return to the fuel tank are

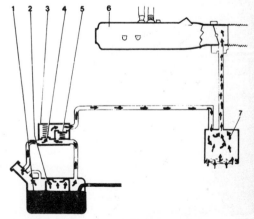

1. Fuel tank
2. Expansion tank
3. Inlet duct
4. Venting filter
5. Pressure reduction valve
6. Inlet manifold
7. Charcoal canister

Fuel evaporative system—fuel injection engines

displaced and drawn into an activated charcoal canister in the engine compartment.

When the engine is at idle or is shut off, the charcoal canister absorbs and stores the vapors from both the tank and the carburetor. Throttling the engine causes the vapors to be drawn out of the canister into the air/fuel mixture bound for the engine. The vapors enter the engine through the intake manifold and are burned in the combustion chambers.

On carbureted models, the float chamber vapors are diverted from the canister to the air cleaner upon acceleration. As a result of these fumes being vented to the air cleaner, an overly rich (proportionally too much fuel for the amount of air present) fuel mixture may develop, leading to starting difficulties-especially in warm weather. A hot-start valve is located between the float chamber and the air cleaner on carbureted models which returns the vapors to the charcoal canister until the engine can handle the extra-rich mixture.

On 1974 and later models, the expansion tank was relocated inside the fuel tank and an equalizing or balance valve is used to regulate pressure buildup in the fuel tank. When the expanding fuel vapors create too much pressure in the tank, the valve opens and allows the vapors to be fed into the charcoal canister. When too much vacuum is present in the fuel tank (due to sudden cooling or low fuel level) a second valve opens and allows air from the venting filter back into the fuel tank to prevent the tank from collapsing. The equalizing valve also prevents fuel from entering the vapor line during hard cornering.

SERVICE

The charcoal canister is located in the engine compartment on all models except the 1800E and 1800ES, on which the canister is located under the left front fender.

On 1970-73 models the canister has a removable foam plastic filter in the bottom which should be replaced every 24,000 miles. The filter is exposed and can be removed from the bottom of the canister when the canister is removed from the car. On 1974 and later models, the entire canister should be replaced every 45,000-48,000 miles, depending on the model and year of the vehicle.On models built after 1979, the canister is non–servicable and requires no maintenance, other than checking lines for kinks or obstructions. If the car has experienced a severe fuel–related problem (continued flooding, polluted or incorrect fuel,etc.) the cannister may need to be replaced. It cannot be cleaned or reconditioned.

Before attempting to remove or service any of

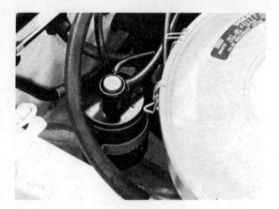

Fuel evaporative control canister—1975 164 shown

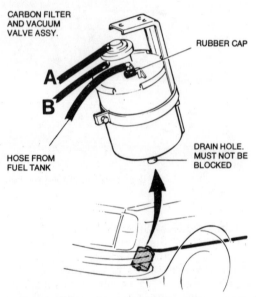

Fuel evaporative control canister—1980 and later models

the charcoal canisters, label each hose and its matching port. Hose placement is critical to the proper operation of the motor. Make sure hoses are reinstalled in their proper place and held firmly with clamps.

To remove the canister on 1970-73 models, disconnect the hoses from the top and side of the canister, loosen the canister bracket bolt and slide the canister out. On 1974 and later models, pull the valve with its hose off the top of the canister, remove the other hoses (if equipped), loosen the clamp screw and slide the canister out of its bracket.

The hoses should be routinely checked for cracks, kinks and restrictions. The ends of the vacuum hoses can become brittle and leak at their connections. The lines to the fuel tank should also be checked periodically for any crushing or kinking under the car, and always after any impact to the underside of the car from solid objects or ice.

Exhaust Gas Recirculation (EGR) System

OPERATION

In order to control emission of NOx, all 1973-74 140 series, and 164E and 1800ES models with automatic transmissions, as well as all 240, 260 series and the 1975 164 were equipped with an exhaust gas recirculation system. 1980 and later USA models are not equipped with EGR systems.

The system consists of a metering valve (EGR valve), a pipe running from the exhaust manifold to the EGR valve, another pipe running from the valve to the intake manifold, and a vacuum hose running from the EGR valve's diaphragm to the intake manifold in front of the throttle valve(s). The valve permits a regulated amount of exhaust gas to enter the inlet duct and mix with the incoming air/fuel mixture.

The only way the EGR valve will open is when vacuum is applied through its vacuum hose. When vacuum is applied, it raises a diaphragm inside the EGR valve. This diaphragm is connected to a plunger inside the EGR valve housing. When the plunger is open, it allows exhaust gases to pass through the pipe between the valve and the intake manifold. When the exhaust gases mix with the air/fuel charge in the combustion chamber, they act to slightly slow the rapid combustion process and lower the overall combustion chamber temperature. This lower combustion temperature prevents the formation of oxides of nitrogen (NOx).

On 1974-75 B20 engines, 1976 B21 and B27 models sold in California and all later models with EGR valves, the EGR system is modified to improve cold start driveability by the addition of a venturi vacuum amplifier system.

The EGR system with vacuum amplifier works as follows: Venturi vacuum at the air intake is used to measure the total air flow. This weak vacuum signal controls the vacuum amplifier which regulates the EGR valve via a solenoid valve. The vacuum amplifier receives inputs both from the strong intake manifold source which is used as a power source, and from the weak air intake source which is to be amplified. The intake vacuum is stored in the vacuum reservoir and is controlled by a check valve in the amplifier. This allows a generous amount of vacuum on tap regardless of variations in engine manifold vacuum.

The amplifier then continues to supply ade-

EGR valve installed—B20F shown, B30F similar

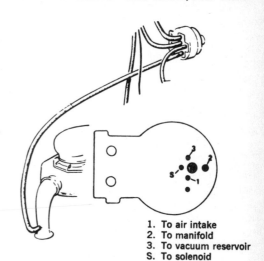

1. To air intake
2. To manifold
3. To vacuum reservoir
S. To solenoid

Vacuum amplifier—B20

quate vacuum at higher speeds and moderate throttle openings, when manifold vacuum normally would drop to an insufficient amount. The EGR system functions as before, except that the exhaust gases are prevented from recirculating at idle and full throttle by a throttle angle sensing micro-switch and an electrically operated solenoid valve, rather than simple vacuum as in 1973. On 1976 and later models, a wax thermostat blocks exhaust gas recirculation until the engine warms to 140°F.

Beginning with the 1975 model year, all Volvos equipped with an EGR system have a reminder light which is actuated by the odometer at 15,000 mile intervals. The light may be reset by pressing a white button at the rear of the odometer.

NOTE: *Models equipped with the Lambda Sond oxygen sensor system do not have EGR valves. 1978-80 California models and 1980 and later 49 states models are not equipped with EGR valves.*

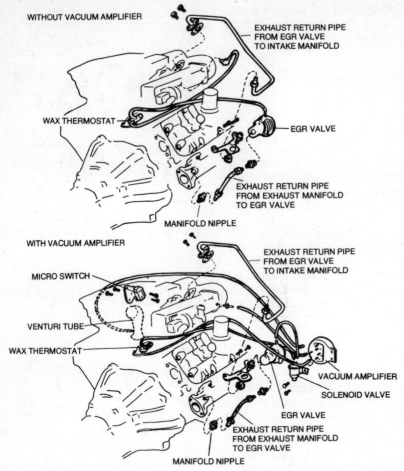

WITHOUT VACUUM AMPLIFIER

EXHAUST RETURN PIPE
FROM EGR VALVE
TO INTAKE MANIFOLD

WAX THERMOSTAT

EGR VALVE

EXHAUST RETURN PIPE
FROM EXHAUST MANIFOLD
TO EGR VALVE

MANIFOLD NIPPLE

WITH VACUUM AMPLIFIER

MICRO SWITCH

EXHAUST RETURN PIPE
FROM EGR VALVE
TO INTAKE MANIFOLD

VENTURI TUBE

WAX THERMOSTAT

VACUUM AMPLIFIER

SOLENOID VALVE

EGR VALVE

EXHAUST RETURN PIPE
FROM EXHAUST MANIFOLD
TO EGR VALVE

MANIFOLD NIPPLE

B27F, B28F EGR system. Top, without vacuum amplifier; below, with vacuum amplifier

SERVICE

Every 12 months or 12,000 miles (1973-74) or 15,000 miles (1975-83), the system must be checked and cleaned. Every 24 months or 24,00 miles (1973-74) or 30,000 miles (1975-83) the EGR must be replaced.

CHECKING EGR VALVE OPERATION

1973 Models
1975 164

The EGR valve and piping conducts exhaust gasses; for this reason, the system components are exposed to high temperatures, corrosion and soot. It is not uncommon for an EGR valve to become plugged with carbon. When this happens, the valve cannot close completely. Since there are times that recirculation is not desirable, having the valve stick open causes a variety of driveability problems including poor mileage, lack of power and rough idle. Checking the EGR valve and replacing it on schedule

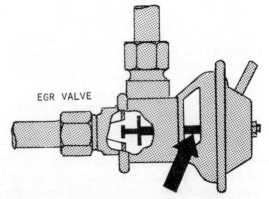

EGR VALVE

Check to see if the rod inside the EGR valve moves in and out

should be a part of your routine maintenance plan.

With the engine warmed up and idling, remove the EGR vacuum hose from the valve and plug it (a wooden golf tee works well), then ap-

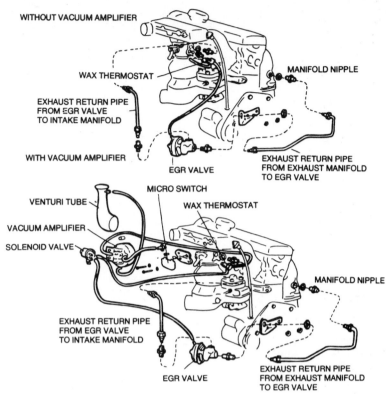

WITHOUT VACUUM AMPLIFIER

WAX THERMOSTAT

MANIFOLD NIPPLE

EXHAUST RETURN PIPE
FROM EGR VALVE
TO INTAKE MANIFOLD

WITH VACUUM AMPLIFIER

EGR VALVE

EXHAUST RETURN PIPE
FROM EXHAUST MANIFOLD
TO EGR VALVE

MICRO SWITCH

VENTURI TUBE

WAX THERMOSTAT

VACUUM AMPLIFIER

SOLENOID VALVE

MANIFOLD NIPPLE

EXHAUST RETURN PIPE
FROM EGR VALVE
TO INTAKE MANIFOLD

EGR VALVE

EXHAUST RETURN PIPE
FROM EXHAUST MANIFOLD
TO EGR VALVE

B21, B23: engines equipped with EGR system. Top, without vacuum amplifier; below, with vacuum amplifier

ply vacuum with a hand-held vacuum pump to the vacuum port on the valve. The engine should stumble or stall, indicating the EGR valve is open. If not, replace the EGR valve.

1974 140 Series
1975 240 Series

1. Start the engine and let it idle.
2. Remove the air intake hose from the vacuum amplifier at connection number 1.
3. Connect a vacuum pump or other suction device to outlet number 1 on the vacuum amplifier.
4. Apply vacuum: the EGR valve should NOT open, i.e. the idle should not stumble or the engine stall.
5. Check that the system holds a vacuum for about 10 seconds.
6. With the vacuum still applied to outlet number 1 on the vacuum amplifier, disconnect the wire from the micro switch at the throttle linkage. The EGR valve should open i.e. the engine should run poorly or stall. The micro-switch "tells" the system that the engine is at idle; by disconnecting the switch, the system reacts as if the engine were under acceleration. The EGR system engages.
7. Reconnnect all components and increase

engine speed. Visually check that the EGR valve opens. Drop the engine to idle: the EGR valve should close.
8. To adjust the micro-switch, unplug the micro-switch electrical connection and hook up a test light between the switch and its electrical connection. Turn on the ignition.
9. Back off the adjustment screws on both the micro switch and the throttle plate. To adjust the throttle plate, turn in its screw until it just touches the stop, then turn it ½ turn more. Secure its locknut.
10. Insert a 0.060 in. (1.5mm) for the 240 series, or a 0.040 in. (1.0mm) for the 140 series, feeler blade under the throttle stop screw. The test light should not light. Turn in the micro-switch screw until the light just turns on. You will hear the switch click. Secure the lock nut, remove the gauge and reconnect the micro-switch wire.

1976-83 Models
Not Equipped with Vacuum Amplifier

1. With the engine cold, check the operation of the wax thermostat. Start the engine and allow it to idle. Manipulate the throttle by hand and check that the EGR valve rod does not

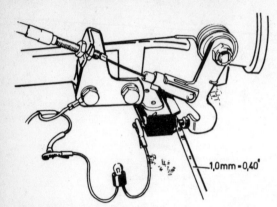

Checking micro switch adjustment— 1974 B20 engine. Measurement should be 0.60 in. for 1975 B20 engine (240 Series)

move in and out. If it does, the thermostat is faulty. It should not operate the EGR valve until the coolant reaches 130-140°F (54–60°C).

2. With the engine warmed up to normal operating temperature — 176°F (80°C) — check that the EGR valve rod does move in and out then the throttle is opened and closed. If not, the wax thermostat, hoses or EGR valve may be at fault.

3. Stop the engine. Disconnect the vacuum hose from the EGR valve. Blow through the hose. If no air passes, the wax thermostat is faulty. If air does pass, either the hose is incorrectly installed or the EGR valve is defective.

4. Finally, connect the EGR vacuum hose and start the engine. Open the throttle to 3000-4000 rpm and then quickly release it. The EGR valve rod should close. If not, replace the EGR valve.

1976-83 Models Equipped with Vacuum Amplifier

NOTE: *Use the illustrations to identify the vacuum amplifier; it will be located in the engine compartment.*

1. With the engine cold — below 130°F (54TC) — coolant temperature, check the operation of the wax thermostat. Disconnect the vacuum hose at the solenoid valve and disconnect the vacuum hose at the vacuum amplifier connection **S**. Draw suction on one of the disconnected hoses. If any air passes, one of the hoses has a vacuum leak or the wax thermostat is faulty. Reconnect the hoses.

2. Start the engine and warm up to normal operating temperature (176°F). Stop the engine. Disconnect the two hoses again and draw suction through either of the hoses. This time the thermostat should be open, and air should pass through. If not, replace the wax thermostat.

3. Connect the hoses. Check the throttle po-

sition sensing micro-switch next. Connect a 12v. test light in series between the upper wire connector and its upper terminal. Switch the ignition to the **ON** position. Pull back the throttle lever and insert a 0.060 in. (1.5mm) feeler gauge between the screw and the lever stop.

When the lever is released and the throttle screw makes contact with the switch plunger, the test light should illuminate. This indicates that current is reaching the solenoid valve, the micro-switch is activating, and the fuse is good. Then repeat by inserting an 0.080 in. (2mm) feeler gauge between the screw and lever stop. This time, the test light should not light and the throttle screw should not make contact with the switch plunger. Adjust as necessary by loosening the locknut on the stopscrew and adjusting for 0.060 in. (1.5mm) clearance.

4. Check the solenoid valve next. With the engine running at idle, disconnect the hose from connection **1**, and create a vacuum. The

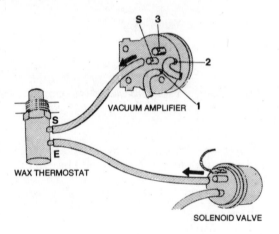

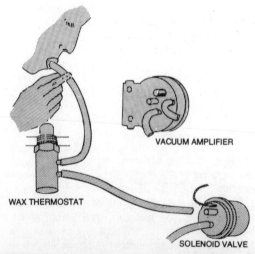

Checking the operation of the wax thermostat—all 1976 and later models

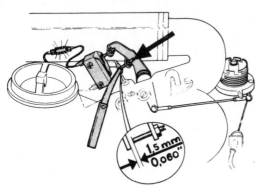

Checking micro switch adjustment—B27F engine shown

EGR valve should remain closed (no change in rpm). If not, the solenoid valve is defective.

5. With the vacuum pump still connected, and engine idling, check that the vacuum reading does not change for 10 seconds. If the reading changes, this indicates a bad amplifier or leaking hoses.

6. Finally, with the engine idling, increase the rpm while observing the EGR valve. If the EGR valve rod does not open, check for clogged venturi or leaking venturi vacuum hose. After increasing engine speed to about 2500 rpm, suddenly release the throttle and check that the EGR valve rod closes. If it does not, the solenoid valve is faulty.

EGR VALVE REMOVAL AND INSTALLATION

The EGR valve simply unbolts from the two pipes it connects. Always use two wrenches to free the couplings or you may bend the pipes. If it is necessary to replace the valve, check the part number stamped on the body of the old valve and install an exact match. An incorrect valve may add to the problems you're trying to cure.

The EGR valve may be cleaned by removing it and tapping it lightly with a soft mallet. This dislodges built up carbon which may be fouling the plunger. Do NOT clean the valve with solvents; this will damage the diaphragm within. Make sure that the ports and pipes are clean and free of carbon. When cleaning or inspecting the EGR valve, hold it in your hand. Mounting it in a vise may deform it and impair its function.

Air Injection Reaction (AIR) System

OPERATION

Many 1975-and later Volvos models are equipped with an air injection reactor system. The system injects filtered air into the exhaust

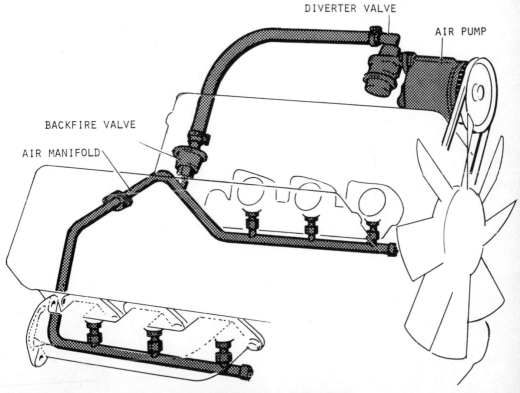

Air injection system—B27F engine

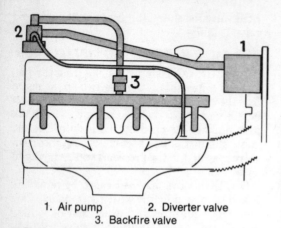

1. Air pump   2. Diverter valve
3. Backfire valve

Air injection system—B20 engine

manifold in order to reduce emissions of carbon monoxide and hydrocarbons. The oxygen in the air reacts with the exhaust gas and promotes further combustion in the exhaust manifold.

The system consists of an air pump (belt-driven), a diverter valve, an anti-backfiring valve, and a separate air manifold which is attached to the exhaust manifold. Under normal conditions, air is pumped from the air pump via

the diverter valve, the backfire valve and the air manifold into the exhaust manifold ports.

The air pump takes in filtered air which is then compressed and discharged to the diverter valve. The diverter valve sends the air through the backfire valve, except during deceleration. The diverter valve also releases some of the air into the atmosphere if the pressure from the pump is too great. The anti-backfire valve is one-way valve which prevents the exhaust gases from flowing back towards the air injection components, but allows the pump air to pass into the air manifold and exhaust manifold.

CHECKING THE AIR SYSTEM

Service the AIR system every 15,000 miles. Make sure the drive belt is in good condition on the air pump. If the belt breaks, the backfire valve must be checked. Make sure all attaching nuts and bolts for the air pump and bracket are secure.

To check the air pump, start the engine and listen for excessive noise from the pump. Remember that the air pump is not completly quiet in normal operation, and it can make a bit of a racket when it's cold. Normally, the noise rises in pitch as engine speed increases. Do not

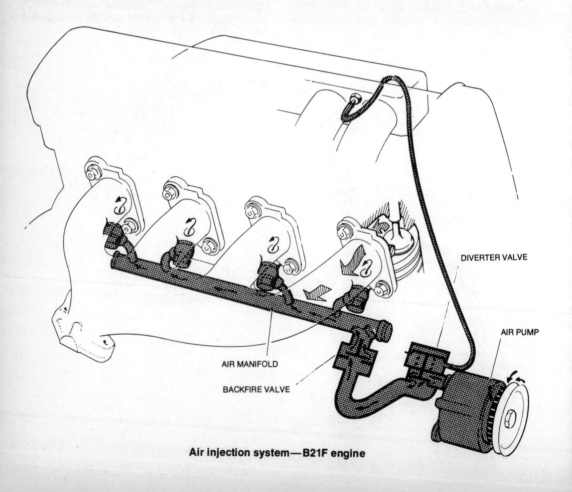

DIVERTER VALVE

AIR PUMP

AIR MANIFOLD

BACKFIRE VALVE

Air injection system—B21F engine

attempt to lubricate or repair the pump: it must be replaced.

To check the backfire valve:

1. Disconnect the hose from the diverter valve.

2. Apply a vacuum to the hose: no air should come through. If it does, replace the backfire valve.

To check the diverter valve:

1. Disconnect and plug the hose from the diverter valve.

2. Run the engine at idle. Air should only be coming out of point **A** in the illustration.

3. Increase the enginen speed to 3000-3500 rpm, then quickly release the throttle. Air should now flow from points **B** in the illustration. If not, replace the diverter valve.

Testing the diverter valve: 1975 models

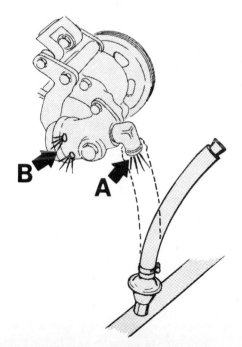

Testing the diverter valve:1976–77 models

Pulsair System

SYSTEM CHECK

Canadian 240 DL Series with B21A, B23E and B21F Engines

Beginning in 1979, Canadian B21A and some B21F engines were fitted with the then new Pulsair air injection system. This system was also incorporated into the Canadian B23E engine in 1983. In the Pulsair, the natural pressure pulses in the engine's exhaust system help to draw fresh air into the exhaust system.

The air is then injected into the end of the exhaust port (as in the air pump system) and the oxygen in the injected air aids in the further burning of emissions. The air pump is eliminated in the Pulsair system. Check valves in the system prevent exhaust gases from entering the air cleaner during the pressure pulses.

To check the operation of the system, disconnect the air hose at the air cleaner. With the engine idling, check that air is being drawn in with the palm of your hand and that no back pressure exists.

Catalytic Converter System

There are two different types of catalytic converters used on Volvos: the oxidation type converter and the three way converter.

All 1975-76 Volvos manufactured for California, 1975 164 models with manual transmission and overdirve for the 49 states, 1977 49 states 240 series and all 1977 260 series, all 1978 49 states models except some 242 DL, 242 GT and 262 C models, and all 1979 49 states 240 models except the 242 GT are equipped

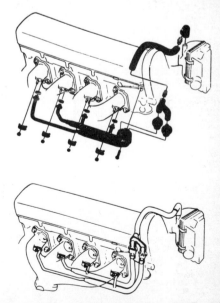

Pulsair system—Canadian B21A/F and B23E models

with the oxidation type converter. The converters are installed in these vehicles to further control emissions of carbon monoxide and hydrocarbons which have resisted the treatment of the air injection system.

The converter is installed in the exhaust system ahead of the muffler. The converter uses platinum and palladium in a substrate or beaded form as the catalyst. The catalyst and the oxygen supplied by the air pump then react with the exhaust gases producing harmless carbon dioxide and water vapor, as well as a minute amount of sulphur dioxide and sulphuric acid.

The converter is designed to last 50,000 miles as long as leaded gasoline is not used. The lead in gasoline will coat the catalytic substrate or beads, preventing the reaction process and rendering the converter ineffective.

At 15,000 mile intervals, the retaining bolts for the converter must be checked for tightness. A service reminder light on the dashboard lights at 15,000 mile intervals. To extinguish the light, press the white reset button at the rear of the odometer.

The 1977 California 240 series, all 1978-80 260 California series, all 1979 49 states 260 series, all 1980 and later (except Diesel) models and the 1979 49 states 242 GT are equipped with three-way catalytic converters.

The purpose of the three-way catalytic converter is to neutralize carbon monoxide, hydrocarbons and oxides of nitrogen in the exhaust gases. The main difference between this converter and the oxidation converter is that the three-way converter is able to process large amounts of oxides of nitrogen (NOx), while the oxidation catalyst cannot.

The operating range of the three way catalyst is limited to a narrow band around the ideal air/fuel mixture for the engine (14.7:1). To keep the mixture within this narrow band, an oxygen sensor is used to monitor the amount of oxygen in the exhaust gases. The readings from the oxygen sensor are transmitted to the ECU (Emissions control unit or fuel injection computer) which fine tunes the air/fuel mixture be-

ing delivered into the engine. See Oxygen Sensor Feedback System (Lambda Sond) for more information on the oxygen sensor system.

As with the oxidation catalytic converter, the use of leaded fuel or fuel additives in the engine will render the three-way catalyst ineffective. Extremely high temperatures within the catalyst will impair or even melt the ceramic insert inside the converter.

Oxygen Sensor Feedback System (Lambda Sond)

This is a self-tuning engine control system, designed to reduce emissions and improve fuel economy. An exhaust gas sensor (oxygen sensor or lambda sensor) is located in the exhaust manifold and monitors the composition of the exhaust gasses leaving the engine. This analysis is fed into a closed-loop feedback system. By reading the oxygen content of the exhaust

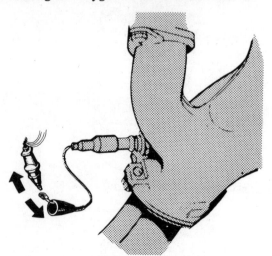

Oxygen sensor location—B21 and B23 engines

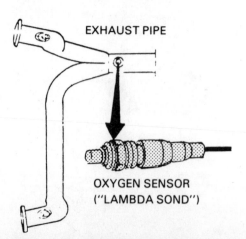

Oxygen sensor location—B27F engine—sensor is mounted above catalytic converter on B28F models

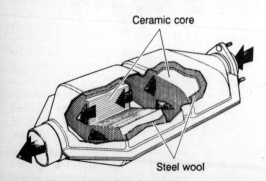

Cross-section of catalytic converter

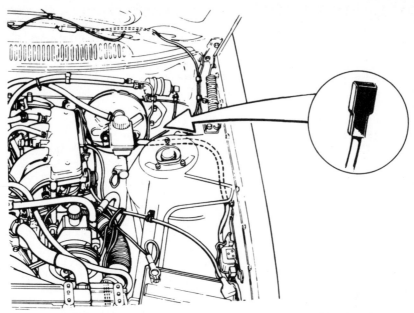

Instrument pick-up connector to test duty cycle on Lambda Sond system

stream, the system continuously adjusts the air/fuel mixture to provide optimum conditions for combustion and efficient breakdown of pollutants by the three-way catalytic converter.

The major components of the system are: the oxygen sensor, the electronic module and the frequency valve. The oxygen sensor is a platinum coated ceramic tube. It is located in the exhaust manifold. The inside is vented to the atmosphere while the outside is connected to the exhaust gas flow. The output from the sensor is fed to the electronic module. This device supplies a control current to the frequency valve.

The frequency valve alters the flow of fuel in the injection system by activating a diaphragm in the fuel pressure regulating valve. By altering the air/fuel flow in the system according to the signal received from the oxygen sensor, the frequency valve keeps the air/fuel mixture within the narrow band needed to allow the three-way converter to operate efficiently. The frequency valve (so called because it operates on a set frequency) functions during what is called its duty cycle.

INSPECTION AND REPLACEMENT OF THE OXYGEN SENSOR

The duty cycle corresponds to the ratio of closed-to-open circuit impulses from the elctronic module. The cycle can be measured in degrees by using a high quality dwell meter which reads up to 70° or more. The dwell meter is connnected to an instrument pick-up connector located on a wire coming from the electronic module. The pick-up connector is located on the

firewall, in the engine compartment to the left of the master cylinder. The dwell meter should be attached to the pick-up and ground.

To check the oxygen sensor, connect the dwell meter to the pick-up and ground and run the engine to normal operating temperature. Start the engine and wait 10 seconds. If the oxygen sensor is defective (or cold) the duty cycle will be 54° for the B21F and 40-50° for the B27F and B28F.

The late model non-maintenance type sensors can only be checked by measuring emissions at the tailpipe with a CO (emissions testing) meter. If the oxygen sensor in the manifold is obviously damaged, it can be replaced by simply disconnecting it and unscrewing it from the manifold. When installing a new sensor, the threads must be coated with anti-seize compound. The unit should be torqued to 40 ft. lbs. Use care in handling the oxygen sensor and its wire; it can be damaged by impact or dropping

On all gasoline powered US and Canadian Volvos through the 1983 model year, the oxygen sensor must be replaced at 30,000 mile intervals. For 1984, Canadian models with the B21A engine were exempt, but all US models require a new sensor every 30,000 miles. In 1985, the only models requiring replacement were the 760GLE (B28F engine) and the 240 Turbo (B21F-Turbo engine). The 1986 760GLE (B28F engine) was the last to require sensor replacement, again at 30,000 miles. All other 1986 and later models have sensors which are considered "life of the car" and do not require replacement unless they fail to function.

RESETTING THE OXYGEN SENSOR SERVICE LIGHT AND SERVICE INDICATOR LIGHT

After the required replacement service is performed on the oxygen sensor system, the service light in the dashboard may be reset. Remove the cover from the special odometer under the dashboard and depress the white button. This will reset the counter for the next 30,000 mile segment. Not all models have oxygen sensor service lights.

Many Volvos, particularly the 700 series,

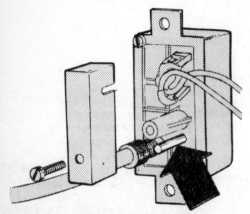

Resetting the EGR valve dashlight: push the white button on counter under the dash. Same counter is used for catalytic converter and oxygen sensor lights

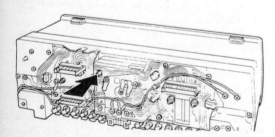

Resetting service reminder light, 740 and 780 models

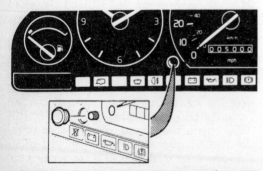

Location of service reminder light reset button, 760 models

have a service reminder light on the dashboard. When the elapsed mileage has reached 5000 miles from the last oil change, the light will come on for two minutes each time the engine is started. After changing the oil and filter and performing the other necessary safety checks, the reminder light may be reset by the following procedures.

On 740 and 780 models, the reset knob is found on the back of the instrument panel. Pressing the knob resets the counter for another 5000 mile increment. Use care in reaching behind the instrument cluster--don't pull any wires loose or disturb other components.

On the 760 model, remove the rubber grommet on the front of the instrument panel. This exposes the head of the reset button within the dash. Use a small screwdriver to depress the knob and reset the counter. Use care not to scratch the face of the dashboard when removing or installing the grommet.

VACUUM DIAGRAMS

Because Volvo was one of the first manufacturers to introduce reliable fuel injection on all their US cars, the underhood area is mercifully free of complicated vacuum hose routing. If the correct routing can not be found either below or in the Positive Crankcase Ventilation section of this chapter, consult the underhood emission decal for the exact routing for your car. The underhood decal may reflect running production changes for a particular engine family.

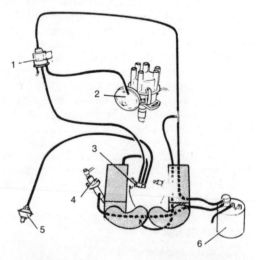

1. Ignition advance solenoid	5. Pressure differential switch
2. Distributor	6. Charcoal canister and vacuum valve
3. Thermal vacuum valve	
4. Start injector pipe	

Vacuum hose connections, B28F and B280F engines

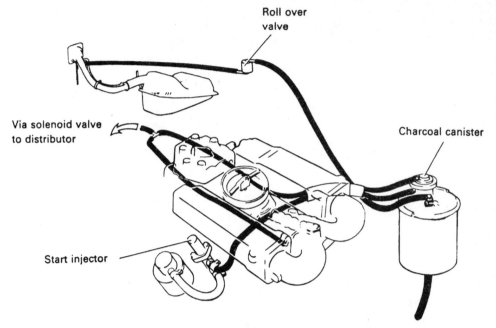

Roll over valve

Via solenoid valve to distributor

Charcoal canister

Start injector

B28 and B280: hose routing for evaporative emissions control system

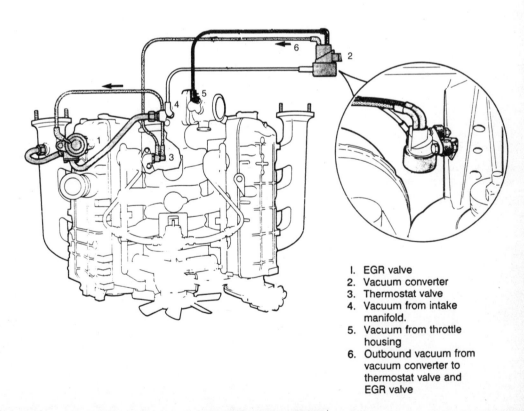

I. EGR valve
2. Vacuum converter
3. Thermostat valve
4. Vacuum from intake manifold.
5. Vacuum from throttle housing
6. Outbound vacuum from vacuum converter to thermostat valve and EGR valve

EGR routing, B280F

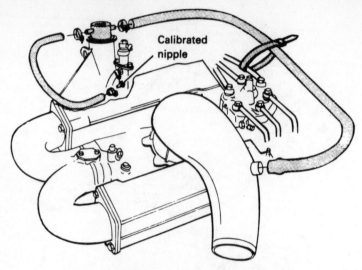

B28F and B280F crankcase ventilation system

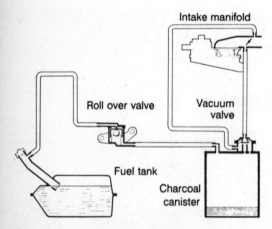

Schematic of evaporative emissions control system. DL and GL shown, others similar

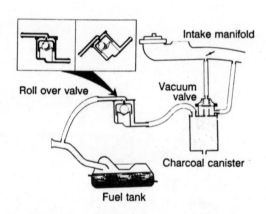

Schematic of evaporative emissions control system. 760 shown, other 700 models similar

Fuel System

5

CARBURETED FUEL SYSTEM

Mechanical Fuel Pump

Carbureted engines are equipped with mechanical fuel pumps. See the end of this chapter for information on the diesel fuel system.

TESTING AND ADJUSTMENT

No adjustments may be made to the fuel pump. Before removing and overhauling the old fuel pump, the following test may be made while the pump is still installed on the engine.

CAUTION: *To avoid accidental ignition of fuel during the test, first remove the coil high tension wire from the distributor and the coil. Disconnect the wire at BOTH ends to eliminate any chance of a stray spark being generated during cranking of the engine.*

1. If a fuel pressure gauge is available, connect the gauge to the engine and crank the engine (with the key or a remote starter switch) until the pressure stops rising and record the highest pressure achieved. If the reading is within the specifications given in the Tune-Up

Troubleshooting Basic Fuel System Problems

Problem	Cause	Solution
Engine cranks, but won't start (or is hard to start) when cold	• Empty fuel tank • Incorrect starting procedure • Defective fuel pump • No fuel in carburetor • Clogged fuel filter • Engine flooded • Defective choke	• Check for fuel in tank • Follow correct procedure • Check pump output • Check for fuel in the carburetor • Replace fuel filter • Wait 15 minutes; try again • Check choke plate
Engine cranks, but is hard to start (or does not start) when hot—(presence of fuel is assumed)	• Defective choke	• Check choke plate
Rough idle or engine runs rough	• Dirt or moisture in fuel • Clogged air filter • Faulty fuel pump	• Replace fuel filter • Replace air filter • Check fuel pump output
Engine stalls or hesitates on acceleration	• Dirt or moisture in the fuel • Dirty carburetor • Defective fuel pump • Incorrect float level, defective accelerator pump	• Replace fuel filter • Clean the carburetor • Check fuel pump output • Check carburetor
Poor gas mileage	• Clogged air filter • Dirty carburetor • Defective choke, faulty carburetor adjustment	• Replace air filter • Clean carburetor • Check carburetor
Engine is flooded (won't start accompanied by smell of raw fuel)	• Improperly adjusted choke or carburetor	• Wait 15 minutes and try again, without pumping gas pedal • If it won't start, check carburetor

Specifications chart in chapter 2, the malfunction is not in the fuel pump.

Check the pressure drop after the engine is stopped. A large pressure drop below the minimum specification indicates leaky valves. If the pump proves to be satisfactory, check the tank and inlet line.

2. If the fuel pressure gauge is not available, disconnect the fuel line at the pump outlet, place a vessel beneath the pump outlet, and crank the engine. A good pump will force the fuel out of the outlet in steady spurts. A worn diaphragm spring may not provide proper pumping action. Check the output through several strokes of the pump, looking for any sign of reduced flow or air bubbles.

3. As a further test, disconnect and plug the fuel line from the tank at the pump, and hold your thumb over the pump inlet. If the pump if functioning properly, a suction should be felt on your thumb when the engine is cranked. No suction indicates that the pump diaphragm is leaking or that the diaphragm linkage is worn.

4. Check the crankcase for gasoline. One quick check is to pull the dipstick and smell the oil; a better check is to examine a large sample (such a pan of recently drained oil) for odor and/or pollution. Gasoline will thin the oil in a fashion very similar to the effect of paint thinner in paint.

A ruptured diaphragm can allow fuel to enter the oil system. This condition must be remedied as soon as possible. Damage to engine bearings can result if the oil is polluted with fuel.

REPLACEMENT

1. Label, disconnect and plug the inlet and outlet lines to the fuel pump.
2. Remove the two fuel pump retaining bolts and carefully pull the pump and old gasket away from the block.

3. Discard the old gasket and position a new one on the pump to be reinstalled.

4. Mount the fuel pump and gasket to the engine block. Be careful to insert the pump lever (rocker arm) into the engine block and align it correctly above the camshaft.

5. While holding the pump securely against the block, install the two fuel pump retaining bolts, and tighten them securely.

6. Unplug and reconnect the fuel lines to the pump. Make sure the correct line is connected to each port.

7. Start the engine and check for fuel leaks. Also check for oil leaks where the pump attaches to the block. Depending on how much fuel was lost with the hoses disconnected, the engine may crank longer than normal before starting.

Electric Fuel Pump

All fuel injected models use similar fuel pumps, although the pumping capacity will change depending on the type of fuel injection and size of the engine. Beginning in the middle of the 1976 production year, a second fuel feed fuel pump was fitted inside the fuel tank and is integral with the fuel tank sender unit.

The purpose of the fuel feed pump is to supply fuel under lower pressure to the main fuel pump. This arrangement reduces the possibility of vapor lock and relieves some of the strain on the external pump. This in-tank pump can be fitted on earlier model continuous (mechanical) fuel injected vehicles.

Because of the need for constant fuel pressure in the continuous fuel injection system, a

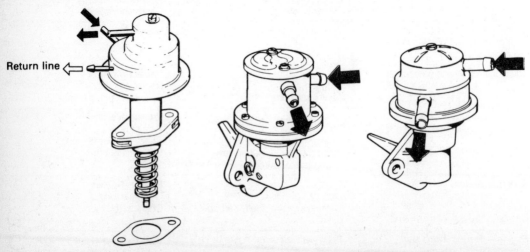

Three types of mechanical fuel pumps used on carbureted Volvos. Arrows show direction of fuel flow. Make sure all hoses are connected to the proper ports

Return line

fuel accumulator is installed between the fuel pump and the engine. The accumulator smoothes out fuel pump pulsing and maintains fuel pressure in the line after the engine is stopped to insure quick start-ups.

On both continuous and electronic fuel injected models, the fuel pump is a wet type, roller fuel pump. As the pump motor spins, the rollers are forced outwards by centrifugal force and ride against the eccentrically shaped pump chambers. Fuel is drawn into the cavities between the rollers and forced outward to the line under pressure.

NOTE: *Volvo states that a no-start condition may occasionally occur when the engine has not been started for an extended period of time. This may be due to the fuel pump sticking in one position because of foreign matter, or corrosion forming on the rotor shaft or commutator and brushes. It is very important to clean the fuel tank pick-up screen or filter at the recommended intervals to prevent water condensation and foreign matter from entering the pump.*

As an additional corrosion prevention measure, add an alcohol solution or gas line antifreeze to the fuel, especially in winter months or if laying up the car for a period of weeks or months. When the pump does become stuck in one position for any of the above reasons, it may be unstuck by lightly rapping on the pump casing with a length of hardwood such as a hammer handle, while the ignition is switched on. This simply loosens the binding material within the pump and allows the motor to turn the pumping mechanism. It is one of the few occasions when a bit of controlled violence will cure an electrical problem.

TESTING AND ADJUSTMENT

No adjustment may be made to the fuel pump. If the pump is not functioning properly, it must be discarded and replaced. To check the function of the fuel pump, the pump should be connected to a pressure gauge. Be careful not to switch the electrical leads. If the pump fails to develop its proper pressure, or if it cannot pump deliver that pressure at its specified amperage, it must be replaced. It is recommended that you consult your dealer or other reputable repair facility for accurate testing of the fuel pump pressure and amperage.

REMOVAL AND INSTALLATION

The fuel pump is located either in front of or beside the fuel tank. On continuous fuel injection models, it is located with the fuel accumulator.

CAUTION: *The fuel system is under pressure. Release pressure slowly and contain*

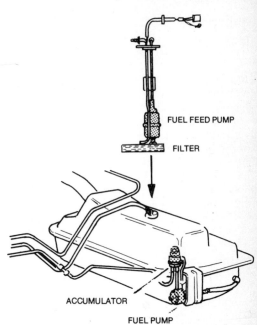

Fuel feed pump used in some 1976 and all 1977 and later USA Volvos

spillage. Observe no smoking/no open flame precautions

1. Remove the gas cap. Remove the electrical lead from the pump as well as the plate to which the pump is mounted if necessary.

2. Clean around the hose connections. After labeling the fuel lines, pinch them shut, loosen the hose clamps and disconnect the lines. Take care not to crush or damage the hoses when pinching them.

3. Loosen the retaining nuts and remove the pump from its rubber mounts.

4. Install the new pump on its rubber mounts and tighten the retaining nuts.

5. Reconnect the fuel lines, tighten the hose clamps, and remove the pinchers.

6. Mount the plate beneath the car and connect the electrical lead.

7. Start the engine and check for leaks.

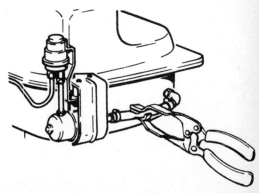

Pinch shut the fuel line when removing the fuel pump

Carburetors

CARBURETOR EMISSIONS COMPONENTS TESTING AND ADJUSTMENT

Carbureted engines have incorporated many pollutant control devices, such as a temperature-regulated fuel jet, an air/fuel mixture pre-heating chamber, and a throttle bypass or overrev valve. Measures have also been taken to improve the operation and driveability of emission controlled engines such as a cold start device, a constant intake air temperature device and a hot start valve. The temperature-regulated fuel mixture is accomplished differently on the Zenith-Stromberg carburetor than on the SU carburetor.

On the Zenith-Stromberg carburetor, a temperature sensitive bimetal spring (in the temperature compensator) actuates an air valve that varies the air supplied the venturi area, maintaining a constant air/fuel ratio. This ratio is maintained despite changing fuel temperature.

Within the SU carburetor, a temperature sensitive bimetal spring raises or lowers an adjustable jet to maintain the proper air/fuel ratio at changing fuel temperatures.

The air/fuel mixture preheating chamber used on pre-1972 models is located between the primary throttles in the carburetors and the secondary throttles in the intake manifold.

TEMPERATURE COMPENSATOR

Zenith-Stromberg Carburetor

If the idle speed drops off sharply during extended periods of idling, especially during warm weather, the temperature compensator may be in need of adjustment or replacement. Use the accompaning diagram to help you.

1. Remove the screws (7) holding the plastic cover (5) to the compensator and remove the cover.

2. With the ambient temperature at or above 85°F (29°C), the valve (3) should be able to be pressed inward with light finger pressure and then return to its position without jamming. If the valve jams and/or is stiff in operation, the temperature compensator should be replaced as a unit. See Temperature Compensator Replacement.

3. If properly adjusted, the valve will begin to open at 70–77°F (21–25°C), and will be fully open at 85°F (29°C). The valve may be adjusted while the temperature compensator is still on the carburetor by loosening one of the cross-slotted screws (8) for the bimetal spring (4), and centering the valve so that it opens and closes at the proper temperature.

If necessary, the temperature compensator

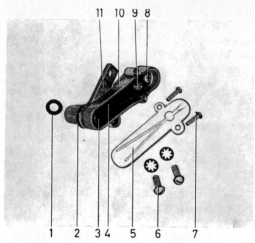

1. Rubber seal
2. Rubber seal
3. Valve
4. Bi-metal spring
5. Cover
6. Screws for temperature compensator
7. Screw for cover
8. Cross-slotted screw
9. Adjusting nut
10. Housing
11. Marking

Temperature compensator—Zenith-Stromberg carburetor

may be removed and isolated at 70–77°F (21–25°C) then adjusted with the nut (9) for the bimetal spring so that the valve is loose in its seat at this temperature.

4. Replace the cover and retaining screws on the compensator and check its operation during idling.

BYPASS VALVE

Zenith-Stromberg Carburetor

If the engine does not return to idle speed soon after the throttle is released, and the throttle control linkage is properly adjusted, the bypass valve may be in need of adjustment or replacement.

1. If the engine refuses to lower its rpm to idle speed when the throttle is released, turn the bypass adjusting screw on the front carburetor to the left, and manually lower the idle.

2. Run the engine briefly up to approximately 2000 rpm, then release the throttle. If the engine returns to idle speed, turn the screw ½ turn further to the left. If the engine does NOT return to idle, replace the bypass valve as a unit. See By-pass Valve Replacement.

3. Remove the air cleaner. While looking into the carburetor bores, observe the air valves. Briefly race the engine and then release the throttle. The air valve of the front carburetor should normally go down to the bridge slower than the air valve of the rear carburetor.

Turn the bypass adjusting screw to the right until the normal function is obtained. If the

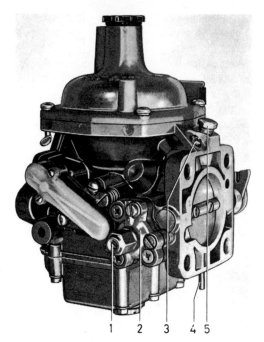

1. Adjusting screw
2. By-pass valve
3. Plug for outlet for speed compensator (air conditioner)
4. Vacuum hose connection for distributor
5. Plug

Zenith-Stromberg carburetor—front left side

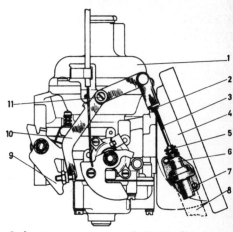

1. Carburetor
2. Locknut
3. Control rod
4. Air cleaner, lower section
5. Rubber seal
6. Hot start valve
7. Attaching rivet
8. Venting filter hose. (Only on vehicle with gas evaporative unit)
9. Throttle lever
10. Valve control
11. Screw for valve control

Hot start valve installation—Zenith-Stromberg carburetor

valve cannot be adjusted so that the front air valve goes down to the bridge slower than the rear air valve, the bypass valve must be replaced as a unit. See By-pass Valve Replacement.

HOT START VALVE

Zenith-Stromberg Carburetor

With the throttle at idle, adjust the valve control of the hot start valve so that the valve is against the carburetor lever with the valve piston in the upper position.

Coat the contact surfaces on the valve and carburetor with high temperature white grease such as Molykote®. Test the operation of the hot start valve by confirming that the engine returns to idle after several brief periods of racing the engine.

SU Carburetor

To adjust the hot start valve, press the control rods down to the bottom position and measure the distance (A) between the rod and the adjusting screw. Adjust the distance to a maximum of 0.04 in. (1mm).

Test the operation of the control rods. Make sure that they do not jam.

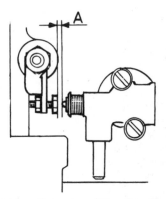

Hot start valve clearance—SU carburetor

CONSTANT (INTAKE) AIR TEMPERATURE DEVICE

If the flap for the constant air temperature device sticks in one position, engine operation will suffer. Normally, the flap is closed to cold air (intake hose) at an ambient temperature of 70–77°F (21–25°C) and closed to hot air (ducted from the exhaust manifold) at 95°–105°F (35–40°C). Depending on the temperature, the flap can remain in a partially open position, blending the warm and cool air to achieve the proper intake air temperature.

1. The operation of the flap may be checked with the housing installed on the car. When the small tab on the flap housing points toward the

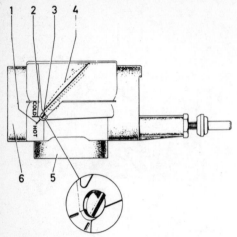

1. HOT = open for warm air
2. COLD = open for cold air
3. Tab
4. Flap
5. Hot air intake
6. Cold air intake

Checking air temperature flap

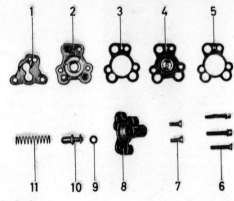

1. Gasket
2. Housing
3. Gasket
4. Diaphragm
5. Gasket
6. Screw for by-pass valve
7. Screw for cover
8. Cover
9. Rubber ring
10. Adjusting screw
11. Spring

By-pass valve disassembled

mark closest to the exhaust heat hose, the flap is open for hot (preheated) air. When the tab points to the mark nearest the cold air intake, the flap is open for cold (outside) air. If the tab indicates that the flap is opening and closing the air sources at the right temperatures, it is operating correctly. If not, check the operation of the flap control thermostat.

2. Disconnect the flap housing from the air intake hoses. Immerse the thermostat in luke-warm water. At a water temperature of 70–77°F (21–25°C), the thermostat should be in its upper (toward the flap housing) position. At 95–105°F (35–40°C), the thermostat should be in its lower position (away from the flap housing). If correct operation cannot be obtained, replace the thermostat and flap housing as a unit.

3. Replace the flap housing and thermostat assembly, making sure that the thermostat is centered in the middle of the air flow. Secure the hose clamp screw on top of the flap.

COMPONENT REPLACEMENT

Temperature Compensator

ZENITH-STROMBERG CARBURETOR

1. Remove the retaining screw (6) and lift off the compensator.

2. Discard the old rubber seals (1,2) and replace them with new ones.

3. Position the compensator to the side of the carburetor and install the retaining screws.

4. Check the operation of the compensator during idle as outlined in Temperature Compensator Testing and Adjustment.

Bypass Valve

ZENITH-STROMBERG CARBURETOR

1. Remove the three retaining screws (6) and lift off the bypass valve.

2. Discard the old bypass valve-to-carburetor housing gasket.

3. Position a new gasket and bypass valve to the carburetor, making sure that the orifices and mating surfaces of the valve and gasket align and install the three retaining screws.

4. Check the operation of the bypass valve as outlined in By-pass Valve Testing and Adjustment".

Hot Start Valve

ZENITH STROMBERG CARBURETOR

The hot start valve on the Zenith-Stromberg carburetor is riveted to the air cleaner. If the valve requires cleaning, it must be done with the assembly in place on the engine.

SU CARBURETOR

1. Remove the two retaining screws and lift off the valve.

2. Discard the old gasket and clean the channels in the carburetor with a low pressure air line.

3. Position the valve and new gasket to the carburetor, making sure that the gasket is aligned properly, then install the two retaining screws.

4. Adjust the position of the control rod and test the operation of the valve as outlined in Hot Start Valve Testing and Adjustment.

1. Channel, connected to air cleaner
2. Channel, connected to floatchamber
3. Gasket (in assembly position)

Hot start valve removal—SU carburetor

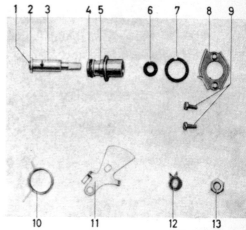

1. Circlip
2. Washer
3. Spindle
4. Rubber ring
5. Housing
6. Rubber seal for spindle
7. Gasket
8. Spring retainer
9. Screws for cold start device
10. Return spring
11. Fast idle screw
12. Tab washer
13. Nut

Cold start device exploded view—SU carburetor

Constant Air Temperature Device Flap Housing

1. Loosen the hose clamps and disconnect the flap housing and thermostat assembly from the hoses for the intake air, heated air, and intake manifold.

2. Install the new flap housing assembly in position and reconnect the three hoses. Make sure that the thermostat is centered in the middle of the intake air flow. Secure the hose clamp screw on top of the flap.

3. Check the operation of the new flap housing as outlined in Constant Air Temperature Device Testing and Adjustment.

Cold Start Device Seals

SU CARBURETOR

1. Pry off the lockwasher (12) for the cold start device and unscrew the channel disc nut (13).

2. Disconnect the return spring (10) and remove the channel disc and spring.

3. Remove the two retaining screws (9) and the spring retainer (8).

4. Lift the cold start device away from the carburetor. Press the spindle (3) out of the cold start device housing (5). Remove the gasket (7), the rubber ring (4), and rubber seal (6) from the spindle, and discard them.

Clean all metal parts with kerosene (not gasoline) and clean the fuel channels with an compressed air.

5. Install a new rubber ring and seal on the housing and oil them with light (10W) engine oil. Install the spindle into the housing.

6. Position the housing assembly, with a new gasket, on the carburetor. Fit the spring retainer and install the retaining screws.

7. Position the return spring in its retainer so that the spring's short end fits into the retainer slot.

8. Hook the channel disc onto the spring's longer end and install the disc on the spindle. Install the channel disc retaining nut and snap on the lockwasher.

Float Adjustment

ZENITH-STROMBERG CARBURETOR

1. Remove the carburetor as outlined above.

2. Invert the carburetor and remove the float chamber.

3. The float is correctly adjusted when the high point of the float is 5/8 in. (16mm) (distance B), and the low point of the float is 1/2 in. (13mm) (distance A) from the sealing surface of the carburetor housing.

4. To adjust the float level, bend the tab at the float chamber inlet valve. Do not bend the arm between the float and the pin.

5. When the proper adjustment has been made, install the float chamber to the housing with a new gasket.

6. Reinstall the carburetor on the intake manifold as explained above.

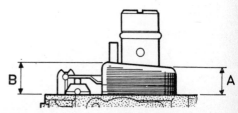

Float level adjustment—Zenith-Stromberg carburetor

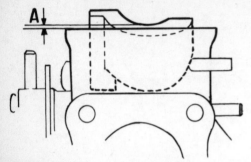

Float level adjustment—SU carburetor

SU CARBURETOR

1. Remove the carburetor as outlined previously.

2. Invert the carburetor and remove the float chamber.

3. The float is correctly adjusted when the distance **A** between the float valley and the housing flange is approximately 0.02–0.06 in. (0.50–1.50mm).

4. The float is adjusted by bending the metal tab at the float chamber inlet valve.

5. When the correct adjustment has been made, install the float chamber to the housing with a new gasket.

6. Install the carburetor as outlined in Carburetor Removal and Installation.

Fast Idle Adjustment

ZENITH-STROMBERG CARBURETOR

Pull out the choke control one inch from the dash. If the choke is adjusted correctly, the mark on the fast idle cam (see illustration)

Fast idle adjustment—Zenith-Stromberg carburetor

should be opposite the centerline of the fast idle screw. Adjust the fast idle with the fast idle screw to 1100–1300 rpm. For cars with dual carburetors, make sure you set the fast idle on both carburetors.

SU CARBURETOR

Pull out the choke control 0.8 in. (20mm) from the dash. Adjust the fast idle (with the fast idle screw) to 1100–1600 rpm. Remember to set both carburetors if so equipped.

Damping Piston Replacement

If the engine stumbles upon acceleration, and the damping cylinders are filled to their proper level with oil, the problem may be with the damping pistons themselves. Unscrew the black knobs on top of the carburetors and remove the damping pistons. If the axial clearance **A** between the bottom of the piston and the retaining clip is not 0.04–0.08 in. (1.0–2.0mm), the piston must be replaced as a unit.

Throttle Linkage Adjustment

On each carburetor, the link rods should maintain a 0.004 in. (0.1mm) – clearance **A** – between the lever and the throttle spindle flange when the throttle control is against the intake manifold bracket. To adjust this clearance, remove the ball-and-socket link from the carburetor stud, and turn the socket on the threaded rod until the adjustment is correct. Remember that you are seeking a clearance measured in thousandths of an inch; the link should not require a great amount of turning.

Carburetor Diaphragm Replacement

ZENITH-STROMBERG CARBURETOR ONLY

The Stromberg carburetor differs from the SU carburetor in that it has a rubber diaphragm attached to the air valve. Vacuum from the intake manifold acts upon the diaphragm to raise and lower the air valve. Obviously, if the

Damping piston clearance

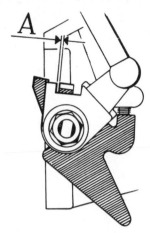

Throttle linkage adjustment—Stromberg carburetor

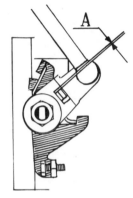

Throttle linkage adjustment—SU carburetor

diaphragm rips (which can happen due to age and/or chemical deterioration), engine performance will suffer measurably. This procedure is done with the carburetor on the engine.

1. Remove the damper piston from the top of the carburetor.

2. Remove the four screws and remove the top of the carburetor.

3. Remove the large spring and remove the air valve complete with rubber diaphragm.

4. Check the diaphragm for rips and brittleness. If no rips or deterioration are evident, reuse the diaphragm.

5. If the diaphragm is ripped or damaged, remove the four screws and remove the diaphragm washer and the diaphragm.

6. Fit a new diaphragm. The diaphragm will fit on the air valve only one way: it has a notch in it which must be inserted in the notch on the air valve.

7. Fit the air valve and diaphragm on the carburetor. You may have to remove the air cleaner to guide the needle on the air valve into its jet. Place the air valve into the carburetor so that the notch in the outside of the diaphragm fits into the notch in the carburetor body.

8. Reinstall the spring and carburetor top. Fill the damper with ATF fluid and install the damper piston.

REMOVAL AND INSTALLATION

Two different types of carburetors have been used on 1970–72 Volvos. A pair of sidedraft Zenith-Stromberg 175 CD2 SE units were used on 1970 140 series models, and on 1970–72 164 models. A pair of sidedraft SU HIF units were used on 1971–72 140 series models.

NOTE: *All wires and hoses should be labeled at the time of removal. The amount of time saved during re–assembly makes the extra effort well worthwhile.*

1. On the Zenith-Stromberg carburetor, disconnect the hot start valve control. Separate the air cleaner halves and remove the inner half from the carburetors.

2. Disconnect the throttle linkage by removing the link rod ball joints from the carburetors. Disconnect the choke cable, taking note of its proper routing and adjustment.

3. Disconnect and plug the fuel lines at the float chambers. Remove the vacuum hose for the distributor. On the SU carburetor, disconnect the hot start valve hose.

4. Remove the four nuts retaining the carburetor to the intake manifold. Remove the carburetors, gaskets, and protection plate. Keep the carburetor vertical and remove it from the engine are. Safely drain the remaining fuel within the bowls of the carburetor and cap the container.

When repairing the carburetor on the workbench, keep the area clean and free from dirt and dust.

To install:

5. Position the protection plate, new gaskets, and carburetor on the intake manifold studs. Install the carburetor retaining nuts and tighten them evenly unitl they are snug against the manifold.

6. Connect the vacuum hoses, fuel hoses, choke, and throttle linkage. On the SU carburetor, connect the hot start valve hose.

7. Install the inner half of the air cleaner to the carburetors. Adjust the idle speed and mixture of the carburetors as outlined in the Tune-Up section of Chapter 2.

8. Fit the air cleaner halves together and, on the Stromberg carburetor, connect the hot start valve control.

CARBURETOR OVERHAUL

Carburetors are relatively complex. Proper performance depends upon the cleanliness and proper adjustment of all internal and external components. In addition to the usual adjustments performed at the regular tune-up inter-

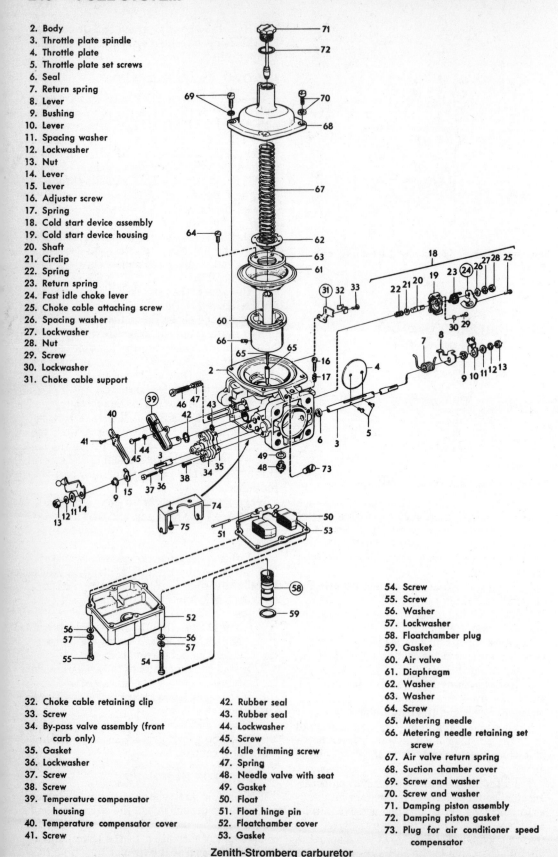

2. Body
3. Throttle plate spindle
4. Throttle plate
5. Throttle plate set screws
6. Seal
7. Return spring
8. Lever
9. Bushing
10. Lever
11. Spacing washer
12. Lockwasher
13. Nut
14. Lever
15. Lever
16. Adjuster screw
17. Spring
18. Cold start device assembly
19. Cold start device housing
20. Shaft
21. Circlip
22. Spring
23. Return spring
24. Fast idle choke lever
25. Choke cable attaching screw
26. Spacing washer
27. Lockwasher
28. Nut
29. Screw
30. Lockwasher
31. Choke cable support

32. Choke cable retaining clip
33. Screw
34. By-pass valve assembly (front carb only)
35. Gasket
36. Lockwasher
37. Screw
38. Screw
39. Temperature compensator housing
40. Temperature compensator cover
41. Screw

42. Rubber seal
43. Rubber seal
44. Lockwasher
45. Screw
46. Idle trimming screw
47. Spring
48. Needle valve with seat
49. Gasket
50. Float
51. Float hinge pin
52. Floatchamber cover
53. Gasket

54. Screw
55. Screw
56. Washer
57. Lockwasher
58. Floatchamber plug
59. Gasket
60. Air valve
61. Diaphragm
62. Washer
63. Washer
64. Screw
65. Metering needle
66. Metering needle retaining set screw
67. Air valve return spring
68. Suction chamber cover
69. Screw and washer
70. Screw and washer
71. Damping piston assembly
72. Damping piston gasket
73. Plug for air conditioner speed compensator

Zenith-Stromberg carburetor

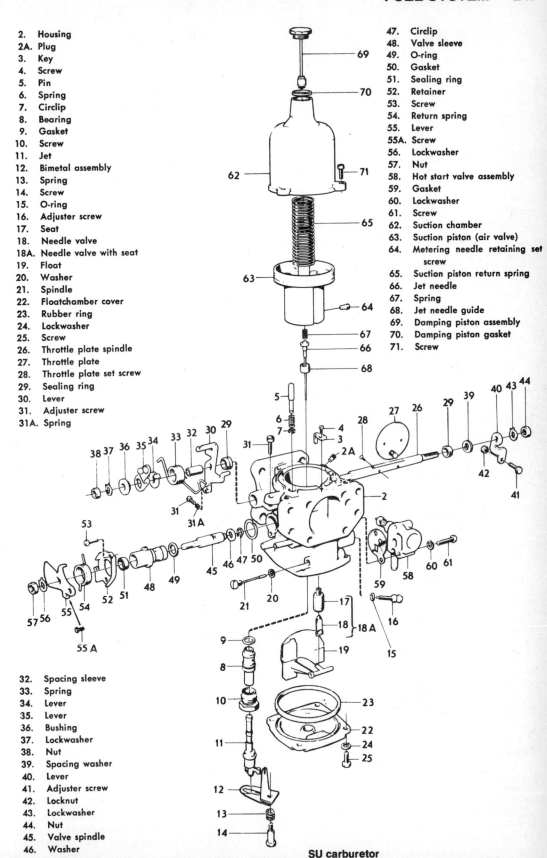

2.	Housing
2A.	Plug
3.	Key
4.	Screw
5.	Pin
6.	Spring
7.	Circlip
8.	Bearing
9.	Gasket
10.	Screw
11.	Jet
12.	Bimetal assembly
13.	Spring
14.	Screw
15.	O-ring
16.	Adjuster screw
17.	Seat
18.	Needle valve
18A.	Needle valve with seat
19.	Float
20.	Washer
21.	Spindle
22.	Floatchamber cover
23.	Rubber ring
24.	Lockwasher
25.	Screw
26.	Throttle plate spindle
27.	Throttle plate
28.	Throttle plate set screw
29.	Sealing ring
30.	Lever
31.	Adjuster screw
31A.	Spring

47.	Circlip
48.	Valve sleeve
49.	O-ring
50.	Gasket
51.	Sealing ring
52.	Retainer
53.	Screw
54.	Return spring
55.	Lever
55A.	Screw
56.	Lockwasher
57.	Nut
58.	Hot start valve assembly
59.	Gasket
60.	Lockwasher
61.	Screw
62.	Suction chamber
63.	Suction piston (air valve)
64.	Metering needle retaining set screw
65.	Suction piston return spring
66.	Jet needle
67.	Spring
68.	Jet needle guide
69.	Damping piston assembly
70.	Damping piston gasket
71.	Screw

32.	Spacing sleeve
33.	Spring
34.	Lever
35.	Lever
36.	Bushing
37.	Lockwasher
38.	Nut
39.	Spacing washer
40.	Lever
41.	Adjuster screw
42.	Locknut
43.	Lockwasher
44.	Nut
45.	Valve spindle
46.	Washer

SU carburetor

vals, it eventually becomes necessary to remove, disassemble, clean, and overhaul the entire carburetor in order to restore its original performance.

To overhaul a carburetor, first purchase the proper rebuilding kit. Read the instructions and study the exploded view of the carburetor thoroughly prior to the actual removal and disassembly.

After reading the detailed carburetor rebuilding instructions, the following general procedure may be used. Remove the carburetor and place it on a clean work table. Disassemble the carburetor by removing the screws securing the upper and lower sections together. Remove the damping piston, air valve, spring, metering needle, fuel jet (SU only), and float assembly.

Soak all metal parts in carburetor cleaning solvent. Scrape all old gasket material from the mating surfaces. After the metal parts have been soaked to remove all gum, varnish, and dirt, rinse them off with a clean, uncontaminated, solvent solution. Blow out all passages with compressed air and allow them to air dry. Do not use drills or wire to clean the passages.

Check the throttle shaft and choke disc for excessive wear. Inspect the float hinge pins for distortion. All non-metal parts that are not being replaced should be wiped clean with a lint-free cloth. After all of the parts have been sufficiently cleaned or replaced, assemble the carburetor using new gaskets and seals, and, on Zenith-Stromberg carburetors, a new air valve diaphragm. If any of the replacement seals in an SU carburetor are cork, they must first be soaked in penetrating oil for a minumum of a half hour to avoid splitting during installation.

Assemble the float chamber and adjust the float height. Assemble the air valve, spring, and metering needle into the upper housing. Join the upper and lower housing together, taking care to properly align the metering needle and fuel jet. When the jet and needle are installed correctly, the air valve should drop to the bridge with a distinctive click. Any binding of these two parts will result in poor carburetor performance. Install the damping piston. Install the carburetor on its manifold with a new gasket. Adjust the choke and throttle linkage, and the idle speed. Run the engine through a full cold start, warm up and hot restart cycle to check for proper function of all carburetor systems. Make adjustments as necessary.

GASOLINE FUEL INJECTION SYSTEM

NOTE: *This book contains testing and service procedures for your car's fuel injection system. More comprehensive testing and diagnosis procedures may be found in CHILTON'S GUIDE TO FUEL INJECTION AND FEEDBACK CARBURETORS, book number 7488, available at your local retailer.*

General information

Fuel injection combined with electronics and various engine sensors provides a precis fuel management system that meets all the demands for improved fuel economy, increased performance and lower tailpipe emissions. A fuel injected engine generally averages ten percent more power and fuel economy (with lower emissions) than a carbureted engine.

Because of its precise control, fuel injection allows the engine to operate at the optimum fuel ratio of 14.7 parts air to 1 part fuel through out the entire range of engine operation — from idle through wide-open throttle. By using an oxygen sensor to measure the content of the exhaust gasses, the on-board computer (control unit or ECU) can adjust the fuel mixture in response to the changing temperature, load and altitude conditions.

It is important to identify all system components, how they work and their relationship to one another before attempting any maintenance or repair on the system. All fuel injection systems are delicate and vulnerable to damage from dust, dirt, water and careless handling. The shock of hitting a cement floor when dropped from waist height can ruin a computer unit. Because of the close tolerances involved within a fuel injector, any particle of rust or dirt in the fuel lines can cause more damage than a well placed grenade.

Many components, while similar in appearance, can vary in their function or electrical properties. Each individual system has some sensors, capabilities and characteristics unique to its own design. Further, injection systems receive constant modifications and improvements during the production run. For these reasons, the careful recording of part numbers and/or engine numbers is essential to obtaining the correct replacement parts.

Safety Precautions

CAUTION: *Whenever working on or around any fuel injection system, always observe these general precautions to prevent the possibility of personal injury and/or damage to the fuel system components.*

• The fuel system is under pressure. Release pressure slowly and contain spillage. Observe no smoking/no open flame precautions.

• Never install or remove battery cables with the key ON or the engine running. Jumper cables should be connected with the key OFF to avoid power surges that can damage electronic control units. Engines equipped with fuel injection units should (where possible) avoid giving or receiving jump starts to avoid the risk of serious damage by electrical arcing.

• Always remove the battery cables before charging the battery. Never use a high output charger on an installed battery. Never use any type of "hot-shot" (24 volt) starting aid.

• Never attach or remove wiring harness connectors with the ignition switch ON, especially to the electronic control unit.

• Always depressurize the fuel system before disconnecting any fuel lines.

• Always use clean rags and tools when working on an open fuel injection system and take extreme care to prevent any dirt from entering the system.

• Wipe all components clean before installation and prepare a clean work area for any disassembly or inspection. Avoid the use of caustic cleaning solvents.

• Avoid any rough handling of components. If a component is dropped or subjected to impact, consider it failed until thoroughly checked for all functions.

• Remove the electronic control unit if the vehicle is to be in an environment with temeratures over 170°F (77°C), such as a paint spray booth. Remove the ECU if any welding is to be done on the car.

Bosch Electronic Fuel Injection
1975 AND EARLIER MODELS

All 1973 and earlier fuel injected models and the 1974–75 164 use the Bosch fuel injection system. Fuel is drawn from the fuel tank by the electric fuel pump and forced through the fuel lines and filter to the pressure regulator.The pressure regulator supplies fuel at a constant pressure of 28 psi to the injectors. The electromagnetic fuel injectors are mounted in the intake ports of the cylinder head.

The duration of fuel injection, and, consequently, fuel quantity, is controlled by engine rpm and load. Engine rpm information is supplied to the electronic brain via the distributor triggering contacts. Engine load information is supplied by the intake air pressure sensor. The electronic brain uses this information to determine the length of time the injectors will remain open. During warm-up periods, the cold start valve injects extra fuel into the intake air stream when the starter is operated. At the same time, the auxiliary air regulator supplies extra air until the engine reaches operating temperature.

When the engine is accelerated, the throttle valve switch sends electrical impulses to the brain to increase the time the injectors are open. When decelerating, the throttle valve switch sends another impulse to the brain, closing off the fuel flow. When engine speed drops to approximately 1,000 rpm, the fuel supply is turned on again, allowing a smooth transition to idle speed.

COMPONENT TESTING, ADJUSTMENT AND REPLACEMENT
Through 1975, B20 and B30 engines

The fuel injection system is repaired simply by replacing the defective component. There are adjustments that can be made to the pressure regulator, throttle valve, throttle valve switch, throttle stop-screw, and the fuel mixture. To make resistance checks, use an ohmmeter and for continuity checks, a 12 V test light. If the control unit is defective, return it to a qualified repair agency and install a new unit.

CONTROL UNIT

The idle mixture may be adjusted with the slotted knob on the control unit. This operation is best performed with the use of a CO meter, which is available on the dealer level. The control unit may be tested only with the help of sophisticated test equipment available, again, only at the dealer level. To replace the control unit:

1. On 1800 series models and 1975 164 models, disconnect the defroster hose, remove the control unit bracket retaining screws, and lower the unit to the floor. On 140 series and 1973–74 164 models, move the passenger's front seat all the way back, unscrew the bolt securing the seat front, move the seat forward while folding the seat bottom to the rear, remove the control unit retaining screws, and draw out the unit.

2. Remove the screw for the cap holding the cable harness to the unit. Pull out the plastic cover strip.

3. Construct a puller out of $5/64$ in. (2mm) welding wire (see illustration) to disconnect the main plug contact. Insert the puller in the rear of the control unit and pull out the plug carefully.

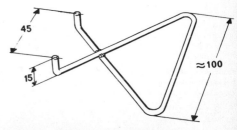

Puller for control unit plug contact

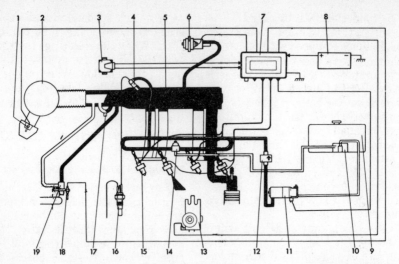

1. Temperature sensor for induction air
2. Air cleaner
3. Throttle valve switch
4. Cold start valve
5. Inlet duct
6. Pressure sensor
7. Control unit (electronic)
8. Battery
9. Fuel tank
10. Fuel filter, suction side
11. Fuel pump
12. Fuel filter, discharge side
13. Triggering contacts in distributor
14. Pressure regulator
15. Injectors
16. Thermal timer contact
17. Idling adjusting screw
18. Temperature sensor for coolant
19. Auxiliary air regulator

Electronic fuel injection—B20F engine

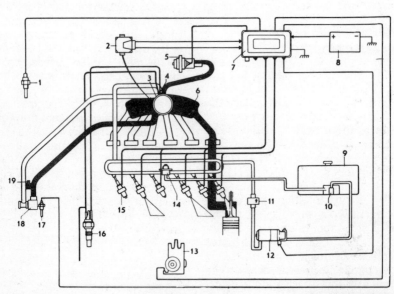

1. Temperature sensor for induction air
2. Throttle valve switch
3. Throttle housing
4. Cold start valve
5. Pressure sensor
6. Inlet duct
7. Control unit (electronic)
8. Battery
9. Fuel tank
10. Fuel filter, suction side
11. Fuel filter, discharge side
12. Fuel pump
13. Triggering contacts in distributor
14. Pressure regulator
15. Injectors
16. Thermal timer contact
17. Temperature sensor for coolant
18. Auxiliary air regulator
19. Idling adjusting screw

Electronic fuel injection—B30F engine

4. Press the plug contact firmly into the new or reconditioned control unit. Fit the plastic cover strip, retaining cap, and screw.

5. Fit the control unit into place and install its retaining screws. Install the remaining components in the reverse order of removal. Have mixture adjusted, if necessary.

PRESSURE REGULATOR

The regulator may be adjusted with its adjusting nut. Pinch and disconnect the flexible fuel hose between the pressure regulator and the header pipe and insert a tee fitting and pressure gauge. Tighten the fuel connections and start the engine. Loosen the locknut and adjust the pressure to 28 psi. If the regulator cannot be adjusted properly, it must be replaced. Remove the tee fitting and gauge, and connect the fuel hoses. Replace the regulator as follows:

1. Place pinch clamps on the three fuel hoses connected to the regulator.

2. Loosen the hose clamps and remove the hoses.

3. On 1970–71 models, remove the regulator from its bracket and replace it with a new one.

4. Connect the fuel hoses to the new regulator, tighten the hose clamps, and remove the pinch clamps.

5. Start the engine and check for fuel leaks.

FUEL INJECTORS

The fuel injectors may be checked for electrical function and sealing only. To check for electrical function, remove the electrical connection and connect an ohmeter across the injector terminals. Resistance should be 2.40 ohms at 68°F (20°C).

Do NOT apply 12 volt current to the injectors. Such voltage would immediately destroy the injector. The internal electric components work on a maximum of three volts.

After following steps 1 and 3–5 below, simply observe the amount of fuel which leaks from the injector with the fuel hose still connected. Acceptable leakage is 5 drops per minute or about one drop every 12 seconds. Excessive dripping delivers too much fuel; the engine runs too rich. Symptoms similar to flooding a carbureted engine may appear. Remove and replace the injectors using the procedure below.

1. On 164 models, remove the air cleaner.

2. Pinch shut the fuel hose to the header pipe.

3. Loosen the hose clamps for the injectors and lift up the header pipe.

4. Remove the plug contacts from the injectors. Disconnect the cable harness from the distributing pipe.

5. Turn the lockrings on the injectors counterclockwise so that they loosen from their bayonet fittings. Lift out the injectors.

6. Place the new injectors, with new washers and new rubber sealing rings, in position and secure them by turning the lockrings clockwise.

7. Connect the cable harness at the distrib-

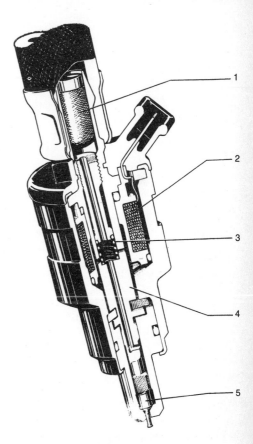

1. Filter
2. Magnetic winding
3. Return spring
4. Magnetic armature
5. Sealing needle

Fuel pressure regulator—1972–73 shown

Cross section of fuel injector

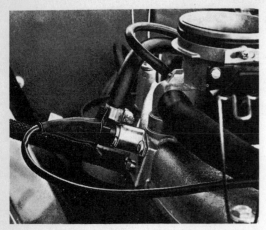

Cold start valve—B30F

uting pipe. Connect the plug contacts to the injectors.

8. Place the header pipe in position, and tighten the hose clamps. Remove the pinch clamps.

9. On 164 models, install the air cleaner.

COLD START VALVE

The cold start valve, mounted on the intake manifold, provides the engine with extr fuel during cold start up. The injection time is governed by the thermal timer which measures coolant temperature and activates the cold start valve electrically. The cold start valve is energized when the temperature of the coolant is below 95°F (35°C). When engaged, the system provides extra fuel for up to 12 seconds, as long as the starter is engaged. To replace the cold start valve:

1. On 164 models, remove the air cleaner.
2. Pinch shut the fuel line to the valve.
3. Remove the plug contact and the fuel hose from the valve.
4. Remove the two retaining screws and the cold start valve from the inlet duct.
5. Place the new cold start valve in position with packing and install the retaining screws.
6. Connect the plug contact and fuel hose to the valve. Remove the pinch clamp.
7. On 164 models, install the air cleaner.

THERMAL TIMER

The thermal timer is a temperature controlled switch controlling current to the cold start valve. In addition to sensing the temperature of the coolant, an internal circuit heats up when the starter is engaged. After a certain temperature is reached, the control circuit to the cold start valve is disconnected. This prevents delivering excessive amounts of fuel to an engine being cranked for long periods. To replace:

1. Drain the cooling system.
CAUTION: *When draining the coolant, keep in mind that cats and dogs are attracted by the ethylene glycol antifreeze, and are quite likely to drink any that is left in an uncovered container or in puddles on the ground. This will prove fatal in sufficient quantity. Always drain the coolant into a sealable container. Coolant should be reused unless it is contaminated or several years old.*

2. Disconnect the plug contacts and unscrew the thermal timer from the cylinder head.

3. Install a new timer and connect the plug contacts.

4. Refill the cooling system.

THROTTLE VALVE SWITCH

The throttle valve switch may be adjusted with an ohmmeter. Connect the ohmmeter to the control unit (contacts 14 and 17 for 4-cylinder, and contacts 9 and 14 for 6-cylinder). Loosen the screws slightly so that the switch may be rotated. Scribe a mark at the upper switch screw on the inlet duct if one is not there already.

Close the throttle valve by turning the switch clockwise as far as it will go. Then, observing the ohmmeter, carefully turn the switch counterclockwise until the ohmmeter registers 0. At this point, the switch is turned a further 1° counterclockwise (½ graduation mark at upper screw), and both switch screws are tightened. Check to make sure that the ohmmeter reading rises to infinity when the throttle valve opens approximately 1°. If it becomes necessary to replace the switch:

1. Disconnect the plug contact from the switch. Remove the two retaining screws and pull the switch straight out of the inlet duct.

2. Fit the new switch to the inlet duct and install the retaining screws. Connect the plug contact.

3. Adjust the switch as outlined above.

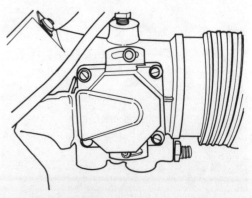

Throttle valve switch, B20F

CHILTON'S
FUEL ECONOMY
& TUNE-UP TIPS

Tune-up • Spark Plug Diagnosis • Emission Controls

Fuel System • Cooling System • Tires and Wheels

General Maintenance

CHILTON'S FUEL ECONOMY & TUNE-UP TIPS

Fuel economy is important to everyone, no matter what kind of vehicle you drive. The maintenance-minded motorist can save both money and fuel using these tips and the periodic maintenance and tune-up procedures in this Repair and Tune-Up Guide.

There are more than 130,000,000 cars and trucks registered for private use in the United States. Each travels an average of 10-12,000 miles per year, and, and in total they consume close to 70 billion gallons of fuel each year. This represents nearly ⅔ of the oil imported by the United States each year. The Federal government's goal is to reduce consumption 10% by 1985. A variety of methods are either already in use or under serious consideration, and they all affect you driving and the cars you will drive. In addition to "down-sizing", the auto industry is using or investigating the use of electronic fuel delivery, electronic engine controls and alternative engines for use in smaller and lighter vehicles, among other alternatives to meet the federally mandated Corporate Average Fuel Economy (CAFE) of 27.5 mpg by 1985. The government, for its part, is considering rationing, mandatory driving curtailments and tax increases on motor vehicle fuel in an effort to reduce consumption. The government's goal of a 10% reduction could be realized — and further government regulation avoided — if every private vehicle could use just 1 less gallon of fuel per week.

How Much Can You Save?

Tests have proven that almost anyone can make at least a 10% reduction in fuel consumption through regular maintenance and tune-ups. When a major manufacturer of spark plugs sur-

---

TUNE-UP

1. Check the cylinder compression to be sure the engine will really benefit from a tune-up and that it is capable of producing good fuel economy. A tune-up will be wasted on an engine in poor mechanical condition.

2. Replace spark plugs regularly. New spark plugs alone can increase fuel economy 3%.

3. Be sure the spark plugs are the correct type (heat range) for your vehicle. See the Tune-Up Specifications.

Heat range refers to the spark plug's ability to conduct heat away from the firing end. It must conduct the heat away in an even pattern to avoid becoming a source of pre-ignition, yet it must also operate hot enough to burn off conductive deposits that could cause misfiring.

The heat range is usually indicated by a number on the spark plug, part of the manufacturer's designation for each individual spark plug. The numbers in bold-face indicate the heat range in each manufacturer's identification system.

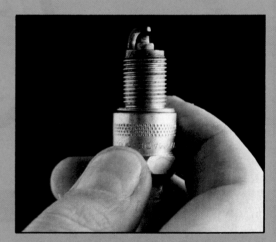

Periodically, check the spark plugs to be sure they are firing efficiently. They are excellent indicators of the internal condition of your engine.

Manufacturer	Typical Designation
AC	R **45** TS
Bosch (old)	WA **145** T30
Bosch (new)	HR **8** Y
Champion	RBL **15** Y
Fram/Autolite	415
Mopar	P-**62** PR
Motorcraft	BRF-**42**
NGK	BP **5** ES-15
Nippondenso	W **16** EP
Prestolite	14GR **5** 2A

On AC, Bosch (new), Champion, Fram/Autolite, Mopar, Motorcraft and Prestolite, a higher number indicates a hotter plug. On Bosch (old), NGK and Nippondenso, a higher number indicates a colder plug.

4. Make sure the spark plugs are properly gapped. See the Tune-Up Specifications in this book.

5. Be sure the spark plugs are firing efficiently. The illustrations on the next 2 pages show you how to "read" the firing end of the spark plug.

6. Check the ignition timing and set it to specifications. Tests show that almost all cars have incorrect ignition timing by more than 2°.

veyed over 6,000 cars nationwide, they found that a tune-up, on cars that needed one, increased fuel economy over 11%. Replacing worn plugs alone, accounted for a 3% increase. The same test also revealed that 8 out of every 10 vehicles will have some maintenance deficiency that will directly affect fuel economy, emissions or performance. Most of this mileage-robbing neglect could be prevented with regular maintenance.

Modern engines require that all of the functioning systems operate properly for maximum efficiency. A malfunction anywhere wastes fuel. You can keep your vehicle running as efficiently and economically as possible, by being aware of your vehicle's operating and performance characteristics. If your vehicle suddenly develops performance or fuel economy problems it could be due to one or more of the following:

PROBLEM	POSSIBLE CAUSE
Engine Idles Rough	Ignition timing, idle mixture, vacuum leak or something amiss in the emission control system.
Hesitates on Acceleration	Dirty carburetor or fuel filter, improper accelerator pump setting, ignition timing or fouled spark plugs.
Starts Hard or Fails to Start	Worn spark plugs, improperly set automatic choke, ice (or water) in fuel system.
Stalls Frequently	Automatic choke improperly adjusted and possible dirty air filter or fuel filter.
Performs Sluggishly	Worn spark plugs, dirty fuel or air filter, ignition timing or automatic choke out of adjustment.

Check spark plug wires on conventional point type ignition for cracks by bending them in a loop around your finger.

Be sure that spark plug wires leading to adjacent cylinders do not run too close together. (Photo courtesy Champion Spark Plug Co.)

7. If your vehicle does not have electronic ignition, check the points, rotor and cap as specified.

8. Check the spark plug wires (used with conventional point-type ignitions) for cracks and burned or broken insulation by bending them in a loop around your finger. Cracked wires decrease fuel efficiency by failing to deliver full voltage to the spark plugs. One misfiring spark plug can cost you as much as 2 mpg.

9. Check the routing of the plug wires. Misfiring can be the result of spark plug leads to adjacent cylinders running parallel to each other and too close together. One wire tends to pick up voltage from the other causing it to fire "out of time".

10. Check all electrical and ignition circuits for voltage drop and resistance.

11. Check the distributor mechanical and/or vacuum advance mechanisms for proper functioning. The vacuum advance can be checked by twisting the distributor plate in the opposite direction of rotation. It should spring back when released.

12. Check and adjust the valve clearance on engines with mechanical lifters. The clearance should be slightly loose rather than too tight.

SPARK PLUG DIAGNOSIS

Normal

APPEARANCE: This plug is typical of one operating normally. The insulator nose varies from a light tan to grayish color with slight electrode wear. The presence of slight deposits is normal on used plugs and will have no adverse effect on engine performance. The spark plug heat range is correct for the engine and the engine is running normally.

CAUSE: Properly running engine.

RECOMMENDATION: Before reinstalling this plug, the electrodes should be cleaned and filed square. Set the gap to specifications. If the plug has been in service for more than 10-12,000 miles, the entire set should probably be replaced with a fresh set of the same heat range.

Oil Deposits

APPEARANCE: The firing end of the plug is covered with a wet, oily coating.

CAUSE: The problem is poor oil control. On high mileage engines, oil is leaking past the rings or valve guides into the combustion chamber. A common cause is also a plugged PCV valve, and a ruptured fuel pump diaphragm can also cause this condition. Oil fouled plugs such as these are often found in new or recently overhauled engines, before normal oil control is achieved, and can be cleaned and reinstalled.

RECOMMENDATION: A hotter spark plug may temporarily relieve the problem, but the engine is probably in need of work.

Incorrect Heat Range

APPEARANCE: The effects of high temperature on a spark plug are indicated by clean white, often blistered insulator. This can also be accompanied by excessive wear of the electrode, and the absence of deposits.

CAUSE: Check for the correct spark plug heat range. A plug which is too hot for the engine can result in overheating. A car operated mostly at high speeds can require a colder plug. Also check ignition timing, cooling system level, fuel mixture and leaking intake manifold.

RECOMMENDATION: If all ignition and engine adjustments are known to be correct, and no other malfunction exists, install spark plugs one heat range colder.

Photos Courtesy Fram Corporation

Carbon Deposits

APPEARANCE: Carbon fouling is easily identified by the presence of dry, soft, black, sooty deposits.

CAUSE: Changing the heat range can often lead to carbon fouling, as can prolonged slow, stop-and-start driving. If the heat range is correct, carbon fouling can be attributed to a rich fuel mixture, sticking choke, clogged air cleaner, worn breaker points, retarded timing or low compression. If only one or two plugs are carbon fouled, check for corroded or cracked wires on the affected plugs. Also look for cracks in the distributor cap between the towers of affected cylinders.

RECOMMENDATION: After the problem is corrected, these plugs can be cleaned and reinstalled if not worn severely.

MMT Fouled

APPEARANCE: Spark plugs fouled by MMT (Methycyclopentadienyl Maganese Tricarbonyl) have reddish, rusty appearance on the insulator and side electrode.

CAUSE: MMT is an anti-knock additive in gasoline used to replace lead. During the combustion process, the MMT leaves a reddish deposit on the insulator and side electrode.

RECOMMENDATION: No engine malfunction is indicated and the deposits will not affect plug performance any more than lead deposits (see Ash Deposits). MMT fouled plugs can be cleaned, regapped and reinstalled.

High Speed Glazing

APPEARANCE: Glazing appears as shiny coating on the plug, either yellow or tan in color.

CAUSE: During hard, fast acceleration, plug temperatures rise suddenly. Deposits from normal combustion have no chance to fluff-off; instead, they melt on the insulator forming an electrically conductive coating which causes misfiring.

RECOMMENDATION: Glazed plugs are not easily cleaned. They should be replaced with a fresh set of plugs of the correct heat range. If the condition recurs, using plugs with a heat range one step colder may cure the problem.

Ash (Lead) Deposits

APPEARANCE: Ash deposits are characterized by light brown or white colored deposits crusted on the side or center electrodes. In some cases it may give the plug a rusty appearance.

CAUSE: Ash deposits are normally derived from oil or fuel additives burned during normal combustion. Normally they are harmless, though excessive amounts can cause misfiring. If deposits are excessive in short mileage, the valve guides may be worn.

RECOMMENDATION: Ash-fouled plugs can be cleaned, gapped and reinstalled.

Detonation

APPEARANCE: Detonation is usually characterized by a broken plug insulator.

CAUSE: A portion of the fuel charge will begin to burn spontaneously, from the increased heat following ignition. The explosion that results applies extreme pressure to engine components, frequently damaging spark plugs and pistons.

Detonation can result by over-advanced ignition timing, inferior gasoline (low octane) lean air/fuel mixture, poor carburetion, engine lugging or an increase in compression ratio due to combustion chamber deposits or engine modification.

RECOMMENDATION: Replace the plugs after correcting the problem.

Photos Courtesy Champion Spark Plug Co.

EMISSION CONTROLS

13. Be aware of the general condition of the emission control system. It contributes to reduced pollution and should be serviced regularly to maintain efficient engine operation.

14. Check all vacuum lines for dried, cracked or brittle conditions. Something as simple as a leaking vacuum hose can cause poor performance and loss of economy.

15. Avoid tampering with the emission control system. Attempting to improve fuel econ-

FUEL SYSTEM

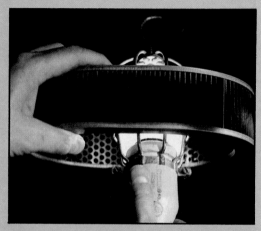

Check the air filter with a light behind it. If you can see light through the filter it can be reused.

Extremely clogged filters should be discarded and replaced with a new one.

18. Replace the air filter regularly. A dirty air filter richens the air/fuel mixture and can increase fuel consumption as much as 10%. Tests show that ⅓ of all vehicles have air filters in need of replacement.

19. Replace the fuel filter at least as often as recommended.

20. Set the idle speed and carburetor mixture to specifications.

21. Check the automatic choke. A sticking or malfunctioning choke wastes gas.

22. During the summer months, adjust the automatic choke for a leaner mixture which will produce faster engine warm-ups.

COOLING SYSTEM

29. Be sure all accessory drive belts are in good condition. Check for cracks or wear.

30. Adjust all accessory drive belts to proper tension.

31. Check all hoses for swollen areas, worn spots, or loose clamps.

32. Check coolant level in the radiator or expansion tank.

33. Be sure the thermostat is operating properly. A stuck thermostat delays engine warm-up and a cold engine uses nearly twice as much fuel as a warm engine.

34. Drain and replace the engine coolant at least as often as recommended. Rust and scale

TIRES & WHEELS

38. Check the tire pressure often with a pencil type gauge. Tests by a major tire manufacturer show that 90% of all vehicles have at least 1 tire improperly inflated. Better mileage can be achieved by over-inflating tires, but never exceed the maximum inflation pressure on the side of the tire.

39. If possible, install radial tires. Radial tires deliver as much as ½ mpg more than bias belted tires.

40. Avoid installing super-wide tires. They only create extra rolling resistance and decrease fuel mileage. Stick to the manufacturer's recommendations.

41. Have the wheels properly balanced.

omy by tampering with emission controls is more likely to worsen fuel economy than improve it. Emission control changes on modern engines are not readily reversible.

16. Clean (or replace) the EGR valve and lines as recommended.

17. Be sure that all vacuum lines and hoses are reconnected properly after working under the hood. An unconnected or misrouted vacuum line can wreak havoc with engine performance.

23. Check for fuel leaks at the carburetor, fuel pump, fuel lines and fuel tank. Be sure all lines and connections are tight.

24. Periodically check the tightness of the carburetor and intake manifold attaching nuts and bolts. These are a common place for vacuum leaks to occur.

25. Clean the carburetor periodically and lubricate the linkage.

26. The condition of the tailpipe can be an excellent indicator of proper engine combustion. After a long drive at highway speeds, the inside of the tailpipe should be a light grey in color. Black or soot on the insides indicates an overly rich mixture.

27. Check the fuel pump pressure. The fuel pump may be supplying more fuel than the engine needs.

28. Use the proper grade of gasoline for your engine. Don't try to compensate for knocking or "pinging" by advancing the ignition timing. This practice will only increase plug temperature and the chances of detonation or pre-ignition with relatively little performance gain.

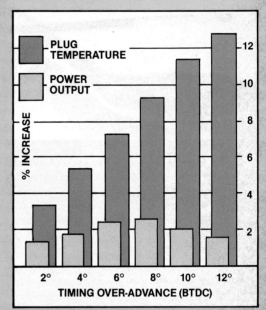

Increasing ignition timing past the specified setting results in a drastic increase in spark plug temperature with increased chance of detonation or preignition. Performance increase is considerably less. (Photo courtesy Champion Spark Plug Co.)

that form in the engine should be flushed out to allow the engine to operate at peak efficiency.

35. Clean the radiator of debris that can decrease cooling efficiency.

36. Install a flex-type or electric cooling fan, if you don't have a clutch type fan. Flex fans use curved plastic blades to push more air at low speeds when more cooling is needed; at high speeds the blades flatten out for less resistance. Electric fans only run when the engine temperature reaches a predetermined level.

37. Check the radiator cap for a worn or cracked gasket. If the cap does not seal properly, the cooling system will not function properly.

42. Be sure the front end is correctly aligned. A misaligned front end actually has wheels going in differed directions. The increased drag can reduce fuel economy by .3 mpg.

43. Correctly adjust the wheel bearings. Wheel bearings that are adjusted too tight increase rolling resistance.

Check tire pressures regularly with a reliable pocket type gauge. Be sure to check the pressure on a cold tire.

GENERAL MAINTENANCE

Check the fluid levels (particularly engine oil) on a regular basis. Be sure to check the oil for grit, water or other contamination.

A vacuum gauge is another excellent indicator of internal engine condition and can also be installed in the dash as a mileage indicator.

44. Periodically check the fluid levels in the engine, power steering pump, master cylinder, automatic transmission and drive axle.

45. Change the oil at the recommended interval and change the filter at every oil change. Dirty oil is thick and causes extra friction between moving parts, cutting efficiency and increasing wear. A worn engine requires more frequent tune-ups and gets progressively worse fuel economy. In general, use the lightest viscosity oil for the driving conditions you will encounter.

46. Use the recommended viscosity fluids in the transmission and axle.

47. Be sure the battery is fully charged for fast starts. A slow starting engine wastes fuel.

48. Be sure battery terminals are clean and tight.

49. Check the battery electrolyte level and add distilled water if necessary.

50. Check the exhaust system for crushed pipes, blockages and leaks.

51. Adjust the brakes. Dragging brakes or brakes that are not releasing create increased drag on the engine.

52. Install a vacuum gauge or miles-per-gallon gauge. These gauges visually indicate engine vacuum in the intake manifold. High vacuum = good mileage and low vacuum = poorer mileage. The gauge can also be an excellent indicator of internal engine conditions.

53. Be sure the clutch is properly adjusted. A slipping clutch wastes fuel.

54. Check and periodically lubricate the heat control valve in the exhaust manifold. A sticking or inoperative valve prevents engine warm-up and wastes gas.

55. Keep accurate records to check fuel economy over a period of time. A sudden drop in fuel economy may signal a need for tune-up or other maintenance.

AUXILIARY AIR REGULATOR

The auxiliary air regulator is found at the front of the cylinder head and has a capillary tube extending into the cooling system. Its functional range is from −13°F to +140°F (−25–+60°C). Depending on the temperature of the coolant, the unit allows additional air into the intake manifold. As the engine heats up, the capillary tube expands and presses back the regulator slide; at 140°F (60°C), the system is completely closed and no additional air is admitted to the system.

To check the operation of the auxiliary air regulator, start the engine and allow it to reach operating temperature, 176°F (80°C). Make a note of the idle speed and then disconnect the hose between the inlet duct and the regulator. While covering the hose opening with your hand, check to see that the idle speed does not drop significantly under the first reading. A drop in idle speed indicates a leak in the regula-

Auxiliary air regulator—B30F

Auxiliary air regulator—B20F

tor, requiring its replacement. Replace the regulator as follows.

1. Drain the cooling system.
CAUTION: *When draining the coolant, keep in mind that cats and dogs are attracted by the ethylene glycol antifreeze, and are quite likely to drink any that is left in an uncovered container or in puddles on the ground. This will prove fatal in sufficient quantity. Always drain the coolant into a sealable container. Coolant should be reused unless it is contaminated or several years old.*
2. Remove the plug contact from the temperature sensor and disconnect the air hoses from the regulator.
3. Remove the two retaining bolts and draw out the regulator.
4. Using a new sealing ring, position the new regulator to the cylinder head and install the retaining bolts.
5. Connect the plug contact and the two air hoses.
6. Refill the cooling system.

INTAKE AIR TEMPERATURE SENSOR

Located in front of the air cleaner, this sensor informs the control unit of changes in air temperature. At air temperatures below 86°F (30°C), the injection interval (duration) increases slightly. To test this sensor, connect an ohmeter across the terminal pins. According to the air temperature, resistance should be: 440Ω @ 50°F (10°C); 300Ω @ 68°F (20°C); 210Ω @ 86°F (30°C); 160Ω @ 104°F (40°C). Acceptable range is ± 40Ω for each listed resistance. To replace the sensor:

1. On 164 models, remove the right drip protection, and the air hose from the right side.
2. Disconnect the four-way plug contact from the sensor.
3. Unscrew the old sensor and install a new one, taking care not to overtighten it.
4. Plug in the four-way contact for the sensor.
5. On 164 models, install the right air hose and drip protection.

COOLANT TEMPERATURE SENSOR

The temperature sensor is located at the front of the cylinder head and informs the control unit of changes in the coolant temperature. This sensor is also tested by checking the resistance with an ohmeter. Ohm readings will vary with coolant temperature as follows: 3,000–4,200Ω @ 50°F (10°C); 2,100–3,100Ω @ 68°F (20°C); 1,400–2,100Ω @ at 86°F (30°C); 1,000–1,400Ω @ 104°F (40°C). Target readings are the middle of the range, but anywhere within the range is acceptable. To replace the coolant sensor:

1. Drain a portion of the cooling system so that the coolant level in the radiator and engine is below the temperature sensor.

CAUTION: *When draining the coolant, keep in mind that cats and dogs are attracted by the ethylene glycol antifreeze, and are quite likely to drink any that is left in an uncovered container or in puddles on the ground. This will prove fatal in sufficient quantity. Always drain the coolant into a sealable container. Coolant should be reused unless it is contaminated or several years old.*

2. Disconnect the plug contact from the sensor.

3. Unscrew the old sensor and install a new one with a new sealing ring.

4. Connect the plug contact.

5. Top up the cooling system.

PRESSURE SENSOR

This device interprets changes in intake air pressure and communicates with the control unit. It is from this unit that the control unit gets its sense of engine load. Generally located on the right front wheel well, the sensor contains mechanical components to read air pressure and a small transformer for sending electrical signals to the brain.

Only the transformer can be checked; there are no mechanical repairs for the sensor. Using an ohmeter, check the resistance between terminals 7 and 15. This measurement of the primary windings should be about 90 ohms. Measure the secondary winding between terminals 8 and 10 and look for about 350 ohms. Any other combination of terminals should yield an infinite resistance, i.e. no connection. If it is necessary to replace the sensor:

1. Disconnect the four-way contact and the air hose from the sensor.

2. Remove the three screws retaining the sensor to the right wheel housing.

3. Transfer the attaching bracket to the new pressure sensor.

4. Position the new sensor to the wheel well and install the retaining screws.

5. Connect the plug contact and the air hose to the sensor.

TRIGGERING CONTACTS

These two contacts are actuated by the distributor camshaft. The electrical message they send to the control unit is used with the air pressure data to determine when injection should begin and how long the injection should last. To inspect or replace the contact unit:

1. Remove the distributor as outlined in chapter 3.

2. Remove the two screws securing the triggering contacts holder to the distributor and then pull out the holder.

3. Lubricate the fiber pieces of the contact breaker lever on the new holder with silicone cam lobe grease.

4. Check to see that the rubber ring is not damaged. Replace if necessary.

5. Install the new holder in the distributor and tighten the retaining screws.

6. Install the distributor as outlined in chapter 3.

CONTINUOUS MECHANICAL FUEL INJECTION (CI)

Bosch continuous fuel injection is standard on all gasoline engine 240 and 260 models, 1974 140 models and all 1980 and later models except the B21F-LH and the B23F-LH. It differs from the electric fuel injection (see above) in that injection takes place continuously. Controlled through variation of the fuel flow rate through the injectors, rather than variation of the fuel injection duration, this system has no electronic computer. It is an electromechanical system that will provide suitable air/fuel mixtures to accommodate differing driving conditions.

The complete system consists of the following components: air/fuel control unit (housing both air flow sensor and fuel distributor), electric fuel pump (and fuel pressure accumulator), fuel filter, control pressure regulator, continuous fuel injectors, auxiliary air valve, cold start injector, thermal time switch, main relay, and a fuel pump relay.

The heart of the system is the air/fuel control unit. It consists of an air flow sensor and a fuel distributor. Intake air flows past the air cleaner and through the air venturi raising (four cylinder) or lowering (V6) the counterbalanced air flow sensor plate. The plate is connected to a pivoting lever which moves the control plunger in the fuel distributor in direct proportion to air flow.

The fuel distributor, which controls and distributes the amount of fuel to the injectors consists of a line pressure regulator, a control plunger, and pressure regulator valves (one for each injector). The line pressure regulator maintains the fuel distributor inlet pressure at about 65 psi. and will recirculate fuel to the tank if pressure exceeds this value. The control plunger (which is connected to the air flow sensor plate) controls the amount of fuel available to each of the pressure regulator valves. The pressure regulator valves maintain a constant fuel pressure differential (1.4 psi) between the inlet and outlet sides of the control plunger. This is independent of the amount of fuel passing through the valves, which varies according to plunger height.

The injectors themselves are spring loaded and calibrated to open at 47–51 psi. They are not electrically operated as on the older electronic fuel injection system.

The control pressure regulator, located on the intake manifold, acts to regulate the fuel/air mixture according to engine temperature. When the engine is cold, the control pressure regulator richens the mixture (4–5 minutes max.). This is accomplished in the following manner; a certain amount of fuel is bled off into a separate control pressure system. The control pressure regulator maintains this fuel at about 52.5 psi. The regulator is connected to the upper side of the fuel distributor control plunger. When the engine temperature is below operat-

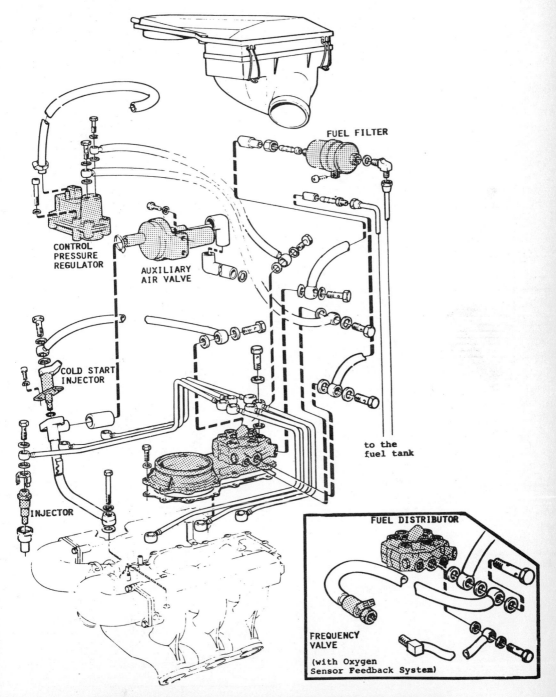

FUEL FILTER

CONTROL
PRESSURE
REGULATOR

AUXILIARY
AIR VALVE

COLD START
INJECTOR

INJECTOR

to the
fuel tank

FUEL DISTRIBUTOR

FREQUENCY
VALVE

(with Oxygen
Sensor Feedback System)

Continuous fuel injection system (mechanical)—B27F engine, B28F similar

ing minimum, a bi-metal spring in the regulator senses this and reduces the fuel pressure on
top of the plunger.

This allows the plunger to rise further and
channel more fuel to the regulator valves and
injectors, thereby richening the mixture. When
the engine warms, the bimetal spring in the
regulator increases the pressure to 52.5 psi,
leaning the mixture back to its normal operating ratio. On V6 models, a vacuum feature is
added to the regulator, whereby low vacuum
situations, such as acceleration, temporarily

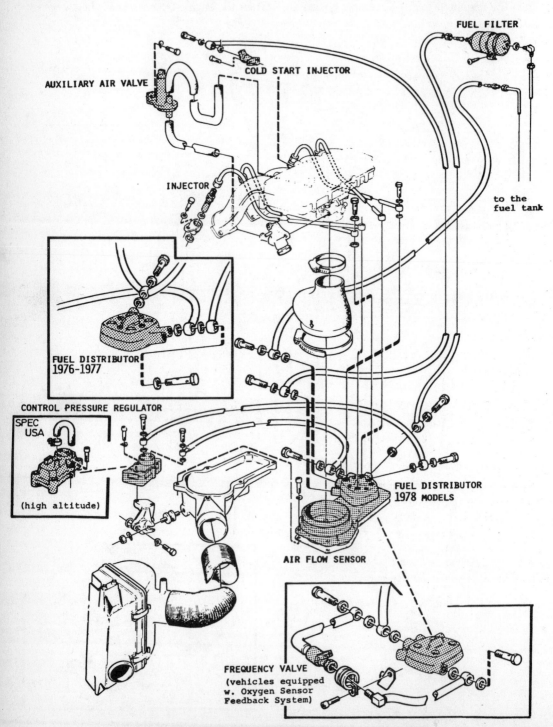

Continuous fuel injection system (mechanical)—B21F engine

lower the control pressure and richen the mixture. At idle, full throttle, and steady state conditions, the vacuum is high and the mixture returns to normal.

The auxiliary air valve provides extra air to mix with the richer mixture during warm-up, thus raising the engine speed and improving cold start driveability. The auxiliary air valve, which also has a temperature sensitive bimetal spring, works directly with the control pressure regulator. At cold startup, the valve is fully open. As the engine warms, an electric coil slowly closes the valve (4–5 minutes max.), blocking off the extra air and eliminating the fast idle speed.

The cold start injector, located on the inlet duct, sprays extra fuel into the intake air stream (during starter operation) when the engine coolant temperature is below 95°F (35°C). It has a maximum spraying duration of 12 seconds.

The thermal time switch, located on the cylinder head, actuates the cold start injector. Its bi-metal spring senses coolant temperature and an electric coil limits the cold start injector spray to 12 seconds.

The fuel accumulator, located adjacent to the fuel pump, has a check valve which keeps residual fuel pressure from dropping below 28 psi

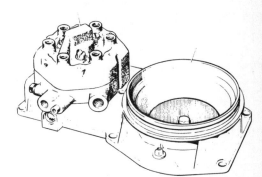

Air/fuel control unit for (6 cylinder) CI system. 'A' is the airflow sensor and 'B' is the fuel distributor

when the engine or fuel pump are shut off. Therefore, the system is always pressurized, preventing vapor lock in hot start situations.

TESTING AND ADJUSTMENT

Resetting

AIR/FUEL CONTROL UNIT

The air-flow sensor plate adjustment is critical. The distance between the sensor plate and the plate stop must be 0–0.02 in. (0–0.5mm).

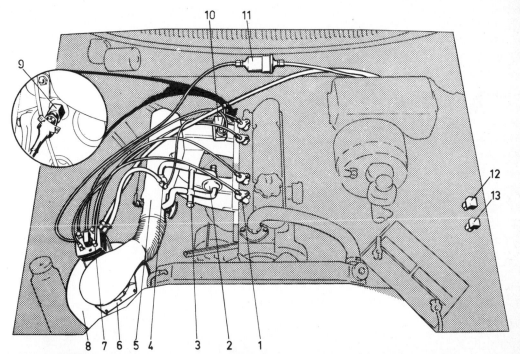

1. Injector
2. Auxiliary air valve
3. Idle adjustment screw
4. Cold start injector
5. Intake manifold
6. Air flow sensor
7. Fuel distributor
8. Air cleaner
9. Thermal time switch
10. Control pressure regulator
11. Fuel filter
12. 13. Safety relay and pump relay

Continuous fuel injection system (mechanical)—B20 engine

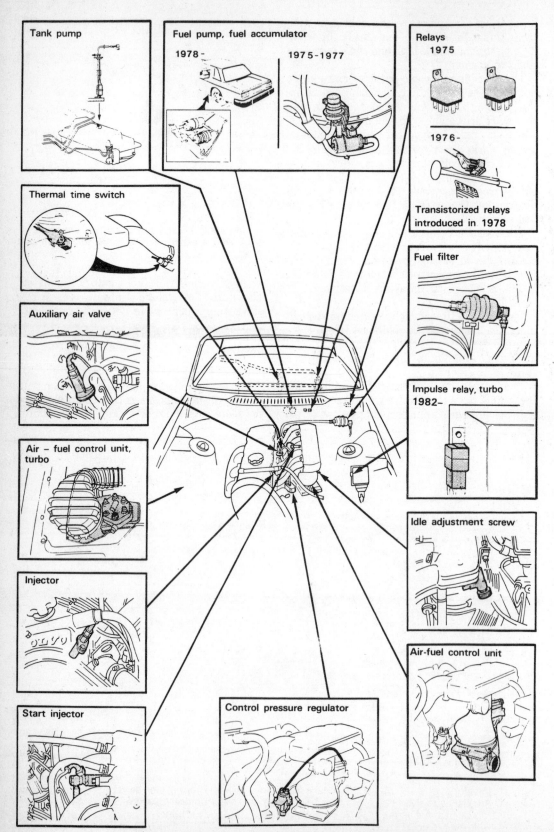

Tank pump

Fuel pump, fuel accumulator
1978 –   1975-1977

Relays
1975

1976 –

Transistorized relays
introduced in 1978

Thermal time switch

Fuel filter

Auxiliary air valve

Impulse relay, turbo
1982–

Air – fuel control unit,
turbo

Idle adjustment screw

Injector

Air-fuel control unit

Start injector

Control pressure regulator

Component location, CI system. 240 shown, others similar

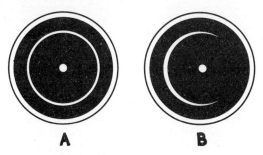

Center the plate on the air-fuel control unit

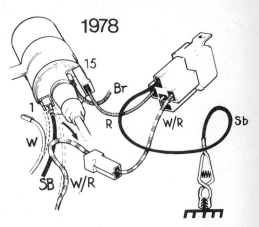

1978

Attach test relay on 1978 and later models

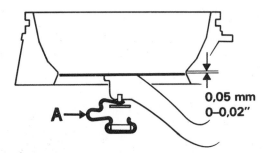

Distance between the sensor plate and the plate stop is adjusted at spring "A" on B21F

The plate must also be centered in the venturi, and must not contact the venturi walls. Loosen the plate center screw to adjust it. The plate should not bind, and although (due to the control pressure) the plate will offer some resistance when depressed, it should return to its rest position when released.

To check the air-flow sensor contact switch, turn the ignition key to the ON position--don't start the motor--and depress (V6) or lift (4-cyl.) the sensor plate by hand. The fuel injectors should buzz, and the fuel pump should activate. If the pump operates, but the injectors do not buzz, check the fuel pressure. If the pump does not operate, check for a short in the air-flow sensor connector. Turn the ignition to OFF before performing any diagnostic work.

FUEL PUMP

If a defective fuel pump is suspected, perform this test. With the ignition switch on, disconnect the wire connector at the air flow sensor. The pump should work. If not, check fuse #7 (1977) or fuses #5 and #7 (1976 and 1978 and later) and voltage across auxiliary air valve terminals. Live terminals indicate a faulty fuel pump or wiring.

WARNING: *The use of the correct special tools or their equivalent is REQUIRED for this procedure. A fuel pressure gauge with a three position valve and T-fitting is required*

to isolate the line, rest, and control pressure readings.

Connect a pressure gauge and T-fitting with 3-way valve inline between the center of the fuel distributor (control pressure fuel line) and the control pressure regulator.

CAUTION: *Disconnect the coil wire (terminal 15) to prevent burning out the coil windings.*

Disconnect the wire connectors at the control pressure regulator and auxiliary air valve. Switch on the ignition and disconnect the wire connector at the air-flow sensor on pre-1978 models, attach test relay as shown on 1978 and later models. The fuel pump should start.

Check the line pressure first. With the T-fitting lever pointing to the fuel distributor, check that the line pressure is 64–75 psi. If insufficient, check fuel lines for leakage, fuel pump for delivery capacity (25.3 fluid ounces in 30 sec.), or low line pressure adjustment. If too high, check for clogged fuel return line or high line pressure adjustment. Line pressure is adjusted along with rest pressure later in this procedure.

Check the control pressure next. With the T-fitting turned at a right angle to the hoses, check the control pressure. Depending on coolant temperature, the control pressure will be somewhere between 18–55 psi, lower for cool temperatures, higher for warm temperatues. If the control pressure is insufficient, try a new pressure regulator. If the pressure is too high, check for a clogged fuel return line, or try a new control pressure regulator. Reconnect the control pressure regulator electrical connector.

After 4–5 minutes, the pressure should equal 44–55 psi. If not, disconnect the electrical connector at the control pressure regulator and check with a 12v test light across the terminals. No voltage indicates a defective (open) wire. Voltage indicates a possible faulty regulator. Then check across the terminals with an ohmmeter. Resistance indicates corroded terminals. No resistance indicates a defective control pressure regulator.

NOTE: *On the B28F engine, the control pressure regulator is equipped with two resistor heaters which are wired in parallel in the regulator wiring circuit. One of the heaters is switched off at temperatures above 60°F (15°C). Correct resistance on this regulator is: 32–38Ω below 55°F (13°C); 16.5–19.5Ω above 65°F (18°C).*

The vacuum function of the control pressure regulator on the V6 engine is checked later in this test.

The auxiliary air valve is checked next. Disconnect the auxiliary air valve hoses. Using a dentist's mirror or similar and a flashlight, check that the valve is partly open at room temperature. Reconnect the wire connector at the valve and, after 4–5 min., the valve should be fully closed. If not, tap on valve and check again. If tapping closes the valve, the valve is OK (engine vibrations will close it in normal operation). If the auxiliary air valve still does not close, disconnect the connector and check the voltage across the wire connector terminals with a 12v test light. No voltage indicates a defective circuit. Next, check across the auxiliary air valve terminals with an ohmmeter. Correct resistance is 40–60 ohms. No resistance indicates a faulty auxiliary air valve.

Check the rest pressure. Connect the wire connector to the air-flow sensor to stop the fuel pump. With the pump stopped, and the pressure guage T-fitting lever at a right angle to the fuel lines, check that the rest pressure is 24 psi, dropping to no less than 14 psi after 10 minutes. The rest pressure and line pressure are adjusted simultaneously by inserting or removing shims between the regulator plunger and plunger cap on the side of the fuel distributor. Shims are available in 0.1mm and 0.5mm sizes. A 0.1mm shim makes a 0.8 psi difference, and a 0.5mm shim makes a 4.3 psi difference on both rest and line pressure.

If the rest pressure drops noticeably within one minute, check for defective control pressure regulator, leaky line pressure regulator or O-ring, a defective fuel pump check valve, or some external fuel leak.

The vacuum function of the V6 control pressure regulator is checked with the pressure gauge and T-fitting installed, and all electrical connectors installed. On a running, warm engine, with the tee fitting positioned at a right angle to the fuel hoses, fuel pressure should be 50–55 psi. When the vacuum hose is disconnected at the regulator, the pressure should drop to 44–50 psi. If not, the regulator is defective.

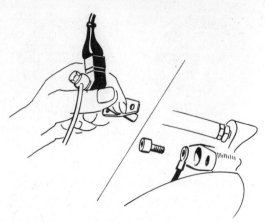

Removing the cold start injector

COLD START INJECTION

Remove the cold start injector from the intake manifold and hold it over a container. For a cold engine — coolant temperature at or less than 90°F (32°C) — the injector should spray during starter operation (max. 12 seconds). If not, check the voltage between the terminals of the injector when the starter is on. Voltage indicates a bad cold start injector. No voltage indicates a faulty thermal time switch or wiring.

With the starter off, disconnect the wire connector at the air-flow sensor on pre-1978 models and attach the test relay as shown (1978 and later models) to operate the fuel pump. Check for cold start injector leakage. Maximum allowable leakage is one drop per minute, less is desirable.

THERMAL TIME SWITCH

Remove the cold start injector and place over a beaker. With the engine fully warmed up — coolant temperature over 95°F (35°C) — the injector should not operate. If it does, the thermal time switch is defective. Reminder: on a cold engine, the start injector should not inject fuel for more than 12 seconds during starter cranking. If it does, the thermal time switch is defective.

CONTINUOUS FUEL INJECTION

The injectors are simple spring-loaded atomizers, designed to open at 47–51 psi on 1974–78 models and 50–54 psi on 1979 and later models. Critical factors are spray pattern, fuel spray quantity, and leakage after the engine is shut off.

To check spray pattern, remove the injectors, one at a time, and hold over a container. Switch the ignition key ON and disconnect the connector at the air-flow sensor to activate the fuel pump. Move the airflow sensor plate. The injector should provide a healthy dose of uniformly

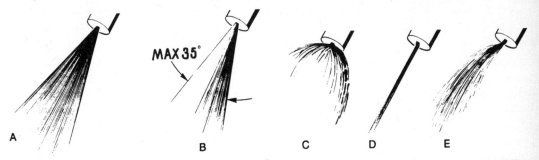

Examples of injector spray patterns. 'A' is proper, 'B' is acceptable; 'C', 'D' and 'E' are unacceptable—the injector must be replaced

atomized fuel at a 15–52° angle in a cone shaped pattern.

To check injection quantity, connect the removed injectors via hoses to 4 (or 6) equal sized containers. Switch on the ignition. Disconnect the connector at the airflow sensor to activate the fuel pump. Run the pump for approximately 30 seconds to pressurize the system. Reconnect the connector to stop the fuel pump. Lift (4-cylinder) or depress (V6) the air-flow sensor plate halfway until one of the beakers fills up. Compare the fuel levels in the containers. If the injection quantity deviates more than 20% between injectors, isolate problem by swapping the lowest and highest quantity injectors and repeating the test. If the same injector still supplies less, clean or replace that injector and fuel supply line. If the other injector is now faulty, the fuel distributor is defective.

The check for injector leak-down (when closed) can now be conducted. Injector leakage beyond slight seepage may be due to the air-flow sensor plate being set to an incorrect height, seizing of fuel distriburtor plunger, or internal leaks in the fuel distributor. Connect the airflow sensor connector to deactivate the fuel pump and switch off the ignition. Check for injector leakage at rest pressure. Move the sensor plate to open the fuel distributor slots. Maximum permissible leakage is one drop per 15 seconds. If all injectors leak, the problem may be excessive rest pressure.

Throttle Linkage Adjustment

On all models, make sure the throttle valve(s) are closed when in the idle position and that they open completely when the accelerator is floored. On the B27F, B28F and B280F engines the throttle valves are located behind the front manifold pipe.

Disconnect the link rod between the throttle valve pulley and the throttle valve, then reconnect it: reconnecting the link should not move the pulley at all. If it does, adjust the link rod at its threaded ends. After reconnecting the link,

have an assistant floor the accelerator pedal: the pulley should rotate and its arm should touch the full throttle stop. If the arm does not touch the stop, adjust the cable at its plastic adjuster. Release the throttle cable and make sure it returns to the idle position. Recheck the link rod.

NOTE: *To adjust the automatic transmission kickdown cable, see Chapter 7.*

BOSCH CONSTANT IDLE SPEED (CIS) SYSTEM

Adjustments

This system, introduced in 1981, controls the engine idle speed by regulating air flow around (bypassing) the throttle valve in the intake manifold. It is used on engines with both mechanical and LH-Jetronic electronic fuel injection systems.

There are five main components in the CIS system:

• The Electronic Control Unit (ECU) processes information from the sensors about engine speed, engine temperature and throttle position. The ECU signals the Air Control Valve to regulate air flow.

• The Air Control Valve, a small electric motor that rotates open or closed depending on the signal from the ECU.

• A micro-switch at the throttle which signals the ECU as the throttle goes back to idle.

• The ignition coil, which provides information to the ECU on engine speed.

• The coolant temperature sensor, which allows the ECU to increase the idle speed when the engine is cold and decrease the idle speed as the engine warms up.

On 1982 and later CIS systems, a micro-switch in the air conditioning control unit signals the ECU to set a higher idle speed when the air conditioning is turned on; this improves air conditioner operation and and eliminates some idle vibration.

On all models except the 760 GLE, the ECU

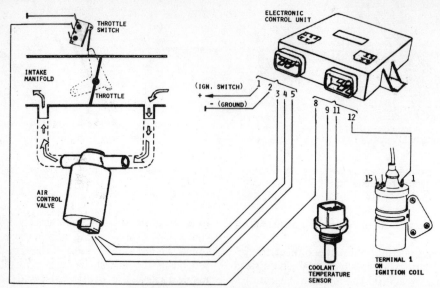

Constant Idle Speed (CIS) components

is mounted inside the right door on the kick panel; on the 760GLE, it is located inside the left door. Air control valves are located next to the intake chamber on the B21, B23, and B28 V6; on the B21F Turbo, the valve is located under the front side of the intake manifold.

Troubleshooting the CIS System

Eliminate all other possible systems faults before investigating faults in the CIS system.

Consult the accompanying chart for possible reasons for an incorrect idle speed.

A common source of problems in the CIS system may be the wires and/or connectors.

There are two connectors, blue at top and black on bottom, at the ECU, and two other ECU connectors at the center and right hand side of the firewall. The air control valve also has a connector at the valve.

If the engine idle speed is considerably lower

CIS Troubleshooting

Symptom	Possible Reasons
Idle varies up and down, more than ±50 rpm for 1981 models, more than ±20 rpm for 1982 and later models.	–CO adjustment incorrect. –Ignition timing incorrect. –Throttle butterfly valve incorrectly adjusted. –Electronic Control Unit faulty. –Air control valve faulty.
Idle speed too high.	–Air control valve sticks. –Bad contact in connector. –Throttle switch incorrectly adjusted. –Temperature sensor faulty or not connected.
No speed control.	–Air control valve sticks. –Bad contact in connector. –Throttle switch incorrectly adjusted. –Electronic Control Unit faulty. –Air control valve faulty.
Engine stalls when braking to stop.	–CO adjustment incorrect. –Ignition timing incorrect. –Throttle butterfly valve incorrectly adjusted. –Bad contact in connector. –Electronic Control Unit faulty. –Low basic rpm.
No rapid idle speed when cold.	–Air control valve sticks. –Electronic Control Unit faulty. –Air control valve faulty. –Coolant temperature sensor faulty.

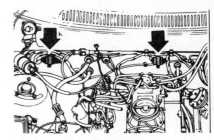

Firewall connectors, CIS system

TEST EQUIPMENT

A good quality volt-ohmmeter, with a range of 0 to approximately 20 volts is necessary to test the CIS system on all models. It is also helpful to have a test light (the type with a pointed contact on the bulb side and an alligator clamp on the other) as this uses more current then a volt-ohmmeter and might in some cases reveal a bad connection better. A tachometer is necessary as is a supply of jumpers, pieces of wire with connectors or alligator clips on both ends. Jumpers are used to connect two terminals of a circuit. Its extremely handy to

ECU location, CIS system. The location on the 760GLE is on the driver's side kick panel

than specified, check the engine vacuum hoses for possible obstructions. The air control valve can be become stuck or obstructed by deposits from the PCV valve and system.

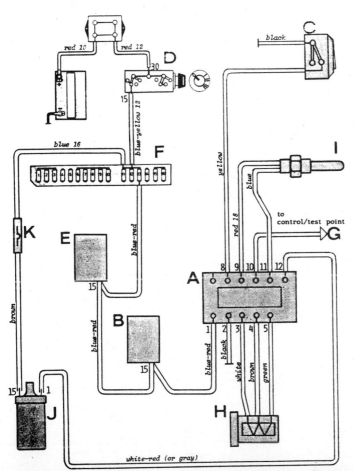

Fuse No. 13:
Instruments
Turn signals
Seat belt warning
CIS System

Legend:
A ECU (Electronic Control Unit)
B Seat belt reminder unit
C Throttle switch
D Ignition switch
E Fuel pump relay
F Fuse box
G Control/test point
H Air control valve
I Coolant temperature sensor
J Ignition coil
K Ballast resistor

CIS wiring schematic for B28F

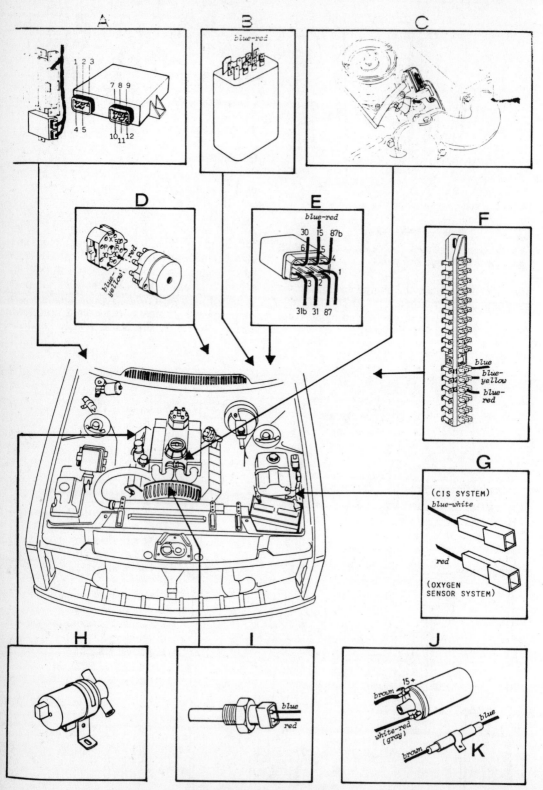

CIS component location, B28F

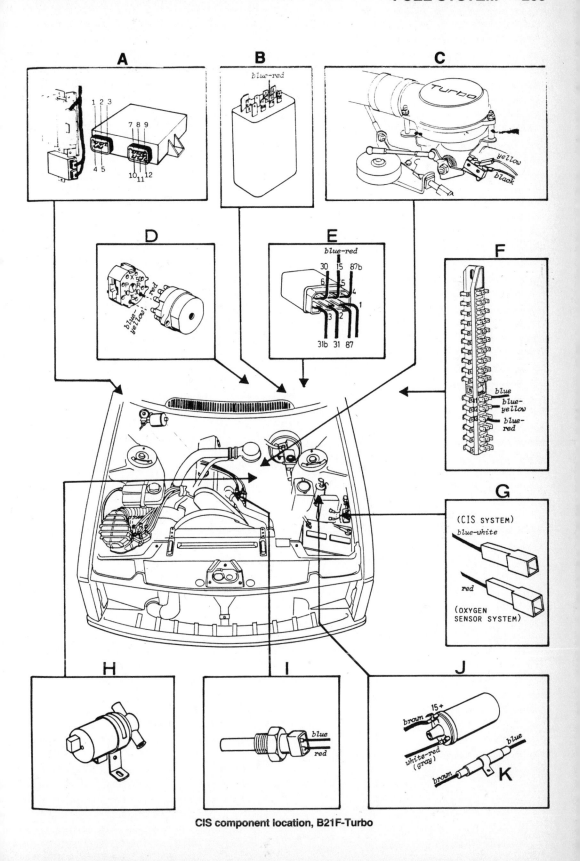

CIS component location, B21F-Turbo

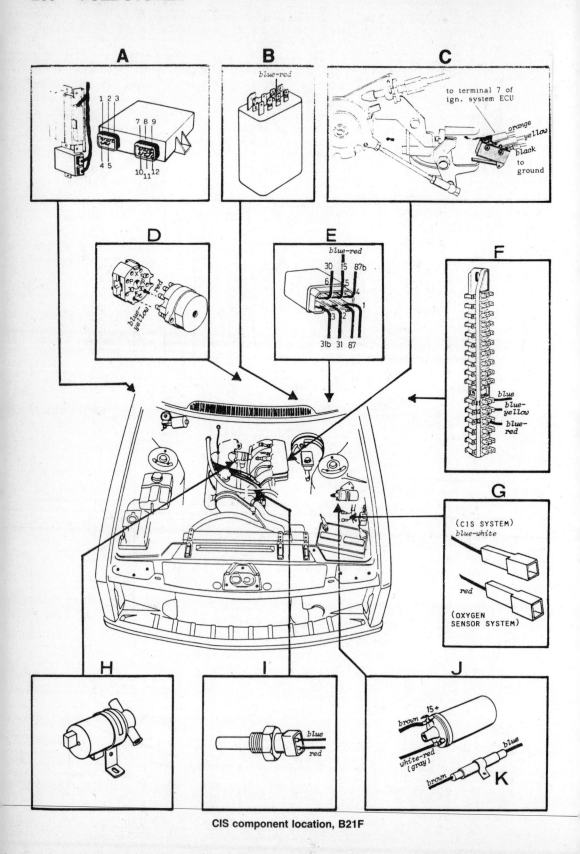

CIS component location, B21F

buy or make jumpers from various colors of wire. Circuits can then be visually identified quickly.

WARNING: *Although the CIS system voltage and currents are low, DO NOT press in the test point between the terminal contacts; just TOUCH the test point to them. Otherwise, the terminal contacts may be damaged.*

Most of the common faults in the CIS system are bad connections in the multipin connectors on the firewall, at the ECU module or at the coolant temperature sensor. If the ECU is not getting correct data from the sensors, it cannot respond properly to the engine conditions of the moment.

TESTING

NOTE: *To prepare for the test, remove the panel that covers the ECU on the kickpanel, and disconnect both connectos at the ECU. Switch the ignition ON, except where noted.*

Current Supply Check

The terminal numbers are marked on the side of the ECU. With the ignition ON, terminal 1 is positive (+) and energized from the ignition switch. Terminal 2 is negative (−) and ground. Connect the voltmeter or test lamp across terminals 1 and 2 in the connector; the voltmeter should read battery voltage and the test lamp should be fully illuminated. If there is no reading, first check an alternate ground, then check fuse No. 13 in the fusebox.

Throttle Switch (Mirco-Switch) Check

Switch the ignition off. Connect the ohmmeter test leads across terminal 8 (blue connector) and terminal 1 (black connector). Check the chart below for ohmmeter and test lamp re-

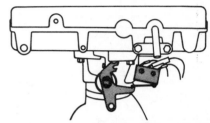

CIS throttle micro switch is located on the throttle linkage

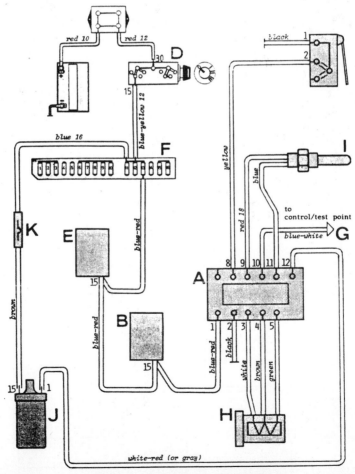

CIS wiring schematic for B21F-Turbo

Throttle Pedal Not Depressed (Idle Position)

1981 models:		
B21F, all	infinite resistance	test lamp NOT illuminated
B28F	zero resistance	test lamp illuminated
1982 models:		
B21F, all	infinite resistance	test lamp NOT illuminated
B28F	infinite resistance	test lamp NOT illuminated
1983 models:		
B21F, all	infinite resistance	test lamp NOT illuminated
B23E	infinite resistance	test lamp NOT illuminated
B28F	infinite resistance	test lamp NOT illuminated

Throttle Pedal Depressed (Above Idle Position)

1981 models:		
B21F, all	zero resistance	test lamp illuminated
B28F	infinite resistance	test lamp NOT illuminated
1982 models:		
B21F, all	zero resistance	test lamp illuminated
B28F	zero resistance	test lamp illuminated
1983 models:		
B21F, all	zero resistance	test lamp illuminated
B23E	zero resistance	test lamp illuminated
B28F	zero resistance	test lamp illuminated

Test conditions for checking the throttle switch

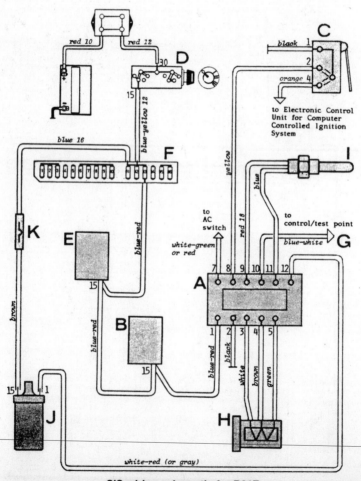

CIS wiring schematic for B21F

sults. If the readings are incorrect, adjust the system according to the instructions below for your particular model.

Coolant Temperature Sensor Check

Use the ohmmeter to test coolant temperature sensor resistance. Connect the meter across terminals 9 and 11 of the connectors. Consult the adjacent charts for resistance readings at specific temperature.

Ignition Signal Check

Connect the tachometer across terminal 12 and any ground point. Start the engine. The tach should show engine speed; if the reading is incorrect or there is no reading at all, check the connectors on the firewall for good contact.

Air Control Valve Check

Connect a jumper wire across terminals 4 and 1, and another jumper across terminals 5 and 2. Start the engine. A high idle speed of 1600 to 2400 prm should be obtained--this indicates that the valve is working properly. If the engine does not develop that high idle speed, the air control valve may be defective. If no fault is found with the air control valve, try a

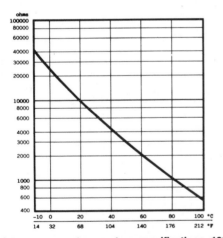

Resistance versus temperature specifications, 1981 B21F and 1981–82 B28F coolant temperature sensor

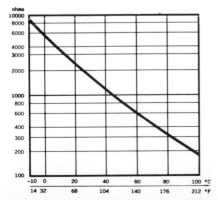

Resistance versus temperature specifications, 1982 B21F coolant temperature sensor

new ECU. Always check all connectors for corrosion and secure fit. Reconnect all connectors and check the overall operations of the CIS system.

Full Throttle Enrichment Switch

NOTE: *The B28F V6 is equipped with two micro switches actuated by throttle control. The second micro switch closes a Lambda-sond (the oxygen sensor) circuit at full throttle to provide richer air/fuel mixture at maximum acceleration. Vehicles sold in high altitude areas have this switch disconnected.*

1. To adjust the switch, loosen the microswitch retaining screws. Turn the switch sideways. The test light should come on, then go out 2.5mm ($^3/_{32}$ in.) before the pulley touches the full throttle stop. Reposition the switch as needed and tighten the retaining screws.

2. To check full throttle enrichment switch operation, disconnect the green wire at the micro-switch. Connect a test light between the micro-switch terminal and the positive battery terminal.

3. Turn the pulley slowly to the full throttle stop. The test light should light up 4mm to 1mm ($^5/_{32}$–$^1/_{32}$ in.) before the pulley touches the stop. Adjust the switch as necessary and reconnect the wiring.

LH-JETRONIC, LH-II JETRONIC and LH-JETRONIC 2.2

The Bosch LH-Jetronic electronic fuel injection system became available on the B21F-LH engine in 1982 and on the B23F-LH in 1983. The complete system contains the following components: L-Jetronic control unit (ECU), airflow sensor, system relay, fuel pump relay, Lambda-sond oxygen sensor, vacuum switch, electric fuel pump, coolant temperature sensor, fuel injectors, and the electronic control unit terminal for the Constant Idle Systems (CIS) if equipped. On the 1983 and later B23F-LH, the fuel injection and the CIS (constant idle speed) systems are both controlled by the same Electronic Control Unit mounted on the right side kick panel.

LH is an abbreviation of a German term which means "hot wire air mass meter". All the LH systems work on the principle of controlling injector duration, but instead of an air flow sensor flap to measure intake air quantity, these systems use a heated platinum wire to measure the air mass. In this manner, altitude influences are eliminated.

A very thin platinum wire is stretched across the air intake opening in the air-flow meter and forms part of a bridging circuit. The intake air flowing over the heated wire cools the wire, changing its electrical resistance according to the temperature. An electronic amplifier in-

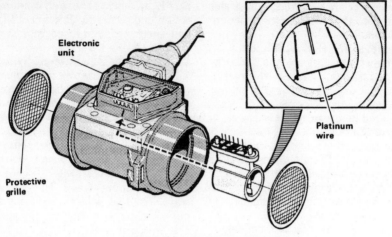

LH-Jetronic air mass meter

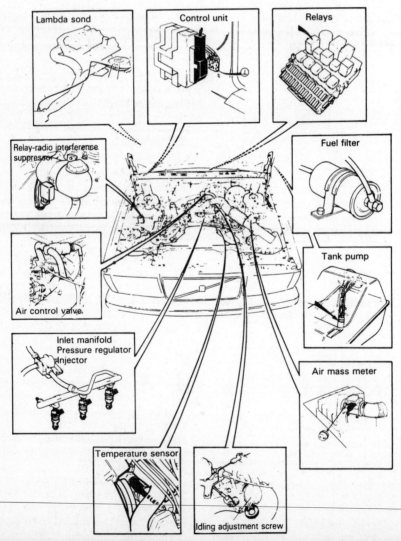

Location of components: B280E/F engines with LH-Jetronic 2.2 Injection systems

stantly responds to any such change and regulates the current to the wire so as to maintain it at a virtually constant temperature. The current necessary to maintain the wire temperature is the measure of the the air mass flowing into the induction system. This measurement is used by the ECU to determine the injector duration (opening time).

Because dirt and impurities may accumulate on the wire and affect the voltage signal, the system is designed to clean the wire each time the engine is shut off. When the engine stops, the wire is heated to 1100–1900°F (593–

1,038°C) for less than one second. This burns off any impurities which could cause false readings.

Testing and Inspection

The components within the fuel injection system are generally very reliable. Outright failure is not common, although reduced function may occur as a result of age and wear. Before jumping into the injection system and its very expensive pieces, check everything else which influences the system. The LH systems depend heavily on all other components being correct.

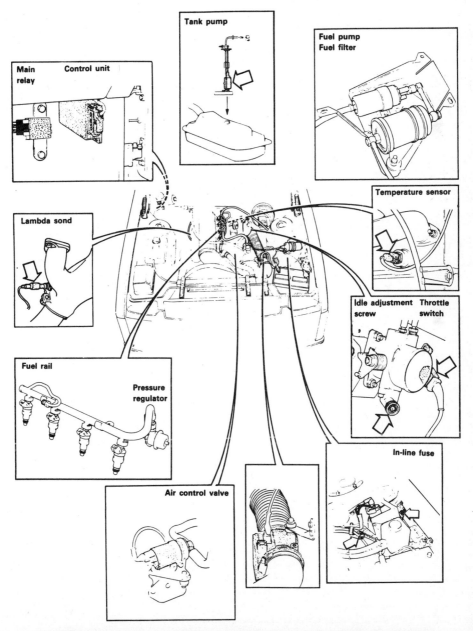

Location of components: B230F engine with LH-Jetronic 2.2 injection systems

It is essential that compression, valve clearance, vacuum routing and flow, and throttle settings be checked and repaired if necessary. Spark plug wires, distributor cap, air filters and electrical connections (including blown fuses) can also cause you to look in the wrong place. A flaw in either the crankcase or evaporative emissions controls can cause hours of misdirected investigation. Simply stated, check the easy things first--repairing a loose ground connector can save you hundreds of dollars.

The fuel injection system is repaired simply be replacing the defective component. There are some adjustments that can be made to some components, but these require a high level of experience and special test equipment. To make resistance checks, use an ohmmeter and for continuity checks, a 12V test light. If the control unit is defective, return it to a qualified repair agency and install a new unit.

It is impossible to test the operation of the ECU without very expensive testing equip-

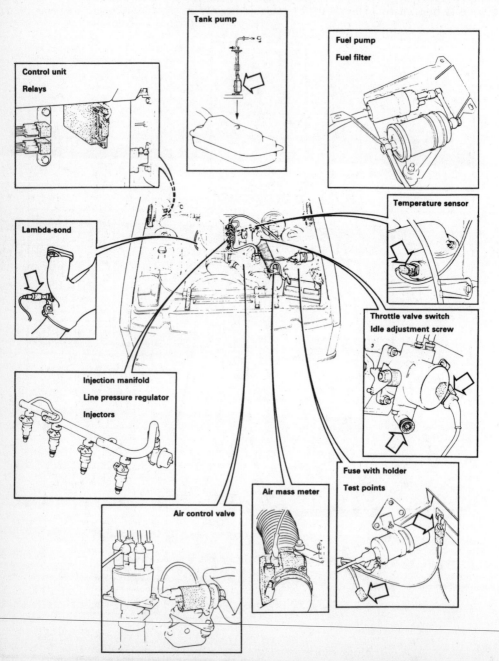

Location of components: B23F engine with LH-Jetronic II injection systems

ment. The easiest way to diagnose a failed ECU is to eliminate all other possibilities by testing the circuits it controls. If all the controlled circuits check good and a performance problem is still evident, the controller must be bad.

NOTE: *ALL OF THE FOLLOWING TESTS ARE PERFORMED WITH THE HARNESS DISCONNECTED FROM THE ECU UNLESS STATED OTHERWISE. THE IGNITION SWITCH MUST BE OFF WHEN REMOVING OR INSTALLING THE CONNECTOR.*

1. With the ignition OFF, remove the right side kick panel and any necessary trim pieces, sill moldings, etc.

2. Carefully release the catches on the ECU and pivot the connector down and away. The connector should come free of the box. If it doesn't, check for the cause of interference; don't force anything.

3. With the connector free, remove the small retaining screws in the connector case. Gently slide the cover a few inches back along the cable. This exposes the body of the connector.

4. The connector numbers are on the body of

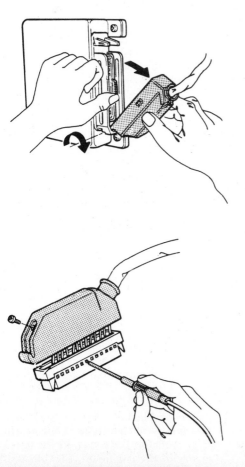

Removal of ECU connector for testing

the connector. Notice the rows of square or rectangular holes along the side of the connector body. These are where you insert the probes of the volt-ohmeter. DO NOT insert the test probes into the front of the connector; this can damage the pins and induce other faults. When testing through the side holes, use only enough pressure to make good contact.

5. When reassembling, work carefully and do not force the body of the plug into the cover. Make sure the wires are not crimped or under undue pressure.

SYSTEM GROUNDS

Connect the ohmeter to a known ground and individually check terminals 11 and 25. On LH-2.2 systems, also check terminals 5 and 19. Resistance should be nearly zero in all cases. If ground checks show high resistance, check the ground connections at the intake manifold.

COOLANT TEMPERATURE SENSOR

Connect the ohmeter between ground and terminal 2. Resistance depends on coolant temperature (see chart). As a reference, if the coolant is at 68°F (20°C), look for readings of 2300–2700 ohms. If the coolant is at 176°F (80°C), expect readings of 300–360 ohms. Hint: if the ohmmage is incorrect, perform the test again at the pins of the sensor. If the readings are now correct, you have a wiring problem, not a sensor problem.

THROTTLE SWITCH (THROTTLE VALVE SWITCH)

With the ohmeter connected between ground and terminal 3, depress the accelerator pedal. The meter should show zero resistance in the idle position and infinite (open) in all other positions. Now connect the ohmeter between ground and terminal 12. Again depress the accelerator pedal; look for zero resistance at full throttle and infinite at all other positions.

Double check any faulty readings at the switch on the intake manifold. If the the values are still wrong, adjust the switch or linkage or replace the switch.

AIR MASS METER: CURRENT SUPPLY AND GROUND

Connect a jumper from terminal 21 to ground and leave in place. On Jetronic 2.2 systems, also jumper connector 17 to ground. Under the hood, gently peel back the rubber cover on the connector to the air mass meter.

On Jetronic II systems, connect the voltmeter between terminal 9 and ground, then between 9 and 36. In both cases the meter should show battery voltage.

For Jetronic 2.2 systems, check between terminals 1 and 5 on the air mass meter, looking for battery voltage. Reinstall the protective

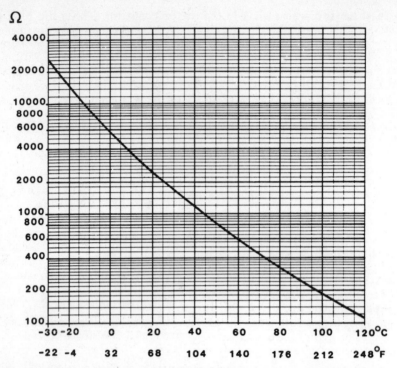

Coolant temperature sensor resistance varies with coolant temperature. B230F with LH-Jetronoic 2.2 injection shown. Others with LH-Jetronic systems are similar ± 100 ohms

rubber boot and remove the ground jumper(s) from the harness.

Now use the ohmeter to check the resistance of the wire in the air mass sensor. For both types of systems, connect the probes to terminals 6 and 7 of the ECU harness (inside the car). Correct resistance is 3.7 ohms. Test the resistance between terminals 6 and 14. Expect a reading between 0 and 1000 ohms, depending the CO setting established at the factory.

AIR MASS METER: BURN-OFF CURRENT

NOTE: *This test is performed with the ECU harness connected.*

Start the engine and allow it to warm up fully. Shut the engine off and peel back the rubber boot at the air mass meter connector.

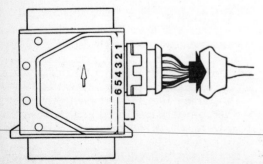

Carefully remove the boot to test the circuits at the air mass meter

On Jetronic II systems, connect the voltmeter between terminals 8 and 36. Restart the motor and accelerate it to at least 2000 rpm. Switch the motor off and observe the voltmeter. After about 5 seconds, the meter should show about 1 volt for about 1 second. This shows that the burn-off cycle has started and finished. Remove the voltmeter and replace the connector boot.

For Jetronic 2.2 systems, connect the voltmeter between terminals 1 and 4. Accelerate the engine above 2100 rpm and then shut it off. After 4 seconds, the meter should deflect for one second. Remove the voltmeter and replace the connector boot.

FUEL INJECTORS

A quick way to check injectors is simply to listen to them. With the engine running, touch a long shaft (such as a screwdriver) to the injector and listen to the opposite end. You should hear a distinct repeated clicking as the injector opens and closes. If one doesn't click, swap it with a known good one elsewhere in the system and reconnect the wires (don't get the wires interchanged). Listen again; if the bad one is still bad, replace it. If the known good one is now bad (and the first bad one now works), there is an electrical fault in the circuit to the injector.

Using an ohmeter, you can check the injector resistance with the engine off. Disconnect the electrical lead to the injector and touch the

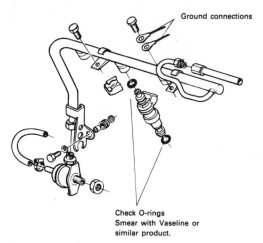

LH-Jetronic injector, 1982 models

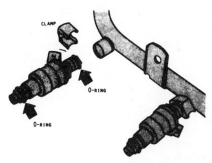

Detail of fuel injector rail, B230F

leads to the two terminals. If the injector temperature is 68°F (20°C), resistance will be 16 ohms. Resistance will rise with injector temperature; its best to do this test on an engine which has not been run in several hours.

DIESEL FUEL SYSTEM

The Volvo diesel engine has indirect fuel injection, which means that the fuel is not inject-

1983 LH-Jetronic injector installation with clamp

ed directly into the combustion chamber but rather is fed into a small pre-combustion chamber in the head. During the compression stroke, air is forced up into the swirl chamber which is connected to the combustion chamber by a narrow channel in the head. The shape of the swirl chamber causes the air to rotate rapidly. This air speed in the swirl chamber promotes even

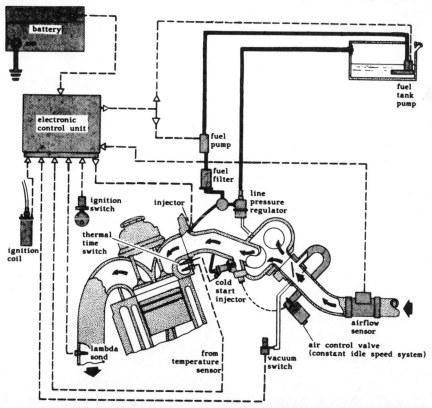

LH-Jetronic fuel and electrical flow diagram

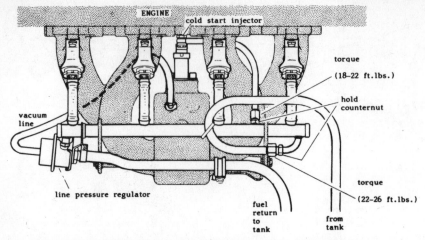

B21 and B23F-LH LH-Jetronic injection manifold, 1982 and later

combustion and is the reason the engine can reach fairly high engine speeds.

Fuel is injected into the swirl chamber just before the piston reaches top dead center and the fuel mixes with the turbulent air for a momentarily. As the piston reaches TDC, it compresses the air/fuel mixture to a ratio of 23:1. This ratio is over twice that of a gasoline engine. The mere act of compressing air to this level generates tremendous heat (1700°F [927°C]), and it is this heat which ignites the air/fuel mixture.

Injection Lines

REMOVAL AND INSTALLATION

If a fuel line under the hood should become damaged or leaky, do not attempt to weld or repair it. Replacement is required in all situations. Before disassembling any of the lines, mark the location of the plastic or metal clamps which bridge the lines. These clamps are important in suppressing vibration which may loosen or damage the lines. Clamps must be reinstalled in the exact positions from which they were removed.

1. Clean all the connections carefully. Re-

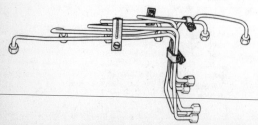

Placement of retaining clamps on diesel fuel injector lines is important

move the vacuum pump, place it to the side and remove the plunger from the cylinder head.

2. Mark the position of all the line clamps, and disconnect ALL the fuel delivery pipes, even if you're only changing one.

3. Remove the clamp(s) holding the pipe(s) to be replaced. Install the new one, but do not tighten the fittings at this point.

4. Reinstall the clamps in their original positions. When the clamps are secure, tighten the pipe fittings to 18 ft. lbs.

5. Making sure that the number one cylinder is on TDC-injection, (the flywheel notch is at the zero mark and the lobes on the camshaft for no. 1 cylinder point upward at equally large angles--you can check the camshaft lobes by looking in through the oil filler hole in the valve cover), reinstall the pump plunger and the vacuum pump.

6. Start the engine and check for leaks. The fuel system will bleed itself of air, but a few seconds will be required until the engine runs smoothly.

Diesel Fuel Injectors

Diesel fuel injectors are prone to plugging due to dirt or water in the system. Because diesel fuel is less refined than gasoline, there is a greater chance of pollutants getting into the fuel system. An inoperative injector can cause very poor fuel mileage, heavier than normal exhaust soot, uneven idle, loss of power and/or overheating and knocking in the cylinder. Don't mistake normal bearing clatter--a generalized noise throughout the engine--for a knocking in a specific cylinder.

REMOVAL AND INSTALLATION

To perform a quick check on the injectors, run the engine at above idle speed. Wrap an ab-

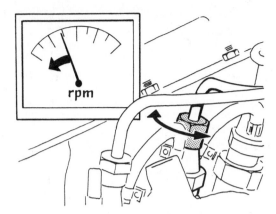

Loosening the cap nut on a properly working diesel injector should lower engine rpm. See text for procedure

sorbant rag around the pipe joint at the injector and loosen the cap nut on the injector. As the pressure in the line leaks off, the cylinder should cease firing and the engine characteristics should change.

If there is no change in engine behavior, the injector or its heat shield may be defective. Injectors cannot be repaired or disassembled; defective injectors must be replaced. If removing or replacing an injector is necessary:

1. Clean all the connections thoroughly before disconnecting anything.

2. Disconnect the fuel delivery pipe(s) at the affected injector(s) and plug the open ends to keep out dirt and dust.

3. Use a 27mm socket and carefully remove the injector from the cylinder head. Remove the heat shield which sits under the injector; it looks like a small, dished washer.

4. Remove any soot or dirt from the sealing surfaces.

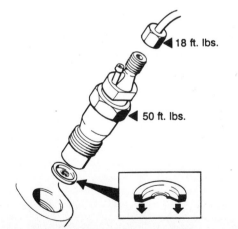

Diesel fuel injector and tightening values; note correct position of heat shield

5. Install new heat shields for each injector removed. Make sure they are installed with the dished side up. An upside-down heat shield will cause symptoms identical to a failed injector.

6. Install the new injector(s) and tighten to 50 ft. lbs. Reconnect the delivery pipes and tighten the connections to 18 ft. lbs.

7. Start the engine and check for leaks.

There is no way to test diesel injectors without an elaborate test bench. Your dealer may have this test equipment. Do not attempt to test the injector by connecting it to its fuel line while out of the engine. You will damage the line by bending it and you run the risk of injury. The injector is under enough pressure that the atomized fuel can penetrate your flesh, inducing blood poisoning.

Fuel Pump/Injection Pump

The fuel pump is also the injection pump and is located on the left rear side of the engine, driven by a belt running off the rear of the camshaft. The pump supplies the engine with more fuel than it can use, the excess fuel being returned to the fuel tank through suction/return lines. The system constantly bleeds itself of air. Because the pump moves such large amounts of fuel, it tends to stay cool and this reduces the chances of vapor lock. The pump is lubricated by the fuel passing through it. Do not use fuel additives unless specifically recommended by Volvo for fear of damaging the pump.

The pump contains a single piston which rotates and distributes fuel to each injector in the correct sequence, much in the same way the distributor on a gasoline engine distributes the spark to the spark plugs.

REMOVAL AND INSTALLATION

WARNING: *The use of the correct special tools or their equivalent is REQUIRED for this procedure. Several special tools are needed to remove and install the pump and to set its timing. If these tools are not available, do not attempt to remove the pump. The Volvo tool numbers are given in the procedure.*

1. Pinch off and remove the two coolant hoses running to the cold start device on the fuel pump.

2. Disconnect the accelerator linkage at the pump and disconnect the wire from the stop valve on the top of the pump. Disconnect the hose coming from the intake manifold.

3. Remove the rear timing belt cover and thoroughly clean the fuel lines and their connections at the injection pump.

4. Disconnect the fuel lines at the pump and plug the open connections to prevent dirt from entering the fuel system.

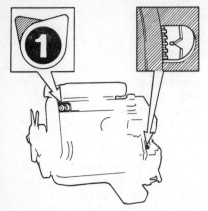

Diesel engine set to TDC-injection. You can view the cam lobes through the oil filler cap

5. Remove the vacuum pump and its plunger.

6. Clean and remove the delivery lines at the fuel injectors. Plug all connections. Remove the lines as a unit and set them aside.

7. Set cylinder no. 1 to TDC injection stroke. At this position, the 0 mark on the flywheel aligns with the pointer and the notch on the injection pump pulley alings with the notch on the pump housing. Both valves on no. 1 cylinder are closed and their camshaft lobes are pointing up at equally large angles.

8. Loosen the retaining bolts for the injection pump, push the pump up, and remove the pump drive belt. Tighten one bolt to hold the pump in the upper position.

9. Loosen the center bolt in the rear camshaft gear while using wrench 5199 to hold the gear. The bolts will be easily accessible if wrench 5201 is used.

NOTE: *The camshaft must not rotate. Loosen the bolt only enough to rotate the gear on the camshaft.*

10. Insert locking pin (No. 5193) into the injection pump gear to lock it in position. Remove the injection pump gear nut and washer.

11. With the pin still in position, use a puller to remove the pump gear.

12. Remove the bolts retaining the front injection pump bracket to the engine, then remove the bolts retaining the pump and remove the pump from the engine.

13. Install the pump on the engine and tighten the bolts only finger tight so that pump position can be adjusted.

14. Set the injection pump so that the mark on pump and the pump bracket align, then tighten the retaining bolts.

15. Make sure the shaft key is correctly installed and install the injection pump gear, washer and nut. Use pin 5193 to hold the gear while tightening the nut.

16. Proceed to Setting the Injection Pump Timing, below.

17. After the injection pump timing is set, fill the pump with clean diesel fuel through the fuel line connection. Make sure you filter the fuel before pouring it into the pump.

18. Install the rear timing gear cover. Connect the fuel lines and fuel delivery pipes. Tighten the fuel line cap nuts and the fuel line banjo bolts to 18 ft. lbs. When installing the fuel lines on the pump, do not mix the banjo bolts: the bolt for the fuel return line has a small hole in it and is marked OUT.

19. Install the vacuum pump and all remaining components. Adjust the accelerator linkage.

SETTING THE INJECTION PUMP TIMING

WARNING: *The use of the correct special tools or their equivalent is REQUIRED for this procedure.*

1. Set cylinder No. 1 to TDC injection stroke. At this position, the 0 mark on the flywheel aligns with the pointer and the notch on the injection pump pulley alings with the notch on the pump housing. Both valves on no. 1 cylinder are closed and their camshaft lobes are pointing up at equally large angles.

2. Disconnect the cold start device on the injection pump by loosening screw **1** in the illustration, pushing the lever forward and rotating the sleeve 90°. Push the lever back against the stop. Do not touch screw **2** in the illustration or the cold start device will have to be reset on a test bench.

3. Loosen the injection pump retaining screws and turn the pump so that the markings on the injection pump and the pump bracket align. Install the lock pin (No. 5193) in the injection pump gear to lock the gear in position. Any pin can be used to lock the gear, however

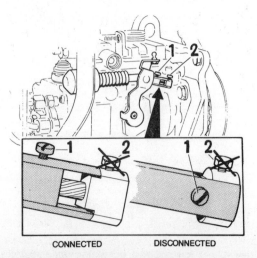

CONNECTED   DISCONNECTED

Disconnect the cold start device

there cannot be any movement of the gear when the pin is installed.

4. Remove the plug in the injection pump distributor and install special holder 5194 and a dial indicator gauge with a measuring range of 0–0.12 in. (0–3mm.) Set the dial gauge at approximately 0.08 in. (2mm).

5. Remove the stop pin and turn the injection pump (using its gear) in its normal direction of rotation until the marks on the injection pump gear and the bracket align.

6. Turn the injection pump gear slightly counterclockwise until the dial gauge indicates its lowest reading. In this position set the dial gauge to zero. Turn the injection pump gear clockwise until the marks on the gear and the bracket align again, then refit the lock pin to lock the gear in position.

7. Install the rear camshaft gear (if removed) and tighten its center bolt only hand tight. Install the drive belt.

8. Adjust the drive belt to the proper tension by moving the pump on its mounts. If you're using the Volvo tension gauge (5197), set the tension gauge to 12.5 and apply tension to the belt until the mark on the plunger of the gauge is flush with the gauge sleeve. Depress the belt heavily with your hand then recheck and adjust the tension.

WARNING: *The dial indicator readings given in the text below are for 1979–1981 US and Canada D24 engines. Specifications*

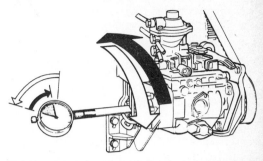

Relationship between pump motion and dial indicator reading when setting the diesel injection pump timing

for other engines are given at the end of the section.

9. Use wrench 5199 (or a suitable substitute) to hold the rear camshaft gear in place and install wrench 5201 with a torque wrench attached on the center bolt. The torque wrench should be installed at a 90° angle to wrench 5201 to give correct readings.

Use wrench 5199 or its substitute to turn the camshaft gear until the dial gauge in the injection pump reads 0.028 in. (0.70mm). Hold the gear in this position and tighten the center bolt to 73 ft. lbs. without moving either the camshaft or the gear.

10. Remove the lock pin and turn the engine over two full turns (one complete four stroke cycle) until the no. 1 cylinder is again on TDC compression stroke. Check the reading on the dial indicator gauge. It should read 0.028 in (0.70mm). If the reading is correct, proceed to step 13.

11. If the reading is less than 0.028 in. (0.70mm), loosen the injection pump retaining screws and turn the pump inward until a reading of 0.028 in. (0.70mm) is obtained. Repeat step 10.

12. If the reading is more than 0.028 in. (0.70mm), loosen the injection pump retaining screws and turn the pump outward until the reading on the gauge is approximately 0.024 in. (0.60mm). Next, turn the pump inward to obtain a reading of 0.028 in (0.70mm) and tighten the retaining bolts. Repeat step 10.

NOTE: *When adjusting, do not tap or knock the pump as this will alter the settings.*

13. Remove the dial indicator and its holder and install the plug. Tighten the plug to 6.5 ft. lbs.

14. Attach the cold start device. Reverse step 1, above. Install all remaining components.

The following are injection pump timing specifications in millimeters of dial indicator reading:
- D20: 0.80
- D24: 0.85

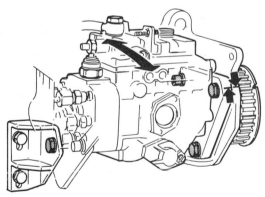

Loosen the injection pump retaining screws and turn the pump so that the markings align

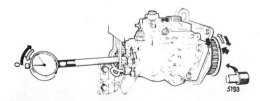

Shown: stop pin, alignment marks on pulley and bracket, dial indicator installed with special adapter 5194

- 1982–83 D24T: 0.80
- 1984–85 D24T: 0.85, Exc. Calif.
- 1984–85 D24T: 0.75 Calif.

Glow plugs (Preheating System)

The preheating system warms the swirl chambers prior to engine start-up. The length of time the plugs are on is determined by the coolant temperature. A coolant temperature sensor sends this data to a control unit which regulates the engagement time of the glow plugs.

When the ignition key is in the ON position, the system is engaged and the dashboard light comes on. After the dash indicator goes out, the plugs remain on for 1–14 seconds, depending on conditions. When the engine starts, the glow plugs are switched off. There is a safety circuit built in which will turn the circuit off after a predetermined amount of time if the engine is not started. This prevents the glow plugs from melting and damaging the engine.

TESTING AND REPLACEMENT

NOTE: *These tests must be carried out with the engine coolant below 100°F (38°C). During any of these tests, remember that the glow plug circuit will shut off after a period of time. It will be necessary to cycle the ignition switch to OFF and then back to ON to continue testing.*

Since the glow plug circuitry uses the normal 12 volt electrical system of the car, it is fairly simple to test with a test light. A voltmeter can also be used.

To check for power to the glow plug, connect the test light to ground and touch the other end to the plug terminal. Turn the key to the ON position and look for both the test lamp and the dashboard indicator to illuminate. If both lamps light, all is well up to the glow plug. If either or both don't light, check the control relay as explained below.

Remove the test lamp and turn the key OFF. Disconnect and remove the ground bar which runs between the glow plugs. Connect one end of the test light to the positive (+) terminal of the battery and touch the other end to the end of one glow plug. If the test light comes on, that plug is good. If the glow plug must be replaced, do so by simply unscrewing it and installing a new one. Reconnect the ground bars between the plugs.

Glow Plug Control Unit (Relay)

On cars with the D24 engine, the control unit is located under the left side of the dashboard. On Turbo models, it is found under the hood on the left shock tower. For D24T vehicles, disconnect the control unit plug and turn the ignition

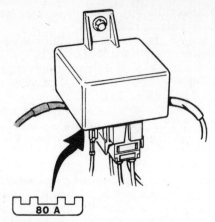

The 80 amp glow plug fuse is located on the bottom of the relay

ON. Ground one end of the test light and check for voltage at terminal 15. If no voltage is present, a wiring fault is present. Also check the terminal of the orange wire. If both the dash indicator and the test light come on, the control unit is failed.

Also with the ignition ON, check for voltage at terminal 30 on the relay; no voltage shows a wiring fault between the battery and the control unit. Check terminal G for voltage; if no voltage is present, check the 80 amp fuse on the bottom of the relay. If voltage is present, the control unit is OK. Remove the test light and reinstall it to the positive battery terminal. Check the control unit ground by touching the test light to terminal 31 (black wire) on the control unit. If the test light does not come on, the unit is not grounded.

On the D24 family, leave the connector on the relay and check for voltage at terminal 15 (blue-with-red wire). No voltage shows a wiring fault between the fuse box and the relay. Under the hood, check the smaller glow plug relay (on the left shock tower) for voltage at terminal 86. Connect the test light to the positive battery terminal and check the glow plug relay for proper ground at terminal 31. If the test lamp lights up, the relay is bad. Remember this is all being done with the engine cold, the ignition ON and within the operating cycle of the glow plugs being on.

Back inside the car, check for voltage at terminal G on the control unit. No voltage indicates a faulty control unit. Connect the test light to the PLUS terminal on the fusebox (+) and check terminal K on the control unit. If the test lamp lights up, you have either a defective dashboard indicator light, a wiring problem between the control unit and the indicator light, or a fault in the printed circuit behind the instrument panel. If the test light does not come on, either the control unit is bad or the wire between the control unit and the temperature sensor is grounded when it shouldn't be.

FUEL TANK

REMOVAL AND INSTALLATION

Generally stated, the only reason to remove the fuel tank should be in cases of physical damage or to gain access to the rear body work for repairs. The tank can be drained in the car by using the fuel pump to pump most of the fuel through the system and collecting it at a disconnected hose near the tank or under the hood. Reconnect and secure the line after draining the system. Its easier if you schedule the work to occur when the tank is nearly empty.

CAUTION: *The fuel system is under pressure. Release pressure slowly and contain spillage. Observe no smoking/no open flame precautions. When performing this work, always have a dry-chemical fire extinguisher handy and know how to use it. Use clean containers large enough to collect all the fuel drained out. Keep drained fuel out of the work area and tightly covered.*

For all cars except the 1988 and later 760 and 780 series, after draining the tank:

1. With the ignition key OFF and all electrical components (radio, heater, etc.) turned off, disconnect the negative battery cable.

2. In the trunk, remove the panels which cover the filler hose. Remove or roll back the trunk carpet or liner and remove the screws holding the access panel in the floor of the trunk.

3. Label and disconnect the filler, overflow and fuel return lines at the tank. It may be necessary to loosen or disconnect some lines at the filler neck as well.

4. Disconnect wiring connectors and grounding connections, labeling as necessary.

5. Block the front wheels, jack the rear end and support the rear of the car with jackstands.

6. Under the car, clamp off and disconnect the hoses between the tank and the body lines. Depending on the model, there may be a mass of hoses around the fuel pump and accumulator. Since some of these components may be bolted to the tank (and be removed with it) look for the fuel lines coming from the body. Identify and disconnect as few lines as possible to make reconnection easier. Label everything.

7. Double check all four sides of the tank and the top surface. There should be no wires or hoses connecting the tank to the car. Check the security of all the plugs or clamps in the fuel lines.

8. Position the jack under center of the tank and use a broad, flat piece of wood between the jack and the bottom of the tank. Raise the jack until it just contacts the tank.

9. Depending on your model, it may be necessary to remove various heat shields or protective covers from the side of the tank or the body. Loosen and remove the tank retaining bolts. The jack should have enough elevation to support the tank in position until all the bolts are removed.

10. With the tank completely free and supported only by the jack, lower the jack about 2 inches and hold that position. Perform a final check for any line or wire still connected and check for possible points of interference in the downward path of the tank.

11. Balance the tank with one hand and slowly release the jack to lower the tank clear of the car. When the tank is clear of the car, the fuel sender and in-tank fuel pump (if so equipped) can be removed by unscrewing the locking ring on the top of the tank. Drain the remaining fuel immediately and store it safely. Remember that fuel vapors (fumes) are highly explosive--get the tank dry as soon as possible and keep it out of enclosed areas where fumes could be trapped.

12. When reinstalling the tank, make sure that the fuel sender and auxiliary pump is properly seated in its mounts and is not resting or binding on anything inside the tank. Make sure that any of the foam rubber insulators on the outside of the tank have not come off. Position the tank on the board and jack as before and elevate it into position. Install the mounts and/or retaining bolts to hold the tank to the car. Remove the jack from the tank area.

13. Reinstall any heat shields or covers which were removed for access.

14. Under the car, remove the plugs from each fuel line and connect it to the proper port on the tank or fuel system. Make sure you get things in the correct place or the car won't run. Make sure each connection is clean and tight, with the proper hose clamps as necessary. Double check for any kinks or points of interference.

15. Using the jack, remove the jackstands and lower the car to the ground. In the trunk, connect the filler, delivery and overflow hoses to the tank. Insure clean tight connections, using new clamps if necessary. If the larger hoses are difficult to fit onto the ports, a light coating of spray silicone inside the hose will ease the job.

16. Reconnect the wiring terminals to the top of the sender unit. Check that the connectors are not corroded or loose. If there is a tank-to-body ground wire, check the body connection for poor contact and/or corrosion and repair if necessary.

17. Check and secure any loosened connections at the fuel filler neck in the fender area. Double check all installation items, paying particular attention to loose hoses or hanging wires, untightened nuts, poor routing of hoses and wires (too tight or rubbing) and tools left in the area. Replace the trunk floor access panel, the trunk floor mat or carpet and install the cover panel over the filler hose.

18. Remove the gas cap and safely deliver clean, fresh fuel into the tank. Use a funnel and pour from a closed container. If you value your paint, don't spill fuel down the bodywork of the car. Replace the gas cap.

19. Reconnect the negative battery cable.

20. Turn the ignition key to the ON position for 5 seconds. Cycle it to OFF and back to ON for another 5 seconds. Turn it OFF and then start the engine. Although the two ON cycles partially primed the system, the engine may crank longer than normal until the correct pressures are developed and fuel reaches the engine.

21. After the engine has started and is running smoothly, shut it off and recheck every hose connection for any sign of leakage or seepage. Remember that the system is once again holding pressure. Be very careful when working around lines and fittings.

760 and 780 Models, 1988 and later

These cars have a saddle type tank designed to fit around the revised rear axle design. The tank is constructed of heavy-duty plastic. The driveshaft runs through a tunnel in the tank and must be removed during tank removal. The tank has several heat shields and safety shields to guard it against damage from heat or driveshaft contact. *The fuel system is under pressure.*

CAUTION: *The fuel system is under pressure. Release pressure slowly and contain spillage. Observe no smoking/no open flame precautions. When performing this work, always have a dry-chemical fire extinguisher handy and know how to use it. Use clean containers large enough to collect all the fuel drained out. Keep drained fuel out of the work area and tightly covered.*

1. Because of a higher degree of sophisticated electronic components, all electrical components (radio, heater fan, etc) must be turned off as well as the ignition switch. Disconnect the negative battery cable. The electrical "spike" caused by this disconnection can destroy components in micro-processing units.

2. In the trunk, disconnect the left side drain hose. Remove the spare tire cover and the trunk mat. Remove the panel and cover for the fuel filler pipe.

3. Remove the access panel over the fuel lev-

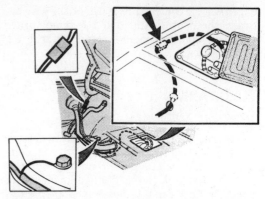

Location of fuel tank electrical connectors, 760 and 780 models

el sender. Disconnect the fuel hoses at the sender and the wire connectors in the trunk. Press the rubber grommet out of the bodywork and remove the wire through the hole.

4. Using a small pump and lengths of hose, drain the tank by sucking fuel out through the filler pipe hole in the fuel sender assembly. This is the only way to drain the tank. Removing the tank with fuel in it is NOT recommended. The added weight of the fuel (approximately 7.2 pounds per gallon) will imbalance the tank and damage the mounts during removal.

5. Block the front wheels, jack the rear end and support the rear of the car with jackstands.

6. From under the car, remove the three bolts holding the heat shield at the front of the tank and remove the shield.

7. Disconnect the front tank attachment by removing the two strap bolts. The outer bolts should be loosened about ⅜ inch but not removed. This will allow you to pull the straps out of the front attachment.

8. Remove the bracket under the tank and remove the nut for tank attachment point on the right side.

9. Gently pull the tank loose from the body. Let the tank rest on the front attachment. The tank is still retained at the rear and cannot come free of the car yet.

10. Mark the front and rear driveshaft (propeller shaft) so that they may be reassembled correctly. Remove the rear flange bolts. Slide the rear driveshaft loose from the splines at the front support bearing.

11. Position a jack under center of the tank and use a broad, flat piece of wood between the jack and the bottom of the tank. Raise the jack until it just contacts the tank.

12. Remove the front tank attachment. Lower the tank slightly and pull it forward. On the top of the tank, remove the hose from the expansion tank port. Remove the tank from the car and remove the shield panels from the tank.

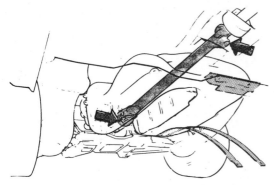

Disconnect rear driveshaft (at points shown by arrows) on 1988–1989 760 and 780 models

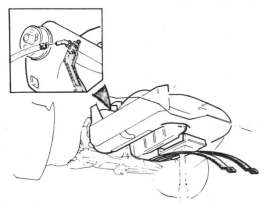

On 1988–1989 760 and 780 models, don't forget the evaporative hose above the tank

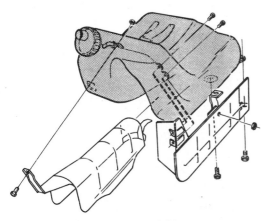

Always reinstall the safety shields

13. Unscrew the locking ring and remove the fuel sender assembly from the tank. Be careful of the wiring harness attached to the top. Remember that fuel vapors (fumes) are highly explosive--get the tank dry as soon as possible and keep it out of enclosed areas where fumes could be trapped.

14. When reinstalling the tank, secure the shield panels to the tank first. Install the fuel sender assembly, making sure it seats properly and is not damaged by hitting the baffles inside the tank during installation. The small arrows on the housing should align with the seam in the top of the tank. Position the wire harness around the tank hose connections.

15. Check that the foam insulator pads on the tank are in place and not crushed. Replace any as needed.

16. Loosen but do not remove the bolts in the rear strap mount. Using the jack and the board, position the tank into the car and fit it into the rear mount.

17. Reconnect the hose to the expansion port on the top of the tank and secure the clamp. Observe the placement of the right side tank mount and move the tank into its final position. Tighten the rear clamp bolts.

18. Install the front tank attachment and tighten the two outer bolts just a few turns. The tank is now resting in its mounts, lower at the front. Remove the jack from the area.

19. Install the drive shaft, observing the matchmarks made earlier. Replace and tighten the rear flange bolts.

20. Install the straps to the front mount, tighten the outer two bolts and then tighten the strap retaining bolts. Reinstall the heat shield over the front tank mount.

21. Reinstall the right side mount and the under-tank bracket.

22. Using the jack, remove the jackstands and lower the car to the ground.

23. Route the harness through the bodywork and into the trunk. Attach the wire to the clip on the sidemember under the trunk. Install the bolt for the ground connector and reconnect the harness and ground.

24. Reconnect the hoses to the tank sender unit, making sure all connections are clean and tight.

25. Remove the gas cap and safely deliver clean, fresh fuel into the tank. Use a funnel and pour from a closed container. If you value your paint, don't spill fuel down the bodywork of the car. Replace the gas cap.

26. Reconnect the negative battery cable.

27. Turn the ignition to the ON position. Listen for the fuel pump running and check for any system leaks. Check that the fuel gauge on the dash is registering properly. Remembering that the system has repressurized itself, attend to leaks or loose connectors.

28. In the trunk, replace the access panel over the fuel sender. Connect the drain hose on the left side and install the protective covers and panel to conceal the fuel filler hoses. Replace the spare tire cover and install the trunk mat.

Chassis Electrical

UNDERSTANDING AND TROUBLESHOOTING ELECTRICAL SYSTEMS

With the rate at which both import and domestic manufacturers are incorporating electronic control systems into their production lines, it won't be long before every new vehicle is equipped with one or more on-board computer. These electronic components (with no moving parts) should theoretically last the life of the vehicle, provided nothing external happens to damage the circuits or memory chips.

While it is true that electronic components should never wear out, in the real world malfunctions do occur. It is also true that any computer-based system is extremely sensitive to electrical voltages and cannot tolerate careless or haphazard testing or service procedures. An inexperienced individual can literally do major damage looking for a minor problem by using the wrong kind of test equipment or connecting test leads or connectors with the ignition switch ON. When selecting test equipment, make sure the manufacturers instructions state that the tester is compatible with whatever type of electronic control system is being serviced. Read all instructions carefully and double check all test points before installing probes or making any test connections.

The following section outlines basic diagnosis techniques for dealing with computerized automotive control systems. Along with a general explanation of the various types of test equipment available to aid in servicing modern electronic automotive systems, basic repair techniques for wiring harnesses and connectors is given. Read the basic information before attempting any repairs or testing on any computerized system, to provide the background of information necessary to avoid the most common and obvious mistakes that can cost both time and money. Although the replacement and testing procedures are simple in themselves, the systems are not, and unless one has a thorough understanding of all components and their function within a particular computerized control system, the logical test sequence these systems demand cannot be followed. Minor malfunctions can make a big difference, so it is important to know how each component affects the operation of the overall electronic system to find the ultimate cause of a problem without replacing good components unnecessarily. It is not enough to use the correct test equipment; the test equipment must be used correctly.

Safety Precautions

CAUTION: *Whenever working on or around any computer based microprocessor control system, always observe these general precautions to prevent the possibility of personal injury or damage to electronic components.*

● Never install or remove battery cables with the key ON or the engine running. Jumper cables should be connected with the key OFF to avoid power surges that can damage electronic control units. Engines equipped with computer controlled systems should avoid both giving and getting jump starts due to the possibility of serious damage to components from arcing in the engine compartment when connections are made with the ignition ON.

● Always remove the battery cables before charging the battery. Never use a high output charger on an installed battery or attempt to use any type of "hot shot" (24 volt) starting aid.

● Exercise care when inserting test probes into connectors to insure good connections without damaging the connector or spreading the pins. Always probe connectors from the rear (wire) side, NOT the pin side, to avoid accidental shorting of terminals during test procedures.

• Never remove or attach wiring harness connectors with the ignition switch ON, especially to an electronic control unit.

• Do not drop any components during service procedures and never apply 12 volts directly to any component (like a solenoid or relay) unless instructed specifically to do so. Some component electrical windings are designed to safely handle only 4 or 5 volts and can be destroyed in seconds if 12 volts are applied directly to the connector.

• Remove the electronic control unit if the vehicle is to be placed in an environment where temperatures exceed approximately 176°F (80°C), such as a paint spray booth or when arc or gas welding near the control unit location in the car.

ORGANIZED TROUBLESHOOTING

When diagnosing a specific problem, organized troubleshooting is a must. The complexity of a modern automobile demands that you approach any problem in a logical, organized manner. There are certain troubleshooting techniques that are standard:

1. Establish when the problem occurs. Does the problem appear only under certain conditions? Were there any noises, odors, or other unusual symptoms?

2. Isolate the problem area. To do this, make some simple tests and observations; then eliminate the systems that are working properly. Check for obvious problems such as broken wires, dirty connections or split or disconnected vacuum hoses. Always check the obvious before assuming something complicated is the cause.

3. Test for problems systematically to determine the cause once the problem area is isolated. Are all the components functioning properly? Is there power going to electrical switches and motors? Is there vacuum at vacuum switches and/or actuators? Is there a mechanical problem such as bent linkage or loose mounting screws? Doing careful, systematic checks will often turn up most causes on the first inspection without wasting time checking components that have little or no relationship to the problem.

4. Test all repairs after the work is done to make sure that the problem is fixed. Some causes can be traced to more than one component, so a careful verification of repair work is important to pick up additional malfunctions that may cause a problem to reappear or a different problem to arise. A blown fuse, for example, is a simple problem that may require more than another fuse to repair. If you don't look for a problem that caused a fuse to blow, for example, a shorted wire may go undetected.

Experience has shown that most problems tend to be the result of a fairly simple and obvious cause, such as loose or corroded connectors or air leaks in the intake system; making careful inspection of components during testing essential to quick and accurate troubleshooting. Special, hand held computerized testers designed specifically for diagnosing the system are available from a variety of aftermarket sources, as well as from the vehicle manufacturer, but care should be taken that any test equipment being used is designed to diagnose that particular computer controlled system accurately without damaging the control unit (ECU) or components being tested.

NOTE: *Pinpointing the exact cause of trouble in an electrical system can sometimes only be accomplished by the use of special test equipment. The following describes commonly used test equipment and explains how to put it to best use in diagnosis. In addition to the information covered below, the manufacturer's instructions booklet provided with the tester should be read and clearly understood before attempting any test procedures.*

TEST EQUIPMENT

Jumper Wires

Jumper wires are simple, yet extremely valuable, pieces of test equipment. Jumper wires are merely wires that are used to bypass sections of a circuit. The simplest type of jumper wire is merely a length of multistrand wire with an alligator clip at each end. Jumper wires are usually fabricated from lengths of standard automotive wire and whatever type of connector (alligator clip, spade connector or pin connector) that is required for the particular vehicle being tested. The well equipped tool box will have several different styles of jumper wires in several different lengths. Some jumper wires are made with three or more terminals coming from a common splice for special purpose testing. In cramped, hard-to-reach areas it is advisable to have insulated boots over the jumper wire terminals in order to prevent accidental grounding, sparks, and possible fire, especially when testing fuel system components.

Jumper wires are used primarily to locate open electrical circuits, on either the ground (-) side of the circuit or on the hot (+) side. If an electrical component fails to operate, connect the jumper wire between the component and a good ground. If the component operates only with the jumper installed, the ground circuit is open. If the ground circuit is good, but the component does not operate, the circuit between the power feed and component is open. You can sometimes connect the jumper wire directly from the battery to the hot terminal of the component, but first make sure the component uses 12 volts in operation. Some electrical components, such as fuel injectors, are designed to operate on about 4 volts and running 12 volts directly to the injector terminals can burn out the wiring. By inserting an inline fuseholder between a set of test leads, a fused jumper wire can be used for bypassing open circuits. Use a 5 amp fuse to provide protection against voltage spikes. When in doubt, use a voltmeter to check the voltage input to the component and measure how much voltage is being applied normally. By moving the jumper wire successively back from the lamp toward the power source, you can isolate the area of the circuit where the open is located. When the component stops functioning, or the power is cut off, the open is in the segment of wire between the jumper and the point previously tested.

CAUTION: *Never use jumpers made from wire that is of lighter gauge than used in the circuit under test. If the jumper wire is of too small gauge, it may overheat and possibly melt. Never use jumpers to bypass high resistance loads (such as motors) in a circuit. Bypassing resistances, in effect, creates a short circuit which may, in turn, cause damage and fire. Never use a jumper for anything other than temporary bypassing of components in a circuit.*

12 Volt Test Light

The 12 volt test light is used to check circuits and components while electrical current is flowing through them. It is used for voltage and ground tests. Twelve volt test lights come in different styles but all have three main parts; a ground clip, a probe, and a light. The most commonly used 12 volt test lights have pick-type probes. To use a 12 volt test light, connect the ground clip to a good ground and probe wherever necessary with the pick. The pick should be sharp so that it can penetrate wire insulation to make contact with the wire, without making a large hole in the insulation. The wrap-around light is handy in hard to reach areas or where it is difficult to support a wire to push a probe pick into it. To use the wrap around light, hook the wire to probed with the hook and pull the trigger. A small pick will be forced through the wire insulation into the wire core.

CAUTION: *Do not use a test light to probe electronic ignition spark plug or coil wires. Never use a pick-type test light to probe wiring on computer controlled systems unless specifically instructed to do so. Any wire insulation that is pierced by the test light probe should be taped and sealed with silicone after testing.*

Like the jumper wire, the 12 volt test light is used to isolate opens in circuits. But, whereas the jumper wire is used to bypass the open to operate the load, the 12 volt test light is used to locate the presence of voltage in a circuit. If the test light glows, you know that there is power up to that point; if the 12 volt test light does not glow when its probe is inserted into the wire or connector, you know that there is an open circuit (no power). Move the test light in successive steps back toward the power source until the light in the handle does glow. When it does glow, the open is between the probe and point previously probed.

NOTE: *The test light does not detect that 12 volts (or any particular amount of voltage) is present; it only detects that some voltage is present. It is advisable before using the test light to touch its terminals across the battery posts to make sure the light is operating properly.*

Self-Powered Test Light

The self-powered test light usually contains a 1.5 volt penlight battery. One type of self-powered test light is similar in design to the 12 volt test light. This type has both the battery and the light in the handle and pick-type probe tip. The second type has the light toward the open tip, so that the light illuminates the contact point. The self-powered test light is dual purpose piece of test equipment. It can be used to test for either open or short circuits when power is isolated from the circuit (continuity test). A powered test light should not be used on any computer controlled system or component unless specifically instructed to do so. Many engine sensors can be destroyed by even this small amount of voltage applied directly to the terminals.

Open Circuit Testing

To use the self-powered test light to check for open circuits, first isolate the circuit from the vehicle's 12 volt power source by disconnecting the battery or wiring harness connector. Connect the test light ground clip to a good ground and probe sections of the circuit sequentially with the test light. (Start from either end of the circuit). If the light is out, the open is between the probe and the circuit ground. If the light is on, the open is between the probe and end of the circuit toward the power source.

Short Circuit Testing

By isolating the circuit both from power and from ground, and using a self-powered test light, you can check for shorts to ground in the circuit. Isolate the circuit from power and ground. Connect the test light ground clip to a good ground and probe any easy-to-reach test point in the circuit. If the light comes on, there is a short somewhere in the circuit. To isolate the short, probe a test point at either end of the isolated circuit (the light should be on). Leave the test light probe connected and open connectors, switches, remove parts, etc., sequentially, until the light goes out. When the light goes out, the short is between the last circuit component opened and the previous circuit opened.

NOTE: *The 1.5 volt battery in the test light does not provide much current. A weak battery may not provide enough power to illuminate the test light even when a complete circuit is made (especially if there are high resistances in the circuit). Always make sure that the test battery is strong. To check the battery, briefly touch the ground clip to the probe; if the light glows brightly the battery is strong enough for testing. Never use a self-powered test light to perform checks for opens or shorts when power is applied to the electrical system under test. The 12 volt vehicle power will quickly burn out the 1.5 volt light bulb in the test light.*

Voltmeter

A voltmeter is used to measure voltage at any point in a circuit, or to measure the voltage drop across any part of a circuit. It can also be used to check continuity in a wire or circuit by indicating current flow from one end to the other. Voltmeters usually have various scales on the meter dial and a selector switch to allow the selection of different voltages. The voltmeter has a positive and a negative lead. To avoid damage to the meter, always connect the negative lead to the negative (-) side of circuit (to ground or nearest the ground side of the circuit) and connect the positive lead to the positive (+) side of the circuit (to the power source or the nearest power source). Note that the negative voltmeter lead will always be black and that the positive voltmeter will always be some color other than black (usually red). Depending on how the voltmeter is connected into the circuit, it has several uses.

A voltmeter can be connected either in parallel or in series with a circuit and it has a very high resistance to current flow. When connected in parallel, only a small amount of current will flow through the voltmeter current path; the rest will flow through the normal circuit current path and the circuit will work normally. When the voltmeter is connected in series with a circuit, only a small amount of current can flow through the circuit. The circuit will not work properly, but the voltmeter reading will show if the circuit is complete or not.

Available Voltage Measurement

Set the voltmeter selector switch to the 20V position and connect the meter negative lead to the negative post of the battery. Connect the positive meter lead to the positive post of the battery and turn the ignition switch ON to provide a load. Read the voltage on the meter or digital display. A well charged battery should register over 12 volts. If the meter reads below 11.5 volts, the battery power may be insufficient to operate the electrical system properly. This test determines voltage available from the battery and should be the first step in any electrical trouble diagnosis procedure. Many electrical problems, especially on computer controlled systems, can be caused by a low state of charge in the battery. Excessive corrosion at the battery cable terminals can cause a poor contact that will prevent proper charging and full battery current flow.

Normal battery voltage is 12 volts when fully charged. When the battery is supplying current to one or more circuits it is said to be "under load". When everything is off the electrical system is under a "no-load" condition. A fully charged battery may show about 12.5 volts at no load; will drop to 12 volts under medium load; and will drop even lower under heavy load. If the battery is partially discharged the voltage decrease under heavy load may be excessive, even though the battery shows 12 volts or more at no load. When allowed to discharge further, the battery's available voltage under load will decrease more severely. For this reason, it is important that the battery be fully charged during all testing procedures to avoid errors in diagnosis and incorrect test results.

Voltage Drop

When current flows through a resistance, the voltage beyond the resistance is reduced (the larger the current, the greater the reduction in voltage). When no current is flowing, there is no voltage drop because there is no current flow. All points in the circuit which are connected to the power source are at the same voltage as the power source. The total voltage drop always equals the total source voltage. In a long circuit with many connectors, a series of small, unwanted voltage drops due to corrosion at the connectors can add up to a total loss of voltage which impairs the operation of the normal loads in the circuit.

INDIRECT COMPUTATION OF VOLTAGE DROPS

1. Set the voltmeter selector switch to the 20 volt position.
2. Connect the meter negative lead to a good ground.

3. Probe all resistances in the circuit with the positive meter lead.

4. Operate the circuit in all modes and observe the voltage readings.

DIRECT MEASUREMENT OF VOLTAGE DROPS

1. Set the voltmeter switch to the 20 volt position.

2. Connect the voltmeter negative lead to the ground side of the resistance load to be measured.

3. Connect the positive lead to the positive side of the resistance or load to be measured.

4. Read the voltage drop directly on the 20 volt scale.

Too high a voltage indicates too high a resistance. If, for example, a blower motor runs too slowly, you can determine if there is too high a resistance in the resistor pack. By taking voltage drop readings in all parts of the circuit, you can isolate the problem. Too low a voltage drop indicates too low a resistance. If, for example, a blower motor runs too fast in the MED and/or LOW position, the problem can be isolated in the resistor pack by taking voltage drop readings in all parts of the circuit to locate a possibly shorted resistor. The maximum allowable voltage drop under load is critical, especially if there is more than one high resistance problem in a circuit because all voltage drops are cumulative. A small drop is normal due to the resistance of the conductors.

HIGH RESISTANCE TESTING

1. Set the voltmeter selector switch to the 4 volt position.

2. Connect the voltmeter positive lead to the positive post of the battery.

3. Turn on the headlights and heater blower to provide a load.

4. Probe various points in the circuit with the negative voltmeter lead.

5. Read the voltage drop on the 4 volt scale. Some average maximum allowable voltage drops are:

FUSE PANEL – 7 volts
IGNITION SWITCH – 5volts
HEADLIGHT SWITCH – 7 volts
IGNITION COIL (+) – 5 volts
ANY OTHER LOAD – 1.3 volts
NOTE: *Voltage drops are all measured while a load is operating; without current flow, there will be no voltage drop.*

Ohmmeter

The ohmmeter is designed to read resistance (ohms) in a circuit or component. Although there are several different styles of ohmmeters, all will usually have a selector switch which permits the measurement of different ranges of re-

sistance (usually the selector switch allows the multiplication of the meter reading by 10, 100, 1000, and 10,000). A calibration knob allows the meter to be set at zero for accurate measurement. Since all ohmmeters are powered by an internal battery (usually 9 volts), the ohmmeter can be used as a self-powered test light. When the ohmmeter is connected, current from the ohmmeter flows through the circuit or component being tested. Since the ohmmeter's internal resistance and voltage are known values, the amount of current flow through the meter depends on the resistance of the circuit or component being tested.

The ohmmeter can be used to perform continuity test for opens or shorts (either by observation of the meter needle or as a self-powered test light), and to read actual resistance in a circuit. It should be noted that the ohmmeter is used to check the resistance of a component or wire while there is no voltage applied to the circuit. Current flow from an outside voltage source (such as the vehicle battery) can damage the ohmmeter, so the circuit or component should be isolated from the vehicle electrical system before any testing is done. Since the ohmmeter uses its own voltage source, either lead can be connected to any test point.

NOTE: *When checking diodes or other solid state components, the ohmmeter leads can only be connected one way in order to measure current flow in a single direction. Make sure the positive (+) and negative (-) terminal connections are as described in the test procedures to verify the one-way diode operation.*

In using the meter for making continuity checks, do not be concerned with the actual resistance readings. Zero resistance, or any resistance readings, indicate continuity in the circuit. Infinite resistance indicates an open in the circuit. A high resistance reading where there should be none indicates a problem in the circuit. Checks for short circuits are made in the same manner as checks for open circuits except that the circuit must be isolated from both power and normal ground. Infinite resistance indicates no continuity to ground, while zero resistance indicates a dead short to ground.

RESISTANCE MEASUREMENT

The batteries in an ohmmeter will weaken with age and temperature, so the ohmmeter must be calibrated or "zeroed" before taking measurements. To zero the meter, place the selector switch in its lowest range and touch the two ohmmeter leads together. Turn the calibration knob until the meter needle is exactly on zero.

NOTE: *All analog (needle) type ohmmeters*

must be zeroed before use, but some digital ohmmeter models are automatically calibrated when the switch is turned on. Self-calibrating digital ohmmeters do not have an adjusting knob, but its a good idea to check for a zero readout before use by touching the leads together. All computer controlled systems require the use of a digital ohmmeter with at least 10 meagohms impedance for testing. Before any test procedures are attempted, make sure the ohmmeter used is compatible with the electrical system or damage to the onboard computer could result.

To measure resistance, first isolate the circuit from the vehicle power source by disconnecting the battery cables or the harness connector. Make sure the key is OFF when disconnecting any components or the battery. Where necessary, also isolate at least one side of the circuit to be checked to avoid reading parallel resistances. Parallel circuit resistances will always give a lower reading than the actual resistance of either of the branches. When measuring the resistance of parallel circuits, the total resistance will always be lower than the smallest resistance in the circuit. Connect the meter leads to both sides of the circuit (wire or component) and read the actual measured ohms on the meter scale. Make sure the selector switch is set to the proper ohm scale for the circuit being tested to avoid misreading the ohmmeter test value.

CAUTION: *Never use an ohmmeter with power applied to the circuit. Like the self-powered test light, the ohmmeter is designed to operate on its own power supply. The normal 12 volt automotive electrical system current could damage the meter.*

Ammeters

An ammeter measures the amount of current flowing through a circuit in units called amperes or amps. Amperes are units of electron flow which indicate how fast the electrons are flowing through the circuit. Since Ohms Law dictates that current flow in a circuit is equal to the circuit voltage divided by the total circuit resistance, increasing voltage also increases the current level (amps). Likewise, any decrease in resistance will increase the amount of amps in a circuit. At normal operating voltage, most circuits have a characteristic amount of amperes, called "current draw" which can be measured using an ammeter. By referring to a specified current draw rating, measuring the amperes, and comparing the two values, one can determine what is happening within the circuit to aid in diagnosis. An open circuit, for example, will not allow any current to flow so the ammeter reading will be zero. More current flows through a heavily loaded circuit or when the charging system is operating.

An ammeter is always connected in series with the circuit being tested. All of the current that normally flows through the circuit must also flow through the ammeter; if there is any other path for the current to follow, the ammeter reading will not be accurate. The ammeter itself has very little resistance to current flow and therefore will not affect the circuit, but it will measure current draw only when the circuit is closed and electricity is flowing. Excessive current draw can blow fuses and drain the battery, while a reduced current draw can cause motors to run slowly, lights to dim and other components to not operate properly. The ammeter can help diagnose these conditions by locating the cause of the high or low reading.

Multimeters

Different combinations of test meters can be built into a single unit designed for specific tests. Some of the more common combination test devices are known as Volt/Amp testers, Tach/Dwell meters, or Digital Multimeters. The Volt/Amp tester is used for charging system, starting system or battery tests and consists of a voltmeter, an ammeter and a variable resistance carbon pile. The voltmeter will usually have at least two ranges for use with 6, 12 and 24 volt systems. The ammeter also has more than one range for testing various levels of battery loads and starter current draw and the carbon pile can be adjusted to offer different amounts of resistance. The Volt/Amp tester has heavy leads to carry large amounts of current and many later models have an inductive ammeter pickup that clamps around the wire to simplify test connections. On some models, the ammeter also has a zero-center scale to allow testing of charging and starting systems without switching leads or polarity. A digital multimeter is a voltmeter, ammeter and ohmmeter combined in an instrument which gives a digital readout. These are often used when testing solid state circuits because of their high input impedance (usually 10 megohms or more).

The tach/dwell meter combines a tachometer and a dwell (cam angle) meter and is a specialized kind of voltmeter. The tachometer scale is marked to show engine speed in rpm and the dwell scale is marked to show degrees of distributor shaft rotation. In most electronic ignition systems, dwell is determined by the control unit, but the dwell meter can also be used to check the duty cycle (operation) of some electronic engine control systems. Some tach/dwell meters are powered by an internal battery, while others take their power from the car battery in use. The battery powered testers usually require calibration much like an ohmmeter before testing.

Special Test Equipment

A variety of diagnostic tools are available to help troubleshoot and repair computerized engine control systems. The most sophisticated of these devices are the console type engine analyzers that usually occupy a garage service bay, but there are several types of aftermarket electronic testers available that will allow quick circuit tests of the engine control system by plugging directly into a special connector located in the engine compartment or under the dashboard. Several tool and equipment manufacturers offer simple, hand held testers that measure various circuit voltage levels on command to check all system components for proper operation. Although these testers usually cost about $300-$500, consider that the average computer control unit (or ECM) can cost just as much and the money saved by not replacing perfectly good sensors or components in an attempt to correct a problem could justify the purchase price of a special diagnostic tester the first time it's used.

These computerized testers can allow quick and easy test measurements while the engine is operating or while the car is being driven. In addition, the on-board computer memory can be read to access any stored trouble codes; in effect allowing the computer to tell you where it hurts and aid trouble diagnosis by pinpointing exactly which circuit or component is malfunctioning. In the same manner, repairs can be tested to make sure the problem has been corrected. The biggest advantage these special testers have is their relatively easy hookups that minimize or eliminate the chances of making the wrong connections and getting false voltage readings or damaging the computer accidentally.

NOTE: *It should be remembered that these testers check voltage levels in circuits; they don't detect mechanical problems or failed components if the circuit voltage falls within the preprogrammed limits stored in the tester PROM unit. Also, most of the hand held testers are designed to work only on one or two systems made by a specific manufacturer.*

A variety of aftermarket testers are available to help diagnose different computerized control systems. Owatonna Tool Company (OTC), for example, markets a device called the OTC Monitor which plugs directly into the assembly line diagnostic link (ALDL). The OTC tester makes diagnosis a simple matter of pressing the correct buttons and, by changing the internal PROM or inserting a different diagnosis cartridge, it will work on any model from full size to subcompact, over a wide range of years. An adapter is supplied with the tester to allow connection to all types of ALDL links, regardless of the number of pin terminals used. By inserting an updated PROM into the OTC tester, it can be easily updated to diagnose any new modifications of computerized control systems.

Wiring Harnesses

The average automobile contains about ½ mile of wiring, with hundreds of individual connections. To protect the many wires from damage and to keep them from becoming a confusing tangle, they are organized into bundles, enclosed in plastic or taped together and called wire harnesses. Different wiring harnesses serve different parts of the vehicle. Individual wires are color coded to help trace them through a harness where sections are hidden from view.

A loose or corroded connection or a replacement wire that is too small for the circuit will add extra resistance and an additional voltage drop to the circuit. A ten percent voltage drop can result in slow or erratic motor operation, for example, even though the circuit is complete. Automotive wiring or circuit conductors can be in any one of three forms:

1. Single strand wire
2. Multistrand wire
3. Printed circuitry

Single strand wire has a solid metal core and is usually used inside such components as alternators, motors, relays and other devices. Multistrand wire has a core made of many small strands of wire twisted together into a single conductor. Most of the wiring in an automotive electrical system is made up of multistrand wire, either as a single conductor or grouped together in a harness. All wiring is color coded on the insulator, either as a solid color or as a colored wire with an identification stripe. A printed circuit is a thin film of copper or other conductor that is printed on an insulator backing. Occasionally, a printed circuit is sandwiched between two sheets of plastic for more protection and flexibility. A complete printed circuit, consisting of conductors, insulating material and connectors for lamps or other components is called a printed circuit board. Printed circuitry is used in place of individual wires or harnesses in places where space is limited, such as behind instrument panels.

Wire Gauge

Since computer controlled automotive electrical systems are very sensitive to changes in resistance, the selection of properly sized wires is critical when systems are repaired. The wire gauge number is an expression of the cross section area of the conductor. The most common system for expressing wire size is the American Wire Gauge (AWG) system.

Wire cross section area is measured in circular mils. A mil is $\frac{1}{1000}$" (0.001"); a circular mil is the area of a circle one mil in diameter. For example, a conductor ¼" in diameter is 0.250 in. or 250 mils. The circular mil cross section area of the wire is 250 squared (250^2) or 62,500 circular mils. Imported car models usually use metric wire gauge designations, which is simply the cross section area of the conductor in square millimeters (mm^2).

Gauge numbers are assigned to conductors of various cross section areas. As gauge number increases, area decreases and the conductor becomes smaller. A 5 gauge conductor is smaller than a 1 gauge conductor and a 10 gauge is smaller than a 5 gauge. As the cross section area of a conductor decreases, resistance increases and so does the gauge number. A conductor with a higher gauge number will carry less current than a conductor with a lower gauge number.

NOTE: *Gauge wire size refers to the size of the conductor, not the size of the complete wire. It is possible to have two wires of the same gauge with different diameters because one may have thicker insulation than the other.*

12 volt automotive electrical systems generally use 10, 12, 14, 16 and 18 gauge wire. Main power distribution circuits and larger accessories usually use 10 and 12 gauge wire. Battery cables are usually 4 or 6 gauge, although 1 and 2 gauge wires are occasionally used. Wire length must also be considered when making repairs to a circuit. As conductor length increases, so does resistance. An 18 gauge wire, for example, can carry a 10 amp load for 10 feet without excessive voltage drop; however if a 15 foot wire is required for the same 10 amp load, it must be a 16 gauge wire.

An electrical schematic shows the electrical current paths when a circuit is operating properly. It is essential to understand how a circuit works before trying to figure out why it doesn't. Schematics break the entire electrical system down into individual circuits and show only one particular circuit. In a schematic, no attempt is made to represent wiring and components as they physically appear on the vehicle; switches and other components are shown as simply as possible. Face views of harness connectors show the cavity or terminal locations in all multi-pin connectors to help locate test points.

If you need to backprobe a connector while it is on the component, the order of the terminals must be mentally reversed. The wire color code can help in this situation, as well as a keyway, lock tab or other reference mark.

NOTE: *Wiring diagrams are not included in this book. As trucks have become more complex and available with longer option lists, wiring diagrams have grown in size and complexity. It has become almost impossible to provide a readable reproduction of a wiring diagram in a book this size. Information on ordering wiring diagrams from the vehicle manufacturer can be found in the owner's manual.*

WIRING REPAIR

Soldering is a quick, efficient method of joining metals permanently. Everyone who has the occasion to make wiring repairs should know how to solder. Electrical connections that are soldered are far less likely to come apart and will conduct electricity much better than connections that are only "pig-tailed" together. The most popular (and preferred) method of soldering is with an electric soldering gun. Soldering irons are available in many sizes and wattage ratings. Irons with higher wattage ratings deliver higher temperatures and recover lost heat faster. A small soldering iron rated for no more than 50 watts is recommended, especially on electrical systems where excess heat can damage the components being soldered.

There are three ingredients necessary for successful soldering; proper flux, good solder and sufficient heat. A soldering flux is necessary to clean the metal of tarnish, prepare it for soldering and to enable the solder to spread into tiny crevices. When soldering, always use a resin flux or resin core solder which is non-corrosive and will not attract moisture once the job is finished. Other types of flux (acid core) will leave a residue that will attract moisture and cause the wires to corrode. Tin is a unique metal with a low melting point. In a molten state, it dissolves and alloys easily with many metals. Solder is made by mixing tin with lead. The most common proportions are 40/60, 50/50 and 60/40, with the percentage of tin listed first. Low priced solders usually contain less tin, making them very difficult for a beginner to use because more heat is required to melt the solder. A common solder is 40/60 which is well suited for all-around general use, but 60/40 melts easier, has more tin for a better joint and is preferred for electrical work.

Soldering Techniques

Successful soldering requires that the metals to be joined be heated to a temperature that will melt the solder—usually 360-460°F (182-238°C). Contrary to popular belief, the purpose of the soldering iron is not to melt the solder itself, but to heat the parts being soldered to a temperature high enough to melt the solder when it is touched to the work. Melting flux-cored solder on the soldering iron will usually destroy the effectiveness of the flux.

NOTE: *Soldering tips are made of copper for good heat conductivity, but must be "tinned" regularly for quick transference of heat to the project and to prevent the solder from sticking to the iron. To "tin" the iron, simply heat it and touch the flux-cored solder to the tip; the solder will flow over the hot tip. Wipe the excess off with a clean rag, but be careful as the iron will be hot.*

After some use, the tip may become pitted. If so, simply dress the tip smooth with a smooth file and "tin" the tip again. An old saying holds that "metals well cleaned are half soldered." Flux-cored solder will remove oxides but rust, bits of insulation and oil or grease must be removed with a wire brush or emery cloth. For maximum strength in soldered parts, the joint must start off clean and tight. Weak joints will result in gaps too wide for the solder to bridge.

If a separate soldering flux is used, it should be brushed or swabbed on only those areas that are to be soldered. Most solders contain a core of flux and separate fluxing is unnecessary. Hold the work to be soldered firmly. It is best to solder on a wooden board, because a metal vise will only rob the piece to be soldered of heat and make it difficult to melt the solder. Hold the soldering tip with the broadest face against the work to be soldered. Apply solder under the tip close to the work, using enough solder to give a heavy film between the iron and the piece being soldered, while moving slowly and making sure the solder melts properly. Keep the work level or the solder will run to the lowest part and favor the thicker parts, because these require more heat to melt the solder. If the soldering tip overheats (the solder coating on the face of the tip burns up), it should be retinned. Once the soldering is completed, let the soldered joint stand until cool. Tape and seal all soldered wire splices after the repair has cooled.

Wire Harness and Connectors

The on-board computer (ECM) wire harness electrically connects the control unit to the various solenoids, switches and sensors used by the control system. Most connectors in the engine compartment or otherwise exposed to the elements are protected against moisture and dirt which could create oxidation and deposits on the terminals. This protection is important because of the very low voltage and current levels used by the computer and sensors. All connectors have a lock which secures the male and female terminals together, with a secondary lock holding the seal and terminal into the connec-

tor. Both terminal locks must be released when disconnecting ECM connectors.

These special connectors are weather-proof and all repairs require the use of a special terminal and the tool required to service it. This tool is used to remove the pin and sleeve terminals. If removal is attempted with an ordinary pick, there is a good chance that the terminal will be bent or deformed. Unlike standard blade type terminals, these terminals cannot be straightened once they are bent. Make certain that the connectors are properly seated and all of the sealing rings in place when connecting leads. On some models, a hinge-type flap provides a backup or secondary locking feature for the terminals. Most secondary locks are used to improve the connector reliability by retaining the terminals if the small terminal lock tangs are not positioned properly.

Molded-on connectors require complete replacement of the connection. This means splicing a new connector assembly into the harness. All splices in on-board computer systems should be soldered to insure proper contact. Use care when probing the connections or replacing terminals in them as it is possible to short between opposite terminals. If this happens to the wrong terminal pair, it is possible to damage certain components. Always use jumper wires between connectors for circuit checking and never probe through weather-proof seals.

Open circuits are often difficult to locate by sight because corrosion or terminal misalignment are hidden by the connectors. Merely wiggling a connector on a sensor or in the wiring harness may correct the open circuit condition. This should always be considered when an open circuit or a failed sensor is indicated. Intermittent problems may also be caused by oxidized or loose connections. When using a circuit tester for diagnosis, always probe connections from the wire side. Be careful not to damage sealed connectors with test probes.

All wiring harnesses should be replaced with identical parts, using the same gauge wire and connectors. When signal wires are spliced into a harness, use wire with high temperature insulation only. With the low voltage and current levels found in the system, it is important that the best possible connection at all wire splices be made by soldering the splices together. It is seldom necessary to replace a complete harness. If replacement is necessary, pay close attention to insure proper harness routing. Secure the harness with suitable plastic wire clamps to prevent vibrations from causing the harness to wear in spots or contact any hot components.

NOTE: *Weatherproof connectors cannot be replaced with standard connectors. Instruc-*

tions are provided with replacement connector and terminal packages. Some wire harnesses have mounting indicators (usually pieces of colored tape) to mark where the harness is to be secured.

In making wiring repairs, it's important that you always replace damaged wires with wires that are the same gauge as the wire being replaced. The heavier the wire, the smaller the gauge number. Wires are color-coded to aid in identification and whenever possible the same color coded wire should be used for replacement. A wire stripping and crimping tool is necessary to install solderless terminal connectors. Test all crimps by pulling on the wires; it should not be possible to pull the wires out of a good crimp.

Wires which are open, exposed or otherwise damaged are repaired by simple splicing. Where possible, if the wiring harness is accessible and the damaged place in the wire can be located, it is best to open the harness and check for all possible damage. In an inaccessible harness, the wire must be bypassed with a new insert, usually taped to the outside of the old harness.

When replacing fusible links, be sure to use fusible link wire, NOT ordinary automotive wire. Make sure the fusible segment is of the same gauge and construction as the one being replaced and double the stripped end when crimping the terminal connector for a good contact. The melted (open) fusible link segment of the wiring harness should be cut off as close to the harness as possible, then a new segment spliced in as described. In the case of a damaged fusible link that feeds two harness wires, the harness connections should be replaced with two fusible link wires so that each circuit will have its own separate protection.

NOTE: *Most of the problems caused in the wiring harness are due to bad ground connections. Always check all vehicle ground connections for corrosion or looseness before performing any power feed checks to eliminate the chance of a bad ground affecting the circuit.*

Repairing Hard Shell Connectors

Unlike molded connectors, the terminal contacts in hard shell connectors can be replaced. Weatherproof hard-shell connectors with the leads molded into the shell have non-replaceable terminal ends. Replacement usually involves the use of a special terminal removal tool that depress the locking tangs (barbs) on the connector terminal and allow the connector to be removed from the rear of the shell. The connector shell should be replaced if it shows any evidence of burning, melting, cracks, or breaks.

Replace individual terminals that are burnt, corroded, distorted or loose.

NOTE: *The insulation crimp must be tight to prevent the insulation from sliding back on the wire when the wire is pulled. The insulation must be visibly compressed under the crimp tabs, and the ends of the crimp should be turned in for a firm grip on the insulation.*

The wire crimp must be made with all wire strands inside the crimp. The terminal must be fully compressed on the wire strands with the ends of the crimp tabs turned in to make a firm grip on the wire. Check all connections with an ohmmeter to insure a good contact. There should be no measurable resistance between the wire and the terminal when connected.

Mechanical Test Equipment

Vacuum Gauge

Most gauges are graduated in inches of mercury (in.Hg), although a device called a manometer reads vacuum in inches of water (in. H_2O). The normal vacuum reading usually varies between 18 and 22 in.Hg at sea level. To test engine vacuum, the vacuum gauge must be connected to a source of manifold vacuum. Many engines have a plug in the intake manifold which can be removed and replaced with an adapter fitting. Connect the vacuum gauge to the fitting with a suitable rubber hose or, if no manifold plug is available, connect the vacuum gauge to any device using manifold vacuum, such as EGR valves, etc. The vacuum gauge can be used to determine if enough vacuum is reaching a component to allow its actuation.

Hand Vacuum Pump

Small, hand-held vacuum pumps come in a variety of designs. Most have a built-in vacuum gauge and allow the component to be tested without removing it from the vehicle. Operate the pump lever or plunger to apply the correct amount of vacuum required for the test specified in the diagnosis routines. The level of vacuum in inches of Mercury (in.Hg) is indicated on the pump gauge. For some testing, an additional vacuum gauge may be necessary.

Intake manifold vacuum is used to operate various systems and devices on late model vehicles. To correctly diagnose and solve problems in vacuum control systems, a vacuum source is necessary for testing. In some cases, vacuum can be taken from the intake manifold when the engine is running, but vacuum is normally provided by a hand vacuum pump. These hand vacuum pumps have a built-in vacuum gauge that allow testing while the device is still attached to the component. For some tests, an additional vacuum gauge may be necessary.

CAUTION: *Some 1987, 1988 and 1989 Volvo 780 and 760 series include an electrically operated Supplemental Restraint System (SRS) or airbag system. The SRS system can deploy during electrical testing if certain steps are not followed. While the airbag and inflator are in the steering column, the system has various other wires and components located under the dash and under the seat.*

If your car is equipped with SRS, observe the following rules when performing electrical diagnosis:

• If you are not absolutely sure of the identity of a component, leave it alone.

• Know where a wire goes before applying voltage or checking resistance.

• Turn the ignition to OFF and disconnect the negative battery cable before disconnecting any electrical connectors inside the car.

• Be sure that the integrity of the SRS wiring is not disturbed during the installation of accessories such as CB radios, phones, audio equipment, etc.

• If the steering wheel must be removed, the bag assembly must first be removed and disconnected from the center of the wheel. Put the unit to the side and DO NOT attempt to check resistance at the inflator.

• On 780 series, ALWAYS disconnect the 4-pin yellow connector at the lower part of the steering column near the center console. The front seat belts are also part of the SRS system. If any diagnostics must be done to the seat belt system, disconnect the seat belt tensioners (grey connectors under the driver's seat) before doing any work.

• On the 760 series, ALWAYS disconnect the 4-pin yellow connector (shown below) before doing ANY electrical diagnostic work.

• Do not disconnect the main lead to the sensor box under the seat.

• Volvo specifically recommends against anyone other than factory-trained personnel

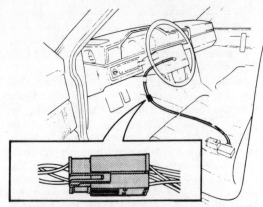

Always disconnect the yellow connector before performing any electrical diagnostic work. 1988 760 with SRS shown

attempting repairs or diagnosis on the SRS system.

HEATING AND AIR CONDITIONING

Heater/Air Conditioner Blower Motor

REMOVAL AND INSTALLATION

1970-72 164 Series

1. Remove the heater unit as outlined in Heater Unit Removal and Installation.

2. Remove the four rubber bushings on the sides of the heater unit.

3. Scribe marks on both sides of the fan housing to ease reassembly. Remove the spring clips and separate the housing halves.

4. Mark the mounting plate's relative position to the fan housing. Straighten the tabs and separate the mounting plate from the housing.

5. Remove the retaining screws and separate the fan motor from the mounting plate.

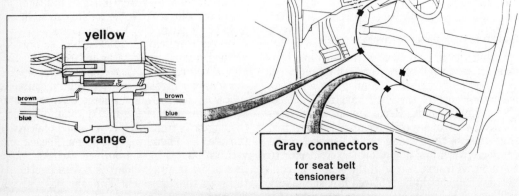

yellow

brown   brown

blue   blue

orange

Gray connectors
for seat belt
tensioners

Location of SRS connectors. 1987 780 shown

6. Reverse the above procedure to install, being careful to apply soft sealer to the housing halves.

1800 Series

NOTE: *The fan motor and fan are replaced as a unit.*

1. Remove the valve cover and place a rag over the rocker arm assembly.

2. On 1970-71 models, remove the pressure regulator bracket from the heater and allow it to hang freely.

3. Disconnect the fan motor wires at the fan terminals.

4. Remove the six retaining screws and remove the fan motor from the heater assembly.

5. Reverse the above procedure to install.

All 1973 140 Series and 164 Models without Air Conditioning

1. Remove the heater unit as outlined in Heater Unit Removal and Installation.

2. Place the unit on its side with the control valve facing upward. Remove the spring clips and separate the housing valves.

3. Lift out the old fan motor and replace it with a new unit, making sure that the support leg without the foot points to the output for the defroster channel. (See illustration).

4. Assemble the heater housing halves with new spring clips, and seal the joint without clips using soft sealing compound.

5. Install the heater unit as outlined in Heater Unit Removal and Installation.

1973 140 Series and Models with Air Conditioning All 1974 and Later Models except 700 series.

In order to remove the blower motor, both the right and left turbines (blower wheels) must first be removed. The heater unit does not have to be removed.

1. Disconnect the negative battery cable.

2. Lift the carpet and remove the central unit side panels.

3. Remove the retaining screws for the control panel and move the panel as far back on the transmission tunnel as the electrical cables will permit.

4. Remove the attaching screws for the rear seat heater ducts and disconnect the ducts from the central unit.

5. Remove the instrument cluster as outlined in Instrument Cluster Removal and Installation.

6. Remove the glovebox by unscrewing the four attaching screws, removing the glovebox door stop, and disconnecting the wires from the glovebox courtesy light. Remove the molded dashboard padding from beneath the glovebox.

7. Disconnect the vacuum hoses to the left and right defroster vacuum motors, then remove the nozzles and both air ducts.

8. Remove the air hoses between the left and right inside air vents.

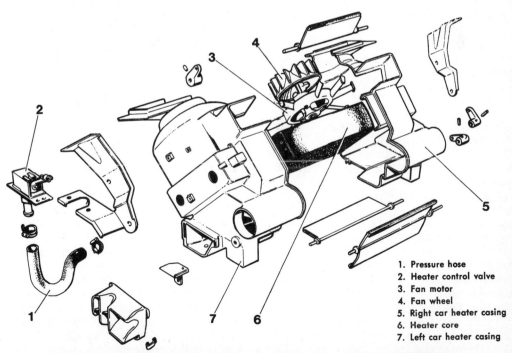

1. Pressure hose
2. Heater control valve
3. Fan motor
4. Fan wheel
5. Right car heater casing
6. Heater core
7. Left car heater casing

Standard heater unit—1973 140 series and 164 models without air conditioning

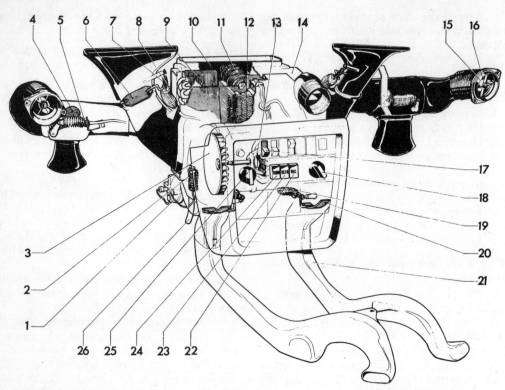

Combination heater—air conditioner unit—1973 140 series and 164 with air conditioning, all 1974 and later models except the 760GLE

1. Heater control valve
2. Capillary tube for heater control valve
3. Turbine
4. Shutter, air vent left floor
5. Vacuum motor
6. Shutter, left defroster nozzle
7. Return spring for vacuum motor
8. Vacuum motor
9. Evaporator (only on vehicles with air conditioning)
10. Air intake cover
11. Vacuum motor for air intake cover
12. Heater core
13. Fan motor
14. Central unit
15. Blow-in valve
16. Shutter knob
17. Air conditioning switch
18. Fan motor switch
19. Vacuum motor
20. Shutter, right air duct, rear floor
21. Air duct to rear floor
22. Knob, air intake cover
23. Knob, defroster shutter
24. Knob, floor shutter
25. Temperature controls
26. Drain hose

9. Remove the clamps on the central unit outer ends and remove the ends.

10. Pry off the locking retainer from the turbines (blower wheels), and remove both left and right turbines.

11. Position the heater control valve capillary tube to one side.

12. Remove the left inner end (blower housing) from the central unit.

13. Unscrew the three retaining screws and remove the fan motor retainer.

14. Disconnect the plug from the fan motor control panel. Release the tabs of the electric cables from the plug contact, remove the rubber grommet, and pull the electric cables down through rightside opening of the central unit.

15. Remove the fan motor from the left opening.

16. When reinstalling, pass the cable through the opening, connect it and replace the rubber grommet.

17. Mount and secure the fan motor. Remember to install the plastic bushings on the fan mounts; failure to do so will make the fan rub the case.

18. Reinstall the inner casing (housing) and hook up the capillary tube.

19. Reinstall the blower wheels and secure the locking clip. Install the outer ends of the central unit and attach their clips.

20. Connect the ductwork to the inside air vents. Reinstall the defroster nozzles and connect the vacuum hoses to the vacuum motors.

21. Replace the molded insulation and reassemble the glovebox.

22. Reinstall the instrument cluster.

23. Connect and secure the rear seat heating ducts. Slide the control panel back towards the dash and into position.

24. Install the central unit side panels. Reconnect the negative battery cable.

740, 760 and 780 series

The 700 series of Volvos may be found equipped with any of three heating and air conditioning systems. The combined unit (CU) is simply a manually operated heater, with or without an air conditioner system. The Automatic Climate Control (ACC) system maintains a constant (preset) temperature in the car by mechanical (vacuum) means, turning on the heater or A/C as necessary. The newer Electronic Climate Control (ECC) system performs the same duties electronically and incorporates an internal self-diagnostic system which will display a signal when it detects a fault. To remove the blower motor:

1. Disconnect the negative battery cable.

2. Remove the panel below the glove compartment. Depending on the model, it may be necessary to remove the glove box.

3. On cars with the CU system, remove the right sill plate and the right kick panel. Carefully disconnect the control unit connector, re-

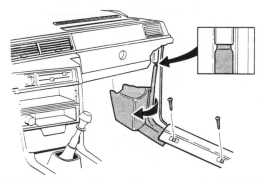

Removal of panels necessary on cars with CU system

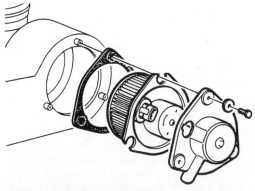

Blower assembly, ECC system

move the mounting screws and remove the control unit with its bracket.

4. Disconnect the wiring to the fan motor, unfasten the screws securing the fan motor, and lower the motor.

3. Remove the motor and fan.

4. To install, reconnect the wiring to the fan motor. Spread a sealer around the mounting face of the fan mounting flange, and install the fan motor. Cars with ECC have a rubber seal between the motor and the fan case; no sealer is required.

5. Reconnect the breather hose to the motor and connect the negative battery cable. Check the fan operation.

6. Reinstall the control unit and secure its connector on cars with the CU system. Replace the right kick panel and the sill plate.

7. Reinstall the panel below the glove compartment and the glove box if removed.

Heater Unit (Complete Assembly)
REMOVAL AND INSTALLATION
1970-72 140 Series, 164

1. Remove the lower radiator hose, open the engine drain plug, and drain the cooling system. Disconnect the negative battery cable.

CAUTION: *When draining the coolant, keep in mind that cats and dogs are attracted by the ethylene glycol antifreeze, and are quite likely to drink any that is left in an uncovered container or in puddles on the ground. This will prove fatal in sufficient quantity. Always drain the coolant into a sealable container. Coolant should be reused unless it is contaminated or several years old.*

2. Remove the hoses to the heater control valve.

3. Remove the heater control panel below the dashboard by removing the two retaining screws. Tilt the top of the panel back so that it loosens from the dashboard clips and clears the hood release.

4. Remove the transmission tunnel mat, defroster hoses, heater control cables, and fan switch wires.

5. Remove the two screws which retain the fuse box to the heater.

6. Remove the control valve, being careful not to damage the copper capillary tube. Loosen the upper hose to the heater.

7. Plug the heater outlets to avoid spilling coolant upon removal. Loosen the heater unit ground cables, remove the four retaining screws, loosen the drain hose, and lift out the heater unit and control valve from their brackets.

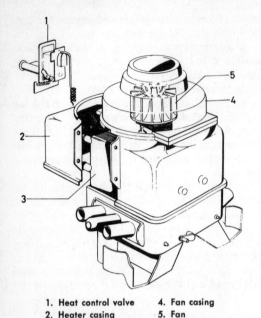

1. Heat control valve   4. Fan casing
2. Heater casing   5. Fan
3. Heater core

1970–72 140 series heater unit. 164 models similar

8. Reverse the above procedure to install. Remember to remove all plugs from lines and ports. When reinstalling, support the unit and handle it carefully so the capillary tube is not damaged. Double check the security of all hose clamps and wiring connectors.

9. Carefully refit the control panel and install its screws. Connect the hoses to the heater control valve.

10. Reconnect the negative battery cable and fill the system with coolant.

1800 Series

1. Disconnect the lower radiator hose, open the engine drain plug, and drain the cooling system. Disconnect the negative battery cable.

CAUTION: *When draining the coolant, keep in mind that cats and dogs are attracted by the ethylene glycol antifreeze, and are quite likely to drink any that is left in an uncovered container or in puddles on the ground. This will prove fatal in sufficient quantity. Always drain the coolant into a sealable container. Coolant should be reused unless it is contaminated or several years old.*

2. Disconnect the heater hoses from the heater core pipe and the control valve pipe. Disconnect the fan motor wires.

3. Disconnect the fresh air intake from the heater.

4. On 1970-71 models, remove the pressure regulator bracket retaining screws and allow the pressure regulator to hang free while still connected to the hoses.

5. Remove the four heater-to-firewall attaching nuts.

6. Remove the defroster hoses. Disconnect the heater control valve and the control cables.

7. Lift out the heater and control valve as a unit.

8. Reverse the above procedure to install.

All 1973 140 Series and 164 Models without Air Conditioning

1. Remove the lower radiator hose, open the engine drain plug, and drain the cooling system. Disconnect the negative battery cable.

CAUTION: *When draining the coolant, keep in mind that cats and dogs are attracted by the ethylene glycol antifreeze, and are quite likely to drink any that is left in an uncovered container or in puddles on the ground. This will prove fatal in sufficient quantity. Always drain the coolant into a sealable container. Coolant should be reused unless it is contaminated or several years old.*

2. Remove the center panel and the left-hand defroster hose.

3. Lift up the driveshaft tunnel mat, disconnect the front and rear attaching screws for the rear seat heater ducts and then remove the ducts.

4. Disconnect the heater control valve and air-mix cables from their shutters.

5. Disconnect and plug the pressure hose at the heater. Also plug the heater pipes to prevent residual coolant from spilling onto the carpet.

6. Remove the attaching screws which secure the left-hand upper bracket to the dashboard and the left-hand lower bracket to the transmission tunnel.

7. Remove the glovebox by unscrewing the four attaching screws, removing the glovebox door stop, and disconnecting the wires from the glovebox courtesy light.

8. Disconnect the defroster and floor heating cables from their levers.

9. Disconnect the fan motor wires at the switch contact plate.

10. Remove the attaching screws which secure the right-hand upper bracket to the dashboard and the right-hand lower bracket to the transmission tunnel.

11. Remove the right-hand defroster hose. Disconnect the hose between the heater and the dashboard circular vents. Lift the heater unit to the right, and then out of the vehicle.

12. Reverse the above procedure to install, taking care to ensure that the air vent rubber seal is properly located, and that the fan motor ground cable is attached at the upper right-hand bracket attaching screw.

1973 140 Series and 164 Models with Air Conditioning
All 1974 and Later Models except 700 series

NOTE: *This procedure does NOT require the discharge of the air conditioning system. Do not disconnect any A/C lines or hoses.*

1. Remove the lower radiator hose, open the engine drain plug, and drain the cooling system. Disconnect the negative battery cable.

CAUTION: *When draining the coolant, keep in mind that cats and dogs are attracted by the ethylene glycol antifreeze, and are quite likely to drink any that is left in an uncovered container or in puddles on the ground. This will prove fatal in sufficient quantity. Always drain the coolant into a sealable container. Coolant should be reused unless it is contaminated or several years old.*

2. Remove the heater hoses from the heater pipes at the engine side of the firewall. Plug the heater pipes.

3. Remove the evaporator hose brackets from their body mounts and disconnect the dryer from its bracket. Position the dryer as close to the firewall as the evaporator hose permits. Do not disconnect any air conditioning lines.

4. Remove the instrument cluster by removing the steering column molded casting, removing the bracket retaining screw and lowering it toward the steering column. Remove the four instrument cluster retaining screws, disconnecting the speedometer cable and tilting the speedometer out of its snap fitting. After moving the cluster forward and disconnecting the electrical plug contacts, lift the cluster out of the vehicle.

5. Remove the air hose between the center unit and the left inner air vent. Remove the hose from the vacuum motor for the left defroster nozzle and the left floor outlet (if equipped).

6. Remove the left-side panel from the central unit.

7. Lift up the driveshaft tunnel mat and disconnect the rear seat heater duct from the central unit.

8. Remove the heater pipes from the firewall.

9. Remove the upper and lower attaching screws for the left support leg. Remove the attaching screws which secure the upper bracket to the dashboard and the lower bracket to the transmission tunnel.

NOTE: *If the upper bracket screw holes are slotted, the screws need only be slackened a few turns.*

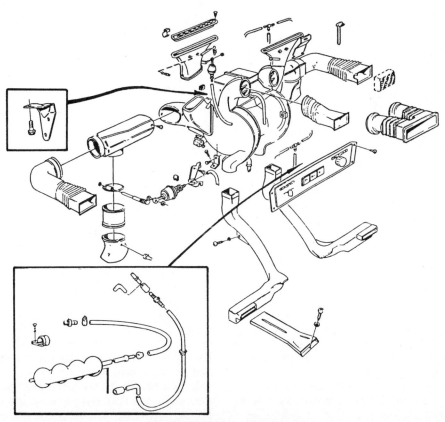

CU system heater components

10. Remove the right-side panel from the central unit.

11. Remove the glovebox by unscrewing the four attaching screws, removing the glovebox door stop, and disconnecting the glovebox courtesy light wires.

12. Remove the right defroster nozzle and the air hose between the central unit and the right inner air vent.

13. Lift up the driveshaft tunnel mat and disconnect the rear seat heater duct from the central unit.

14. Remove the upper and lower attaching screws from the right support leg. Remove the lower attaching screws for the control panel.

15. Disconnect the fan motor wires and the ground wires from the control panel.

16. Disconnect the yellow cable from its plug contact.

17. Separate the halves of the vacuum hose connector and disconnect the vacuum tank hose at the connector.

18. Position the control panel as far back on the transmission tunnel as the cables permit.

19. Remove the screws which attach the upper brackets to the firewall and the lower brackets to the transmission tunnel.

20. Remove the thermostat clamp from the central unit, and the two evaporator cover retaining clamps.

21. Without disconnecting any of the refrigerant lines, remove the evaporator from the central unit, placing it on the right-hand side of the firewall.

22. Remove the molded dashboard padding from beneath the glovebox if it's in the way.

23. Remove the retaining clamps for the right outer vent duct, and remove the duct. Pry off the locking retainer for the turbine (blower), and remove the turbine. Remove the clamps which retain the blower housing (inner end) to the central unit and remove the housing.

24. Remove the passenger's front seat (if it's in the way) and lift the central unit forward and onto the floor of the vehicle. Be careful not to place undue stress on the connected refrigerant lines.

25. When reinstalling the central unit, lift it onto the right floor and install the rubber seal for the air intake. Lift the unit into position and insert the upper left bracket over the dashboard screws. Install the rightside bracket screws and tighten the left ones.

26. Install the evaporator, cover it and secure the clamps. Carefully reinstall the thermostat on the loser flange.

27. Use a sealing compound around the evaporator pipes and the thermostat line as necessary.

28. Install the ducts for the heater hoses to the dashboard.

29. Install the tunnel brackets and the drain hose.

30. Install the right inner end of the unit and the vacuum hose for the floor shutter.

31. Install the turbine wheel (fan) and the outer end of the central unit. Make sure the clips are reinstalled properly.

32. Install the air duct between the central unit and the right inner air outlet.

33. Install the right defroster nozzle and connect its vacuum hose.

34. Install the glove box, the air duct to the right side vent, and the air ducts to the rear floor.

35. Connect the air duct for the left inner air vent, connect and adjust the left defroster nozzle and attach its vacuum line.

36. Replace the instrument cluster.

37. Reassemble the vacuum connectors and connect the hoses to the vacuum tank.

38. Reconnect the yellow wire to the contact unit and the contact to the control unit.

39. Install the ground wires, tighten the instrument cluster and the support legs.

40. Reinstall the control panel, the insulation pads and the side panels.

41. Connect the heater hoses to the ports on the control unit. Install the firewall panel and clamp down the air conditioning hoses and dryer in the engine compartment.

42. Refill the engine coolant.

43. Double check all installation items, paying particular attention to loose hoses or hanging wires, untightened nuts, poor routing of hoses and wires (too tight or rubbing) and tools left in the area.

44. Reconnect the battery and check the function of the system components.

Heater Core
REMOVAL AND INSTALLATION
1970-72 140 Series, 164

1. Remove the heater unit as outlined in Heater Unit Removal and Installation.

2. Remove the four rubber bushings on the sides of the heater unit.

3. Scribe marks on both sides of the fan housing to facilitate assembly. Remove the spring clips and separate the housing halves.

4. Separate the heater core from the housing half, taking care not to damage the sensitive body of the control valve.

5. Reverse the above procedure to install, being careful to apply soft sealer to the housing halves.

1800 Series

1. Remove the heater unit as outlined in Heater Unit Removal and Installation.

2. Remove the fan motor.

3. Remove the screws securing the heater housing halves together and then separate the halves.

4. Remove the heater core from the housing.

5. Install the new or reconditioned core in the housing. Check the operation of the shutters for binding or looseness.

6. Install the thermostat capillary tube on the core.

7. Apply new soft sealing compound to the housing halves prior to assembly.

8. Reinstall the fan motor and install the heater unit as explained in "Heater Unit Removal and Installation".

1973 140 Series and 164 without Air Conditioning

1. Remove the heater unit as outlined in Heater Unit Removal and Installation.

2. Place the unit on its side with the control valve facing upward. Remove the spring clips and separate the housing halves.

3. Disconnect the capillary tube from the heater core and then lift out the core.

4. Reverse the above procedure to install, being careful to transfer the foam plastic packing to the new heater core, and to install the fragile capillary tube carefully on the core.

1973 140 Series, 164 with Air Conditioning, All 1974 and Later Models except 700 series.

1. Remove the heater-air conditioner unit as outlined under Heater Unit Removal and Installation.

2. Remove the left outer end of the central unit. Remove the locking retainer and the turbine (blower wheel).

3. Remove the two retaining screws for the left transmission tunnel bracket.

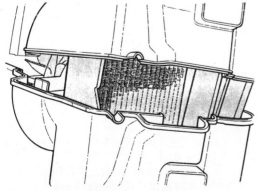

Use care in separating case halves

4. Remove the lockring for the left intake shutter shaft.

5. Remove the three retaining screws and lift off the inner end.

6. Remove the three retaining screws for the fan motor retainer.

7. Disconnect the heater hoses at the heater core.

8. Remove the clamps which retain the central unit halves together, lift off the left half, and remove the heater core.

9. Reverse the above procedure to install, taking care to transfer the foam plastic packing to the new heater core.

740, 760 and 780 Series

On vehicles equipped with ACC (Automatic Climate Control), a thermal switch is located on the outlet hose from the heater core. It switches on and starts the fan motor only when the water temperature exceeds approximately 95°F (35°C). This prevents cold air from being blown into the passenger compartment during winter. The thermal switch is bypassed in the DE-FROST position.

740 MODELS

These vehicles use the standard unit system (CU) with or without the air conditioning system (CU + AC).

NOTE: *PLEASE RE-READ THE AIR CONDITIONING SECTION IN CHAPTER ONE SO THAT THE SYSTEM MAY BE DISCHARGED PROPERLY. ALWAYS WEAR EYE PROTECTION AND GLOVES WHEN DISCHARGING THE SYSTEM. OBSERVE NO SMOKING/NO OPEN FLAME RULES.*

1. Disconnect the negative battery cable and the throttle cable from the pulley. Discharge the air conditioning system (if equipped).

2. Using 2 hose clamps, attach one to the water valve inlet hose and the other to the heater core inlet hose, to pinch off the cooling system.

3. Disconnect the hose from the water valve.

4. From the left side of the dash, remove the lower panel. Remove the hose from the panel air vent.

5. At the control panel, move the selector to the FLOOR position. Place a rag below the water valve.

6. Remove the following items:
   a. The accelerator pedal.
   b. The ignition system control unit and bracket.
   c. The cruise control connector (if equipped).
   d. The water valve hose and the grommet.

7. Remove both hoses from the water valve and the clip from the water valve control cable.

8. To remove the water valve, turn it right, pull it out and disconnect the cable.

9. Remove the heater core cover and the heater core.

10. Install the heater core and the cover. Connect the water valve.

11. Install the water valve control cable clip, turn the valve left, adjust the cable and install the clip. Connect the hoses to the water valve and the heater core.

12. Install the following items:

a. The grommet and the water valve.

b. The cruise control connector (if equipped).

c. The ignition system bracket and control unit.

d. The accelerator pedal.

13. Connect the hose to the panel vent below the dash and the lower panel.

14. Connect the throttle cable to the pulley.

15. Refill the cooling system and recharge the air conditioning system (if equipped).

16. Start the vehicle, allow it to reach normal operating temperatures, check the system operation and for leaks.

760 AND 780 MODELS

NOTE: *The following procedure is for vehicles equipped with the Climate Unit (CU) and Automatic Climate Control (ACC) systems.*

1. Disconnect the negative battery cable.

2. Drain the cooling system or pinch the heater hoses to prevent coolant from leaking when the core is removed.

CAUTION: *When draining the coolant, keep in mind that cats and dogs are attracted by the ethylene glycol antifreeze, and are quite likely to drink any that is left in an uncovered container or in puddles on the ground. This will prove fatal in sufficient quantity. Always drain the coolant into a sealable container. Coolant should be reused unless it is contaminated or several years old.*

3. Remove the ashtray, the ashtray holder, the cigarette lighter and console's storage compartment.

NOTE: *Two screws are located under the plastic cover.*

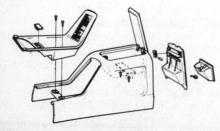

760GLE center console assembly

4. Remove the console assembly from the gearshift lever and the parking brake.

5. Disconnect the electrical connector. Remove the rear ash tray, the console and light.

6. Remove the screws beneath the plastic cover in the bottom of the storage compartment and the parking brake console.

7. From the left side of the passenger compartment, remove the panel from under the dashboard.

8. Pull down the floor mat and remove the side panel screws, front and rear edges.

9. From the right side of the passenger compartment, remove the panel from under the glove compartment and the glove compartment box with lighting.

10. Pull down the floor mat on the right side and remove the side panel screws, front and rear edge.

11. Remove the radio compartment screws.

12. Remove the screws from the heater control, the radio compartment console and the control panel.

13. Loosen the central electrical unit and remove the mount it from the dash.

14. Remove the center dash panel, the distribution duct screw and the air duct-to-panel vents/distribution duct screws.

15. Remove the screws holding the air ducts top-to-rear seats and the air distribution duct section-to-rear seat ducts.

16. Remove the vacuum hoses from the vacuum motors and the hose from the aspirator (if equipped with an ACC unit).

17. Remove the distribution unit from the vehicle.

18. Remove the retaining clips and the heater core assembly.

19. If the vacuum motors must be replaced, remove the panel from the distribution unit and replace the vacuum motor.

20. Install the heater core assembly and the retaining clips.

21. Install the distribution unit into the vehicle.

22. Connect the vacuum hoses to the vacuum motors and the hose to the aspirator (if equipped with an ACC unit).

23. Install the air ducts top-to-rear seats and the air distribution duct section-to-rear seat ducts.

24. Install the center dash panel, the distribution duct screw and the air duct-to-panel vents/distribution duct screws.

25. Install the central electrical unit and the mount to the dash.

26. Install the heater control, the radio compartment console and the control panel.

27. Install the radio compartment screws.

28. At the right side of the passenger com-

partment, install the panel under the glove compartment and the glove box.

29. Install the side panel screws.

30. At the left side of the passenger compartment, install the panel under the dashboard.

31. Install the plastic cover in the bottom of the storage compartment and the parking brake console.

32. Connect the electrical connector. Install the rear ash tray, the console and light.

33. Install the console assembly to the gearshift lever and the parking brake.

34. Install the ashtray holder, the ashtray, the cigarette lighter and console's storage compartment.

35. Remove the heater hose clamps, refill the cooling system and charge the air conditioning system.

36. Connect the negative battery cable. Start the engine, allow it to reach normal operating

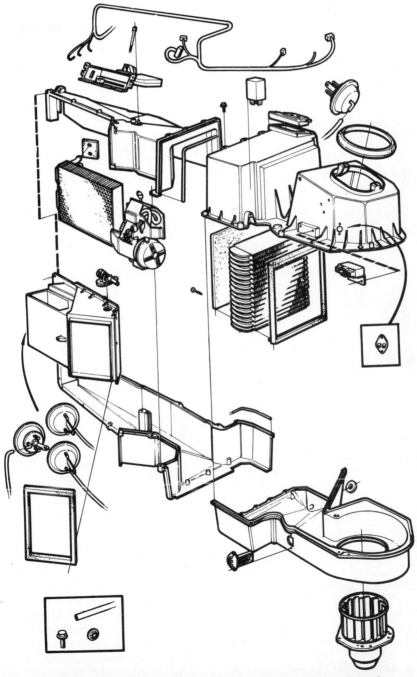

760GLE climate control unit assembly with Automatic Climate Control

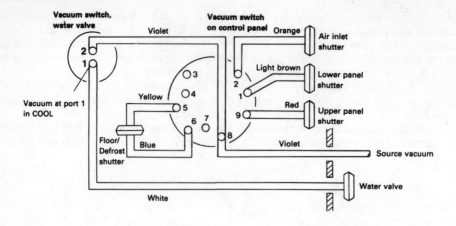

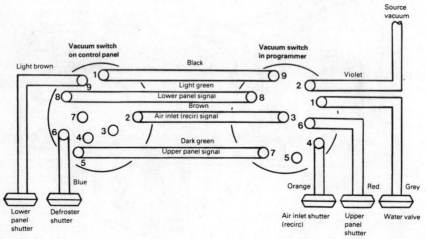

Vacuum routing for CU and ACC systems. Above: CU with air conditioning. Below: ACC system

temperatures, check the system operation and check the system for leaks.

760 AND 780 MODELS

NOTE: *The following procedure is for vehicles equipped with the Electronic Climate Control (ECC) system. It requires removal of the complete dashboard. Do not attempt this repair if you are not at ease with complicated, lengthy tasks.*

CAUTION: *If the vehicle is equipped with the SRS (airbag) system, observe all safety precautions outlined earlier in this chapter before beginning disassembly.*

1. Disconnect the negative battery cable.

2. Using hose clamp tools, pinch off the heater hoses at the heater core and disconnect the hoses from the core. Remove the heater core cover plate.

3. Remove the dashboard by performing the following procedures:

a. From the right side, remove the lower glove box panel, the glove box, the footwell panel and the windshield pillar (A-pillar) inner trim. Disconnect the solar sensor electrical connector and pull out the cable ties.

b. From the left side, remove the lower steering wheel sound-proofing, the knee bolster (leave the bracket attached to the bolster), the footwell panel and the A-pillar panel.

c. From the left side, remove the defroster grille, the plastic fusebox screws, the ashtray, the dashboard-to-center console screws, the parking brake-to-console screws (move console rearward) and the lower center console screws (located below the ashtray).

NOTE: *Before performing the next procedure, be sure the front wheels are in the straight ahead position.*

d. If not an SRS vehicle, remove the steering wheel, the steering wheel adjustment assembly (Allen wrench), the upper steering column cover panels and the steering column combination switch assembly.

e. If an SRS vehicle, remove the steering column adjuster (Allen wrench), the steering column covers, the air bag assembly (Torx head wrench), the steering wheel center bolt, the plastic tape label screw from the steering wheel hub (use the lock screw, label attached, to lock the contact reel through the steering wheel hub hole) and lift off the steering wheel. Remove the contact reel and the steering column combination switch assembly.

NOTE: *After securing the contact reel, do not turn the steering wheel for it will shear off the contact reel pin.*

f. From the left side of the steering column, use fingers to push out the light switch panel. Remove the small trim mouldings and the light switch.

g. From the right side of the steering column, use fingers to push out the switch pan-

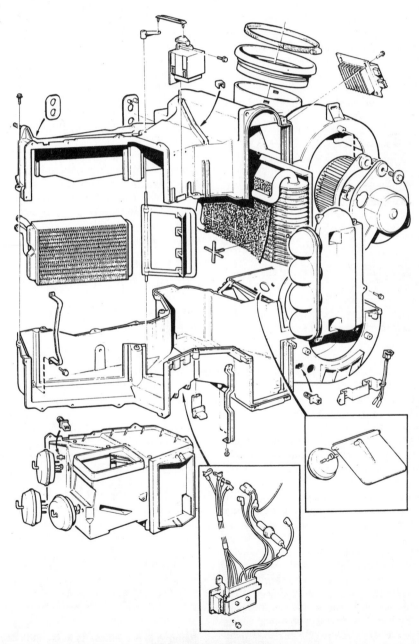

ECC system components

el. Remove the ECC control panel, the radio console and the small trim moulding.

h. Remove the outer air vent grille by lifting it upwards, grasp it at the bottom and pull it upwards to release it. Remove the instrument panel cover-to-dash screws and the cover.

i. Remove the combined instrument assembly-to-dash screws (2 screws are next to the steering column) and the assembly; disconnect any electrical connectors and/or vacuum hoses.

k. From the rear of the dashboard, cut the cable ties.

l. At the dashboard-to-firewall area, turn the retaining clips ⅓ turn (to release), pull the dash out slightly and pass the fuse box through the opening. Disconnect the cable harnesses from the dashboard and carefully lift it from the vehicle.

4. Remove the lower duct from the left side of the heater/air conditioning housing. Disconnect the vacuum hoses from the diaphragms and the electrical connector. Remove the heater core cover-to-housing screws and the cover.

5. Remove the heater core-to-housing bracket and carefully remove the heater core.

6. Install the heater core and the bracket.

7. Install the heater core cover to the housing. Connect the electrical connector and the vacuum hoses. Install the lower duct to the housing assembly.

8. Install the dash by performing the following procedures:

a. Install the dash, connect the cable harnesses, pass the fuse box through the opening. Secure the dash clips by turning them ⅓ turn.

b. Install the combined instrument assembly to the dash. Install the instrument panel cover and the outer air vent grille.

c. Install the small trim molding, the radio console, the ECC control panel and the right side switch panel.

d. At the left side of the steering column, install the light switch, the small trim moldings and the light switch panel.

e. If an SRS vehicle, install the steering column combination switch assembly and the contact reel. Install the steering wheel and remove the lock screw. Install the steering wheel center bolt, the air bag assembly and the steering column adjuster.

f. If not an SRS vehicle, install the steering column combination switch assembly, the steering column covers, the steering wheel adjustment assembly and the steering wheel.

g. At the left side, install the lower center console screw, the parking brake-to-console screws, the dashboard-to-center console

screws, the ashtray, the plastic fusebox screws and the defroster grille.

h. At the left side, install the A-pillar trim, the footwell panel, the knee bolster (with bracket) and the lower steering wheel sound-proofing.

i. At the right side, connect the solar sensor electrical connector, install the A-pillar trim, the footwell panel, the glove box and the lower glove box panel.

9. Install the heater core cover plate and connect the heater hoses to the heater core.

10. Refill the cooling system. Connect the negative battery cable.

11. Start the engine, allow it to reach normal operating temperatures. Check the heater operation and the system for leaks.

Heater Controls/Control Panel
REMOVAL AND INSTALLATION

While reasonably simple to remove, the control panel is connected to the various systems by a cluster of wires, cables and vacuum hoses. Use caution during removal and installation not to damage or crimp these items. Label items as they are disconnected. Work gently and don't force the panel into position; cables and linkages must move smoothly throughout their entire range of travel.

1975 and Later 200 Series

1. Disconnect the negative lead to the battery.

2. Remove the soundproofing and and side panels on both sides of the center dash.

3. Remove the radio.

4. Loosen and remove the screws holding the control panel cover and move the cover aside.

5. Remove the control panel; carefully move it away from the dash as far as possible. Repairs

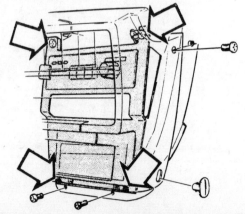

Remove these screws to loosen the heater control panel

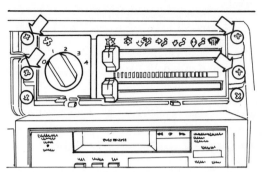

On the 700 Series, heater controls are held in by four screws

or replacements can now be performed on the back of the control panel. If it is necessary to replace a lever assembly, note that the knob on the front pulls off, allowing the lever to slip through the slot. Any needed adjustments should be performed (to cables etc.) at this time.

6. Carefully refit the control panel to the dash.

7. Install the cover panel and secure it.

8. Reinstall the radio.

9. Install the soundproofing and side panels; reconnect the negative battery cable.

700 Series

1. Disconnect the negative battery cable.

2. Carefully remove the trim panel surrounding the heater controls. It will break if you force it.

3. Remove the four screws holding the controls to the dash; slide the unit free. Depending on whether the car has the CU, ACC or ECC system, the control unit will have a mass of cables and vacuum lines attached. Label everything as you disconnect items.

4. When reassembling, use care to prevent kinks in the vacuum hoses.

Evaporator Core
REMOVAL AND INSTALLATION

The evaporator is made of aluminum and consists of chambers which are separated by fins. The refrigerant flowing into the evaporator, expands, boils and absorbs heat from the surrounding air. As a result, water condenses on the fins and is drained off through a hose at the bottom of the evaporator housing.

NOTE: *PLEASE RE-READ THE AIR CONDITIONING SECTION IN CHAPTER ONE SO THAT THE SYSTEM MAY BE DISCHARGED PROPERLY. ALWAYS WEAR EYE PROTECTION AND GLOVES*

WHEN DISCHARGING THE SYSTEM. OBSERVE NO SMOKING/NO OPEN FLAME RULES.

200 Series

1. Following the instructions given above, remove the heater/air conditioning assembly from the vehicle.

2. Place the assembly on a cleared area and remove or disconnect the following:

   a. The upper hose from the heater core.

   b. The air inlet rubber seal from the top of the housing.

   c. The REC shutter clips from the left side.

   d. The rubber seals from both defroster vents.

   e. All clips from both the outer blower motor casings and remove the casings from the assembly.

3. Remove the blower wheel locking clips from both sides and the blower wheels.

4. Remove the heater core drain hose, the vacuum tank assembly, the vacuum tank bracket screws from the left side, the REC shutter spring and the heater housing clips.

5. Remove or disconnect the blower motor screws, the heater control valve capillary tube from the attachment and the vacuum hoses from the T-joint.

6. Carefully separate the heater/air conditioning housing at the center seam.

7. Remove the blower motor, evaporator and the heater core assembly.

8. Install the heater core, the evaporator and the blower motor.

9. Using sealant, coat the heater/air conditioning housing halves and assemble the housings.

10. Install or connect the vacuum hoses to the

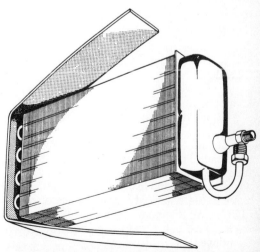

Air conditioning evaporator. 240 shown, others similar. Always reinstall the protective cover

T-joint and the heater control valve capillary tube.

11. Install the heater/air conditioning housing clips, the REC shutter spring, the vacuum tank bracket, the vacuum tank and the heater core drain hose.

12. Install the blower motor wheels and the blower motor wheel clips to both sides.

13. Install or connect the following items:

a. The clips to both the outer blower motor casings and the assembly casings.

b. The rubber seals to both defroster vents.

c. The REC shutter clips to the left side.

d. The air inlet rubber seal to the top of the housing.

e. The upper hose from the heater core.

14. Install the heater/air conditioning assembly into the vehicle.

15. Connect the evaporator lines to the evaporator, refill the cooling system and charge the air coniditicing system.

16. Start the engine and check the system operation.

740 and 760 Models w/Climate Unit (CU) and Automatic Climate Control (ACC)

1. Disconnect the negative battery cable and the throttle cable from the pulley. Safely discharge the refrigerant from the air conditioning system.

2. Disconnect, cap or plug the evaporator connections in the engine compartment.

3. Using 2 hose clamps, attach one to the water valve inlet hose and the other to the heater core inlet hose, pinching off the cooling system.

4. Disconnect the hose from the water valve.

5. Remove the lower panel from the left side of the dash. Remove the hose from the panel air vent.

6. At the control panel, move the selector to the FLOOR position.

7. Remove the following items:

a. The accelerator pedal.

b. The ignition system control unit and bracket.

c. The cruise control connector (if equipped).

8. Remove the evaporator cover and the evaporator.

9. Install the evaporator and the cover.

10. Install the water valve control cable clip, turn the valve to the left (counterclockwise), adjust the cable and install the clip. Connect the hoses to the water valve and the heater core.

11. Install the following items:

a. The cruise control connector (if equipped).

b. The ignition system bracket and control unit.

c. The accelerator pedal.

13. Connect the hose the panel vent below the dash and the lower panel.

14. Connect the throttle cable to the pulley.

15. Refill the cooling system and recharge the air conditioning system.

16. Start the vehicle, allow it to reach normal operating temperatures, check the system operation and for leaks.

760 and 780 Models w/Electronic Climate Control (ECC)

1. Disconnect the negative battery cable.

2. Safely discharge the air conditioning system.

3. Disconnect the electrical connector and unscrew the receiver/drier from the wheel house.

4. Disconnect the electrical connectors from the firewall. Remove the cover plate and the foam rubber seal.

5. Remove the lower glove box panel and the glove box.

6. Disconnect the vacuum lines from the tank and remove the evaporator cover.

7. Carefully pull out the evaporator.

8. Carefully position the evaporator into the housing.

9. Install the evaporator cover and connect the vacuum lines to the tank.

10. Install the foam rubber seal and the cover plate at the firewall.

11. Connect the air conditioning lines and the vacuum lines.

12. Install and connect the receiver/drier at the wheel house.

13. Charge the air conditioning system.

14. Start the engine and check the operation of the air conditioning system.

RADIO

Removal and Installation
ANALOG (DIAL TYPE) TUNERS TO 1980

1. Disconnect the negative battery cable.

2. Remove the radio control knobs by pulling them straight out. Remove the control shaft retaining nuts.

3. Disconnect the speaker wires, the power lead (either at the fuse box or at the in-line fuse connection), and the antenna cable from its jack on the radio.

4. Remove the hardware which attaches the radio to its mounting (support) bracket(s) and slide it back and down from the dash.

5. Reverse the above procedure to install. Don't overtighten the shaft nuts and make sure the wiring is firmly connected before reinstalling the radio unit.

DIGITAL TUNERS
1980 and LATER

On most of the 200 series and some of the earliest 700 series, the radio is held in by two clips in the console. Remove the side covers and locate the two access holes (one on each side) in line with the radio case. Insert a small probe or very small screwdriver into each hole and push gently. This releases the clip and the radio may be removed from the front of the console.

Later models have the same style clips, but they are released by inserting a thin, flat probe down each side of the radio from the front. Again, release the clips and slide the radio free. Disconnect the wiring before pulling the radio too far from the dash.

The newest radios are the easiest to remove, with the releases being built into the front of the case. Simply push the tabs with your fingers and remove the radio.

WARNING: *Although these radios are the simplest to remove, many have a security code programmed into the circuitry. Once reinstalled, the radio will not work if the correct code is not entered. The radio should not be removed or disconnected if the user code is not available.*

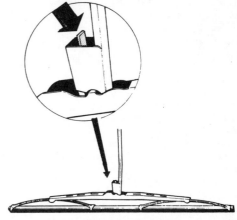

Wiper blade replacement through 1983

WINDSHIELD WIPERS

Blade and Arm

REMOVAL AND INSTALLATION

Wiper Blades
Cars through 1983

1. Lift the arm and blade clear of the glass.
2. Press in the locking tab on the back of the wiper arm.
3. Remove the blade assembly from the arm. A little side to side motion can help to loosen the blade assembly.
4. When reinstalling, make sure the new blade seats on the arm with a distinct click. If it doesn't click, it isn't on properly and will fly off at the height of a thunderstorm.

Wiper Blades
1984 Models and Later

1. Lift the wiper arm and blade clear of the glass. Hold the blade assembly at right angles to the arm.
2. Pinch in the end of the plastic clip at the back of the arm.
3. Slide the blade assembly down the arm until it clears the "U" at the end.
4. Move the blade slightly to the side and remove it from the arm.
5. When reinstalling, pay attention! It is possible to get the blade on the arm backwards, resulting in strange positioning against the glass.

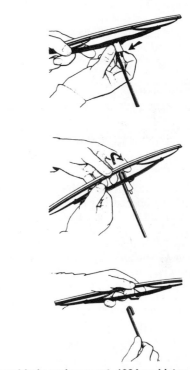

Wiper blade replacement, 1984 and later

The blade should seat on the arm with a distinct click and should then be able to be folded down parallel to the arm so that it sits flush against the glass over its entire length.

Wiper Arms
All models

1. Pry up or lift the plastic or metal spindle cover at the base of the arm.
2. Unscrew and remove the axle nut.
3. Gently lift the blade and arm from the glass and remove the arm from the drive axle.
4. When reassembling, tighten the axle nut to 10-13 ft. lbs. Do not overtighten or the

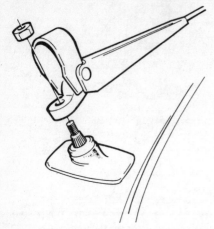

Lift the cover for access to the wipe axle nut

splines will be damaged. Make sure the the wiper blade will be in the correct position on the glass before tightening the nut.

Windshield Wiper Motor

REMOVAL AND INSTALLATION

1800 Series
Complete Windshield Wiper Unit

1. Disconnect the negative battery cable.
2. Remove the wiper arm and blade assemblies. Unscrew the wiper arm shaft nuts and lift off the washers and rubber seals.
3. Disconnect the electrical wires at the wiper motor.
4. Remove the two wiper motor retaining bolts and lower the motor and linkage assembly out from under the dash.
5. Reverse the above procedure to install.

1970-72 140 Series, 164 Models

1. Disconnect the negative battery cable.
2. Remove the wiper arm and blade assemblies.

3. Remove the molded panel from under the dash.
4. Remove the heater switch.
5. Remove the instrument cluster as outlined in Instrument Cluster Removal and Installation.
6. Remove the intermediate defroster nozzle and disconnect the hoses.
7. Remove the retaining bolts and lower the wiper motor.
8. Install the motor and secure the retaining bolts.
9. Replace the defroster nozzle and connect its hoses.
10. Reinstall the instrument cluster.
11. Install the heater switch and the molded panel below the dash.
12. Reinstall the wiper arm and blade assemblies, making sure that the blades will be correctly positioned on the glass.

1973-75 Series, 164 Models and 240 Series

1. Disconnect the negative battery cable.
2. Disconnect the drive link from the wiper motor lever by unsnapping the locking tab underneath the dashboard.
3. Open the hood and disconnect the plug contact from the motor, located on the firewall.
4. Remove the three attaching screws and lift out the motor.
5. When reinstalling, take care to transfer the rubber seal, rubber damper, and spacer sleeves to the new motor. Position the motor and secure its mounting screws. Connect the plug.
6. Under the dash, connect the drive link and make sure it is locked in place.
7. Reconnect the negative battery cable.

All 1976 and Later Models — 200 Series

NOTE: *This procedure includes wiper drive link removal and installation.*

1. Disconnect the negative battery cable.
2. Remove the right side-panel and remove

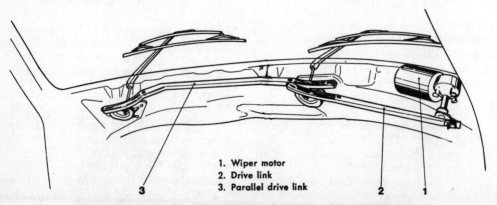

1. Wiper motor
2. Drive link
3. Parallel drive link

Windshield wiper unit—1973–75 140 series, 164 models and 240 series

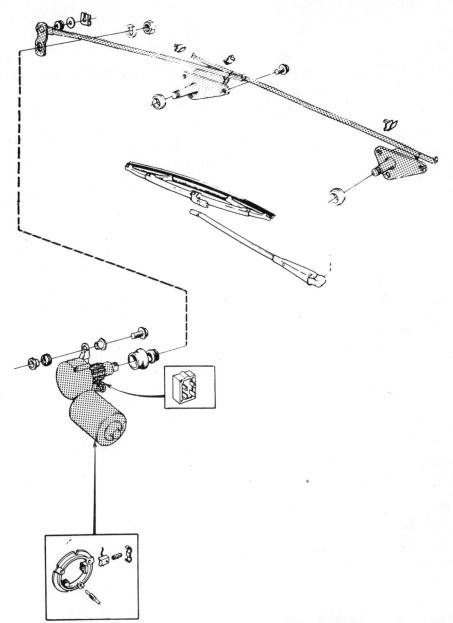

Windshield wiper assembly—1976 and later except the 760GLE

the panel under the dashboard (beneath the glove box).

3. Remove the defroster hoses and remove the glove box.

4. Remove the wiper arms.

5. Disconnect the wiper assembly and lift it out through the glove box opening.

6. Reverse the above procedure to install.

700 Series

1. Disconnect the negative battery cable

2. Remove the wiper arms and remove the rubber boot at the base of the arm.

3. Lift the hood to its uppermost position by pushing the catch on the hood hinges.

3. Release the washer hoses from the clips along the edge of the cowl. Unscrew the cowl retaining bolts. Older cars may use plastic clips instead of bolts to hold the cowl in place. Lower the hood to its normal position.

4. Remove the cowl by pulling it forward and then rotating the front edge upward. Close the hood.

5. Unscrew the bolts which hold the linkage assembly. One of the bolts is hidden beneath a rubber cap.

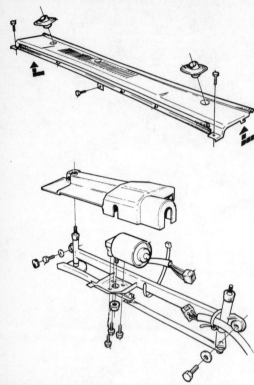

Cowl removal and linkage assembly, 700 Series

6. Remove the cover from the wiper motor, cut the cable tie and disconnect the plug to the motor.

7. Unscrew the spindle nut on the motor and the three bolts holding the motor to the linkage. Lift the motor free of the linkage.

8. When reassembling, make sure the wipers are in the park position.

9. After the motor is secure on the linkage and the linkage is mounted on the car, visually check for any possible interference between the moving parts and the wiring. Always reinstall the wire tie on the motor harness.

10. Make sure the cowl is properly seated before installing the bolts. Install the washer hoses in their clips, replace the rubber boots and install the wiper arms. Connect the negative battery cable.

Wiper Linkage

REMOVAL AND INSTALLATION

1970-72 140 Series, 164

1. Disconnect the negative battery cable.
2. Remove the wiper motor as described above.
3. Disconnect the heater control cable.
4. Remove the fuse box from its bracket and allow it to hang free.
5. On carbureted versions, remove the choke cable.

6. Remove the attaching screws for the wiper frame and lower the frame.
7. Reverse the above procedures to install.

1974-75 140 Series, 164 Models and 240 Series

DRIVE LINK

1. On vehicles equipped with a combination heater-air conditioner unit, remove the glovebox and the right defroster nozzle.
2. Remove the right side panel and the defroster hoses.
3. Remove the locking tab for the wiper motor lever connection, loosen the nut for the cable stretcher, and remove the drive link.
4. When reassembling, carefully place the cable around the wiper arm drive segment. Make sure the cable nipple is inserted in the recess.

PARALLEL DRIVE LINK

1. On vehicles equipped with a combination heater-air conditioner unit, remove the glovebox and the right defroster nozzle.
2. Remove the right-hand side panel and the defroster hoses.
3. Remove the drive link by releasing the locking tab for the wiper motor lever connection and loosening the cable stretcher.
4. Remove each cable stretcher nut and disconnect both ends of the cable from their wiper arm drive segments.
5. Lift forward and remove the parallel drive link.
6. Reverse the above procedure to install, taking care to place each cable end around its wiper drive arm segment. The cable nipple must be inserted in the segment recess.

CABLE

1. Remove the drive link and parallel drive link as described above.
2. Pry up and remove the cable retaining lockwasher. Remove the old cable.
3. Position the new cable on its wiper arm drive segments and secure it with a new retaining lockwasher.
4. Install the cable stretcher on the drive link. The tensioning nut should not be tightened until the drive link and parallel drive link are installed.
5. Install the drive link and parallel drive link. Tighten the tensioning nut.

Tailgate Windshield Wiper

REMOVAL AND INSTALLATION

200 Series

1. Disconnect the negative battery cable.
2. Remove the upholstered finish panel on the inside of the tailgate.

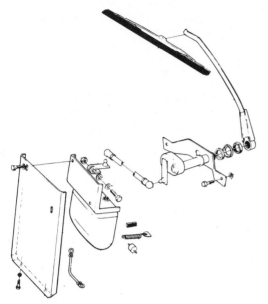

200 Series rear wiper assembly

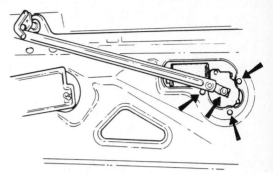

Rear wiper motor, 700 Series. Arrows show fasteners to be removed

3. Remove the bolts for the wiper motor protection plate.

4. Disconnect the ball-and-socket wiper arm link at the motor.

5. Fold the protection plate aside and lift out the wiper motor.

6. Mark the wires and disconnect them at the motor.

NOTE: *The brushes in the motor are replaceable. Remove the motor cover, unhook the brush springs and remove the brushes from the holders. Be careful not to damage the brush holders. Install the new brushes and attach the springs.*

7. When reinstalling, make certain that the motor is in the park position before installing. Connect the wiring to the motor and install the motor and the protection plate.

8. Reattach the connecting link to the motor and install the retaining screws for the protection plate.

9. Install the trim panel on the inside of the tailgate and connect the negative battery cable.

700 Series

1. Disconnect negative battery cable.

2. Remove the inner trim pad on the tailgate.

3. Loosen and remove the center nut on the motor and remove the linkage from the motor.

4. Remove the bolts holding the motor and remove the motor. Disconnect the wiring from the motor.

5. When reassembling, make certain that the motor is in the park position.

6. Attach the wiring and mount the motor to the door.

7. Attach the linkage to the motor and tighten the center nut.

8. Replace the trim pad and atttach the negative battery cable.

Headlight Wiper Blades
REMOVAL AND INSTLLATION

The small blades for the headlight wipers found on the 700 Series are removed in the same fashion as the windshield wiper blades. Pull the wiper away from the light, lift the spindle cover, remove the shaft nut and remove the blade and arm. It is necessary to disconnect the washer tube from the blade assembly when removing the arm.

During installation, place the wiper blade below the park stop on the light. Tighten the shaft nut and reposition the blade above the stop. The blade should rest firmly on the stop. Don't forget to reattach the washer line.

Headlight Wiper Motor
REMOVAL AND INSTALLATION
740 and 760 models

1. Remove the wiper arm.

2. Disconnect wiring connector and the ground wire (2 separate connectors) for the motor. Connectors for both left and right motors may be located near the left fender

3. Loosen the nut on the motor shaft, slide off the plastic tubing and remove the motor.

4. Reassemble in reverse order. Make sure the motor is in the park position before installation. Insure a secure fit on all wiring connectors.

780 Models

1. Remove the wiper arm.

2. Disconnect wiring connector and the ground wire (2 separate connectors) for the motor. Connectors for both left and right motors may be located near the left fender.

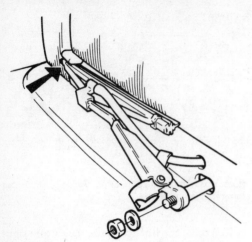

Headlight wiper system. Blade stop is shown by arrow

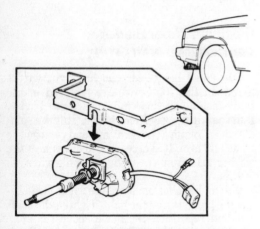

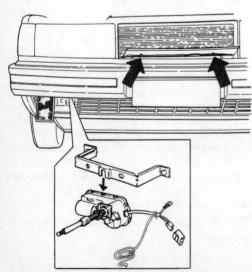

Headlight wiper assemblies. Above: 740 and 760 models. Below: Right side of 780. Large arrows show wire harness clips to be released during removal

3. Pull the wiring through the grommet in the front side panel.

For the LEFT wiper motor:

a. Remove the foglight or auxiliary light cluster and turn aside.

b. Loosen the nut on the motor shaft, remove the plastic tubing, and remove the motor through the front side panel.

c. Reassemble in reverse order. Make sure the motor is in the park position before installation. Insure a secure fit on all wiring connectors.

For the RIGHT wiper motor:

a. Tie a five foot piece of string to the wiring connectors. This will ease reinstallation.

b. Remove the grille.

c. Carefully lift the lower part of the spoiler and release the two clips holding the wiring harness.

d. Pull the wiring through the front of the spoiler, allowing the string to follow the wire path. When the wiring is clear of the spoiler, untie the string but allow it to remain in place in the car.

e. Remove the foglight or auxiliary light cluster and turn aside.

f. Loosen the nut on the motor shaft, remove the plastic tubing, and remove the motor.

g. When reassembling, remove the sleeves from the terminals of the new motor.

h. Install the motor and tie the string to the wiring harness. Position and attach the foglight assembly.

i. Using the string, pull the wiring through the spoiler and into position. Install new cable ties and/or clips as necessary; the cables and pipes across the front of the car must be held in place.

j. Reinstall the grille.

k. Remove the string and connect the electrical connectors, making sure they are clean and tight. Reinstall the wiper arm.

INSTRUMENTS AND SWITCHES

Instrument Cluster

REMOVAL AND INSTALLATION

A voltage stabilizer feeds a 10 V current to both the temperature gauges and the fuel gauge. Electrical malfunctions in these gauges must be checked with an ohmmeter, not a 12 V test light. If malfunctions occur simultaneously in all three of the gauges that are fed by the stabilizer, the stabilizer itself is probably malfunctioning. When replacing the voltage stabilizer, the new unit must fit in the same position as the old one. If the stabilizer is not located correctly in the dash, the voltage output may be altered.

1800 Series

The 1800 series Volvos are equipped with a tachometer, coolant temperature gauge, oil temperature gauge, speedometer (with odometer, tripmeter, and warning lamps), fuel gauge, oil pressure gauge, and clock. Each of these instruments must be remove separately.

When replacing an instrument, first disconnect the negative battery cable, then disconnect the electrical connectors at the back of the gauge. Remove the retaining nuts and attaching bracket and pull the instrument straight out of the dash.

1970-72 140 Series, 164 Models

1. Disconnect the negative battery cable.
2. Remove the two screws holding the control panel.
3. Remove the two retaining screws and lower the molded panel beneath the dashboard.
4. Pull the upper section of the cluster outward so it loosens from its retaining clips. Loosen the panel from the hood release mechanism.
5. Move the control panel--with the short side first--through the dashboard opening.
6. Disconnect the heater controls and the speedometer cable. Remove the flange nuts for the instruments.
7. Rotate the instrument cluster slightly, so that the electrical connections may be removed from the back.
8. Lift out the cluster from the dashboard.
9. When reinstalling, remember to hook up the electrical connections before placing the unit into the dash.
10. Secure the flange nuts on the instruments and reconnect the speedometer and heater control cables.
11. Place the panel through the dash opening and engage the retaining clips.
12. Replace the molded panel under the dash, install the retaining screws for the instrument cluster and connect the negative battery cable.

200 series

1. Disconnect the negative battery cable.
2. Remove the molded plastic casings from the steering column.
3. Remove the bracket retaining screw and lower the bracket toward the steering column.
4. Remove the cluster attaching screws.
5. Disconnect the speedometer cable.
6. Tilt the cluster out of its snap fitting and disconnect the plug. On vehicles equipped with a tachometer, disconnect the tachometer sending wire.
7. Lift the cluster out of the dashboard.

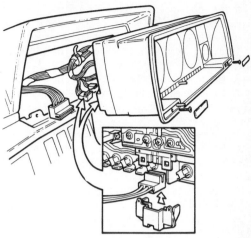

Instrument cluster, 700 series. Note screws under small cover panels

8. When reinstalling, make sure wiring and speedometer cable is reconnected before replacing the cluster. Also make sure the cluster engages its snap fittings when placed in the dash.
9. Install the cluster attaching screws and replace the bracket and retaining screw.
10. Install the molded plastic casings on the steering column and connect the negative battery cable.

700 Series

1. Remove the soundproofing above the foot pedals.
2. Remove the two cover panels and screws holding the instrument panel.
3. On 1982-1986 and some 1987 models, cut the cable tie next to the air duct.
4. Lift the instrument cluster away from the dashboard.
5. Remove the connector seal on the back of the cluster and remove the electrical connectors.
6. When reinstalling, remember to hook up all the wiring before installation. Always use a new connector seal.
7. If the wiring harness was cut away from the air duct (step 3, above) always re-tie it to prevent chafing. Use a new wire tie and anchor securely.
8. Install the two retaining screws and replace the covers.
9. Install the soundproofing panel.

Windshield Wiper Switch/Turn Signal Switch

REMOVAL AND INSTALLATION

CAUTION: *This procedure requires removal of the steering wheel. If the vehicle is equipped with the SRS (airbag) system, refer to the safety precautions listed earlier in this chapter. DO NOT remove the wheel until these precautions have been followed.*

1. Turn the steering wheel to the straight ahead position.

2. Remove the center pad from the wheel.

3. Remove the steering wheel retaining bolt. If possible, matchmark the wheel and steering shaft.

If the vehicle is equipped with SRS, pull out the locking screw and the long tape label from its station in the steering wheel hub. Use the lock screw (with the tape flag attached) to lock the contact reel through the hole in the steering wheel hub. Do not turn the steering wheel once the bolt is removed; the pin in the contact reel will shear.

4. Remove the steering wheel and the upper and lower steering column casings.

5. To remove the wiper switch, simply remove the screws holding it to the column and unplug the connector. The turn signal switch is on the opposite side and is also held to the column by two or three screws.

6. When reassembling, remember to check the position of all the wires so that nothing is pinched in casings.

7. Reinstall the column casings and then reinstall the steering wheel. Check that the steering wheel position is true to the position of the wheels.

If the vehicle is SRS equipped, do not turn the steering wheel until the center bolt is reinstalled and tight; doing so will shear the pin in the contact reel. Remove the locking bolt with

its flag and store it in the extra hole on the left side of the wheel.

8. Tighten the steering wheel bolt to 24 ft. lbs. Reinstall the center pad.

9. If equipped with the SRS system, make the necessary connections to reactivate the system.

Rear Window Wiper Switch

The tailgate washer/wiper controls are mounted on the same control stalk as the front wipers. The components are not individually replaceable for the rear system. To replace the switch assembly, follow the directions given for Windshield Wiper Switch, Removal and Installation.

Headlight Switch (Lighting Selector)
REMOVAL AND INSTALLATION
200 Series and Earlier Cars

1. Disconnect the negative battery cable.

2. Disconnect the hose from the left side dash vent.

3. Carefully remove the trim below the vent, remove the screws holding the vent in place and remove the vent assembly.

4. Using a very small screwdriver, loosen the set-screw holding the selector knob onto the shaft. If no set screw is evident, simply pull on the knob until it comes free of the shaft.

5. Remove the shaft nut from the switch and remove the switch through the back of the dash. Remove the plug from the back of the switch assembly.

6. When reassembling, remember to connect the new switch to the wiring harness and remember to tighten the small set-screw holding the knob to the shaft. Reconnect the battery and check the switch function.

700 Series

1. Remove the selector knob by pulling it free of the shaft.

2. Disconnect the wiring connector by reaching under the dash. It may be necessary to loosen or remove the under dash pad to gain access.

3. Remove the shaft nut from the switch and

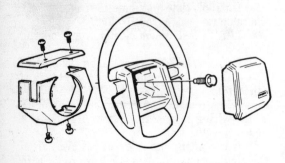

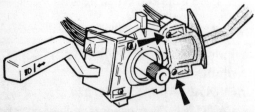

Steering wheel removal is necessary for access to wiper and turn signal switches. Non-SRS 700 series shown

Detail of headlight selector switch, 700 series

remove the switch through the back of the dash.

4. Reassemble in reverse order.

Rocker Switches
REMOVAL AND INSTALLATION

The dash or console mounted rocker switches are easily removed. Depending on the model, it may be necessary to remove the trim panel surrounding the switch. After this is done, reach behind the switch and disconnect the wire harness running to the switch. While your hand is back there, grasp each side of the switch, compress the retaining clips and remove the switch through the front of the panel.

If length allows, the wire harness may be brought out through the panel (after the switch is removed) for circuit testing. When reinstalling, make sure the wiring is properly routed and not crimped or pinched. The switch should engage the panel with a definite click when in place. Reinstall the trim panel.

Ignition Switch
REMOVAL AND INSTALLATION

On all models, the ignition keylock is mounted on the steering column and incorporates a steering wheel lock to deter car theft. The lock is attached to the steering column by shearbolts, whose heads break off when the proper tightness is reached. Removing the lock requires removing these bolts, either by cutting slots in their tops and using a screwdriver to extract them, or by drilling them out. If they are drilled out, the lock housing will probably be damaged. On many models, removing the ignition lock also requires loosening or removing the steering column. Because of the complexity of these operations, repairs are best left to a professional repair facility.

If your diagnosis of an electrical problem shows a failed ignition switch, the electrical part at the rear of the assembly can be changed on all 1975 and later models.

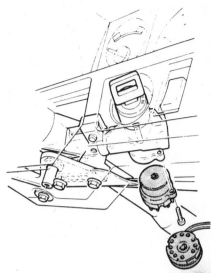
Electrical contacts on back of ignition switch are replaceable. 700 series shown, others similar

CAUTION: *If the vehicle is equipped with the SRS (airbag) system, refer to the safety precautions listed earlier in this chapter.*

Disconnect the negative battery cable and gain access to the back of the ignition switch by removing panels and covers as necessary. Remove the round multi-wire connector at the back of the switch, then unfasten and remove the electrical unit (sometimes called the start contact) from the back of the lock assembly.

This unit is generally held on with two small screws, but they are in a difficult location and an awkward position--have patience. When reassembling, make certain that the new unit is properly seated against the pin from the ignition lock. Also insure that the wiring connector is firmly attached to the new start contact.

With this two part system, the only time you need to deal with the lock assembly is in cases of key and lock problems such as broken keys or binding tumblers within the lock.

Speedometer Cable
REMOVAL AND INSTALLATION

On all cars through the 200 series, the speedometer is cable driven by the transmission. The cable is connected to a drive gear in the transmission case and connects to the dashboard unit which interprets the number of cable revolutions into an expression of speed and distance.

The speedometer cable is unscrewed from the rear of the speedometer (it may be necessary to remove the instrument cluster for access) and from the transmission case. When installing a new cable, seat the ends of the inner cable in

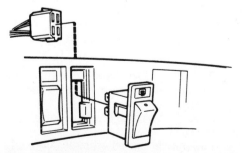
Rocker switch removal

both the speedometer and transmission. Cable routing is critical; at no point should the bends in the cable be any sharper than a 4 inch radius. A crimped or binding cable can cause noise, vibration and possible damage to the speedometer unit.

NOTE: *A tamper-proof seal is installed on all 1977 and later models, on both the speedometer connection and the transmission connection. The speedometer connection has a plastic collar which must be broken to remove the cable. The retaining bolt for the transmission side of the cable is covered by a plastic cap which must be broken in order to remove the bolt.*

The 700 series does not have a mechanical cable. This series uses an electric inductive pickup in the differential to generate speed data. The number of electrical pulses varies with the speed; the speedometer unit transforms the pulses into a readable display of speed.

An inoperative speedometer in these cars is really an electrical problem requiring the usual checking of fuses, grounds, connectors and wiring. The sensor mounted in the differential works on a critical internal clearance; it should not be removed or loosened for testing.

LIGHTING

Headlights

Headlights, like any other lighting device, can fail due to broken filaments. The front of any car is the worst possible location for a lighting device, since it is subject to impact, extreme temperature change and extensive vibration-- all of which shorten the life of the light. The front of the car is also where good lighting is needed the most, so it is not uncommon to have to replace a headlight during ownership of a vehicle.

There are two general styles of headlamp, sealed beam and replacable bulb types. The sealed beam is by far the most common and includes all the circular and rectangular lamps found on most cars built through the early 1980s. The sealed beam is so named because it includes the lamp (filament), the reflector and the lens in one sealed unit. Sealed beams are available in several standard sizes and shapes.

The replacable bulb is the newer technology. Using a small halogen bulb, only the lamp is replaced, while the lens and reflector are part of the body of the car. This is generally the style found on the "European" or wrap-around lighting systems. While the replacement bulbs are more expensive than sealed beams, they tend to produce more and better light. The fixed lenses and reflectors can be engineered to allow better frontal styling and better light distribution for a particular vehicle.

It is quite possible to replace a headlight of either type without affecting the alignment (aim) of the light. Sealed beams mount into a bracket (bucket) to which springs are attached. The adjusting screws control the position of the bucket which in turn aims the light. Replaceable bulbs simply fit into the back of the reflector; the reflector and lens are aimed by separate adjusting screws. Take a moment before disassembly to identify the large adjusting screws (generally two for each lamp) and don't change their settings.

With the exception of the oldest cars, sealed beams are always removed from the front of the car. Start with the outer trim pieces and work your way in to the lamp and its retainer. Bulb type units are usually replaced from the back of the reflector under the hood.

REMOVAL AND INSTALLATION

Sealed Beam

CAUTION: *Trim and headlight components can have sharp edges. Work carefully and wear gloves when changing headlights. Never push on the lens of a headlight or attempt to pry it into position.*

140 SERIES

1. Open the hood and remove the headlight plug by pulling it straight out.
2. Loosen the three screws so that the plastic headlight retainers can be removed.
3. Remove the sealed beam from the engine compartment.
4. Reverse the above procedure to install, and recheck headlight alignment.

164 SERIES

1. Remove the headlight outer trim rim by pulling it upward and away from the car.
2. Loosen the three small screws a few turns so that the inner trim ring may be rotated and removed. Don't remove the screws and don't turn the two larger adjusting screws.
3. Pull out the sealed beam slightly and remove the wiring connector at the rear.
4. Reverse the above procedure to install, and recheck headlight alignment.

1800 SERIES

1. Remove the headlight outer chrome rim by removing the retaining screw at the lower part of the rim.
2. Remove the three screws holding the inner rim.
3. Pull out the sealed beam slightly and remove the headlight connector.

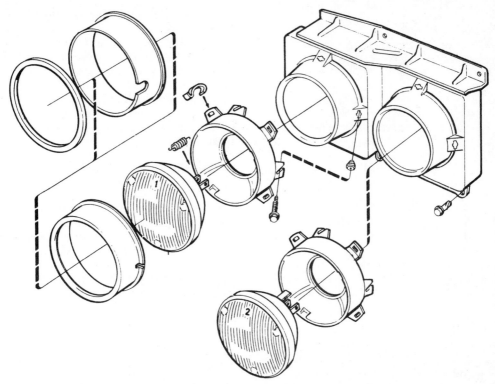

Headlighting assembly, 200 series with dual round lamps

4. Reverse the above procedure to install, and recheck the headlight alignment.

200 SERIES and EARLY 700 SERIES

1. Disconnect the negative battery cable.

2. Raise the hood and turn the two plastic screws which retain the headlight trim ½ turn and remove the headlight trim.

3. For cars with single round headlamps, turn the chromed headlight retainer slightly counterclockwise, remove the retainer and lift out the headlight.

For cars with dual round headlamps, unsnap the four clips and remove the headlight retainer and the headlight.

For cars with dual rectangular headlamps, remove the four small screws holding the retainer. Remove the retainer and the headlamp.

4. Disconnect the electrical connector and dispose of the old headlamp.

5. Installation is the reverse of removal.

NOTE: *In 1986, the 760 series introduced a different type of trim retaining clip. Instead of turning two plastic screws, locate the clip*

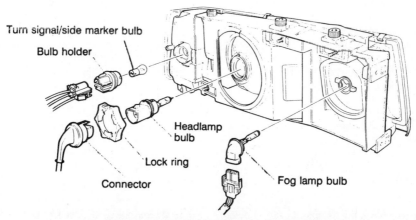

Front lighting assembly, 760 Others similar after 1986

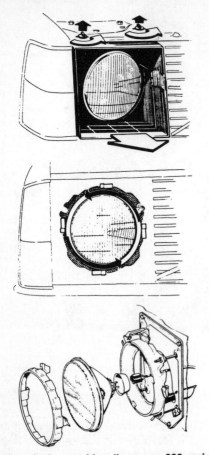

Removing single round headlamps on 200 series

in the top center of the trim panel, squeeze the two sides together and pull it upwards to release the trim.

Replaceable Bulb; 200 Series after 1985, all 700 series after 1987

Note: *On 780 models, it may be necessary to remove the washer fluid fill tube to gain access to the bulb holder.*

1. Make sure the headlights are off and the ignition is off.

2. Working from under the hood, release the clip and remove the wire connector from the back of the lamp assembly.

3. Unscrew and remove the large locking ring on the back of the headlamp.

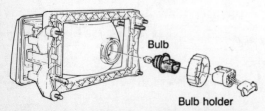

Detail of replaceable bulb headlight. 780 shown, others similar

4. Remove the bulb and its holder; replace them as a unit

WARNING: *When installing new bulbs, never touch the glass bulb with your fingers. The grease will develop a hot spot on the bulb and radically shorten its life.*

5. When reinstalling, make sure that the bulb sits properly in the reflector assembly. Tighten the locking ring and reattach the wiring connector.

Signal and Marker Lights

REMOVAL AND INSTALLATION

Front Turn Signal and Marker Lights

The turn signals and side marker lights are generally reached by removing the lens. Front lenses through 1984-85 are retained by two screws; remove the screws and the lens. Don't lose the rubber gasket under the lens as it serves to keep water out of the lamp. With the lens off, the bulb can be removed with a half-turn counterclockwise. Wear gloves or wrap the bulb in a rag when removing as old bulbs frequently shatter when turned. Install the new bulb and turn the lights on to check bulb function. Replace the gasket and the lens, but don't overtighten the mounting screws--you can crack the lens.

In the mid-1980s, the government required sealed lighting units to prevent moisture intrusion. If no mounting screws are visible on the front of the lens, the bulb is reached from under the hood. After identifying the proper lamp, simply grasp the base of the socket, turn it counterclockwise and remove the bulb and socket from the housing. Using gloves or a rag, remove the bulb from the socket either with a

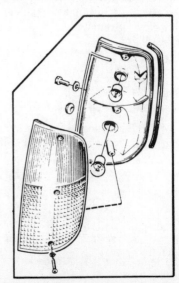

Front sidemarker and turn signal bulbs, prior to 1986

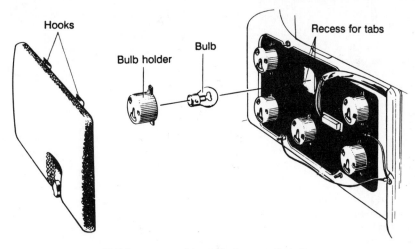

Tail lamp assembly; 240 shown, all similar

turn to the left or, for smaller lamps, by pulling the the bulb straight out. After installing the new bulb, turn the lights on to check the bulb function before replacing the socket in the housing. After the socket is in the housing, lock it in place with a half-turn clockwise.

Rear Turn Signal, Brake, Parking and Marker Lights

With the exception of station wagons through 1980, all rear light bulbs are reached from the inside of the trunk. Until 1981 the station wagons required the removal of the lens from the outside. With the lens off, the bulb is removed with a ¼-twist counterclockwise.

Since Volvo uses a multi-lamp arrangement at the rear, it is prudent to identify which light is inoperative before being confronted with an array of six or eight lamp holders inside the trunk. Remove the interior cover panel either by unscrewing the knob (if so equipped) or by popping the panel off with a small screwdriver.

NOTE: *To reach the left side rear lamps on station wagons built after 1980, it is necessary to remove the spare tire and its cover.*

After the cover is removed:

1. Locate the bulb holder for the appropriate bulb and turn it about ¼-turn counterclockwise.

2. Remove the bulb holder and replace the bulb. Make sure that the new bulb is an exact match for the old one and is properly seated in the holder.

3. Reinstall the bulb and holder. Note that one of the guide tabs on the bulb holder is wider than the other two; it can only be installed in one position.

4. Check the function of the bulb by turning on the appropriate lights.

5. Replace the cover(s) and, on wagons, replace the spare tire and cover.

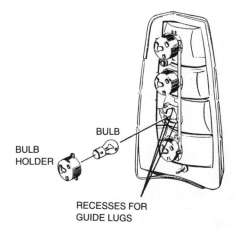

Tail lamp assembly; station wagons after 1980

TRAILER WIRING

Wiring the car for towing is fairly easy. There are a number of good wiring kits available and these should be used, rather than trying to design your own. All trailers will need brake lights and turn signals as well as tail lights and side marker lights. Most states require extra marker lights for overly wide trailers. Also, most states have recently required back-up lights for trailers, and most trailer manufacturers have been building trailers with back-up lights for several years.

Additionally, some Class I, most Class II and just about all Class III trailers will have electric brakes.

Add to this number an accessories wire, to operate trailer internal equipment or to charge the trailer's battery, and you can have as many as seven wires in the harness.

Determine the equipment on your trailer and buy the wiring kit necessary. The kit will contain all the wires needed, plus a plug adapter set which included the female plug, mounted on the bumper or hitch, and the male plug, wired into, or plugged into the trailer harness.

When installing the kit, follow the manufacturer's instructions. The color coding of the wires is standard throughout the industry.

One point to note, some domestic vehicles, and most imported vehicles, have separate turn signals. On most domestic vehicles, the brake lights and rear turn signals operate with the same bulb. For those vehicles with separate turn signals, you can purchase an isolation unit so that the brake lights won't blink whenever the turn signals are operated, or, you can go to your local electronics supply house and buy four diodes to wire in series with the brake and turn signal bulbs. Diodes will isolate the brake and turn signals. The choice is yours. The isolation units are simple and quick to install, but far more expensive than the diodes. The diodes, however, require more work to install properly, since they require the cutting of each bulb's wire and soldering in place of the diode.

One final point, the best kits are those with a spring loaded cover on the vehicle mounted socket. This cover prevents dirt and moisture from corroding the terminals. Never let the vehicle socket hang loosely. Always mount it securely to the bumper or hitch.

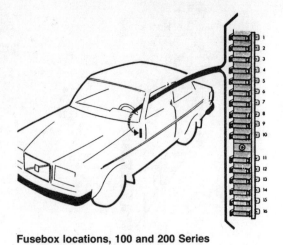

Fusebox locations, 100 and 200 Series

Fusebox location, all 700 Series except 88–89 760

CIRCUIT PROTECTION

Fuses

LOCATION AND REPLACEMENT

All electrical equipment is protected from overloading by fuses. Each fuse has an amperage rating that will allow it to transmit a predetermined amount of current before its filament melts, thereby stopping the excessive current flow. By providing this engineered "weak spot" in the circuit, the first failure will occur at a known location (the fuse), eliminating hours of tracing wiring harnesses to locate a problem.

If a fuse blows repeatedly, the trouble is probably in the electrical component that the fuse protects. Never replace a fuse with another of a higher ampere rating. Sometimes a fuse will blow when all of the electrical equipment protected by the fuse is operating, especially under severe weather conditions. For this reason, it is wise to carry a few spare fuses of each type in the car.

When tracking down an inoperative electrical circuit, follow a logical pattern. Wiring itself is rarely the problem on modern cars. Your time is better spent checking the fuse, the component(s) in the circuit, the circuit grounds and

the wiring connectors. Remember that in some cases a fuse can look good but not be capable of passing an electrical load. Either remove the fuse and check it with an ohmeter or simply replace it with a new one. Always have the ignition switched off when removing and replacing fuses. On all models, the circuit that each fuse protects is given either on the fuse box cover or in the owners manual. Volvo fuseboxes are located as follows:

• 1970-71 100 Series: Behind a snap-out panel in the dashboard above the transmission tunnel.

• 1972 100 Series: Over the transmission tunnel, behind the control panel for the clock, rear defroster and emergency flashers. Remove the two retaining screws at the upper corners of the panel and tilt the panel down.

• 1800 Series: Under the dashboard, to the driver's left.

• 1973 and later 100 and 200 Series: Behind a swing-out cover on the lower part of the left front pillar.

• 1984 through 1987 740 and 760 Series and all 780: Behind the ashtray in the center con-

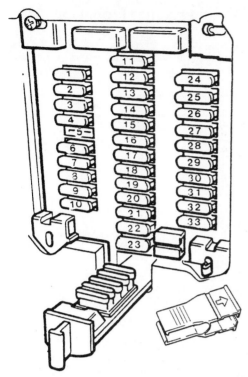

Fusebox, 88–89 760 Series

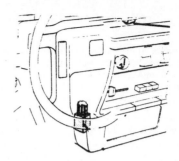

Turn signal flasher location, 100 and 200 Series

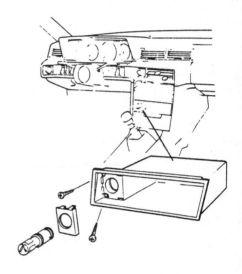

Access to relay panel on all 700 Series

sole. Remove the ashtray by pulling it out and pressing down on the tongue. Lift the cover marked "Electrical Fuses". The fuses can be pulled straight up from the fusebox using either your fingers or the fuse puller provided.

• 1988-89 760 Series: On the left end of the dashboard, behind a swing-out panel. Spare fuses are located in a small tray which pulls out from the bottom of the fusebox

NOTE: *On certain models with electronic fuel injection, an additional fuse for the fuel pump is housed in the engine compartment on the left wheel well.*

Diesel glow plug circuits have a separate fuse located on the bottom of the glow plug relay under the hood.

Turn Signal Flasher/Relay
LOCATION AND REPLACEMENT

The flasher unit on 100 series and P1800 series is located behind the instrument cluster. It simply unplugs from its mount and is replaced easily.

On all subsequent models--200 and 700 Series--the flasher or relay is located behind the center console. The 200 Series cars use a single unit which is located to the left and below the heater controls panel. Removal of various console sidepanels may be necessary for access.

The 700 Series use a central relay console located behind the ashtray. To gain access to the relay panel:

1. Remove the ashtray and its holder.
2. Remove the cigarette lighter and its cover.
3. Unscrew the case retaining screws (for the ashtray casing) and remove the casing.
4. Depress the catch and slide the relay board towards you.

Troubleshooting Basic Turn Signal and Flasher Problems

Most problems in the turn signals or flasher system, can be reduced to defective flashers or bulbs, which are easily replaced. Occasionally, problems in the turn signals are traced to the switch in the steering column, which will require professional service.

F = Front   R = Rear   ● = Lights off   ○ = Lights on

Problem		Solution
Turn signals light, but do not flash		• Replace the flasher
No turn signals light on either side		• Check the fuse. Replace if defective. • Check the flasher by substitution • Check for open circuit, short circuit or poor ground
Both turn signals on one side don't work		• Check for bad bulbs • Check for bad ground in both housings
One turn signal light on one side doesn't work		• Check and/or replace bulb • Check for corrosion in socket. Clean contacts. • Check for poor ground at socket
Turn signal flashes too fast or too slow		• Check any bulb on the side flashing too fast. A heavy-duty bulb is probably installed in place of a regular bulb. • Check the bulb flashing too slow. A standard bulb was probably installed in place of a heavy-duty bulb. • Check for loose connections or corrosion at the bulb socket
Indicator lights don't work in either direction		• Check if the turn signals are working • Check the dash indicator lights • Check the flasher by substitution

One indicator light doesn't light		• On systems with 1 dash indicator: See if the lights work on the same side. Often the filaments have been reversed in systems combining stoplights with taillights and turn signals.
		    Check the flasher by substitution
		• On systems with 2 indicators: Check the bulbs on the same side
		    Check the indicator light bulb
		    Check the flasher by substitution

Troubleshooting Basic Dash Gauge Problems

Problem	Cause	Solution
Coolant Temperature Gauge		
Gauge reads erratically or not at all	• Loose or dirty connections • Defective sending unit • Defective gauge	• Clean/tighten connections • Bi-metal gauge: remove the wire from the sending unit. Ground the wire for an instant. If the gauge registers, replace the sending unit. • Magnetic gauge: disconnect the wire at the sending unit. With ignition ON gauge should register COLD. Ground the wire; gauge should register HOT.
Ammeter Gauge—Turn Headlights ON (do not start engine). Note reaction		
Ammeter shows charge Ammeter shows discharge Ammeter does not move	• Connections reversed on gauge • Ammeter is OK • Loose connections or faulty wiring • Defective gauge	• Reinstall connections • Nothing • Check/correct wiring • Replace gauge
Oil Pressure Gauge		
Gauge does not register or is inaccurate	• On mechanical gauge, Bourdon tube may be bent or kinked • Low oil pressure • Defective gauge • Defective wiring • Defective sending unit	• Check tube for kinks or bends preventing oil from reaching the gauge • Remove sending unit. Idle the engine briefly. If no oil flows from sending unit hole, problem is in engine. • Remove the wire from the sending unit and ground it for an instant with the ignition ON. A good gauge will go to the top of the scale. • Check the wiring to the gauge. If it's OK and the gauge doesn't register when grounded, replace the gauge. • If the wiring is OK and the gauge functions when grounded, replace the sending unit
All Gauges		
All gauges do not operate All gauges read low or erratically All gauges pegged	• Blown fuse • Defective instrument regulator • Defective or dirty instrument voltage regulator • Loss of ground between instrument voltage regulator and car • Defective instrument regulator	• Replace fuse • Replace instrument voltage regulator • Clean contacts or replace • Check ground • Replace regulator
Warning Lights		
Light(s) do not come on when ignition is ON, but engine is not started Light comes on with engine running	• Defective bulb • Defective wire • Defective sending unit • Problem in individual system • Defective sending unit	• Replace bulb • Check wire from light to sending unit • Disconnect the wire from the sending unit and ground it. Replace the sending unit if the light comes on with the ignition ON. • Check system • Check sending unit (see above)

Troubleshooting the Heater

Problem	Cause	Solution
Blower motor will not turn at any speed	• Blown fuse • Loose connection • Defective ground • Faulty switch • Faulty motor • Faulty resistor	• Replace fuse • Inspect and tighten • Clean and tighten • Replace switch • Replace motor • Replace resistor
Blower motor turns at one speed only	• Faulty switch • Faulty resistor	• Replace switch • Replace resistor
Blower motor turns but does not circulate air	• Intake blocked • Fan not secured to the motor shaft	• Clean intake • Tighten security
Heater will not heat	• Coolant does not reach proper temperature • Heater core blocked internally • Heater core air-bound • Blend-air door not in proper position	• Check and replace thermostat if necessary • Flush or replace core if necessary • Purge air from core • Adjust cable
Heater will not defrost	• Control cable adjustment incorrect • Defroster hose damaged	• Adjust control cable • Replace defroster hose

Troubleshooting Basic Windshield Wiper Problems

Problem	Cause	Solution
Electric Wipers		
Wipers do not operate— Wiper motor heats up or hums	• Internal motor defect • Bent or damaged linkage • Arms improperly installed on linking pivots	• Replace motor • Repair or replace linkage • Position linkage in park and reinstall wiper arms
Wipers do not operate— No current to motor	• Fuse or circuit breaker blown • Loose, open or broken wiring • Defective switch • Defective or corroded terminals • No ground circuit for motor or switch	• Replace fuse or circuit breaker • Repair wiring and connections • Replace switch • Replace or clean terminals • Repair ground circuits
Wipers do not operate— Motor runs	• Linkage disconnected or broken	• Connect wiper linkage or replace broken linkage
Vacuum Wipers		
Wipers do not operate	• Control switch or cable inoperative • Loss of engine vacuum to wiper motor (broken hoses, low engine vacuum, defective vacuum/fuel pump) • Linkage broken or disconnected • Defective wiper motor	• Repair or replace switch or cable • Check vacuum lines, engine vacuum and fuel pump • Repair linkage • Replace wiper motor
Wipers stop on engine acceleration	• Leaking vacuum hoses • Dry windshield • Oversize wiper blades • Defective vacuum/fuel pump	• Repair or replace hoses • Wet windshield with washers • Replace with proper size wiper blades • Replace pump

Troubleshooting Basic Lighting Problems

Problem	Cause	Solution
Lights		
One or more lights don't work, but others do	• Defective bulb(s) • Blown fuse(s) • Dirty fuse clips or light sockets • Poor ground circuit	• Replace bulb(s) • Replace fuse(s) • Clean connections • Run ground wire from light socket housing to car frame
Lights burn out quickly	• Incorrect voltage regulator setting or defective regulator • Poor battery/alternator connections	• Replace voltage regulator • Check battery/alternator connections
Lights go dim	• Low/discharged battery • Alternator not charging • Corroded sockets or connections • Low voltage output	• Check battery • Check drive belt tension; repair or replace alternator • Clean bulb and socket contacts and connections • Replace voltage regulator
Lights flicker	• Loose connection • Poor ground • Circuit breaker operating (short circuit)	• Tighten all connections • Run ground wire from light housing to car frame • Check connections and look for bare wires
Lights "flare"—Some flare is normal on acceleration—if excessive, see "Lights Burn Out Quickly"	• High voltage setting	• Replace voltage regulator
Lights glare—approaching drivers are blinded	• Lights adjusted too high • Rear springs or shocks sagging • Rear tires soft	• Have headlights aimed • Check rear springs/shocks • Check/correct rear tire pressure
Turn Signals		
Turn signals don't work in either direction	• Blown fuse • Defective flasher • Loose connection	• Replace fuse • Replace flasher • Check/tighten all connections
Right (or left) turn signal only won't work	• Bulb burned out • Right (or left) indicator bulb burned out • Short circuit	• Replace bulb • Check/replace indicator bulb • Check/repair wiring
Flasher rate too slow or too fast	• Incorrect wattage bulb • Incorrect flasher	• Flasher bulb • Replace flasher (use a variable load flasher if you pull a trailer)
Indicator lights do not flash (burn steadily)	• Burned out bulb • Defective flasher	• Replace bulb • Replace flasher
Indicator lights do not light at all	• Burned out indicator bulb • Defective flasher	• Replace indicator bulb • Replace flasher

Drive Train

7

UNDERSTANDING THE MANUAL TRANSMISSION

Because of the way an internal combustion engine breathes, it can produce torque, or twisting force, only within a narrow speed range. Most modern, overhead valve engines must turn at about 2,500 rpm to produce their peak torque. By 4,500 rpm they are producing so little torque that continued increases in engine speed produce no power increases.

The manual transmission and clutch are employed to vary the relationship between engine speed and the speed of the wheels so that adequate engine power can be produced under all circumstances. The clutch allows engine torque to be applied to the transmission input shaft gradually, due to mechanical slippage. The car can, consequently, be started smoothly from a full stop.

The transmission changes the ratio between the rotating speeds of the engine and the wheels by the use of gears. On cars, 4-speed or 5-speed transmissions are most common. The lower gears allow full engine power to be applied to the rear wheels during acceleration at low speeds.

The transmission contains a mainshaft which passes all the way through the transmission, from the clutch to the driveshaft. This shaft is separated at one point, so that front and rear portions can turn at different speeds.

Power is transmitted by a countershaft in the lower gears and reverse. The gears of the countershaft mesh with gears on the mainshaft, allowing power to be carried from one to the other. All the countershaft gears are integral with that shaft, while several of the mainshaft gears can either rotate independently of the shaft or be locked to it. Shifting from one gear to the next causes one of the gears to be freed from rotating with the shaft and locks another to it. Gears are locked and unlocked by internal dog clutches which slide between the center of the gear and the shaft. The forward gears usually employ synchronizers; friction members which smoothly bring gear and shaft to the same speed before the toothed dog clutches are engaged.

The clutch is operating properly if:

1. It will stall the engine when released with the vehicle held stationary.

2. The shift lever can be moved freely between 1st and reverse gears when the vehicle is stationary and the clutch disengaged.

Transmission Application

The transmission type designation, serial number and part number are stamped on a metal plate which is riveted to the underside of the case on manual transmissions or the left side on automatic transmissions.

Manual transmissions installed in 1970–89 Volvos are the M40/M41, M45/M46, M400/M410 and the M47 models. Except for the 5-speed M47 introduced in 1987, all are fully synchronized 4-speed transmissions with all forward gears in constant mesh. The M41, M46 and M410 units are equipped with Laycock-deNormanville overdrive units, and except for the overdrive engaging switch and push plate, are identical to their M40, M45 and M400 counterparts.

The M40 transmission is installed as standard equipment on 140 series and the 1975 240 series models. The M41 overdrive unit is optional on the 140 series and the 1975 240 series, and standard equipment on most 1800E and all 1800ES models. The M400 transmission is standard equipment on 164 models. The M410 overdrive unit is optional on 164 models, and was installed on some early 1970 1800E models. The M45 transmission is standard on 1976 and later 240 series models and the 1980 and later DL. The M46 overdrive unit is optional on 1976–80 240 models and the 1980 and later DL

Troubleshooting the Manual Transmission

Problem	Cause	Solution
Transmission shifts hard	• Clutch adjustment incorrect • Clutch linkage or cable binding • Shift rail binding	• Adjust clutch • Lubricate or repair as necessary • Check for mispositioned selector arm roll pin, loose cover bolts, worn shift rail bores, worn shift rail, distorted oil seal, or extension housing not aligned with case. Repair as necessary.
	• Internal bind in transmission caused by shift forks, selector plates, or synchronizer assemblies • Clutch housing misalignment • Incorrect lubricant • Block rings and/or cone seats worn	• Remove, dissemble and inspect transmission. Replace worn or damaged components as necessary. • Check runout at rear face of clutch housing • Drain and refill transmission • Blocking ring to gear clutch tooth face clearance must be 0.030 inch or greater. If clearance is correct it may still be necessary to inspect blocking rings and cone seats for excessive wear. Repair as necessary.
Gear clash when shifting from one gear to another	• Clutch adjustment incorrect • Clutch linkage or cable binding • Clutch housing misalignment • Lubricant level low or incorrect lubricant • Gearshift components, or synchronizer assemblies worn or damaged	• Adjust clutch • Lubricate or repair as necessary • Check runout at rear of clutch housing • Drain and refill transmission and check for lubricant leaks if level was low. Repair as necessary. • Remove, disassemble and inspect transmission. Replace worn or damaged components as necessary.
Transmission noisy	• Lubricant level low or incorrect lubricant • Clutch housing-to-engine, or transmission-to-clutch housing bolts loose • Dirt, chips, foreign material in transmission • Gearshift mechanism, transmission gears, or bearing components worn or damaged • Clutch housing misalignment	• Drain and refill transmission. If lubricant level was low, check for leaks and repair as necessary. • Check and correct bolt torque as necessary • Drain, flush, and refill transmission • Remove, disassemble and inspect transmission. Replace worn or damaged components as necessary. • Check runout at rear face of clutch housing
Jumps out of gear	• Clutch housing misalignment • Gearshift lever loose • Offset lever nylon insert worn or lever attaching nut loose • Gearshift mechanism, shift forks, selector plates, interlock plate, selector arm, shift rail, detent plugs, springs or shift cover worn or damaged • Clutch shaft or roller bearings worn or damaged	• Check runout at rear face of clutch housing • Check lever for worn fork. Tighten loose attaching bolts. • Remove gearshift lever and check for loose offset lever nut or worn insert. Repair or replace as necessary. • Remove, disassemble and inspect transmission cover assembly. Replace worn or damaged components as necessary. • Replace clutch shaft or roller bearings as necessary

Troubleshooting the Manual Transmission (cont.)

Problem	Cause	Solution
Jumps out of gear (cont.)	• Gear teeth worn or tapered, synchronizer assemblies worn or damaged, excessive end play caused by worn thrust washers or output shaft gears • Pilot bushing worn	• Remove, disassemble, and inspect transmission. Replace worn or damaged components as necessary. • Replace pilot bushing
Will not shift into one gear	• Gearshift selector plates, interlock plate, or selector arm, worn, damaged, or incorrectly assembled • Shift rail detent plunger worn, spring broken, or plug loose • Gearshift lever worn or damaged • Synchronizer sleeves or hubs, damaged or worn	• Remove, disassemble, and inspect transmission cover assembly. Repair or replace components as necessary. • Tighten plug or replace worn or damaged components as necessary • Replace gearshift lever • Remove, disassemble and inspect transmission. Replace worn or damaged components.
Locked in one gear—cannot be shifted out	• Shift rail(s) worn or broken, shifter fork bent, setscrew loose, center detent plug missing or worn • Broken gear teeth on countershaft gear, clutch shaft, or reverse idler gear Gearshift lever broken or worn, shift mechanism in cover incorrectly assembled or broken, worn damaged gear train components	• Inspect and replace worn or damaged parts • Inspect and replace damaged part • Disassemble transmission. Replace damaged parts or assemble correctly.

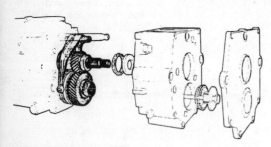

M45 + 5th gear = M47

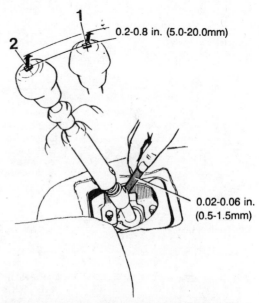

0.2-0.8 in. (5.0-20.0mm)

0.02-0.06 in. (0.5-1.5mm)

Adjust the detent plate for the correct clearance

and standard on 260 series models and the 1980 and later GL, GLE, Diesel, GT Coupe and 760 GLE.

In 1982 the M46 became the standard unit for all models with manual transmission and in 1987 the 240, 740 and 760 Turbo received the 5-speed M47. The M47 continues through 1989 in the 240 series and the 740 Turbo. The 1989 740 GL uses the M46 transmission.

Adjustments

LINKAGE

Shift linkage adjustments are neither necessary nor possible on Volvo manual transmissions. The linkage is mounted internally and is permanently bathed in oil.

On 1970–71 140 series, the shift lever mounts directly in the top of the transmission. This configuration, although providing for more direct shifting action, required the use of a long wand-like shift lever with long throws required to change gears. This situation was remedied on 1972 and later 140 series cars, as well as all 164 and 1800 series and all later models, with the implementation of an inboard mounted, intermediate shifter rod. This rod allows the use of a much shorter, sportier shift lever and shorter throws between gears.

On these models the reverse gear detent clearance is the only adjustment that can be made to the shift linkage. When properly adjusted, first and second gears can be easily selected and the shift lever has about ½ inch of sideways freeplay in either gear.

Remove the shift lever cover, the trim frame and if necessary, the ash tray assembly. Engage first gear and adjust the clearance between the detent plate and the gear shift lever. Also check the clearance with second gear engaged. Clearance should be 0.02–0.06 in. (0.5–1.5mm).

Back-up Light Switch
REMOVAL AND INSTALLATION
M45/M46 transmissions through 1984

1. Remove the gearshift boot. Remove the left side cover panel from the center console and disconnect the reverse light connector.
2. Bend a piece of stiff wire into a large 'S' shape and slide it down the right side of the transmission tunnel. This will be used to keep the wire harness from vanishing into an impossible location.
3. Safely elevate the front of the car and support it on jackstands.
4. Gain access to the switch and disconnect the wiring.
5. Install the new switch and, using the S-hook, position the cable properly and resecure it to the gearshift carrier rod.
6. Lower the vehicle and attach the connector for the reverse lights.
7. Remove the S-hook, reinstall the left side panel on the console and the shift boot.

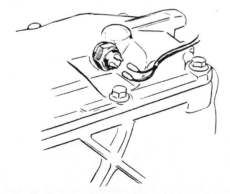

Location of reverse switch on M45/M46 and M47 transmissions

6-cylinder Engines wit M45/M46 and M47 Transmissions

1. Raise and support the front end on jackstands.
2. Remove the wiring and replace the switch.

700 series w/ 4-cylinder Gasoline or Diesel Engines

1. Elevate the car front and rear and support on jackstands.
2. Matchmark and remove the front driveshaft from the transmission or overdrive unit; lower the shaft out of the way.
3. Position and support the transmission with a jack or transmission hoist.
4. Loosen, but do not separate the exhaust joint at the right side of the transmission case.
5. Carefully remove the transmission crossmember from the body.
6. Lower the rear end of the gearbox.
7. Disconnect the wiring from the switch. Thoroughly clean the area around the switch before removing it.
8. After replacing the switch and connecting the wiring, check its function before reassembling everything.
9. Raise the gearbox back into position and install the crossmember. Position and tighten the exhaust joint.
10. Reinstall the driveshaft. Lower the car from its stands.

Transmission
REMOVAL AND INSTALLATION

The transmission assembly may be removed with the engine installed in the vehicle.

140 Series and 1975 240 Series

1. If possible, support the engine with a hoist or support apparatus such as Volvo tool 2727. The purpose of supporting the rear of the engine is to prevent damage to the fan, radiator or front engine mounts by limiting the downward travel of the engine when the transmission crossmember is removed.

If no lifting apparatus is available, place a jack with a protective wooden block beneath the engine oil pan. Do not place the jack under the flywheel (clutch) housing.
2. Lift up the gearshift boot, unscrew the protective cover, and remove the gear shift lever from the transmission.
3. Safely elevate the car at a height which will allow removal of the transmission. Remove the drain plug from the transmission and drain the oil.
4. Slowly loosen the nuts for the transmission crossmember. Make sure that the support-

ing apparatus or the jack supports the rear of the engine in place.
Remove the crossmember.

Disconnect the front universal joint from the transmission (or overdrive) output shaft flange. Disconnect the speedometer cable. Disconnect the rear engine mount and the exhaust pipe bracket.

5. Allow the rear of the engine to drop 0.8 in. (2mm). Disconnect the back-up light wires, and the wires for the overdrive, if so equipped.

6. Remove the four bolts which retain the transmission to the flywheel (clutch) housing. It may be necessary to use a universal (swivel) joint on the wrench to gain access to the two upper bolts.

CAUTION: *The transmission is heavy! Support its weight with a second jack or hoist before removing. Do not allow the transmission to hang partially removed on the shaft.*

7. To remove the transmission, pull it straight out to the rear. While the transmission is removed, inspect the condition of the clutch and the throwout bearing. Replace the throwout bearing if it is scored or if it has been emitting metal-to-metal noises.

8. When reinstalling, be careful to install two guide pins in the flywheel (clutch) housing. This will aid in aligning the transmission input shaft with the clutch spline when the transmission is being fitted to the flywheel housing.

The transmission must be supported on the jack and pushed straight in to the clutch assembly. Again, do not allow the transmission to hang partially installed; the input shaft may bend.

9. Install two of the transmission retaining bolts. After two transmission-to-flywheel housing bolts are installed, the guide pins may be removed and the remaining two bolts installed. Torque the transmission-to-flywheel housing bolts to 45 ft. lbs. Fill the transmission with oil to the proper level.

10. Reconnect the wiring for the overdrive unit and/or the reverse lights. Elevate the rear of the engine about 0.8 in. (2mm) until it is in its original position.

11. Reinstall the exhaust pipe bracket, the rear engine mount and reconnect the speedometer cable. Attach the driveshaft to the transmission or overdrive unit.

12. Reattach the support crossmember. Double check all installation items, paying particular attention to loose hoses or hanging wires, untightened nuts, poor routing of hoses and wires (too tight or rubbing) and tools left in the work area.

13. Lower the car from its stands. Inside the car, reinstall the shift lever mechanism, the protective cover and the shifter boot.

14. Remove the hoist or support apparatus from the engine area.

164 Series

1. If possible, support the engine with a hoist or support apparatus such as Volvo tool 2727. The purpose of supporting the rear of the engine is to prevent damage to the fan, radiator or front engine mounts by limiting the downward travel of the engine when the transmission crossmember is removed.

If no lifting apparatus is available, place a jack with a protective wooden block beneath the engine oil pan. Do not place the jack under the flywheel (clutch) housing.

2. Lift up the gearshift boot, unscrew the protective cover, and remove the gear shift lever from the transmission.

3. Safely elevate the car at a height which will allow removal of the transmission. Remove the drain plug from the transmission and drain the oil.

4. Remove the upper radiator bolts and the exhaust manifold flange nuts. Disconnect the negative battery cable, the throttle shaft and clutch cable from the flywheel (clutch) housing.

5. Slowly loosen the nuts for the transmission support crossmember. Making sure that the rear of the engine remains supported, remove the crossmember.

6. Disconnect the exhaust pipe bracket and the speedometer cable. Disconnect the front universal joint from the transmission (or overdrive) output shaft flange.

7. Lower the rear of the engine approximately 1.8 in. (46mm). Disconnect the back-up light wires and the wires for the overdrive, if so equipped.

CAUTION: *The transmission is heavy. Support its weight with a second jack or hoist before removing. Do not allow the transmission to hang partially removed on the shaft.*

8. Place a hydraulic floor jack beneath the transmission. Remove the bolts which retain the transmission and flywheel (clutch) housing assembly to the engine. Leave the starter connected but position it to one side. Remove the transmission by pulling it straight to the rear.

9. Prior to assembly, inspect the condition of the clutch and the throwout bearing. Replace the bearing if it is scored or noisy in operation.

10. When reassembling, do not allow the gearbox to hang on the shaft partially installed. Support the transmission on the jack and slide it straight forward into the flywheel assembly. Install the retaining bolts and torque them to 45 ft. lbs.

11. Reattach the starter if necessary. Fill the transmission oil to the proper level. Reconnect the overdrive and/or reverse light wiring.

12. Elevate the rear of the engine until it is in its original position.

13. Reinstall the exhaust pipe bracket and reconnect the speedometer cable. Attach the driveshaft to the transmission or overdrive unit.

14. Reattach the support crossmember. Reconnect the clutch cable, the throttle shaft and the negative battery cable.

15. Replace the upper radiator bolts and the exhaust manifold flange nuts. Double check all installation items, paying particular attention to loose hoses or hanging wires, untightened nuts, poor routing of hoses and wires (too tight or rubbing) and tools left in the work area.

16. Lower the car from its stands. Inside the car, reinstall the shift lever mechanism, the protective cover and the shifter boot.

17. Remove the hoist or support apparatus from the engine area.

1800 Series (M41)

1. Remove the storage console from the transmission tunnel. Lift up the shifter boot, unscrew the protective cover and remove the gear shift lever.

2. Disconnect the negative battery cable. Remove the radiator attaching bolts.

3. Jack up the vehicle sufficiently to allow removal of the transmission. Install jackstands. Remove the lower drain plug and drain the transmission oil.

4. Remove the bolts which retain the driveshaft to the flange, and remove the attaching bolts for the support bearings. Pull the driveshaft approximately ½ in. (13mm) to the rear.

5. Place a jack, with a protective wooden block, beneath the oil pan of the engine.

6. Disconnect the exhaust pipe bracket and the speedometer. Remove the rear engine mount. Slowly loosen the nuts for the transmission support crossmember making sure that the jack supports the rear of the engine.

7. Lower the engine approximately 0.8 in. (2mm). Disconnect the electric cables from the transmission.

CAUTION: *The transmission is heavy. Support its weight with a second jack or hoist before removing. Do not allow the transmission to hang partially removed on the shaft.*

8. Remove the four bolts which secure the transmission to the flywheel (clutch) housing. It may be necessary to use a universal joint to gain access to the two upper bolts. Support the weight of the transmission with another jack and pull the unit straight out to the rear.

9. To remove the transmission, pull it straight out to the rear. While the transmission is removed, inspect the condition of the clutch and the throwout bearing. Replace the

throwout bearing if it is scored or if it has been emitting metal-to-metal noises.

10. When reinstalling, be careful to install two guide pins in the flywheel (clutch) housing. This will aid in aligning the transmission input shaft with the clutch spline when the transmission is being fitted to the flywheel housing.

The transmission must be supported on the jack and pushed straight in to the clutch assembly. Again, do not allow the transmission to hang partially installed; the input shaft may bend.

11. Install two of the transmission retaining bolts. After two transmission-to-flywheel housing bolts are installed, the guide pins may be removed and the remaining two bolts installed. Torque the transmission-to-flywheel housing bolts to 45 ft. lbs. Fill the transmission with oil to the proper level.

12. Reconnect the wiring for the overdrive unit and/or the reverse lights. Elevate the rear of the engine about 0.8 in. (2mm) until it is in its original position.

13. Reinstall the exhaust pipe bracket, the rear engine mount and reconnect the speedometer cable. Attach the driveshaft to the transmission or overdrive unit.

14. Reattach the support crossmember. Double check all installation items, paying particular attention to loose hoses or hanging wires, untightened nuts, poor routing of hoses and wires (too tight or rubbing) and tools left in the work area.

15. Lower the car from its stands. Inside the car, reinstall the shift lever mechanism, the protective cover and the shifter boot.

16. Reinstall the radiator attaching bolts and connect the negative battery cable.

1800 Series (M410)

1. Disconnect the upper and lower radiator hoses and drain the cooling system. Disconnect the heater hoses and the air intake hose. Pull up the rubber boot, unscrew the protective cover and remove the gearshift lever.

CAUTION: *When draining the coolant, keep in mind that cats and dogs are attracted by the ethylene glycol antifreeze, and are quite likely to drink any that is left in an uncovered container or in puddles on the ground. This will prove fatal in sufficient quantity. Always drain the coolant into a sealable container. Coolant should be reused unless it is contaminated or several years old.*

2. Raise the vehicle sufficiently to remove the transmission, and install jackstands. Disconnect the driveshaft, exhaust pipe bracket, clutch cable, and the electrical wires for the backup light and the overdrive.

3. Place a hydraulic floor jack beneath the

transmission, and remove the transmission support crossmember.

4. Place a protective wooden block between the rear of the engine and the firewall. Lower the jack and the rear of the engine until the engine contacts the wooden block.

CAUTION: *The transmission is heavy! Support its weight with a second jack or hoist before removing. Do not allow the transmission to hang partially removed on the shaft.*

5. Remove the bolts which secure the flywheel (clutch) housing to the engine. Leave the starter connected but position it to one side. Remove the transmission by pulling it straight to the rear.

6. Prior to installation, inspect the condition of the clutch and throwout bearing. Replace the bearing if it is scored or has been noisy in operation.

7. After reinstalling the transmission, tighten the mounting bolts to 45 ft. lbs. Secure the starter to the bellhousing. Fill the transmission with oil to the proper level.

8. Raise the motor to its proper position and support it on the jack until the transmission crossmember is in place. Once secure, remove the block of wood from the firewall area.

9. Reattach the driveshaft, the exhaust pipe bracket, the clutch cable and the wiring for the overdrive and the reverse lights.

10. Double check all installation items, paying particular attention to loose hoses or hanging wires, untightened nuts, poor routing of hoses and wires (too tight or rubbing) and tools left in the work area. Lower the vehicle to the ground.

11. Reinstall the heater hoses, the air intake and the upper and lower radiator hoses. Fill the cooling system with the proper amount of fluid.

12. Inside the car, install the shifter mechanism, the protective cover and the shift boot.

1976 and Later 200 Series

1. Disconnect the battery. At the firewall, disconnect the back-up light connector.

2. Jack up the front of the car and install jackstands. Under the car, loosen the setscrew and drive out the pin for the shifter rod. Disconnect the shift lever from the rod.

3. Inside the car, pull up the shift boot. Remove the fork for the reverse gear detent. Remove the snapring and lift up the shifter. If overdrive-equipped, disconnect the engaging switch wire.

4. On 240 Series and 1980 and later GL and DL models, disconnect the clutch cable and return spring at the fork. On 260 Series and 1980 and later GLE, Diesel, GT and Coupe models, remove the bolts retaining the slave cylinder to the flywheel housing and tie the cylinder back out of the way (do not disconnect any hoses).

5. Disconnect the exhaust pipe bracket(s) from the flywheel cover. Remove the oil pan splash guard.

6. Using a floor jack and a block of wood, support the engine beneath the oil pan. Remove the transmission support crossmember.

7. Disconnect the driveshaft. Disconnect the speedometer cable. If so equipped, disconnect the overdrive wire.

8. Remove the starter retaining bolts and pull the starter free of the flywheel housing. Leave the starter wiring connected and secure the starter out of the way.

CAUTION: *The transmission is heavy. Support its weight with a second jack or hoist before removing. Do not allow the transmission to hang partially removed on the shaft.*

9. Support the transmission using another floor jack. Remove the flywheel (bell) housing-to-engine bolts and remove the transmission by pulling it straight back.

10. Prior to installation, inspect the condition of the clutch and throwout bearing. Replace the bearing if it is scored or has been noisy in operation.

11. After reinstalling the transmission, tighten the mounting bolts to 30 ft. lbs. Secure the starter to the bellhousing. Fill the transmission with oil to the proper level.

12. Connect the drive shaft, the speedometer cable and if necessary, the overdrive wiring.

13. Reinstall the transmission cross member. When secure, remove the jack from beneath the engine. Replace the splash guard and attach the exhaust bracket to the bell housing.

14. Depending on the model, either reconnect the clutch cable and return spring to the fork or remount the hydraulic clutch cylinder to the bell housing.

15. Inside the car, connect the shifter and the reverse gear detent fork. Connect the wiring for the overdrive switch and install the shift boot and cover.

16. Under the car, connect the shifter rod to the shift lever. Don't forget to tighten the setscrew.

17. Connect the reverse light wiring and attach the negative battery cable.

700 Series with M46 or M47

1. If possible, support the engine with a hoist or support apparatus such as Volvo tool 5006. The purpose of supporting the rear of the engine is to prevent damage to the fan, radiator or front engine mounts by limiting the downward travel of the engine when the transmission crossmember is removed.

If no lifting apparatus is available, place a jack with a protective wooden block beneath the engine oil pan. Do not place the jack under the flywheel (clutch) housing.

2. Disconnect the battery ground cable. Remove the ash tray and holder assembly. Remove the trim box around the gear shift lever.

3. Disconnect the shift lever cover from the floor. Remove the snapring at the base of the shift lever.

4. Jack up the car and safely support it with jackstands. From underneath the car, disconnect the gear shift rod at the gear shift lever. Remove the lock screw, and press out the pivot

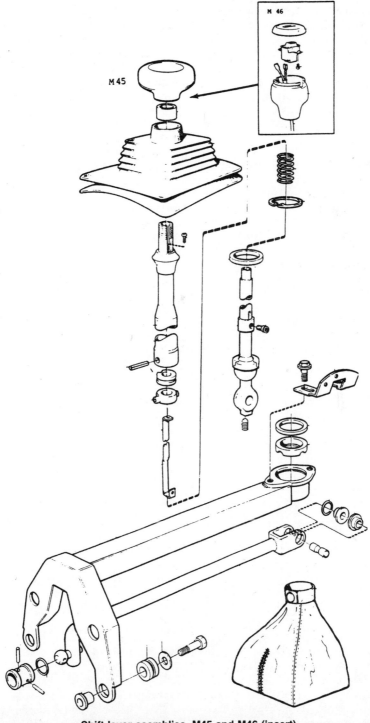

M 46

M 45

Shift lever asemblies, M45 and M46 (insert)

pin. Push up on the shift lever, and pull it up and out of the car.

5. Matchmark the driveshaft and transmission flanges for later assembly. Disconnect the driveshaft from the transmission.

6. Separate the exhaust pipe at the joint under the car. Detach the bracket from the front end of the exhaust pipe (near the bend).

7. Unbolt the transmission crossmember; at the same time, detach it from the rear support (rubber bushing).

8. Remove the rear support from the transmission.

NOTE: *On B200 and B230 engines, lower the engine until ½ inch remains between the distributor cap and the firewall.*

9. Tag and disconnect the electrical connectors from the overdrive, back-up light connector and the solenoid.

10. Cut the plastic clamp at the gear shift assembly from the wiring harness.

11. Remove the starter motor retaining bolts. On models with the B28 family of V6 engines, remove the cover plate under the bellhousing and the cover plate from the other starter motor opening.

12. On B28F models (hydraulic clutch), remove the slave cylinder from the bellhousing and upper bolts holding the bellhousing. On D24T models, (mechanical clutch), detach the clutch cable from the release fork and the bellhousing. Remove the upper retaining bolts from the bell housing.

CAUTION: *The transmission is heavy. Support its weight with a second jack or hoist before removing. Do not allow the transmission to hang partially removed on the shaft.*

13. Place a transmission jack or a hydraulic floor jack underneath the gearbox so that the transmission is resting on the jack pad. *It is very helpful here to have another person steadying and guiding the transmission on the jack as it is lowered.*

Remove the lower bolts holding the bellhousing, and carefully lower the transmission a few inches as you roll it back so the input shaft will clear. Stop the jack and make sure all wires and linkage are disconnected, then lower the transmission the rest of the way.

14. When sliding the transmission into place, make sure the release bearing is correctly positioned in the shift fork, and that the input shaft is aligned in the clutch disc.

15. Install the upper bolts in the bellhousing. Raise the end of the gearbox and attach the gear carrier lever.

16. Attach the slave cylinder or clutch cable to its mounts. Adjust clutch clearance on D24T

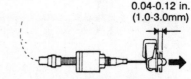

0.04-0.12 in.
(1.0-3.0mm)

Correct free play in cable operated clutch

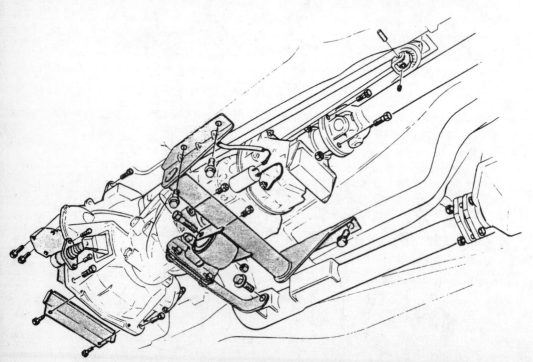

Transmission removal, 700 Series. B28 engine with M46 transmission shown

models to 0.04–0.12 in. (1–3mm) between the release fork and bearing.

17. Reinstall the starter motor. On B28 engines, reinstall the cover for the other starter hole.

18. Remount the gear lever carrier to the gearbox. Secure the connectors for the reverse lights, the solenoid and (on M46) the overdrive unit.

19. Replace the transmission crossmember. On B200/B230 engines, elevate the motor back to its normal position.

20. Tighten the exhaust pipe joint, attach its bracket and attach the gearshift rod to the gearshift lever.

21. Install and tighten the driveshaft. Refill the transmission with the proper amount of oil.

22. Connect the gearshift rod to the gear shift lever. Inside the car, mount and secure the shifter assembly.

23. Double check all installation items, paying particular attention to loose hoses or hanging wires, untightened nuts, poor routing of hoses and wires (too tight or rubbing) and tools left in the work area.

24. Lower the car to the ground. Install the ashtray, interior trim and shifter boot.

25. Reconnect the negative battery cable.

Overdrive

The overdrive unit for the M41, M46 and M410 transmissions is a planetary gear type and is mounted on the rear of the transmission. When the overdrive is in the direct drive position (overdrive switched off), power from the transmission mainshaft is transmitted through the freewheel rollers and uni-directional clutch to the overdrive output shaft.

When the car is backing up or during periods of engine braking, torque is transmitted through the clutch sliding member which is held by spring pressure against the tapered portion of the output shaft.

When the overdrive is actuated, the clutch sliding member is pressed by hydraulic pressure against the brake disc (ring), which locks the sun wheel. As a result, the output shaft of the overdrive rotates at a higher speed than the mainshaft, thereby accomplishing a 20% reduction in engine speed in relation to vehicle speed.

REMOVAL AND INSTALLATION

To prevent internal damage and facilitate removal, the vehicle should first be driven in 4th gear with the overdrive engaged, and then coasted for a few seconds with the overdrive disengaged and the clutch pedal depressed. This can be done with the rear wheels elevated and

the car on jackstands BUT make certain that the stands are properly located and on a very firm base. The overdrive unit can be removed with the transmission in the car.

The internal workings of the overdrive are similar to an automatic transmission. The need for special pressure and clearance measuring tools puts this repair outside the scope of this book. Disassembly and internal repair of the overdrive is best left your dealer or professional repair facility.

1. Safely elevate the front of the car and support it on jackstands. Disconnect the negative battery cable.

2. Disconnect the driveshaft from the overdrive flange.

3. Support the engine from below with a jack. Use a block of wood to protect the oil pan.

4. Remove the transmission crossmember and lower the engine/transmission assembly about an inch. On the B200/B230 engines, check that the distributor does not hit the firewall.

5. Disconnect the wiring at the overdrive solenoid.

6. Position a second jack or transmission dolly under the overdrive unit. Remove the bolts holding the overdrive to the transmission and pull the overdrive unit straight back until free of the transmission output shaft.

7. When reinstalling, make sure that the overdrive unit is fitted straight onto the transmission shaft. At no time should it hang on the shaft partially installed.

8. Install the retaining bolts and torque to 5–8 ft. lbs. Reconnect the solenoid wiring. Raise the motor back to its proper position and install the transmission crossmember.

9. Reconnect the driveshaft to the output flange, lower the car to the ground and reconnect the battery cable. If the overdrive was drained, refill the unit with the correct amount of oil. M41 and M410 units use SAE 80W/90 gear oil. M46 units use automatic transmission

Remove the bolts and separate the overdrive unit from the intermediate flange

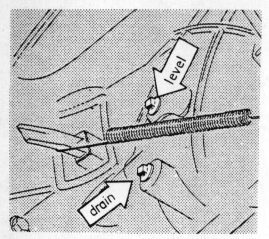

Check the overdrive fluid at the upper port

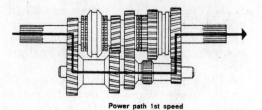

Power path 1st speed

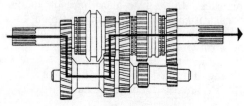

Power path 2nd speed

fluid. Recheck the oil level and top up if needed after 10–15 miles of driving. The oil level should be to the edge of the filler (upper) hole.

Overdrive Solenoid

REMOVAL AND INSTALLATION

NOTE: *The solenoid and operating valve are one unit, and are replaced together.*

1. Disconnect the wire clips from the solenoid unit.

2. Unscrew the solenoid from the side of the overdrive unit.

3. When installing, use a new seal and new O-rings. Immerse the O-rings in automatic transmission fluid prior to installation. Screw the solenoid into the overdrive by hand until snug. Using a crow's-foot open-end wrench attachment on a torque wrench, torque the solenoid unit to 37 ft. lbs.. Attach the wire clips, check overdrive oil level and check operation.

Transmission Overhaul

The procedures below refer to a manual gearbox which is removed from the car. If the unit has been removed with the overdrive attached, remove the overdrive unit before carrying out these procedures.

WARNING: *The use of the correct special tools or their equivalent is REQUIRED for this procedure. Do not begin repairs unless equipped with bearing pullers, hub pullers, snaring pliers, and variously sized bearing drivers and installation tools. Access to a press will also be required.*

M40/M41 Transmissions

1. Mount the gearbox securely on the workbench or attach to a transmission stand.
2. Unscrew the bolts for the gearbox cover

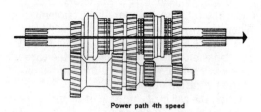

Power path 3rd speed

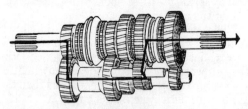

Power path 4th speed

Power path reverse

Power routing, M40/M41 Transmission

and remove the cover. Remove the spring and interlock (detent) balls for the shift rails.

3. Remove the cover over the shift rails and remove the selector fork bolts.

4. Slide the selector fork backwards to the 1st gear position. Drive the retaining pin out

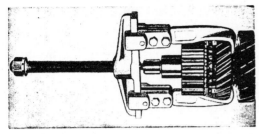

Removing the front synchronizer on M40/M41 transmissions

slightly, but do not allow it to foul the 1st gear. Move the selector fork forward enough to allow the pin to pass in front of the gear. Drive the pin out completely and remove it.

5. Slide out the selector rails. Hold the forks so that they maintain position and do not jam the rails. Remove the forks.

6. Remove the bolts for the rear cover. Turn the cover so that it does not lock the shaft for the idler and reverse gears. Drive out the shaft for the idler gear. The idler gear will fall to the bottom of the gearbox.

NOTE: *The shaft must be driven out rearward.*

7. Pull out the mainshaft.

8. Remove the bolts and remove the cover over the input shaft. Gently pry out the oil seal from the cover.

9. Drive out the input shaft. It may be necessary to remove the circlip and press the bearing off the shaft.

10. Remove the idler gear from the bottom of the case. Using a puller of the correct size (Volvo 2878 or similar), remove the shaft for the reverse gear. When the shaft is free, remove the reverse gear and other parts from the case.

11. Disassemble the mainshaft as follows:

a. If the transmission is equipped with overdrive, remove the circlip and press off the rotor for the overdrive oil pump. Remove the circlip for the mainshaft rear bearing.

If not equipped with overdrive, counterhold the end flange and remove the flange nut.

b. Slide the engaging sleeve for 1st and 2nd gear forward. Place the shaft in a press and support it under 1st gear. Press out the shaft.

c. Remove the synchronizer, thrust washer, engaging sleeves, inserts and springs from the shaft. Take note of the order of assembly of the parts; make notes or diagrams to help you during reassembly.

d. Remove the snapring on the front of the shaft. Pull off the synchronizer hub and 3rd gear using a puller. Remove the thrust washer.

e. Remove the snapring, the thrust washer, 2nd gear, the synchronizer and spring.

f. Remove the oil seal from the rear cover and remove the speedometer gear. It may be necessary to remove the snaprings and press out the bearing.

12. When disassembled check each gear carefully, looking for any signs of cracking or chipping particularly in the tooth areas. ANY sign of damage requires replacement of the gear. Check the synchronizers and selector sleeves for excessive blunting of points or edges. Inspect all the bearings for scoring or cracks on the balls or races. Inspect the shift rails for excessive wear at the indentations.

13. Reassemble the mainshaft. Press the bearing into the rear cover and fit the snapring. Use a snapring which fits securely into the groove; select a different thickness if the ring is loose in fit.

14. For a gearbox without overdrive:

a. Place the speedometer gear on the bearing in the rear cover. Use a drift of the proper size and press in the oil seal.

b. Install the parts for the 1st and 2nd gear synchronizer on the mainshaft. Make sure the springs are installed correctly.

c. Install the synchronizer, 1st gear and the thrust washer. Place the rear cover on the shaft. Make sure that the speedometer gear is properly positioned.

d. Fit on the flange and use a sleeve to press on the cover and the flange. Using a counter hold on the flange, install the washer and nut for the flange and tighten the nut.

For a gearbox with overdrive:

a. Place the rear cover and bearing on a supporting sleeve. Install the thrust washer, 1st gear and synchronizer.

b. Press in the shaft. Select a snapring of the proper thickness and install it on the shaft.

c. Install the locking key, the rotor for the oil pump and the snapring.

15. Install the synchronizer, 2nd gear and thrust washer onto the shaft. Again, select a circlip which fits snugly in the groove and install it.

16. Install the thrust washer, 3rd gear and synchronizer on the shaft. Assemble the 3–4 synchronizer hub and install the snaprings. Install the synchronizer assembly on the mainshaft and select a snug fitting lockring to hold it in place.

17. After the mainshaft is assembled, install the reverse gear and shaft. The reverse shaft is mounted so that it projects $9/32$ in. (7mm) outside the transmission case.

18. Using a mandrel of the proper size (Volvo 2907 or similar), place the spacing washers and

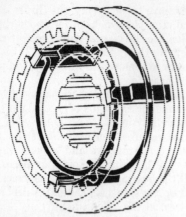

Synchronizer springs must be properly placed during reassembly. M40/M41 shown

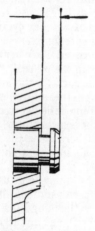

The reverse shaft will project beyond the case. Dimension shown by arrows is $^9/_{32}$ in.

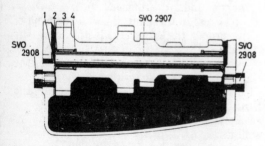

1. Thrust washer   3. Needle bearing
2. Spacing washer   4. Spacing washer

Installing the idler gear in M40/M41 transmissions. Volvo special tools shown

needles (24 in each bearing) in position. Use grease to hold the needles in position.

19. Using grease to hold them in place, attach the washers to the housing and guide them into position. (A centering plug such as Volvo 2908

is very helpful here.) Lay the idler gear in the bottom of the gear housing.

20. Using a drift, press the bearing onto the input shaft. Lock it in place with a snapring. Again using grease to hold them in place, position the 14 bearing rollers in position in the input shaft. Press the input shaft into position in the housing and then press the oil seal into the cover.

21. Place the cover over the input shaft. Don't forget the O-rings for the bolts.

22. Place the mainshaft within the case. Turn the rear cover so that the counter shaft can be installed.

23. Gently turn the transmission upside down. Install the counter shaft from the rear and hold against the mandrel with your hand. Make sure the thrust washers (held in place by the grease) don't fall out of place. Install the idler gear.

24. If the transmission does not couple to an overdrive unit, install the rear cover. If an overdrive unit is used, install it with new hardware.

25. Reinstall the shift rails and forks. Move the selector fork over the rear position when installing the new lock pin. Install the cover over the shift rails.

NOTE: *If the end caps at the front of the case were removed, they should be reinstalled. Note that the center cap should project about 0.16 in (4mm) beyond the housing.*

26. Install the interlock balls and springs. Install the gearbox cover.

27. Check the operation of the gearbox by testing each gear for smooth engagement and release.

M400/M410 Transmissions

1. Mount the gearbox securely on the workbench or attach to a transmission stand.

2. Unscrew the bolts for the gearbox cover and remove the cover. Remove the spring and interlock (detent) balls for the shift forks.

3. Remove the bolts for the selector forks. Push the rails backwards and drive out the tensioning pin in the flange of the rails.

4. Hold the selector forks so they don't jam on the rails and remove the rails. Remove the selector forks.

5. Install a counterhold (Volvo 2985 or similar) between the input shaft and the front synchronizer. Remove the bolt and remove the mainshaft rear bearing

6. Remove the release bearing. Loosen the bolts and remove the cover for the input shaft. Then remove the bolts for the clutch casing and remove the casing.

7. Remove the circlip and, using a bearing puller (Volvo 2982 or similar), remove the bear-

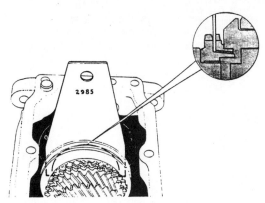

Use Volvo special tool 2985 or similar to counter-hold the mainshaft

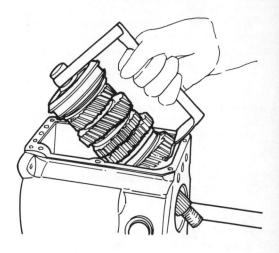

Volvo tool for removing and carrying the main-shaft assembly

ing for the input shaft. Remove the counterhold device.

8. Turn the transmission upside down. Using a metal drift placed in the center hole, carefully drive the intermediate shaft forward until the front gear just touches the end of the housing.

Now drive the intermediate shaft backwards until the rear bearing outer ring releases.

NOTE: *The intermediate shaft may snag on the fitting for the reverse shaft. It may be necessary to guide the shaft to one side.*

9. Place the transmission in its normal upright position. Pull out the input shaft and remove the synchronizer. Remove the thrust washer from the rear end of the mainshaft. Fit a lifting tool (Volvo 2829 or similar) onto the mainshaft. Push the 1st–2nd engaging sleeve backwards and lift the mainshaft clear of the case.

10. Lift the intermediate shaft. Using an appropriate drift, drive the outer ring for the intermediate shaft front bearing out of its mount. Pull off the inner rings – front and rear – with the appropriate pullers.

11. Using Volvo puller 2830 or similar, remove the reverse shaft and take out the reverse gear.

12. Drive out the sealing ring from the front and rear covers with a drift.

13. To disassemble the mainshaft:

   a. Remove the lifting tool and then remove 1st gear, the needle bearing and the synchronizer.

   b. Remove the engaging sleeves for the synchronizers. Remove the circlips for the sychronizer hubs.

   c. Place the shaft in a press and support it below the gears. Press off 2nd gear and the 1st–2nd synchronizing hub.

   d. Reverse the shaft and again place it in the press, supported below the gear. Press off 3rd gear and the 3rd–4th synchronizer hub.

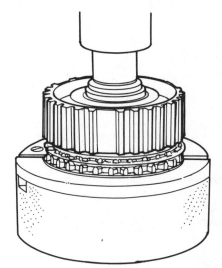

Disassembling the mainshaft in a press. Volvo tool shown

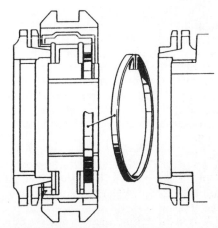

Install the resilient ring correctly

14. After the shaft is disassembled, clean all the parts in solvent. Examine the gears carefully for any signs of cracks or scoring, particularly in the tooth areas. Check the synchronizers for excessive wear, and examine the bearings closely for any sign of scoring or cracks.

To rebuild the mainshaft:

a. Assemble the 1st–2nd and 3rd–4th synchronizers. Fit the snaprings correctly and place the resilient ring in the hub for the 3rd–4th synchronizer.

b. Use a small screwdriver to center the ring and install the cone into the synchronizer. Make sure the flanges fit properly into the grooves. Assemble the complete synchronizer and 3rd gear. Turning the gear will make it easier to fit the resilient ring in place.

c. Support the sychronizer and gear on a press. Insert the needle bearing and press in the mainshaft. Turn the gear during installation to check that the gear and needle bearing fit correctly. Select a circlip which is snug in the groove and install it.

d. Assemble the 1st–2nd synchronizer, cone, 2nd gear and needle bearing on the press. Make sure the gear ring on the engaging sleeve faces forward and that the flanges fit correctly within the grooves of the cone.

Press in the mainshaft. While installing, turn 2nd gear to prevent binding. Select a circlip which is snug in the groove and install it.

e. Install 1st gear with its needle bearing and synchronizer onto the mainshaft. Install the lifting device.

15. Using appropriate drifts, install the sealing rings into the front cover. Press the bearing onto the input shaft. Note that the ball holder should face inwards. Press the rear bearing inner ring onto the intermediate shaft.

16. Place the gear lever for the reverse shaft onto the bearing pin in the transmission housing. Install the reverse gear and shaft. The shaft should be level with the housing or a maximum of 0.08 in. (2mm) underneath.

17. Place the intermediate shaft in the bottom of the case. Install the mainshaft in the case; remove the lifting tool and fit the thrust washers onto the mainshaft.

18. Install the rear bearing onto the mainshaft. The ball holder should face inwards. Using a bearing press, set the bearing into the housing.

19. Install the needle bearing on the input shaft. Install the loose cone for the 3rd–4th synchronizer. Place it correctly so that the flanges fit into the grooves. Push the input shaft into the housing and onto the pin of the mainshaft.

20. Turn the transmission upside down. Press the front bearing inner ring onto the intermediate shaft with suitable bearing drivers. Drive in the outer rings until they are about 0.10 in. (2.5mm) above the face of the case.

21. Turn the transmission so that the front end is up and install the clutch casing and the front cover with new gaskets.

22. Turn the transmission so that the rear end is upward. Install the new gasket and place a 0.028 in. (0.7mm) shim on the rear bearing outer ring. Using either a dial indicator or other accurate means, determine the amount of vertical play (axial) in the intermediate shaft. If using the dial indicator, press down on the center of the shaft and turn it; set the dial to zero when the shaft is at its lowest point.

Press the intermediate shaft upwards (a small screwdriver through the oil level hole does this easily) and turn it. Record the dial reading when the shaft is at its highest point.

23. Subtract 0.0024 in. (0.06mm) from the highest reading and select shims equal to this difference. Remove the measuring equipment and insert the shims; the thickest shim should be against the rear cover. Recheck the end play; final measurements should be 0.0012–0.004 in. (0.03–0.10mm).

24. Reinstall the selector forks, flanges and selector rails. Make sure the flange for the reverse gear fits properly in the gear lever. Install the retaining bolts and install new tensioning pins.

25. Install the intermediate flange and a new gasket. Install the overdrive unit if so equipped.

26. Place the interlocking balls and springs in position. Install the transmission cover with a new gasket. Install the speedometer gear and the clutch release bearing.

27. Check the operation of the gearbox by testing each gear for smooth engagement and release.

For M400/M410, use a dial indicator to measure the dial play of the intermediate shaft

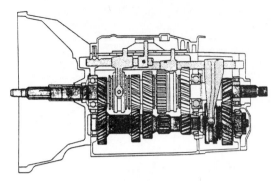

Power transfer in 5th gear (M47)

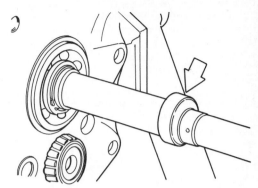

Eccentric for overdrive oil pump. Be sure to catch the small locking pin during removal

M45/M46 and M47 Transmissions

1. Mount the gearbox securely on the workbench or attach to a transmission stand.

2. Unscrew the bolts for the gearbox cover and remove the cover. Remove the spring and interlock (detent) ball for the shift forks. Remove the reverse light switch and the overdrive switch (except M47).

3. Remove the selector plate assembly and the return spring. Remove the gasket and clean the gasket surface.

4. Remove the glide washers for the selector plate assembly. Remove the locking pin for the shifter.

5. On M46 units, remove the overdrive unit.

6. Remove the gearshift carrier assembly.

7. Remove the sleeve for the gearshift rod joint. Tap out the rear pin in the gearshift rod, rotate the rod and remove the front pin. Remove the gearshift rod.

8. Unbolt and remove the intermediate housing; remove the gasket and shims.

9. Remove the gear selector rails, the shifter and the shift forks.

10. On M46 units, remove the eccentric for the overdrive oil pump by removing the lock ring and pulling off the eccentric. Catch the locking key as it falls clear.

11. Remove the lock ring and spacer for the mainshaft bearing.

12. Install a counterhold (Volvo 2985 or similar) between the input shaft and the front synchronizer. Remove the spacer ring and remove the mainshaft bearing. Remove the bearing thrust washer.

13. Remove the clutch fork, spacer and release bearing. Then remove the bolts for the clutch casing (bell housing) and remove the casing.

14. Remove the outer races for the intermediate shaft bearings. On cast iron housings, tap the shaft backwards until the rear outer bearing race comes free. Then knock the shaft forward until the front outer race can be removed.

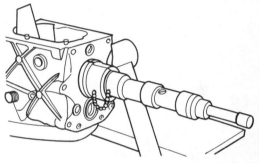

Removing the mainshaft bearing with Volvo tools. Note the use of a counterholding tool inside the case

On aluminum cases (How can you tell? Use a magnet!) tap the shaft only enough to expose the race, then affix a puller (Volvo 5177 or similar) and extract the race. Continued thumping on the shaft will crack the case. Don't risk it.

15. Pull out the input shaft and remove the 4th gear synchronizer ring.

16. Lift out the main shaft.

17. Lift out the intermediate shaft, and on M47 units, the intermediate shaft extension.

18. Using a punch, tap the reverse gear shaft backwards and remove the gear and shaft.

19. Remove the reverse gear shift fork and remove the seal for the selector rail.

20. Using a suitable puller, remove the intermediate shaft bearings from the shaft.

21. Remove 1st gear and its synchronizer ring from the mainshaft.

22. Remove the lock ring for the 1st–2nd synchronizer hub. Using a press, support the hub and press the hub and gear off the shaft.

23. Remove the lock ring for the 3rd–4th synchronizer hub. Using a press, support the hub and press the hub and gear off the shaft. On M47 units, remove the 5th gear synchronizer, hub and gear.

24. Remove the locking ring and spacer ring for the input shaft bearing.

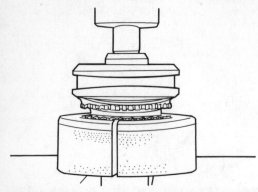

Removing the synchronizer hub and gear. Note use of special tool to support assembly properly

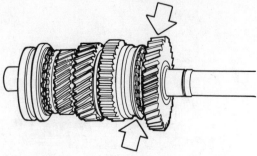

Correct position of 1st gear and synchronizer on the mainshaft

25. Again using the press and supporting the bearing, remove the bearing on the input shaft.

26. Remove the rubber ring from the gear-shift rod joint.

27. Remove the gearshift rod bushings and the bell housing seal.

28. Disconnect the sychronizer hubs by pushing the hubs out of the sleeves. Clean all parts in solvent and examine the gears carefully for any signs of cracks or scoring, particularly in the tooth areas. Check the synchronizers for excessive wear, and examine the bearings closely for any sign of scoring or cracks.

29. Begin reassembly by building up the synchronizer hubs. Position the hub in the sleeve so that slots align with the chamfered teeth within the sleeve. Insert the dogs (three in each synchro) and lock them in place with the springs.

30. Using the proper drivers, install the bell housing seal, position a new rubber ring in the shifter joint and install new bushings on the gearshift rod. Use grease to retain the rubber ring on the right side of the shifter rod.

31. Install a new seal for the selector rail in the case.

32. Using the press, assemble the 3rd gear and its synchronizer ring and install the assembly with the 3rd–4th synchronizer hub onto the main shaft. Repeat the procedure for the 2nd gear and synchronizer hub and install it with the 1st–2nd synchronizer onto the mainshaft. On M47 units, assemble 5th gear and its attendant synchronizer parts onto the intermediate shaft. Don't forget the locking rings (circlips) for each assembly.

33. Install the 1st gear and synchronizer ring onto the mainshaft.

34. Using a drift of the correct size, install the two intermediate shaft bearings onto the shaft.

NOTE: *The bearings for the small end of the intermediate shaft are different for diesel applications. Make sure you use the correct bearing for your application.*

Installing the bearing on the intermediate shaft. Volvo tool shown

35. Install the bearing on the input shaft. Install the lock ring on the input shaft but DO NOT install the spacer ring at this time. It will be installed later in the procedure.

Follow this sub-procedure only if transmission case is aluminum:

a. Position the intermediate shaft in its housing. Position the outer races for the intermediate shaft bearings in the case.

b. Install the bell housing with its gasket and torque its bolts to 30 ft. lbs.

c. Turn the transmission to a vertical position. Eliminate any play in the intermediate shaft bearings by tapping the bearing race until the clearance is gone and the shaft does not rotate easily.

d. Using an accurate metric depth gauge, measure the distance between the (intermediate shaft bearing) outer race and the rear surface of the case.

e. Calculate the thickness of shims for the intermediate shaft. Keep all your measurements and calculations in millimeters; replacement shims are not referenced in inch units.

Start with the depth just measured--let's

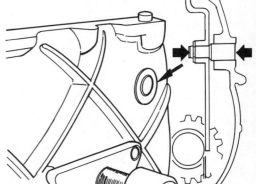

Adjust the clearance between reverse gear and its shift fork to 0.004–0.040 in. (0.10–1.00mm) by moving the mounting pin

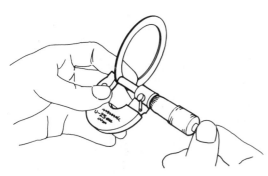

Use a metric depth gauge to take necessary measurements, then select correct shim(s) based on calculations

say 1.50mm--and add 0.25mm for the gasket thickness. (1.50 + 0.25 = 1.75mm) The shaft free play spec is 0.03–0.08mm, so add that to your total. (1.75 + 0.03 to 0.08 = 1.78 to 1.83mm). Since shims are available only in multiples of 5, we choose in our example shims totalling 1.80mm.

Select the shims and set them aside; don't install them yet.

f. Since this was only for the purposes of preliminary measurement, remove the bellhousing and its gasket, remove the outer races for the intermediate shaft bearings and lift out the intermediate shaft.

36. Install the reverse gear shifter and lock ring. Install reverse gear and its shaft.

37. Check and adjust the position of the reverse gear shaft in the case. It should be 0.002 in. (0.05mm) below the housing face.

38. Adjust the clearance between reverse gear and the shift fork. Correct clearance is 0.004–0.04 in. (0.1–1.0mm). Perform adjustments by tapping the shift fork pivot pin with a punch to move it.

39. Position the intermediate shaft (and its extension for M47) in the bottom of the transmission case.

40. Position the main shaft in its housing.

41. Put the thrust washer and bearing on the mainshaft. The bearing should have its positioning ring in place.

42. Using Volvo tool 2831 or similar, press the mainshaft bearing into position. Press so that reverse gear is loaded towards the center of the transmission. Make sure that gears do not contact each other and cause damage.

43. Install the lock ring for the mainshaft bearing.

44. For M46 units, place the locking key in the mainshaft keyway and install the overdrive oil pump eccentric and its locking ring.

45. Coat the bearing with grease and install the roller bearing into the input shaft.

46. Place the 4th gear synchronizer ring in the hub.

47. Attach the input shaft to the mainshaft and push it in all the way. Lift up the intermediate shaft so that the bearings are correctly positioned in the housing.

48. Pull out the input shaft so that the spacer ring can be positioned on the bearing. Push the shaft back in; the spacer should lie against the housing.

49. Install the outer races for the intermediate shaft bearings. On units in aluminum cases, use a drift of the correct diameter.

50. Using a metric depth gauge, measure the distance between the front end of the input shaft bearing and the front surface of the case. Record this number. Now measure the distance between the surface of the bell housing and the bottom of the bearing case. The following calculation will compute the necessary thickness of the shims for the input shaft.

Start with the distance from the bell housing surface to the bottom of the bearing seat--for example, let's say 5.60mm--and add to it the known thickness of the gasket, 0.25mm. (5.60 + 0.25 = 5.85) From the result, subtract the distance between the front of the input shaft

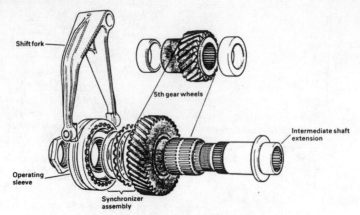

Shift fork

5th gear wheels

Intermediate shaft
extension

Operating
sleeve

Synchronizer
assembly

5th gear components, M47

bearing and the front of the case--for our example, 4.71mm. (5.85 − 4.71 = 1.04) Now subtract the allowable freeplay in the shaft--0.01 to 0.15mm--to get the final shim thickness. (1.04 − 0.01 to 0.15 = 1.03 to 0.89). The nearest shim thickness to our need is 0.90mm.

51. Install the bell housing with its gasket; for aluminum cases, install the clutch fork and spacer. Tighten the bolts to 30 ft. lbs.

52. Install the clutch release (throw-out) bearing.

53. Turn the transmission to a vertical position. For aluminum cased units, remove any free play in the intermediate shaft by using a drift to tap the bearing race until the shaft has noticeable drag when turning.

For units with iron cases, measure the distance between the outer race of the intermediate shaft bearing and the surface of the housing. To this measurement, add the known thickness of the gasket, 0.25mm. Subtract the allowable clearance, 0.025 to 0.10mm, and choose the shim or combination of shims closest to the total.

54. For both iron and aluminum cases, determine and select shims for the mainshaft in the following manner:

a. Measure the distance between the front of the mainshaft bearing and the surface of the transmission case. Also measure the distance between the rear cover surface and the bottom of the bearing seat.

b. Beginning with the rear measurement (cover-to-bearing seat), add the known thickness of the gasket, 0.25mm.

c. From that total, subtract the front bearing-to-case surface measurement.

d. From that result, subtract the allowable clearance (freeplay), 0.01 to 0.20mm. Select the shim closest to the total.

55. Install the shift forks; make sure the lugs are in their correct position. Install the shifter and the gear selection rails.

56. Position the gasket and shim pack for the intermediate shaft. (For aluminum cases, this shim thickness was computed in step 35. For iron units, it was computed in step 53).

57. Position the mainshaft shim pack in the intermediate housing or, on M45, the rear cover.

58. Install the cover (M45) or the housing (M46), and secure with the two lower bolts finger tight. On M45 units, install the drive flange and tighten the bolts to 65–75 ft. lbs. On M45, install the speedometer gear and O-ring at this time.

59. Install the gearshift rod and carrier. Tighten the bolts to 30 ft. lbs.

60. Install and tighten remaining bolts for rear cover or intermediate housing. Correct torque is 30 ft. lbs.

61. Install the lock pin for the shifter, install the selector plate assembly and the return spring.

62. Install the gearshift lever (without its lockscrew and lockring) on the transmission. Hold the selector plate assembly with the palm of your hand and move the shifter through all the gears. Check for proper engagement and release of each gear. Make necessary corrections before proceeding. Remove the shifter.

63. Install the detent ball and spring; install a new gasket for the top cover.

64. Install the top cover and tighten the bolts to 15 ft. lbs.

65. Reinstall the overdrive switch, the reverse light switch and the wiring at the solenoid. The unit may be refilled with oil now or after installation in the car.

Clutch

The purpose of the clutch is to disconnect and connect engine power at the transmission. A car at rest requires a lot of engine torque to get all that weight moving. An internal combustion engine does not develop a high starting torque (unlike steam engines), so it must be allowed to operate without any load until it builds up enough torque to move the car. Torque increases with engine rpm. The clutch allows the engine to build up torque by physically disconnecting the engine from the transmission, relieving the engine of any load or resistance. The transfer of engine power to the transmission (the load) must be smooth and gradual; if it weren't, drive line components would wear out or break quickly. This gradual power transfer is made possible by gradually releasing the clutch pedal. The clutch disc and pressure plate are the connecting link between the engine and transmission. When the clutch pedal is released, the disc and plate contact each other (clutch engagement), physically joining the engine and transmission. When the pedal is pushed in, the disc and plate separate (the clutch is disengaged), disconnecting the engine from the transmission.

The clutch assembly consists of the flywheel, the clutch disc, the clutch pressure plate, the throwout bearing and fork, the actuating linkage and the pedal. The flywheel and clutch pressure plate (driving members) are connected to the engine crankshaft and rotate with it. The clutch disc is located between the flywheel and pressure plate, and splined to the transmission shaft. A driving member is one that is attached to the engine and transfers engine power to a driven member (clutch disc) on the transmission shaft. A driving member (pressure plate) rotates (drives) a driven member (clutch disc) on contact and, in so doing, turns the transmission shaft. There is a circular diaphragm spring within the pressure plate cover (transmission side). In a relaxed state (when the clutch pedal is fully released), this spring is convex; that is, it is dished outward toward the transmission. Pushing in the clutch pedal actuates an attached linkage rod. Connected to the other end of this rod is the throwout bearing fork. The throwout bearing is attached to the fork. When the clutch pedal is depressed, the clutch linkage

Troubleshooting Basic Clutch Problems

Problem	Cause
Excessive clutch noise	Throwout bearing noises are more audible at the lower end of pedal travel. The usual causes are: • Riding the clutch • Too little pedal free-play • Lack of bearing lubrication A bad clutch shaft pilot bearing will make a high pitched squeal, when the clutch is disengaged and the transmission is in gear or within the first 2″ of pedal travel. The bearing must be replaced. Noise from the clutch linkage is a clicking or snapping that can be heard or felt as the pedal is moved completely up or down. This usually requires lubrication. Transmitted engine noises are amplified by the clutch housing and heard in the passenger compartment. They are usually the result of insufficient pedal free-play and can be changed by manipulating the clutch pedal.
Clutch slips (the car does not move as it should when the clutch is engaged)	This is usually most noticeable when pulling away from a standing start. A severe test is to start the engine, apply the brakes, shift into high gear and SLOWLY release the clutch pedal. A healthy clutch will stall the engine. If it slips it may be due to: • A worn pressure plate or clutch plate • Oil soaked clutch plate • Insufficient pedal free-play
Clutch drags or fails to release	The clutch disc and some transmission gears spin briefly after clutch disengagement. Under normal conditions in average temperatures, 3 seconds is maximum spin-time. Failure to release properly can be caused by: • Too light transmission lubricant or low lubricant level • Improperly adjusted clutch linkage
Low clutch life	Low clutch life is usually a result of poor driving habits or heavy duty use. Riding the clutch, pulling heavy loads, holding the car on a grade with the clutch instead of the brakes and rapid clutch engagement all contribute to low clutch life.

pushes the fork and bearing forward to contact the diaphragm spring of the pressure plate. The outer edges of the spring are secured to the pressure plate and are pivoted on rings so that when the center of the spring is compressed by the throwout bearing, the outer edges bow outward and, by so doing, pull the pressure plate in the same direction — away from the clutch disc. This action separates the disc from the plate, disengaging the clutch and allowing the transmission to be shifted into another gear. A coil type clutch return spring attached to the clutch pedal arm permits full release of the pedal. Releasing the pedal pulls the throwout bearing away from the diaphragm spring resulting in a reversal of spring position. As bearing pressure is gradually released from the spring center, the outer edges of the spring bow outward, pushing the pressure plate into closer contact with the clutch disc. As the disc and plate move closer together, friction between the two increases and slippage is reduced until, when full spring pressure is applied (by fully releasing the pedal), The speed of the disc and plate are the same. This stops all slipping, creating a direct connection between the plate and disc which results in the transfer of power from the engine to the transmission. The clutch disc is now rotating with the pressure plate at engine speed and, because it is splined to the transmission shaft, the shaft now turns at the same engine speed. Understanding clutch operation can be rather difficult at first; if you're still confused after reading this, consider the following analogy. The action of the diaphragm spring can be compared to that of an oil can bottom. The bottom of an oil can is shaped very much like the clutch diaphragm spring and pushing in on the can bottom and then releasing it produces a similar effect. As mentioned earlier, the clutch pedal return spring permits full release of the pedal and reduces linkage slack due to wear. As the linkage wears, clutch free-pedal travel will increase and free-travel will decrease as the clutch wears. Free-travel is actually throwout bearing lash.

The diaphragm spring type clutches used are available in two different designs: flat diaphragm springs or bent spring. The bent fingers are bent back to create a centrifugal boost ensuring quick re-engagement at higher engine speeds. This design enables pressure plate load to increase as the clutch disc wears and makes low pedal effort possible even with a heavy-duty clutch. The throwout bearing used with the bent finger design is 1¼ in. (31.75mm) long and is shorter than the bearing used with the flat finger design. These bearings are not interchangeable. If the longer bearing is used with the bent finger clutch, free-pedal travel will not exist. This results in clutch slippage and rapid wear.

The transmission varies the gear ratio between the engine and rear wheels. It can be shifted to change engine speed as driving conditions and loads change. The transmission allows disengaging and reversing power from the engine to the wheels.

CAUTION: *The clutch driven disc contains asbestos, which has been determined to be a cancer causing agent. Never clean clutch surfaces with compressed air! Avoid inhaling dust from any clutch surface!*

When cleaning clutch surfaces, use a commercially available brake cleaning fluid.

All 1970 and later model Volvos are equipped with Borg and Beck or Fichtel and Sachs diaphragm spring clutches. The 140, 240, 1800 series, DL.GL, GT, and Diesel models use an 8½ in. (216mm) clutch disc. The carburetor equipped 164, 260, GLE, Coupe, and the 760 GLE uses a 9 in. (229mm) clutch disc. The 260, GLE, Coupe, and the 760 GLE with the B28F V6 and later 700 series use a hydraulically operated clutch, incorporating a clutch master cylinder and slave cylinder. There is no effective adjustment in this type of system. All other models use a cable operated clutch.

Adjustment

CABLE ACTUATED CLUTCHES

NOTE: *No adjustment is possible on the hydraulic clutch.*

1. Loosen the locknut for the fork on the clutch cable.

2. Make the necessary adjustment and tighten the locknut. The free play (A) at the fork should be 3–5mm for all 4-cylinder engines except the Turbo, 1–3mm for the Gas and Diesel Turbo engines, and 4–5mm for the 164.

3. If this adjustment is insufficient, or if a new cable is installed, the sleeve attachment to the flywheel housing should be adjusted with the adjusting nuts. The freeplay adjusted at the fork will be noticeable as freeplay in the pedal.

REMOVAL AND INSTALLATION

Sections are identified by transmission model. See manual transmission identification paragraph at the beginning of this chapter to identify the transmission in your vehicle.

M40, M41 Transmissions

1. Remove the transmission as outlined in the applicable Transmission Removal and Installation procedure.

2. Remove the upper bolt for the starter motor.

3. Remove the throwout bearing. Disconnect

the clutch cable at the release lever (fork) and loosen the cable sleeve at its bracket.

4. Remove the bolts which retain the flywheel (clutch) housing to the engine, and lift off the housing.

5. Remove the bolt for the release fork ball joint, remove the ball and the release fork.

6. Scribe alignment marks on the clutch and flywheel. In order to prevent warpage, slowly loosen the bolts holding the clutch to the flywheel in a diagonal pattern. Remove the bolts and lift off the clutch and pressure plate.

7. Inspect the clutch assembly as outlined under Clutch Inspection.

8. When ready to install, wash the pressure plate and flywheel with solvent to remove any traces of oil, and wipe them clean with a cloth.

9. Position the clutch assembly (the longest side of the hub facing backward) to the flywheel and align the bolt holes. Insert a pilot shaft (centering mandrel), or an input shaft from an old transmission of the same type, through the clutch assembly and flywheel. This centers the assembly and pilot bearing.

10. Install the six bolts which retain the clutch assembly to the flywheel and tighten them in a diagonal pattern, a few turns at a time. After all the bolt are tightened, remove the pilot shaft (centering mandrel).

11. Install the ball and release fork in the flywheel housing.

12. Place the upper starter bolt in the housing. Position the housing to the engine and first install the four upper bolts (11mm), then the lower starter bolts, and finally the two lower bolts (10mm).

13. Insert the cable sleeve in its bracket and install the rear nut. Connect the cable at the release lever (fork), and install the throwout bearing.

14. Install the nut for the upper starter motor bolt.

15. Install the transmission as outlined in the applicable Transmission Removal and Installation section.

16. Adjust the clutch pedal free travel.

M45, M46 and M47 Transmissions

1. Remove the transmission as outlined under "Removal and Installation".

2. Scribe alignment marks on the clutch and flywheel. In order to prevent warpage, slowly loosen the bolts holding the clutch to the flywheel in a diagonal pattern. Remove the bolts and lift off the clutch and pressure plate.

3. Inspect the clutch assembly as outlined under Clutch Inspection.

4. When ready to install, wash the pressure plate and flywheel with solvent to remove any traces of oil, and wipe them clean with a cloth.

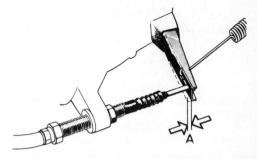

Clutch free play adjustment, manual (non-hydraulic) clutches. Locknut at center, adjusting nut at left

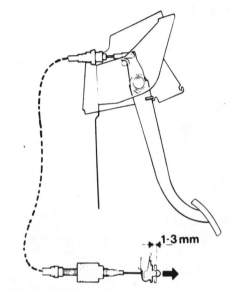

Clutch free play clearance—Turbo engines

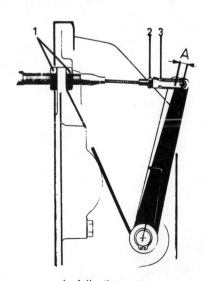

1. Adjusting nuts
2. Locknut
3. Fork

Clutch free play adjustment—164 model

5. Position the clutch assembly (the longest side of the hub facing backward or away from the engine) to the flywheel and align the bolt holes. Insert a pilot shaft (centering mandrel), or an input shaft from an old transmission of the same type, through the clutch assembly and flywheel. This centers the assembly and pilot bearing.

6. Install the six bolts which retain the clutch assembly to the flywheel and tighten them in a diagonal pattern, a few turns at a time. After all the bolt are tightened, remove the pilot shaft (centering mandrel).

7. Install the transmission as outlined under "Removal and Installation".

8. On the models so equipped, bleed the clutch hydraulic system, if necessary.

M400, M410 Transmissions

1. Remove the transmission as outlined in the "Removal and Installation" section.

2. Scribe alignment marks on the clutch and flywheel. In order to prevent warpage, slowly loosen the bolts which retain the clutch assembly to the flywheel diagonally in rotation. Remove the bolts and lift off the clutch and pressure plate.

3. Inspect the clutch assembly as outlined under Clutch Inspection.

4. When ready to install, wash the pressure

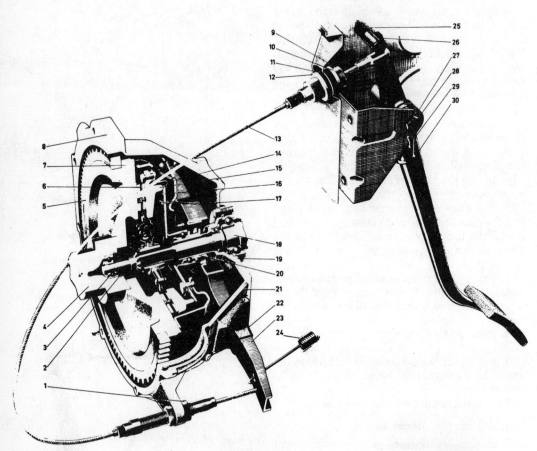

1. Adjusting nuts	11. Rubber bushing	21. Holding plate
2. Circlip	12. Washer	22. Dust cover
3. Support bearing in crank-shaft	13. Clutch wire	23. Release fork
	14. Retainer	24. Return spring
4. Crankshaft	15. Pressure plate	25. Pedal stop
5. Flywheel	16. Thrust spring	26. Rubber sleeve
6. Clutch plate	17. Support rings	27. Bracket
7. Clutch cover	18. Clutch plate shaft (input shaft transmission)	28. Screw for pedal shaft
8. Flywheel housing		29. Return spring
9. Nut	19. Cover, transmission	30. Clutch pedal
10. Washer	20. Throw-out bearing	

Clutch and clutch controls—140 series, 1800 series

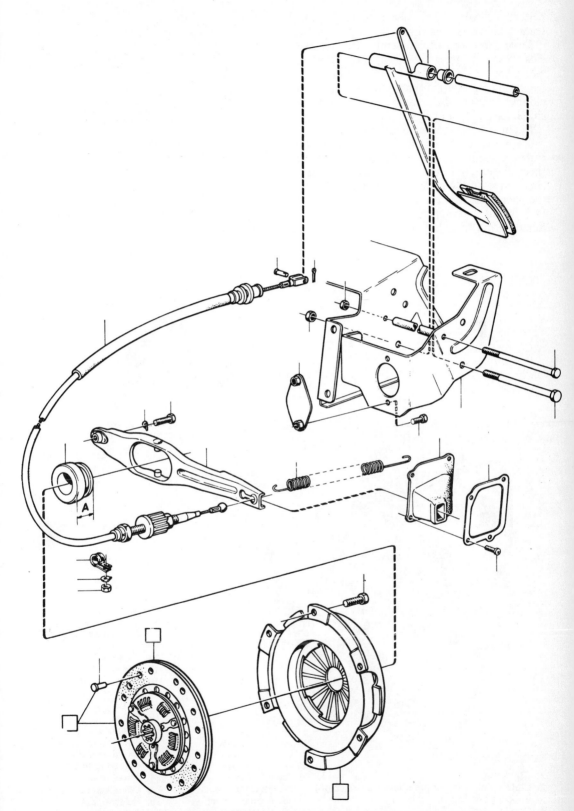

Clutch and clutch controls—240 series, 1980 and later DL, GL, GT and Diesel models

plate and flywheel with solvent to remove any traces of oil, and wipe them clean with a cloth.

5. Position the clutch assembly (the longest side of the hub facing backward) to the flywheel and align the bolt holes. Insert a pilot shaft (centering mandrel), or an input shaft from an old transmission of the same type, through the clutch assembly and flywheel so that the flywheel pilot bearing is centered.

6. Install the six bolts which retain the clutch assembly to the flywheel, and tighten them diagonally in rotation, a few turns at a time. After all the bolts are tightened, remove the pilot shaft (centering mandrel).

7. Install the transmission as outlined in the Removal and Installation section.

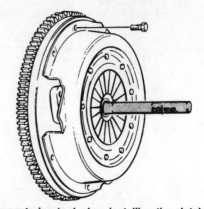

Use a centering tool when installing the clutch and pressure plate

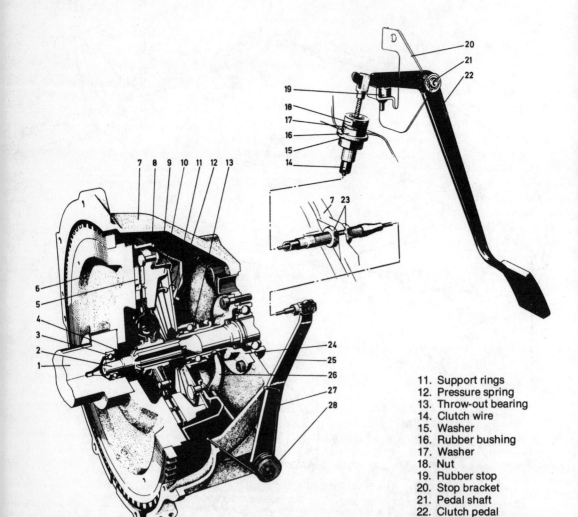

1. Crankshaft
2. Clutch plate shaft (input shaft, transmission)
3. Support bearing in crankshaft
4. Circlip
5. Clutch plate
6. Flywheel
7. Flywheel housing
8. Clutch cover
9. Retainer
10. Thrust plate
11. Support rings
12. Pressure spring
13. Throw-out bearing
14. Clutch wire
15. Washer
16. Rubber bushing
17. Washer
18. Nut
19. Rubber stop
20. Stop bracket
21. Pedal shaft
22. Clutch pedal
23. Adjusting nuts
24. Cover, transmission
25. Lever and release shaft
26. Release fork
27. Return spring
28. Washer

Clutch and clutch controls—164 models

CLUTCH INSPECTION

Check the pressure plate for heat damage, cracks, scoring, or other damage to the friction surface. Check the curvature of the pressure plate with a steel ruler.

Place the ruler diagonally over the pressure plate friction surface and measure the distance between the straight edge of the ruler and the inner diameter of the pressure plate. This measurement must not be greater than 0.008 in. (0.2mm). In addition, there must be no clearance between the straight edge of the ruler and the outer diameter of the pressure plate. This check should be made at several points. Additionally, inspect the tips of the diaphragm springs (fingers) for any sign of wear.

Replace the clutch as a unit (disc, pressure plate and throwout bearing) if any fault is found.

Check the throwout bearing by rotating it several times while applying finger pressure, so that the ball bearings roll against the inside of the races. If the bearing does not turn easily or if it binds at any point, replace it as a unit. Also make sure that the bearing slides easily on the guide sleeve from the transmission.

Inspect the clutch disc for signs of slippage (burns) or oil contamination. Make sure the rivets are not loose and that the clutch contact surfaces are well above the rivet heads. The thickness of the disc above the rivet heads is the "remaining life" of the disc; always replace the disc if in doubt.

When reassembling, apply grease to the splines and end shaft, the throwout bearing and the pivot ball and seat of the clutch fork.

Clutch Master Cylinder

REMOVAL AND INSTALLATION

1. Drain the clutch reservoir with a bulb syringe. Be careful not to drip brake fluid on any painted surfaces.
2. Remove the underdash panel and remove the lockring and pin from the clutch pedal.
3. Remove the hose from the master cylinder. Use a clean jar to collect spillage.
4. Remove the two retaining bolts and remove the master cylinder.
5. When reinstalling, make sure that the clearance (free play) between the pushrod and

Always check the pressure plate for warpage. Distance between arrows must not exceed 0.008 in. (0.20mm)

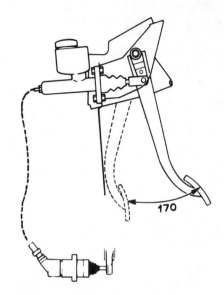

Clutch master cylinder and slave cylinder location—V6 models. Clutch travel is about 6.7 in. (170 mm)

piston is 0.04 in. (1mm). Make certain the hose is correctly threaded and secure. Top up the fluid and bleed the system as explained below.

Clutch Slave Cylinder

REMOVAL AND INSTALLATION

1. Raise and support the front end on jackstands.
2. Disconnect the fluid line at the cylinder.
3. Unbolt the cylinder from the flywheel housing.
4. Installation is the reverse of removal. Be sure to bleed the system after installation.

Hydraulic Clutch Bleeding

The hydraulic clutch system should be bled any time the hoses have been loosened or any component replaced. The bleeding process is quite simple and eliminates any air which has become trapped within the lines.

Add brake fluid to the reservoir. Attach a length of hose to the bleeder nipple on the slave cylinder (at the transmission) and put the other end in a clear glass jar. Put enough brake fluid in the jar to cover the end of the hose.

Have an assistant press the clutch pedal to the floor and open the bleed screw on the slave cylinder. Close off the bleeder while the pedal is still depressed and repeat the process with another application of the clutch pedal. As the bleeder is released each time, observe the fluid in the jar. When no bubbles are coming out of the hose, the system is bled. Secure the fitting, remove the hose and jar, and top up the brake fluid to its proper level.

AUTOMATIC TRANSMISSION

Understanding Automatic Transmissions

The automatic transmission allows engine torque and power to be transmitted to the rear wheels within a narrow range of engine operating speeds. The transmission will allow the engine to turn fast enough to produce plenty of power and torque at very low speeds, while keeping it at a sensible rpm at high vehicle speeds. The transmission performs this job entirely without driver assistance. The transmission uses a light fluid as the medium for the transmission of power. This fluid also works in the operation of various hydraulic control circuits and as a lubricant. Because the transmission fluid performs all of these three functions, trouble within the unit can easily travel from one part to another. For this reason, and because of the complexity and unusual operating principles of the transmission, a very sound understanding of the basic principles of operation will simplify troubleshooting.

THE TORQUE CONVERTER

The torque converter replaces the conventional clutch. It has three functions:

1. It allows the engine to idle with the vehicle at a standstill, even with the transmission in gear.

2. It allows the transmission to shift from range to range smoothly, without requiring that the driver close the throttle during the shift.

3. It multiplies engine torque to an increasing extent as vehicle speed drops and throttle opening is increased. This has the effect of making the transmission more responsive and reduces the amount of shifting required.

The torque converter is a metal case which is shaped lika sphere that has been flattened on opposite sides. It is bolted to the rear end of the engine's crankshaft. Generally, the entire metal case rotates at engine speed and serves as the engine's flywheel.

The case contains three sets of blades. One set is attached directly to the case. This set forms the torus or pump. Another set is directly connected to the output shaft, and forms the turbine. The third set is mounted on a hub which, in turn, is mounted on a stationary shaft through a one-way clutch. This third set is known as the stator.

A pump, which is driven by the converter hub at engine speed, keeps the torque converter full of transmission fluid at all times. Fluid flows continuously through the unit to provide cooling.

Under low-speed acceleration, the torque converter functions as follows:

The torus is turning faster than the turbine. It picks up fluid at the center of the converter and, through centrifugal force, slings it outward. Since the outer edge of the converter moves faster than the portions at the center, the fluid picks up speed.

The fluid then enters the outer edge of the turbine blades. It then travels back toward the center of the converter case along the turbine blades. In impinging upon the turbine blades, the fluid loses the energy picked up in the torus.

If the fluid were now to immediately be returned directly into the torus, both halves of the converter would have to turn at approximately the same speed at all times, and torque input and output would both be the same.

In flowing through the torus and turbine, the fluid picks up two types of flow, or flow in two spearate directions. It flows through the turbine blades, and it spins with the engine. The stator, whose blades are stationary when the vehicle is being accelerated at low speeds, converts one type of flow into another. Instead of allowing the fluid to flow straight back into the torus, the stator's curved blades turn the fluid almost 90° toward the direction of rotation of the engine. Thus the fluid does not flow as fast toward the torus, but is already spinning when the torus picks it up. This has the effect of allowing the torus to turn much faster than the turbine. This difference in speed may be compared to the difference in speed between the smaller and larger gears in any gear train. The result is that engine power output is higher, and engine torque is multiplied.

As the speed of the turbine increases, the fluid spins faster and faster in the direction of engine rotation. As a result, the ability of the stator to redirect the fluid flow is reduced. Under cruising conditions, the stator is eventually forced to rotate on its one-way clutch in the direction of engine rotation. Under these conditions, the torque converter begins to behave almost like a solid shaft, with the torus and turbine speeds being almost equal.

THE PLANETARY GEARBOX

The ability of the torque converter to multiply engine torque is limited. Also, the unit tends to be more efficient when the turine is rotating at relatively high speeds. Therefore, a planetary gearbox is used to carry the power output of the turbine to the driveshaft.

Planetary gears function very similarly to conventional transmission gears. However, their construction is different in that three elements make up one gear system, and, in that all three elements are different from one another.

The three elements are: an outer gear that is shaped like a hoop, with teeth cut into the inner surface; a sun gear, mounted on a shaft and located at the very center of the outer gear; and a set of three planet gears, held by pins in a ring-like planet carrier, meshing with both the sun gear and the outer gear. Either the outer gear or the sun gear may be held stationary, providing more than one possible torque multiplication factor for each set of gears. Also, if all three gears are forced to rotate at the same speed, the gearset forms, in effect, a solid shaft.

Most modern automatics use the planetary gears to provide either a single reduction ratio of about 1.8:1, or two reduction gears: a low of about 2.5:1, and an intermediate of about 1.5:1. Bands and clutches are used to hold various portions of the gearsets to the transmission case or to the shaft on which they are mounted. Shifting is accomplished, then, by changing the portion of each planetary gearset which is held to the tranmission case or to the shaft.

THE SERVOS AND ACCUMULATORS

The servos are hydraulic pistons and cylinders. They resemble the hydraulic actuators used on many familiar machines, such as bulldozers. Hydraulic fluid enters the cylinder, under pressure, and forces the piston to move to engage the band or clutches.

The accumulators are used to cushion the engagement of the servos. The transmission fluid must pass through the accumulator on the way to the servo. The accumulator housing contains a thin piston which is sprung away from the discharge passage of the accumulator. When fluid passes through the accumulator on the way to the servo, it must move the piston against spring pressure, and this action smooths out the action of the servo.

THE HYDRAULIC CONTROL SYSTEM

The hydraulic pressure used to operate the servos comes from the main transmission oil pump. This fluid is channeled to the various servos through the shift valves. There is generally a manual shift valve which is operated by the tranmission selector lever and an automatic shift valvee for each automatic upshift the transmission provides: i.e., 2-speed automatics have a low-high shift valve, while 3-speeds have a 1–2 valve, and a 2–3 vavle.

There are two pressures which effect the operation of these valves. One is the governor pressure which is affected by vehicle speed. The other is the modulator pressure which is affected by intake manifold vacuum or throttle position. Governor pressure rises with an increase in vehicle speed, and modulator pressure rises as the throttle is opened wider. By responding to these two pressures, the shift valves cause the upshift points to be delayed with increased throttle opening to make the best use of the engine's power output.

Most transmissions also make use of an auxiliary circuit for downshifting. This circuit may be actuated by the throttle linkage or the vacuum line which actuates the modulator, or by a cable or solenoid. It applies pressure to a special downshift surface on the shift valve or valves.

The transmission modulator also governs the line pressure, used to actuate the servos. In this way, the clutches and bands will be actuated with a force matching the torque output of the engine.

The transmission used on 1975 and earlier models is a 3-speed, dual-range, Borg-Warner model 35. The BW 35 consists of a three element torque converter coupling, planetary gear set, and a valve control system. A similar Borg-Warner (BW) 55 or Aisin-Warner (AW) 55 (made in Japan under license) is used beginning in the 1976 and later models. The AW70 and the heavy duty AW71 are 4-speed automatic transmissions available since 1982. The AW71 is used with the higher torque B23F/B230F Turbo and the B28/B280 V6 engines.

The ZF (Zahnrad Fabrik) 4HP22 was introduced in 1985. It is a four speed automatic gearbox with a lock-up clutch. This clutch locks in place when the transmission is in fourth gear, effectively making fourth an overdrive. While the ZF22 was introduced on the D24 engine, it is also found coupled to some late model B230F engines.

The transmission type designation, serial number and part number are stamped on a metal plate which is riveted to the left side of the case on automatic transmissions.

Fluid Pan

REMOVAL AND INSTALLATION

CAUTION: *If the vehicle has been driven within the last 3–5 hours the fluid may be scalding hot. Use extreme caution when draining fluid or handling components.*

1970-75 BW 35

1. Place the transmission selector in PARK.
2. Raise the vehicle and place jackstands underneath.
3. The drain plug is located on the pan. Place a container underneath to catch the fluid.
4. After the fluid has stopped draining, remove the 15 pan retaining bolts and remove the pan and gasket.
5. Inspect the magnetic element in the pan for metal shavings or chips. Also remove any

Troubleshooting Basic Automatic Transmission Problems

Problem	Cause	Solution
Fluid leakage	• Defective pan gasket	• Replace gasket or tighten pan bolts
	• Loose filler tube	• Tighten tube nut
	• Loose extension housing to transmission case	• Tighten bolts
	• Converter housing area leakage	• Have transmission checked professionally
Fluid flows out the oil filler tube	• High fluid level	• Check and correct fluid level
	• Breather vent clogged	• Open breather vent
	• Clogged oil filter or screen	• Replace filter or clean screen (change fluid also)
	• Internal fluid leakage	• Have transmission checked professionally
Transmission overheats (this is usually accompanied by a strong burned odor to the fluid)	• Low fluid level	• Check and correct fluid level
	• Fluid cooler lines clogged	• Drain and refill transmission. If this doesn't cure the problem, have cooler lines cleared or replaced.
	• Heavy pulling or hauling with insufficient cooling	• Install a transmission oil cooler
	• Faulty oil pump, internal slippage	• Have transmission checked professionally
Buzzing or whining noise	• Low fluid level	• Check and correct fluid level
	• Defective torque converter, scored gears	• Have transmission checked professionally
No forward or reverse gears or slippage in one or more gears	• Low fluid level	• Check and correct fluid level
	• Defective vacuum or linkage controls, internal clutch or band failure	• Have unit checked professionally
Delayed or erratic shift	• Low fluid level	• Check and correct fluid level
	• Broken vacuum lines	• Repair or replace lines
	• Internal malfunction	• Have transmission checked professionally

Transmission Fluid Indications

The appearance and odor of the transmission fluid can give valuable clues to the overall condition of the transmission. Always note the appearance of the fluid when you check the fluid level or change the fluid. Rub a small amount of fluid between your fingers to feel for grit and smell the fluid on the dipstick.

If the fluid appears:	It indicates:
Clear and red colored	• Normal operation
Discolored (extremely dark red or brownish) or smells burned	• Band or clutch pack failure, usually caused by an overheated transmission. Hauling very heavy loads with insufficient power or failure to change the fluid, often result in overheating. Do not confuse this appearance with newer fluids that have a darker red color and a strong odor (though not a burned odor).
Foamy or aerated (light in color and full of bubbles)	• The level is too high (gear train is churning oil) • An internal air leak (air is mixing with the fluid). Have the transmission checked professionally.
Solid residue in the fluid	• Defective bands, clutch pack or bearings. Bits of band material or metal abrasives are clinging to the dipstick. Have the transmission checked professionally.
Varnish coating on the dipstick	• The transmission fluid is overheating

Lockup Torque Converter Service Diagnosis

Problem	Cause	Solution

No lockup	• Faulty oil pump
	• Sticking governor valve
	• Valve body malfunction
	    (a) Stuck switch valve
	    (b) Stuck lockup valve
	    (c) Stuck fail-safe valve
	• Failed locking clutch
	• Leaking turbine hub seal
	• Faulty input shaft or seal ring
		• Replace oil pump
		• Repair or replace as necessary
		• Repair or replace valve body or its internal components as necessary
		
		• Replace torque converter
		• Replace torque converter
		• Repair or replace as necessary

Will not unlock	• Sticking governor valve
	• Valve body malfunction
	    (a) Stuck switch valve
	    (b) Stuck lockup valve
	    (c) Stuck fail-safe valve
		• Repair or replace as necessary
		• Repair or replace valve body or its internal components as necessary

Stays locked up at too low a speed in direct	• Sticking governor valve
	• Valve body malfunction
	    (a) Stuck switch valve
	    (b) Stuck lockup valve
	    (c) Stuck fail-safe valve
		• Repair or replace as necessary
		• Repair or replace valve body or its internal components as necessary

Locks up or drags in low or second	• Faulty oil pump
	• Valve body malfunction
	    (a) Stuck switch valve
	    (b) Stuck fail-safe valve
		• Replace oil pump
		• Repair or replace valve body or its internal components as necessary

Sluggish or stalls in reverse	• Faulty oil pump
	• Plugged cooler, cooler lines or fittings
	• Valve body malfunction
	    (a) Stuck switch valve
	    (b) Faulty input shaft or seal ring
		• Replace oil pump as necessary
		• Flush or replace cooler and flush lines and fittings
		• Repair or replace valve body or its internal components as necessary

Loud chatter during lockup engagement (cold)	• Faulty torque converter • Failed locking clutch • Leaking turbine hub seal	• Replace torque converter • Replace torque converter • Replace torque converter
Vibration or shudder during lockup engagement	• Faulty oil pump • Valve body malfunction • Faulty torque converter • Engine needs tune-up	• Repair or replace oil pump as necessary • Repair or replace valve body or its internal components as necessary • Replace torque converter • Tune engine
Vibration after lockup engagement	• Faulty torque converter • Exhaust system strikes underbody • Engine needs tune-up • Throttle linkage misadjusted	• Replace torque converter • Align exhaust system • Tune engine • Adjust throttle linkage
Vibration when revved in neutral Overheating: oil blows out of dip stick tube or pump seal	• Torque converter out of balance • Plugged cooler, cooler lines or fittings • Stuck switch valve	• Replace torque converter • Flush or replace cooler and flush lines and fittings • Repair switch valve in valve body or replace valve body
Shudder after lockup engagement	• Faulty oil pump • Plugged cooler, cooler lines or fittings • Valve body malfunction • Faulty torque converter • Fail locking clutch • Exhaust system strikes underbody • Engine needs tune-up • Throttle linkage misadjusted	• Replace oil pump • Flush or replace cooler and flush lines and fittings • Repair or replace valve body or its internal components as necessary • Replace torque converter • Replace torque converter • Align exhaust system • Tune engine • Adjust throttle linkage

sludge or gum from the bottom of the pan. Clean the mating surfaces of the transmission case and pan.

6. Position the pan (with a new gasket) to the case and install the 15 retaining bolts. Tighten all the bolts only finger tight first, then tighten them to 8–13 ft. lbs. in an alternating pattern across the pan. Coat the threads of the drain plug with sealing or locking compound such as Loctite®. Install the plug and a new plug gasket and torque to 8–10 ft. lbs..

7. Remove the jackstands and lower the vehicle. Refer to the capacities chart and fill the transmission to the proper level (between the MAX and MIN marks for a cold transmission) with type **F** automatic transmission fluid.

1976 and Later BW55, AW55, AW70, AW71 and ZF22

1. Raise the car and place jackstands underneath.

2. On older models, the dipstick tube doubles as the filler tube, and when removed, the drain plug. If no drain plug is evident in the pan, disconnect the tube from the side of the pan, and drain the transmission. The ZF22 has a drain plug in the bottom of the pan as do the later BW and AW units.

3. Remove the 14 pan bolts and lower the pan and gasket. Some fluid will remain in the pan. On the ZF22, note the two different types of retaining clips; the ones with the rounded edges mount at the corners of the pan.

4. Inspect the magnet (located adjacent to the filter screen) for metal particles. Check the filter screen for the pump. Remove any gum or sludge from the bottom of the pan. Clean and dry the pan and install a new gasket.

5. Position the pan and install the bolts finger tight. Then tighten them to 4–7 ft. lbs. in an alternating pattern across the pan.

6. Connect the dipstick tube if removed and tighten to 59–74 ft. lbs.

7. Remove the jackstands and lower the car.

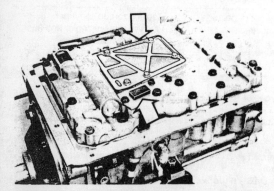

AW55/BW55 transmission. Arrows show location of magnet and strainer screen

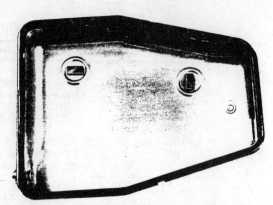

Oil pan to ZF 4HP22 transmission. Note correct placement of magnets when reinstalling

Refer to the capacities chart and fill the transmission to the proper level with ATF Type F.

FILTER (PUMP STRAINER) SERVICE

1. Remove the pan as outlined above.

2. Remove the bolts which retain the front pump wire-mesh strainer to the valve body, and lower the strainer.

3. Clean the strainers in an alcohol-based solvent solution.

4. Position the strainers to the valve body and install the retaining screws and bolts. Torque the bolts to 1.7–2.5 ft. lbs. (BW 35) or 3.7–4.4 ft. lbs. (BW55, AW55, AW70 and AW71).

5. Install the pan with a new gasket as outlined in the "Removal and Installation" section.

Adjustments

FRONT BAND ADJUSTMENT

BW 35

1. Remove the pan as outlined in the Pan Removal and Installation section.

2. Insert a 6mm gauge block between the adjusting bolt and the servo cylinder. Tighten the bolt with an inch-pound torque wrench to 10 in. lbs.

3. Adjust the position of the adjusting bolt spring. It should be 1–2 threads from the lever.

4. Remove the gauge block and torque wrench. Make sure that the long end of the adjusing bolt spring is inserted in the cam for the front brake band.

5. Install the pan as outlined in the Pan Removal and Installation section.

REAR BAND ADJUSTMENT

BW 35

1. An access hole is provided in the right side of the transmission tunnel. On some 140 series and 164 models, it is necessary to disconnect

.250" Gauge Block   Ten (10) In. Lbs. Torque

Front band adjustment—BW 35

the right heater duct. Lift up the carpet and position it to one side. Remove the rubber plug from the access hole.

2. Loosen the locknut from the adjusting screw located on the right side of the transmission case.

3. Using a $\frac{5}{16}$ in. square socket and a foot-pound torque wrench, tighten the adjusting screw to 10 ft. lbs.; then back off the adjusting screw one complete turn.

4. Without disturbing the adjustment, tighten the locknut.

5. Install the rubber plug, fit the carpet, and install the heater duct if removed.

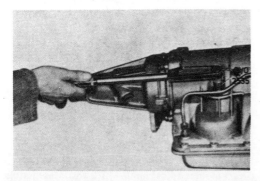

Rear band adjustment—BW 35

The BW55, AW55, AW70, AW71 and ZF22 transmissions are equipped with a multi-disc (band) system which does not require any adjustment. No provision is made for band adjustment, even at overhaul.

SHIFT LINKAGE ADJUSTMENT

1970–71 140 Series and 164 (with BW 35)

1. Disconnect the pull rod from the selector shaft lever. Place the selector lever in NEUTRAL.

2. Place the lever on the transmission in the central position. Adjust the length of the pull rod so that, on 140 series models, the ball socket can easily be snapped onto the lever ball, and so that, on 164 models, the pin can easily be pushed through the yoke and lever.

When the pull rod is adjusted correctly, the distance to the link in the NEUTRAL position should be equal to the distance to the link in the DRIVE position.

3. Make sure that the gear indicator points correctly on the scale (quadrant). Adjustments are made to the cable sleeve at the indicator.

4. Make sure that the output shaft is locked with the control lever in the PARK position.

5. Connect the pull rod to the selector shaft lever.

1971–73 1800 Series

1. Check to make sure that the transmission lever and the lever at the linkage bracket are parallel. If necessary, adjust the length of the lower control rod.

2. Disconnect the upper control rod from the intermediate lever. Place the gear selector in N.

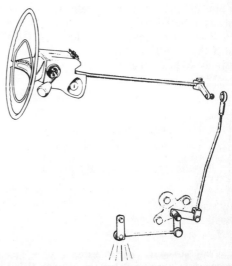

Gear selector linkage adjustment—1970 140 series, 164

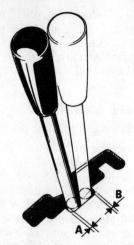

Gear selector adjustment—1800 series

Also set the transmission lever to its third (neutral) position. Adjust the length of the upper control rod so that the ball socket aligns with the ball stud. Connect the control rod to the lever.

3. If the upper control rod adjustment is correct, the distances to the inhibitor plate in Neutral and Drive (A and B) should be equal.

4. Make sure that the output shaft is locked with the selector lever in the Park position.

1972–73 140 Series and 164

1. Disconnect the shift rod from the transmission lever. Place both the transmission lever and the gear selector lever in the **2** position.

2. Adjust the length of the shift control rod so that a small clearance (distance B) of 1mm is obtained between the gear selector lever inhibitor and the inhibitor plate when the shift control rod is connected to the transmission lever.

3. Position the gear selector lever in **DRIVE** and make sure that a similar small clearance (distance A) of 1mm exists between the lever in-

hibitor and the inhibitor plate. Disconnect the shift control rod from the transmission lever and adjust if necessary.

4. Lock the control rod bolt with its safety clasp and tighten the locknut. Make sure that the control rod lug follows with the transmission lever.

5. After moving the transmission lever to the **PARK** and **1** positions, make sure that the clearances **A** and **B** remain the same. In addition, make sure that the output shaft is locked with the selector lever in the **PARK** position.

1972–75 140 Series
164 Models
240 Series with BW 35

1. Disconnect the shift rod from the transmission lever. Place both the transmission lever and the gear selector lever in the **2** position.

2. Adjust the length of the shift control rod so that a small clearance (distance B) of 1mm is obtained between the gear selector lever inhibitor and the inhibitor plate, when the shift control rod is connected to the transmission lever.

3. Position the gear selector lever in **DRIVE** and make sure that a similar small clearance (distance A) of 1mm exists between the lever inhibitor and the inhibitor plate. Disconnect the shift control rod from the transmission lever and adjust, if necessary.

4. Lock the control rod bolt with its safety clasp and tighten the locknut. Make sure that the control rod lug follows with the transmission lever.

5. After moving the transmission lever to the **PARK** and **1** positions, make sure that the clearances **A** and **B** remain the same.

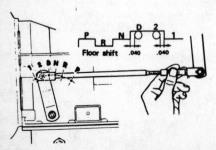

Adjusting automatic transmission gear selector. Clearance in position D toward position N is the same as the clearance in position 2 toward position 1. Adjust at the bottom end of the gear selector

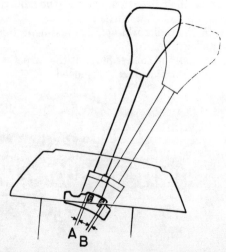

Gear selector adjustment—1972 and later models except 1800 series

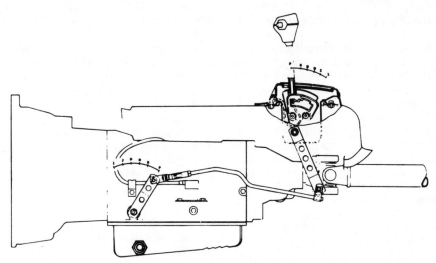

Shortened shaft linkage and closer control console—AW70/AW71 automatics

1976 and Later Models Except 700 Series

1. With the engine off, check that the distance between the **D** position and its forward stop is equal to the distance between the **2** position and its rearward stop when the gear selector is moved. If you are not sure, remove the gear quadrant cover, and measure.

2. If adjustment is necessary, a rough setting is made by loosening the locknut and rotating the clevis on the control rod to the transmission. A fine adjustment can be made by rotating the knurled sleeve between the control rod locknut and the pivot from the gear selector lever. Increasing the rod length will decrease clearance between the **D** position and its forward stop, and vice versa. Maximum permissable length of exposed thread between the locknut and the control rod is 28mm.

700 Series with AW70/71 or ZF22

NOTE: *Before adjusting shift linkage, make sure the starter motor operates only in P or N positions; that the back-up light illuminate only in R and that the shift lever is vertical in P with the car level.*

1. Place the shift lever in **P**.
2. Loosen the locknuts on the adjustment and reaction rods (on the linkage under the car).
3. Make sure the shift lever is in **P**. Turn the drivshaft until it locks in position.
4. Position the gear linkage lever (A) vertically and tighten the locknut. (The gear selector lever may hit the dashboard if the linkage lever is positioned too far backwards.)
5. Press the reaction rod arm backwards until a slight resistance is felt. Tighten the locknut to 3.5 ft. lbs. This is just enough to hold it it in

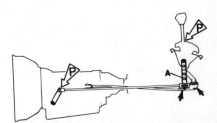

760GLE automatic transmission gear linkage. "A" is adjusting rod arm; arrows point to locknuts on the adjustment rod (left) and the reaction rod (right) arms.

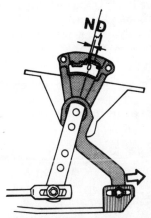

Checking clearance between "D" and "N", and 1st. and 2nd.

place and still allow adjustment; it will be fully tightened later in the procedure.

6. Move the shift selector to **D** and:
   a. For AW70/71 transmissions: Check the freeplay in **D** when the lever is gently moved towards **N**. The play should be noticeable and less than or equal to the freeplay in **2** when the lever is moved gently towards **1**. If the

play is correct, tighten the locknut to 15 ft. lbs.

If the lever is rigid in position **2** (no freeplay), move the reaction lever forward about 2.5mm. If the lever is rigid in position **D**, move the reaction lever backwards about 2.5mm. Again check freeplay and, if correct, tighten the locknut to 15 ft. lbs.

b. For ZF22 transmissions: Check the freeplay in **D** when the lever is gently moved towards **N**. The play should be noticeable and less than or equal to the freeplay in 3 when moved towards **2**. If the play is correct, tighten the locknut to 15 ft. lbs.

If the lever is rigid (no freeplay) in position **3**, move the reaction lever forward about 2.5mm. If the lever is rigid in the **D** position, move the lever backwards about 2.5mm. Recheck the freeplay and if correct, tighten the locknut to 15 ft. lbs.

7. Recheck that the starter engages only in **P** or **N** and that the reverse lights illuminate only in **R**. On certain cars, the reverse lights may not engage after the shift linkage is adjusted; in this case, adjust the reaction lever slightly forward, thereby reducing the play in **D** when moved towards **N**.

THROTTLE AND DOWNSHIFT CABLE ADJUSTMENT

1970–75 Models

Correct adjustment of the throttle cable is imperative for the proper shifting of the transmission. Connect a tachometer to the engine and an oil pressure gauge to the rear of the transmission (as shown) for this adjustment.

PROCEDURE A

1. Warm up the engine and check the idle speed against specifications in the Tune-Up Chart. Make sure that the throttle cable and ca-

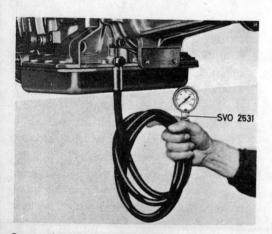

Connecting oil pressure gauge

ble housing (outer sheath) are attached correctly.

2. On dual carburetor engines, the threaded sleeve should be screwed to within $\frac{1}{32}$ in. (0.8mm) of the crimped stop on the cable.

CAUTION: *Firmly apply the handbrake and block all four wheels. The next test requires momentary acceleration in gear.*

3. With one foot firmly on the brake pedal and the accelerator fully depressed, make sure that the carburetor is at the full-open stopped position and that the line pressure reading is 160 psi minimum.

PROCEDURE B

If the cable stop has been damaged, the adjustment disturbed, or if the transmission is not functioning properly, the throttle cable must be adjusted as follows:

1. Firmly apply the parking brake and place blocks in front and in back of the wheels.

2. Place the gear selector in **D**. Note the line pressure readings at 700 rpm and 1200 rpm. The line pressure increase between the two readings should be a minimum of 15 psi and a maximum of 20 psi for B20 engines, and 25–30 psi for B30 engines.

3. If the pressure increase is below the standard, the effective length of the outer cable (cable housing) must be increased.

If the pressure increase is above specification, shorten the effective length of the cable.

The length of the outer cable is determined by the adjuster. Adjust it and retest as necessary.

PROCEDURE C

If the cable itself has been damaged and is in need of replacement, the transmission oil pan must be removed. Refer to "Fluid Pan Removal and Installation". Adjust the new cable as follows:

NOTE: *Do not attempt to lubricate the new cable; it is pre-lubricated.*

1. With the pan removed, observe the position of the throttle cable cam (in the transmission) in relation to the accelerator pedal position.

2. With the accelerator fully released and the carburetor lever at the idle stop, the heel of the cam must contact the full diameter of the downshift valve, taking up all of the slack in the inner throttle cable.

3. With the accelerator fully depressed and the carburetor lever at the full- open stop, the constant radius area of the cam must be the point of contact with the downshift valve.

4. Make sure that the outer cable (cable housing) is correctly positioned in its adjuster.

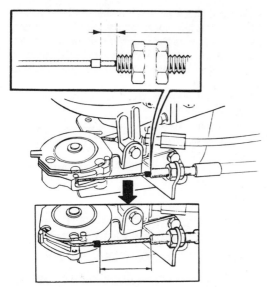

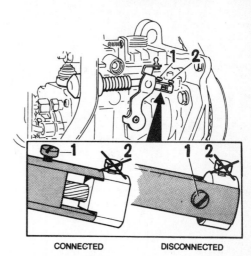

CONNECTED   DISCONNECTED

Diesel engine throttle linkage adjustment—disconnecting the cold start device

Cable adjustments for AW70/71 and ZF22 transmissions

1976 and Later Models Except Diesel

1. The throttle plate angle and throttle cable must be adjusted first. Disconnect the cable at the control pulley and the linkage rod at the throttle shaft.

2. Set the throttle plate angle by loosening the adjusting screw locknut and backing off the screw. Turn in the screw until it just makes contact and then one additional turn. Tighten the locknut.

3. Adjust the linkage rod so that it fits onto the throttle shaft pulley ball without moving the cable pulley. Attach the throttle cable to the pulley and adjust the cable sheath so that the cable is stretched but does not move the cable pulley. Fully depress the gas pedal and check that the pulley contacts the full throttle stop.

4. With the transmission cable hooked up, check that there is 0.010–0.040 in. (0.25–0.60mm) clearance between the cable clip and the adjusting sheath. The cable should be stretched at idle.

5. Pull out the cable about ½ in. (13mm) and release. A distinct click should be heard from the transmission as the throttle cam returns to its initial position. Depress the gas pedal again to wide open throttle. Check that the transmission cable moves about 2 in. (50mm). Adjust as necessary at the adjusting sheath.

Diesel

If the engine is cold, the cold start device must be disengaged before the linkage can be adjusted. To disengage the cold start device, loosen screw (1) in the illustration, push the lever forward and turn the sleeve 90°

WARNING: *Do not touch screw (2) in the illustration, or the cold start device will have to be reset on the test bench.*

To adjust the linkage:

1. Disconnect the link rod lever on the injection pump by unsnapping the plastic clamp on the ball joint of the link rod and pulling the lever off the socket on the accelerator arm.

2. Turn the plastic cable adjuster until the cable is stretched out but does not cause the pulley to move from its idle stop.

3. Have an assistant press the accelerator pedal to the floor and check to see that the pulley notch touches the maximum speed stop.

For manual transmission models, proceed to step 7.

4. To adjust the kickdown cable on models with automatic transmission, have an assistant press the accelerator pedal to the floor and measure how much inner cable is exposed on the kickdown cable. It should be exposed approximately 2.05 in. (52mm) between the end positions.

5. Return the accelerator pedal to idle posi-

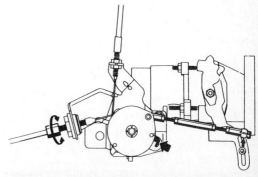

Adjusting throttle linkage. Disconnect the link rod lever and adjust the cable at its plastic adjuster

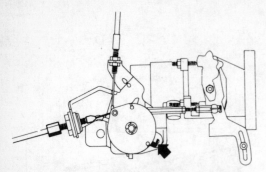

Depress the accelerator pedal and make sure the pulley notch touches the maximum speed stop

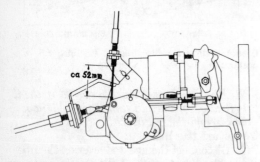

Adjusting the kickdown cable—automatic transmission models

tion. The kickdown cable should be stretched and the distance between the kickdown cable clip and the cable sheath should be 0.01–0.04 in. (0.25–1.00mm).

6. If either of these measurements are not correct, adjust them at the threaded end of the cable sheath.

7. On all models, connect the link rod to the injection pump accelerator arm.

8. Have an assistant floor the accelerator pedal and adjust the link rod length so that the injection pump accelerator arm touches the maximum speed adjusting screw.

9. Return the accelerator pedal to the idle po-

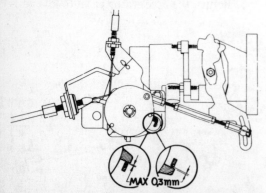

A maximum clearance of 0.012 in. (0.3 mm) is permitted between the pulley and the maximum speed stop

sition and check to see that the accelerator arm touches the idle speed adjusting screw. If not, loosen and move the link rod ball joint in its oblong slot on the accelerator arm until the arm touches the idle speed adjusting screw. Tighten the ball joint.

10. Repeat steps 8 and 9 until the linkage is correctly adjusted.

NOTE: *A maximum clearance of 0.012 in. (0.3mm) is permitted between the pulley and the maximum speed stop.*

11. Reconnect the cold start device, if disconnected.

Neutral Safety (Start Inhibitor) Switch and Reverse Light Switch.

ADJUSTMENT AND/OR REPLACEMENT

The neutral safety switch also serves to illuminate the reverse lights. On the earlier models, the switch is found in the transmission case. The system was later simplified and refined; from the mid-1970s onward, the switch is found on the left side of the gearshift selector.

Some switches can be adjusted by moving them on their slotted mounts or threads. Others are fixed in position and can only be removed and replaced.

1970–72 Models

1. Check the adjustment of the gear selector as outlined above. Place the gear selector in DRIVE and firmly apply the parking brake.

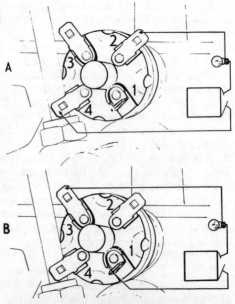

A. Bulb connected to back-up light contacts
B. Bulb connected to starter inhibitor contacts

Neutral safety switch adjustment—1970–71

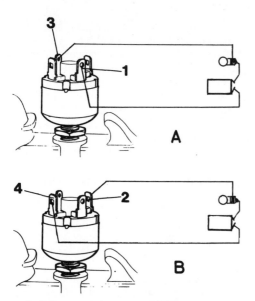

A. Bulb connected to starter inhibitor contacts
B. Bulb connected to back-up light contacts

Neutral safety switch adjustment—1972

2. On 1972 140 series and 164 models, remove the shift lever from the transmission.

3. Loosen the locknut for the switch. Label or diagram the position of the wires on the switch and disconnect the electrical leads. Unscrew the switch until it is held in by just a few threads.

4. On 1970–71 models, connect a 12 volt test light to the back-up light terminals (2 and 4) and screw in the switch until the test light goes out. Disconnect the light and mark this position on the switch and transmission with a pencil. Connect the test light to the start inhibitor terminals (1 and 3) and screw out the switch until the light goes on. Disconnect the light and also mark this position. The proper adjustment is midway between these two marks.

5. On 1972 models, connect a 12 volt test light to start inhibitor terminals (1 and 3), and screw in the switch until the test light goes out. Disconnect the light and mark this position on the switch and transmission with a pencil. Connect the test light to the back-up light terminals (2 and 4) and screw out the switch until the light goes on. Disconnect the light and also mark this position. The proper adjustment is midway between these two marks.

6. When the proper adjustment is achieved, tighten the locknut; take care not to disturb the adjustment. Connect the four electrical leads.

7. On 1972 140 series and 164 models, reinstall the control lever on the transmission.

8. Block the wheels so that the car cannot move either forward or backward. Make sure that the engine can only be started with the

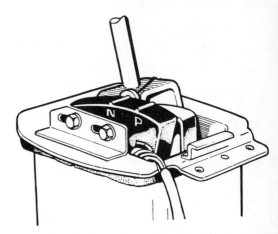

Adjustable neutral safety switch must be properly aligned with the shifter

gear selector in Neutral or Park. Make sure that the back-up lights operate only when the selector is placed in Reverse.

1976 and Later Models, 200 Series

Some early 1976 models have a non-adjustable neutral switch located on the side of the case. All subsequent production models have an adjustable switch, located beneath the shifter quadrant in the tunnel. To adjust:

1. Remove the shifter quadrant cover.

2. Place the shifter lever in Park. Check that the round switch contact centers over the indicating line for **P**. If not, loosen the two switch mounting screws and align the switch.

3. Place the shifter lever in Neutral. Repeat the check and adjust as necessary.

4. If it is necessary to replace the switch, simply remove the two mounting screws and disconnect the wiring connector. Install the new switch and reconnect the wiring.

5. Check that the engine starts only in Park or Neutral, and that the back-up lights work only in Reverse.

200 and 700 Series with AW/BW 55, AW70/71 and ZF22 Transmissions.

1. Remove the ashtray and panel in the center console.

2. For 1982 through 1984 models:

   a. Remove the left half of the selector faceplate. Do this by removing the two screws hidden under the brush.

   b. Remove the non-adjustable switch from the shifter segment. Separate the connector and remove the switch.

   c. Install the new switch and connect the wiring. Make sure that the tab on the shifter enters the slot on the switch. Don't forget the prism which fits onto the top of the new switch.

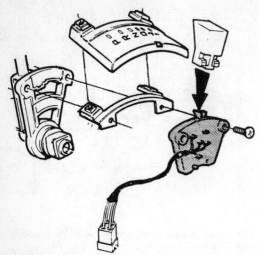

Removing shifter faceplate and holder, 1985 and later cars

d. Press the rubber seal into place and replace the selector faceplate. Install the two screws under the brush.

3. For 1985 and later models:

a. Remove the faceplate with the gear position symbols.

b. Remove the non-adjustable switch from the shifter segment. Separate the connector and remove the switch.

c. Install the new switch and connect the wiring. Make sure that the tab on the shifter enters the slot on the switch. Don't forget the prism which fits onto the top of the new switch.

d. Reinstall the holder and the shifter faceplate.

4. Install the panel and the ashtray in the center console.

Automatic Transmission

REMOVAL AND INSTALLATION

CAUTION: *If the vehicle has been driven within the last 3–5 hours, the transmission oil can be scalding hot. Use extreme care when draining the oil or handling components.*

1800 Series

1. Disconnect the battery ground and lift off the windshield washer container.

2. Disconnect the throttle cable from the lever and bracket.

3. Remove the radiator attaching bolts.

4. Raise the vehicle and support front and rear on jackstands.

5. Drain the oil into a clean container.

6. Disconnect the driveshaft from the transmission flange.

7. Disconnect the oil cooler pipes and remove the sump reinforcing bracket.

8. Remove the converter attaching bolts.

9. Place a jack or transmission dolly with holding fixture under the transmission.

10. Remove the shift control rods, shift lever bracket and rear crossmember.

11. Disconnect the front muffler clamp and the speedometer cable from the case.

12. Lower the jack until the filler pipe touches the firewall.

13. Disconnect all electrical connections at the case.

14. Remove the two upper bolts from the converter housing, the filler pipe and the two remaining converter housing bolts.

15. Lower the jack and pull the transmission to the rear to clear the guide pins.

NOTE: *The transmission must not be tilted forward or the converter will slide off the input shaft.*

16. Install the transmission by balancing it on the jack or dolly and loading it straight onto the engine.

17. Install the two upper bolts for the converter housing, the filler pipe and two of the housing bolts. Torque the converter-to-drive plate bolts to 27 ft. lbs.

18. Connect the wiring to the transmission switches.

19. Elevate the jack and place the transmission in its final position. Install the speedometer cable and secure the front muffler clamp.

20. Install the rear crossmember, the shift lever bracket and the shift control rods. Tighten the crossmember bolts to 18 ft. lbs. Once the crossmember is secure, the jack may be removed.

21. Install the remaining converter housing bolts, the sump reinforcement and connect the oil cooler pipes.

22. Attach the driveshaft and refill the oil in the transmission.

23. Lower the vehicle from its stands and install the radiator attaching bolts.

24. Attach the throttle cable to the lever and bracket and adjust if necessary.

25. Replace the windshield washer container and attach the negative battery cable.

140 Series

1. Disconnect the negative battery cable. Remove the dipstick and filler pipe clamp.

2. Remove the bracket and throttle cable from the dashboard and throttle control.

3. Disconnect the exhaust pipe at the manifold flange.

4. Raise the car and support on jackstands at the front and rear axles.

5. Drain the fluid into a clean container.

6. Disconnect the driveshaft from the transmission flange.

7. Disconnect the selector lever controls (shift linkage) and the pan reinforcing bracket.

8. Remove the converter attaching bolts.

9. Support the transmission with a jack or a transmission dolly and holding fixture.

10. Remove the rear crossmember.

11. Disconnect the exhaust pipe and rear engine mount brackets.

12. Remove the speedometer cable and filler pipe.

13. Install a wooden block between the engine and firewall; lower the jack until the engine contacts the block.

14. Make sure no tension is put on the battery cable.

15. Disconnect all electrical wiring at the transmission case.

16. Disconnect the starter cable and remove the starter.

17. Remove the converter housing bolts.

18. Pull the transmission backwards to clear the guide pins.

19. When reinstalling, load the transmission straight onto the engine and install the converter housing bolts. Tighten the converter-to-drive plate bolts to 27 ft. lbs.

20. Install the starter and connect its cable; hook up all other wiring to the transmission case.

21. Using the jack, elevate the transmission and engine into their proper position. Install the speedometer cable and the filler pipe.

22. Reconnect the exhaust pipe and the rear engine mount brackets.

23. Install the rear crossmember and tighten its bolts to 18 ft. lbs. When the crossmember is secure, the jack may be removed.

24. Install the converter attaching bolts. Connect the selector lever controls and the pan reinforcing bracket.

25. Connect the driveshaft to the transmission flange.

26. Lower the car from its stands and refill the transmission fluid.

27. Reconnect the exhaust pipe at the manifold flange.

28. Reinstall the bracket and throttle cable and adjust if necessary.

29. Install the dipstick and filler pipe.

30. Reconnect the negative battery cable.

164 and 1975 240 Series

1. Disconnect the negative battery cable. Remove the dipstick and filler pipe clamp.

2. Remove the bracket and throttle cable from the dashboard and throttle control.

3. Disconnect the exhaust pipe at the manifold flange.

4. Raise the car and support on jackstands at the front and rear axles.

5. Drain the fluid into a clean container.

6. Disconnect the driveshaft from the transmission flange.

7. Disconnect the selector lever controls (shift linkage) and the pan reinforcing bracket.

8. Remove the converter attaching bolts.

9. Support the transmission with a jack or a transmission dolly and holding fixture.

10. Remove the rear crossmember.

11. Disconnect the exhaust pipe brackets and remove the speedometer cable from the case.

12. Remove the filler pipe.

13. Install a wooden block between the engine and firewall; lower the jack until the engine contacts the block.

14. Make sure no tension is put on the battery cable.

15. Disconnect all electrical wiring at the transmission case.

16. Disconnect the starter cable and remove the starter.

17. Remove the converter housing bolts.

18. Pull the transmission backwards to clear the guide pins.

19. When reinstalling, load the transmission straight onto the engine and install the converter housing bolts. Tighten the converter-to-drive plate bolts to 35 ft. lbs.

20. Install the starter and connect its cable; hook up all other wiring to the transmission case.

21. Using the jack, elevate the transmission and engine into their proper position. Install the speedometer cable and the filler pipe.

22. Reconnect the exhaust pipe and the rear engine mount brackets.

23. Install the rear crossmember and tighten its bolts to 18 ft. lbs. When the crossmember is secure, the jack may be removed.

24. Install the converter attaching bolts. Connect the selector lever controls and the pan reinforcing bracket.

25. Connect the driveshaft to the transmission flange.

26. Lower the car from its stands and refill the transmission fluid.

27. Reconnect the exhaust pipe at the manifold flange.

28. Reinstall the bracket and throttle cable and adjust if necessary.

29. Install the dipstick and filler pipe.

30. Reconnect the negative battery cable.

1976 and Later 240, DL series

1. Disconnect the negative battery cable. Remove the dipstick and filler pipe clamp.

2. Remove the bracket and throttle cable from the dashboard and throttle control.

3. Disconnect the exhaust pipe at the manifold flange.

4. Raise the car and support on jackstands at the front and rear axles.

5. Drain the fluid into a clean container.

6. Disconnect the driveshaft from the transmission flange.

7. Disconnect the selector lever controls (shift linkage) and the pan reinforcing bracket.

8. Remove the converter attaching bolts.

9. Support the transmission with a jack or a transmission dolly and holding fixture.

10. Remove the rear crossmember.

11. Disconnect the exhaust pipe brackets and remove the speedometer cable from the case.

12. Remove the filler pipe.

13. Install a wooden block between the engine and firewall; lower the jack until the engine contacts the block.

14. Make sure no tension is put on the battery cable.

15. Disconnect all electrical wiring at the transmission case.

16. Disconnect the starter cable and remove the starter.

17. Remove the converter housing bolts.

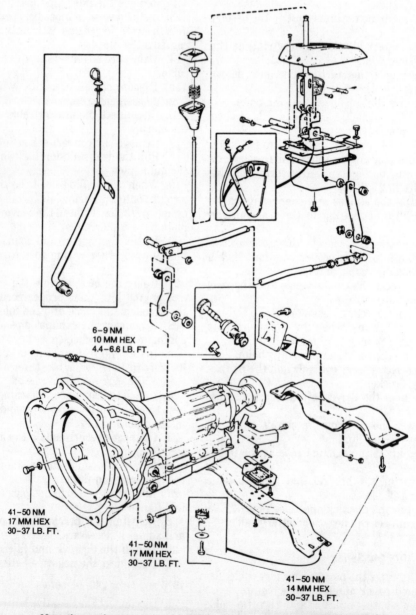

6–9 NM
10 MM HEX
4.4–6.6 LB. FT.

41–50 NM
17 MM HEX
30–37 LB. FT.

41–50 NM
17 MM HEX
30–37 LB. FT.

41–50 NM
14 MM HEX
30–37 LB. FT.

Mounting and components for BW55, AW55—AW70 and AW71 similar

18. Pull the transmission backwards to clear the guide pins.

19. When reinstalling, load the transmission straight onto the engine and install the converter housing bolts. Tighten the converter-to-drive plate bolts to 35 ft. lbs.

20. Install the starter and connect its cable; hook up all other wiring to the transmission case.

21. Using the jack, elevate the transmission and engine into their proper position. Install the speedometer cable and the filler pipe.

22. Reconnect the exhaust pipe and the rear engine mount brackets.

23. Install the rear crossmember and tighten its bolts to 18 ft. lbs. When the crossmember is secure, the jack may be removed.

24. Install the converter attaching bolts. Connect the selector lever controls and the pan reinforcing bracket.

25. Connect the driveshaft to the transmission flange.

26. Lower the car from its stands and refill the transmission fluid.

27. Reconnect the exhaust pipe at the manifold flange.

28. Reinstall the bracket and throttle cable and adjust if necessary.

29. Install the dipstick and filler pipe.

30. Reconnect the negative battery cable.

All 260, GL Series

1. Disconnect the negative battery cable and remove the air cleaner.

2. Disconnect the throttle cable.

3. Remove the two upper converter housing bolts.

4. Remove the filler pipe.

5. Raise the vehicle, support it front and rear

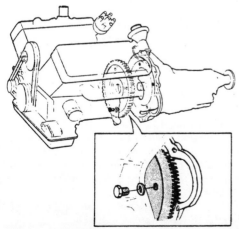

Access to coupling flange bolts on AW/BW 55 and AW 70/71 transmissions

with jackstands and drain the transmission oil into a clean container.

6. Remove the splash shield (8 bolts).

7. Disconnect the front muffler from the rubber hanger.

8. Disconnect the driveshaft from the transmission flange.

9. Remove the exhaust pipe brackets at the rear of the transmission.

10. Remove the rear crossmember.

11. Remove the rear engine support and exhaust pipe bracket.

12. Remove the speedometer cable.

13. Disconnect the cooler lines at the transmission.

14. Remove the electrical connections from the transmission.

15. Remove neutral start switch, if mounted on the case.

16. Remove shift control rod.

17. Remove the engine-to-transmission cover plate.

18. Remove the starter motor and cover.

19. Remove the converter-to-drive plate bolts.

20. Position a jack or a transmission dolly with holding fixture under transmission.

21. Remove the two lower converter housing bolts.

22. Pull the transmission back and down to clear the guide pins.

23. When reinstalling , support the transmission on the jack and position at the rear of the engine. Attach the transmission and install and tighten the starter and bolts.

24. Connect the oil filler pipe at the lower end but do NOT tighten the nut yet.

25. Install the upper retaining bolts for the case and tighten them to 35 ft. lbs. Install the bracket and nuts for the oil filler pipe.

26. Now tighten the lower nut for the oil pipe. Correct torque is 60–70 ft. lbs.

27. Attach the converter to drive plate bolts and torque them to 35 ft. lbs.

28. Install the cover plate for the alternate starter position. Install the lower cover plate and tighten the bolts only to 5–6 ft. lbs.

29. Move the gear selector into position 2 (second form the front) and attach the front end of the control rod.

30. Attach the rear end of the control rod. Rough adjustments may be done by turning the entire assembly; fine adjustments are done only by turning the serrated sleeve. Maximum visible thread is 1⅛ in. or 29mm.

31. Check the control rod adjustment. The freeplay from D to its forward stop should be the same as from 2 to its rearward stop. Adjust linkage as necessary to establish this freeplay.

32. Install the neutral safety switch if it is mounted in the case.

33. Install the oil cooler pipes.

34. Attach the driveshaft to the drive flange on the transmission.

35. Install the exhaust pipe bracket, the rear engine mount and the speedometer cable.

36. Install the transmission crossmember and tighten its bolts to 35 ft. lbs.

37. Install and tighten the exhaust pipe clamps and the rubber muffler hanger.

38. Install the splash guard under the engine.

39. Attach the throttle cable to the bracket and adjust as necessary. Check the full throttle adjustment; the pulley should touch the stop with the accelerator pedal floored. Adjust the transmission cable as outlined previously in this chapter.

40. Install the air cleaner, fill the transmission with the correct amount of fluid and lower the car to the ground.

700 Series

1. Place the gear selector in the **P** position; if equipped with ZF 22, place selector in **N**.

2. Disconnect the kickdown cable at the throttle pulley on the engine. Disconnect the battery ground cable.

3. Disconnect the oil filler tube at the oil pan, and drain the transmission oil.

CAUTION: *The oil will be scalding hot if the car was recently driven.*

4. Disconnect the control rod at the transmission lever, and disconnect the reaction rod at the transmission housing.

5. On the AW 71 transmission, disconnect the wire at the solenoid (slightly to the rear of the transmission-to-driveshaft flange).

6. Matchmark the transmission-to-driveshaft flange and unbolt the driveshaft.

7. Place a jack or transmission dolly under the transmission and support the unit. Remem-

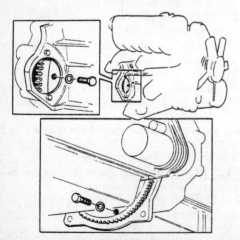

Access to coupling flange bolts on ZF 22 transmission. D24 and D24T engines shown above; B23 and B230 below

ber that the transmission will be heavier at the front end than the rear. Remove the transmission crossmember assembly.

8. Disconnect the exhaust pipe at the joint and remove the exhaust pipe bracket from the exhaust pipe. Remove the rear engine mount with the exhaust pipe bracket.

9. On D24T models, remove the starter motor. On B28F V6 models, remove the bolts retaining the starter motor.

10. Remove the cover for the alternate starter motor location on B28F models. Remove the cover plate at the torque coverter housing bottom on B28F models.

11. Disconnect the oil cooler lines at the transmission.

12. Remove the two upper bolts at the torque converter cover. Remove the oil filler tube.

NOTE: *It is helpful to have another person steadying and guiding the transmission during the removal process.*

14. Remove the two lower bellhousing screws.

15. Remove the screws retaining the torque converter to the drive plate. Pry the torque converter back from the drive plate with a small pry bar.

16. Slowly lower the transmission as you pull it back to clear the input shaft. Do not tilt the transmission forward, or the torque converter may slide off.

17. When reinstalling, install the two lower bolts in the casing as soon as the transmission is in place. For B28 motors, adjust the panel between the starter motor and torque converter casing and install the bolts for the starter.

18. Mount the oil filler tube at the oil pan but do not tighten the nut.

19. Install the tube bracket and the two upper bolts in the converter casing. Now tighten the nut for the oil tube to 65 ft. lbs.

19. Install the bolts for the coupling flange; tighten the bolts hand-tight first, then tighten in a criss-cross pattern to 32 ft. lbs.

20. Reinstall the rear engine mount with the exhaust pipe bracket and reconnect the exhaust system.

21. Reinstall the transmission crossmember; when it is securely bolted in place, the supporting jack may be removed.

22. Reinstall the driveshaft.

23. Making sure that both the transmission linkage and the shift selector in the car are in the PARK position (NEUTRAL for ZF 22 transmission), attach the actuator rod and the reaction rod. Adjust the shift linkage as necessary.

24. On AW71 models, install and connect the wiring to the solenoid valve.

25. Connect the kickdown cable at the throttle pulley. Adjust the cable if necessary.

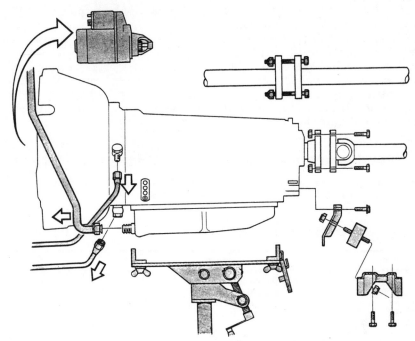

Removal of external parts on ZF 22 transmission

26. Fill the transmission with oil. Attach the negative battery cable.

DRIVELINE

The driveshaft is a two-piece tubular unit, connected by an intermediate universal joint. The rear end of the front section of the driveshaft contains a splined sleeve. A splined shaft forming one of the yokes for the intermediate U-joint fits into this sleeve.

The front section is supported by a bearing contained in an insulated rubber housing attached to the bottom of the driveshaft tunnel. The front section is connected to the transmission flange, and the rear section is connected to the differential housing flange by universal joints.

Each joint consists of a spider with four ground trunnions carried in the flange yokes by needle bearings.

Driveshaft and Universal Joints
REMOVAL AND INSTALLATION

1. Jack up the vehicle and install safety stands.
2. Mark the relative positions of the driveshaft yokes on the transmission and differential housing flanges for purposes of assembly.

Remove the nuts and bolts which retain the front and rear driveshaft sections to the transmission and differential housing flanges.

Remove the support bearing housing from the driveshaft tunnel, and lower the driveshaft and universal joint assembly as a unit.

3. Pry up the lock washer and remove the support bearing retaining nut. Pull off the rear section of the drivshaft with the intermediate universal joint and splined shaft of the front section. The support bearing may now be pressed off from the driveshaft.

4. Remove the support bearing from its housing.

5. For removal of the universal joints from the driveshaft, consult Universal Joint Overhaul.

6. Inspect the driveshaft sections for straightness. Using a dial indicator, or rolling the shafts along a flat surface, make sure that

Universal joint

the driveshaft out-of-round does not exceed 0.010 in. (0.25mm). Do not attempt to straighten a damaged shaft. Any shaft exceeding 0.010 in. (0.25mm) out-of-round will cause substantial vibration, and must be replaced. Also, inspect the support bearing by pressing the races against each other by hand, and turning them in opposite directions. If the bearing binds at any point, it must be discarded and replaced.

7. Install the support bearing into its housing.

8. Press the support bearing and housing onto the front driveshaft section. Push the splined shaft of the rear section (with the intermediate universal joint and rear driveshaft section) into the splined sleeve of the front section. Install the retaining nut and lock washer for the support bearing.

Troubleshooting Basic Driveshaft and Rear Axle Problems

When abnormal vibrations or noises are detected in the driveshaft area, this chart can be used to help diagnose possible causes. Remember that other components such as wheels, tires, rear axle and suspension can also produce similar conditions.

BASIC DRIVESHAFT PROBLEMS

Problem	Cause	Solution
Shudder as car accelerates from stop or low speed	• Loose U-joint • Defective center bearing	• Replace U-joint • Replace center bearing
Loud clunk in driveshaft when shifting gears	• Worn U-joints	• Replace U-joints
Roughness or vibration at any speed	• Out-of-balance, bent or dented driveshaft • Worn U-joints • U-joint clamp bolts loose	• Balance or replace driveshaft • Replace U-joints • Tighten U-joint clamp bolts
Squeaking noise at low speeds	• Lack of U-joint lubrication	• Lubricate U-joint; if problem persists, replace U-joint
Knock or clicking noise	• U-joint or driveshaft hitting frame tunnel • Worn CV joint	• Correct overloaded condition • Replace CV joint

BASIC REAR AXLE PROBLEMS

First, determine when the noise is most noticeable.

Drive Noise: Produced under vehicle acceleration.

Coast Noise: Produced while the car coasts with a closed throttle.

Float Noise: Occurs while maintaining constant car speed (just enough to keep speed constant) on a level road.

Road Noise

Brick or rough surfaced concrete roads produce noises that seem to come from the rear axle. Road noise is usually identical in Drive or Coast and driving on a different type of road will tell whether the road is the problem.

Tire Noise

Tire noises are often mistaken for rear axle problems. Snow treads or unevenly worn tires produce vibrations seeming to originate elsewhere. **Temporarily** inflating the tires to 40 lbs will significantly alter tire noise, but will have no effect on rear axle noises (which normally cease below about 30 mph).

Engine/Transmission Noise

Determine at what speed the noise is most pronounced, then stop the car in a quiet place. With the transmission in Neutral, run the engine through speeds corresponding to road speeds where the noise was noticed. Noises produced with the car standing still are coming from the engine or transmission.

Front Wheel Bearings

While holding the car speed steady, lightly apply the footbrake; this will often decease bearing noise, as some of the load is taken from the bearing.

Rear Axle Noises

Eliminating other possible sources can narrow the cause to the rear axle, which normally produces noise from worn gears or bearings. Gear noises tend to peak in a narrow speed range, while bearing noises will usually vary in pitch with engine speeds.

NOISE DIAGNOSIS

The Noise Is	Most Probably Produced By
• Identical under Drive or Coast	• Road surface, tires or front wheel bearings
• Different depending on road surface	• Road surface or tires
• Lower as the car speed is lowered	• Tires
• Similar with car standing or moving	• Engine or transmission
• A vibration	• Unbalanced tires, rear wheel bearing, unbalanced driveshaft or worn U-joint
• A knock or click about every 2 tire revolutions	• Rear wheel bearing
• Most pronounced on turns	• Damaged differential gears
• A steady low-pitched whirring or scraping, starting at low speeds	• Damaged or worn pinion bearing
• A chattering vibration on turns	• Wrong differential lubricant or worn clutch plates (limited slip rear axle)
• Noticed only in Drive, Coast or Float conditions	• Worn ring gear and/or pinion gear

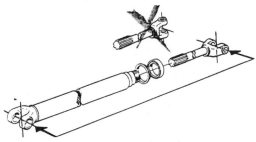

Correct relative placement of yokes is essential to eliminating driveline vibrations

NOTE: *Pay particular attention to the placement of the yokes at the end of the shaft. They must be in the same alignment front and rear or driveline vibration will be induced.*

9. Taking note of the alignment marks made prior to removal, position the driveshaft and universal joint assembly to its flange and install but do not tighten its retaining nuts and bolts.

Position the support bearing housing to the driveshaft tunnel and install the retaining nut. Tighten the nuts which retain the driveshaft sections to the transmission and differential housing flanges to a torque of 25–30 ft. lbs.

10. Remove the safety stands and lower the vehicle. Road test the car and check for driveline vibrations.

UNIVERSAL JOINT OVERHAUL

1. Remove the driveshaft and universal joint assembly as outlined above.
2. Clean off the dirt from the surrounding area and remove the snaprings, which secure the needle bearings in the yokes, with a snapring pliers. If the rings are difficult to loos-

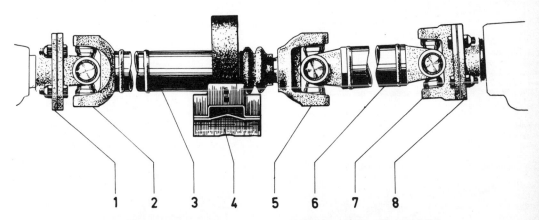

1. Flange on transmission
2. Front universal joint
3. Front section of propeller shaft
4. Support bearing
5. Intermediate universal joint
6. Rear propeller shaft
7. Rear universal joint
8. Flange on rear axle

Typical drive shaft

en, apply rust penetrant and tap the ring lightly with a hammer and punch.

3. Lightly mount the shaft in a vise and adjust its position so that the yoke is supported by the jaws. If at all possible, do not tighten the vise onto the tubular shaft; it can be easily deformed.

4. Using a plastic mallet, tap on the shaft flange until the bearing cup(s) protrude about 0.2 in. (5mm). Do not tap on the tubular shaft.

5. Leaving the flange clamped in the vise, lift the driveshaft and insert a piece of wood or a hammer handle under the shaft. Gently press down on the driveshaft; this will lever the bearing cap upwards.

Once all are removed, clean the seats in the driveshaft and flange. Clean the spider and needle bearings completely. Check the contact surfaces for wear. Replace any worn or broken parts. If the old needle bearings and spider are to be reused, fill them with molybdenum disulfide chassis grease, and make sure that the rubber seals are not damaged. If new needle bearings are used, fill them half-way with the grease.

6. Remove the bearing caps and seals from the new spider. Make sure that the needle bearings and seals are in place within the cups.

7. Position the spider into the flange yoke.

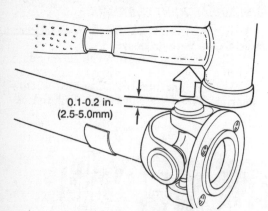

Gently tap the flange to raise the bearing cup

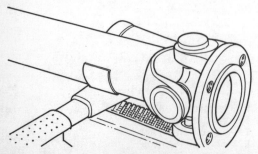

Press down on the shaft when supported from underneath to further free bearing cups

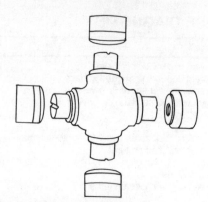

Make sure the needle bearings are in place inside the cups before installation

Place one of the bearing cups on the spider and tap the cup until it is firmly seated.

8. Using the vise and a sleeve of proper size, press the cup into place in the yoke. The cup should project through the yoke about 0.1–0.2 in. (2.5–5.0mm). Install the snapring (circlip). Make sure the spider is centered within the yoke.

9. Repeat the previous pressing operation on the opposite side of the flange yoke. Note that when the second bearing cup is pressed into place, the first bearing cup is pressed against its snapring.

10. Fit the spider into the driveshaft yoke. Place and press each bearing cup into place following the procedures above.

11. Release the assembly from the vise. Check the new joint for free motion in all dimensions. If any stiffness or binding is present, remount the assembly in the vise (as described previously) and LIGHTLY tap the spider ends with a plastic mallet.

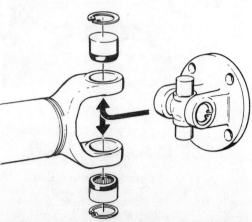

Positioning the flange and new joint into the driveshaft

Center Bearing

REMOVAL AND INSTALLATION

The center support bearing must rotate freely with no noise or binding. It not a serviceable component; if it is noisy or binds it must be replaced. Use of a press with the appropriate blocks and sleeves is required for replacement.

1800 and 140/160 Series

1. Remove the driveshaft as outlined previously.
2. Separate the front and rear shafts and loosen the cover for the support bearing. Remove the complete bearing.
3. Using a press if necessary, remove the bearing from the rubber housing. Before installing the new bearing, make sure all seating surfaces are clean.
4. Install the new bearing into the rubber mount and reassemble the shaft into the bearing.

200 Series

1. Remove the front driveshaft and center bearing assembly as outlined above.
2. Press the bearing out of the rubber mount. The bearing will stay attached to the driveshaft.
3. Using a drift or a press if necessary, remove the bearing from the driveshaft. Take care not to damage the dust cover around the bearing.
4. Install the new bearing by pressing it onto the shaft. Install the rubber mount. Observe correct placement of the bearing within the mount.
5. Reassemble the driveshaft halves. If the splines are dry, lightly coat them with grease.

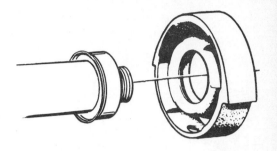
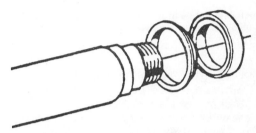

Disassembly of the center bearing and dust cover, 200 Series

6. When reinstalling the driveshaft and central bearing in the car, check that the spring and washer are positioned correctly in the rubber mount. Also make sure that the bearing is centered in its mounts before final tightening.

700 Series

1. Remove the front driveshaft section as outlined above.
2. Remove the protective rubber boot and, using a sleeve of suitable size, mount the shaft in a press and remove the shaft from the bearing assembly.
3. Remove the bearing from the "cage" by using the press and a sleeve.

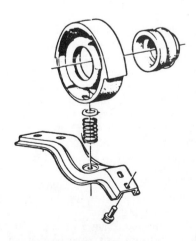

Drive shaft center bearing

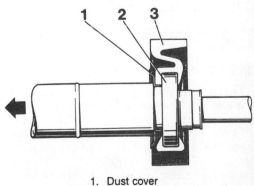

1. Dust cover
2. Bearing
3. Rubber mount

Install the bearing correctly in the rubber mount

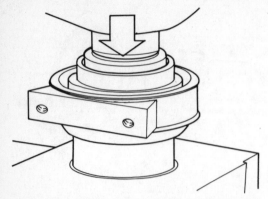

Installing the bearing into the cage on 700 Series. Volvo tools shown above and below bearing

WARNING: *There are five different types of bearings used on 1980 through 1984 Volvos. When buying the new bearing, have the old one along for comparison and make sure the replacement is identical in every respect.*

4. Install the new bearing into the cage. Support the cage as necessary and use a drift when pressing the bearing into place.

5. Tap the protective ring (dust cover) onto the driveshaft, then use the press as needed to install the bearing assembly onto the shaft. Install the rear dust cover, tapping it evenly so that it seats straight.

6. Check the bearing for free motion, silent operation and lack of binding.

7. Install the rubber boot on the back part of the bearing. Lubricate it with a light coat of petroleum jelly. Make sure the boot is properly held in place.

8. Making sure that the yokes are placed in identical positions, reassemble the front and rear driveshaft halves. Install the small rubber boot (if any) on the rear driveshaft section.

9. Reinstall the driveshaft as outlined previously.

REAR AXLE

Understanding Rear Axles

The rear axle is a special type of transmission that reduces the speed of the drive from the engine and transmission and divides the power to the rear wheels. Power enters the rear axle from the driveshaft via the companion flange. The flange is mounted on the drive pinion shaft. The drive pinion shaft and gear which carry the power into the differential turn at engine speed. The gear on the end of the pinion shaft drives a large ring gear the axis of rotation of which is 90° away from the of the pinion. The

pinion and gear reduce the gear ratio of the axle, and change the direction of rotation to turn the axle shafts which drive both wheels. The rear axle gear ratio is found by dividing the number of pinion gear teeth into the number of ring gear teeth.

The ring gear drives the differential case. The case provides the two mounting points for the ends of a pinion shaft on which are mounted two pinion gears. The pinion gears drive the two side gears, one of which is located on the inner end of each axle shaft.

By driving the axle shafts through the arrangement, the differential allows the outer drive wheel to turn faster than the inner drive wheel in a turn.

The main drive pinion and the side bearings, which bear the weight of the differential case, are shimmed to provide proper bearing preload, and to position the pinion and ring gears properly.

NOTE: *The proper adjustment of the relationship of the ring and pinion gears is critical. It should be attempted only by those with extensive equipment and/or experience.*

Limited-slip differentials include clutches which tend to link each axle shaft to the differential case. Clutches may be engaged either by spring action or by pressure produced by the torque on the axles during a turn. During turning on a dry pavement, the effects of the clutches are overcome, and each wheel turns at the required speed. When slippage occurs at either wheel, however, the clutches will transmit some of the power to the wheel which has the greater amount of traction. Because of the presence of clutches, limited-slip units require a special lubricant.

Determining Axle Ratio

The drive axle is said to have a certain axle ratio. This number (usually a whole number and a decimal fraction) is actually a comparison of the number of gear teeth on the ring gear and the pinion gear. For example, a 4.11 rear means that theoretically, there are 4.11 teeth on the ring gear and one tooth on the pinion gear or, put another way, the driveshaft must turn 4.11 times to turn the wheels once. Actually, on a 4.11 rear, there might be 37 teeth on the ring gear and 9 teeth on the pinion gear. By dividing the number of teeth on the pinion gear into the number of teeth on the ring gear, the numerical axle ratio (4.11) is obtained. This also provides a good method of ascertaining exactly what axle ratio one is dealing with.

Another method of determining gear ratio is to jack up and support the car so that both rear wheels are off the ground. Make a chalk mark

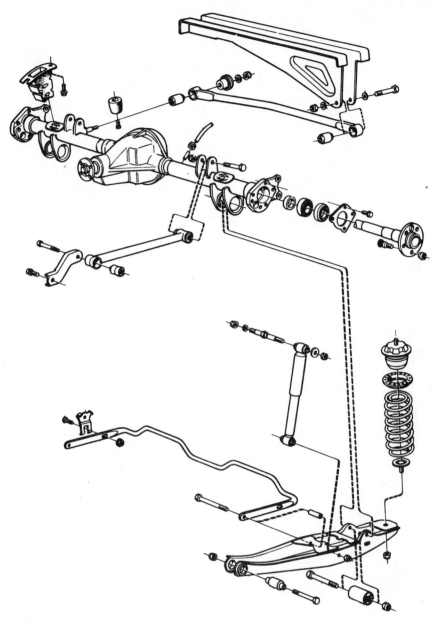

Rear suspension—240, 260 series

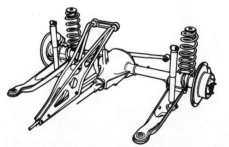

760GLE series rear axle. Sub-frame is a ladder-like assembly above the differential

on the rear wheel and the driveshaft. Put the transmission in neutral. Turn the rear wheel one complete turn and count the number of turns that the driveshaft makes. The number of turns that the driveshaft makes in one complete revolution of the rear wheel is an approximation of the rear axle ratio.

All 1970–87 Volvos use a solid rear axle housing carried in two support arms. Two torque rods, connected between the axle shaft tubes and the body, limit the rear axle wind-up. A track bar (Panhard rod) controls lateral move-

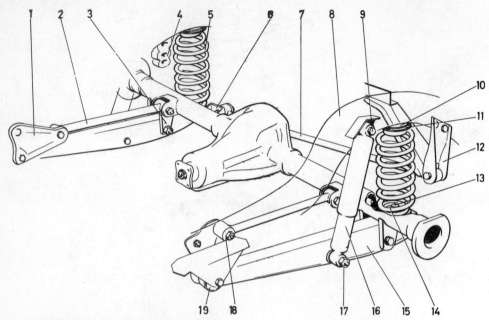

1. Bracket
2. Support stay
3. Bracket
4. Rubber buffer
5. Rear spring
6. Bracket
7. Track bar

8. Rear side-member
9. Shock absorber upper attachment
10. Washer
11. Rubber spacer
12. Bracket
13. Screw, lower spring attachment

14. Washer
15. Support arm
16. Shock absorber
17. Shock absorber lower attachment
18. Front support stay attachment
19. Front bushing support arm

Rear suspension assembly—140 series, 164

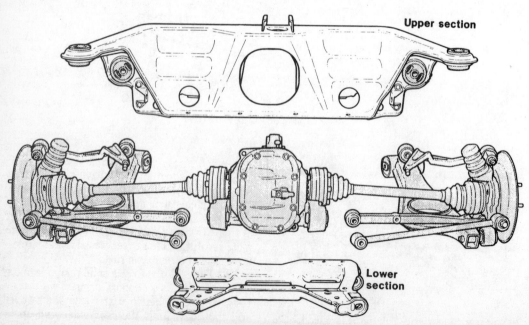

Upper section

Lower section

Volvo Multi-Link Suspension

ment of the axle housing. The 760GLE also incorporates a triagulated dual-ladder sub-frame to connect the axle unit to the unibody.

In 1988, the 760 4 door sedan and the 780 model introduced Volvo's Multi-Link suspension system. This independently suspends each rear wheel, allowing improved ride and roadholding as well as allowing each rear wheel to be aligned separately.

Final drive is of the hypoid design, with the drive pinion lying below the ring gear. On the solid axle models, each axle shaft is indexed into a splined sleeve for the differential side gears, and supported at its outer end in a tapered roller bearing. Bearing clearance is not adjustable by use of shims as on earlier model Volvos, but instead is determined by bearing thickness. Both sides of the axle bearings are protected by oil seals.

On vehicles with the Multi-Link suspension, the axles are actually halfshafts, bolted to the differential. Each halfshaft has a constant velocity (CV) joint at each end, allowing a full range of motion as the car passes over bumps and depressions.

Some special 1976 and later models are equipped with limited slip differentials for better traction.

The identification plate showing the final drive ratio, the part number and the serial number of the differential can be found on a plate attached to the axle tube or the housing.

Determining Gear Ratio

Determining the axle ratio of any given axle can be a very useful tool to the contemporary car owner. Axle ratios are a major factor in a vehicle's fuel mileage, so the car buyer of today should know both what he or she is looking for, and what the salesperson is talking about. Knowledge of axle ratios is also valuable to the owner/mechanic who is shopping through salvage yards for a used axle, or who is changing ratios by changing rear axles.

The rear axle is said to have a certain ratio, say 4.11. It is called a "4.11 rear" although the 4.11 actually means 4.11 to 1 (4.11:1). This means that the driveshaft will turn 4.11 times for every turn of the rear wheels.

The number 4.11 is determined by dividing the number of teeth on the pinion gear into the number of teeth on the ring gear. In the case of a 4.11 rear, there could be 9 teeth on the pinion and 37 teeth on the ring gear (37 divided by 9 = 4.11). Counting the teeth provides a sure way, although troublesome, of determining the ratio for your car. The axle must be drained and the rear cover removed to do this, and then the teeth counted.

A much easier method is to jack up the car and safely support it with jackstands, so BOTH rear wheels are off the ground. Block the front wheels and put the transmission in NEUTRAL. Make a chalk mark on the rear wheel and one on the driveshaft. Turn the rear wheel exactly one revolution and count the number of turns that the driveshaft makes. (Having an assistant to count one or the other is extremely helpful). The number of turns the driveshaft makes in one complete revolution of the rear wheel is a close approximation of the rear axle ratio.

Axle Shaft, Bearing and Oil Seal
REMOVAL AND INSTALLATION

CAUTION: *This procedure requires removal of the rear brake pads or shoes. Brake pads and shoes contain asbestos, which has been determined to a cancer causing agent. Never clean the brake surfaces with compressed air! Avoid inhaling and dust from brake surfaces! When cleaning brakes, use commercially available brake cleaning fluids.*

All Except Multi-Link Suspension

1. Raise the vehicle and support it on jackstands.
2. Remove the applicable wheel.
3. If equipped with drum brakes, remove the shoes, springs and hardware. If equipped with disc brakes:

   a. On models through 1975, place a wooden block beneath the brake pedal, plug the master cylinder reservoir vent hole, then remove and plug the brake line from the caliper. Be careful not to allow any brake fluid to spill onto the disc or pads. Remove the two bolts which retain the brake caliper to the axle housing, and lift off the caliper. Lift off the brake disc.

   b. On 1976 and later models, detach the brake line and bracket from the rear axle, then remove the mounting bolts and remove the caliper. Use a piece of stiff wire to hang the caliper, with brake line still attached, out of the way. Do not allow the caliper to hang by the brake line. Release the parking brake shoes as explained in Chapter 9.

4. On all models, remove the thrust washer bolts through the holes in the axle shaft flange. Using a puller (slide hammer), remove the axle shaft, bearing and oil seal assembly. If a slide hammer is not available, the brake disc may be bolted onto the axle backwards (remember to mount the nuts tapered side out) and used to pull the axle free.

5. Remove the inner oil seal (1974-on) with a suitable puller or small prybar.

6. Using a press, remove the axle shaft bear-

Remove the axle shaft with a slide hammer

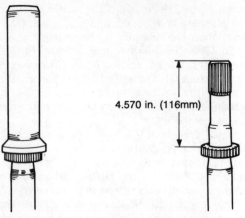

4.570 in. (116mm)

Placement of gear is critical. If at all possible, use Volvo tool shown (No. 2412) or exact substitute

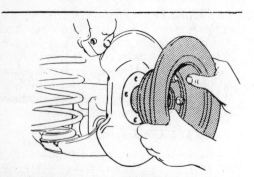

Alternate methods of removing the axles

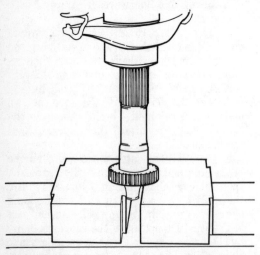

Removing the sender wheel from the axle of certain 700 Series

ing and its locking ring from the axle shaft. Remove and discard the old oil seal.

NOTE: *Some 700 series axles contain a toothed wheel used for sending speed data to the engine and other systems. This wheel must be removed in a press before removing the axle bearing and seal.*

7. The new bearing must be packed with grease before installation. The preferred method is with a bearing packer (a low cost tool available at most automotive supply shops) but it may be done by hand if necessary. The bearing must be packed from one side until the grease comes out the other side.

It is very important that the bearing be completely packed with grease before installation.

8. Fill the space between the lips of the new oil seal with wheel bearing grease. Position the new seal on the axle shaft. Using a press, install the bearing with a new locking ring, onto the axle shaft.

WARNING: *When reinstalling the additional toothed gear on axles for 700 series, the gear must be installed precisely 116mm onto the shaft. The acceptable margin is ± 0.1mm. If at all possible, use Volvo tool 2412 which will allow precise location of this gear. If this gear is not properly located, the car may not run properly.*

9. Install the inner oil seal (1974-on) in the axle shaft housing using a seal installation tool (such as Volvo 5009 or similar) and drift.

10. Install the axle shaft into the housing, rotating it so that it aligns with the differential. Install the bolts for the thrust washer and tighten to 36 ft. lbs.

11. Install the brake disc, caliper and pads. If equipped with drum brakes, reinstall the shoes, springs and hardware.

12. Install the wheel and lower the car to the ground. Retighten the lug nuts with the car on the ground.

Vehicles with Multi-Link Suspension

Because of the nature of the Multi-Link suspension, component position and bolt tightening values (torque) are critical to ride quality and rear wheel alignment. When installing components, exact location must be achieved--

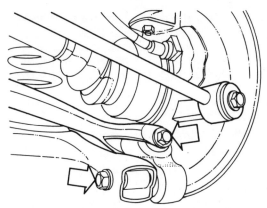

Upper arrow shows bolt for support arm. Lower link bolt shown by lower arrow

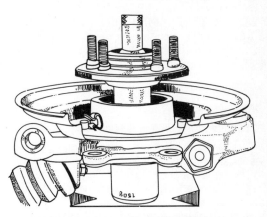

Use correct tools when installing the hub. Volvo tools shown above and below the hub

close doesn't count. Tightening specifications must be followed exactly or component function will be impaired.

WARNING: *The use of the correct special tools or their equivalent is REQUIRED for this procedure.*

1. Safely elevate the car on jackstands. Make sure the rear stands don't interfere with any of the suspension arms.

2. Remove the wheel on the appropriate side. Remove the brake caliper mounting bolts and use a piece of wire to hang the caliper out of the way.

3. Mark the position of the brake disc relative to its small locating pin, then remove the disc. Remove the brake shoes.

4. Disconnect and remove the handbrake cable from the wheelbearing housing.

5. Remove the retaining bolt for the support arm at the housing. Tap the support arm loose.

6. Remove the nut and bolt holding the lower link arm to the housing.

7. Remove the retaining bolt for the track rod (Panhard rod) at the bearing housing and use a small claw-type puller to remove the track rod.

8. Loosen and remove the large nut holding the end of the driveshaft within the bearing housing.

9. Remove the retaining nut for the upper link at the bearing housing. The wheel bearing housing can now be removed as a unit.

NOTE: *There are shims between the bearing housing and the upper link arm. Collect them when the housing is removed.*

10. Mount the housing assembly in a vise. Using Volvo tool 5340 or similar, apply a counterhold between the hub and bearing housing. Press out the hub with a proper sized drift.

11. With the hub removed, the circlip holding the bearing in the housing can be removed. Press the bearing out of the housing.

12. Use a bearing puller (such as Volvo 2722 or similar) and a counterhold (Volvo 5310 or similar) to pull the inner ring off the hub.

13. To reinstall, press in the new bearing using a drift and counterhold and install the circlip.

14. Using a counterhold below the inner ring, press the hub into place.

WARNING: *If the counterhold (support) is not used, the wheel bearing will be destroyed during the hub installation.*

15. Install the wheel bearing housing onto the driveshaft and install the driveshaft retaining nut. Get the nut secure but don't try to torque it--that will be done later.

16. Install the shims between the upper link and the wheel bearing housing and then install the retaining nut at the upper link.

17. Pull the wheel bearing housing outwards at the top and tighten the upper link arm nut to 85 ft. lbs. This pulling out is essential to insure correct wheel alignment when completed.

18. Tilt the bearing housing outwards at the bottom (as necessary) to refit the lower link arm and it retaining bolt. When in place, pull the bottom of the bearing housing inwards (towards the center of the car) and tighten the link arm to 36 ft.lbs. PLUS an additional 90° of rotation.

19. Install the support arm and its bolt. Tighten the nut to 44 ft. lbs. PLUS an additional 90° of rotation.

20. Install the track rod (Panhard rod) and tighten to 63 ft. lbs.

21. Reinstall the handbrake cable at the bearing housing.

22. Reinstall the brake shoes, the brake disc as marked and the brake caliper. Tighten the caliper mounting bolts to 44 ft. lbs.

23. Install the wheel, tightening the lugs to 60–62 ft. lbs. Lower the car to the ground.

24. Tighten the driveshaft nut to 103 ft.lbs PLUS 60° of rotation.

Halfshafts

REMOVAL AND INSTALLATION

700 Series with Multi-link Suspension

1. Loosen the lug nuts for the appropriate wheel. Loosen the large halfshaft retaining nut in the center of the wheel bearing housing.

2. Block the front wheels and safely elevate and support the rear of the car.

3. Remove the wheel and remove the halfshaft retaining nut.

4. At the center of the car, remove the eight bolts holding the upper and lower sections of the final drive housing.

5. Remove the bolts holding the halfshaft to the final drive unit (differential) and remove the shaft from the wheelbearing housing.

6. When the shaft is removed, inspect the rubber boots for any sign of splitting or cracking. The boots must be intact and waterproof or the joint within is at risk. A light coat of silicone or vinyl protectant applied to a CV boot will extend its life.

7. When reinstalling, fit the threaded end (at the wheel) first, then position and secure the inboard end. Always use new, lightly oiled bolts and tighten them to 70 ft. lbs.

8. Reinstall the lower section of the final drive housing. Before tightening the eight mounting bolts, install two long 12mm bolts (or 2 12mm drifts) in the centering holes and align the panel. This is essential to insure correct wheel alignment when finished.

9. Tighten the eight mounting bolts to 52 ft. lbs. PLUS 30° of rotation.

10. Use a new, lightly oiled halfshaft retaining nut and install it on the threaded end of the shaft. Tighten it until it is snug but do not attempt to apply final tightening.

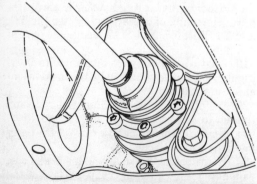

The halfshaft mounts to the final drive with six bolts

11. Install the wheel, tightening the lugs to 60–62 ft. lbs. Lower the car to the ground.

12. Apply the hand brake and tighten the halfshaft nut to 103 ft.lbs. PLUS 60° of rotation. Double check the wheel lugs for correct tightness.

Pinion Seal

REMOVAL AND INSTALLATION

All Except Multi-Link Suspension

1. Disconnect the driveshaft at the final drive unit (differential).

2. Loosen and remove the large center nut in the center of the pinion flange. The use of a counterhold device is highly recommended. (Volvo 5149 or similar)

3. Use a puller to remove the flange from the housing.

4. Remove the old seal from the inside of the casing and discard it. Prepare the new seal by greasing the lip area and greasing the small spring to hold it in place during installation.

5. Install the seal using suitable drivers; do not crimp or gouge the seal during installation.

6. With an installation tool (Volvo 5156 or similar), reinstall the flange in the housing.

7. Check the serial number on the rear axle. If it begins with an "S", follow step 7b, below. If it does NOT contain an S prefix, continue with 7a below.

    a. Install the center nut and tighten it to 145–180 ft. lbs. Use a counterhold to hold the flange while tightening.

    b. Axles denoted by the S prefix in their serial number contain a compression sleeve within the differential housing. On these cars, install the center nut and carefully tighten it to 1.3 ft. lbs.(finger tight only). Make sure that the brakes are not applied and turn the flange at about 1 revolution per second so as to tighten the nut.   As an alternative, the nut may be tightened with a wrench to at least 130 ft. lbs.

8. Reinstall the driveshaft. Check the oil level within the final drive and top up as necessary.

Vehicles with Multi-Link Suspension

1. Matchmark the driveshaft flange and the final drive (differential) flange. Remove the bolts and separate the shaft from the final drive.

2. Loosen and remove the large center nut in the center of the pinion flange. The use of a counterhold device is highly recommended. (Volvo 5149 or similar). Remove the one additonal bolt from the flange. This bolt is a weight which serves to balance the rotational forces of the driveshaft.

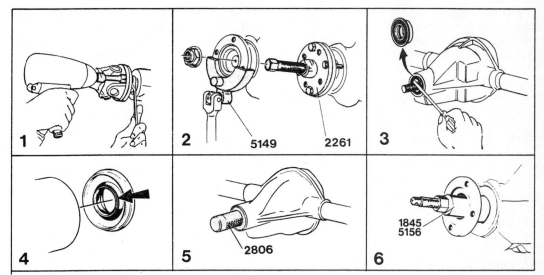

Removing and replacing pinion seal. Volvo tool numbers shown. Refer to text for complete procedure

3. Matchmark or etch reference marks on the flange and its center shaft.

4. Drain the oil from the housing.

5. Use a puller to remove the flange from the housing.

6. Remove the old seal from the inside of the casing and discard it. Prepare the new seal by greasing the lip area and greasing the small spring to hold it in place during installation. The use of a seal puller such as Volvo 5069 is highly recommended.

7. Install the seal using suitable drivers; do not crimp or gouge the seal during installation.

8. Position the flange so that the marks align. With an installation tool (Volvo 5156 or similar), reinstall the flange in the housing.

9. Install a new, lightly oiled center nut and tighten it to 132–145 ft. lbs.

WARNING: *Do not overtighten the center nut. The pinion bearings will become over-adjusted and fail prematurely.*

10. Install the bolt for weight in its original position.

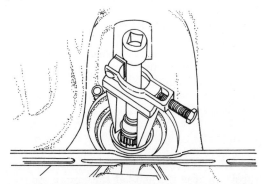

Use a bearing puller to withdraw the seal. Volvo tool 5069 shown

11. Install the driveshaft, observing correct placement as shown by the matchmarks. Use new nuts and bolts and tighten them to 36 ft. lbs.

12. Refill the final drive unit with oil.

Axle Housing — Complete Unit
REMOVAL AND INSTALLATION

WARNING: *This operation requires removal of a substantial amount of weight from the rear of the car. The vehicle may become front heavy; make sure that floorstands or lifting arms are properly positioned to support the vehicle with the rear axle removed.*

The use of an axle cradle or two floor jacks is required. Because of the size and weight of the axle assemble, it cannot be safely controlled and supported on a single jack.

1800 Series and 140/160 Series

1. Elevate the car and support it firmly with stands. Do not place the stands in the area of the axle or rear suspension. Locate the stands at the jack points on the body or on the frame. With the car elevated and securely supported, remove the rear wheels.

2. Using the jacks or cradle, elevate the rear axle slightly--just enough to take the tension off its upper mounts. Loosen and remove the upper attaching bolts for the shock absorbers.

3. Disconnect the handbrake cables from the levers and brackets on the backing plates.

4. Disconnect the driveshaft from the flange on the pinion.

5. Remove the brake pipe connector from the rear axle housing. Plug the open lines.

6. Loosen the front attaching bolts for the

support arms about one turn. Unscrew the rear bolts for the torque rods.

7. Remove the track rod (Panhard rod) from its mount on the rear axle case and remove the lower attaching bolts for the springs.

8. Lower the jacks or cradle until the support arms release from the springs. Loosen the bolts holding the rear axle to the support arms.

9. Lower the jacks or cradle and remove the axle assembly by pulling it forwards.

10. When reinstalling, position the unit on its jacks or cradle in place under the car. Loosely reconnect the bolts for the support arms and torque rods.

11. Elevate the axle assembly until the track rod mount on the axle is at the same height as the attachment on the body. Install the track rod and secure its bolts.

12. Install the attaching bolts for the springs. Tighten the nuts for the support arms and torque rods.

13. Remove the plugs and reinstall the brake lines and retainers to the axle housing. Carefully connect the lines.

14. Attach the driveshaft to the pinion flange.

15. Install the upper bolts for the shock absorbers. Reinstall the handbrake cables into the brackets and levers.

16. Double check all nut and bolt attachments. If all are secure and tightened, the jacks or cradle may be slowly lowered and removed from the area.

17. Bleed the brake system and adjust the handbrake.

18. Reinstall the rear wheels and lower the vehicle to the ground.

19. Tighten the wheel lugs to 70–100 ft. lbs.

240/260 Series

1. Elevate the car and support it firmly with stands. Do not place the stands in the area of the axle or rear suspension. Locate the stands at the jack points on the body or on the frame. With the car elevated and securely supported, remove the rear wheels.

2. Remove the rear axle vent hose and the brake line brackets. Do not loosen any brake lines; they will be left intact.

3. Remove the brake calipers and secure them to the upper spring mount with a piece of stiff wire.

4. Remove the brake discs and parking brake shoes.

5. Remove the thrust washer bolts through the holes in the axle shaft flange. Using a puller (slide hammer), remove the axle shaft, bearing and oil seal assembly. If a slide hammer is not available, the brake disc may be bolted onto the

axle backwards (remember to mount the nuts tapered side out) and used to pull the axle free.

6. Position the jacks or cradle below the rear axle so that the axle is supported but not elevated.

7. If the exhaust system runs under the axle housing, disconnect the first joint forward of the axle, disconnect any hangers or brackets behind the axle and remove the rear section of the exhaust system.

8. Disconnect the two reaction rods which run from the top of the axle housing to the bodywork.

9. Disconnect the panhard rod from the rear axle.

10. Loosen and remove the bolts attaching the driveshaft to the pinion flange.

11. Separate the handbrake cables from the rear axle.

12. Remove the bolts which hold the lower mount of the shock absorber. Then remove the adjacent bolt which holds the anti-roll bar (sway bar).

13. Loosen, but do not remove, the trailing arm bolts at the front of the trailing arm. Lower the jacks or cradle and allow the axle assemble to pivot downwards on the trailing arms. When clear of the car and well supported on the jacks or cradle, remove the trailing arm mounts at the axle housing. Remove the axle assembly from under the car.

14. When reinstalling, position the axle unit under the vehicle and attach the trailing arm mounts. Tighten the bolts only enough to hold and still allow motion.

15. Elevate the rear axle and align the springs to their upper mounts. Install the anti-roll bar bolts and the bolts for the lower shock absorber mounts

16. Attach the torque rods to their mounts and attach the Panhard rod to its mount. Tighten these bolts only enough to hold and still allow motion.

17. Replace the handbrake cable brackets.

18. Install the driveshaft to the pinion flange and secure the bolts.

19. If the rear exhaust section was removed, reinstall it.

20. Reinstall the axles in their housings and secure the thrust washer bolts.

21. Install the parking brake shoes, the brake discs and the brake calipers. Tighten the caliper mounting bolts to 42 ft. lbs.

22. Replace the wheels and lower the vehicle to the ground. Tighten the wheel lugs to 83 ft. lbs.

23. With the weight of the vehicle on the wheels, tighten the bolts at the torque rod-to-axle mount, the panhard rod-to-axle mount and the front mounts of the trailing arms.

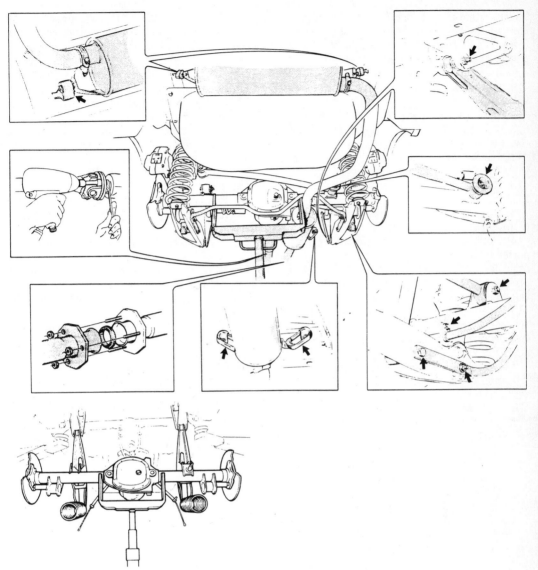

Points of reference for axle removal on 240 and 260 Series

740/760 Series without Multi-Link Suspension

1. Elevate the car and support it firmly with stands. Do not place the stands in the area of the axle or rear suspension. Locate the stands at the jack points on the body or on the frame. With the car elevated and securely supported, remove the rear wheels.

2. Remove the brake calipers and secure them to the upper spring mount with a piece of stiff wire.

3. Remove the brake discs and parking brake shoes. Disconnect the cables from the parking brake levers and remove the bolts for the pressure plate.

4. Remove the parking brake cable and the mounting brackets on the rear axle.

5. Position the jacks or cradle below the rear axle so that the axle is supported but not elevated.

6. Remove the thrust washer bolts through the holes in the axle shaft flange. Using a puller (slide hammer), remove the axle shaft, bearing and oil seal assembly. If a slide hammer is not available, the brake disc may be bolted onto the axle backwards (remember to mount the nuts tapered side out) and used to pull the axle free.

7. Disconnect the lower torque rod from the rear axle housing.

8. Raise the jacks or cradle slightly. If the ex-

haust system runs under the axle housing, disconnect the first joint forward of the axle, disconnect any hangers or brackets behind the axle and remove the rear section of the exhaust system.

9. Disconnect the Panhard rod from the rear axle.

10. Remove the connector for the speedometer transmitter and, if equipped, the connectors for the ETC system.

11. Loosen and remove the bolts attaching the driveshaft to the pinion flange.

12. Remove the upper torque rod from the rear axle.

13. Remove the bolts which hold the lower mount of the shock absorber.

14. Double check that the axle is firmly supported by the jacks or cradle. Remove the front brackets for the support arms. Pry the support arms loose from the front mounts and remove the rear axle assembly from under the car.

15. Once the axle assembly is clear of the car, remove the anti-roll bar (sway bar). Mark the support arms for the left and right sides and remove the arms from the axle housing.

When reinstalling, make sure the left and right markings are observed. Fit the bushings within the clamps and fit the clamps.

16. Tighten the clamps in a criss-cross pattern to 33 ft.lbs and reinstall the anti-roll bar if so equipped.

17. Position the axle on its jacks or cradle and elevate it so the support arms align with both their front mounts and the spring seats.

18. Install the front brackets for the support arms and tighten the two bolts to 35 ft. lbs. Tighten the nut to 62 ft. lbs.

19. Install the lower shock absorber bolts and tighten to 62 ft. lbs.

20. Reinstall the driveshaft to the pinion flange. Connect the wiring for the ETC sensor and/or the speedometer sensor.

21. Attach the Panhard rod to the axle and tighten it to 62 ft. lbs.

22. Reinstall the exhaust system as necessary. It will be helpful to elevate the axle to gain clearance.

23. Reinstall the upper torque rod but do not tighten it now.

24. Loosely fit the lower torque rod to its frame. If you loosen the frame to position the bolts, the frame must be tightened before the rod bolts are tightened.

25. Reinstall the parking brake cable to the brake levers. Check the boots at the backing plates.

26. Replace the axles.

27. Reinstall the parking brake shoes, the brake discs and the brake calipers. Tighten the caliper mounting bolts to 42 ft. lbs.

28. Install the rear wheels, remove the jacks or cradle and lower the car to the ground.

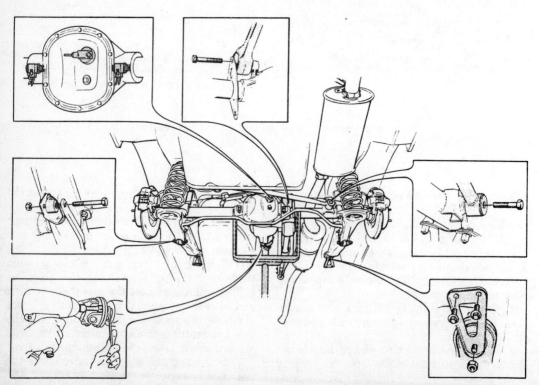

Points of reference for axle removal on 740/760 Series without Multi-Link suspension

29. With the weight of the car on the ground, tighten both torque rods (upper and lower) to 100 ft. lbs. If this is not done with the axle loaded, the bushings will turn when the axle moves up or down.

30. Adjust the parking brake cable. Check the oil level in the axle housing and top up as necessary.

760/780 with Multi-Link Suspension

Because of the nature of the Multi-Link suspension, component position and bolt tightening values (torque) are critical to ride quality and rear wheel alignment. When installing components, exact location must be achieved--close doesn't count. Tightening specifications must be followed exactly or component function will be impaired.

1. Elevate the car and support it firmly with stands. Do not place the stands in the area of the axle or rear suspension. Locate the stands at the jack points on the body or on the frame.

With the car elevated and securely supported, remove the rear wheels.

2. On one side only, remove the bolt holding the support arm to the wheel bearing housing. Drive out the support arm.

3. Remove the nut and bolt holding the lower link arm to the wheel bearing housing.

4. Remove the bolts holding the track rod (Panhard rod) to the wheel bearing housing. Use a puller and a long bolt to move the rod away from the housing.

5. Remove the eight bolts joining the upper and lower sections of the rear axle housing.

6. Swing the lower part of the wheel bearing housing outwards and swing down the lower part of the axle housing. It will still have the two arms attached to it and will be attached to the car by the arms on the opposite side.

7. Matchmark the flanges at the rear of the driveshaft. Remove the four bolts and lower the driveshaft.

8. Place a jack or cradle under the center of

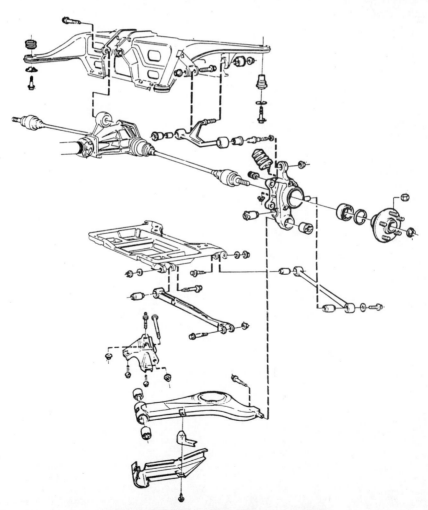

Detail of Multi-Link final drive components

the final drive (differential) unit. Elevate the jack and support the unit.

9. Remove the three bolts holding the final drive to the upper housing.

10. Lower the final drive slightly. Remove the wiring to the impulse sender.

11. Remove the bolts holding the axles to the final drive. Carefully lower the final drive unit and remove it from under the car.

12. When reinstalling, raise the final drive unit almost to its final position under the car and connect the impulse sender cable. Tighten the bolt to 7 ft. lbs.

13. Raise the unit to its final position and install the three bolts to the upper housing. Tighten the bolts to 117 ft. lbs. When the bolts are secure, the jack or cradle may be removed.

14. Attach the halfshafts to the final drive. Tighten the bolts to 22 ft. lbs. PLUS 90°of rotation.

15. Remount the driveshaft to the pinion flange, tightening the bolts to 36 ft. lbs. Remember to observe the matchmarks made earlier and position the driveshaft properly.

16. Raise the lower section of the axle housing. Loosely install the eight bolts which retain it to the upper housing. Before tightening the eight mounting bolts, install two long 12mm bolts (or 2 12mm drifts) in the centering holes and align the panel. This is essential to insure correct wheel alignment when finished.

17. Tighten the eight bolts to 52 ft. lbs. PLUS an additional 30° of rotation.

18. Position and install the lower link arm on the wheelbearing housing. Before tightening the nut and bolt, pull the housing in towards the center of the car. When all the play is out of the mount, tighten the link bolt to 36 ft.lbs PLUS 90° of rotation.

19. Reconnect the support arm and tighten its bolt to 44 ft. lbs. PLUS 90° of rotation.

20. Install the track rod and tighten to 62 ft. lbs.

21. Install the wheels and lower the car from its stands. Tighten the wheels to 62 ft. lbs. Check the oil level in the final drive and top up as necessary.

FRONT SUSPENSION

All 140 series, 164, and 1800 series model Volvos use a coil spring, independent front suspension incorporating upper and lower control arms bolted to each side of the rigid front frame member. The coil springs and telescopic double-acting shock absorbers are bolted to the lower control arms at the bottom and seat in the crossmember at the top. A pair of steering knuckles are carried in ball joints between the upper and lower control arms. A stabilizer bar is attached to the lower control arm and to the body.

All 200 series and later model Volvos use a coil spring independent front suspension with a pair of MacPherson type struts located between a sheet metal tower at the top and the lower control arm at the bottom.

The MacPherson strut design incorporates the coil spring, shock absorber and wheel spindle into a single assembly, eliminating the need for an upper control arm. The MacPherson strut design provides for generous vertical suspension travel allowing the use of softer springs. The strut design is, however, extremely sensitive to front wheel imbalance and the slightest imbalance often leads to front end wobble.

On the earlier cars with front struts, the caster angle of the front suspension is fixed and cannot be adjusted. (The angle is determined by the placement of the components; if the caster is found to be out of specification during an

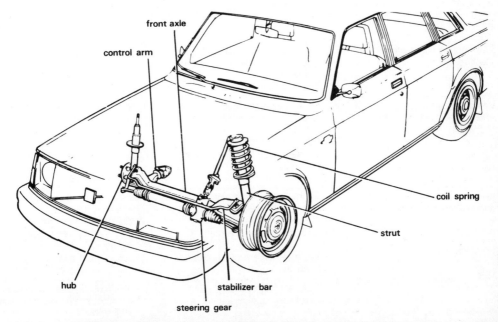

Component location, 200 and 700 Series with MacPherson suspension

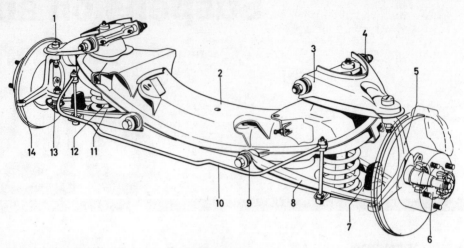

1. Upper ball joint
2. Front cross member
3. Upper control arm
4. Upper control arm bushing
5. Steering knuckle
6. Hub
7. Rubber buffer
8. Lower control arm
9. Lower control arm bushing
10. Stabilizer
11. Coil spring
12. Shock absorber
13. Lower ball joint
14. Steering arm

Front suspension assembly—140 series, 164 shown. 1800 series similar

Troubleshooting Basic Steering and Suspension Problems

Problem	Cause	Solution
Hard steering (steering wheel is hard to turn)	• Low or uneven tire pressure • Loose power steering pump drive belt • Low or incorrect power steering fluid • Incorrect front end alignment • Defective power steering pump • Bent or poorly lubricated front end parts	• Inflate tires to correct pressure • Adjust belt • Add fluid as necessary • Have front end alignment checked/adjusted • Check pump • Lubricate and/or replace defective parts
Loose steering (too much play in the steering wheel)	• Loose wheel bearings • Loose or worn steering linkage • Faulty shocks • Worn ball joints	• Adjust wheel bearings • Replace worn parts • Replace shocks • Replace ball joints
Car veers or wanders (car pulls to one side with hands off the steering wheel)	• Incorrect tire pressure • Improper front end alignment • Loose wheel bearings • Loose or bent front end components • Faulty shocks	• Inflate tires to correct pressure • Have front end alignment checked/adjusted • Adjust wheel bearings • Replace worn components • Replace shocks
Wheel oscillation or vibration transmitted through steering wheel	• Improper tire pressures • Tires out of balance • Loose wheel bearings • Improper front end alignment • Worn or bent front end components	• Inflate tires to correct pressure • Have tires balanced • Adjust wheel bearings • Have front end alignment checked/adjusted • Replace worn parts
Uneven tire wear	• Incorrect tire pressure • Front end out of alignment • Tires out of balance	• Inflate tires to correct pressure • Have front end alignment checked/adjusted • Have tires balanced

alignment, bent components must be identified and replaced.) Later cars including the 700 Series have slotted upper mounts which allow a small range of caster adjustment.

Coil Spring

REMOVAL AND INSTALLATION

140 Series, 164

1. Remove the hub cap and loosen the lug nuts a few turns.
2. Firmly apply the parking brake and place blocks in back of the rear wheels. Jack up the front of the car and place jackstands in back of the front jacking points. Remove the front wheels.
3. Remove the shock absorber.
4. Remove the cotter pin and ball nut; disconnect the steering rod from the steering knuckle. Loosen the clamp for the flexible brake hoses. Remove the stabilizer attachment from the lower control arm.
5. Place a jack under the lower control arm. Raise the jack to unload the lower control arm. Remove the cotter pins and loosen the nuts for the upper and lower ball joints; then rap with a hammer until they loosen from the spindle. Remove the nuts and lower the jack slightly.
6. Remove the steering knuckle with the front brake caliper and disc still connected to the brake lines. In order not to stretch the brake lines, place the brake unit on a milk crate or other suitable stand.

CAUTION: *Do not attempt to remove the spring until it is fully extended. As an added safety measure, a chain may be attached to the lower spring coil and secured to the frame.*

7. Slowly lower the jack and the lower control arm to the fullest extent. Remove the spring and rubber spacer.
8. To install the spring, place a jack directly beneath the spring attachment point on the lower control arm. Place the spring with the rubber spacer in position, and lift up the lower control arm with the jack so that the steering knuckle and brake unit assembly may be installed.
9. Install and tighten the upper and lower ball joint nuts. Connect the stabilizer to its attachment on the lower control arm.
10. Install the shock absorber.
11. With the wheel pointing straight ahead, and the lower control arm unloaded, connect the steering rod to the steering knuckle and install the ball nut and cotter pin.
12. Clamp the brake hoses to the stabilizer bolt.
13. Install the wheel. Remove the jackstands

and lower the car. Tighten the lug nuts to 85–90 ft. lbs. and install the hub cap.

1800 Series

1. Remove the hub cap and loosen the lug nuts a few turns.
2. Firmly apply the parking brake and place blocks in back of the rear wheels.
3. Jack up the front of the car and place jackstands beneath the front crossmember. Remove the wheel.
4. Remove the shock absorber.
5. Position a jack directly beneath the lower spring attachment on the lower control arm, and raise the jack until the upper control arm rubber buffer is lifted.
6. Disconnect the stabilizer from the lower control arm. Remove the cotter pin and ball nut from the lower ball joint.

CAUTION: *Do not attempt to remove the spring until it is fully extended. As an added safety measure, a chain may be attached to the lower spring coil and secured to the frame.*

7. Slowly lower the jack and the lower control arm. If the lower ball joint does not release when the jack is lowered, it must be pressed out with a press tool (Volvo 2281 or similar). When the lower control arm is lowered sufficiently, carefully remove the spring, rubber spacer and washer assembly.
8. When reinstalling, take care to place the rubber spacer and washer correctly on top of the spring, prior to installation. Position the jack under the lower arm and place the spring in its seat.
9. Slowly raise the jack and lower arm. As the spring comes into position, make sure it seats properly at the top and reconnect and tighten the lower ball joint. Install a new cotter pin when the nut is secure.
10. Reconnect the stabilizer to the lower control arm.
11. Install the shock absorber.
12. Install the wheel. Lower the car from its stands and tighten the wheel lugs to 75 ft. lbs.

200 and 700 Series (MacPherson Strut)

WARNING: *The use of the correct special tools or their equivalent is REQUIRED for this procedure.*

To remove the spring, a coil spring compressor must be used. Under no circumstances should you attempt to lower and disassemble the strut assembly without the proper spring compressor. Serious injury could result.

Spring compressors can be rented from many repair and supply shops.

1. Remove the hub cap and loosen the lug nuts a few turns.

2. Firmly apply the parking brake and place blocks in back of the rear wheels.

3. Install the spring compressor on the spring directly beneath the upper mount. Make sure that at least 3 coils of the spring are between the tool attachment points. Tighten the tool and compress the spring.

4. Jack up the front of the car at the center of the front crossmember. When the wheels are 2–3 in. (50–75mm) off the ground, the car is high enough. Place jackstands beneath the front jacking points.

Remove the floor jack from the crossmember, and reposition it beneath the lower control arm to provide support at the outer end. Remove the wheel.

5. Using a ball joint puller, disconnect the steering rod from the steering arm.

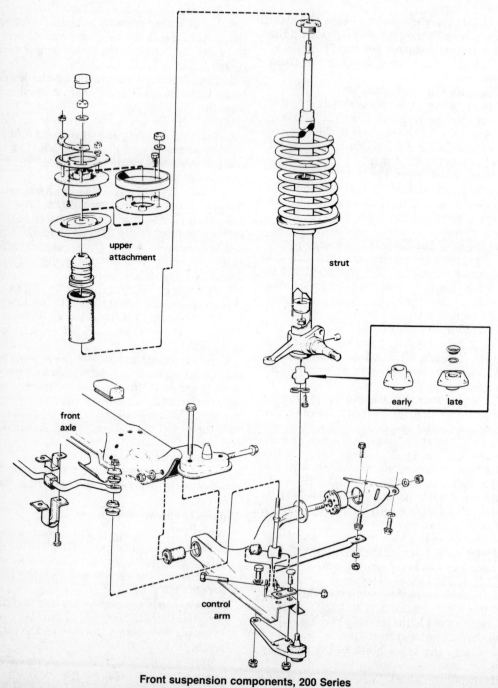

upper attachment

strut

early   late

front axle

control arm

Front suspension components, 200 Series

6. Disconnect the stabilizer bar at the upper link.

7. Remove the bolt holding the brake line bracket to the fender well.

8. Open the hood and remove the cover from the top of the strut assembly upper mount. Mark the position of the upper mounts relative to their holes.

9. While keeping the strut from turning, loosen and remove the nut for the upper strut mount.

10. Before lowering the strut assembly, wire or tie the strut to some stationary component (or use a holding fixture such as Volvo 5045) to prevent the strut from traveling down too far and damaging the hydraulic brake lines.

Lower the jack supporting the lower arm and allow the strut to tilt out at about a 60° angle. At this angle, the top of the strut assembly should just protrude past the wheel well, allowing removal of the strut components from the top. Take great care to control the descent of the strut and prevent damage to the fender.

11. Lift off the spring seat, rubber bumper, and the shock absorber protector. On 700 series, the upper spring mount must be removed from the shaft. Remove the coil spring and compressor assembly from the strut.

12. Slowly relieve the tension on the compressor and remove it from the spring. Place the compressor on the replacement spring (making sure at least 3 coils separate the attachment points as before) and compress.

NOTE: *If the spring compressor does not have enough travel to fully release the spring tension, it will be necessary to use another sandwich type compressor to remove the original compressor once the spring is out of the car.*

13. Position the new spring and compressor on the strut assembly. On 700 Series, install the upper spring mount. Make sure the spring end is properly aligned with the lower mount.

NOTE: *Make sure that the compressor bolts face downwards.*

14. Install the rubber bumper and the shock absorber protector. Position the spring seat on the spring, making sure it is aligned with the spring.

15. Carefully lift and guide the strut assembly into its upper attachment in the spring tower. Connect the stabilizer bar to the stabilizer link.

16. Guide the shock absorber spindle into the upper attachment and raise the jack beneath the lower control arm. Install the washer and nut on top of the shock absorber spindle. Position the upper mount according to marks made during removal.

Tighten the upper mounting bolts. The smaller outer nuts should be tightened to 15–25

Removing the coil spring—240, 260 series and 1980 and later models. The entire strut does not have to be removed to remove the coil spring

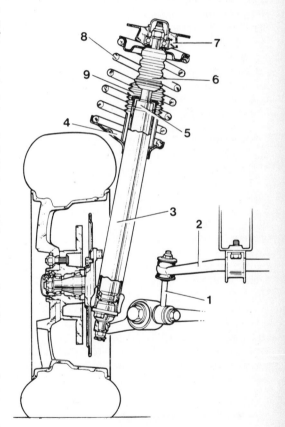

1. Anti-roll bar (sway bar) link
2. Anti-roll bar (sway bar)
3. Spring strut tube
4. Spring lower seat
5. Shock absorber
6. Rubber bumper
7. Upper mount
8. Coil spring
9. Rubber bellows

Front suspension detail, 700 Series

ft. lbs. The large center nut should be tightened to 90–100 ft. lbs. Install the cover.

17. Attach the brake line bracket to its mount. Make sure that the brake lines sit properly in their mounts. Tighten the nut holding the stabilizer bar to the link. Connect the steering rod at the steering arm.

18. Release the coil spring compressor and install the wheel and tire assembly. Remove the jackstands and lower the car. Bounce the suspension a few times and then road test.

Shock Absorbers

The purpose of the shock absorber is simply to limit the motion of the spring during compression (bump) and rebound cycles. If the car were not equipped with these motion dampers, the up and down motion of the car would multiply until the vehicle was alternately trying to leap off the ground and to pound itself into the pavement.

Contrary to popular rumor, the shocks do not affect the ride height of the car nor do they affect the ride quality except for limiting the pitch or bounce of the car. These factors are controlled by other suspension components such as springs and tires. The simplest test of the shock absorbers is simply to push down on one corner of the unladen car and release it.

Observe the motion of the body as it is released. In most cases, it will come up beyond its original rest position, dip back below it and settle quickly to rest. This shows that the damper is slowing and controlling the spring action. Any tendency to excessive pitch (up-and-down) motion or failure to return to rest within 2–3 cycles is a sign of poor function within the shock absorber.

While each shock absorber can be replaced individually, it is recommended that they be changed as a pair (both front or both rear) to maintain equal response on both sides of the car. Chances are quite good that if one has failed, its mate is weak also.

REMOVAL AND INSTALLATION

140 and 164 Series

1. Remove the upper nut, washer, and outer rubber bushing.

2. Remove the two lower attaching bolts beneath the lower control arm, and pull the shock absorber assembly down and out.

3. Test the damping action of the shock absorber. Secure the bottom of the shock in a vise and extend and compress the shaft. Definite resistance should be felt in each direction, al-

though the amount of effort required in each direction may be greatly different.

If the shock absorber is operating properly and is being reinstalled, be sure to use new rubber bushings on top.

4. Position the inner washer, spacing sleeve, and inner rubber bushing on top of the shock absorber.

5. Position the shock to its upper and lower attachments, and install the lower attaching bolts.

6. Install the outer rubber bushing, washer, and the upper nut on top of the unit. Tighten the upper nut until it makes firm contact with the spacing sleeve.

1800 Series

1. Remove the upper nut, washer, and outer rubber bushing from the top of the shock absorber.

2. Remove the lower nut, washer, and outer rubber bushing from beneath the shock absorber.

3. Remove the two lower attaching bolts from beneath the lower control arm, and pull the shock absorber assembly down and out.

4. Test the damping action of the shock absorber. Secure the bottom of the shock in a vise and extend and compress the shaft. Definite resistance should be felt in each direction, although the amount of effort required in each direction may be greatly different.

If the shock absorber is operating properly and is being reinstalled, be sure to use new rubber bushings on top.

5. Place the shock absorber through the lower control arm and install the two lower bolts.

6. Install the lower nut, washer and bushing.

7. Install the upper bushing, washer and nut.

200 and 700 Series (MacPherson Strut)

WARNING: *The use of the correct special tools or their equivalent is REQUIRED for this procedure.*

To remove the spring, a coil spring compressor must be used. Under no circumstances should you attempt to lower and disassemble the strut assembly without the proper spring compressor. Serious injury could result.

Spring compressors can be rented from many repair and supply shops.

1. Remove the hub cap and loosen the lug nuts a few turns.

2. Firmly apply the parking brake and place blocks in back of the rear wheels.

3. Install the spring compressor on the spring directly beneath the upper mount. Make sure that at least 3 coils of the spring are be-

tween the tool attachment points. Tighten the tool and compress the spring.

4. Jack up the front of the car at the center of the front crossmember. When the wheels are 2–3 in. (50–75mm) off the ground, the car is high enough. Place jackstands beneath the front jacking points.

Remove the floor jack from the crossmember, and reposition it beneath the lower control arm to provide support at the outer end. Remove the wheel.

5. Using a ball joint puller, disconnect the steering rod from the steering arm.

6. Disconnect the stabilizer bar at the upper link.

7. Remove the bolt holding the brake line bracket to the fender well.

8. Open the hood and remove the cover from the top of the strut assembly upper mount. Mark the position of the upper mounts relative to their holes.

9. While keeping the strut from turning, loosen and remove the nut for the upper strut mount.

10. Before lowering the strut assembly, wire or tie the strut to some stationary component (or use a holding fixture such as Volvo 5045) to prevent the strut from traveling down too far and damaging the hydraulic brake lines.

Lower the jack supporting the lower arm and allow the strut to tilt out at about a 60° angle. At this angle, the top of the strut assembly should just protrude past the wheel well, allowing removal of the strut components from the top. Take great care to control the descent of the strut and prevent damage to the fender.

11. Lift off the spring seat, rubber bumper, and the shock absorber protector. On 700 series, the upper spring mount must be removed from the shaft. Remove the coil spring and compressor assembly from the strut.

12. While keeping the strut outer tube from turning, remove the upper shock absorber retaining nut.

NOTE: *The shock absorber unit is a sealed unit. It cannot be repaired or overhauled.*

13. Pull the shock absorber unit out of the outer tube (casing).

NOTE: *On some models, gas type shock absorbers are used. A special tool (such as Volvo 5173 or similar) must be used to remove and install the unit.*

14. Install the new shock absorber unit into the outer tube and install the retaining nut. You can stop the outer tube from turning with the nut by holding the tube at the weld with a pair of locking pliers.

15. Pull the shock absorber shaft to its uppermost position.

16. Position the spring and compressor on the strut assembly. On 700 Series, install the upper spring mount. Make sure the spring end is properly aligned with the lower mount.

NOTE: *Make sure that the compressor bolts face as they did during removal.*

17. Install the rubber bumper and the shock absorber protector. Position the spring seat on the spring, making sure it is aligned with the spring.

15. Carefully lift and guide the strut assembly into its upper attachment in the spring tower. Connect the stabilizer bar to the stabilizer link.

18. Guide the shock absorber spindle into the upper attachment and raise the jack beneath the lower control arm. Install the washer and nut on top of the shock absorber spindle. Position the upper mount according to marks made during removal.

Tighten the upper mounting bolts. The smaller outer nuts should be tightened to 15–25 ft. lbs. The large center nut should be tightened to 90–100 ft. lbs. Install the cover.

19. Attach the brake line bracket to its mount. Make sure that the brake lines sit properly in their mounts. Tighten the nut holding the stabilizer bar to the link. Connect the steering rod at the steering arm.

20. Release the coil spring compressor and install the wheel and tire assembly. Remove the jackstands and lower the car. Bounce the suspension a few times and then road test.

Upper Ball Joint
INSPECTION
140 Series, 164 Models and 1800 Series

If the upper ball joint is worn, the wheel and tire assembly will exhibit excessive play when the joint is unloaded. Place a jack beneath the lower control arm and lift the wheel until clear of the ground. Make sure that the upper control arm is not making contact with the rubber stop.

Firmly grasp the top and bottom of the tire and try to rock it in and out; that is, intermittently push the top of the tire towards the engine compartment, then pull it away from the car, while simultaneously doing the opposite to the bottom of the tire. Replace the upper ball joint if the radial play of the wheel and tire assembly is excessive.

NOTE: *Do not confuse possible wheel bearing play with ball joint play. It is advisable that the wheel bearing adjustment procedure in Chapter Nine be followed prior to replacing the ball joint.*

REMOVAL AND INSTALLATION
140 and 160 Series

1. Remove the hub cap and loosen the lug nuts a few turns.

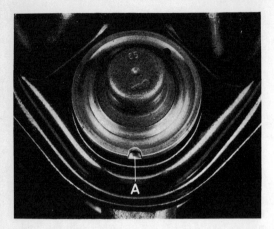

Locating the upper ball joint, 140 and 160 Series

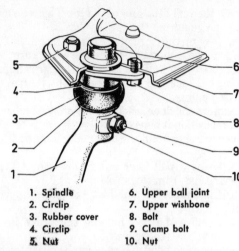

1. Spindle	6. Upper ball joint
2. Circlip	7. Upper wishbone
3. Rubber cover	8. Bolt
4. Circlip	9. Clamp bolt
5. Nut	10. Nut

Upper ball joint attachment—1800 series

2. Jack up the front of the vehicle and place safety stands beneath the front jacking points. Remove the wheel.

3. Loosen, but do not remove the nut for the upper ball joint. With a hammer, tap around the ball joint stud on the steering knuckle until it loosens. Remove the nut, and safety wire the upper end of the steering knuckle to the stabilizer bar to avoid straining the flexible brake hoses.

4. Loosen the nut for the upper control arm shaft ½ turn. Lift up the control arm slightly and press out the old ball joint with a press tool and a sleeve.

5. Make sure that the rubber cover of the new ball joint is filled with multipurpose grease. Bend the pin end over the slot, and make sure that the grease forces its way out.

6. Press the ball joint into the upper control arm using the press tool, a sleeve, and a drift. It is imperative that the ball joint be aligned so that the slot comes into line with the longitudinal shaft of the control arm (either internally or externally) as the pin has maximum movement along this line.

7. Lower the upper control arm to its operating position, and tighten the shaft nuts to 40–45 ft. lbs. Remove the safety wire and place the steering knuckle in position. Install and tighten the ball nut to 60–70 ft. lbs. If the pin rotates during tightening, clamp it firmly with a screw vise.

8. Install the wheel. Remove the safety stands and lower the vehicle. Tighten the lug nuts to 85–90 ft. lbs., and install the hub cap.

1800 Series

1. Remove the hub cap and loosen the lug nuts a few turns.

2. Jack up the front of the vehicle and place safety stands beneath the lower control arms. Remove the wheel.

3. Remove the two nuts (5) and bolts (8) which hold the ball joint to the upper control arm. Lift the upper control arm up and out of the way.

4. Remove the clamping nut (10) and bolt (9) which secure the ball joint to the steering knuckle. Remove the upper ball joint, sealing washers, and rubber cover assembly.

5. Make sure that the rubber cover of the new ball joint is filled with multipurpose grease. If the old ball joint is being reused, make sure that the rubber cover is not damaged, and fill it with grease.

6. After making sure that the sleeve and sealing washers (circlips) are positioned properly, place the ball joint assembly on the steering knuckle and install the clamping nut and bolt.

7. Lower the upper control arm into position over the ball joint and install the attaching nuts and bolts.

8. Install the wheel. Remove the safety stands and lower the vehicle. Tighten the lug nuts to 85–90 ft. lbs., and install the hub cap.

Lower Ball Joint

INSPECTION

140 Series, 164 Models, 1800 Series

If the lower ball joint is worn, measurement (A) taken from the ball stud to the cover of the ball joint will exceed to the maximum allowable length. The check is made with the vehicle standing on the ground, wheels pointing straight ahead.

Two types of lower ball joints have been used on late model Volvos; only one uses a pressure spring inside. The maximum allowable length of the spring type ball joint is 4.5 in. (114mm) for the 140 series and 164, and 4.4 in. (112mm) for the 1800 series. The maximum allowable

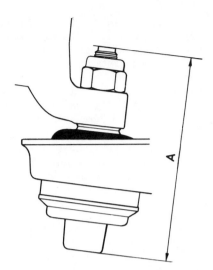

Spring type lower ball joint maximum allowable length

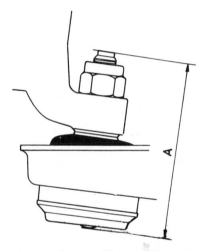

Non-spring type lower ball joint maximum allowable length

length for the non-spring type ball joint is 3.91 in. (99mm) for the 140 series and 164, and 3.76 in. (96mm) for the 1800 series.

240, 260 Series 1980 and Later Models

To check the lower ball joints, place a jack under the lower control arm as close to the wheel as possible. Raise the jack just enough to bring the tire clear of the ground and check ball joint play with the loaded weight of the car on the jack. Check the play with a tire iron or some suitable pry bar but be careful not to damage the rubber dust cover. Maximum allowable play is 0.118 in. (3mm).

REMOVAL AND INSTALLATION

140 and 160 Series

1. Remove the hub cap and loosen the lug nuts a few turns.

2. Jack up the front of the vehicle and place jackstands beneath the front jacking points. Remove the wheel.

3. Remove the brake lines from their bracket at the stabilizer bolt. Remove the cotter pin and stud nut, and press the steering rod ball stud from the steering knuckle.

4. Remove the cotter pins and loosen but do not remove the nuts for both the upper and lower ball joints. Tap with a hammer until the ball joints loosen from the spindle. Place a jack beneath the lower control arm and raise it to unload the control arm. Remove the ball joint nuts.

5. Remove the steering knuckle with the front brakes still connected to the brake lines. In order not to stretch the brake lines, place the brake unit on a milk crate or other stand.

6. Press the lower ball joint out of the lower control arm with a press tool and sleeve.

7. Make sure that the rubber cover of the new ball joint is filled with multipurpose grease. Bend the pin end to the side, and make sure that the
grease forces its way out.

8. To install, press the lower ball joint into its control arm with a press tool, sleeve and drift. Make sure that the ball joint is not loose in the control arm.

9. Position the steering kncukle and brake unit assembly between the upper and lower control arms and tighten the ball joint stud nuts to 60–70 ft. lbs. (upper ball joint), and 75–90 ft. lbs. (lower ball joint). If the pins rotate during tightening, clamp them firmly with a screw vise.

10. Install the steering rod ball stud into the steering knuckle and tighten the stud nut. Lower the jack slightly and, with the front wheels pointing straight ahead, attach the brake lines to their bracket at the stabilizer bolt.

11. Install the wheel. Remove the jackstands and lower the vehicle. Tighten the lug nuts to 85–90 ft. lbs., and install the hub cap.

1800 Series

1. Remove the hub cap and loosen the lug nuts a few turns.

2. Jack up the front of the car and place safety stands under the lower control arms. Remove the wheel.

3. Remove the four nuts (6) and bolts (8) which retain the ball joint to the lower control arm. Remove the cotter pin and ball stud nut which secure the steering knuckle to the ball joint.

4. Disconnect and plug the brake hoses at their retainer. Remove the ball joint from the steering knuckle by lightly tapping its attachment with a hammer.

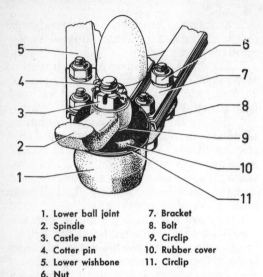

1. Lower ball joint
2. Spindle
3. Castle nut
4. Cotter pin
5. Lower wishbone
6. Nut
7. Bracket
8. Bolt
9. Circlip
10. Rubber cover
11. Circlip

Lower ball joint attachment—1800 series

5. Make sure that the rubber cover of the new ball joint is filled with multipurpose (universal) grease.

6. Place the ball joint, sealing washers (circlip), and sleeve into position on the steering knuckle and install the ball stud nut. Tighten the nut to 35–40 ft. lbs.

7. Place the ball joint and steering knuckle assembly into position on the lower control arm and install the four retaining nuts and bolts.

8. Unplug and connect the brake hoses. Bleed the brake system.

9. Install the wheel and tire assembly. Remove the safety stands and lower the vehicle. Tighten the lug nuts to 85–90 ft. lbs. and install the hub cap.

240, 260 Series Early Production Models

WARNING: *The use of the correct special tools or their equivalent is REQUIRED for this procedure.*

To remove the spring, a coil spring compressor must be used. Under no circumstances should you attempt to lower and disassemble the strut assembly without the proper spring compressor. Serious injury could result.

Spring compressors can be rented from many repair and supply shops.

1. Remove the hub cap and loosen the lug nuts a few turns.

2. Firmly apply the parking brake and place blocks in back of the rear wheels.

3. Install the spring compressor on the spring directly beneath the upper mount. Make sure that at least 3 coils of the spring are between the tool attachment points. Tighten the tool and compress the spring.

4. Jack up the front of the car at the center of the front crossmember. When the wheels are 2–3 in. (50–75mm) off the ground, the car is high enough. Place jackstands beneath the front jacking points.

Remove the floor jack from the crossmember, and reposition it beneath the lower control arm to provide support at the outer end. Remove the wheel.

5. Using a ball joint puller, disconnect the steering rod from the steering arm.

6. Disconnect the stabilizer bar at the upper link.

7. Remove the bolt holding the brake line bracket to the fender well.

8. Open the hood and remove the cover from the top of the strut assembly upper mount. Mark the position of the upper mounts relative to their holes.

9. While keeping the strut from turning, loosen and remove the nut for the upper strut mount.

10. Before lowering the strut assembly, wire or tie the strut to some stationary component (or use a holding fixture such as Volvo 5045) to prevent the strut from traveling down too far and damaging the hydraulic brake lines.

Lower the jack supporting the lower arm and allow the strut to tilt out at about a 60° angle. At this angle, the top of the strut assembly should just protrude past the wheel well, allowing removal of the strut components from the top. Take great care to control the descent of the strut and prevent damage to the fender.

11. Lift off the spring seat, rubber bumper, and the shock absorber protector. Remove the coil spring and compressor assembly from the strut.

12. While keeping the strut outer tube from turning, remove the upper shock absorber retaining nut.

13. Pull the shock absorber unit out of the outer tube (casing).

NOTE: *On some models, gas type shock absorbers are used. A special tool (such as Volvo 5173 or similar) must be used to remove and install the unit.*

14. Loosen the ball joint retaining nut, located inside the shock absorber tube. Grasp the outer tube at the weld (with a pair of locking pliers or a pipe wrench) and loosen the nut with a 19mm socket and a long extension, until the joint bracket comes loose.

15. Using a drift and hammer, loosen the cone-shaped part of the ball joint from the strut assembly.

16. Coat the inside of the 19mm socket with vaseline or bearing grease. (The grease will keep the nut within the socket after loosening.) Remove the ball joint retaining nut.

17. Wire the top of the strut assembly to the tower, and allow the strut to hang vertically. Disconnect the ball joint from the bottom of the strut assembly. Take care not to damage the brake hoses. Then disconnect the ball joint from the lower control arm.

18. Attach the new ball joint to the lower control arm.

NOTE: *Make sure the new ball joint stud is free of grease, or the stud could be tightened too far into the cone making the rubber bellows stick to the strut.*

19. Remove the wire and lift the strut assembly into position. Install the ball joint nut, and tighten to 30–50 ft. lbs. Stop the outer tube from turning by holding it at the weld.

20. Install the shock absorber and retaining nut. Tighten to 30–50 ft. lbs. Pull the shock absorber shaft to its uppermost position.

21. Position the spring and compressor on the strut assembly. Make sure the spring end is properly aligned with the lower mount.

NOTE: *Make sure that the compressor bolts face as they did during removal.*

22. Install the rubber bumper and the shock absorber protector. Position the spring seat on the spring, making sure it is aligned with the spring.

23. Carefully lift and guide the strut assembly into its upper attachment in the spring tower. Connect the stabilizer bar to the stabilizer link.

24. Guide the shock absorber spindle into the upper attachment and raise the jack beneath the lower control arm. Install the washer and nut on top of the shock absorber spindle. Position the upper mount according to marks made during removal.

Tighten the upper mounting bolts. The smaller outer nuts should be tightened to 15–25 ft. lbs. The large center nut should be tightened to 90–100 ft. lbs. Install the cover.

25. Attach the brake line bracket to its mount. Make sure that the brake lines sit properly in their mounts. Tighten the nut holding the stabilizer bar to the link. Connect the steering rod at the steering arm.

26. Release the coil spring compressor and install the wheel and tire assembly. Remove the jackstands and lower the car. Bounce the suspension a few times and then road test.

240 and 260 Series
Late Production Models

1. Jack up the front of the car and install jackstands beneath the front jacking attachments.

2. Remove the wheel.

3. Reach in between the spring coils and loosen the lower shock absorber retaining nut a few turns. On car built after 1978, this is NOT necessary as the shock absorber does not rest against the ball joint mount.

4. Remove the four bolts (12mm) retaining the ball joint seat to the bottom of the strut.

5. Remove the three nuts (19mm) retaining the ball joint to the lower control arm.

6. Place the ball joint and attachment assembly in a vise and remove the 19mm nut from the ball joint stud. Then drive out the old ball joint.

7. Install the new ball joint in the attachment and tighten the stud nut to 35–50 ft. lbs.

NOTE: *On 1979 and later models with power steering, the ball joints are different for the left and right side. Compared to previous years, the ball joint is 0.393 in. (10mm) forward in the control rod attachment.*

It is therefore most important that these ball joints are installed on the correct side.

8. Attach the ball joint assembly to the strut. Always use new locking bolts or washers. Tighten to 15–20 ft. lbs.

9. Attach the ball joint assembly to the control arm. Tighten to 70–95 ft. lbs.

10. Tighten the shock absorber retaining nut if it had been loosened. Install the wheel. Lower the car and road test.

700 Series

1. Jack up the front end of the car, support on stands and remove the wheel.

2. Remove the bolt connecting the anti-roll bar (sway bar) link to the control arm.

3. Remove the cotter pin for the ball joint stud, and remove the nut.

4. Using a ball joint puller, press out the ball joint from the control arm. Make sure the puller is located directly in line with the stud, and that the rubber grease boot is not damaged by the puller.

5. Remove the bolts holding the ball joint to the spring strut. Press the control arm down and remove the ball joint.

6. When installing the new ball joint, always use new bolts and coat all threads with a liquid thread sealer. Torque bolts to 22 ft.lb., checking that the bolt heads sit flat on the ball joint, then tighten an additional 90° of rotation.

7. Install the nut holding the control arm ball joint stud and tighten to 44 ft. lbs. Always use a new cotter pin on the ball joint stud.

8. Install the anti-roll bar link.

9. Install the wheel and lower the car to the ground.

Sway Bar

The sway bar, variously called the anti-roll bar or stabilizer bar, serves to control the sideways roll of the body during cornering. While the bar itself rarely fails, the links and bushings

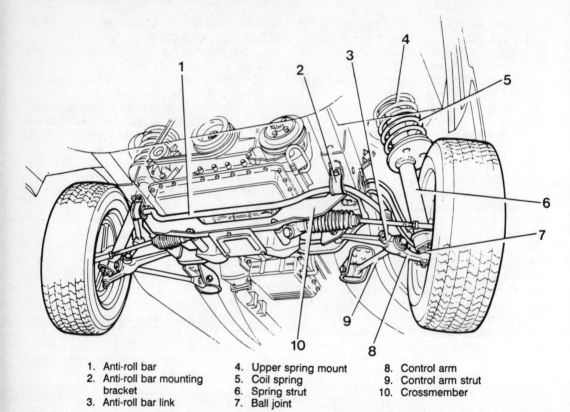

1. Anti-roll bar
2. Anti-roll bar mounting bracket
3. Anti-roll bar link
4. Upper spring mount
5. Coil spring
6. Spring strut
7. Ball joint
8. Control arm
9. Control arm strut
10. Crossmember

Front suspension component location, 7800 Series

around it are prone to wear. If the bar is not rigidly mounted to the car, it cannot do its job properly.

Sway bars of different diameters (thicknesses) can stiffen or soften the roll characteristics of a vehicle. Bushings are easily replaced and well worth the effort in terms of restoring proper cornering manners to your car.

REMOVAL AND INSTALLATION

All Models

1. Loosen the front wheel nuts a few turns. Elevate the front end and position jackstands under the front control arms. On the 700 Series, position the jackstands underneath the jacking attachments.

2. Lower the car onto the stands and make sure the stands are properly supporting the control arms.

3. Remove the wheels. Remove the underside splashguard panel if so equipped.

4. Loosen and remove the upper nut holding the sway bar to the link.

5. Remove the upper link nut on the opposite side. The bar now hangs by its two forward brackets.

6. Remove the bolts for the two retaining brackets and remove the bar.

7. If the link bushings are worn, remove the lower link bolts and remove the entire link. Inspect all the bushings for compression or elongation. Replace any that are not almost perfect. The two U-shaped bushings from the front brackets are particularly prone to deforming.

8. After replacing bushings as needed, reconnect the lower link to the arm on each side.

9. Hold the bar in position and install the front brackets with their bushings. Make sure the slot in the bushing faces forward.

10. Install the bar to the link on one side of the car but do not tighten more than a few turns. Connect the bar to the link on the opposite side and install the bushings and nut.

11. Tighten each upper link nut until 1.65 in. (42mm) can be measured between the outer surfaces of the upper and lower washers.

12. Reinstall the underside splash panel if necessary, and install the wheel.

13. Lower the car to the ground and snug the wheel lugs.

Strut rod

The front strut rods, also called the radius rod or control arm strut, serve to locate the lower control arm and prevent fore-and-aft movement. Except for impact damage, the rods rarely fail. The rubber bushings on each end are prone to fatigue and wear and may need to be replaced after a few years.

Loosen the rod-to-body bolt but don't remove it. Remove the nut at the control arm. This is sometimes easier said than done; the control arm bolt can be very tight. Once the front nut is loosened, the back mount may be removed and the rod placed on a workbench.

If the bushings are to be replaced, press them free of their mounts and install the new ones. Reinstall the rod, attaching the rear bolt first. Make sure the front bushings seat properly in the control arm and that the front nut draws tight against its washer.

Upper Control Arm
REMOVAL AND INSTALLATION

NOTE: *On all models, always fully install the control arm, bounce the suspension several times, and THEN tighten the control arm-to-control arm shaft nuts.*

1800 Series

1. Loosen the front wheel lugs, raise the car, support it on jackstands under the lower control arm and remove the wheel.
2. Remove the control arm-to-cross shaft nuts and clamps.
3. Remove the nuts at the spindle end, the bolts for the ball joint and lift off the control arm.
4. Position the new control arm and ball joint assembly. Fit the clamps and torque the nuts to 14–18 ft. lbs.
5. Reassemble the other parts.

140 and 160 Series

1. Loosen the wheel lugs, raise the front end, support it on jackstands and remove the wheel.
2. Loosen, but do not remove, the upper ball joint nut. Remove the ball joint by tapping on the steering knuckle around the ball joint pin.
3. Remove the nut and suspend the upper end of the knuckle to avoid straining the brake hose.
4. Disconnect the control arm from the cross shaft. Take note of the number and position of the shims.
5. Place the new control arm in position and attach the bolts by hand. Fit the shims into their exact previous positions.
6. Tighten the nuts for the crossshaft to 40–45 ft. lbs.
7. Reinstall the upper ball joint in the steering knuckle and tighten the nut.
8. Install the wheel. Lower the vehicle and tighten the lugs to 85–90 ft. lbs.

Lower Control Arm
REMOVAL AND INSTALLATION

NOTE: *On all models, always fully install the control arm, bounce the suspension several times, and THEN tighten the control arm to crossmember mounting nuts or bolts.*

1800 Series

1. Loosen the wheel lugs, raise and support the front end and remove the wheels.
2. Remove the shock absorber.
3. Place a jack under the lower control arm at the spring. Raise the jack until the control arm rubber stop rises.
4. Disconnect the stabilizer bar from the lower control arm.
5. Remove the lower ball joint.
6. Slowly lower the jack and remove the spring when all tension is relieved.
CAUTION: *The spring is under considerable pressure. The use of a spring compressor or safety chain is advised.*
7. Disconnect the control arm from the cross shaft and remove.
8. Install the new arm on the cross shaft. Position the spring and raise the control arm into place.
9. Connect the lower ball joint and the stabilizer bar to the lower control arm.
10. Install the shock absorber.
11. Install the wheel, lower the car and tighten the wheel lugs.

140, 164 Series

1. Loosen the wheel lugs, raise and support the car and remove the wheels.
2. Remove shock absorber.
3. Disconnect the tie rod from the steering arm with a separator tool.
4. Loosen the brake hose clamp and remove the stabilizer.
5. Place a jack under the lower control arm and support it.
6. Loosen the ball joint nuts and tap around the ball joints with a hammer until they loosen from the knuckle.
7. Remove the nuts, lower the jack slightly and remove the knuckle with the front brake unit. Suspend or position this assembly out of the way.
8. Lower the jack slowly and carefully and, when all tension is relieved, remove the spring.
CAUTION: *The spring is under considerable pressure. It is advisable to use a spring compressor or safety chain when removing the spring.*
9. Remove the control arm shaft nut, turn the relay rod with the tie rod (so that the con-

trol arm shaft is free) and remove the control arm shaft.

10. Remove the control arm.

11. When reinstalling, pay attention to the correct order of spacers, rings and washers on the shaft. Their order and placement is important. Install the control arm in place and tighten the nut to 95–110 ft. lbs.

12. Place the spring in position and elevate the arm with the jack.

13. Attach the steering knuckle and connect and tighten the ball joints.

14. Install the brake hose clamps. Connect the tie rod to the steering rod.

15. Reinstall the shock absorber.

16. Install the wheel, lower the car and tighten the lug nuts to 85–90 ft. lbs.

240 and 260 Series

1. Jack up the car, support on stands and remove the wheels.

2. Disconnect the stabilizer (sway bar) link at the control arm.

3. Remove the ball joint from the control arm. (Helpful tips can be found in "Lower Ball Joint Removal and Installation" in this chapter.)

4. Remove the control arm rear attachment plate.

5. Remove the control arm front retaining bolt.

6. Remove the control arm.

7. If bushings are to be replaced, note that the right and left bushings are not interchangeable. The right side bushing should be turned so that the small slots point horizontally when installed.

8. Install the bracket onto the control arm. The nut should be tightened only enough to hold securely. The washer should be able to be turned with your fingers after the nut is on.

9. Attach the control arm. Install the front retaining bolt and nut; tighten the nut only a few turns onto the bolt.

10. Guide the stabilizer link into position. Attach it loosely with its nut and bolt.

11. Install the ball joint and its mount. Tighten the three mounting bolts to 75–95 ft. lbs.

12. Install the rear bracket to the car. Tighten the three bolts to 25–35 ft. lbs.

13. Tighten the stabilizer link.

14. Install the wheels and lower the car to the ground. Roll the car back and forth several times while bouncing the front end up and down. This "normalizes" the front suspension and allows the control arm to seek its final position.

15. Tighten the rear mount nut to 38–44 ft. lbs. Tighten the front mount to 55 ft. lbs.

700 Series

1. Jack the car, support it on safety stands and remove the wheel.

2. Remove the cotter pin from the ball joint and remove the ball joint nut.

3. Disconnect the stabilizer (sway bar) link at the control arm.

4. Disconnect the strut bolt and remove the front bushing.

5. Use a ball joint puller and separate the ball joint from the control arm. Make sure the puller is properly located and that the rubber boot is not damaged during removal.

6. Unbolt the control arm at the crossmember and remove the arm.

7. If the bushings are to be replaced, use a press and support the arm from below. The new bushings should always be pressed in from the front side of the arm.

8. Fit the control arm over the end of the strut rod. Install the arm in the crossmember but do not fully tighten the nut.

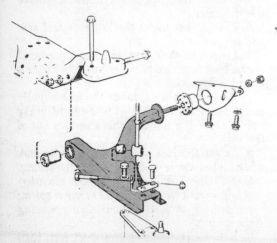

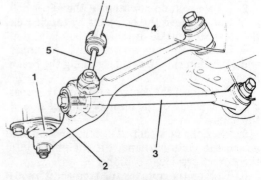

1. Ball joint
2. Control arm
3. Control arm strut
4. Anti-roll bar

Lower control arm detail, 200 Series   **Control arm detail, 700 Series**

9. Install the ball joint in the control arm. Tighten the nut to 44 ft. lbs. Install a new cotter pin.

10. Install the bushing, washer and bolt for the strut rod. tighten the bolt to 70 ft. lbs.

11. Attach the stabilizer link to the control arm and tighten it to 63 ft. lbs.

12. Install the wheels and lower the car to the ground. Roll the car back and forth several times while bouncing the front end up and down. This "normalizes" the front suspension and allows the control arm to seek its final position.

13. Tighten the control arm-to-crossmember bolt to 63 ft. lbs. Tighten the wheel lugs evenly to 63 ft. lbs.

Front Wheel Bearings

REPLACEMENT

CAUTION: *This procedure requires removal of the brakes. Brake pads and shoes contain asbestos, which has been determined to a cancer causing agent. Never clean the brake surfaces with compressed air! Avoid inhaling and dust from brake surfaces! When cleaning brakes, use commercially available brake cleaning fluids.*
WARNING: *The use of the correct special tools or their equivalent is REQUIRED for this procedure.*

All models except 700 Series

1. Loosen the wheel nuts, elevate the car and safely support it with jackstands under the lower control arms.

2. Plug the vent hole in the brake fluid reservoir to prevent spillage and leakage.

3. Remove the wheels. Disconnect the brake hose at its joint to the metal pipe. Catch any spilled fluid and plug the open lines.

4. Remove the attaching bolts and remove the brake caliper. Note the position of any shims in the mounting.

5. Remove the grease cap. Remove the cotter pin, the castle nut and mount a hub puller onto the disc.

6. Pull the hub off. The outer bearing will come off with it; the inner bearing may stay on the stub axle. If this happens, simply use a bearing puller of the correct size to remove the bearing from the axle.

7. Remove the brake disc from the hub. Bearings can now be inspected and cleaned. Clean all the components thoroughly, including the inside of the hub. Every trace of the old grease must be removed.

After cleaning, inspect all the parts. Look carefully for any signs of imperfect surfaces, cracking, bluing or looseness. Check the match-

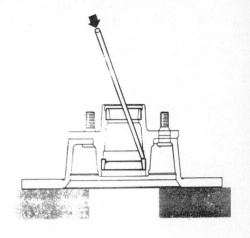

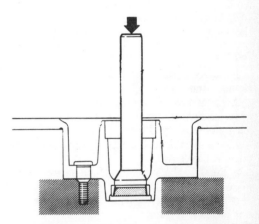

Above: Removing inner bearing race with a drift. Below: Removing outer race with a bearing removal tool

ing surface or race on which the rollers run. Any sign of imperfection requires replacement.

After the bearings have been cleaned, inspected and are totally dry, repack them using a quality bearing or multi-purpose grease. Each bearing must be fully packed; the use of a bearing packer is highly recommended although the job can be done by hand if close attention is paid. The space inside the hub should also be packed; remember that the stub axle comes through here--don't pack it solid.

If it is necessary to replace the races, they should be removed from the hub using tools which match the full diameter of the race. Use of a punch or drift may cause damage. The seals, made of pressed felt, should be soaked in light engine oil before installation.

8. Place the inner bearing in position within the hub. Using the correct sized drift, install the inner seal.

9. Install the hub onto the stub axle and fit the outer bearing in place. Install the washer and castle nut.

10. Adjust the front wheel bearings by spinning the hub and simultaneously tightening the center nut to 50 ft. lbs. Then loosen the center nut two flats on the center nut.

If the nut recess (groove) doesn't line up with the cotter pin hole, loosen the nut just a bit until it aligns. Install a new cotter pin and check that the hub spins freely without excess sideplay.

11. Install the brake disc on the hub.

12. Fill the grease cap half full with bearing grease and install the cap.

13. Reinstall the caliper, observing shim placement as noted during removal.

14. Remove the plugs and connect the brake lines.

15. Bleed the brakes and remove the plug from the reservoir vent hole.

16. Install the wheel and lower the vehicle to the ground. Final tighten the wheel lugs.

700 Series

1. Safely elevate and support the front end. Remove the wheel.

2. Loosen the retaining bolts and remove the brake caliper. Hang the caliper out of the way with a piece of stiff wire.

3. Pry off the grease cap. Remove the cotter pin and castle nut.

4. Remove the brake disc. The outer bearing will come off with the disc. Use a bearing puller to remove the inner bearing from the spindle if it is difficult to remove.

NOTE: *On 1988–89 760 and 780 cars with Multi-Link rear suspension, the brake disc will be a separate item. Removing the disc will expose the hub lock nut, which must be removed. Both wheel bearings are found inside the hub.*

5. With the disc supported on blocks of wood, remove the inner seal with a seal puller. The inner bearing race may be removed with a long brass punch. The outer race may be removed with the use of the proper size driver.

The bearings can now be inspected and cleaned. Clean all the components thoroughly, including the inside of the disc. Every trace of the old grease must be removed.

After cleaning, inspect all the parts. Look carefully for any signs of imperfect surfaces, cracking, bluing, rust or looseness. Check the matching surface or race on which the rollers run. Any sign of imperfection requires replacement.

After the bearings have been cleaned, inspected and are totally dry, repack them using a quality bearing or multi-purpose grease. Each bearing must be fully packed; the use of a bearing packer is highly recommended although the job can be done by hand if close attention is

paid. The space inside the disc should also be packed; remember that the spindle comes through here--don't pack it solid.

6. If the races were removed, install them into the disc using drivers of proper size. Make sure they install straight and are not cocked or out of place. For 1988–89 760 and 780 with Multi-Link rear suspension, the bearings install into the hub, not the disc.

7. Install the inner bearing with a new seal into the brake disc or hub. Smear the seal lip with grease.

8. Install the disc, the outer bearing and the castle nut. For 1988–89 760 and 780 with Multi-Link rear suspension, install the hub and with a NEW locknut. Do not reuse the old nut; bearing damage may result. Tighten the new nut to 74 ft. lbs. PLUS an additional 45° of rotation.

9. Install the brake caliper. Volvo recommends the use of new retaining bolts. The bolts should be tightened to 74 ft. lbs.

10. Adjust the front wheel bearing by spinning the disc several times and then tightening the nut to 42 ft. lbs. Loosen the nut ½ turn, then retighten to 12 in. lbs. This is just enough to hold the bearing in place but not enough to develop any side loading.

11. Install a new cotter pin. If the hole in the spindle doesn't align with the castle nut, tighten the nut just until the hole and slot align.

12. Install the grease cap. Install the wheel.

13. Lower the car to the ground and tighten the wheel to 63 ft. lbs.

Spindle (Stub axle)
REPLACEMENT

CAUTION: *This procedure requires removal of the brakes. Brake pads and shoes contain asbestos, which has been determined to a cancer causing agent. Never clean the brake surfaces with compressed air! Avoid inhaling and dust from brake surfaces! When cleaning brakes, use commercially available brake cleaning fluids.*

WARNING: *The use of the correct special tools or their equivalent is REQUIRED for this procedure.*

1800 Series

1. Loosen the wheel nuts, elevate the car and safely support it with jackstands under the lower control arms.

2. Plug the vent hole in the brake fluid reservoir to prevent spillage and leakage.

3. Remove the wheels. Disconnect the brake hose at its joint to the metal pipe. Catch any spilled fluid and plug the open lines.

4. Remove the attaching bolts and remove

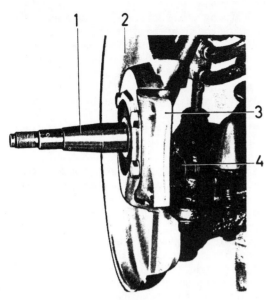

1. Stub axle
2. Protective plate (splash shield)
3. Retainer
4. Steering arm

P1800 Series, front axle detail

the brake caliper. Note the position of any shims in the mounting.

5. Remove the grease cap. Remove the cotter pin, the castle nut and mount a hub puller onto the disc.

6. Pull the hub off. The outer bearing will come off with it; the inner bearing may stay on the stub axle. If this happens, simply use a bearing puller of the correct size to remove the bearing from the axle.

7. Remove the four bolts and separate the splash shield, retainer and steering arm from the knuckle.

8. Loosen and remove the upper and lower ball joints.

9. Lift out the stub axle and steering knuckle assembly.

10. Since the wheel bearings have been removed and exposed, they should be cleaned and repacked before reinstallation. When reassembling, fit the stub axle into position and and attach the upper and lower ball joints.

11. Assemble and connect the retainer, steering arm and splash shield to the steering knuckle/stub axle assembly.

12. Place the inner bearing in position within the hub. Using the correct sized drift, install the inner seal.

13. Install the hub onto the stub axle and fit the outer bearing in place. Install the washer and castle nut.

14. Adjust the front wheel bearings by spin-

ning the hub and simultaneously tightening the center nut to 50 ft. lbs. Then loosen the center nut two flats on the center nut.

If the nut recess (groove) doesn't line up with the cotter pin hole, loosen the nut just a bit until it aligns. Install a new cotter pin and check that the hub spins freely without excess sideplay.

15. Install the brake disc on the hub.

16. Fill the grease cap half full with bearing grease and install the cap.

17. Reinstall the caliper, observing shim placement as noted during removal.

18. Remove the plugs and connect the brake lines.

19. Bleed the brakes and remove the plug from the reservoir vent hole.

20. Install the wheel and lower the vehicle to the ground. Final tighten the wheel lugs.

140 and 160 Series

1. Safely elevate and support the car on jackstands. Remove the front wheel.

2. Remove the front brake caliper; use stiff wire and hang the caliper out of the way.

3. Remove the grease cap. Remove the cotter pin, the castle nut and mount a hub puller onto the disc.

4. Pull the hub off. The outer bearing will come off with it; the inner bearing may stay on the stub axle. If this happens, simply use a bearing puller of the correct size to remove the bearing race from the axle.

5. Use a ball joint separator and remove the steering rod from the steering arm. Volvo tool 2294 is recommended.

6. Loosen, but do not remove, the nuts for the ball joints. Tap on the housing with a hammer until the ball joint shafts loosen in their mounts.

7. Use a floor jack and elevate the control arm slightly. Remove the nuts for the ball joints and remove the steering knuckle/stub axle assembly.

8. Since the wheel bearings have been removed and exposed, they should be cleaned and repacked before reinstallation. When reassembling, fit the stub axle into position and and attach the upper and lower ball joints.

9. Attach the steering rod onto the steering arm.

10. Place the inner bearing in position within the hub. Using the correct sized drift, install the inner seal.

11. Install the hub onto the stub axle and fit the outer bearing in place. Install the washer and castle nut.

12. Adjust the front wheel bearings by spinning the hub and simultaneously tightening the

center nut to 50 ft. lbs. Then loosen the center nut two flats on the center nut.

If the nut recess (groove) doesn't line up with the cotter pin hole, loosen the nut just a bit until it aligns. Install a new cotter pin and check that the hub spins freely without excess sideplay.

13. Install the brake disc on the hub.

14. Fill the grease cap half full with bearing grease and install the cap.

15. Reinstall the caliper.

16. Install the wheel and lower the vehicle to the ground. Final tighten the wheel lugs.

200 Series

CAUTION: *This procedure requires removal of the brakes. Brake pads and shoes contain asbestos, which has been determined to a cancer causing agent. Never clean the brake surfaces with compressed air! Avoid inhaling and dust from brake surfaces! When cleaning brakes, use commercially available brake cleaning fluids.*

WARNING: *The use of the correct special tools or their equivalent is REQUIRED for this procedure.*

To remove the spring, a coil spring compressor must be used. Under no circumstances should you attempt to lower and disassemble the strut assembly without the proper spring compressor. Serious injury could result.

1. Loosen the wheel nuts, elevate the car and safely support it with jackstands under jack points or frame.

2. Plug the vent hole in the brake fluid reservoir to prevent spillage and leakage.

3. Remove the wheels. Disconnect the brake line bracket but don't disconnect the hoses.

4. Remove the attaching bolts and remove the brake caliper. Note the position of any shims in the mounting. Use wire to support the caliper out of the way.

5. Remove the grease cap. Remove the cotter pin, the castle nut and mount a hub puller onto the disc.

6. Pull the hub off. The outer bearing and disc will come off with it; the inner bearing may stay on the stub axle. If this happens, simply use a bearing puller of the correct size to remove the bearing from the axle.

7. Place a floor jack beneath the control arm to support it but do not locate it under the lower ball joint.

8. Install the spring compressor on the spring directly beneath the upper mount. Make sure that at least 3 coils of the spring are between the tool attachment points. Tighten the tool and compress the spring.

9. Using a ball joint puller, disconnect the steering rod from the steering arm.

10. Disconnect the stabilizer bar at the upper link.

11. Open the hood and remove the cover from the top of the strut assembly upper mount. Mark the position of the upper mounts relative to their holes.

12. While keeping the strut from turning, loosen and remove the nut for the upper strut mount.

13. Before lowering the strut assembly, wire or tie the strut to some stationary component (or use a holding fixture such as Volvo 5045) to prevent the strut from traveling down too far.

Lower the jack supporting the lower arm and allow the strut to tilt out at about a 60° angle. At this angle, the top of the strut assembly should just protrude past the wheel well, allowing removal of the strut components from the top. Take great care to control the descent of the strut and prevent damage to the fender.

14. Lift off the spring seat, rubber bumper, and the shock absorber protector. Remove the coil spring and compressor assembly from the strut.

15. If the same spring is to be reused, it may be left within the compressor and put aside until reassembly.

16. While keeping the strut outer tube from turning, remove the upper shock absorber retaining nut.

17. Pull the shock absorber unit out of the outer tube (casing).

NOTE: *On some models, gas type shock absorbers are used. A special tool (such as Volvo 5173 or similar) must be used to remove and install the unit.*

18. Remove the lower ball joint nut and mount. Please consult the section in this chapter for "Lower Ball Joint Removal and Installation" for specific instructions regarding early or later production cars.

19. With the lower ball joint disconnected, the strut assembly may be removed from the car. It is a one piece assembly consisting of the shock absorber tube, the lower spring seat and the spindle (stub axle).

The components are not individually replaceable; any failure requires a complete replacement unit.

20. When reinstalling, position the new unit and install the lower ball joint, following the correct procedure for early or late production cars. Support the upper part of the assembly as before to prevent damage.

21. Install the shock absorber unit into the outer tube and install the retaining nut. You can stop the outer tube from turning with the

nut by holding the tube at the weld with a pair of locking pliers.

22. Pull the shock absorber shaft to its uppermost position.

23. Position the spring and compressor on the strut assembly. Make sure the spring end is properly aligned with the lower mount.

24. Install the rubber bumper and the shock absorber protector. Position the spring seat on the spring, making sure it is aligned with the spring.

25. Carefully lift and guide the strut assembly into its upper attachment in the spring tower. Connect the stabilizer bar to the stabilizer link.

26. Guide the shock absorber spindle into the upper attachment and raise the jack beneath the lower control arm. Install the washer and nut on top of the shock absorber spindle. Position the upper mount according to marks made during removal.

Tighten the upper mounting bolts. The smaller outer nuts should be tightened to 15–25 ft. lbs. The large center nut should be tightened to 90–100 ft. lbs. Install the cover.

27. Attach the brake line bracket to its mount. Make sure that the brake lines sit properly in their mounts. Tighten the nut holding the stabilizer bar to the link. Connect the steering rod at the steering arm.

28. Slowly release the coil spring compressor, allow the spring to seat and remove the compressor.

29. Inspect the front wheel bearings as outlined under "Front Wheel Bearings Removal and Installation" in this chapter. Repack the bearings if necessary and always replace the seals.

30. Place the inner bearing in position within the hub. Using the correct sized drift, install the inner seal.

31. Install the hub onto the stub axle and fit the outer bearing in place. Install the washer and castle nut.

32. Adjust the front wheel bearings by spinning the hub and simultaneously tightening the center nut to 50 ft. lbs. Then loosen the center nut two flats on the center nut.

If the nut recess (groove) doesn't line up with the cotter pin hole, loosen the nut just a bit until it aligns. Install a new cotter pin and check that the hub spins freely without excess sideplay.

33. Install the brake disc on the hub.

34. Fill the grease cap half full with bearing grease and install the cap.

35. Reinstall the caliper, observing shim placement as noted during removal.

36. Reinstall the brake hose mounting bracket. Check that the brake lines are not stretched or kinked.

37. Remove the jack from under the control arm. Remove the plug from the reservoir vent hole.

38. Install the wheel and lower the vehicle to the ground. Final tighten the wheel lugs.

700 Series

1. Safely elevate and support the front end. Remove the wheel.

2. Loosen the retaining bolts and remove the brake caliper. Hang the caliper out of the way with a piece of stiff wire.

3. Pry off the grease cap. Remove the cotter pin and castle nut.

4. Remove the brake disc. The outer bearing will come off with the disc. Use a bearing puller to remove the inner bearing from the spindle if it is difficult to remove.

NOTE: *On 1988–89 760 and 780 cars with Multi-Link rear suspension, the brake disc will be a separate item. Removing the disc will expose the hub lock nut, which must be removed. Both wheel bearings are found inside the hub.*

5. Position a jack under the lower control arm to support it, but don't place it under the lower ball joint.

6. Install the spring compressor on the spring directly beneath the upper mount. Make sure that at least 3 coils of the spring are between the tool attachment points. Tighten the tool and compress the spring.

7. Using a ball joint puller, disconnect the steering rod from the steering arm.

8. Disconnect the stabilizer bar at the upper link.

9. Remove the bolt holding the brake line bracket to the fender well.

10. Open the hood and remove the cover from the top of the strut assembly upper mount. Mark the position of the upper mounts relative to their holes.

11. While keeping the strut from turning, loosen and remove the nut for the upper strut mount.

12. Before lowering the strut assembly, wire or tie the strut to some stationary component (or use a holding fixture such as Volvo 5045) to prevent the strut from traveling down too far and causing damage.

Lower the jack supporting the lower arm and allow the strut to tilt out at about a 60° angle. At this angle, the top of the strut assembly should just protrude past the wheel well, allowing removal of the strut components from the top. Take great care to control the descent of the strut and prevent damage to the fender.

13. Lift off the spring seat, rubber bumper, and the shock absorber protector. Remove the upper spring mount from the shaft. If the same

spring is to be reinstalled, it may be left within the compressor and put aside.

14. While keeping the strut outer tube from turning, remove the upper shock absorber retaining nut.

15. Pull the shock absorber unit out of the outer tube (casing).

NOTE: *On some models, gas type shock absorbers are used. A special tool (such as Volvo 5173 or similar) must be used to remove and install the unit.*

16. Remove the cotter pin for the lower ball joint stud, and remove the nut.

17. Using a ball joint separator, press out the ball joint from the control arm. Make sure the puller is located directly in line with the stud, and that the rubber grease boot is not damaged by the puller.

18. Remove the bolts holding the ball joint to the spring strut. Press the control arm down and remove the ball joint.

19. With the lower ball joint disconnected, the strut assembly may be removed from the car. It is a one piece assembly consisting of the shock absorber tube, the lower spring seat and the spindle (stub axle).

The components are not individually replaceable; any failure requires a complete replacement unit.

20. When reinstalling, position the new unit and install the lower ball joint. Tighten the retaining nut to 44 ft. lbs. Support the upper part of the assembly as before to prevent damage.

21. Install the shock absorber unit into the outer tube and install the retaining nut. You can stop the outer tube from turning with the nut by holding the tube at the weld with a pair of locking pliers.

22. Pull the shock absorber shaft to its uppermost position.

23. Position the spring and compressor on the strut assembly. Install the upper spring mount. Make sure the spring end is properly aligned with the lower mount.

NOTE: *Make sure that the compressor bolts face as they did during removal.*

24. Install the rubber bumper and the shock absorber protector. Position the spring seat on the spring, making sure it is aligned with the spring.

25. Carefully lift and guide the strut assembly into its upper attachment in the spring tower. Connect the stabilizer bar to the stabilizer link.

26. Guide the shock absorber spindle into the upper attachment and raise the jack beneath the lower control arm. Install the washer and nut on top of the shock absorber spindle. Position the upper mount according to marks made during removal.

Tighten the upper mounting bolts. The

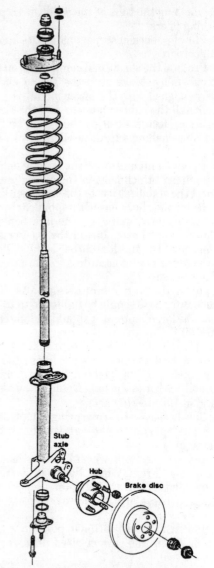

Front hub and stub axle assembly, 700 Series with Multi-Link suspension

smaller outer nuts should be tightened to 15–25 ft. lbs. The large center nut should be tightened to 90–100 ft. lbs. Install the cover.

27. Attach the brake line bracket to its mount. Make sure that the brake lines sit properly in their mounts. Tighten the nut holding the stabilizer bar to the link. Connect the steering rod at the steering arm.

28. Slowly release the coil spring compressor and remove it from the car.

29. Inspect the front wheel bearings as outlined under "Front Wheel Bearings – Removal and Installation" in this chapter. Repack the bearings if necessary and always replace the seals.

30. Place the inner bearing in position within

the hub or disc. Using the correct sized drift, install the inner seal.

31. Install the disc, the outer bearing and the castle nut. For 1988–89 760 and 780 with Multi-Link rear suspension, install the hub and with a NEW locknut. Do not reuse the old nut; bearing damage may result. Tighten the new nut to 74 ft.lbs PLUS an additional 45° of rotation.

32. Install the brake caliper. Volvo recommends the use of new retaining bolts. The bolts should be tightened to 74 ft. lbs.

32. Adjust the front wheel bearing by spinning the disc several times and then tightening the nut to 42 ft. lbs. Loosen the nut ½ turn, then retighten to one ft.lb. This is just enough to hold the bearing in place but not enough to develop any side loading.

33. Install a new cotter pin. If the hole in the spindle doesn't align with the castle nut, tighten the nut just until the hole and slot align.

34. Install the grease cap. Install the wheel.

35. Lower the car to the ground and tighten the wheel to 63 ft. lbs.

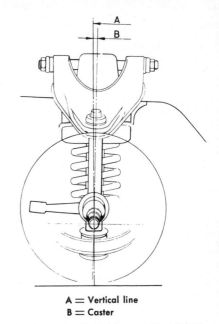

A = Vertical line
B = Caster

Caster angle—not adjustable on 200 and 700 Series

Front End Alignment

Alignment of the front wheels is essential if your car is to go, stop and turn as designed. Alignment can be altered by collision, overloading, poor repair or bent components.

If you are diagnosing bizarre handling and/or poor road manners, the first place to look is the tires. Although the tires may wear as a result of an alignment problem, worn or poorly inflated tires can make you chase alignment problems which don't exist.

Once you have eliminated all other causes, unload everything from the trunk except the spare tire, set the tire pressures to the correct level and take the car to a reputable alignment facility. Since the alignment settings are measured in very small increments, it is almost impossible for the home mechanic to accurately determine the settings. The explanations that follow will help you understand the three dimensions of alignment: caster, camber and toe.

CASTER

Caster is the tilting of the steering axis either forward or backward from the vertical, when viewed from the side of the vehicle. A backward tilt is said to be positive and a forward tilt is said to be negative. Changes in caster affect the straight line tendency of the vehicle and the "return to center" of the steering after a turn. If the camber is radically different between the left and right wheels (such as after hitting a major pothole), the car will exhibit a nasty pull to one side.

On the 140, 160 and 1800 Series Volvos, caster is adjustable through the use of shims which reposition the suspension components in the correct direction. The later 200 and 700 Series Volvos do not allow adjustment; replacement of bent components is required.

CAMBER

Camber is the tilting of the wheels from the vertical (leaning in or out) when viewed from

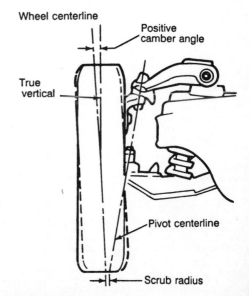

Wheel centerline

Positive camber angle

True vertical

Pivot centerline

Scrub radius

Camber angle

Wheel Alignment

Year	Model	Caster Range (deg)	Camber Range (deg)	Toe-in (in.)	Steering Axis Inclination (at 0° camber)	Wheel Pivot Ratio (deg)	
						Inner Wheel	Outer Wheel
1970–71	140 series 164	0–1P	0–½P	0–0.16	7.5	20	21.5–23.5
1970–71	1800 series	0–1P	0–½P	0–0.16	8.0	20	21.5–23.5
1972	140 series 164	0–1P	0–½P	0.080–0.20	7.5	20	21.5–23.5
1972–73	1800 series	①	0–½P	0–0.12	8.0	20	21.5–23.5
1973	140 series 164	1½P–2P	0–½P	0.08–0.20	7.5	20	21.5–23.5
1974	140 series, 164	1½P–2½P ②	0–½P	0–0.063	7.5	20	21.5–23.5
1975	240 series	2P–3P	1P–1½P	③	12	20	20.8
1975	164	½P–1½P	¾N–1¼N	0.063–0.188	7.5	20	21.5–23.5
1976–77	240 series, 260 series	2P–3P	1P–1½P	0.18–0.30	12	20	20.8
1978	240, 260 series	2P–3P	1P–1½P	0.12–0.24 ④	12	20	20.8

Year	Model						
1979	240, 260 series	2P–3P ⑤	0–1N ⑥	0.12–0.24 ④	12	20	20.8
1980–83	All models except GLT, 760 GLE	2P–3P ⑤	1P–1½P	0.18–0.24 ⑦	12	20	20.8
1980–83	GLT	2P–3P ⑤	¼P–¾P	0.18–0.24 ⑦	12	20	20.8
1983	760 GLE	5P	13/32P	0.10–0.18	—	—	—
1984	DL, GL	3P–4P	1P–1½P ⑥	0.06–0.18	12	20	20.8
1984	GLT, GLE	3P–4P	¼–¾P ⑥	0.06–0.18	12	20	20.8
1984–87	740, 760, 780 series	4½–5½	2/10N–8/10P	0.10–0.18	—	—	—
1985–89	240 series all models	3P–4P	¼P–¾P ⑥	0.06–0.18	12	20	20.8
1988–89	760, 780	4½P–5½P	2/10N–8/10P	0.00–0.025	—	—	—

P Positive   N Negative
① 0–1P—165HR15 Tires
  2P–2½P—185/70HR15 Tires
② w/power steering, caster is 2P–3P
③ w/manual steering—0.171–0.183 in.
  w/power steering—0.114–0.126 in.
④ Power steering—0.06–0.18
⑤ Power steering—3P–4P
⑥ Must not exceed ½° difference between sides
⑦ Power steering—0.12–0.18 in.

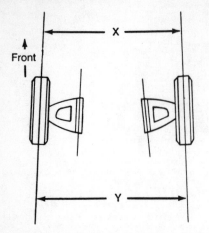

Toe-In is how much closer the fronts of the tires are than the rear of the tires (Y–X)

the front of the vehicle. When the wheels tilt outward at the top, the camber is said to be positive. When the wheels tilt inward at the top the camber is said to be negative. The amount of tilt is measured in degrees from the vertical. This measurement is called camber angle.

Camber affects the position of the tire on the road surface during vertical suspension movement and cornering. Changes in camber affect the handling and ride qualities of the car as well as tire wear. Many tire wear patterns indicate camber related problems from misalignment, overloading or poor driving habits.

Camber is adjustable on the 100, 200, and 1800 families of Volvos. On the 700 Series, the position is fixed by the correct location of the suspension components. Any camber reading outside of specification requires replacement of bent parts.

TOE

Toe is the turning in or out (parallelism) of the wheels. The actual amount of toe setting is normally only a fraction of an inch. The purpose of toe-in (or out) specification is to ensure parallel rolling of the wheels. Toe-in also serves to offset the small deflections of the steering support system which occur when the vehicle is rolling forward.

Changing the toe setting will radically affect the overall "feel" of the steering, the behavior of the car under braking, tire wear and even fuel economy. Excessive toe (in or out) causes excessive drag or scrubbing on the tires.

Toe is adjustable on all Volvos. It is generally measured in decimal inches or degrees. It is adjusted by loosening the locknut on each tierod end and turning the rod until the correct reading is achieved. The rods left and right must remain equal in length during all adjustments.

REAR SUSPENSION

All Volvos except the 1988–89 760 and 780 use a coil spring rear suspension. The solid rear axle is suspended from the rigid frame member by a pair of support arms and damped by a pair of double-acting telescopic shock absorbers. A pair of torque rods control rear axle wind-up and a track rod limits the lateral movement of the rear axle in relation to the car. A rear stabilizer bar, attached to both rear support (trailing) arms, is installed on certain models.

In 1988, the 760 4 door sedan and the 780 model introduced Volvo's Multi-Link suspension system. This independently suspends each rear wheel, allowing improved ride and roadholding as well as allowing each rear wheel to be aligned separately. The rear suspension is two-way adjustable, allowing setting of camber and toe at the rear wheels. Caster is fixed by the design of the suspension and cannot be altered except by replacement of damaged parts.

Multi-Link suspensions require alignment any time the suspension components are disassembled. Position of components is critical as are torque values when retightening bolts. Multi-link repairs are discussed separately at the end of this section.

Coil Springs
REMOVAL AND INSTALLATION
140, 160 Series and all 200 Series

WARNING: *The use of the correct special tools or their equivalent is REQUIRED for this procedure.*

To remove the spring, a coil spring compressor must be used. Under no circumstances should you attempt to remove the spring without the proper spring compressor. Serious injury could result.

1. Remove the hub cap and loosen the lug nuts a few turns. Jack up the car and place jackstands in front of the rear jacking points. Remove the wheel.

2. Place a hydraulic jack beneath the rear axle housing and raise the housing sufficiently to compress the spring. Install the spring compressor and tighten it to hold the spring in its compressed position. Make sure there are at least three coils of spring between the attachment points of the compressor. Loosen the nuts for the upper and lower spring attachments.

CAUTION: *The spring is compressed under several hundred pounds of pressure! When it is freed from its lower attachment, it will attempt to suddenly return to its extended position. It is therefore imperative that the axle housing be lowered with extreme care until the spring is extended. As an added safety measure, a chain may be attached to the lower spring coil and secured to the axle housing.*

3. Disconnect the shock absorber at its upper attachment. Carefully lower the jack and axle housing until the spring is extended. Remove the spring.

4. To install, position the retaining bolt and inner washer for the upper attachment inside the spring. While holding the outer washer and rubber spacer to the upper body attachment, install the spring and inner washer to the upper attachment (sandwiching the rubber spacer). Tighten the retaining bolt.

5. Raise the jack and secure the bottom of the spring to its lower attachment with the washer and retaining bolt. Slowly remove the spring compressor.

6. Connect the shock absorber to its upper attachment. Install the wheel.

7. Remove the jackstands and lower the car. Tighten the lug nuts to 85–90 ft. lbs. and install the hub cap.

1800 Series

1. Remove the hub cap and loosen the lug nuts a few turns. Place blocks in front of the front wheels. Jack up the rear of the car and place jackstands in front of the rear jacking points.

2. Remove the wheel and release the parking brake.

3. Place a hydraulic jack beneath the rear axle housing and raise the jack and axle housing sufficiently to unload the downward travel limiter (shock absorber band). Install the spring compressor and tighten it enough to hold the spring in a partially compressed position.

4. Disconnect the shock absorber at its lower attachment. Also disconnect the suspension travel limiter (shock absorber band) at its upper attachment.

CAUTION: *Do not attempt to remove the spring until it is extended. As an added safety measure, a chain may be attached to the lower spring coil and secured to the axle housing.*

5. Carefully lower the jack and axle housing until the spring is extended. Remove the spring and rubber spacer.

6. To install, fit the rubber spacer to the top of the spring and position the spring into it upper attachment. Secure the bottom of the spring into its lower attachment, making sure that the rubber cushion on the axle housing is positioned correctly.

7. Raise the jack sufficiently so that the shock absorber may be connected to its lower attachment. Connect the suspension travel limiter to its upper attachment. Slowly remove the spring compressor.

8. Install the wheel and tire assembly. Remove the jackstands and lower the car. Tighten the lug nuts to 85–90 ft. lbs., and install the hub cap.

700 Series except Multi-Link suspension

1. Loosen the lug nuts a few turns. Place blocks in front of the front wheels. Jack up the rear of the car and place jackstands in front of the rear jacking points.

2. Remove the wheel. Remove the rear caliper and support it out of the way with a piece of wire. Do not allow it to hang by its hose.

3. Place a jack under the rear axle and elevate the axle just enough to take the tension off the lower shock absorber mount.

4. As a safety precaution, install a spring compressor on the spring and tighten it enough to hold it in a partially compressed position. Loosen and remove the lower shock absorber bolt.

5. Lower the rear axle to unload the spring. Remove the upper bolt, washers and rubber spacer. Remove the spring.

6. When installing, fit the rubber spacer and washer to the new spring. Make sure that the recess in the spacer is properly seated.

7. Press and secure the lower washer to the rubber spacer.

8. Attach the spring to the upper mount. Tighten the nut to 35 ft. lbs. Position the spring in the lower (trailing) arm.

9. Raise the rear axle with the jack and install the lower shock absorber bolt. Tighten it to 63 ft. lbs.

10. Use new mounting bolts and install the rear brake caliper. Tighten the mounting bolts to 43 ft. lbs. Install the wheel and lower the car to the ground. Final tighten the lugs to 63 ft. lbs.

On the 700 Series, the lower washer must be secure against the upper spacer

Shock Absorbers

REMOVAL AND INSTALLATION

140, 160 Series and all 200 Series

1. Remove the hub cap and loosen the lug nuts a few turns. Place blocks in front of the front wheels. Jack up the rear of the car and place jackstands in front of the rear jacking points. Remove the wheel.

2. Remove the nuts and bolts which retain the shock absorber to its upper and lower attachments and remove the shock absorber. Make sure that the spacing sleeve (inside the axle support arm for the lower attachment) is not misplaced.

3. The damping effect of the shock absorber may be tested by securing the lower attachment in a vise and extending and compressing it. A properly operating shock absorber should offer about three times as much resistance to extending the unit as to compressing it.

Replace the shock absorber if any impaired function is found. Also replace it if any leakage is present or if the rubber bushings are damaged.

4. To install, position the shock absorber to its upper and lower attachments. Make sure that the spcing sleeve is installed inside the axle support (trailing) arm and is aligned with the lower attachment bolt hole.

5. Install the retaining nuts and bolts and tighten to 63 ft. lbs. On 240 and 260 Series, the shock fits inside the support arm. On all 140 and 164 models, the shock attaches on the outboard side of the support arm.

6. Install the wheel and tire assembly. Re-

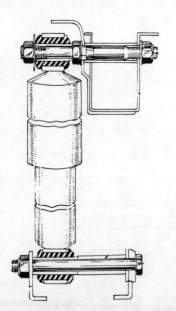

Rear shock absorber and mounts, 200 Series

move the jackstands and lower the car. Tighten the lug nuts to 85–90 ft. lbs., and install the hub cap.

1800 Series

1. Fold the rear seat back forward. On 1800E models, remove the upholstery for the shelf under the rear window, and on 1800ES models fold back the carpet for the cargo bed, which will reveal the shock absorber upper attaching points.

2. Remove the upper nut, washers, and outer rubber bushing from the top of the shock absorber.

3. Under the car, remove the lower nut, washer, and outer rubber bushing from the bottom of the shock absorber.

4. Compress and remove the shock absorber.

5. Test the damping action of the shock absorber. Extending the unit should offer about three times as much resistance as compressing the unit. If the shock absorber is operating properly and is being reinstalled, be sure to use new rubber bushings.

6. Install inner washers and new rubber bushings, if removed, on the unit. Compress the shock absorber and position it to its upper and lower attachments.

7. Install the outer nut, washers, and new rubber bushings first to the top and then to the bottom of the shock absorber.

8. Replace the package shelf upholstery or the cargo bed carpet to its original position.

700 Series except Multi-Link suspension.

1. Loosen the lug nuts a few turns. Place blocks in front of the front wheels. Jack up the rear of the car and place jackstands in front of the rear jacking points.

2. Remove the wheel. (While not absolutely necessary, access is improved.)

3. Place a jack under the rear axle and elevate the axle just enough to take the tension off the lower shock absorber mount.

4. Remove the lower shock absorber bolt.

5. In the spare tire well, locate and remove the rubber plug which covers the access hole to the upper shock mount.

WARNING: *Remember the car is on jackstands. Do not climb into the trunk or the car may become imbalanced and fall off the stands. Work from the side of the car and reach into the trunk.*

6. Remove the upper bolt and remove the shock absorber.

7. Install the new unit by first tightening the upper bolt and then the lower one. Tighten both bolts to 63 ft. lbs. Replace the rubber plug in the spare tire well.

8. Lower the rear axle and remove the jack.

9. Install the wheel and lower the vehicle. Tighten the wheel lugs to 63 ft. lbs.

Trailing Arms
REMOVAL AND INSTALLATION

In all cases (except Multi-Link suspension), replacing the trailing arm requires removal of the axle assembly. The reader is referred to "Axle Housing Complete Unit, Removal and Installation" in Chapter 7. When the axle assembly is removed, the trailing arm is simply unbolted and removed. Check the arm carefully for any deformation or rusting. Also check all the bushings for any sign of wear or elongation.

Sway Bar

The sway bar, variously called the anti-roll bar or stabilizer bar, serves to control the sideways roll of the body during cornering. While the bar itself rarely fails, the links and bushings around it are prone to wear. If the bar is not rigidly mounted to the car, it cannot do its job properly.

REMOVAL AND INSTALLATION
All 200 and 700 Series so equipped

1. Safely jack and support the rear of the vehicle. Place the stands at the rear jacking points. While not absolutely necessary, the job may be easier if the wheels are removed.
2. Use a floor jack to raise the rear axle just enough to unload the lower shock absorber mount. Remove the lower shock retaining bolt.
3. Remove the nut holding the sway bar to the bracket.
4. On the other side of the car, remove the shock retaining bolt and the nut holding the sway bar to the bracket.
5. When installing the new bar, install both the bracket nut and the lower shock retaining bolt hand tight on one side. Then install the nut and bolt hand tight on the other side.
6. Once all four mounting points are snug,

tighten the bracket nuts to 35 ft.lbs and the shock absorber bolts to 63 ft. lbs.
7. Remove the jack from the axle. Install the wheels if removed and lower the car to the ground. Tighten the wheel lugs to 85–90 ft. lbs. (200 Series) or 63 ft. lbs. (700 Series).

Multi-Link Rear Suspension 1988–89 760 and 780

NOTE: *Multi-Link suspensions require alignment any time the suspension components are disassembled. Position of components is critical as are torque values when retightening bolts.*

COMPONENT REMOVAL AND INSTALLATION
Spring, Shock Absorber and Support arm

NOTE: *It is important that the car be parked in a straight-ahead position with no side loadings in the suspension. After the car is in the work area, roll it forward and backwards 6–8 ft. and make sure the front and rear wheels point straight.*

1. Safely elevate and support both ends of the car. Make sure the front supports are placed as far forward as possible. Check that the rear supports will not interfere with the support arm.
2. Remove the wheels. Loosen and remove the bolts holding the protective cover (guard) to the arm and remove the guard.
3. At the front of the arm, remove the two retaining bolts which hold the bracket (for the support arm) to the frame. Don't attempt to remove the through bolt (eye bolt).
4. Remove the retaining bolt at the rear of the support arm.
5. Separate the rear end of the support arm from the wheel bearing housing.
6. Using either Volvo tool 5972 or two floor jacks, support the arm at the front and rear

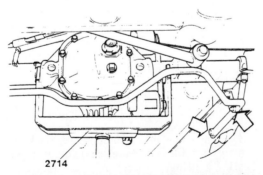

2714

Arrows show location of rear sway bar bolts. Note use of cradle to support rear axle. Volvo tool shown

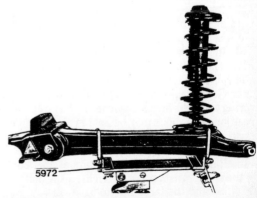

5972

Use of Volvo tool to support the lower arm on Multi-Link suspensions

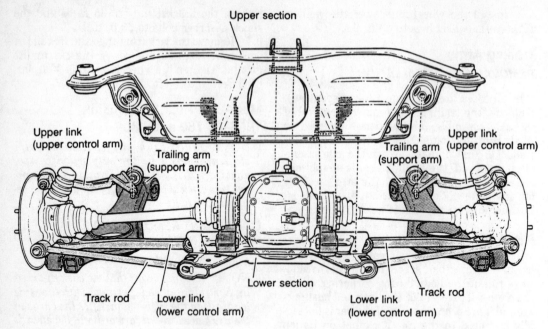

Components of Multi-Link suspension

ends. Elevate the jacks just enough to relieve the tension on the shock absorber.

7. Remove the retaining bolt at the top of the shock abosorber.

8. Lower the jacks slowly; the arm will come free with the spring and shock attached.

9. Remove the spring and the upper and lower rubber seats. Unbolt the shock absorber from the arm. If the support arm is to be replaced, unbolt and remove the bracket at the front of the arm. Take note of the relationship between the bracket and the arm; the bracket correctly mounts one way only.

10. When installing, install the support arm bracket in the correct position and tighten the nut to 91 ft.lbs PLUS 120° of rotation.

11. Install the shock absorber on the arm and tighten the bottom mount to 41 ft. lbs.

12. Install the bottom spring seat on the support arm. Take care to properly locate the grooves in the seat.

13. Install the spring and the top rubber seat. Place the assembled support arm on the jacks and raise into position.

14. Gently raise the jacks and compress the spring until the shock absorber is in the correct position. The shock may be held in place temporarily with a drift or screwdriver in the hole. Insert the bolt and tighten it to 62 ft. lbs.

15. Reinstall the mounting bolts at the front of the support arm bracket. Tighten the bolts to 35 ft.lbs and the large nut to 51 ft. lbs.

16. At the rear of the support arm, tap the arm into place on the wheel bearing housing.

Tighten the bolt to 44 ft.lbs. PLUS 90° of rotation. Do not overtighten this fitting.

17. Reinstall the protective cover on the control arm. Install the wheel.

18. Lower the car to the ground and final tighten the lugs to 62 ft. lbs.

19. Have the rear alignment checked and adjusted if necessary.

Upper Control Arm

CAUTION: *The following procedure requires removal of the brakes. Brake pads and shoes contain asbestos, which has been determined to a cancer causing agent. Never clean the brake surfaces with compressed air! Avoid inhaling and dust from brake surfaces! When cleaning brakes, use commercially available brake cleaning fluids.*

1. Safely elevate and support both ends of the car. Make sure the front supports are placed as far forward as possible. Check that the rear supports will not interfere with the support arm.

2. Remove the wheels. Remove the brake caliper and tie it with wire out of the way. Do not allow it to hang by its hose.

3. Remove the bolt holding the lower support arm to the wheel bearing housing and tap the support arm loose.

4. Remove the nut and bolt holding the lower control arm (intermediate arm) to the wheel bearing housing.

5. Remove the bolt attaching the track rod to the wheel bearing housing. Use a small bearing

puller and a long 12mm bolt to disconnect the track rod.

6. Remove the nut which holds the upper control arm to the wheel bearing housing. Collect and note the location of the spacers between the upper control arm and the bearing housing. They are alignment shims and must be reinstalled properly.

7. At the rear of the upper control arm, remove the nut holding it to the rear axle member (support).

8. At the front of the upper control arm, remove the nut and bolt which holds it to the rear axle member.

9. Use a pair of adjustable pliers to remove the control arm from the car.

10. Install the new arm and install the nuts and bolts holding it to the rear axle member. Install both the front and rear mounts.

11. Install the spacers at the wheel bearing housing, position the arm and install the nut holding the arm to the housing.

12. Inboard, (at the rear axle support) tighten the rearmost nut to 62 ft. lbs. Tighten the front nut and bolt to 51 ft.lbs. PLUS 60° of rotation.

13. Pull the top of the wheel bearing housing outwards (away from the center of the car). This is essential for correct wheel alignment.

14. Tighten the upper control arm nut (at the bearing housing) to 84 ft. lbs.

15. Pull the wheel bearing housing outward and install the lower control arm with its bolt and nut, but do not tighten it.

16. Pull the wheel bearing housing inwards (towards the center of the car). This is essential for correct wheel alignment.

17. Tighten the control arm nut to 37 ft. lbs. PLUS 90° of rotation.

18. Reinstall the support arm; tighten its mount to 44 ft. lbs. PLUS 90° of rotation.

19. Install the track rod and tighten to 62 ft. lbs.

20. Install the brake caliper, tightening its mounting bolts to 44 ft. lbs.

21. Install the wheel. Lower the car to the ground and tighten the wheel lugs to 62 ft. lbs.

22. Have the rear alignment checked and adjusted if necessary.

Rear Wheel Alignment

The tracking of the rear wheels is as important as the tracking of the front. Any misalignment at the rear will give the car a loose or "slippery" feel under cornering. All the handling and tire wear conditions discussed under front end alignment apply equally to the rear; at the rear they are often harder to diagnose and cure.

On all but the Multi-Link rear suspensions,

the position of the rear wheels is fixed in all three dimensions by the correct location of the components. Any tire or handling problems not traced to other causes will require replacement of suspension parts. The alignment dimensions--caster, camber and toe--can be measured on an alignment rack but are not adjustable.

It should be noted that any time the rear wheel alignment is checked, the front must also be checked and set. Ideally this is done on a four wheel alignment machine which will provide data on the comparative front and rear track as well as each front and each rear wheel.

Simultaneous four wheel alignment capability is REQUIRED for cars with Multi-Link rear suspension. Failure to use the proper equipment may result in the rear wheels having a mind of their own and steering in other directions than the driver might like. This "rear steer" effect can feel like roller skating on an ice rink; find an alignment shop with the proper equipment and get it done right. Volvo dealers are required by the manufacturer to have the proper equipment.

The Multi-Link suspension is adjusted for camber and toe through the use of eccentric bolts in the suspension links. The camber adjuster is located on the inboard end of the lower link. The toe adjuster is located at the inboard end of the track rod. Neither should be adjusted by anyone who is not using a four wheel alignment machine and the specifications book.

An additional adjustment controls toe variation. Although the toe setting can be numerically correct with the car at rest, it can change as a function of load and suspension motion. This very minor change can greatly upset the handling of the car. By inserting precisely sized shims between the upper control arm and the wheel bearing housing, this minor variation can be further controlled. This is particularly handy if the car constantly has a load in the trunk or constantly carries several people. The rear suspension can be fine-tuned for the best road manners under given load conditions.

STEERING

Steering Wheel
REMOVAL AND INSTALLATION

NOTE: *The use of a knock-off type steering wheel puller or the use of a hammer may damage the collapsible column.*

1970–71 140 Series, 164 Models

1. Disconnect the negative battery cable.
2. Remove the retaining screw from the up-

per half of the molded turn signal switch housing and the three retaining screws from the lower half. Remove both halves from the column.

3. Remove the two screws which retain the horn ring to the steering wheel. Turn and lift up the horn ring and disconnect the plug contact.

4. Remove the steering wheel nut.

5. With the front wheels pointing straight ahead, and the steering wheel centered, install the steering wheel puller (Volvo tool 2711 or similar) and pull off the steering wheel.

6. To install, make sure that the front wheels are pointing straight ahead, then place the centered steering wheel on the column and install the nut. Tighten the steering wheel nut to 25–30 ft. lbs.

7. Connect the horn plug contact and install the horn ring.

8. First install the lower and then the upper turn signal housing halves and their retaining screws.

9. Connect the negative battery cable and check the operation of the horn.

1972 140 Series, 164 Models

1. Disconnect the negative battery cable.

2. Remove the retaining screw for the upper half of the molded turn signal switch housing and lift off the housing.

3. Pry up and remove the impact protection from the horn ring. Disconnect the plug contact for the horn and remove the four retaining screws for the horn ring. Lift off the horn ring, noting the positions of the various springs and washers.

4. Remove the steering wheel nut.

5. With the front wheels pointing straight ahead, and the steering wheel centered, install a steering wheel puller (Volvo tool 2972 or similar) and pull off the steering wheel.

Troubleshooting the Steering Column

Problem	Cause	Solution
Will not lock	• Lockbolt spring broken or defective	• Replace lock bolt spring
High effort (required to turn ignition key and lock cylinder)	• Lock cylinder defective • Ignition switch defective • Rack preload spring broken or deformed • Burr on lock sector, lock rack, housing, support or remote rod coupling • Bent sector shaft • Defective lock rack • Remote rod bent, deformed • Ignition switch mounting bracket bent • Distorted coupling slot in lock rack (tilt column)	• Replace lock cylinder • Replace ignition switch • Replace preload spring • Remove burr • Replace shaft • Replace lock rack • Replace rod • Straighten or replace • Replace lock rack
Will stick in "start"	• Remote rod deformed • Ignition switch mounting bracket bent	• Straighten or replace • Straighten or replace
Key cannot be removed in "off-lock"	• Ignition switch is not adjusted correctly • Defective lock cylinder	• Adjust switch • Replace lock cylinder
Lock cylinder can be removed without depressing retainer	• Lock cylinder with defective retainer • Burr over retainer slot in housing cover or on cylinder retainer	• Replace lock cylinder • Remove burr
High effort on lock cylinder between "off" and "off-lock"	• Distorted lock rack • Burr on tang of shift gate (automatic column) • Gearshift linkage not adjusted	• Replace lock rack • Remove burr • Adjust linkage
Noise in column	• One click when in "off-lock" position and the steering wheel is moved (all except automatic column) • Coupling bolts not tightened	• Normal—lock bolt is seating • Tighten pinch bolts

Troubleshooting the Steering Column (cont.)

Problem	Cause	Solution
Noise in column (cont.)	• Lack of grease on bearings or bearing surfaces	• Lubricate with chassis grease
	• Upper shaft bearing worn or broken	• Replace bearing assembly
	• Lower shaft bearing worn or broken	• Replace bearing. Check shaft and replace if scored.
	• Column not correctly aligned	• Align column
	• Coupling pulled apart	• Replace coupling
	• Broken coupling lower joint	• Repair or replace joint and align column
	• Steering shaft snap ring not seated	• Replace ring. Check for proper seating in groove.
	• Shroud loose on shift bowl. Housing loose on jacket—will be noticed with ignition in "off-lock" and when torque is applied to steering wheel.	• Position shroud over lugs on shift bowl. Tighten mounting screws.
High steering shaft effort	• Column misaligned	• Align column
	• Defective upper or lower bearing	• Replace as required
	• Tight steering shaft universal joint	• Repair or replace
	• Flash on I.D. of shift tube at plastic joint (tilt column only)	• Replace shift tube
	• Upper or lower bearing seized	• Replace bearings
Lash in mounted column assembly	• Column mounting bracket bolts loose	• Tighten bolts
	• Broken weld nuts on column jacket	• Replace column jacket
	• Column capsule bracket sheared	• Replace bracket assembly
	• Column bracket to column jacket mounting bolts loose	• Tighten to specified torque
	• Loose lock shoes in housing (tilt column only)	• Replace shoes
	• Loose pivot pins (tilt column only)	• Replace pivot pins and support
	• Loose lock shoe pin (tilt column only)	• Replace pin and housing
	• Loose support screws (tilt column only)	• Tighten screws
Housing loose (tilt column only)	• Excessive clearance between holes in support or housing and pivot pin diameters	• Replace pivot pins and support
	• Housing support-screws loose	• Tighten screws
Steering wheel loose—every other tilt position (tilt column only)	• Loose fit between lock shoe and lock shoe pivot pin	• Replace lock shoes and pivot pin
Steering column not locking in any tilt position (tilt column only)	• Lock shoe seized on pivot pin	• Replace lock shoes and pin
	• Lock shoe grooves have burrs or are filled with foreign material	• Clean or replace lock shoes
	• Lock shoe springs weak or broken	• Replace springs
Noise when tilting column (tilt column only)	• Upper tilt bumpers worn	• Replace tilt bumper
	• Tilt spring rubbing in housing	• Lubricate with chassis grease
One click when in "off-lock" position and the steering wheel is moved	• Seating of lock bolt	• None. Click is normal characteristic sound produced by lock bolt as it seats.
High shift effort (automatic and tilt column only)	• Column not correctly aligned	• Align column
	• Lower bearing not aligned correctly	• Assemble correctly
	• Lack of grease on seal or lower bearing areas	• Lubricate with chassis grease
Improper transmission shifting—automatic and tilt column only	• Sheared shift tube joint	• Replace shift tube
	• Improper transmission gearshift linkage adjustment	• Adjust linkage
	• Loose lower shift lever	• Replace shift tube

Troubleshooting the Turn Signal Switch

Problem	Cause	Solution
Turn signal will not cancel	• Loose switch mounting screws • Switch or anchor bosses broken • Broken, missing or out of position detent, or cancelling spring	• Tighten screws • Replace switch • Reposition springs or replace switch as required
Turn signal difficult to operate	• Turn signal lever loose • Switch yoke broken or distorted • Loose or misplaced springs • Foreign parts and/or materials in switch • Switch mounted loosely	• Tighten mounting screws • Replace switch • Reposition springs or replace switch • Remove foreign parts and/or material • Tighten mounting screws
Turn signal will not indicate lane change	• Broken lane change pressure pad or spring hanger • Broken, missing or misplaced lane change spring • Jammed wires	• Replace switch • Replace or reposition as required • Loosen mounting screws, reposition wires and retighten screws
Turn signal will not stay in turn position	• Foreign material or loose parts impeding movement of switch yoke • Defective switch	• Remove material and/or parts • Replace switch
Hazard switch cannot be pulled out	• Foreign material between hazard support cancelling leg and yoke	• Remove foreign material. No foreign material impeding function of hazard switch—replace turn signal switch.
No turn signal lights	• Inoperative turn signal flasher • Defective or blown fuse • Loose chassis to column harness connector • Disconnect column to chassis connector. Connect new switch to chassis and operate switch by hand. If vehicle lights now operate normally, signal switch is inoperative • If vehicle lights do not operate, check chassis wiring for opens, grounds, etc.	• Replace turn signal flasher • Replace fuse • Connect securely • Replace signal switch • Repair chassis wiring as required
Instrument panel turn indicator lights on but not flashing	• Burned out or damaged front or rear turn signal bulb • If vehicle lights do not operate, check light sockets for high resistance connections, the chassis wiring for opens, grounds, etc. • Inoperative flasher • Loose chassis to column harness connection • Inoperative turn signal switch • To determine if turn signal switch is defective, substitute new switch into circuit and operate switch by hand. If the vehicle's lights operate normally, signal switch is inoperative.	• Replace bulb • Repair chassis wiring as required • Replace flasher • Connect securely • Replace turn signal switch • Replace turn signal switch
Stop light not on when turn indicated	• Loose column to chassis connection • Disconnect column to chassis connector. Connect new switch into system without removing old.	• Connect securely • Replace signal switch

Troubleshooting the Turn Signal Switch (cont.)

Problem	Cause	Solution
Stop light not on when turn indicated (cont.)	Operate switch by hand. If brake lights work with switch in the turn position, signal switch is defective. • If brake lights do not work, check connector to stop light sockets for grounds, opens, etc.	• Repair connector to stop light circuits using service manual as guide
Turn indicator panel lights not flashing	• Burned out bulbs • High resistance to ground at bulb socket • Opens, ground in wiring harness from front turn signal bulb socket to indicator lights	• Replace bulbs • Replace socket • Locate and repair as required
Turn signal lights flash very slowly	• High resistance ground at light sockets • Incorrect capacity turn signal flasher or bulb • If flashing rate is still extremely slow, check chassis wiring harness from the connector to light sockets for high resistance • Loose chassis to column harness connection • Disconnect column to chassis connector. Connect new switch into system without removing old. Operate switch by hand. If flashing occurs at normal rate, the signal switch is defective.	• Repair high resistance grounds at light sockets • Replace turn signal flasher or bulb • Locate and repair as required • Connect securely • Replace turn signal switch
Hazard signal lights will not flash—turn signal functions normally	• Blow fuse • Inoperative hazard warning flasher • Loose chassis-to-column harness connection • Disconnect column to chassis connector. Connect new switch into system without removing old. Depress the hazard warning lights. If they now work normally, turn signal switch is defective. • If lights do not flash, check wiring harness "K" lead for open between hazard flasher and connector. If open, fuse block is defective	• Replace fuse • Replace hazard warning flasher in fuse panel • Conect securely • Replace turn signal switch • Repair or replace brown wire or connector as required

Troubleshooting the Ignition Switch

Problem	Cause	Solution
Ignition switch electrically inoperative	• Loose or defective switch connector • Feed wire open (fusible link) • Defective ignition switch	• Tighten or replace connector • Repair or replace • Replace ignition switch
Engine will not crank	• Ignition switch not adjusted properly	• Adjust switch
Ignition switch wil not actuate mechanically	• Defective ignition switch • Defective lock sector • Defective remote rod	• Replace switch • Replace lock sector • Replace remote rod
Ignition switch cannot be adjusted correctly	• Remote rod deformed	• Repair, straighten or replace

Troubleshooting the Power Steering Gear

Problem	Cause	Solution
Hissing noise in steering gear	• There is some noise in all power steering systems. One of the most common is a hissing sound most evident at standstill parking. There is no relationship between this noise and performance of the steering. Hiss may be expected when steering wheel is at end of travel or when slowly turning at standstill.	• Slight hiss is normal and in no way affects steering. Do not replace valve unless hiss is extremely objectionable. A replacement valve will also exhibit slight noise and is not always a cure. Investigate clearance around flexible coupling rivets. Be sure steering shaft and gear are aligned so flexible coupling rotates in a flat plane and is not distorted as shaft rotates. Any metal-to-metal contacts through flexible coupling will transmit valve hiss into passenger compartment through the steering column.
Rattle or chuckle noise in steering gear	• Gear loose on frame	• Check gear-to-frame mounting screws. Tighten screws to 88 N·m (65 foot pounds) torque.
	• Steering linkage looseness	• Check linkage pivot points for wear. Replace if necessary.
	• Pressure hose touching other parts of car	• Adjust hose position. Do not bend tubing by hand.
	• Loose pitman shaft over center adjustment	• Adjust to specifications
	NOTE: A slight rattle may occur on turns because of increased clearance off the "high point." This is normal and clearance must not be reduced below specified limits to eliminate this slight rattle.	
	• Loose pitman arm	• Tighten pitman arm nut to specifications
Squawk noise in steering gear when turning or recovering from a turn	• Damper O-ring on valve spool cut	• Replace damper O-ring
Poor return of steering wheel to center	• Tires not properly inflated	• Inflate to specified pressure
	• Lack of lubrication in linkage and ball joints	• Lube linkage and ball joints
	• Lower coupling flange rubbing against steering gear adjuster plug	• Loosen pinch bolt and assemble properly
	• Steering gear to column misalignment	• Align steering column
	• Improper front wheel alignment	• Check and adjust as necessary
	• Steering linkage binding	• Replace pivots
	• Ball joints binding	• Replace ball joints
	• Steering wheel rubbing against housing	• Align housing
	• Tight or frozen steering shaft bearings	• Replace bearings
	• Sticking or plugged valve spool	• Remove and clean or replace valve
	• Steering gear adjustments over specifications	• Check adjustment with gear out of car. Adjust as required.
	• Kink in return hose	• Replace hose
Car leads to one side or the other (keep in mind road condition and wind. Test car in both directions on flat road)	• Front end misaligned	• Adjust to specifications
	• Unbalanced steering gear valve	• Replace valve
	NOTE: If this is cause, steering effort will be very light in direction of lead and normal or heavier in opposite direction	

Troubleshooting the Power Steering Gear (cont.)

Problem	Cause	Solution
Momentary increase in effort when turning wheel fast to right or left	• Low oil level • Pump belt slipping • High internal leakage	• Add power steering fluid as required • Tighten or replace belt • Check pump pressure. (See pressure test)
Steering wheel surges or jerks when turning with engine running especially during parking	• Low oil level • Loose pump belt • Steering linkage hitting engine oil pan at full turn • Insufficient pump pressure • Pump flow control valve sticking	• Fill as required • Adjust tension to specification • Correct clearance • Check pump pressure. (See pressure test). Replace relief valve if defective. • Inspect for varnish or damage, replace if necessary
Excessive wheel kickback or loose steering	• Air in system • Steering gear loose on frame • Steering linkage joints worn enough to be loose • Worn poppet valve • Loose thrust bearing preload adjustment • Excessive overcenter lash	• Add oil to pump reservoir and bleed by operating steering. Check hose connectors for proper torque and adjust as required. • Tighten attaching screws to specified torque • Replace loose pivots • Replace poppet valve • Adjust to specification with gear out of vehicle • Adjust to specification with gear out of car
Hard steering or lack of assist	• Loose pump belt • Low oil level **NOTE:** Low oil level will also result in excessive pump noise • Steering gear to column misalignment • Lower coupling flange rubbing against steering gear adjuster plug • Tires not properly inflated	• Adjust belt tension to specification • Fill to proper level. If excessively low, check all lines and joints for evidence of external leakage. Tighten loose connectors. • Align steering column • Loosen pinch bolt and assemble properly • Inflate to recommended pressure
Foamy milky power steering fluid, low fluid level and possible low pressure	• Air in the fluid, and loss of fluid due to internal pump leakage causing overflow	• Check for leak and correct. Bleed system. Extremely cold temperatures will cause system aeriation should the oil level be low. If oil level is correct and pump still foams, remove pump from vehicle and separate reservoir from housing. Check welsh plug and housing for cracks. If plug is loose or housing is cracked, replace housing.
Low pressure due to steering pump	• Flow control valve stuck or inoperative • Pressure plate not flat against cam ring	• Remove burrs or dirt or replace. Flush system. • Correct
Low pressure due to steering gear	• Pressure loss in cylinder due to worn piston ring or badly worn housing bore • Leakage at valve rings, valve body-to-worm seal	• Remove gear from car for disassembly and inspection of ring and housing bore • Remove gear from car for disassembly and replace seals

Troubleshooting the Manual Steering Gear

Problem	Cause	Solution
Hard or erratic steering	• Incorrect tire pressure	• Inflate tires to recommended pressures
	• Insufficient or incorrect lubrication	• Lubricate as required (refer to Maintenance Section)
	• Suspension, or steering linkage parts damaged or misaligned	• Repair or replace parts as necessary
	• Improper front wheel alignment	• Adjust incorrect wheel alignment angles
	• Incorrect steering gear adjustment	• Adjust steering gear
	• Sagging springs	• Replace springs
Play or looseness in steering	• Steering wheel loose	• Inspect shaft spines and repair as necessary. Tighten attaching nut and stake in place.
	• Steering linkage or attaching parts loose or worn	• Tighten, adjust, or replace faulty components
	• Pitman arm loose	• Inspect shaft splines and repair as necessary. Tighten attaching nut and stake in place
	• Steering gear attaching bolts loose	• Tighten bolts
	• Loose or worn wheel bearings	• Adjust or replace bearings
	• Steering gear adjustment incorrect or parts badly worn	• Adjust gear or replace defective parts
Wheel shimmy or tramp	• Improper tire pressure	• Inflate tires to recommended pressures
	• Wheels, tires, or brake rotors out-of-balance or out-of-round	• Inspect and replace or balance parts
	• Inoperative, worn, or loose shock absorbers or mounting parts	• Repair or replace shocks or mountings
	• Loose or worn steering or suspension parts	• Tighten or replace as necessary
	• Loose or worn wheel bearings	• Adjust or replace bearings
	• Incorrect steering gear adjustments	• Adjust steering gear
	• Incorrect front wheel alignment	• Correct front wheel alignment
Tire wear	• Improper tire pressure	• Inflate tires to recommended pressures
	• Failure to rotate tires	• Rotate tires
	• Brakes grabbing	• Adjust or repair brakes
	• Incorrect front wheel alignment	• Align incorrect angles
	• Broken or damaged steering and suspension parts	• Repair or replace defective parts
	• Wheel runout	• Replace faulty wheel
	• Excessive speed on turns	• Make driver aware of conditions
Vehicle leads to one side	• Improper tire pressures	• Inflate tires to recommended pressures
	• Front tires with uneven tread depth, wear pattern, or different cord design (i.e., one bias ply and one belted or radial tire on front wheels)	• Install tires of same cord construction and reasonably even tread depth, design, and wear pattern
	• Incorrect front wheel alignment	• Align incorrect angles
	• Brakes dragging	• Adjust or repair brakes
	• Pulling due to uneven tire construction	• Replace faulty tire

Troubleshooting the Power Steering Pump

Problem	Cause	Solution
Chirp noise in steering pump	• Loose belt	• Adjust belt tension to specification
Belt squeal (particularly noticeable at full wheel travel and stand still parking)	• Loose belt	• Adjust belt tension to specification
Growl noise in steering pump	• Excessive back pressure in hoses or steering gear caused by restriction	• Locate restriction and correct. Replace part if necessary.
Growl noise in steering pump (particularly noticeable at stand still parking)	• Scored pressure plates, thrust plate or rotor • Extreme wear of cam ring	• Replace parts and flush system • Replace parts
Groan noise in steering pump	• Low oil level • Air in the oil. Poor pressure hose connection.	• Fill reservoir to proper level • Tighten connector to specified torque. Bleed system by operating steering from right to left—full turn.
Rattle noise in steering pump	• Vanes not installed properly • Vanes sticking in rotor slots	• Install properly • Free up by removing burrs, varnish, or dirt
Swish noise in steering pump	• Defective flow control valve	• Replace part
Whine noise in steering pump	• Pump shaft bearing scored	• Replace housing and shaft. Flush system.
Hard steering or lack of assist	• Loose pump belt • Low oil level in reservoir **NOTE:** Low oil level will also result in excessive pump noise • Steering gear to column misalignment • Lower coupling flange rubbing against steering gear adjuster plug • Tires not properly inflated	• Adjust belt tension to specification • Fill to proper level. If excessively low, check all lines and joints for evidence of external leakage. Tighten loose connectors. • Align steering column • Loosen pinch bolt and assemble properly • Inflate to recommended pressure
Foaming milky power steering fluid, low fluid level and possible low pressure	• Air in the fluid, and loss of fluid due to internal pump leakage causing overflow	• Check for leaks and correct. Bleed system. Extremely cold temperatures will cause system aeriation should the oil level be low. If oil level is correct and pump still foams, remove pump from vehicle and separate reservoir from body. Check welsh plug and body for cracks. If plug is loose or body is cracked, replace body.
Low pump pressure	• Flow control valve stuck or inoperative • Pressure plate not flat against cam ring	• Remove burrs or dirt or replace. Flush system. • Correct
Momentary increase in effort when turning wheel fast to right or left	• Low oil level in pump • Pump belt slipping • High internal leakage	• Add power steering fluid as required • Tighten or replace belt • Check pump pressure. (See pressure test)
Steering wheel surges or jerks when turning with engine running especially during parking	• Low oil level • Loose pump belt • Steering linkage hitting engine oil pan at full turn • Insufficient pump pressure	• Fill as required • Adjust tension to specification • Correct clearance • Check pump pressure. (See pressure test). Replace flow control valve if defective.

Troubleshooting the Power Steering Pump (cont.)

Problem	Cause	Solution
Steering wheel surges or jerks when turning with engine running especially during parking (cont.)	• Sticking flow control valve	• Inspect for varnish or damage, replace if necessary
Excessive wheel kickback or loose steering	• Air in system	• Add oil to pump reservoir and bleed by operating steering. Check hose connectors for proper torque and adjust as required.
Low pump pressure	• Extreme wear of cam ring • Scored pressure plate, thrust plate, or rotor • Vanes not installed properly • Vanes sticking in rotor slots • Cracked or broken thrust or pressure plate	• Replace parts. Flush system. • Replace parts. Flush system. • Install properly • Freeup by removing burrs, varnish, or dirt • Replace part

6. Remove the turn signal switch flange.

7. To install, make sure that the front wheels are pointing straight ahead, then position the turn signal switch flange into the column and place the centered steering wheel on the column. Install the steering wheel nut and tighten to 20-30 ft. lbs.

8. Making sure the springs and washers are positioned correctly, install the horn ring on the steering wheel and tighten the four retaining screws. Connect the horn plug contact.

9. Install the upper turn signal housing half.

10. Connect the negative battery cable and test the operation of the horn.

1800 Series

1. Disconnect the negative battery cable.

2. Pry off the steering wheel impact pad.

3. Disconnect the horn plug contact. Remove the three retaining screws and lift off the horn ring, (if so equipped) noting the placement of the springs and washers.

4. Bend back the lockring washer and remove the steering wheel nut. Mark the relative positions of the steering wheel to the column. Loosen the horn wire.

5. Install the steering wheel puller and pull off the wheel.

6. To install, place the steering wheel on the column so that the alignment marks made prior to removal line up. Install the nut and tighten to 20–30 ft. lbs.

7. Connect the horn plug contact, and install the horn ring, springs, and washers with the three retaining screws (if so equipped).

8. Snap on the impact pad.

9. Connect the negative cable and test the operation of the horn.

All 100 and 200 Series, 1973 and later.

1. Disconnect the negative battery cable.

2. Remove the retaining screws for the upper half of the molded turn signal housing and lift off the housing.

3. Pry off the steering wheel impact pad.

4. Disconnect the horn plug contact.

5. Remove the steering wheel nut.

NOTE: *Due to a change in the cone angle of this steering shaft, a puller is not needed on 1979 and later models.*

6. With the front wheels pointing straight ahead and the steering wheel centered, install a steering wheel puller. On 164 models, use an outside circumference type (Volvo 5003 or similar) and pull off the steering wheel.

On 140, 240, and 260 models, use a universal type puller (Volvo 2263 or similar).

7. To install, make sure that the front wheels are pointing straight ahead and place the centered steering wheel on the column. Keep the plug contact on the left side and install the nut. Tighten it to 20–30 ft. lbs.

8. Connect the horn plug contact and install the impact pad.

9. Install the upper turn signal housing half.

10. Connect the negative battery cable and test the operation of the horn.

700 Series without Supplemental Restraint System (SRS)

1. Disconnect the negative battery cable.

2. Gently pry up the lower edge of the steering wheel center pad and remove it.

3. Unscrew the steering wheel center nut and remove the steering wheel.

4. When installing the steering wheel, torque the center to 26 ft. lbs.

5. Install the center pad and snap it into place. Reconnect the negative battery cable.

760 and 780 with Supplemental Restraint System

Some 1987-88 and 1989 Volvo 780 and 760 series include an electrically operated Supplemental Restraint System (SRS) or airbag system. The SRS system can deploy during electrical testing or other work if certain steps are not followed. While the airbag and inflator are in the steering column, the system has various other wires and components located under the dash and under the seat.

If your car is equipped with SRS, observe the following rules when performing any work in or around the steering column or dashboard:

• If you are not absolutely sure of the identity of a component, leave it alone.

• Know where a wire goes before applying voltage or checking resistance.

• Turn the ignition to OFF and disconnect the negative battery cable before disconnecting any electrical connectors inside the car.

• Be sure that the integrity of the SRS wiring is not disturbed during the installation of accessories such as CB radios, phones, audio equipment, etc.

• If the steering wheel must be removed, the bag assembly must first be removed and disconnected from the center of the wheel. Put the unit to the side and DO NOT attempt to check resistance at the inflator.

• On 780 series, ALWAYS disconnect the 4-pin yellow connector at the lower part of the steering column near the center console. The front seat belts are also part of the SRS system. If any diagnostics must be done to the seat belt system, disconnect the seat belt tensioners (grey connectors under the driver's seat) before doing any work.

• On the 760 series, ALWAYS disconnect the 4-pin yellow connector.

• Do not disconnect the main lead to the sensor box under the seat.

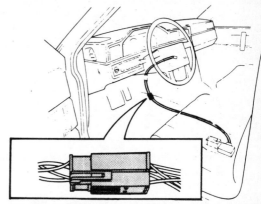

Always disconnect the yellow connector before performing any electrical diagnostic work. 1988 760 with SRS shown

•Volvo specifically recommends against anyone other than factory-trained personnel attempting repairs or diagnosis on the SRS system.

To remove the steering wheel:

1. Park the car with the front wheels and the steering wheel straight.

2. Switch off the ignition and disconnect the negative battery cable. Disconnect the yellow connector in the SRS harness.

3. Remove the 3mm Allen screw holding the steering wheel adjuster.

4. Remove the five screws in the lower cover and remove the covers.

5. Remove the two Torx® screws (TX 27) from the back side of the steering wheel. This will free the airbag assembly in the center pad of the wheel. Disconnect the wire at the bag unit and set it aside.

6. Remove the bolt in the center of the steering wheel but leave the wheel in place.

7. Remove the lock screw (at the end of the plastic label) from its storage position in the wheel hub. Install the lock screw through the steering wheel hub to lock the contact reel. Do

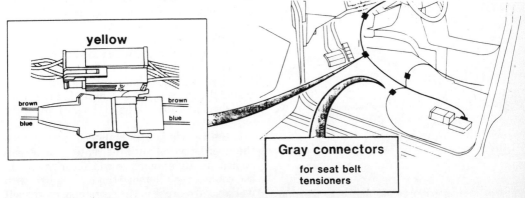

Location of SRS connectors. 1987 780 shown

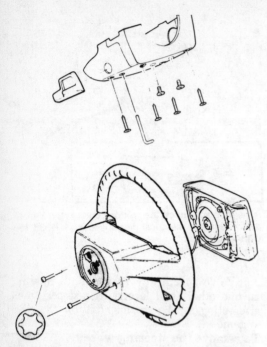

Location of retaining bolts on SRS equipped vehicles

not turn the wheel after the lock screw is in place; the pin in the contact reel will shear.

8. Lift off the steering wheel.

9. When reinstalling, feed the wire through the steering wheel and place the wheel in position. Make sure the pin on the contact reel aligns with the center of the hole in the steering wheel.

10. Install the center bolt for the steering wheel and tighten finger tight only.

11. Remove the lock screw from the contact reel. Rewind the flag and store it in its compartment.

12. Tighten the steering wheel center nut to 24 ft. lbs.

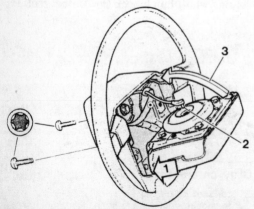

Steps in reassembling airbag unit onto steering wheel

13. Place the lower part of the airbag assembly on the steering wheel (1). Connect the electrical connector and insure that it clicks into position (2). Align the bag assembly and rotate it up into place (3). Install the two Torx® screws through the back of the wheel and tighten them to 6 ft. lbs.

14. Make sure that the steering wheel can be turned freely and that the column ignition lock functions correctly.

15. Reinstall the steering wheel covers and the wheel adjustor handle. Connect the yellow connectors in the SRS system. Connect the negative battery cable.

Combination Switch (Windshield Wiper Switch/Turn Signal Switch)

REMOVAL AND INSTALLATION

CAUTION: *This procedure requires removal of the steering wheel. If the vehicle is equipped with the SRS (airbag) system, refer to the safety precautions listed earlier in this chapter. DO NOT remove the wheel until these precautions have been followed.*

1. Turn the steering wheel to the straight ahead position.

2. Remove the center pad from the wheel.

3. Remove the steering wheel retaining bolt. If possible, matchmark the wheel and steering shaft.

If the vehicle is equipped with SRS, pull out the locking screw and the long tape label from its station in the steering wheel hub. Use the lock screw (with the tape flag attached) to lock the contact reel through the hole in the steering wheel hub. Do not turn the steering wheel once the bolt is removed; the pin in the contact reel will shear.

4. Remove the steering wheel and the upper and lower steering column casings.

5. To remove the wiper switch, simply remove the screws holding it to the column and unplug the connector. The turn signal switch is on the opposite side and is also held to the column by two or three screws.

6. When reassembling, remember to check the position of all the wires so that nothing is pinched in casings.

7. Reinstall the column casings and then reinstall the steering wheel. Check that the steering wheel position is true to the position of the wheels.

If the vehicle is SRS equipped, do not turn the steering wheel until the center bolt is reinstalled and tight; doing so will shear the pin in the contact reel. Remove the locking bolt with its flag and store it in the extra hole on the left side of the wheel.

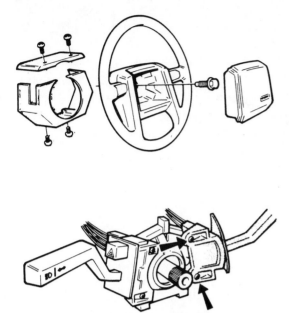

Steering wheel removal is necessary for access to wiper and turn signal switches. Non-SRS 700 series shown

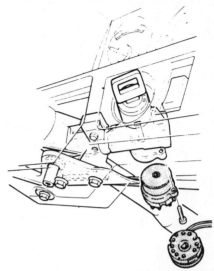

Electrical contacts on back of ignition switch are replaceable. 700 series shown, others similar

8. Tighten the steering wheel bolt to 24 ft. lbs. Reinstall the center pad.

9. If equipped with the SRS system, make the necessary connections to reactivate the system.

Ignition Switch

REMOVAL AND INSTALLATION

On all models, the ignition keylock is mounted on the steering column and incorporates a steering wheel lock to deter car theft. The lock is attached to the steering column by shearbolts, whose heads break off when the proper tightness is reached. Removing the lock requires removing these bolts, either by cutting slots in their tops and using a screwdriver to extract them, or by drilling them out.

If they are drilled out, the lock housing will probably be damaged. On many models, removing the ignition lock also requires loosening or removing the steering column. Because of the complexity of these operations, repairs are best left to a professional repair facility.

If your diagnosis of an problem shows a failed ignition switch, the electrical part at the rear of the assembly can be changed on all 1975 and later models.

CAUTION: *If the vehicle is equipped with the SRS (airbag) system, refer to the safety precautions listed earlier in this chapter.*

Disconnect the negative battery cable and gain access to the back of the ignition switch by removing panels and covers as necessary. Remove the round multi-wire connector at the back of the switch, then unfasten and remove the electrical unit (sometimes called the start contact) from the back of the lock assembly.

This unit is generally held on with two small screws, but they are in a difficult location and an awkward position--have patience. When reassembling, make certain that the new unit is properly seated against the pin from the ignition lock. Also insure that the wiring connector is firmly attached to the new start contact.

Steering Column Upper Shaft

REMOVAL AND INSTALLATION

1800 Series

1. Disconnect the negative battery cable. Remove the clamping bolt at the base of the column.

2. Remove the steering wheel. Remove the flange, the turn signal switch, the spring and the bearing seat.

3. Disconnect the lock ring (circlip) and pull down the spring and lower bearing seat.

4. Pull the column out of the casing. Use the steering wheel to help you pull.

5. To reinstall, insert the column in the casing and make sure the parts of the lower bearing are in place.

6. Run the horn cable into position. Push the steering column into position in the flange (at the lower joint) and install the clamping bolt and lock ring.

7. At the upper end, replace the bearing seat and spring, the flange and the turn signal switch.

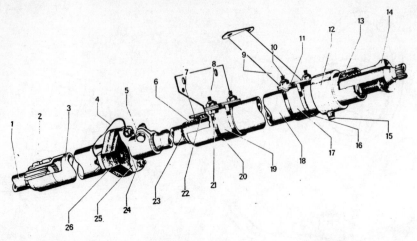

1. Steering cam	10. Shear bolt	19. Clamp
2. Nut	11. Spacer	20. Rubber bushing
3. Sleeve	12. Steering lock mount	21. Bolt
4. Ground wire.	13. Upper bearing	22. Lower bearing
5. Clamp bolt	14. Flange	23. Lock ring
6. Spring	15. Bolt	24. Nut
7. Seat	16. Rubber bushing	25. Flange
8. Lower mount	17. Clamp	26. Rubber coupling disc.
9. Upper mount	18. Steering column casing	

Steering column components, 1800 Series

8. Reinstall the steering wheel and check the function of the steering column lock. Reconnect the battery cable and check the function of the turn signals.

100 Series

1. Disconnect the negative battery cable.
2. Remove the steering wheel. Remove the flange, the turn signal switch, the spring and the bearing seat.
3. Separate the sleeve (holding the upper and lower columns) located near the floor.
4. Pull the column free of the casing.
5. When assembling, insert the steering shaft and position it in the sleeve. Tighten the sleeve nut to 30 ft. lbs. and bend the lock tab into one of the slots.

6. At the upper end, replace the bearing seat and spring, the flange and the turn signal switch.
7. Reinstall the steering wheel and check the function of the steering column lock. Reconnect the battery cable and check the function of the turn signals.

200 Series

1. Disconnect the negative battery cable.
2. Under the hood, remove the clamping bolt at the shaft joint.
3. Remove the steering wheel.
4. Remove the plastic column covers.
5. Disconnect the wiring and remove the turn signal and wiper controls.
6. Remove the housing which holds the

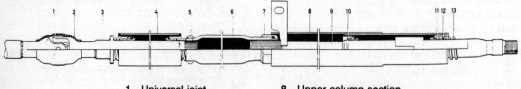

1. Universal joint	8. Upper column section
2. Rubber seal	9. Upper column casing
3. Lower column section	10. Ring
4. Lower column casing	11. Bearing
5. Rivet	12. Seat
6. Sleeve	13. Spring
7. Nut	

Steering column components, 164 Model

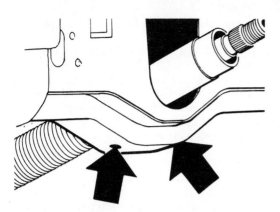

Location of shear-head bolts on 200 Series

switches. Remove the spring and race for the upper bearing.

7. Find the two bolts for the steering lock. They will not have heads on them. Drill holes exactly in the center of the bolts and use a screw extractor to remove the bolts.

8. Remove the rubber grommet for the steering shaft at the firewall.

9. Push the steering shaft in through the firewall until clear of the lower part of the dashboard. Pull the shaft back into the driver's compartment.

10. Disconnect the steering lock from the shaft. Either install it on the new shaft or install the new lock on the present shaft.

11. When reassembling, install the rubber grommet onto the end of the shaft. Push the column into place and fit it through the firewall. Position the column so the steering lock projects through the hole in the panel.

12. Attach the joint to the shaft and tighten the nut and bolt.

13. Install new shear bolts, but DO NOT break them. Later adjustment may be required.

14. Install the rubber grommet in the firewall.

15. At the upper end, install the switch bracket. Don't forget to connect the ground wire to one of the screws.

16. Install the turn signal switch, wiper switch and connect the wiring.

17. Install the race and spring for the upper bearing. Replace the plastic column covers.

18. Check that the front wheels point straight ahead and install the steering wheel. Tighten the nut to 25 ft. lbs.

19. Turn the steering wheel and check for free rotation and no binding or rubbing. Make any needed adjustments before continuing.

20. Tighten the lower attachment bolts and then tighten the shear bolts. Keep turning the bolts until the heads break off.

21. Reconnect the battery cable and check the operation of the horn, turn signals and wipers.

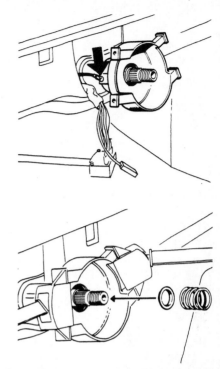

When reassembling steering column on 200 Series, remember to attach the ground wire (above) and install the bearing race correctly (below)

700 Series

CAUTION: *If the vehicle is equipped with the SRS (airbag) system, refer to the safety precautions listed earlier in this chapter.*

1. Disconnect the negative battery cable.

2. Under the hood, disconnect the upper steering shaft clamp bolt and snap ring. Then disconnect the lower steering shaft clamp bolt and snapring.

3. Push the steering shaft towards the firewall to free it from the clamp joint.

WARNING: *On SRS equipped vehicles, refer to the specific removal procedures listed under "Steering Wheel, Removal and Installation" in this chapter.*

4. Remove the steering wheel and remove the upper and lower plastic covers around the steering column.

5. Remove the horn wire, disconnect the wiring to the wiper and turn signal switches and remove the switches.

6. Remove the panel under the column and remove the heater hose. Remove the panel around the ignition switch and the heater controls. Be careful not to scratch the trim.

7. Find the two bolts for the steering lock. They will not have heads on them. Drill holes exactly in the center of the bolts and use a screw extractor to remove the bolts.

8. Remove the single bolt in the support bar.

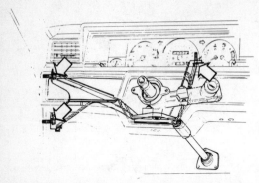

Location of support bracket bolts on 700 Series

9. At the floorboard, remove the three screws for the lower bearing plate

10. Under the dash, loosen (but do not remove) the three bolts for the steering column support bracket. One bolt is located high, about behind the speedometer; the other two are on the extreme left side of the dash.

11. Insert the key and turn it to position II (ON). Remove the retaining screw. Press in the locking tab and withdraw the lock assembly. Remove the key and disconnect the wiring from the switch.

12. Carefully pull down on the support bracket and lift out the steering column guide. Remove the steering column.

13. Check the length of the steering column. The collapsible coupling must be intact. Correct overall length of the shaft is 28.63 in. ± 0.04 in. (727mm ± 1mm). If the shaft isn't the correct length, replace it.

14. When installing, place the shaft within the guide and insert into place in the dash. If the shaft was disassembled or replaced, remember to fit the triangular bearing plate onto the bottom of the shaft.

15. Install new shear bolts. Snug them to hold but DO NOT break them yet. Install the single bolt into the bottom of the support bar.

16. Insert the key in the ignition lock and turn it to II. Press the lock tab down and place the lock in position. Make sure that it bottoms correctly in its housing. Tighten the retaining screw and check the operation of the key and column lock assembly.

17. Tighten the bolts for the steering column support.

18. Install the lower bearing plate at the floorboard.

19. Double check placement of the column in the dash. Make any necessary adjustments in position. Make sure no wiring or cables are snagged or pulled out of place.

20. Tighten the two shear bolts until the heads break off.

21. Install the wiper and turn signal switches.

Connect the switch wiring and connect the horn wire.

22. Install the uppper and lower steering column covers.

23. Replace the trim panel for the ignition switch and the heater controls. Install the heater hose and reinstall the lower panel.

24. Under the hood, attach the upper joint to the upper steering shaft. Tighten the bolt to 15 ft. lbs. Tighten the lower joint to the same value. Install the snaprings.

WARNING: *On SRS equipped vehicles, refer to the specific installation procedures listed under "Steering Wheel, Removal and Installation" in this chapter.*

25. Install the steering wheel and tighten the center nut to 25 ft. lbs. Install the center pad.

26. If the vehicle is SRS equipped, reconnect the harness connectors. Attach and secure the negative battery cable.

Steering Linkage
REMOVAL AND INSTALLATION
140 Series, 164 Models, 1800 Series

Bent or damaged steering rods and tie rods must be replaced, never straightened. All components of the steering linkage, including the pitman arm and idler arm (on worm and roller steering types), are connected by means of ball joints. Ball joints cannot be disassembled or adjusted, so they must also be replaced when damaged. They should also be replaced if the rubber seal is broken and the joint contaminated.

The ball joints of the steering rods are made in unit with the rods, therefore the entire rod assembly must be replaced when the ball joint becomes unserviceable. Maximum permissible axial (vertical) play is 0.120 in. (3mm). After removing the cotter pins and ball stud nuts, use a ball joint separator and press the balljoint out of its connecting socket.

The ball joints on the tie rod may be replaced individually. After the ball joint is disconnected, the lock nut on the tie rod is loosened and the clamp bolt released. The ball joint is then screwed out of the tie rod, taking note of the number of turns. The new ball joint is screwed in exactly the same number of turns, and the clamp bolt and lock nut tightened.

After reconditioning the rods and joints, the wheel alignment must be adjusted.

The pitman arm, relay arm (idler arm) and various other steering links are removed in straightforward manner. Remove the cotter pin and lock nut from the appropriate ball joints and separate the joints. In the case of the pitman arm arm, bend up the lock tab at the nut

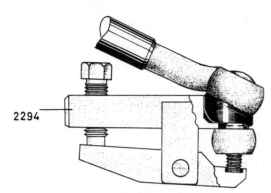

Ball joint separator. Volvo tool shown

and remove the nut. The arm may need gentle tapping to come free of the splines on the steering box. Keep the following general rules in mind:

1. Always use the correct tool to separate ball joints. Improper tools will damage the joint or rip the boot.

2. Keep the mating surfaces of rods and joints clean.

3. If the relay rod was removed, tighten its mounting nut to 55 ft. lbs.

4. Do not disturb the position of the front wheels when any component is disconnected.

5. Always have the alignment checked and adjusted after any steering repair.

All 200 and 700 Series

These models are equipped with rack and pinion steering (manual or power). Rack and pinion systems save space and weight, improve steering response and eliminate most of the rods and linkage under the car.

Two different units are used, either ZF manual or power steering or CAM manual or power steering. On all types, the tie rod ends are removed by disconnecting the ball joint at the steering knuckle, loosening the locknut and unscrewing the tie rod end from the tie rod. Count every full turn needed to remove the tie rod end from the tie rod and install the new tie rod end that exact number of turns. Tighten the locknut and attach the ball joint at the steering knuckle. Have the alignment checked and reset if necessary. If close attention was paid to the exact number of turns of each tie rod end, the alignment should not be far off specification.

When servicing the tie rods, check the rubber bellows for cracks or leaks. The bellows can be replaced by removing the tie rod end, loosening the clamps and pulling the bellows off the tie rod. On both manual and power steering CAM gear boxes, the rack is filled with gear oil. On both manual and power steering ZF gear boxes, the rack is packed with special fluid grease.

Manual Steering Gear
REMOVAL AND INSTALLATION
1800, 140, 164 Series

1. Jack up the front end of the vehicle and support on jackstands.

2. Release the bolt at the lower steering coupling flange. Remove the nuts and push the lower part of the flange as far down as possible on the guide bolt.

3. Remove the lock nut for the pitman arm. Matchmark the arm and the shaft for ease of reassembly. Pull off the pitman arm with a pitman arm puller (Volvo tool 2370 or equivalent). When the puller has been set in place, turn the wheels completely to the left.

4. Remove the nuts and bolts and lift off the steering gearbox.

5. Make sure the steering gearbox is in its centered postion. (Alternate position is full left.) Reinstall the steering gear in position and secure the mounting bolts.

6. Set the wheels so they match the setting of the steering gearbox, i.e. centered or full left, and place the steering wheel in the same position. Secure both halves of the lower flange. Check that the flange splines coincide with the shaft splines.

7. Install the pitman arm to the steering gearbox. If the steering gear and pitman arm are matchmarked, make sure the marks align and reinstall the arm.

If the gear and arm are not marked, follow the procedure below:

a. Turn the steering wheel fully to the left.

b. Turn the steering wheel fully to the right (until it binds) and count the number of turns the wheel makes from left lock to right

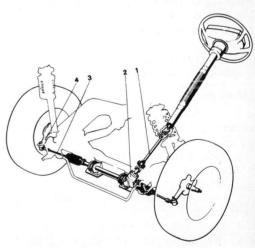

1. Steering shaft   3. Steering rod
2. Steering gear   4. Steering arm

Manual steering assembly—240, 260 series and 1980 and later models

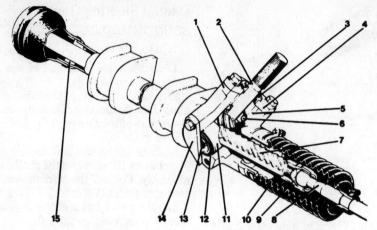

1. Housing
2. Pinion
3. Seal
4. Pinion cover
5. Spacer sleeve
6. Upper Pinion bearing
7. Rack
8. Steering rod
9. Inner ball joint
10. Rubber bellow
11. Pre-tensioning piston
12. O-ring
13. Spring
14. Cover
15. Bushing

Manual steering gear assembly (cam gear)—rack and pinion type

lock. Measure the turns carefully and approximate any fractional turns (½, ¼, etc).

c. Beginning at right lock, return the wheel one half of the number of turns it took to get there. This will put the steering gear box at its centered position.

d. Set the left wheel straight ahead.

e. Connect the pitman arm to the steering box.

f. Lower the car to the ground and check that the wheels are straight ahead. If it is necessary to adjust the wheels, remember to use the correct tool when removing the pitman arm from the shaft.

8. Tighten the pitman arm bolt to 110 ft. lbs.

9. Lower the car to the ground and road test for proper steering alignment.

200 Series

1. Remove the lock bolt and nut from the column flange. Bend apart the flange slightly with a screwdriver.

2. Jack up the front end. The stands should be positioned at the jack supports. Remove the front wheels.

3. Disconnect the tie rod ends, using a ball joint puller.

4. Remove the splash guard.

5. Disconnect the steering gear from the front axle member (beam).

6. Disconnect the steering gear at the steering shaft flange. Remove the steering gear. Save the dowel pins.

7. Install rubber spacers and plates for the steering gear attachment points.

8. Position the steering gear and guide the pinion shaft into the steering shaft. The recess on the pinion shaft should be aligned towards the lock bolt opening in the shaft.

9. Attach the steering gear to the front axle member. Check that the U-bolts are aligned in the plate slots. Install flat washers and nuts. Tighten the nuts to 10–18 ft. lbs.

10. Install the splash guard.

11. Connect the steering rods to the steering arms. Tighten the nuts to 44 ft. lbs.

12. Install the front wheels and lower the vehicle.

13. Install the lock bolt for the steering shaft flange. Tighten the bolt to 18 ft. lbs.

14. Have the alignment checked and reset if needed.

Power Steering Gear
REMOVAL AND INSTALLATION
1800, 140, 164 Series

1. Jack up the front end and support on jackstands.

2. Drain the oil from the steering pump as follows:

a. Position a pan under the pump and remove the drain bolt from the pump.

b. Turn the steering wheel to full left lock. Remove the cover on the fluid reservoir.

c. Start the engine and allow it to run for a MAXIMUM of 10 seconds. This will run the

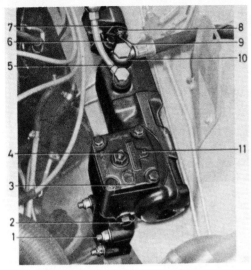

1. Bolt	6. Clamping bolt
2. Drain plug	7. Flange
3. Steering box	8. Nut
4. Adjusting screw	9. Screw
5. Delivery line (early	10. Return line
prod.)	11. Bleeder screw

Power steering gear installed—164, 140 series.

pump and remove the fluid from the lines and reservoir. DO NOT run the engine without fluid in the system; the pump will become damaged.

d. Stop the engine and turn the wheel from lock to lock until all the oil has run out. Reinstall the drain plug.

3. Remove the lock nut for the pitman arm. Disconnect the pitman arm with a pitman arm puller. When attaching the puller, turn the wheels fully to the right.

4. Disconnect the oil lines from the steering housing after cleaning the connections. Loosen the clamping bolt.

5. Remove the attaching bolts and pull the steering gear forwards.

6. When reinstalling, place the steering gear in the middle position. A slight increase in resistance should be felt. The line-up marks on the steering spindle and gear housing should coincide.

7. Check to make sure that the steering wheel is pointing the front wheels straight ahead.

8. Install the steering gear shaft into the lower steering column section. Install and tighten the attaching bolts. Tighten the clamping bolt. Connect the oil lines. The longer line should run in a curve to the rear and be held with a clamp.

9. Point the front wheels straight and install the pitman arm. Torque the nut to 125–141 ft. lbs.

10. Fill the reservoir with Type A automatic transmission fluid and bleed the system as outlined under Power Steering System Bleeding.

200 Series

1. Disconnect the steering column shaft flange at the steering gearbox. Remove the clamp screw and pry the flange open.

2. Jack up the front end. Position jackstands at the front jack supports. Remove the front wheels.

3. Use a ball joint separator and disconnect the tie rods at the outer ends.

4. Remove the splash guard.

5. Disconnect the hydraulic hoses at the steering gear. Install protective plugs in the hose connections.

NOTE: *On late model 260 cars, the hose clamp on the crossmember must be removed.*

6. Remove the bolts holding the steering gear. Remove the steering gear from its mounts and save the spacers.

7. Remove the steering gear from the car by pulling it down until it is free from the steering shaft flange. Then remove the unit through the left side of the vehicle. Save the dowel pins.

8. When reinstalling, position the steering gear and attach the pinion shaft to the steering shaft flange. Take care to align the recess for the lock bolt.

9. Install right side U-bolt and bracket, but do NOT tighten the nuts.

10. Install left side retaining bolts, and tighten. Tighten the U-bolts.

11. Connect the steering rods to the steering arms.

12. Install the lock bolt on the steering column flange.

13. Connect the return and pressure hoses to the steering gear. On late model 260s, secure the hose clamp to the crossmember.

14. Fill the reservoir with Type A automatic transmission fluid and bleed the system as outlined under Power Steering System Bleeding.

700 Series

1. Elevate the front end and safely support on jackstands. Place the stands at the front jacking points. Block the rear wheels.

2. Remove the splashguard and the small jacking panel on the front crossmember.

3. Disconnect the lower steering shaft from the steering gear.

4. At the lower universal joint, remove the snaprings and loosen the upper clamp bolt. Then remove the lower clamp bolt and slide the joint up on the shaft.

5. Use a ball joint separator and disconnect the tie rods at the outer ends.

6. Disconnect the fluid lines from the steer-

ing gear. Catch the spilled fluid in a pan and install plugs in the lines.

7. Remove the sway bar mounting brackets from the side members and move them out of the way. Remove the steering gear retaining bolts and lower the assembly out of the car.

8. When reinstalling, position the rack in position and install the retaining bolts. Tighten them to 32 ft. lbs.

9. Install the sway bar mounting brackets.

10. Use new copper washers and connect the fluid lines to the assembly.

11. Connect the tie rods and tighten their nuts to 44 ft. lbs.

12. Slide the lower universal joint down the shaft and into position. Tighten the lower clamp bolt first, then the upper. Both bolts are tightened to 15 ft. lbs. Install the snaprings.

13. Reinstall the jacking plate and the splashguard.

14. Lower the car to the ground. Fill the reservoir with ATF. Start the engine and smoothly turn the steering wheel from lock to lock 3 or 4 times; recheck the fluid level in the reservoir.

Power Steering Pump
REMOVAL AND INSTALLATION
1800 and 140/160 Series

1. Remove all dirt and grease from around the line connections at the pump.

2. Using a container to catch any power steering fluid that might run out, disconnect the lines, and plug them to prevent dirt from entering the system.

3. Remove the tensioning bolt and the attaching bolts.

4. Clear the pump of the fan belt and lift it out.

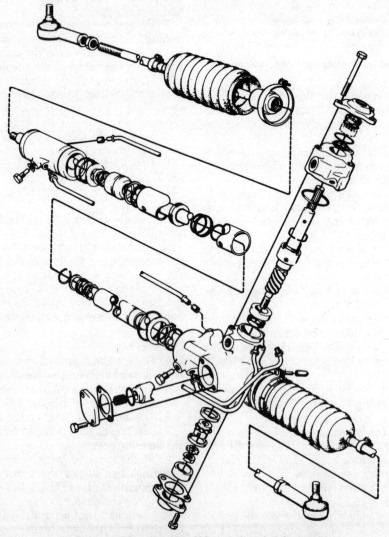

Power steering gear assembly—rack and pinion type

5. If a new pump is to be used, the old brackets, fittings, and pulley must be transferred to the new unit. The pulley may be removed with a puller and pressed onto the new pump shaft with a press tool. Under no circumstances should the pulley be hammered on; this will damage the pump bearings.

6. To install, place the pump in position and loosely fit the attaching bolts. Connect the lines to the pump with new seals.

7. Place the fan belt onto the pulley and adjust the fan belt tension.

8. Tighten the tensioning bolt and the attaching bolts.

9. Fill the reservoir with Type A automatic transmission fluid and bleed the system as outlined under Power Steering System Bleeding.

200 Series

1. Remove all dirt and grease from around the line connections at the pump.

2. Using a container to catch any power steering fluid that might run out, disconnect the lines, and plug them to prevent dirt from entering the system.

3. Remove the tensioner locking screws on both sides of the pump and remove the drive belt.

4. Turn the pump up and remove the three bolts holding the bracket to the engine block. Remove the pump and bracket.

5. If the pump is being replaced with a new one, remove the nut and pulley from the old pump and transfer it to the new one. Separate the bracket and tensioner from the pump and install them loosely on the new pump.

6. Place the pump in position on the engine and install the retaining bolts and spacer.

7. Install the drive belt and install the tensioner lock.

8. Adjust the belt tension and then tighten the nuts of the long bolts.

9. Use new copper washers and reconnect the fluid lines to the pump.

10. Fill the reservoir with Type A or Dexron®II automatic transmission fluid and bleed the system as outlined under Power Steering System Bleeding.

700 Series

1. Remove the splashguard from under the engine.

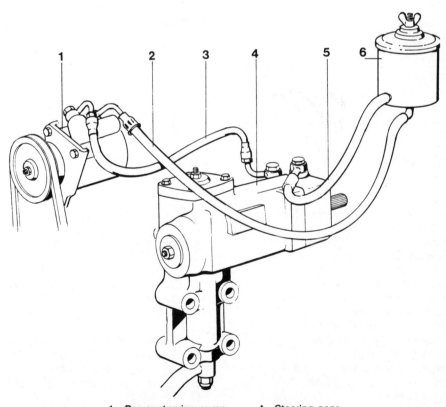

1. Power steering pump
2. Suction line
3. Delivery line
4. Steering gear
5. Return line
6. Reservoir

Power steering system, 140 and 160 Series

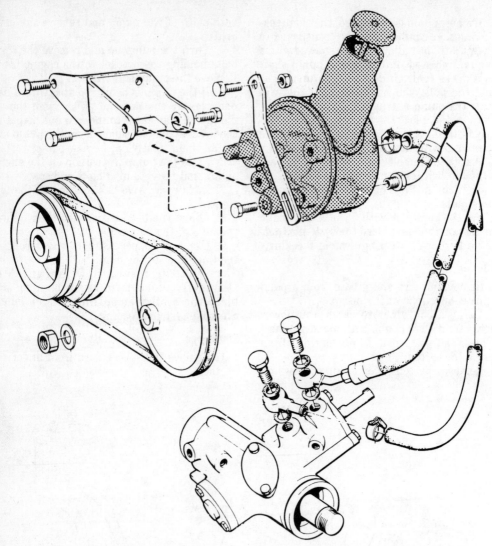

Power steering system on 260 model. Saginaw pump with integrated reservoir shown

2. Loosen the belt tensioner. Remove the mounting bracket and bolt.

3. Disconnect the lines at or near the pump. Depending on the type of pump, it may be necessary to disconnect the rubber hose(s) from the metal pipes instead of removing the lines at the pump body. Use a catch pan under the car for spillage and plug the lines and fittings immediately to avoid contamination.

4. Remove the large retaining bolt and remove the drive belt from the pump.

5. Lower the pump slightly and disconnect the filler hose from the pump. Remove the pump from the car.

6. If the pump is to be replaced with a new one, transfer the pulley, the mounting bracket and the washers to the new pump.

Install the mounting bracket on the new

pump; make sure the thick washer is between the bracket and the pump body. Install the pulley; remember that the conical face of the washer must be to the outside.

7. Reconnect the filler hose to the pump.

8. Position the pump and install the retaining bolts loosely.

9. Install the mounting bracket and belt. Adjust the belt tension.

10. Tighten the lower retaining bolts.

11. Reconnect the fluid hoses to the pump. Use new washers and/or hose clamps. Tighten the banjo fittings (if any) to 31 ft. lbs.

12. Fill the fluid reservoir and start the engine. Slowly turn the wheel lock to lock once or twice and check for leaks. Top the fluid to the proper level.

13. Reinstall the splashguard. The power

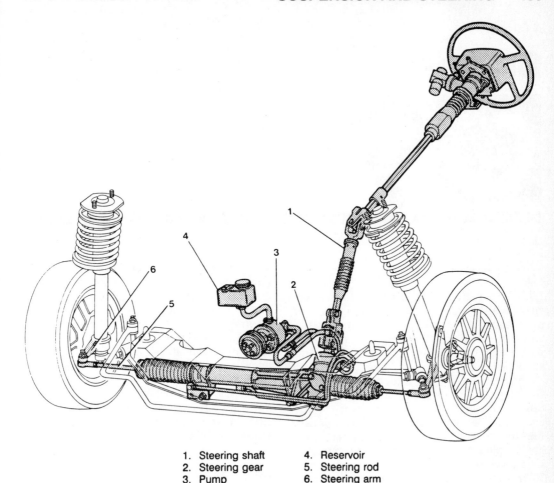

1. Steering shaft
2. Steering gear
3. Pump
4. Reservoir
5. Steering rod
6. Steering arm

Power steering system, 700 Series

steering system is self-bleeding; no external bleeding is required.

POWER STEERING SYSTEM BLEEDING

Bleeding removes any air which become trapped within the fluid system. The system should be bled every time any hose or component has been loosened or removed. The system should also be bled if it has run low on fluid during operation.

1. Fill the reservoir with the proper type of fluid. Raise the front wheels off the ground, and install safety stands. Place the transmission in neutral and apply the parking brake.

2. Keeping a can of fluid within easy reach, start the engine and fill the reservoir as the level drops.

3. When the reservoir level has stopped dropping, slowly turn the steering wheel from lock to lock several times. Fill the reservoir if necessary.

4. Locate the bleeder screw (non-rack and pinion steering models only) on the power steering gearbox. Open the bleeder screw about ¾ turn, and close it when oil starts flowing out.

5. Continue to turn the steering wheel slowly until the fluid in the reservoir is free of air bubbles.

6. Stop the engine and observe the oil level in the reservoir. If the oil level rises more than ¼ in. (6mm) past the level mark, air still remains in the system. Continue bleeding until the level rise is correct.

7. Remove the safety stands and lower the car.

Brakes

9

BRAKE SYSTEM

All Volvos are equipped with a four wheel power-assisted disc brake system. Volvo was one of the first manufacturers to commit to the four wheel disc system on all of its cars. Disc brakes offer better stopping, ease of repair and simplified construction.

The calipers are manufactured either by Girling or ATE, so when ordering disc pads or caliper rebuilding kits, you must identify which you have. The name of the manufacturer is cast into the metal of the caliper. The brake discs are one piece castings. The discs on some models are vented for quicker heat dispersion.

Whenever adding to or replacing the brake fluid, it is imperative that the fluid be of SAE 70 R3 (SAE J 1703) quality or better. Fluid meeting DOT 3 or DOT 4 specifications is also acceptable. Using inferior brake fluids may result in premature failure of the hydraulic components or in impaired braking function. Fluids not meeting specifications may not withstand the great temperatures generated at the disc and caliper during braking. If the fluid boils within the lines, the pedal will feel spongy and give little response at the wheels.

Brake fluid is said to be hygroscopic, meaning to attract moisture. Water is the absolute last substance you want in the brake system, as it causes corrosion and can ruin seals. Any time it is necessary to add brake fluid, always use a fresh can. That half full can on the shelf has been through many heating and cooling cycles in the last six months; enough moisture has condensed out of the air within the can to pollute the fluid. You can use this old fluid for cleaning components during disassembly, but don't introduce any into the fluid system. Avoid mixing brake fluids from different manufacturers and never reuse old brake fluid.

In 1987, Volvo introduced its Anti-lock Braking System (ABS) on models in the 700 Series.

This system prevents wheel lock-up (skidding) during hard braking, thus allowing the car to be steered during an emergency situation. (A wheel which is not turning will not provide steering response.) The ABS system uses a combination of mechanical, electronic and hydraulic components to sense impending lock-up at each wheel and meter the brake fluid flow to the wheels.

There are certain differences in repair procedures for ABS and non-ABS components. The ABS procedures, if different, are explained separately at the end of each repair section.

ABS SYSTEM

The ABS system comprises many components including sensors, pulse-wheels, the hydraulic modulator and the Electronic Control Unit (ECU). The ECU is the "brains" of the system while the modulator performs the actual work of controlling the fluid flow to each wheel. Testing of the system requires specific dealer-only equipment. The hydraulic unit, located either in the trunk or under the hood, is connected to a maze of brake lines. Don't attempt to loosen, bleed or repair anything at this unit.

Under very hard braking, you may hear unusual sounds from the hydraulic modualtor; this is quite normal and is simply a result of the unit doing its job.

The ABS warning light on the dash should not be confused with the brake warning light. If the ABS light comes on, it indicates a fault in the Anti-Lock system, not the main braking system. The car can be safely driven, but will not have the benefit of the ABS system. If the brake warning light comes on, the braking system may be impaired due to fluid loss in the system. In this case braking may be reduced; diagnosis and repair is required immediately and caution should be used when driving.

Troubleshooting the Brake System

Problem	Cause	Solution
Low brake pedal (excessive pedal travel required for braking action.)	• Excessive clearance between rear linings and drums caused by inoperative automatic adjusters	• Make 10 to 15 alternate forward and reverse brake stops to adjust brakes. If brake pedal does not come up, repair or replace adjuster parts as necessary.
	• Worn rear brakelining	• Inspect and replace lining if worn beyond minimum thickness specification
	• Bent, distorted brakeshoes, front or rear	• Replace brakeshoes in axle sets
	• Air in hydraulic system	• Remove air from system. Refer to Brake Bleeding.
Low brake pedal (pedal may go to floor with steady pressure applied.)	• Fluid leak in hydraulic system	• Fill master cylinder to fill line; have helper apply brakes and check calipers, wheel cylinders, differential valve tubes, hoses and fittings for leaks. Repair or replace as necessary.
	• Air in hydraulic system	• Remove air from system. Refer to Brake Bleeding.
	• Incorrect or non-recommended brake fluid (fluid evaporates at below normal temp).	• Flush hydraulic system with clean brake fluid. Refill with correct-type fluid.
	• Master cylinder piston seals worn, or master cylinder bore is scored, worn or corroded	• Repair or replace master cylinder
Low brake pedal (pedal goes to floor on first application—o.k. on subsequent applications.)	• Disc brake pads sticking on abutment surfaces of anchor plate. Caused by a build-up of dirt, rust, or corrosion on abutment surfaces	• Clean abutment surfaces
Fading brake pedal (pedal height decreases with steady pressure applied.)	• Fluid leak in hydraulic system	• Fill master cylinder reservoirs to fill mark, have helper apply brakes, check calipers, wheel cylinders, differential valve, tubes, hoses, and fittings for fluid leaks. Repair or replace parts as necessary.
	• Master cylinder piston seals worn, or master cylinder bore is scored, worn or corroded	• Repair or replace master cylinder
Decreasing brake pedal travel (pedal travel required for braking action decreases and may be accompanied by a hard pedal.)	• Caliper or wheel cylinder pistons sticking or seized	• Repair or replace the calipers, or wheel cylinders
	• Master cylinder compensator ports blocked (preventing fluid return to reservoirs) or pistons sticking or seized in master cylinder bore	• Repair or replace the master cylinder
	• Power brake unit binding internally	• Test unit according to the following procedure: (a) Shift transmission into neutral and start engine (b) Increase engine speed to 1500 rpm, close throttle and fully depress brake pedal (c) Slow release brake pedal and stop engine (d) Have helper remove vacuum check valve and hose from power unit. Observe for backward movement of brake pedal. (e) If the pedal moves backward, the power unit has an internal bind—replace power unit

Troubleshooting the Brake System (cont.)

Problem	Cause	Solution
Spongy brake pedal (pedal has abnormally soft, springy, spongy feel when depressed.)	• Air in hydraulic system • Brakeshoes bent or distorted • Brakelining not yet seated with drums and rotors • Rear drum brakes not properly adjusted	• Remove air from system. Refer to Brake Bleeding. • Replace brakeshoes • Burnish brakes • Adjust brakes
Hard brake pedal (excessive pedal pressure required to stop vehicle. May be accompanied by brake fade.)	• Loose or leaking power brake unit vacuum hose • Incorrect or poor quality brakelining • Bent, broken, distorted brakeshoes • Calipers binding or dragging on mounting pins. Rear brakeshoes dragging on support plate. • Caliper, wheel cylinder, or master cylinder pistons sticking or seized • Power brake unit vacuum check valve malfunction • Power brake unit has internal bind • Master cylinder compensator ports (at bottom of reservoirs) blocked by dirt, scale, rust, or have small burrs (blocked ports prevent fluid return to reservoirs). • Brake hoses, tubes, fittings clogged or restricted • Brake fluid contaminated with improper fluids (motor oil, transmission fluid, causing rubber components to swell and stick in bores • Low engine vacuum	• Tighten connections or replace leaking hose • Replace with lining in axle sets • Replace brakeshoes • Replace mounting pins and bushings. Clean rust or burrs from rear brake support plate ledges and lubricate ledges with molydisulfide grease. **NOTE:** If ledges are deeply grooved or scored, do not attempt to sand or grind them smooth—replace support plate. • Repair or replace parts as necessary • Test valve according to the following procedure: (a) Start engine, increase engine speed to 1500 rpm, close throttle and immediately stop engine (b) Wait at least 90 seconds then depress brake pedal (c) If brakes are not vacuum assisted for 2 or more applications, check valve is faulty • Test unit according to the following procedure: (a) With engine stopped, apply brakes several times to exhaust all vacuum in system (b) Shift transmission into neutral, depress brake pedal and start engine (c) If pedal height decreases with foot pressure and less pressure is required to hold pedal in applied position, power unit vacuum system is operating normally. Test power unit. If power unit exhibits a bind condition, replace the power unit. • Repair or replace master cylinder **CAUTION:** Do not attempt to clean blocked ports with wire, pencils, or similar implements. Use compressed air only. • Use compressed air to check or unclog parts. Replace any damaged parts. • Replace all rubber components, combination valve and hoses. Flush entire brake system with DOT 3 brake fluid or equivalent. • Adjust or repair engine

Troubleshooting the Brake System (cont.)

Problem	Cause	Solution
Grabbing brakes (severe reaction to brake pedal pressure.)	• Brakelining(s) contaminated by grease or brake fluid	• Determine and correct cause of contamination and replace brakeshoes in axle sets
	• Parking brake cables incorrectly adjusted or seized	• Adjust cables. Replace seized cables.
	• Incorrect brakelining or lining loose on brakeshoes	• Replace brakeshoes in axle sets
	• Caliper anchor plate bolts loose	• Tighten bolts
	• Rear brakeshoes binding on support plate ledges	• Clean and lubricate ledges. Replace support plate(s) if ledges are deeply grooved. Do not attempt to smooth ledges by grinding.
	• Incorrect or missing power brake reaction disc	• Install correct disc
	• Rear brake support plates loose	• Tighten mounting bolts
Dragging brakes (slow or incomplete release of brakes)	• Brake pedal binding at pivot	• Loosen and lubricate
	• Power brake unit has internal bind	• Inspect for internal bind. Replace unit if internal bind exists.
	• Parking brake cables incorrrectly adjusted or seized	• Adjust cables. Replace seized cables.
	• Rear brakeshoe return springs weak or broken	• Replace return springs. Replace brakeshoe if necessary in axle sets.
	• Automatic adjusters malfunctioning	• Repair or replace adjuster parts as required
	• Caliper, wheel cylinder or master cylinder pistons sticking or seized	• Repair or replace parts as necessary
	• Master cylinder compensating ports blocked (fluid does not return to reservoirs).	• Use compressed air to clear ports. Do not use wire, pencils, or similar objects to open blocked ports.
Vehicle moves to one side when brakes are applied	• Incorrect front tire pressure	• Inflate to recommended cold (reduced load) inflation pressure
	• Worn or damaged wheel bearings	• Replace worn or damaged bearings
	• Brakelining on one side contaminated	• Determine and correct cause of contamination and replace brakelining in axle sets
	• Brakeshoes on one side bent, distorted, or lining loose on shoe	• Replace brakeshoes in axle sets
	• Support plate bent or loose on one side	• Tighten or replace support plate
	• Brakelining not yet seated with drums or rotors	• Burnish brakelining
	• Caliper anchor plate loose on one side	• Tighten anchor plate bolts
	• Caliper piston sticking or seized	• Repair or replace caliper
	• Brakelinings water soaked	• Drive vehicle with brakes lightly applied to dry linings
	• Loose suspension component attaching or mounting bolts	• Tighten suspension bolts. Replace worn suspension components.
	• Brake combination valve failure	• Replace combination valve
Chatter or shudder when brakes are applied (pedal pulsation and roughness may also occur.)	• Brakeshoes distorted, bent, contaminated, or worn	• Replace brakeshoes in axle sets
	• Caliper anchor plate or support plate loose	• Tighten mounting bolts
	• Excessive thickness variation of rotor(s)	• Refinish or replace rotors in axle sets
Noisy brakes (squealing, clicking, scraping sound when brakes are applied.)	• Bent, broken, distorted brakeshoes	• Replace brakeshoes in axle sets
	• Excessive rust on outer edge of rotor braking surface	• Remove rust

Troubleshooting the Brake System (cont.)

Problem	Cause	Solution
Noisy brakes (squealing, clicking, scraping sound when brakes are applied.) (cont.)	• Brakelining worn out—shoes contacting drum of rotor	• Replace brakeshoes and lining in axle sets. Refinish or replace drums or rotors.
	• Broken or loose holddown or return springs	• Replace parts as necessary
	• Rough or dry drum brake support plate ledges	• Lubricate support plate ledges
	• Cracked, grooved, or scored rotor(s) or drum(s)	• Replace rotor(s) or drum(s). Replace brakeshoes and lining in axle sets if necessary.
	• Incorrect brakelining and/or shoes (front or rear).	• Install specified shoe and lining assemblies
Pulsating brake pedal	• Out of round drums or excessive lateral runout in disc brake rotor(s)	• Refinish or replace drums, re-index rotors or replace

Adjustment

Disc brakes are inherently self adjusting. The only adjustment needed will be for the parking brakes, which are small brake shoes located in the hub drum of the rear disc brake rotors. See the end of this chapter for procedures.

Brake Light Switch
REMOVAL AND INSTALLATION

The switch controlling the brake lights is located at the brake pedal. As the pedal moves from its rest position, the switch engages and turns on the brake lights. To change the switch, simply unplug the connectors at the switch, unscrew the locknut and remove the switch.

After installing the new switch, it must be adjusted so that the switch engages (brake lights come on) after 3/8–1/2 in. (9–12mm) of pedal travel. With the brake pedal in the released position, the distance (A) between the brass hub of the switch and the pedal lever should be 0.08–0.24 in. (2–6mm). To adjust, loosen the attaching screws for the switch bracket and move the switch in the required direction.

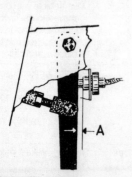

Stop light switch adjustment

Master Cylinder
REMOVAL AND INSTALLATION
1970–73 140 Series

1. To prevent brake fluid from spilling onto and damaging the paint, place a protective cover over the fender apron, and rags beneath the master cylinder.

2. Disconnect the brake lines from the master cylinder and plug them immediately.

3. Remove the two nuts which retain the master cylinder and reservoir assembly to the vacuum booster, and lift the assembly forward, being careful not to spill any fluid on the fender. Empty out and discard the brake fluid.

CAUTION: *Do not depress the brake pedal while the master cylinder is removed.*

4. In order for the master cylinder to function properly when installed to the vacuum booster, the adjusting nut for the thrust rod of the booster must not prevent the primary piston of the master cylinder from returning to its resting position.

A clearance (C) of 0.020–0.059 in. (0.5–1.5mm) is required between the thrust rod and primary piston with the master cylinder installed. The clearance may be adjusted by rotating the adjusting nut for the booster thrust rod in the required direction.

To determine what the clearance (C) will be when the master cylinder and booster are connected, first measure the distance (A) between the face of the attaching flange and the center of the primary piston on the master cylinder, then measure the distance (B) that the thrust rod protrudes from the fixed surface of the booster (making sure that the thrust rod is depressed fully with a partial vacuum existing in the booster). When measurement (B) is sub-

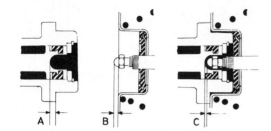

Adjusting the brake booster thrust rod— 1970–73 140 series

tracted from measurement (A), clearance (C) should be obtained. If not, adjust the length of the thrust rod by turning the adjusting screw to suit. After the final adjustment is obtained, apply a few drops of locking compound to the adjusting nut.

5. Position the master cylinder and reservoir assembly onto the studs for the booster, and install the washers and nuts. Tighten the nuts to 17 ft. lbs.

6. Remove the plugs and connect the brake lines.

7. Bleed the entire brake system.

1974 140 and 164
1800 Series
All 200 Series
All 700 Series

1. To prevent brake fluid from spilling onto and damaging the paint, place a protective cover over the fender apron, and rags beneath the master cylinder.

2. Label and disconnect the brake lines from the master cylinder and plug them immediately. If the vehicle has a hydraulic clutch, disconnect its line from the fluid reservoir. Plug it and secure the line out of the way.

3. Remove the two nuts which retain the master cylinder and reservoir assembly to the vacuum booster, and lift the assembly forward, being careful not to spill any fluid on the fender. Empty out and discard the brake fluid.

CAUTION: *Do not depress the brake pedal while the master cylinder is removed!*

4. To install, place a new sealing rim (if equipped) onto the sealing flange of the master cylinder. Position the master cylinder and reservoir assembly onto the booster studs, and install the washer and nuts. Tighten the nuts to 8.6–10.8 ft. lbs.

5. Remove the plugs and loosely connect the brake lines. Have a helper depress the brake pedal to remove air from the cylinder. Tighten the nuts for the lines when the brake fluid (free of air bubbles) is forced out. Reconnect the lines for the hydraulic clutch if so equipped.

6. Bleed the entire brake system. If the car has a hydraulic clutch, bleed the clutch system.

MASTER CYLINDER OVERHAUL

164, 1800 Series

1. Remove the master cylinder from the booster as outlined above.

2. Firmly fasten the flange of the master cylinder in a vise.

3. Position both hands beneath the reservoir and pull it free of its rubber seals. Remove the filler cap and strainer from the reservoir, as well as the rubber seals and nuts (if so equipped) from the cylinder.

4. Remove the stop screw. Using a pair of snapring pliers, remove the snapring from the primary piston and shake out the pistons.

5. Discard both the primary and secondary pistons.

6. Clean all reusable metal parts in clean brake fluid or methylated alcohol. The parts must be thoroughly dried with filtered, water-free compressed air, or air dried. All cleaning alcohol must be removed from the parts, as it lowers the boiling temperature of brake fluid.

If the inside of the cylinder is scored or scratched, the cylinder must be replaced. Minor pitting and corrosion may be removed by honing. Remember to flush the cylinder clean after honing, and make sure that the passages are clear. Check the cylinder bore for excessive wear.

7. Make sure that the new rubber seals, a new brass washer and back-up ring are installed on the new secondary piston. Make sure

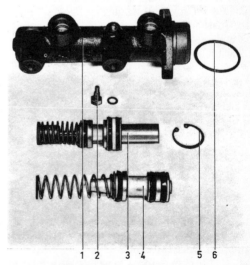

1. Cylinder housing   4. Secondary piston
2. Stop screw   5. Circlip
3. Primary piston   6. Sealing ring

Master cylinder disassembled— 164, 1800 series

that the rubber seals are pointing in the right direction.

8. Coat the cylinder bore with brake fluid and dip the secondary piston and seals in brake fluid prior to installation. Install the secondary piston and spring in the bore, taking care not to damage the rubber seals.

9. Make sure that the new rubber seals, metal washers, plastic washer, back-up ring, sleeve, and springs are installed on the new primary piston. Make sure that the seals are facing in the right direction.

10. On 1800 models, compress the primary piston spring and tighten the screw for the sleeve until it bottoms. Torque the screw to 1.5–2.2 ft. lbs.

11. Dip the primary piston assembly in brake fluid and install it in the bore, taking care not to damage the rubber seals. While holding the piston in the bore, install the snapring.

12. Check that the hole for the stop screw is clear, and install the new stop screw and sealing washer. Torque the screw to 3.5–5.7 ft. lbs. on all 164 and 1800 series.

13. Check the movement of the pistons and make sure that the flow-through holes are clear. The equalizing hole is checked by inserting a 25 gauge (1800) or 22 gauge (164) soft copper wire through it and making sure that it is not blocked by the secondary piston seal. If it is blocked, the master cylinder will not function properly and must be reassembled.

14. Install the nuts (if so equipped), new rubber seals and washers onto the master cylinder at the reservoir connections. After making sure that the venting hole in the cap is open, install the cleaned strainer and cap. Press the reservoir into the master cylinder by hand.

15. Install the master cylinder as outlined in the applicable Master Cylinder Removal and Installation section.

140 Series
All 200 Series
All 700 Series except ABS system

1. Remove the master cylinder from the booster as outlined previously.

2. Firmly fasten the flange of the master cylinder in a vise.

3. Position both hands beneath the reservoir and pull it free of its rubber seals. Remove the filler cap and strainer from the reservoir, as well as the rubber seals and nuts (if so equipped) from the cylinder.

4. Remove the stop screw. Using a pair of snapring pliers, remove the snapring from the primary piston and shake out the piston.

5. Remove both the seal from the secondary piston, taking care not to damage or score the

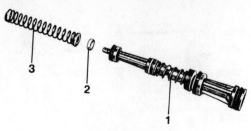

1. Piston assembly
2. Spring seat
3. Spring

Master cylinder piston assembly—240, 260 and 1980 and later models

surfaces of the plunger. The old primary piston should be discarded and replaced.

6. Clean all reusable metal parts in clean brake fluid or methylated alcohol. The parts may be allowed to thoroughly air dry, or compressed air may be used. All alcohol must be removed from the parts, as alcohol lowers the boiling temperature of brake fluid.

If the outside of the cylinder is scored or scratched, the cylinder must be replaced. Minor pitting or corrosion may be removed by honing. Remember to flush the cylinder clean after honing, and make sure that the passages are clear. Check the piston for damage and proper clearance in the bore.

7. Install new seals on the secondary piston, making sure that they are positioned in the proper direction.

8. Coat the cylinder bore with brake fluid and dip the secondary piston and seals in brake fluid prior to installation. Slide the spring, spring plate, and washer onto the secondary piston and install the assembly in the bore, taking care not to damage the seals. Dip the new primary piston and seal assembly in brake fluid. Press the primary piston assembly into the bore and install a new washer and snapring.

9. Make sure that the hole for the stop screw is clear and install the new top screw and sealing washer.

10. Check the movement of the pistons and make sure that the flow-through holes are clear. The equalizing hole (140 series only) is checked by inserting a 25 gauge soft copper wire through it and making sure that it is not blocked by the secondary piston seal. If it is blocked, then the master cylinder in incorrectly assembled, and you must take it through the numbers again.

11. Install the nuts (if so equipped), new rubber seals, and washers onto the master cylinder at the reservoir connections. After making sure that the venting hole in the cap is open, install the cleaned strainer and cap. Press the reservoir into the master cylinder by hand.

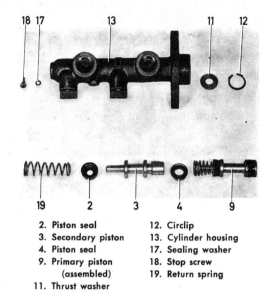

2. Piston seal	12. Circlip
3. Secondary piston	13. Cylinder housing
4. Piston seal	17. Sealing washer
9. Primary piston	18. Stop screw
(assembled)	19. Return spring
11. Thrust washer	

Master cylinder disassembled (with type 1 secondary piston)—140 series

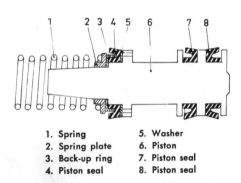

1. Spring	5. Washer
2. Spring plate	6. Piston
3. Back-up ring	7. Piston seal
4. Piston seal	8. Piston seal

Type 2 secondary piston—140 series

12. Install the master cylinder as outlined in the applicable Master Cylinder Removal and Installation section.

ABS System Master cylinder overhaul

1. Remove the master cylinder as described previously. Drain and remove the fluid reservoir. Remove the two seals between the reservoir and the cylinder.

2. Remove the washer in the front hole of the cylinder.

3. To disassemble the master cylinder, press the pistons into the cylinder while using a pair of long-nosed pliers to remove the locking pin through the front hole.

4. After the lock pin is removed, remove the lock ring for the pistons and remove the pistons.

5. Clean all reusable metal parts in methylated alcohol. The parts may be allowed to thoroughly air dry, or compressed air may be used. All alcohol must be removed from the parts, as alcohol lowers the boiling temperature of brake fluid.

If the bore of the cylinder is scored or scratched, the cylinder must be replaced. Minor pitting or corrosion may be removed by honing. Remember to flush the cylinder clean after honing, and make sure that the passages are clear. Check the piston for damage and proper clearance in the bore.

6. Install the pistons into the cylinder. Turn the oval opening of the front stage so that it faces the fluid reservoir hole.

7. Press the pistons in to the bottom of the cylinder and install the lock pin through the front hole. Release the pistons and check that the lock pin holds the front stage.

8. Press the pistons inward again and install the lock ring.

9. Install the washer in the front hole and re-install the two sealing rings. Use new rings if any damage is seen.

10. Install the master cylinder as outlined previously.

11. Bleed the brakes.

Brake Booster

All models are equipped with a mechanical tandem type power booster device located between the brake pedal and the master cylinder. Either intake manifold vacuum (models through 1974) or a camshaft driven vacuum pump (1975 and later models) is used to supply power to the booster. When the brake pedal is pushed, the vacuum acts on a diaphragm inside the booster; this in effect amplifies the brake pedal pressure.

REMOVAL AND INSTALLATION

1. Remove the master cylinder, following previously listed procedures. On 140 Series, remove the ignition coil if it is in the way.

2. Disconnect the vacuum hose and the check valve from the brake booster. The check valve is a press fit and may be removed with gentle prying.

3. On 700 Series, loosen the fuel filter from its mounts and move it aside. Remove the vacuum pump.

4. Disconnect the link from the brake pedal. Remove the bracket with the clutch pedal stop.

5. Remove the retaining nuts (4), pull the power booster forward and disconnect fork from the link arm.

6. The brake booster is non-servicable; any failure requires replacement of the complete unit. To reinstall, transfer any necessary parts to the new unit. Remember to transfer the rubber seal for the check valve. Make sure it is properly seated in its groove.

7. Install a new sealing ring on the booster.

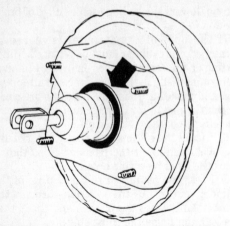

Remember to install the seal when installing the power brake booster

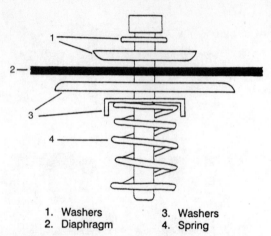

1. Washers   3. Washers
2. Diaphragm   4. Spring

Assembly of internal parts of vacuum pump for gasoline engines. Correct placement of washers is important

(The DBA 9 in. (228mm) booster found on some 200 Series does not have a ring; it requires sealing compound to be applied to the firewall.)

8. Attach the brake booster to the firewall. Connect the brake rod to the pedal. Secure the soundproofing under the dash.

9. Install the master cylinder following the procedures outlined previously. Connect the check valve and the vacuum hose.

10. On 700 Series, reinstall the fuel filter and the vacuum pump. On 200 series, reinstall the ignition coil if it was removed.

11. Bleed the brake system completely.

Vacuum Pumps

REMOVAL AND INSTALLATION

Gasoline engines

1. Disconnect the hose from the vacuum pump. Remove the four bolts and remove the pump from the engine.

2. Remove the upper cover, the seal, and the valve springs. Note and MARK the valve positions; they face in different directions in the cover. Remove the valves and the seals below them.

3. Matchmark the upper and lower halves of the pump assembly. This is essential for proper reassembly. A felt-tip marker works well. Remove the eight screws and separate the halves of the pump.

4. Remove the center screw, the washer, the diaphragm, the washers and the spring.

5. Remove the lower cover and the axle (pivot) pin for the pump arm. Place a shim such as a feeler gauge between the arm and the lever; this will prevent the arm from bending during removal of the pin.

6. Remove the pump rod and lever arm. Clean the parts and check them for damage.

Pay close attention to the condition of the needle bearing for the pump arm.

7. To reassemble, fit the pump rod and lever arm into the housing and press in the axle pin. Use a shim to support the bracket while pressing the pin in. Put a drop of locking compound onto the ends of the pin to secure it.

8. Reinstall the bottom cover and seal.

9. Assemble onto the center screw the washers, the diaphragm, the other washers and the spring. Make certain the washers are in the correct position.

10. Hold the pump upside down and fit the screw with the parts on it. Make sure everything lines up and seats properly.

11. Reassemble the pump halves; use the matchmarks to position the halves.

12. Install the seals.

13. Observe the marks made during removal and install the valves. Make sure they face in different directions.

14. Install the valve springs, the seal and the cover.

15. Use a new gasket and install the vacuum pump to the motor. Connect the vacuum hoses.

Diesel Engines

1. Remove the hoses from the pump body. Remove the retaining bolts and lift the pump from the cylinder head. Remove the plunger from the cylinder head and thoroughly clean the pump.

2. Matchmark the pump body and the cover. This is essential to correct reassembly.

3. Remove the screws (1), the cover (2) and the gasket (3). Lift out the intermediate piece (11), the filler piece (10), both valves (12 and 13) and all three washers (14).

4. Use a valve spring compressor tool (Volvo 6052 or similar) to press the diaphragm rod

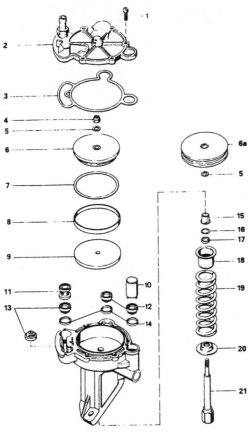

1. Screws
2. Cover
3. Gasket
4. Nut
5. Washer
6. Piston
6a. One-piece piston
7. O-ring
8. Piston ring
9. Plunger disc
10. Filler piece
11. Intermediate piece
12. Valve
13. Valve
14. Washers
15. Bushing
16. O-ring
17. Washer
18. Spring cup
19. Spring
20. Spring plate
21. Diaphragm rod

Vacuum pump for diesel engine

spring down about 0.4 in. (10mm). Unscrew the nut (4) while holding the hexagonal head of the rod stationary.

5. Release the compressor tool and remove the diaphragm rod (21), the washer (17), the O-ring (16) and the bushing (15).

6. Use the diaphragm rod to press out the plunger (6 or 6a) and the plunger disc (9). Re-

move the O-ring (7) and the piston ring (8). (6a is a one-piece
plunger; it will not have an O-ring or piston ring.)

7. Clean all reusable parts and inspect for damage. The intermediate piece should be 0.59–0.60 in. (15.0–15.2mm) in height. The filler piece should be 1.02–1.03 in. (25.9–26.1mm) in height. Replace any worn or faulty parts.

8. Lubricate any new components with engine oil. Install the bushing (15), the O-ring (16) and the washer (17).

9. Lubricate the diaphragm rod (21) and install it along with the spring plate (20), the spring (19) and the spring cup.

10. Use the compressor tool and tension the spring so that the threaded end of the diaphragm rod extends about 0.2 in. (5mm) above the pump flange surface. Align the rod so that it is perpendicular to the flange.

11. Install the piston plate (9) on the diaphragm rod. Make sure the **APG** mark faces out.

12. Lightly lubricate the piston bore; insert the piston with its piston ring and O-ring (6,7, 8 or 6a) and be very careful not to damage the piston ring.

NOTE: *On pumps with one-piece pistons (6a), insert the tapered end of the piston on top of the small washer (5).*

13. Install a new lock-nut (4) and washer (5) onto the end of the diaphragm rod.

14. Relieve the tension on the spring so that the bottom of the rod contacts the housing. Hold the rod stationary and tighten the locknut to 7 ft. lbs.

15. In the pump body, install the three washers (14), the two valves (12 and 13), the intermediate piece (11) and the filler piece (10).

NOTE: *After rebuilding the pump, the inlet valve is sealed by the large gasket (3), not by a separate smaller gasket.*

16. Install a new gasket (3) on the housing, install the cover (2) and tighten the screws in a diagonal pattern to 22–37 ft. lbs.

17. Install the plunger and vacuum pump on the cylinder head. Tighten the mounting bolts and connect the vacuum hoses.

Valves

REMOVAL AND INSTALLATION

System Warning Valve

The brake system warning valve is located near the master cylinder in the engine compartment on 1973–77 models. On 1978 and later models it is located under a bolt on the front axle member. The 700 Series vehicles without ABS have the unit mounted on the left front shock tower. The valve is centered by hydraulic

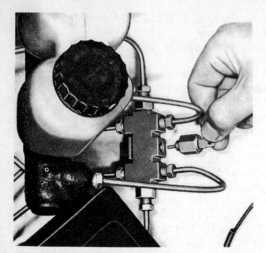

Removing brake warning switch

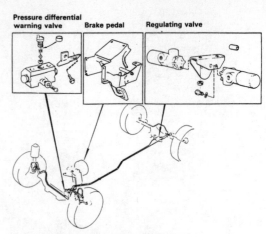

Pressure differential warning valve   Brake pedal   Regulating valve

Component location, 200 Series

pressure from the primary circuit on one side and the secondary circuit on the other.

When a hydraulic imbalance occurs, such as a leak in one of the calipers, the valve will move off-center toward the system with the lower pressure. When the valve moves off-center, it closes a circuit to a warning light on the dashboard, warning the driver of the imbalance. Sometimes, the valve will actuate the warning light when one of the systems is bled during normal maintenance. When this happens, the valve has to be reset.

Cars with ABS do not use this system. The pressure sensing circuit is built into the hydraulic unit. In case of system leakage, a sensor within the cap of the brake fluid reservoir will close a switch and illuminate the dash warning light.

If the valve must be replaced:

1. Place a rag beneath the valve to catch the brake fluid, loosen the pipe connections, label and disconnect the six brake lines. Disconnect the electrical plug contact, and lift out the valve.

2. Connect the new warning valve in the and connect the plug contact.

3. Bleed the entire brake system.

VALVE RESETTING

1800, 100 and 200 Series.

1. Disconnect the plug contact and screw out the warning switch so that the pistons inside the valve may return to their normal position.

2. Repair and bleed the faulty hydraulic circuit.

3. Screw in the warning switch and tighten it to a torque of 10–14 ft. lbs. Connect the plug contact.

4. When the system has been bled, depress the brake pedal firmly (simulating a hard stop)

for about a minute. Check that there has been no leakage at the warning switch threads. If any leakage--no matter how slight--is found, replace the valve assembly.

NOTE: *The non-ABS 700 Series vehicles do not require this procedure. The valve will self-center once equal pressures have been restored within the system.*

Brake System Proportioning Valves 1800, 100 and 200 Series

Each of the brake circuits has a proportioning (relief) valve located inline between the rear wheels. The purpose of this valve is to ensure that brake pressure on all four wheels compen-

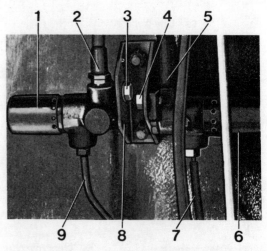

1. Left brake valve
2. Brake hose to left rear wheel
3. Attaching screw
4. Attaching screw
5. Brake hose to right rear wheel
6. Right brake valve
7. From the master cylinder
8. Bracket
9. From the master cylinder secondary circuit

Brake proportioning valves installed

sates for the change in weight distribution under varied braking conditions.

The harder the brakes are applied, the more weight there is on the front wheels. The valve regulates the hydraulic pressure to the rear wheels so that under hard braking conditions they receive a smaller percentage of the total braking effort. This prevents premature rear wheel lockup and possible skidding or loss of control.

VALVE REPLACEMENT

Sophisticated pressure testing equipment is required to troubleshoot the dual hydraulic system in order to determine if the proportioning valve(s) are in need of replacement. However, if the car is demonstrating signs of rear wheel lock-up under moderate to heavy braking and other variables such as tire pressure, tread depth, etc., have been ruled out, the valve(s) may be at fault. The valves are not rebuildable and must be replaced as a unit.

To replace the valve:

1. At the proportioning valve, disconnect and plug the brake lines coming from the front of the car.

2. Loosen the connection for the flexible brake hose to the rear wheel a maximum of ¼ turn. This will allow some flex in the hose during removal.

3. Remove the bolt(s) which retain the valve to the underbody, and unscrew the valve from the rear brake hose.

4. To install the valve, place a new seal on it, and screw the valve onto the rear brake hose and hand tighten. Secure the valve to the underbody with the retaining bolts(s).

5. Connect the brake lines from the front of the car and tighten both connections, making sure that there is no tension on the flexible rear hose.

6. Snug the connection to the rear brake hose, but do not overtighten.

7. Bleed the brake system.

Brake Hoses

REMOVAL AND INSTALLATION

Metal lines and rubber brake hoses should be checked frequently for leaks and external damage. Metal lines are particularly prone to crushing and kinking under the car. Any such deformation can restrict the proper flow of fluid and therefore impair braking at the wheels. Rubber hoses should be checked for cracking or scraping; such damage can create a weak spot in the hose and it could fail under pressure.

Any time the lines are removed or disconnected, extreme cleanliness must be observed. The slightest bit of dirt in the system can plug a

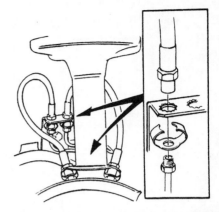

Detail of brake hose connections at front calipers

fluid port and render the brakes defective. Clean all joints and connections before disassembly (use a stiff brush and clean brake fluid) and plug the lines as soon as they are disconnected. New lines and hoses should be blown or flushed clean before installation to remove any contamination. To replace a line or hose:

1. Clean the surrounding area on the joints to be disconnected.

2. To reduce fluid spillage during the repair, either plug the vent hole in the reservoir cap or substitute another cap without a vent hole.

3. Disconnect the hose or line to be replaced. If disconnecting rubber hoses at the brake caliper, label or identify each hose so that they may be replaced in the same location. Plug the line ends as soon as the joint is disconnected.

4. Install the new line paying close attention to the proper routing and installation of any retaining clips. Make sure the new line will not rub against any other parts. Brake lines must be at least ⅜ inch away from the steering column.

NOTE: *If the new line requires bending, do so gently using a pipe bending tool. Do not attempt to bend the tubing by hand; it will kink the pipe and render it useless.*

5. Remove the line plugs and tighten the line connections at both ends.

6. Bleed the brake system beginning with the wheel closest to the replaced line or hose.

Bleeding the Hydraulic System

Whenever a spongy brake pedal indicates that there is air in the system, or when any part of the hydraulic system has been removed for service, the system must be bled. In addition, if the level in the master cylinder reservoir is allowed to go below the minimum mark for too long a period of time, air may enter the system, necessitating bleeding.

If only one brake caliper or wheel cylinder is removed for servicing, it is usually necessary to

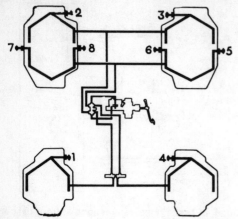

Bleeding sequence, 140 and 164 Series with Gir-ling brakes

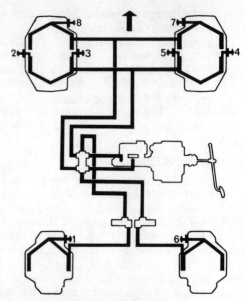

Bleeding sequence—1800 series

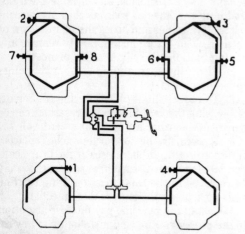

Bleeding sequence, 140 and 164 Series with ATE brakes

bleed only that unit. If, however, the master cylinder, warning valve, or any of the main brake lines are removed, the entire system must be bled.

Be careful not to spill any brake fluid onto the brake surfaces (disc, pads, drum and linings) and, of course, the paint work. When bleeding the entire system, the rear of the car should be raised higher than the front. Only use brake fluid bearing the designation SAE 1703 (SAE 70 R3), or DOT 4. Never reuse old brake fluid.

NOTE: *The following procedure is acceptable for cars with and without ABS.*

1. Check to make sure that there are not mats or other materials obstructing the travel of the brake pedal. During bleeding, the full pedal travel should be 6 in. (150mm) for the 140, 240 260 series and later models, and 5.5 in. (140mm) for the 164 and 1800 series (providing that both circuits are bled simultaneously).

2. Clean the cap and the top of the master cylinder reservoir, and make sure that the vent hole in the cap is open. Fill the reservoir to the maximum mark. Never allow the level to dip below the minimum mark during bleeding, as this will allow air into the system.

3. If only one brake caliper or line was removed, it will usually suffice to bleed only that wheel. Otherwise, prepare to bleed the entire system beginning at the left front wheel.

4. Remove the protective cap for the bleeder screw, and fit a $5/16$ line wrench on the nipple. Install a tight plastic hose onto the nipple, and insert the other end of the hose into a glass bottle containing clean brake fluid. The hose must hang down below the surface of the fluid, or air will be sucked into the system when the brake pedal is released.

5. Open the bleeder screw a maximum of ½ turn. Have a helper slowly depress the brake pedal until it bottoms, pause a second or two, and then quickly release the pedal. This should be repeated until the fluid flowing into the bottle is completely free of air bubbles. During this procedure you should check the master cylinder reservoir frequently and top up the fluid level as needed.

Have your helper press the pedal to the bottom of its travel and hold it there while you tighten the bleeder screw. Install the protective cap.

NOTE: *On the 240, 260 series and the 1980 and later models, when bleeding the front brakes, connect bleeder hoses to all three bleeder nipples (two on the 760 GLE), submerge the hoses in brake fluid and open the nipples. Keeping the reservoir full, pump the*

Bleeding the front calipers—240, 260 and 1980 and later models. Bleed all three nipples (two on the 760GLE) at once

brake pedal until no bubbles appear, hold the pedal down and close the nipple.

6. If the entire system is to be bled, follow the above procedure for the remaining nipples at the right front, left rear and right rear wheel IN THAT ORDER. Generally, it is sufficient to bleed each circuit once. However, if the pedal continues to feel spongy, repeat the bleeding sequence. Remember to keep the master cylinder reservoir level above the minimum mark.

7. Fill the reservoir with the specified brake fluid to the maximum mark.

8. With the bleeder valves closed and the master cylinder topped off, turn the ignition ON but do not start the engine. Apply moderate force to the brake pedal simulating a hard stop. The pedal must travel no more than 2.4 in. (61mm) without ABS; 2.17 in. (55mm) with ABS. The brake warning light (and ABS light) must stay off.

Switch off the ignition and continue to bleed the system until the pedal travel and/or the brake warning light tests are satisfied.

9. Top off the reservoir and install the cap. Remember to put the rubber caps onto the bleeder nipples at each caliper.

FRONT DISC BRAKES

Brake Pads

INSPECTION

The front brake pads may be inspected without removal. With the front end elevated and supported, remove the wheel(s). Unlock the steering column lock and turn the wheel so that the brake caliper is out from under the fender.

View the pads--inner and outer--through the cut-out in the center of the caliper.Remember to look at the thickness of the pad friction material (the part that actully presses on the disc) rather than the thickness of the backing plate which does not change with wear.

Remember that you are looking at the profile of the pad, not the whole thing. Brake pads can wear on a taper which may not be visible through the window. It is also not possible to check the contact surface for cracking or scoring from this position. This quick check can be helpful only as a reference; detailed inspection requires pad removal.

REMOVAL AND INSTALLATION

CAUTION: *Brake pads and shoes contain asbestos, which has been determined to a cancer causing agent. Never clean the brake surfaces with compressed air! Avoid inhaling and dust from brake surfaces! When cleaning brakes, use commercially available brake cleaning fluids.*

Girling Brakes
All vehicles except 700 Series

1. Remove the hub caps and loosen the lug nuts a few turns.

2. Raise the vehicle and place jackstands beneath the rear axle and the front jack attachments. Remove the wheels.

3. Remove the hairpin-shaped locking clips together with the damping springs for the brake pads. Pull out the pads. Discard them if they are worn down to a lining thickness of ⅛ in. (3mm) or less. If they are reusable, mark them for ease of assembly.

4. Carefully clean out the pad cavity. Replace any damaged dust covers. If any dirt has contaminated the cylinders, the caliper must be removed for overhaul. Inspect the brake disc as described under Brake Discs Inspection and Replacement.

5. Carefully depress the pistons in their cylinders so that the new pads will fit. This may be done with a large pair of pliers or a C-clamp, but extra care must be exercised not to damage the rubber piston seals, the pistons, or the new pads themselves.

A piston depressing tool (Volvo 2809) is available from the dealer that accomplishes the job without danger to the caliper components. Remember that when the pistons are depressed in their bores, brake fluid is displaced causing the level in the master cylinder to rise, and perhaps, overflow.

6. Install the new pads and secure them with first one lock pin, then the other pin with the damping springs. Install new locking clips on the lock pins. Make sure that the pads are able

to move and that the linings do not project outside of the brake disc.

NOTE: *If the Girling calipers were fitted with plates between the brake pads and the caliper, reinstall the plates. If, instead of plates, round damper washers were used, refit them with their smaller contact face towards the pad. Never use glue or grease and do not attempt to use plates and washers at the same time. Not all Girling calipers use plates or washers.*

7. Depress the brake pedal several times and make sure that the movement feels normal. The first brake pedal application may result in a very "long" pedal due to the pistons being retracted. Always make several brake applications before starting the vehicle. Bleeding is not usually necessary after pad replacement.

8. Install the wheel. Remove the jackstands and lower the vehicle. Tighten the lug nuts to 80–90 ft. lbs. and install the hub cap.

NOTE: *Braking should be moderate for the first 5 miles or so until the new pads seat correctly. The new pads will bed best if put through several moderate heating and cooling cycles. Avoid hard braking until the brakes have experienced several long, slow stops with time to cool in between. Taking the time to properly bed the brakes will yield quieter operation, more efficient stopping and contribute to extended brake life.*

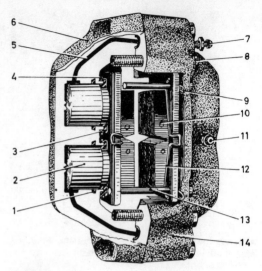

1. Sealing ring　　　　8. Bolt
2. Piston　　　　　　　9. Retaining clip
3. Rubber dust cover　10. Brake pad
4. Retaining ring　　 11. Lower bleeder nipple
5. Channel　　　　　 12. Damping spring
6. Outer half　　　　 13. Retaining pin
7. Upper bleeder nipple 14. Inner half

Girling front caliper—all except 700 Series

700 Series

1. Loosen the lugs one or two turns, raise the vehicle and place on jackstands.
2. Remove the wheels.
3. Remove the bolt in the lower guide pin and loosen the upper bolt a few turns. Hold the guide pin with a 17mm wrench.
4. Lift up the caliper and remove the brake pads.

WARNING: : *Do not depress the brake pedal when the caliper is removed.*

5. Carefully clean out the pad cavity. Replace any damaged parts. If any dirt has contaminated the cylinders, the caliper must be removed for overhaul. Inspect the brake disc as described under Brake Discs Inspection and Replacement.

6. Carefully depress the pistons in their cylinders with pliers. Be careful not to damage the dust covers.

NOTE: *Remove some brake fluid when depressing pistons or brake fluid reservoir may overflow.*

7. Check the condition of the boots on the guide pins and replace them if they are cracked or broken. Check the guide pins; clean them with solvent (never with sandpaper or a wire

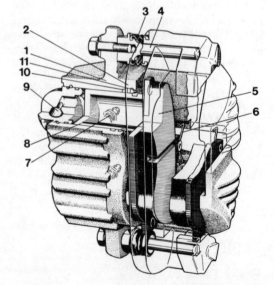

1. Caliper　　　　　 7. Bleeder screw
2. Holder　　　　　 8. Piston
3. Rubber bellows　 9. Brake fluid inlet
4. Guide pin　　　 10. Sealing ring
5. Brake lining　　 11. Dust cover
6. Spring

Girling front caliper, 700 Series

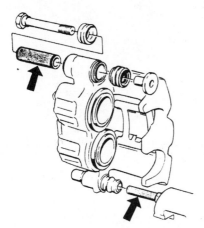

Arrows show slide points to be lubricated on 700 Series front calipers

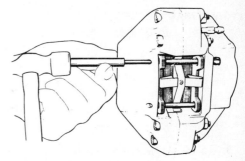

Removing guide pin—ATE brakes

brush) and coat them with a silicone high-temperature grease.

8. Install the new brake pads and reposition the caliper. Always use a new bolt and made sure that the springs on the brake pads are correctly positioned. Tighten the bolt in the lower guide pin to 25 ft. lbs.

9. Depress the brake pedal several times and make sure that the movement feels normal. The first brake pedal application may result in a very "long" pedal due to the pistons being retracted. Always make several brake applications before starting the vehicle. Bleeding is not usually necessary after pad replacement.

10. Install the wheel. Remove the jackstands and lower the vehicle. Tighten the lug nuts to 60 ft. lbs. and install the hub cap.

NOTE: *Braking should be moderate for the first 5 miles or so until the new pads seat correctly. The new pads will bed best if put through several moderate heating and cooling cycles. Avoid hard braking until the brakes have experienced several long, slow stops with time to cool in between. Taking the time to properly bed the brakes will yield quieter operation, more efficient stopping and contribute to extended brake life.*

ATE Brakes

1. Remove the hub caps and loosen the lug nuts a few turns.

2. Raise the vehicle and place jack stands beneath the rear axle and the front jack attachments.

3. Using a $^9/_{64}$ in. (3.5mm) drift, tap out the upper guide pin for the pads, remove and discard the tensioning spring. Tap out the lower pin. Pull out the pads and inspect them. Discard them if they are worn down to a lining thickness of ⅛ in. (3mm) or less. If they are reusable, mark them for ease of assembly.

4. Carefully clean out the pad cavities. Replace any damaged dust covers. If any dirt has contaminated the cylinders, the caliper must be removed for overhaul. Inspect the brake disc as described under Brake Disc Inspection and Replacement.

5. Carefully depress the pistons in their cylinders so that the new pads will fit. This may be done with a large pair of pliers or a C-clamp, but extra care must be exercised not to damage the rubber piston seals, the pistons, or the new pads themselves. A piston depressing tool (Volvo 2809) is available from the dealer that accomplishes the job without danger to the caliper components.

Remember that when the pistons are depressed in their bores, brake fluid is displaced, causing the level in the master cylinder to rise, and perhaps, overflow.

6. Install the new pads. Using only a hammer, tap one of the guide pins into position. Place a new tensioning spring into position, and while pushing it in against the pads tap the other guide pin into position. Make sure that the pads can move.

7. Depress the brake pedal several times and make sure that the movement feels normal. The first brake pedal application may result in a very "long" pedal due to the pistons being retracted. Always make several brake applications before starting the vehicle. Bleeding is not usually necessary after pad replacement.

8. Install the wheel. Remove the jackstands and lower the vehicle. Tighten the lug nuts to 80–90 ft. lbs. and install the hub cap.

NOTE: *Braking should be moderate for the first 5 miles or so until the new pads seat correctly. The new pads will bed best if put through several moderate heating and cooling cycles. Avoid hard braking until the brakes have experienced several long, slow stops with time to cool in between. Taking the time to properly bed the brakes will yield quieter operation, more efficient stopping and contribute to extended brake life.*

Front Brake Caliper

REMOVAL AND INSTALLATION

1. Loosen the lug nuts a few turns. Block the reservoir cap vent hole to reduce leakage of brake fluid when the lines are disconnected. Firmly apply the parking brake.

2. Raise the front end and place jackstands beneath the front jack attachments. Remove the wheel.

3. On 140 series and 164 models, remove the brake hose retaining clip from the stabilizer bar and disconnect the lower hose and brake line from their connection underneath the car. Disconnect the upper hose from the caliper. Plug all brake connections to prevent leakage.

4. On 1800, 200 and 700 Series, label and disconnect the brake lines at the caliper and plug them.

5. Remove the two caliper attaching bolts and lift the unit off the retainer.

6. To install, first check the mating surfaces of the caliper and its retainer to make sure that they are clean and not damaged. Always use new retaining bolts and lightly coat the threads with a locking compound.

Position the caliper to its retainer over the disc and install the two attaching bolts. For all vehicles except 700 Series, tighten the bolts to 65–70 ft. lbs. The mounting bolts on 700 Series cars should be tightened only to 25 ft. lbs.

Install the brake pads (if not already done), making sure that the caliper is parallel to the disc and that the disc can rotate freely in the brake pads.

7. On 140 series and 164 models, connect the lower brake hose and the brake line to their inboard connection and install the brake hose retaining clip to the stabilizer bar. Connect the upper brake hose to the caliper.

8. On 1800, 240, 260 and 700 Series, connect both brake lines to the caliper.

9. Unplug the reservoir cap vent hole. Install the wheel and lower the car to the ground. Tighten the lug nuts to 80–90 ft. lbs.

10. Bleed the brake system as outlined under Bleeding Hydraulic System.

OVERHAUL

NOTE: *The following procedure applies to front and rear calipers of both Girling and ATE design.*

1. Remove the brake caliper and pads from the car as outlined previously.

2. Remove the retaining rings and the rubber dust covers. Place a wooden block (1) between the pistons. Using compressed air applied through the brake line port, force the pistons toward the wooden block. Remove the

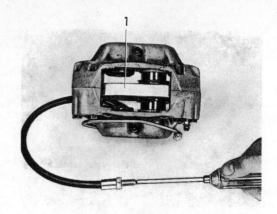

1. Wooden disc

Removing the pistons from the front caliper with wooden block and compressed air

pistons from their bores, taking care not to burr or scratch them.

NOTE: *Compressed air is the only reliable way to force out the pistons. Do not attempt to lever or pry out the pistons. The metal will become gouged and function will be impaired.*

3. Remove the sealing rings with a blunt plastic tool. Be careful not to damage the edges of the grooves. Screw out the bleeder nipple(s), and on front calipers, remove the external connecting line if still attached.

WARNING: *Do not attempt to separate the caliper halves. Assembling the halves requires special pressure testing equipment. Overhaul can be completed without splitting the caliper.*

4. Clean all reusable metal parts in clean brake fluid or methylated alcohol. Dry all parts

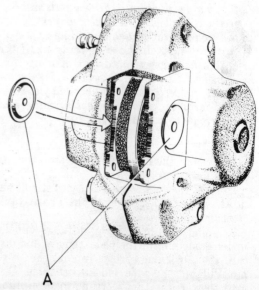

Girling calipers (rear) fitted with round damper washers

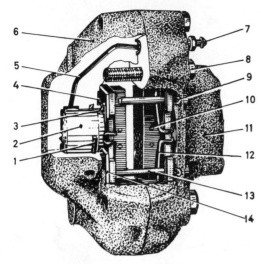

1. Sealing ring
2. Piston
3. Rubber dust cover
4. Retaining ring
5. Channel
6. Outer half
7. Bleeder nipple

8. Bolt
9. Retaining clip
10. Brake pad
11. Inner half
12. Damping spring
13. Retaining pin
14. Washer

Girling Rear Caliper

5. Coat the mating surfaces of the pistons and cylinder with fresh brake fluid.

6. Install new sealing rings in the cylinders.

7. On Girling brakes and ATE front brakes, press the pistons into their bores with the large end facing inward. Make sure that the pistons are installed straight and are not scratched in the process.

8. On ATE rear brakes, make sure that the pistons are in the proper positions to prevent brake squeal. The piston notches should incline 20° in relation to the lower guide area on the caliper.

Check the location of the piston with a template such as Volvo tool 2919. When the template is placed against the one recess, the distance (A) to the other recess may be no greater then 0.039 in. (1mm). If the location of the piston needs adjusting, use Volvo tool 2918 or similar and press it against the piston. Force out the shoes by screwing in the handle. Turn the piston in the required direction, release the tool and remeasure with the template. Repeat this operation for the other piston.

9. Place the new rubber dust covers on the

with compressed air or allow to air dry. Make sure that all of the passages are clear. All alcohol must be removed from the parts.

If any of the cylinders are scored or scratched, the entire housing must be replaced. Minor scratching may be removed from the pistons by fine polishing. Replace any piston that is damaged or worn.

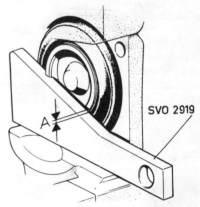

Checking location of rear caliper pistons—Ate brakes

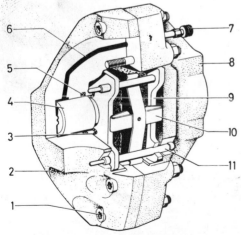

1. Bolt
2. Outer half
3. Rubber dust cover
4. Piston
5. Sealing ring
6. Channel

7. Bleeder nipple
8. Inner half
9. Brake pad
10. Damping spring
11. Guide pin

ATE rear caliper

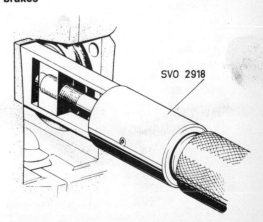

Adjusting location of rear caliper pistons—ATE brakes

pistons and housing. Install the new retaining rings.

10. Screw in the bleeder nipples(s).

11. Install the assembled caliper, then install the brake pads. Connect the brake line(s).

12. Add brake fluid to the reservoir to replace that lost during removal. Bleed the brake system.

Brake Disc (Rotor)

REMOVAL AND INSTALLATION

All Vehicles except 700 Series

1. Loosen the lug nuts a few turns. Elevate the car and safely support on jackstands.

2. Remove the wheel.

3. Remove the brake pads and remove the brake caliper. Do not disconnect the brake hose running to the caliper; use a piece of stiff wire and hang the caliper out of the way.

4. Loosen and remove the small retaining screws on the face of the disc. They will be difficult to loosen; don't strip the heads.

5. Remove the brake disc. It may be necessary to tap on the disc with a rubber or rawhide mallet to loosen it from its place. Don't use a metal hammer; you can crack the disc.

6. When reassembling, make sure the disc sits squarely on the mount and install the retaining screws.

7. Install the brake caliper and pads. Check that the disc can turn freely and that the caliper is properly seated. Since the brake line was not disconnected, it should not be necessary to bleed the brakes.

8. Reinstall the wheel and lower the car to the ground. Final tighten the lugs to 80–90 ft. lbs.

700 Series

1. Loosen the lug nuts a few turns. Elevate the car and safely support on jackstands.

2. Remove the wheel.

3. Remove the brake pads and remove the brake caliper. Do not disconnect the brake hose running to the caliper; use a piece of stiff wire and hang the caliper out of the way.

4. Use a 10mm Allen wrench to disconnect the caliper bracket.

5. Remove the center grease cap, the cotter pin and the castle nut.

6. Remove the outer wheel bearing and place in a clean, protected location.

7. Remove the brake disc and the inner wheel bearing. It may be necessary to use a bearing puller (Volvo 2722 or similar) if the inner bearing is difficult to remove. Place the bearing in a clean, protected location. Remove the inner bearing seal if it remains in the hub.

NOTE: *Cars with ABS have the pulse wheel*

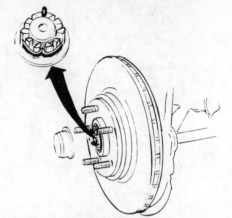

Always use a new cotter pin when reinstalling the disc. Bend the ends as shown

mounted within the disc. This toothed wheel must be removed and transferred to a new rotor if one is being installed. Use a universal gear puller and carefully lift off the pulse wheel. Use a bearing installation tool and a press to install the pulse wheel on the new disc.

8. When reassembling, the wheel bearings must be cleaned and repacked. The reader is referred to the Front Wheel Bearings--700 Series section of Chapter 8.

9. Install the inner bearing in the hub. Using a seal installation tool, install a new grease seal. Make sure the face of the seal is even with the hub.

10. Install the brake disc, the outer bearing and the castle nut. Rotate the disc while tightening the nut to 41 ft. lbs. Loosen the nut ½ turn.

11. Tighten the nut to 13 in. lbs. (finger tight) and install a new cotter pin. If the cotter pin will not go throught the nut into the hole, tighten the nut slightly.

12. Install the brake caliper. Use new attaching bolts and tighten them to 72 ft. lbs. Install the brake pads.

13. Install the wheel and lower the vehicle to the ground. Final tighten the wheel lugs to 60 ft. lbs.

INSPECTION

Front and Rear Discs

The brake disc may be inspected without removal, however viewing the back (inner) face of the disc is difficult. Ideally, the caliper should be removed allowing full access to both faces of the disc. Run-out mesurements must be taken with the disc mounted on the car and the wheel bearings properly adjusted.

The friction surface on both sides of the disc should be examined for surface deviations such

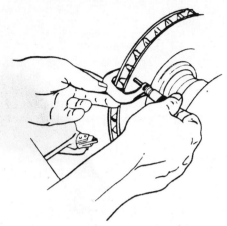

Use a micrometer to measure brake disc thickness

as scoring or corrosion. Minor radial scratches and small rust spots may be removed by resurfacing or fine polishing the disc. The lateral run-out of the disc must not exceed 0.004 in. (0.1mm) for the front, and 0.060 in. (0.15mm) for the rear, measured at the outer edge of the disc. Do not mistake a faulty wheel bearing adjustment, or an improperly mounted disc for lateral runout.

Actual disc thickness, which varies from model to model (see specifications), should not vary more than 0.0012 in. (0.03mm) when taken at several points on the same disc. If the disc is worn at any point to less than the minimum permissible thickness (see specifications), it must be replaced. A brake disc which is too thin cannot handle the heat generated by braking. If the disc cracks under braking, the wheel can lock instantly, causing loss of control and a possible collision.

After the disc has been resurfaced, measure the thickness to insure it is still above the minimum specification. A resurfaced disc should be washed in solvent inside and out to remove any metal filings which could get caught in the wheel bearings. Dry the disc thoroughly and re-pack the wheel bearings and inner hub. A new set of brake pads is highly recommended when installing a new or reconditioned disc.

REAR DISC BRAKES

Brake Pads

INSPECTION

The rear brake pads may be inspected without removal. With the rear end elevated and supported and the front wheels blocked, remove the wheel(s). View the pads--inner and outer--through the cut-out in the center of the caliper. Remember to look at the thickness of the pad friction material (the part that actually presses on the disc) rather than the thickness of the backing plate which does not change with wear.

Remember that you are looking at the profile of the pad, not the whole thing. Brake pads can wear on a taper which may not be visible through the window. It is also not possible to check the contact surface for cracking or scoring from this position. This quick check can be helpful only as a reference; detailed inspection requires pad removal.

REMOVAL AND INSTALLATION

CAUTION: *Brake pads and shoes contain asbestos, which has been determined to a cancer causing agent. Never clean the brake surfaces with compressed air! Avoid inhaling and dust from brake surfaces! When cleaning brakes, use commercially available brake cleaning fluids.*

The rear brake pads for all models are removed following the same procedures as the front pads. Identify the type of caliper--ATE or Girling--and refer to the instructions for front brake pad removal earlier in this chapter.

In 1988, with the introduction of the Multi-Link rear suspension, Volvo redesigned the rear caliper and disc on certain 700 Series cars. The rear caliper is virtually identical to the fronts but before it can be swung up (on its upper pivot) it may be necessary to push the piston back. Do this by inserting a screwdriver into the recess between the outer pad and the caliper and gently moving the caliper. Remember that doing this may cause the brake fluid reservoir to overflow.

Reinstall the pads following the directions given earlier under Front Disc Brakes--Removal and Installation. Remember that the rear brakes must also be bedded in the first few miles of driving.

Brake Caliper
REMOVAL AND INSTALLATION
All Models

1. Loosen the lug nuts a few turns. Block the reservoir cap vent to reduce fluid loss.
2. Place blocks in front of the front wheels. Raise the rear of the car and place jackstands beneath the rear axle. Release the parking brake and remove the wheel(s).
3. Some vehicles have a protective cover over the caliper. It is easily removed by loosening its mounting bolt. Disconnect the brake line at the joint near the shock absorber or inner fender well (not at the caliper). Plug the line.
4. Remove the brake pads. Remove the two

caliper attaching bolts and lift the caliper off the retainer. The brake hose may now be removed from the caliper.

5. To install, first check the mating surfaces of the caliper and its retainer to make sure that they are clean and not damaged. Coat the threads of the attaching bolts with locking compound.

Attach the brake hose to the caliper and position the caliper to its retainer. Install two new attaching bolts. Tighten the bolts to 42 ft. lbs. Make sure that the caliper is parallel to the disc, and that the disc can rotate freely in the brake pads. If the protective cover was removed, replace it.

6. Connect the brake hose to the system. Unplug the reservoir cap hole.

7. Install the wheel. Remove the jackstands and lower the car. Tighten the lug nuts to 80–90 ft. lbs. (700 Series: 63 ft. lbs.).

8. Bleed the rear brake caliper as outlined under Bleeding Hydraulic System.

NOTE: *Once the calipers have been removed, they may be overhauled following the procedures listed earlier in this chapter.*

Brake Disc
REMOVAL AND INSTALLATION

The rear discs are removed in the same manner as the front discs. After removing the wheel, brake pads and caliper, hang the caliper out of the way. The disc will have the small retaining screws on the face; loosen them and the disc will come free.

Late model 700 Series with Multi-Link rear suspension have a small stud threaded into the disc. While helping to locate the wheel, this stud also retains the disc to the hub. Loosen it and the disc comes free. Note that it is NOT necessary to loosen the large center hub nut to remove the disc. Please don't.

Although the outer part of the rear disc serves as the contact surface for the hydraulic (foot) brakes, the inner surface is the contact surface for the cable operated emergency/parking brake. If you plan to have the discs refaced, also check the condition of the inner face. It generally stays in good shape, but can become scored from dust and grit. The maximum allowable diameter for this drum is 6.32 in. (160.5mm). Diameters in excess of this measurement require discarding the disc.

PARKING/EMERGENCY BRAKE

The cable operated emergency brake is a complete separate brake system acting only on the rear wheels. When the lever in the car is pulled up, cables running to the rear of the car actuate 2 sets of brake shoes. These shoes expand against the machined surface inside the rear brake disc. Thus, the car still has (limited) stopping ability even if the entire hydraulic brake system fails.

Because of the many advances in design and engineering, and the government regulations requiring dual hydraulic brake systems, the odds of a total hydraulic failure are probably longer than your chances of hitting the lottery in three states on your birthday. The system must, however, remain in proper repair and adjustment so that it will hold the car when parked and be available for emergency use if needed.

Cables
ADJUSTMENT
1800, 140 and 160 Series

The parking brake should be fully engaged when the lever is pulled up to the third or fourth notch. If it is not, adjust as follows:

1. Apply the parking brake. Remove the rear hub caps and loosen the lug nuts a few turns.

2. Place blocks in front of the front wheels. Jack up the rear end and place jackstands beneath the rear axle. Remove the wheel. Release the parking brake.

3. Make sure that the brake pads are not stuck on the discs. Disconnect the parking brake cable from the actuating lever. This keeps the pre-tension off the brakes while you adjust them.

4. Rotate the disc until the adjusting screw hole aligns with the serrations (ridges) on the adjusting wheel inside the disc. Insert a screwdriver, and adjust the shoes by moving the handle of the screwdriver upward. When the disc cannot be rotated easily, stop adjusting the shoes.

Turn the adjusting screw back 4 or 5 serrations. Turn the disc in its normal direction of rotation and make sure that the shoes do not drag. A slight brushing is permissible, but if there is heavy drag, back off the adjusting screw 2 or 3 serrations more. Connect the cable to the lever.

5. Repeat the adjusting procedure for the other wheel.

6. Apply the parking brake lever and make sure that the parking brake is fully engaged with the lever at the third or fourth notch. If the brakes are properly adjusted but don't apply fully, adjust the cable:

   a. Locate the cable yoke assembly under the car. It is the device that pulls simultaneously on both the left and right brake cables.

   b. Loosen the two locknuts on the thread-

1. Inside support attachment
2. Rubber cover
3. Lever
4. Shaft
5. Pull rod
6. Block
7. Cable
8. Rubber cover
9. Front attachment
10. Cable sleeve

11. Attachment
12. Brake drum
13. Brake shoe (secondary shoe)
14. Return spring
15. Adjusting device
16. Lever
17. Movable rod
18. Anchor bolt
19. Return spring
20. Rear attachment

21. Rubber cable guide
22. Pawl
23. Ratchet segment
24. Rivet
25. Outside support attachment
26. Warning valve switch
27. Push rod
28. Parking brake lever
29. Spring
30. Push button

Parking brake assembly—1970–74 models

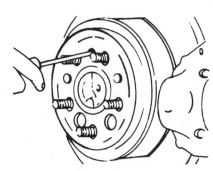

Adjusting the parking brake through the access hole in the rear hub

ed shaft. The shaft will probably be dirty and rusted. Be prepared to clean the threads.

c. Tighten the adjusting nut (the one that bears on the spring) a few turns and recheck the lever in the car. Continue adjusting until the brakes are fully applied at the third or fourth notch.

d. Tighten both locknuts. While you're under there, clean the pulley wheel and apply a light coat of oil to its axle.

NOTE: *Do not attempt to adjust the emergency brake only by tightening the cable. The brake shoes must be properly adjusted before the cable is tightened.*

7. Install the wheels. Remove the jackstands and lower the car. Tighten the lug nuts to 80–90 ft. lbs.

200 Series.

1. Apply the parking brake. Remove the rear hub caps and loosen the lug nuts a few turns.

2. Place blocks in front of the front wheels. Jack up the rear end and place jackstands beneath the rear axle. Remove the wheel. Release the parking brake.

3. Make sure that the brake pads are not stuck on the discs.

4. Rotate the disc until the adjusting screw hole aligns with the serrations (ridges) on the adjusting wheel inside the disc. Insert a screwdriver and adjust the shoes by moving the handle of the screwdriver upward. When the disc cannot be rotated easily, stop adjusting the shoes.

Turn the adjusting screw back 4 or 5 serrations. Turn the disc in its normal direction of rotation and make sure that the shoes do not drag. A slight brushing is permissible, but if there is heavy drag, back off the adjusting screw 2 or 3 serrations more.

5. Repeat the adjusting procedure for the other wheel.

6. Apply the parking brake lever and make sure that the parking brake is fully engaged with the lever at the second and eighth notch. If the brakes are properly adjusted but don't apply fully, adjust the cable:

a. Remove the rear ashtray at the rear of the console to gain access to the cable adjuster.

b. Use a 17mm socket with an extension to turn the nut on the adjuster. Tighten the adjuster a few turns and recheck the adjuster in the car. Continue adjusting until the brakes are firmly applied between the second and eighth notch.

c. Reinstall the rear ashtray.

NOTE: *Do not attempt to adjust the emergency brake only by tightening the cable. The brake shoes must be properly adjusted before the cable is tightened.*

7. Install the wheels. Remove the jackstands and lower the car. Tighten the lug nuts to 80–90 ft. lbs.

700 Series

1. Remove the ash tray and holder from the rear of the handbrake cover.

2. Use a screwdriver and hammer to tap the spring sleeve clear of the adjusting screw.

3. Hold the end of the threaded shaft with a pair of pliers; use an open end wrench to adjust the nut a few turns. Check the brake lever and

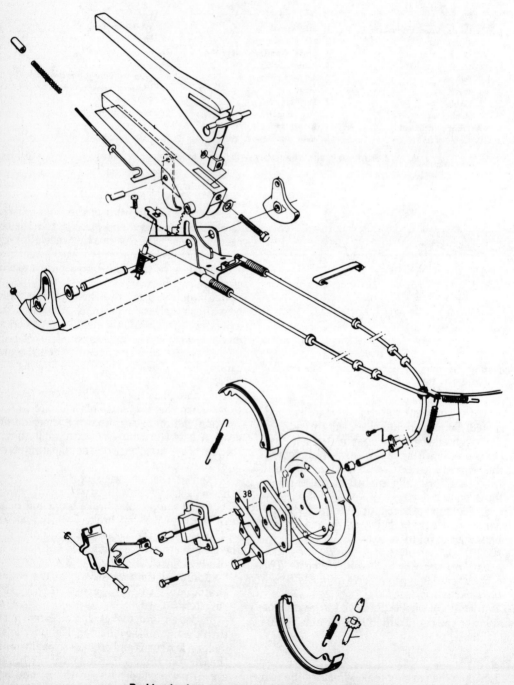

Parking brake assembly—1975 and later models

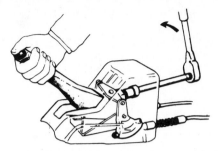

Adjust the cable so that the brakes are fully applied between the second and eighth notches

continue to adjust until brake application is achieved between the second and fifth notches.

NOTE: *The system is designed so that the first two notches DO NOT activate the brakes. Don't overtighten the cable.*

4. Check that the spring sleeve is in its original position and reinstall the ashtray and holder.

REMOVAL AND INSTALLATION

1800, 140 and 160 Series

1. Apply the parking brake and loosen the rear wheel lugs a few turns.

2. Safely elevate and support the rear of the vehicle and block the front wheels. Remove the rear wheels.

3. Under the center of the car, loosen the locknuts on the adjusting yoke and loosen the brake adjustment. This relieves some of the tension from the cables.

4. Remove the bolt which is the axle for the pivot (pulley) wheel.

CAUTION: *Although the tension has been lessened, the yoke and cables may spring free suddenly!*

5. Working your way from the front to the rear of each side, remove the rubber boot and retaining nut at the frontmost cable mount and remove the carrier bracket farther back on the frame member.

6. At each rear wheel, compress the spring to relive tension on the arm (Volvo tool 2742 or similar) and remove the lock pin holding the cable to the brake arm. Some cars may have a locking device over the pin; pry it up to gain access.

7. Remove the return spring with the washers. Loosen the retaining nut holding the cable casing to the mount. When both sides are free, remove the cable to the front of the car.

8. Before installing the new cable, properly adjust the shoes at the rear wheels as outlined previously. Install the carriers onto the new cable.

9. Attach the cable to the rear mount and tighten the retaining nut. Do this on each side.

10. Install the spring and washers. Compress the spring and install the lock pin which holds the cable to the brake arm. The lock pin should be lightly oiled before installation.

11. Working towards the front of the car, install the carriers onto the frame member and install the front mount and rubber boot. The boots must be properly seated to keep dirt and water out of the cable casing.

12. Clean and lubricate the pulley wheel and its center pin. Catch the cable on the wheel and install the wheel into the adjusting yoke. Install the center bolt and nut.

13. Adjust the yoke as described previously in this section.

14. Refit the wheels, lower the car to the ground and final tighten the lugs to 80–90 ft. lbs.

200 Series

1. Remove the console covering the parking brake lever assembly. Loosen the adjusting screw to relieve tension on the cables.

NOTE: *The brake cables cross under the car. The cable to the left rear wheel is on the right side of the lever and vice-versa. Know which cable you're changing before proceeding.*

2. Remove the retaining nut for the cable to be changed; it may be necessary to use a small screwdriver to keep the cable from turning.

3. Lift up the front of the rear seat cushion. Move the carpet aside and remove the clamps holding the cable to the floor. Pop the rubber grommet out of the floor pan.

4. Loosen the lugs a few turns; safely elevate and support the rear of the car. Remove the rear wheels.

5. If the vehicle has guard plates over the rear calipers, remove them.

6. Remove the clamp holding the brake line to the rear axle.

7. Remove the caliper mounting bolts and remove the caliper; use stiff wire to hang the caliper out of the way.

WARNING: *Be careful! The brake line is still attached to the caliper--don't bend it!*

8. Remove the brake disc. The hub is be-

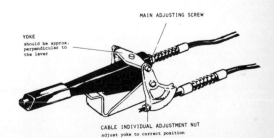

Brake lever assembly, double cable system

tween you and the brake shoes, but you can work around it. Don't attempt to remove the hub.

9. Use a pair of brake spring pliers and remove the retaining spring. Remove the brake shoes; take note of the placement of the adjuster.

10. Press out the lock pin that holds the cable to the lever.

11. Under the car, just ahead of the spring, re-

Brake Specifications

All measurements given are (in.) unless noted

Year	Model	Lug Nut Torque (ft. lbs.)	Master Cylinder Bore	Brake Disc Minimum Thickness	Brake Disc Maximum Run-Out	Brake Disc Diameter Front Disc	Brake Disc Diameter Rear Disc	Minimum Lining Thickness Front	Minimum Lining Thickness Rear
1970–72	140 Series	70–100	0.882	0.457 ① 0.331 ②	0.004 ① 0.006 ②	10.7	11.63	0.125	0.125
	164	70–100	0.950	0.457 ① 0.331 ②	0.004 ① 0.006 ②	10.7	11.63	0.125	0.125
	1800 E/ES	70–100	0.882	0.520 ① 0.330 ②	0.004 ① 0.006 ②	10.6	11.63	0.125	0.125
1973	140 Series	70–100	0.882 ③	0.457 ① 0.331 ②	0.004 ① 0.006 ②	10.7	11.63	0.125	0.125
	164	70–100	0.950 ④	0.900 ① 0.331 ②	0.004 ① 0.006 ②	10.7	11.63	0.125	0.125
	1800 ES	70–100	0.882	0.520 ① 0.331 ②	0.004 ① 0.006 ②	10.6	11.63	0.125	0.125
1974	140 Series	70–100	0.875	0.457 ① 0.331 ②	0.004 ① 0.006 ②	10.7	11.63	0.125	0.125
	164	70–100	0.875	0.900 ① 0.331 ②	0.004 ① 0.006 ②	10.7	11.6	0.125	0.125
1975	240 Series	70–100	0.877	0.557 ① 0.331 ②	0.004 ① 0.006 ②	10.35	11.06	0.125	0.125
	164	70–100	0.875	0.900 ① 0.331 ②	0.004 ① 0.006 ②	10.7	11.63	0.125	0.125
1976–83	240 Series, DL, GL, GT, Turbo	88	0.878	0.557 ① 0.331 ②	0.004 ① 0.006 ②	10.35	11.06	0.125	0.125
	260 Series, GLE, Coupe, Diesel	88	0.878	0.900 ① 0.331 ②	0.004 ① 0.006 ②	10.35	11.06	0.125	0.125
	760 GLE	63	0.878	0.551 ① 0.378 ②	0.003 ① 0.004 ②	11.02	11.06	0.118	0.078
84–89	240 Series	63	0.88	0.500 ⑤ 0.803 ⑥ 0.330 ②	0.004 ① 0.004 ① 0.004 ②	10.33	11.06	0.120	0.012
84–89 84–87	740 and 760	63	0.878 ⑦ 0.938 ⑧	0.433 ⑤ 0.790 ⑥ 0.330 ②	0.003 ① 0.004 ②	11.03 ⑤ 11.31 ⑥	11.06	0.118	0.078
88–89	760 & 780	63	0.878 ⑦ 0.938 ⑧	0.433 ⑤ 0.790 ⑥ 0.315 ②	0.003 ① 0.080 ②	11.03 ⑤ 11.31 ⑥	11.06	0.118	0.078

① Front
② Rear
③ Master cylinder bore is 0.875 starting from chassis nos; 377809 on 142, 403575 on 144, and 194933 on 145
④ Master cylinder bore is 0.875 starting from chassis no. 79021
⑤ Front—solid disc
⑥ Front—vented disc
⑦ Early type
⑧ Late type

move the retaining bolt holding the cable mount to the car. Withdraw the cable and plastic collar. Pull out the conplete cable from the center support and the floor pan.

12. Install the new cable by inserting the plastic collar through bracket. Fit the rubber seal at the brake backing plate.

13. Route the cable through the center support and through the hole in the floor panel.

NOTE: *Remember that the cables cross each other. The left side cable should go through the hole on the right of the driveshaft and vice versa. Additionally, the cable from the left rear wheel should cross UNDER the right side cable at the center support.*

14. Install the cable into the plastic collar and attach the retaining nut.

15. Lubricate the lock pin and the moving parts of the mechanism at each wheel. Attach the cable and install the lock pin. If the pin has a locking device, bend it back into position.

16. Install the brake shoes with the lower attaching spring. Once in place, install the adjuster and the upper attaching spring.

17. Install the brake disc. Make sure it turns freely without dragging on the brake shoes. Adjust the shoes if needed.

18. Carefully position and secure the brake caliper. Attach the clamp which holds the brake line to the rear axle.

19. Refit the caliper guard if so equipped.

20. Adjust the shoes as outlined under, Brake Cables--Adjustment.

21. Install the rubber grommet in the floor pan. Make sure it is properly seated.

22. Place the end of the cable into the lever assembly. Install the clamp holding the cable to the floor and replace the carpet and rear seat cushion.

23. At the lever assembly, screw in the nut until the end of the cable projects at least ¼ in. (6mm) beyond the nut. Adjust the cable tension until the crosspiece on the top of the lever is square to the lever (when applied).

24. Adjust the main adjusting screw to get full application of the brakes between two and eight notches on the lever.

25. Reinstall the console assembly over the parking brake mechanism. Reinstall the wheel(s) and lower the vehicle.

700 Series

SHORT CABLE, RIGHT SIDE

1. Jack up the rear of the car and safely support it with jackstands.

2. Remove the right rear wheel. Remove the right brake caliper and hang it from the coil spring with a wire. Remove the brake disc. Unhook the rear return spring and remove the brake shoes.

3. Push out the pin holding the cable to the brake lever. Remove the rubber boot from the backing plate and remove the boot from the cable.

4. Remove the spring clip, pin and cable from the back of the differential housing. Remove the cable guide on the differential by removing the top bolt from the housing cover. Remove the cable.

5. Install the boot on the new cable. Check the boots for wear or damage and replace if necessary. Install the cable and position it through the hole in the backing plate. Make sure the boot sits correctly on the backing plate.

6. Smear the contact surfaces of the brake levers with a thin layer of heat-resistance graphite grease. Connect the cable to the lever and install the pin.

NOTE: *The arrow stamped on the lever should face upwards and point outwards.*

7. Push the cable through and place the lever in position behind the rear axle flange.

8. Install the cable guide on the axle. Connect the cable to the equalizer using the pin and spring clip.

9. Install the brake shoes and rear return spring. Install the brake disc and caliper. Use new bolts, and torque to 43 ft. lbs. Make sure the disc rotates freely. Adjust the parking brake. Install the wheel and lower the car.

LONG CABLE, LEFT SIDE

1. Remove the center console.

2. Loosen the parking brake adjusting screw. Remove the cable lock ring and remove the cable. Pull out the cable from the spring sleeve.

3. Jack up the rear end of the car and safely support it on jackstands. Remove the left rear wheel.

4. Remove the left rear brake caliper and hang it from the coil spring with a piece of wire. Remove the brake disc and rear return spring. Remove the brake shoes.

5. Push out the pin holding the cable to the lever. Remove the rubber boot from the backing plate, and remove the boot from the cable.

6. Pull out the cable from the backing plate and the equalizer on top of the rear axle.

7. Remove the cable clamp on the sub-frame (above the driveshaft) and the cable.

8. Install the new cable through the grommet in the floor; check that the grommet sits correctly. Clamp the cable to the sub-frame.

9. Smear the contact surfaces of the brake levers with a thin layer of heat-resistance graphite grease. Connect the cable to the lever and install the pin.

NOTE: *The arrow stamped on the lever should face upwards and point outwards.*

10. Push the cable through and place the lever in position behind the rear axle flange.

11. Install the cable guide on the axle. Connect the cable to the equalizer using the pin and spring clip.

12. Install the brake shoes and rear return spring. Install the brake disc and caliper. Use new bolts, and torque to 43 ft. lbs. Make sure the disc rotates freely. Adjust the parking brake. Install the wheel and lower the car.

Parking Brake Shoe
REPLACEMENT

1. Using the appropriate procedure under, Brake Cable--Adjustment, gain access to the adjuster and loosen it so that the tension is removed from the cable.

2. Elevate and safely support the rear end.

3. On 200 series, remove the brake line-to-axle clamp.

4. Remove the caliper and hang it out of the way. Be careful not to crimp hoses or lines.

5. Remove the disc. The hub is between you and the brake shoes but you can work around it. Don't attempt to remove the hub.

6. Using brake spring pliers, remove one retaining spring from the shoe assembly. (700 Series have only one spring.) Remove the shoes from the car, taking note of the location and placement of the adjuster.

7. Assemble the shoes with one spring and install onto the car. Install the other retaining spring, except 700 Series.

8. Install the brake disc. Check that the disc turns freely without binding on the shoes.

9. Reinstall the brake caliper. Always use new retaining bolts and tighten them to 42 ft. lbs.

10. On 200 Series, reinstall the brake line-to-axle clamp.

11. Adjust the brake shoes (except 700 Series) and then the brake cables as described in Brake Cables--Adjustment.

12. Reinstall the wheels and lower the car to the ground. Check the emergency brake for proper holding and adjust the cables as necessary.

EXTERIOR

Doors

REMOVAL AND INSTALLATION

CAUTION: *The door(s) are heavy! Provide proper support for the door when removing. Do not allow the door to sag while partially attached and do not subject the door to impact or twisting movements.*

140 and 160 Series
1800 Series

1. Remove the door panel (inner trim pad) following the instructions given in Door Panel Removal and Installation later in this chapter.

2. Remove/disconnect the door stop mechanism. On 1800 Series, simply drive or drill the pivot pin free at the pillar; the arm will then be free of the body. For 140 and 160 Series, unbolt the bracket from the pillar.

3. Open the door until the hinge bolts can be easily reached. Remember that the door stop is disconnected; don't open the door too far or you may damage paint or metalwork.

4. Remove the retaining bolts holding the

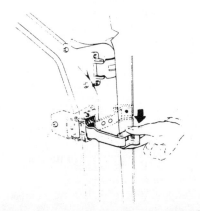

Removal of the door stop bracket on 100 and early 200 Series

hinge to the body. Have a helper hold the door and support it during removal. Once the door is free of the body, the hinges may be removed from the door if desired.

5. When reinstalling, place the door in position and seat the hinge bolts finger tight. When the bolts are tight enough to hold the door in place, but loose enough to allow adjustment, close the door and check the alignment of the door seams. All the seams (gaps) should be even in width; the leading edge gap should be the same width as the trailing edge gap, and the weather strip should be evenly compressed around the door.

The door is three-way adjustable on its hinges. The door may be moved fore-and-aft or up and down on its hinge mounts. If adjustment towards or away from the body is necessary, shims may be placed (or removed) between the hinge and the body.

6. After the door is positioned correctly, tighten the mounting bolts and recheck the door fit.

7. Reinstall the door stop mechanism and check its function.

8. Reinstall the door trim pad.

200 and 700 Series

1. Disconnect any wiring harnesses running into the door. This may be done either inside the door (remove the door liner) or under the dash inside the pillar. Make sure the wiring harness will not catch or bind as the door is removed from the car.

2. On the earlier 200 Series, remove the bolt holding the door stop bracket to the body. Later cars have the stop included in the lower hinge.

3. Have a helper support the door; loosen and remove the four bolts holding the hinge to the door.

4. When reinstalling, have your helper position the door and install the hinge bolts. If the hinges were not removed from the body, the

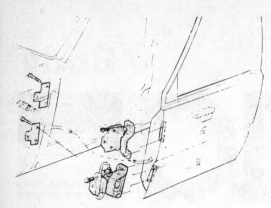

Hinge detail-700 Series

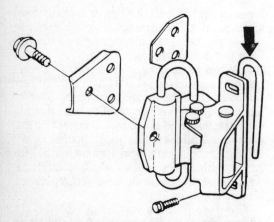

Lower hinge assembly on 700 and late 200 Series. Arrow shows placement of shim for lateral adjustment

door should be in alignment. If not, the hinge-to-body bolts must be loosened just enough to allow the door to be moved into postion. Tighten all the hinge bolts and check the final fit.

5. If the door stop bracket was removed, re-install it.

6. Connect the wiring harness and check the function of electrical components in the door.

DOOR ALIGNMENT/ADJUSTMENT

As explained above, the primary door adjustments are carried out at the hinge bolts at the forward end of each door. Further adjustment for closed position and for smoothness of latching may be made at the latch plate or striker. This piece is located at the rear edge of the door and is attached to the bodywork of the car; it is the piece the door engages when closed.

Although the striker or latchplate is different on various models, the procedure for adjusting is the same:

1. Loosen the large phillips screw(s) holding the striker. Know in advance that these bolts will be very tight--an impact screwdriver is a very handy tool for this job--make sure you use the correct size bit.

2. With the bolts just loose enough to allow the striker to move if necessary, hold the outer door handle in the released position and close the door. The striker will move into the correct location to match the doorlatch. Open the door and tighen the mounting bolts. The striker may be adjusted towards or away from the center of the car, thereby pulling the door tighter to the body if needed. The 140 and 160 Series require a 1.5° inward angle on the front strikers and a 2.5° inward angle on the rear stikers.

NOTE: *Do not attempt to correct height variations (sag) by adjusting the striker.*

3. After the striker bolts have been tightened, open and close the door several times. Observe the motion of the door as it engages the striker; it should continue its straight-in motion and not deflect up or down as it hits the striker.

Check the feel of the latch during opening and closing. It must be smooth and linear, without any trace of grinding or binding during engagement and release.

It may be necessary to repeat the striker adjustment procedure several times (and possibly adjust the hinges) before the correct door-to-body match is produced.

Hood

REMOVAL AND INSTALLATION

1800 Series

1. Raise the hood. Remove the outer part of the air cleaner. This will allow access to the right side hinge bolt. Unbolt the hood support and lower but do not latch the hood.

2. Using a pair of pliers, remove the lower clamps on the radiator grille. Lift the grille clear of the car by pulling it out at the lower edge first.

3. Loosen and remove the hood hinge bolts. Lift the hood clear of the car.

4. When reinstalling, line the hood up by viewing the seam between the hood and the bodywork--the gap should be even all around. With the hinge bolts finger tight, the hood may be moved on the hinges to align it. Vertical adjustment is adjusted by installing shims between the hood and the hinges.

5. Tighten the bolts and check the fit and latching--adjust as needed.

6. Reinstall the grille and its clamps.

7. Raise the hood and install the hood prop. Install the outer part of the air cleaner.

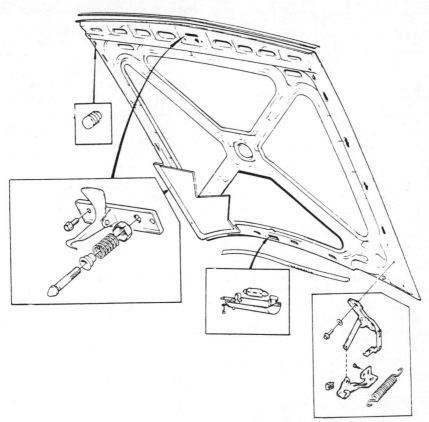

Hood components. 200 Series shown; 100 and 700 Series are similar

All Other Models

1. Raise the hood. Disconnect any electrical or fluid lines between the hood and the body.

2. Have a helper support the hood so it doesn't damage the body during removal. Remove the hinge-to-hood bolts on each side and lift the hood clear of the car.

NOTE: *Hoods are getting lighter; take great care not to bend or dimple the hood. Store it on pads and cover it to protect it while off the car.*

3. When reinstalling, position the hood and install the bolts just tight enough to hold it in position. Lower the hood and check the alignment--the gap should be even all around. With the hinge bolts finger tight, the hood may be moved on the hinges to align it. Vertical adjustment is adjusted by installing shims between the hood and the hinges.

4. Tighten the bolts and recheck the fit and latching--adjust as necessary.

5. Reconnect any electrical or fluid lines between the hood and body.

ADJUSTMENT

For all Volvo products, the hood is adjustable at the hinges as discussed above. Additionally, the hood latch is adjustable by loosening the two bolts holding the latch to the hood and moving it for-and-aft as necessary to get the correct match. Any side to side adjustment must be done at the hinges.

The closed height of the hood is adjustable by turning the hood stops--rubber bumpers mounted either on the bodywork (early cars) or on the hood itself. These rubber stops allow the hood to be brought into alignment with the height of the fenders on either side. It should also be noted that if one of these cushions is missing, the hood can make a rattle or banging noise which is often mistaken for suspension noise.

Trunk Lid

REMOVAL AND INSTALLATION

2-Door and 4-Door models

1. Open the trunk lid. Have a helper support the lid; remove the retaining clip for the gas shock (which holds the lid open) and disconnect it from the lid. On 1800 Series, the lid is held open by two torsion rods. They need not be disconnected to remove the trunk lid.

2. Disconnect any wiring to the trunk lid at

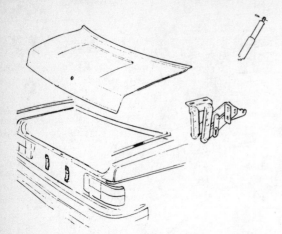

Trunk lid and hinge detail, 200 Series

the nearest connector. Make sure the wiring will not bind when the lid is removed.

3. Remove the bolts which hold the hinges to the trunk lid and lift the lid clear of the car. Use caution not to warp or dimple the lid. The hinges may then be unbolted from the body if desired, but this may require removing some cover panels for access to the bolts. On the 1800 Series, the hinges and torsion rods are removed as a unit.

4. When reinstalling, the lid is placed in position and the bolts tightend only snug. Check the lid-to-body match and adjust the trunk lid as necessary.

5. Reconnect the gas shock to the trunk lid and reconnect the wiring, if any.

Wagon (5-door) models except 1800 ES

CAUTION: *Because of the size and weight of the cargo door, this procedure REQUIRES two people during removal and installation.*

1. Disconnect the negative battery cable.

2. Remove the inner cover panel on the cargo door. Disconnect any electrical connectors within the door. On the 145 model, remove the left license plate lamp and its electrical cable. Tag or identify the connectors for ease of reassembly.

3. Pull the harness through the hole in the top of the door.

4. Have your helper support the door; disconnect the gas shock(s) from the door. On the 145, disconnect the mechanical support on the opposite side as well.

5. With the door well supported, remove the door-to-hinge bolts on each side at the top. On the 740, one of the bolts is beneath a rubber plug which must be removed. Carry the door away from the car and store on pads.

6. When reinstalling, install the bolts snug but not tight; check the alignment of the door in relation to the body and adjust the door as necessary. When the alignment is correct, tighten the hinge bolts.

Left-right alignment is critical on the cargo door. Take your time and work for an even fit.

7. Connect the gas shock(s) to the door.

8. Feed the wire harness through the hole at the top of the door and into position. Connect the wires to the proper points. On the 145 Series, reinstall the left license plate light.

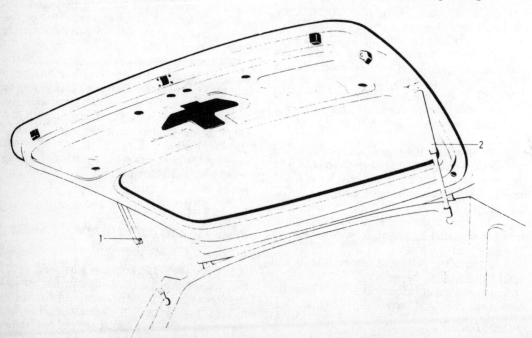

Tailgate on Model 145. (1) is the mechanical arm, (2) gas shock

1800 ES

The hatch of the 1800 ES is all glass, with the hinges and latch mounted on rubber bushings. After disconnecting the wire for the defroster and removing the gas shock, the glass is removed by simply unbolting the hinge nuts and lifting the glass clear.

Extreme care must be taken not to hit or scratch the glass during removal. When reinstalling, correct placement of the rubber seals must be observedto avoid shattering the glass. At no time should any steel component come into direct contact with the glass. The mounting bolts should be tightened just enough to hold with no attempt at overtightening.

ALIGNMENT

All Models

Both trunk lids and wagon doors are adjustable on their hinges due to slotted holes. The trunk lids are also adjustable by loosening the hinge-to-body bolts and repositioning the hinge vertically. The 1800 ES has only minimal adjustment in the glass mounts.

Wagon cargo doors have additional adjustors on the sides of the door. Loosen their screws a few turns and close the door. The adjustor should seek the correct position for smooth operation. Because of the curve of the body and roofline, the wagon door needs to be checked carefully for alignment to the body. Seams should be straight and even and panels should be flush with no obvious high or low points.

Final adjustments are made at the latch (on the lid) and the striker (on the body). Each can be loosened and moved on its mounts to control tightness and ease of operation. It is recommended to start by loosening the striker only; close the lid and let the striker seek its position.(This maddening little job can drive you off the deep end after a few cycles of loosen it, tighten it, open it, close it.) Continue adjusting until the latch has no bind in its operation, the key turns freely and the weatherstrip is evenly compressed around the door.

Bumpers

REMOVAL AND INSTALLATION

140, 160 and 1800 Series

Both the front and rear bumpers of these cars are composed of various sections bolted together. The bumpers are mounted to the car on four support brackets (1800 ES: six brackets). The retaining nuts and bolts are loosened and removed; the bumper may then be removed from the car as a unit and disassembled into component parts on the workbench.

The retaining bolts are reached from under the car (behind the bumper). It may be easier to elevate and support the car before beginning. The bumper bolts are sure to be rusted solid-- have a healthy supply of penetrating oil at hand. The steel bumpers are reasonably heavy-- don't drop one on yourself while lying under the car.

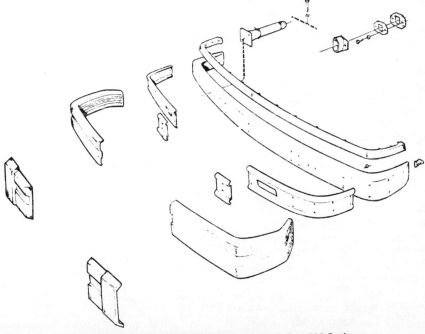

Front bumper components, USA and Canadian 200 Series

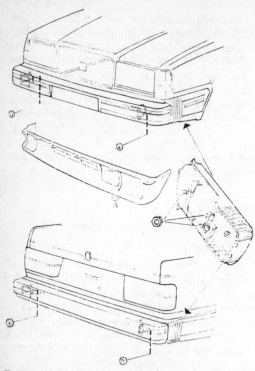

Front and rear bumpers, 700 Series

When reinstalling the bumper, make sure that it aligns properly with the bodywork. Since it runs the full width of the car, the slightest mounting error can make it look crooked.

200 and 700 Series

As government regulations tightened in the early and mid 1970s, bumpers were redesigned to include impact absorbsion. This is generally accomplished through the use of gas-filled shock absorbers which allow the bumper to move inward under light impact. The design of the bumpers changed to accomodate the shocks; bumpers are now steel or aluminum beams bolted to the shocks with a plastic cover on the outside. For both front and rear bumpers on cars built after model year 1974:

1. Loosen the sides of the bumper cover by either removing the nuts or releasing the plastic clip. The nuts will be found inside the trunk or on the inside of the front fender. On certain models, the front air dam (spoiler) must be removed before removing the front bumper.

2. Under the car, identify the bolts which hold the bumper assembly to the shock absorbers. Loosen them a few turns and wiggle the bumper outwards, checking that it will come free without damage.

3. Remove the bolts on one side. Either allow the bumper to rest on the ground or support it on a box until the other side is free.

4. Remove the bolts on the other side and remove the bumper. Take note of any spacers which may have been placed for alignment.

5. With the bumper removed, the shocks may be unbolted and replaced if needed.

CAUTION: *Gas filled shocks must not be discarded in the trash. Take them to your dealer or a reputable body shop so that they may be properly drilled and vented before disposal. Do not attempt to drill the shocks yourself--injury can result.*

6. When reinstalling, make sure the bumper lines up straight to the body work. Install the retaining bolts and tighten them.

7. Secure the side mounts of the bumper cover with the proper nuts or clips. Reinstall the air dam if it was removed.

Grille

REMOVAL AND INSTALLATION

1800 Series

1. Using a pair of pliers, loosen the lower clamps.

2. Lift out the grille by swinging the lower part out first.

3. When reinstalling, place the upper edge in position first and make sure the clips seat properly.

4. Install the lower clamps. Place the clamp above the hole and press it into place.

140 and 160 Series

The aluminum grille is removed simply by removing the retaining screws. Use care not to crush the metal or mar the polished finish on the grille.

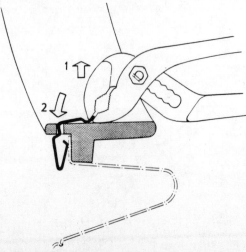

The correct way to remove the lower grille clips on 1800 Series

200 and 700 Series

The plastic grilles on these cars are retained by a variety of plastic clips and screws. With the hood raised, remove all the retaining hardware and lift the grille clear of the car. On later cars, be careful of any wires and/or tubing running between the grille and the radiator. Do not force the grille into position or it will crack; work carefully and make sure everything lines up before tightening the mounting hardware.

Standard Equipment Fog Lights
REMOVAL AND INSTALLLATION
160 Series

1. Inside the engine compartment, remove the screw and the plastic cover over the back of the lighting units.
2. Disconnect the wire from the fog light.
3. Squeeze the holder together and pull it straight back, releasing the bulb.
4. Remove the old bulb and install the new one. Make sure the bulb is properly seated; the guides on the bulb will only allow it to lock in place in one position.
   WARNING: *Do not touch the glass part of the bulb with your fingers. If this should happen accidentally, clean the lamp with alcohol and dry it with a lint- free cloth. Grease on the glass will cause hot spots and shorten the life of the bulb.*
5. Refit the holder and connect the wire. Install the plastic cover and its screw.

200 Series

While the 200 Series does not have integrated front fog lights (they can be added as separate units), in the mid-80s the cars began arriving with rear fog lights. Although these lamps appear to be the same as the red tail lights, they use a higher intensity (wattage) lamp.

The lamp is changed in identical fashion to a tail light bulb but care must be used in purchasing the replacement. The bulb will have identifying codes on its base and these codes should be matched exactly when replacing the lamp.

700 Series

Cars in the 700 Series may have front fog lamps either integrated into the headlight assembly or installed as separate units below the bumper. The integrated type requires only a quarter turn counter-clockwise to release the socket from the lamp assembly, although you may have to remove the washer reservoir to gain access. With the socket removed, release the side catches and remove the lamp. When installing the new lamp, hold it only by the base and do not touch the glass with your fingers.

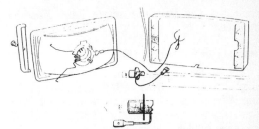

Bulb replacement on fog light mounted below the bumper

Make sure it is correctly positioned within the lens housing.

To change the bulb in a separatly mounted foglight:

1. Remove the screw in the vertical plastic retainer on each side of the foglight lens and remove the retainers.
2. Carefully lift the glass lens assembly out of the plastic mount. There are wires attached to the back of it.
3. Disconnect the wires to the lamp and the ground connection. Note that the connectors are different; they will only reassemble in the correct manner.
4. On the back of the lens, push down on the ends of the spring clip and spread the clip out from under its holder. Swing the clip out of the way.
5. Pull the bulb out of the reflector. Install the new bulb in the reflector and make sure that the square notch in the bulb flange fits over the guide on the reflector.
   WARNING: *Do not touch the glass part of the bulb with your fingers. If this should happen accidentally, clean the lamp with alcohol and dry it with a lint- free cloth. Grease on the glass will cause hot spots and shorten the life of the bulb.*
6. Swing the spring clip over the bulb and secure it in its clamps.
7. Reconnect the wiring to the ground and the bulb.
8. Place the reflector assembly back in the plastic housing and install the vertical retainers. Install the screws but do not overtighten.

The rear fog lights on all 700 Series are integrated into the tailamp assemblies. The bulbs are changed in identical fashion to the tail light bulbs, but care should be used in purchasing replacements. Note the code on the base of the bulb and obtain a replacement lamp of the same wattage.

Outside Mirrors
REMOVAL AND INSTALLATION

The manual mirrors on all Volvos do not offer replaceable glass. If the mirror is cracked or damaged, the complete mirror head must be replaced.

Manual Mirrors through 1979

The outside chromed mirrors on all Volvos may either be removed with its stalk by unbolting it from the door or may be removed from the stalk by unscrewing the pivot bolt behind the glass holder. Use the correct size screwdriver and don't strip the heads of the screws during removal.

Manual Mirrors after 1979, including Manual Remote Control

1. Depending on the type of mirror, remove either the small screw in the back of the adjusting tab (inside the door) or remove the rubber boot over the adjusting lever.

2. Remove the adjuster mechanism and its covers. On the cable adjuster type, remove the bolt which holds the adjuster head to the door frame.

3. Remove the mounting bolts holding the

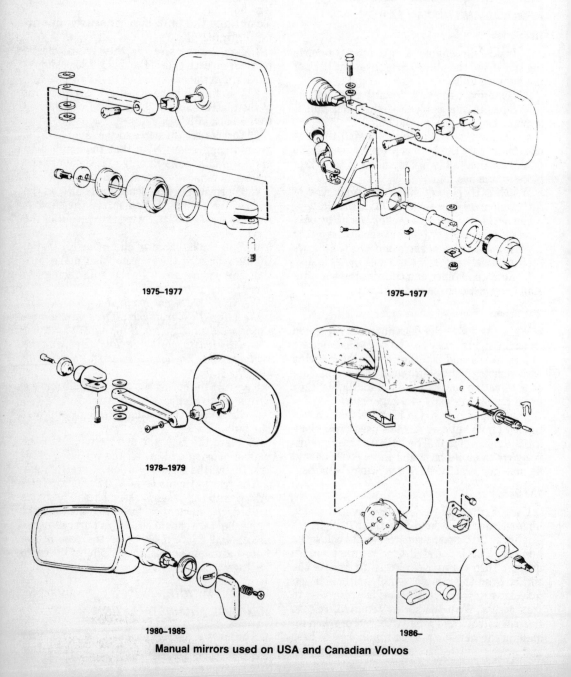

1975–1977

1975–1977

1978–1979

1980–1985

1986–

Manual mirrors used on USA and Canadian Volvos

mirror to the door frame. Support the mirror while doing this or it will fall when released. The adjusting cable must be fed through the door frame when removing.

4. When reinstalling, support the mirror during installation of the retaining screws. Make sure that any insulation or padding is put back in its correct location to reduce wind noise. If replacing a cable type mirror, thread the cable into position before securing the mounting bolts.

5. Install the adjuster tab or secure the cable retainer.

6. Attach any trim pieces and install either the locking screw or the rubber boot.

Electric mirrors

GLASS REPLACEMENT, 1975-85

NOTE: *This repair is best done inside under warm and dry conditions. The performance of the adhesive may be affected in other locations.*

1. Pry the glass off the backing plate with a screwdriver or similar tool.

2. Clean the holder with alcohol; make sure all the old adhesive is removed.

3. Install the new piece of tape onto the mirror holder (backing plate). Make sure the tape is centered. If any air bubbles are trapped under the tape, puncture them with a pin.

4. Remove the backing paper(s) from the new glass. Align the mirror and press it into place against the tape. Pay attention...you only get one chance to mount the mirror straight.

GLASS REPLACEMENT, 1986 AND LATER

1. With the mirror attached to the car, push in on the bottom of the glass until the cogs (teeth) can be seen through the hole in the bottom of the housing.

2. Use a small thin screwdriver to reach through the hole and slide the cogs to the right. Lift the mirror glass out.

3. Install the new glass, making sure the guides on the back of the mirror are in place.

4. Use the screwdriver to slide the cogs to the left and lock the glass in place.

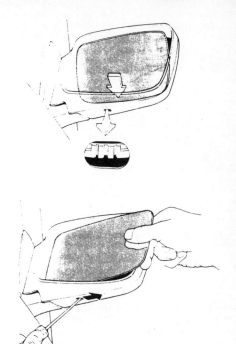

Removing the mirror glass, 1986 and later models

MOTOR REPLACEMENT, 1975-85

1. Remove the mirror from the door.

a. For cars prior to 1980, remove the inner trim panel on the door. Disconnect the wiring harness running to the mirror. 1980 and later cars have the connector under the dash next to the fuse box.

b. Remove the bolts holding the mirror assembly to the door and support the mirror while threading the wiring through the openings.

2. Remove the glass and pry off the plastic plug under the swivel point of the mirror "neck".

3. Tag or diagram the wiring on the back of the motor. Unplug the connectors.

Replacement of the mirror glasss, 1975–85. (A) is shows the position of the tape before installing the new glass

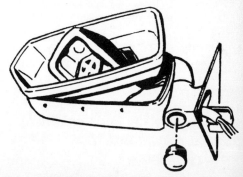

Replacement of the mirror motor on the 1975–1985 models requires removing the mirror from the door

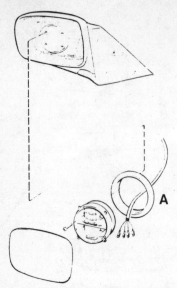

Replacement of the mirror motor, 1986 and later models. The dust cover (A) must be transferred to the new motor.

4. Remove the plastic washer and pull out the wires. Remove the rubber cap on the motor and remove the mounting screws for the motor.

5. Install the rubber cap on the new motor. Place the new motor in position and insert the wiring through the flange. Tighten the motor screws.

6. Install the wiring and replace the plastic covering.

7. Replace the plug in the swivel point. Use a light adhesive to hold it in place.

8. Mount the mirror to the door, connect the wiring harness and reinstall the door pad.

MOTOR REPLACEMENT, 1986 AND LATER

1. Remove the glass as discussed previously.

2. Remove the mounting screws holding the motor to the mirror frame.

3. Label or diagram the wiring on the back of the motor and disconnect the wiring. The round dust cover on the back of the motor must be tranferred to the new motor.

4. Connect the wires to the new motor. Mount the motor and tighten the retaining screws.

5. Install the mirror glass.

INTERIOR

Door Panels (Trim Pads or Liners)
REMOVAL AND INSTALLATION

1800, 140 and 160 Series

1. On 140 and 160 models, remove the armrest. It is retained by one or more screws, some hidden under plastic cover. Pop off the covers, remove the screws and, on the 160 Series, turn the plastic ring at the front several turns to the left.

Push the armrest forwards so that the hook at the front edge disengages. Remove the armrest.

2. Remove the window winder. Position the winder so that the arm points down. Push in on the hub of the winder, then push down on it. This should loosen the spring clip holding the winder onto the axle.

An alternate method is to straighten a paper clip and bend a small "J" onto the bottom. Use it to reach between the winder and the door panel, snag the clip and pull it out. When doing this, keep your other hand over the top of the winder. Otherwise, when the clip comes free it will fly to an undisclsosed location, never to be seen again.

3. The door panel is removed by gently prying the edge away from the door. Use a broad flat tool inserted between the panel and the metal of the door. The idea is to separate the clips without damage so they may be reused.

4. Proceed around the door until all the clips are released. Remove the door panel by lifting up to free the lip at the window edge.

NOTE: *Inside the door is either a paper or plastic moisture barrier. It may be removed for access to the door parts but it must not be ripped or torn. Should it become damaged, either replace it (plastic replacements are available for paper liners) or repair it with water-*

One method of removing the spring clip behind the window winder

CHILTON'S
AUTO BODY
REPAIR TIPS

Tools and Materials • Step-by-Step Illustrated Procedures
How To Repair Dents, Scratches and Rust Holes
Spray Painting and Refinishing Tips

With a little practice, basic body repair procedures can be mastered by any do-it-yourself mechanic. The step-by-step repairs shown here can be applied to almost any type of auto body repair.

TOOLS & MATERIALS

You may already have basic tools, such as hammers and electric drills. Other tools unique to body repair — body hammers, grinding attachments, sanding blocks, dent puller, half-round plastic file and plastic spreaders — are relatively inexpensive and can be obtained wherever auto parts or auto body repair parts are sold. Portable air compressors and paint spray guns can be purchased or rented.

Auto Body Repair Kits

The best and most often used products are available to the do-it-yourselfer in kit form, from major manufacturers of auto body repair products. The same manufacturers also merchandise the individual products for use by pros.

Kits are available to make a wide variety of repairs, including holes, dents and scratches and fiberglass, and offer the advantage of buying the materials you'll need for the job. There is little waste or chance of materials going bad from not being used. Many kits may also contain basic body-working tools such as body files, sanding blocks and spreaders. Check the contents of the kit before buying your tools.

BODY REPAIR TIPS

Safety

Many of the products associated with auto body repair and refinishing contain toxic chemicals. Read all labels before opening containers and store them in a safe place and manner.

• Wear eye protection (safety goggles) when using power tools or when performing any operation that involves

the removal of any type of material.

• Wear lung protection (disposable mask or respirator) when grinding, sanding or painting.

Sanding

1 Sand off paint before using a dent puller. When using a non-adhesive sanding disc, cover the back of the disc with an overlapping layer or two of masking tape and trim the edges. The disc will last considerably longer.

2 Use the circular motion of the sanding disc to grind *into* the edge of the repair. Grinding or sanding away from the jagged edge will only tear the sandpaper.

3 Use the palm of your hand flat on the panel to detect high and low spots. Do not use your fingertips. Slide your hand slowly back and forth.

WORKING WITH BODY FILLER

Mixing The Filler

Cleanliness and proper mixing and application are extremely important. Use a clean piece of plastic or glass or a disposable artist's palette to mix body filler.

1 Allow plenty of time and follow directions. No useful purpose will be served by adding more hardener to make it cure (set-up) faster. Less hardener means more curing time, but the mixture dries harder; more hardener means less curing time but a softer mixture.

2 Both the hardener and the filler should be thoroughly kneaded or stirred before mixing. Hardener should be a solid paste and dispense like thin toothpaste. Body filler should be smooth, and free of lumps or thick spots.

Getting the proper amount of hardener in the filler is the trickiest part of preparing the filler. Use the same amount of hardener in cold or warm weather. For contour filler (thick coats), a bead of hardener twice the diameter of the filler is about right. There's about a 15% margin on either side, but, if in doubt use less hardener.

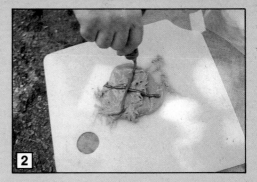

3 Mix the body filler and hardener by wiping across the mixing surface, picking the mixture up and wiping it again. Colder weather requires longer mixing times. Do not mix in a circular motion; this will trap air bubbles which will become holes in the cured filler.

Applying The Filler

1 For best results, filler should not be applied over ¼" thick.

Apply the filler in several coats. Build it up to above the level of the repair surface so that it can be sanded or grated down.

The first coat of filler must be pressed on with a firm wiping motion.

Apply the filler in one direction only. Working the filler back and forth will either pull it off the metal or trap air bubbles.

REPAIRING DENTS

Before you start, take a few minutes to study the damaged area. Try to visualize the shape of the panel before it was damaged. If the damage is on the left fender, look at the right fender and use it as a guide. If there is access to the panel from behind, you can reshape it with a body hammer. If not, you'll have to use a dent puller. Go slowly and work the metal a little at a time. Get the panel as straight as possible before applying filler.

1 This dent is typical of one that can be pulled out or hammered out from behind. Remove the headlight cover, headlight assembly and turn signal housing.

2 Drill a series of holes ½ the size of the end of the dent puller along the stress line. Make some trial pulls and assess the results. If necessary, drill more holes and try again. Do not hurry.

3 If possible, use a body hammer and block to shape the metal back to its original contours. Get the metal back as close to its original shape as possible. Don't depend on body filler to fill dents.

4 Using an 80-grit grinding disc on an electric drill, grind the paint from the surrounding area down to bare metal. Use a new grinding pad to prevent heat buildup that will warp metal.

5 The area should look like this when you're finished grinding. Knock the drill holes in and tape over small openings to keep plastic filler out.

6 Mix the body filler (see Body Repair Tips). Spread the body filler evenly over the entire area (see Body Repair Tips). Be sure to cover the area completely.

7 Let the body filler dry until the surface can just be scratched with your fingernail. Knock the high spots from the body filler with a body file ("Cheese-grater"). Check frequently with the palm of your hand for high and low spots.

8 Check to be sure that trim pieces that will be installed later will fit exactly. Sand the area with 40-grit paper.

9 If you wind up with low spots, you may have to apply another layer of filler.

10 Knock the high spots off with 40-grit paper. When you are satisfied with the contours of the repair, apply a thin coat of filler to cover pin holes and scratches.

11 Block sand the area with 40-grit paper to a smooth finish. Pay particular attention to body lines and ridges that must be well-defined.

12 Sand the area with 400 paper and then finish with a scuff pad. The finished repair is ready for priming and painting (see Painting Tips).

Materials and photos courtesy of Ritt Jones Auto Body, Prospect Park, PA.

REPAIRING RUST HOLES

There are many ways to repair rust holes. The fiberglass cloth kit shown here is one of the most cost efficient for the owner because it provides a strong repair that resists cracking and moisture and is relatively easy to use. It can be used on large and small holes (with or without backing) and can be applied over contoured areas. Remember, however, that short of replacing an entire panel, no repair is a guarantee that the rust will not return.

1 Remove any trim that will be in the way. Clean away all loose debris. Cut away all the rusted metal. But be sure to leave enough metal to retain the contour or body shape.

2 Grind away all traces of rust with a 24-grit grinding disc. Be sure to grind back 3-4 inches from the edge of the hole down to bare metal and be sure all traces of paint, primer and rust are removed.

3 Block sand the area with 80 or 100 grit sandpaper to get a clear, shiny surface and feathered paint edge. Tap the edges of the hole inward with a ball peen hammer.

4 If you are going to use release film, cut a piece about 2-3″ larger than the area you have sanded. Place the film over the repair and mark the sanded area on the film. Avoid any unnecessary wrinkling of the film.

5 Cut 2 pieces of fiberglass matte to match the shape of the repair. One piece should be about 1″ smaller than the sanded area and the second piece should be 1″ smaller than the first. Mix enough filler and hardener to saturate the fiberglass material (see Body Repair Tips).

6 Lay the release sheet on a flat surface and spread an even layer of filler, large enough to cover the repair. Lay the smaller piece of fiberglass cloth in the center of the sheet and spread another layer of filler over the fiberglass cloth. Repeat the operation for the larger piece of cloth.

7 Place the repair material over the repair area, with the release film facing outward. Use a spreader and work from the center outward to smooth the material, following the body contours. Be sure to remove all air bubbles.

8 Wait until the repair has dried tack-free and peel off the release sheet. The ideal working temperature is 60°-90° F. Cooler or warmer temperatures or high humidity may require additional curing time. Wait longer, if in doubt.

9 Sand and feather-edge the entire area. The initial sanding can be done with a sanding disc on an electric drill if care is used. Finish the sanding with a block sander. Low spots can be filled with body filler; this may require several applications.

10 When the filler can just be scratched with a fingernail, knock the high spots down with a body file and smooth the entire area with 80-grit. Feather the filled areas into the surrounding areas.

11 When the area is sanded smooth, mix some topcoat and hardener and apply it directly with a spreader. This will give a smooth finish and prevent the glass matte from showing through the paint.

12 Block sand the topcoat smooth with finishing sandpaper (200 grit), and 400 grit. The repair is ready for masking, priming and painting (see Painting Tips).

Materials and photos courtesy Marson Corporation, Chelsea, Massachusetts

PAINTING TIPS

Preparation

1 SANDING — Use a 400 or 600 grit wet or dry sandpaper. Wet-sand the area with a ¼ sheet of sandpaper soaked in clean water. Keep the paper wet while sanding. Sand the area until the repaired area tapers into the original finish.

2 CLEANING — Wash the area to be painted thoroughly with water and a clean rag. Rinse it thoroughly and wipe the surface dry until you're sure it's completely free of dirt, dust, fingerprints, wax, detergent or other foreign matter.

3 MASKING — Protect any areas you don't want to overspray by covering them with masking tape and newspaper. Be careful not get fingerprints on the area to be painted.

4 PRIMING — All exposed metal should be primed before painting. Primer protects the metal and provides an excellent surface for paint adhesion. When the primer is dry, wet-sand the area again with 600 grit wet-sandpaper. Clean the area again after sanding.

Painting Techniques

Paint applied from either a spray gun or a spray can (for small areas) will provide good results. Experiment on an old piece of metal to get the right combination before you begin painting.

SPRAYING VISCOSITY (SPRAY GUN ONLY) — Paint should be thinned to spraying viscosity according to the directions on the can. Use only the recommended thinner or reducer and the same amount of reduction regardless of temperature.

AIR PRESSURE (SPRAY GUN ONLY) — This is extremely important. Be sure you are using the proper recommended pressure.

TEMPERATURE — The surface to be painted should be approximately the same temperature as the surrounding air. Applying warm paint to a cold surface, or vice versa, will completely upset the paint characteristics.

THICKNESS — Spray with smooth strokes. In general, the thicker the coat of paint, the longer the drying time. Apply several thin coats about 30 seconds apart. The paint should remain wet long enough to flow out and no longer; heavier coats will only produce sags or wrinkles. Spray a light (fog) coat, followed by heavier color coats.

DISTANCE — The ideal spraying distance is 8″-12″ from the gun or can to the surface. Shorter distances will produce ripples, while greater distances will result in orange peel, dry film and poor color match and loss of material due to overspray.

OVERLAPPING — The gun or can should be kept at right angles to the surface at all times. Work to a wet edge at an even speed, using a 50% overlap and direct the center of the spray at the lower or nearest edge of the previous stroke.

RUBBING OUT (BLENDING) FRESH PAINT — Let the paint dry thoroughly. Runs or imperfections can be sanded out, primed and repainted.

Don't be in too big a hurry to remove the masking. This only produces paint ridges. When the finish has dried for at least a week, apply a small amount of fine grade rubbing compound with a clean, wet cloth. Use lots of water and blend the new paint with the surrounding area.

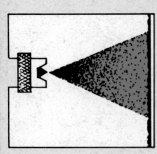

WRONG

Thin coat. Stroke too fast, not enough overlap, gun too far away.

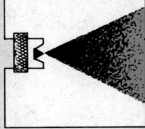

CORRECT

Medium coat. Proper distance, good stroke, proper overlap.

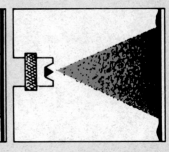

WRONG

Heavy coat. Stroke too slow, too much overlap, gun too close.

proof tape. It must be reinstalled intact after any door repairs

5. Before reinstalling the door panel, check every clip to insure that it is properly located and not damaged. Replace any that are unusable.

6. Position the door panel onto the top of the door and seat the lip at the window rail. It may require gentle tapping to seat properly.

7. Making sure each clip aligns with its hole, proceed around the door and tap each clip into place.

8. Fit the spring clip onto the window winder so that the open end points along the long part of the winder. Place the winder onto the axle--it was pointing down when you removed it--and give it a sharp tap. The winder will move into place and the clip will lock onto the slot in the axle.

9. On 140 and 160 Series, reinstall the armrest. Don't forget the plastic screw covers if any were removed.

200 Series

1. Remove the door pocket by turning the three studs 90° and lifting off the pocket.

2. Remove the armrest. The screws may be concealed behind plastic covers.

3. Remove the plastic housing around the inner latch release (door handle).

4. Remove the window winder. Do this by lifting up the small trim strip at the base of the winder. Remove the concealed screw and the winder may be pulled free.

5. Unscrew the lock button from the shaft.

6. The door panel is removed by gently prying the edge away from the door. Use a broad flat tool inserted between the panel and the metal of the door. The idea is to separate the clips without damage so they may be reused.

7. Proceed around the door until all the clips are released. Remove the door panel by lifting up to free the lip at the window edge. Be prepared to disconnect any wiring encountered within the door (courtesy lights, speakers, etc) during removal.

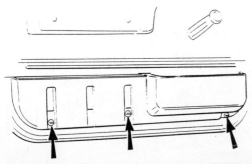

Turn the clips 90° to release the side pockets on 200 Series

NOTE: *Inside the door is a plastic moisture barrier. It may be removed for access to the door parts but it must not be ripped or torn. Should it become damaged, either replace it or repair it with waterproof tape. It must be reinstalled intact after any door repairs*

8. Before reinstalling the door panel, check every clip to insure that it is properly located and not damaged. Replace any that are unusable.

9. Position the door panel onto the top of the door and seat the lip at the window rail. It may require gentle tapping to seat properly.

10. Making sure each clip aligns with its hole, proceed around the door and tap each clip into place.

11. Install the window winder, the lock button and the release handle housing.

12. Reinstall the armrest and the door pocket.

700 Series

1. Carefully pry the trim strip loose from the face of handgrip. Remove the two concealed screws and remove the handgrip. If the car has manually operated windows, remove the window winder.

2. Remove the speaker grille and speaker. On 740 and 760 models, the grille is part of the longer panel held on by two concealed screws. The separate grille on the 780 is held by two screws located under the plastic trim at the lower end. Disconnect wiring at the nearest connectors as access is gained.

3. On 740/760, remove the lock button. On 780 Series, remove the two large plastic clips at the bottom of the door panel.

4. On 780 remove the two screws located just below the arm rest (just behind the line of the door release lever) and remove the knob from the release lever.

5. On 780 models lift the panel up and away from the door. For 740/760 models, the door panel is removed by gently prying the edge away from the door. Use a broad flat tool inserted between the panel and the metal of the door. The idea is to separate the clips without damage so they may be reused. Proceed around the door until all the clips are released. Remove the door panel by lifting up to free the lip at the window edge.

NOTE: *Inside the door is a plastic moisture barrier. It may be removed for access to the door parts but it must not be ripped or torn. Should it become damaged, replace it or repair it with waterproof tape. It must be reinstalled intact after any door repairs*

6. On 780 Series, remove the housing which surrounds the door release lever after the panel is removed. This will make reinstallation much easier.

7. Before reinstalling the door panel, check every clip (740 and 760) to insure that it is properly located and not damaged. Replace any that are unusable.

8. Position the door panel onto the top of the door and seat the lip at the window rail. It may require gentle tapping to seat properly. Making sure each clip aligns with its hole, proceed around the door and tap each clip into place.

Connect the wiring harnesses as the components move into place.

9. For the 780, install the two large clips at the bottom of the panel and the two screws under the armrest.

10. Install the speaker and grille and connect the wiring.

11. Install the door release housing and knob on the 780 Series.

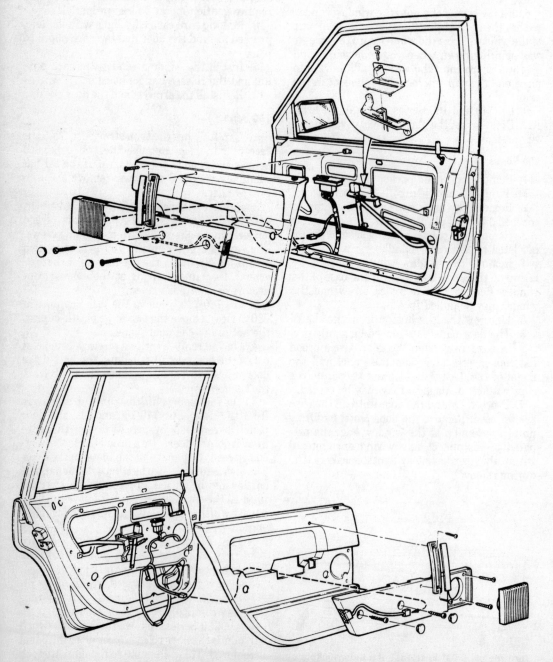

Front and rear door components, 760 GLE. 740 doors similar

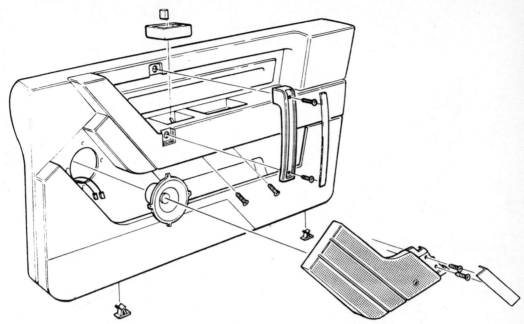

Front door panel components, 780

12. Install the handgrip and install the cover strip. If the window winder was removed, reinstall it.

Door Locks

REMOVAL AND INSTALLATION

1800

1. Remove the inner door panel and the moisture barrier.

2. Disconnect the spring at the top of the latch linkage.

3. Remove the one screw and two nuts holing the door handle to the door and lift the handle away from the door.

4. With the handle removed, the two screws in the back of the assembly may be removed. Remove the circlip at the back of the lock cylinder and the lock may be removed from the pushbutton assembly.

5. After reassembling the lock and handle as-

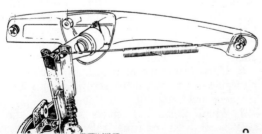

1800 door handle assembly. View is from inside the door

sembly, position it on the car and install the nuts and bolt. Make sure the actuating tab engages the linkage properly. Check the operation of the latch and door lock before replacing the moisture barrier and door panel.

140 and 160 Series

The door locks on these vehicles are removed simply by removing the door panel and the moisture barrier and unscrewing the retaining screw for the lock. The retaining screw is located on the rear edge of the door. When reinstalling the lock, make sure the tab on the back of the lock engages the latch properly.

200 Series

1. Remove the inner door liner and the moisture barrier.

2a. For cars with manual locks, the lock cylinder is held within the door by a clip which slides across the back of the cylinder. On 1979 and older cars, the clip can be slid free. Later cars use the same clip, but it is retained to the door with two small screws which must be removed to free the clip.

2b. On cars with electric locks, the left door lock has a collar surrounding it. This electrical fitting causes all the doors to lock when the key is used in the driver's door. The retainer on this switch may be opened by prying up the plastic catch; the switch may then be removed from the lock cylinder.

3. When reinstalling, make sure the lock cylinder engages the latch mechanism properly. If

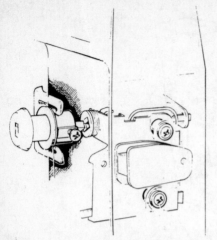

200 Series door lock assembly with pre-1979 retaining clip

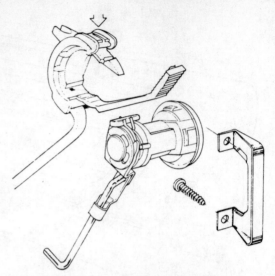

Driver's door lock assembly, all 700 Series

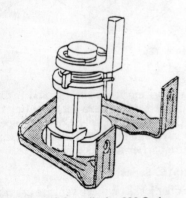

Updated lock retaining clip for 200 Series

replacing the lock on a 1979 or older car, the bracket must be replaced with the updated type. The new bracket stiffens the face of the door panel around the lock face.

4. If the car has electric locks, make sure the switch collar is in its correct position and the clip is secure.

5. Reinstall the moisture barrier and the inner door panel.

700 Series

1. Remove the door trim pad and the moisture barrier.

2. The back of the lock cylinder has a rod connected to it. Disconnect the rod by swinging the clip away from the shaft and then separating the shaft from the lock. Don't break or deform the clip during removal.

3. If removing the left door lock, loosen the electrical switch around the lock by releasing the plastic catch on the collar. Remove the switch from the lock.

4. Remove the two screws holding the lock

retaining bracket. Remove the bracket and remove the lock from the door.

5. When reassembling, make sure the rod is properly attached and secure. Install the retaining bracket and its two screws.

6. Reinstall the switch on the left door lock and make sure it is properly positioned and secure.

7. Check the operation of the keylock and the power locks.

8. Install the moisture barrier and the door panel.

Door Glass and Regulator
REMOVAL AND INSTALLATION
1800

1. Remove the door pad and moisture barrier.

2. In the upper center of the door, remove the two screws holding the upper window stop. Remove the stop from inside the door.

3. Fit the window winder onto the axle and wind the window to the top of its travel, then lower it about a quarter turn. Hold the glass while doing this to keep it in position.

4. Hold the glass with two hands; slide the glass rearwards and lean the top of the glass inward (toward the center of the car). This will unhook the glass from the lifting mechanism.

5. Lower the lift mechanism and lift the glass out of the door.

6. If the lifting mechanism (regulator) is to be replaced, remove the five screws holding it to the door and lift it out of the door.

7. When reinstalling, make sure that the glass is centered and runs easily in the guides. The rear guide (track) is adjustable to get a weathertight seal on the glass.

8. With all mechanical components, including the upper stop installed, test the window through the full range of motion. There should be no binding or resistance and the glass should remain square to the door during its travel.

9. Reinstall the moisture barrier and the door pad.

140 and 160 Series

1. Lower the window almost to its bottom position.

2. Remove the door pad and the moisture barrier.

3. Remove the screws which hold the bracket for the front vertical track and remove the bracket. (This step is omitted for rear doors.)

4. Remove the sealing strip which runs around the door frame.

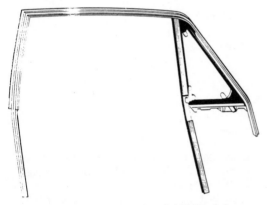

Upper door frame from 140 and 164 front door

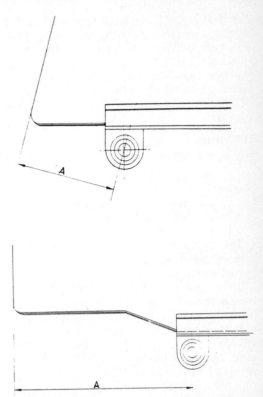

Correct placement of glass in lower channel (Above: Front glass, lower: Rear glass) See text for dimension A

5. Remove the attaching screws which hold the door frame to the door. Screws are located on both the front and rear edges of the door.

6. Lift the door frame straight up and out of the door.

7. Remove the guide roller at the upper edge of the door.

8. Support the window within the door and remove the locking springs holding the sliding rails to the lift arms. Don't allow the window to fall or get misplaced within the door.

9. Lift the window off the pins in the winder and remove the glass from the door.

10. If the regulator is to be removed from the car, remove the retaining bolts and remove the mechanism.

11. When refitting the glass into the carrier, make sure that the correct spacing is maintained. The distance (A) is 3.1 in. (80mm) for front windows and 6.7 in. (170mm) for the rear glass.

12. Reconnect the glass to the regulator pins and install the locking springs.

13. Install the upper guide roller.

14. Reinstall the door frame and secure the front and rear retaining screws. Make sure that the glass and the frame align properly. Install the sealing strip around the frame.

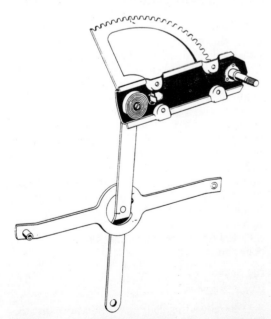

Winding mechanism (regulator) for 140 and 160 Series

15. Install the lower track bracket. Run the window through the full up and down travel and check for any signs of binding or resistance. Check also that the glass is even in its match to the door frame and is not under any abnormal tension, particularly in the closed position.

16. Reinstall the moisture barrier and the door pad.

200 Series
MANUAL WINDOWS

1. Remove the door pad and the moisture barrier.

2. If the glass is to be replaced or removed, remove the safety catches from the pins on the two lower arms and lift out the glass.

The regulator can be removed without removing the glass, but the glass must be supported within the door.

3. To remove the regulator (lift mechanism), remove the safety clips from the pins on the two lower arms. Remove the five bolts holding the regulator to the door and remove the regulator.

4. When reassembling, be careful not to scratch or knock the glass while fitting the new regulator into the door. Make certain the safety clips are firmly seated on the pins.

ELECTRIC WINDOWS

1. Remove the door pad and the moisture barrier.

2. If the glass is to be replaced or removed, remove the safety catches from the pins on the two lower arms and lift out the glass.

The regulator can be removed without removing the glass, but the glass must be supported within the door.

3. Disconnect the wiring for the motor. On cars through model year 1979, the wiring must be disconnected at the fusebox. 1980 and later models may be disconnected at the armrest control panel.

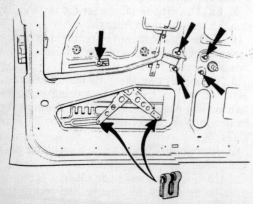

Retaining bolts for manual window regulator on 200 Series. Retaining clip on lower rails is used on all 200 and 700 Series

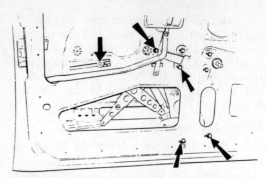

Retaining bolts for power window regulators on 200 Series

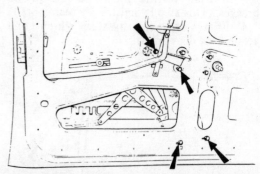

Loosen only these four bolts to adjust binding in 200 Series electric windows

4. Remove the five bolts holding the regulator and remove the regulator from the door.

5. When reinstalling, tighten the mounting screws just enough to hold position and no more. Attach the glass to the regulator with the safety clips and make sure they are properly seated.

6. Hook up the electrical connections and check the operation of the motor. Run the window up and down, checking for evenness of motion and smoothness of operation. The four frontmost mounting bolts can be loosened to eliminate binding. Loosen the screws and operate the window up and down. As the regulator seeks its best position, tighten the bolts to hold it in place. It should take 5 seconds for the window to open fully.

7. Raise the window to its stopped position. Loosen the stop (at the forward edge of the regulator) and raise the window as far as it will go. Readjust the stop to mesh with the gears and tighten it in place.

8. Reinstall the moisture barrier and the door pad.

700 Series
MANUAL WINDOWS

1. Remove the door pad and the moisture barrier.

2. If the glass is to be replaced or removed,

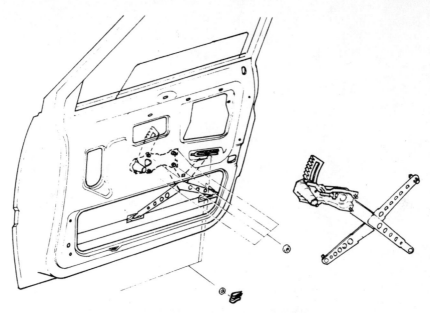

Manual window regulator, 700 Series

remove the safety catches from the pins on the two lower arms and lift out the glass. It may be necessary to remove the lower channel from the glass.

The regulator can be removed without removing the glass, but the glass must be supported within the door.

NOTE: *If replacing the glass in a rear door, the front window track must be removed. Loosen the two bolts in the edge of the door and the track will come free.*

3. To remove the regulator (lift mechanism), remove the safety clips from the pins on the two lower arms. Remove the five bolts holding the regulator to the door and remove the regulator.

4. When reassembling, be careful not to scratch or knock the glass while fitting the new regulator into the door. Make certain the safety clips are firmly seated on the pins.

5. If installing new glass, a new piece of cushioning tape must be placed in the lower channel.

6. After reinstallation, check the travel of the glass and eliminate and binding or stiffness. Loosen the upper stop bolt (located just forward of the spring for the door release) and wind the window to its full up position. Press the bolt rearwards and retighten it.

ELECTRIC WINDOWS

WARNING: *The use of the correct special tools or their equivalent is REQUIRED for this procedure.*

1. Remove the door pad and the moisture barrier.

2. If the glass is to be replaced or removed, remove the safety catches from the pins on the two lower arms and lift out the glass. It may be necessary to remove the lower channel from the glass.

The regulator can be removed without removing the glass, but the glass must be supported within the door.

NOTE: *If replacing the glass in a rear door, the front window track must be removed. Loosen the two bolts in the edge of the door and the track will come free.*

3. Label or diagram the wiring at the motor and disconnect the wiring using Volvo tool 6351 or similar to disconnect the terminals.

4. To remove the regulator (lift mechanism), remove the safety clips from the pins on the two lower arms and the upper arm. Remove the four bolts holding the regulator to the door and remove the regulator.

5. When reassembling, be careful not to scratch or knock the glass while fitting the new regulator into the door. Make certain the safety clips are firmly seated on the pins.

6. If installing new glass, a new piece of cushioning tape must be placed in the lower channel.

7. Reconnect the wiring to the motor making certain that correct positioning is obtained.

8. After reinstallation, check the travel of the glass and eliminate and binding or stiffness. Loosen the upper stop bolt (located just forward of the spring for the door release) and press it forward. Wind the window to its full up position. Press the bolt rearwards and retighten it.

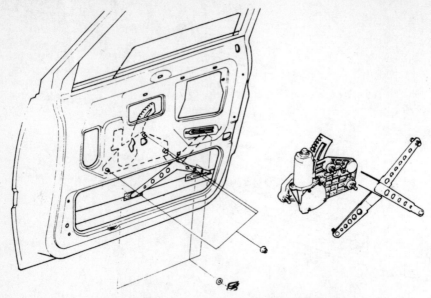

Electric window regulator and motor, 700 Series

Seats
REMOVAL AND INSTALLATION
Manual seats
1800, 140 and 160 Series

The front seats are retained to the car by bolts (usually four) into the floor rails. In most cases these are easily seen and removed, allowing the seat and its tracks to be removed from the car. On 140 and 160 Series, it may be easier to remove the bottom cushion (push down, release the clips and lift the cushion off) and then remove the seat frame from the tracks. During removal of the seat be alert for any wiring running to or under the seat which may become fouled or damaged.

If the seat itself is to be worked on out of the car, it is very helpful the support it on crates or sawhorses; the design of the seat makes it awkward to manipulate and topheavy if set upright on the ground. Seat removal is also a good time to perform a thorough cleaning inside the car as a large open area is created. The amount of loose change found under the seats usually makes this project worthwhile.

When reinstalling the seat, note that the elevation and rake (tilt) of the seat may be adjusted by selecting alternate bolt holes. Once the seat has been examined and the mounting system is understood, a little experimentation can yield a most comfortable seating position.

Manual Seats
200 and 700 Series

The front seat and its rails may be unbolted from the floor of the car. Many cars have heated seats; it will be necessary to disconnect the wiring harness for this system before removing the seat.

On the early 760 Series, it is necessary to remove the seat belt anchor from the side of the seat. Remove the screw in the rear of the side pocket, lift the pocket out of the way and remove the seat belt bolt.

After all the retaining bolts are removed, the front seats in the 700 Series are removed by sliding the seat to the rear of its track and lifting upwards to free the seat from the catches.

The rear seat cushion is removed by pressing down directly over the retaining clips (freeing the hook from the loop) and lifting the cushion clear. The rear seat backrest is held by catches which hold the upper bar in place. These catches can be released with a screwdriver; don't bend them anymore than needed or reassembly will be very difficult.

When reassembling the rear seat, always in-

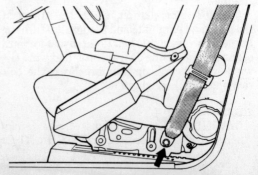

Seat belt retaining bolt on early model 760

stall the backrest first. Make sure that every clip engages properly and is firmly closed.

Power Seats
All Models so equipped.

1. Disconnect the negative battery cable.
2. Remove the plastic rail covers as necessary and remove the front bolts holding the seat tracks to the car. Loosen but do not remove the bolts at the rear of the tracks.
3. Gently elevate the front of the seat; identify and label the wiring running to the seat components. Disconnect the seat wiring connectors.

WARNING: *Do not disconnect any wiring for other components. Many other units may be found under the seat--leave them connected at all times.*

4. Remove the rear mounting bolts and lift the seat clear of the car. It will be heavy--a helper inside the car can ease removal.
5. Either support the seat on crates or a clean workbench or place the seat on a clean blanket to protect it.

Power Seat Motors
REMOVAL AND INSTALLATION

1. Disconnect the negative battery cable.
2. Remove the seat from the car following the procedure outlined previously.

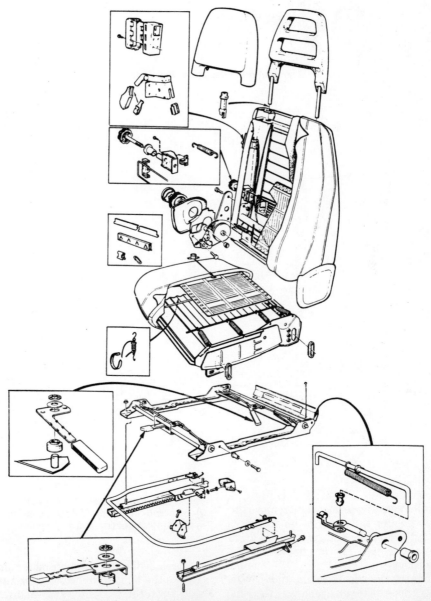

Detail of front seat components, 200 Series with manual seats

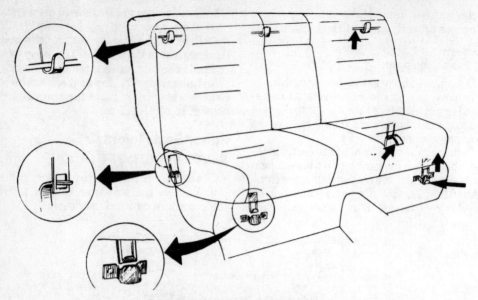

Rear seat retaining clips, 700 Series

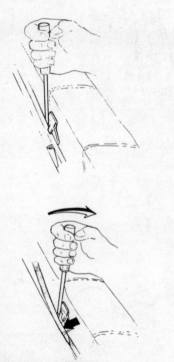

Rear seatback clips, 200 Series

3. Turn the seat upside down and remove the four screws holding the motor to its bracket.

4. Lift out the motor and remove the drive cable from the motor. Use care not to kink or crease the cable.

5. Disconnect the wiring to the motor. On 780 models, this may require removing the pins from the connector case.

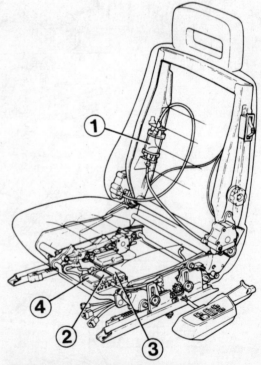

Power seat from model 780. 1) Backrest tilt motor 2) Fore-and-aft motor 3) Front section elevation motor 4) Rear section elevation motor

To remove the fore-and-aft motor on the 780, remove the middle connector from the control unit. Open the connector and remove the wiring at the terminals.

6. When reinstalling, make sure the wiring is properly located and secure in its connector. Fit the cable into the motor and install the retainer if any.

7. Install the motor and final check the wiring. Make sure it is out of the way of any moving parts.

8. Reinstall the seat in the car, connect the wiring harnesses and connect the negative battery cable. Check the operation of the seat.

NOTE: *The motor controlling the seatback tilt is within the seatback. Access to this motor involves removal of the seatback and disassembly of upholstery pieces. If trouble is experienced with this motor, repair by trained personnel is recommended.*

How to Remove Stains from Fabric Interior

For rest results, spots and stains should be removed as soon as possible. Never use gasoline, lacquer thinner, acetone, nail polish remover or bleach. Use a 3′ x 3″ piece of cheesecloth. Squeeze most of the liquid from the fabric and wipe the stained fabric from the outside of the stain toward the center with a lifting motion. Turn the cheesecloth as soon as one side becomes soiled. When using water to remove a stain, be sure to wash the entire section after the spot has been removed to avoid water stains. Encrusted spots can be broken up with a dull knife and vacuumed before removing the stain.

Type of Stain	How to Remove It
Surface spots	Brush the spots out with a small hand brush or use a commercial preparation such as K2R to lift the stain.
Mildew	Clean around the mildew with warm suds. Rinse in cold water and soak the mildew area in a solution of 1 part table salt and 2 parts water. Wash with upholstery cleaner.
Water stains	Water stains in fabric materials can be removed with a solution made from 1 cup of table salt dissolved in 1 quart of water. Vigorously scrub the solution into the stain and rinse with clear water. Water stains in nylon or other synthetic fabrics should be removed with a commercial type spot remover.
Chewing gum, tar, crayons, shoe polish (greasy stains)	Do not use a cleaner that will soften gum or tar. Harden the deposit with an ice cube and scrape away as much as possible with a dull knife. Moisten the remainder with cleaning fluid and scrub clean.
Ice cream, candy	Most candy has a sugar base and can be removed with a cloth wrung out in warm water. Oily candy, after cleaning with warm water, should be cleaned with upholstery cleaner. Rinse with warm water and clean the remainder with cleaning fluid.
Wine, alcohol, egg, milk, soft drink (non-greasy stains)	Do not use soap. Scrub the stain with a cloth wrung out in warm water. Remove the remainder with cleaning fluid.
Grease, oil, lipstick, butter and related stains	Use a spot remover to avoid leaving a ring. Work from the outisde of the stain to the center and dry with a clean cloth when the spot is gone.
Headliners (cloth)	Mix a solution of warm water and foam upholstery cleaner to give thick suds. Use only foam—liquid may streak or spot. Clean the entire headliner in one operation using a circular motion with a natural sponge.
Headliner (vinyl)	Use a vinyl cleaner with a sponge and wipe clean with a dry cloth.
Seats and door panels	Mix 1 pint upholstery cleaner in 1 gallon of water. Do not soak the fabric around the buttons.
Leather or vinyl fabric	Use a multi-purpose cleaner full strength and a stiff brush. Let stand 2 minutes and scrub thoroughly. Wipe with a clean, soft rag.
Nylon or synthetic fabrics	For normal stains, use the same procedures you would for washing cloth upholstery. If the fabric is extremely dirty, use a multi-purpose cleaner full strength with a stiff scrub brush. Scrub thoroughly in all directions and wipe with a cotton towel or soft rag.

Mechanic's Data

General Conversion Table

Multiply By	To Convert	To	
		LENGTH	
2.54	Inches	Centimeters	.3937
25.4	Inches	Millimeters	.03937
30.48	Feet	Centimeters	.0328
.304	Feet	Meters	3.28
.914	Yards	Meters	1.094
1.609	Miles	Kilometers	.621
		VOLUME	
.473	Pints	Liters	2.11
.946	Quarts	Liters	1.06
3.785	Gallons	Liters	.264
.016	Cubic inches	Liters	61.02
16.39	Cubic inches	Cubic cms.	.061
28.3	Cubic feet	Liters	.0353
		MASS (Weight)	
28.35	Ounces	Grams	.035
.4536	Pounds	Kilograms	2.20
—	To obtain	From	Multiply by

Multiply By	To Convert	To	
		AREA	
.645	Square inches	Square cms.	.155
.836	Square yds.	Square meters	1.196
		FORCE	
4.448	Pounds	Newtons	.225
.138	Ft./lbs.	Kilogram/meters	7.23
1.36	Ft./lbs.	Newton-meters	.737
.112	In./lbs.	Newton-meters	8.844
		PRESSURE	
.068	Psi	Atmospheres	14.7
6.89	Psi	Kilopascals	.145
		OTHER	
1.104	Horsepower (DIN)	Horsepower (SAE)	.9861
.746	Horsepower (SAE)	Kilowatts (KW)	1.34
1.60	Mph	Km/h	.625
.425	Mpg	Km/1	2.35
—	To obtain	From	Multiply by

Tap Drill Sizes

National Coarse or U.S.S.

Screw & Tap Size	Threads Per Inch	Use Drill Number
No. 5	40	.39
No. 6	32	.36
No. 8	32	.29
No. 10	24	.25
No. 12	24	.17
1/4	20	8
5/16	18	F
3/8	16	5/16
7/16	14	U
1/2	13	27/64
9/16	12	31/64
5/8	11	17/32
3/4	10	21/32
7/8	9	49/64

National Coarse or U.S.S.

Screw & Tap Size	Threads Per Inch	Use Drill Number
1	8	7/8
1 1/8	7	63/64
1 1/4	7	17/64
1 1/2	6	1 11/32

National Fine or S.A.E.

Screw & Tap Size	Threads Per Inch	Use Drill Number
No. 5	44	.37
No. 6	40	.33
No. 8	36	.29
No. 10	32	.21

National Fine or S.A.E.

Screw & Tap Size	Threads Per Inch	Use Drill Number
No. 12	28	15
1/4	28	3
6/16	24	1
3/8	24	Q
7/16	20	W
1/2	20	29/64
9/16	18	33/64
5/8	18	37/64
3/4	16	11/16
7/8	14	13/16
1 1/8	12	1 3/64
1 1/4	12	1 11/64
1 1/2	12	1 27/64

Drill Sizes In Decimal Equivalents

Inch	Decimal	Wire	mm
1/64	.0156		.39
	.0157		.4
	.0160	78	
	.0165		.42
	.0173		.44
	.0177		.45
	.0180	77	
	.0181		.46
	.0189		.48
	.0197		.5
	.0200	76	
	.0210	75	
	.0217		.55
	.0225	74	
	.0236		.6
	.0240	73	
	.0250	72	
	.0256		.65
	.0260	71	
	.0276		.7
	.0280	70	
	.0292	69	
	.0295		.75
	.0310	68	
1/32	.0312		.79
	.0315		.8
	.0320	67	
	.0330	66	
	.0335		.85
	.0350	65	
	.0354		.9
	.0360	64	
	.0370	63	
	.0374		.95
	.0380	62	
	.0390	61	
	.0394		1.0
	.0400	60	
	.0410	59	
	.0413		1.05
	.0420	58	
	.0430	57	
	.0433		1.1
	.0453		1.15
3/64	.0465	56	
	.0469		1.19
	.0472		1.2
	.0492		1.25
	.0512		1.3
	.0520	55	
	.0531		1.35
	.0550	54	
	.0551		1.4
	.0571		1.45
	.0591		1.5
	.0595	53	
	.0610		1.55
1/16	.0625		1.59
	.0630		1.6
	.0635	52	
	.0650		1.65
	.0669		1.7
	.0670	51	
	.0689		1.75
	.0700	50	
	.0709		1.8
	.0728		1.85

Inch	Decimal	Wire	mm
	.0730	49	
	.0748		1.9
	.0760	48	
	.0768		1.95
5/64	.0781		1.98
	.0785	47	
	.0787		2.0
	.0807		2.05
	.0810	46	
	.0820	45	
	.0827		2.1
	.0846		2.15
	.0860	44	
	.0866		2.2
	.0886		2.25
	.0890	43	
	.0906		2.3
	.0925		2.35
	.0935	42	
3/32	.0938		2.38
	.0945		2.4
	.0960	41	
	.0965		2.45
	.0980	40	
	.0981		2.5
	.0995	39	
	.1015	38	
	.1024		2.6
	.1040	37	
	.1063		2.7
	.1065	36	
	.1083		2.75
7/64	.1094		2.77
	.1100	35	
	.1102		2.8
	.1110	34	
	.1130	33	
	.1142		2.9
	.1160	32	
	.1181		3.0
	.1200	31	
	.1220		3.1
1/8	.1250		3.17
	.1260		3.2
	.1280		3.25
	.1285	30	
	.1299		3.3
	.1339		3.4
	.1360	29	
	.1378		3.5
	.1405	28	
9/64	.1406		3.57
	.1417		3.6
	.1440	27	
	.1457		3.7
	.1470	26	
	.1476		3.75
	.1495	25	
	.1496		3.8
	.1520	24	
	.1535		3.9
	.1540	23	
5/32	.1562		3.96
	.1570	22	
	.1575		4.0
	.1590	21	
	.1610	20	

Inch	Decimal	Wire & Letter	mm
	.1614		4.1
	.1654		4.2
	.1660	19	
	.1673		4.25
	.1693		4.3
	.1695	18	
11/64	.1719		4.36
	.1730	17	
	.1732		4.4
	.1770	16	
	.1772		4.5
	.1800	15	
	.1811		4.6
	.1820	14	
	.1850	13	
	.1850		4.7
	.1870		4.75
3/16	.1875		4.76
	.1890		4.8
	.1890	12	
	.1910	11	
	.1929		4.9
	.1935	10	
	.1960	9	
	.1969		5.0
	.1990	8	
	.2008		5.1
	.2010	7	
13/64	.2031		5.16
	.2040	6	
	.2047		5.2
	.2055	5	
	.2067		5.25
	.2087		5.3
	.2090	4	
	.2126		5.4
	.2130	3	
	.2165		5.5
7/32	.2188		5.55
	.2205		5.6
	.2210	2	
	.2244		5.7
	.2264		5.75
	.2280	1	
	.2283		5.8
	.2323		5.9
	.2340	A	
15/64	.2344		5.95
	.2362		6.0
	.2380	B	
	.2402		6.1
	.2420	C	
	.2441		6.2
	.2460	D	
	.2461		6.25
	.2480		6.3
1/4	.2500	E	6.35
	.2520		6.
	.2559		6.5
	.2570	F	
	.2598		6.6
	.2610	G	
	.2638		6.7
17/64	.2656		6.74
	.2657		6.75
	.2660	H	
	.2677		6.8

Inch	Decimal	Letter	mm
	.2717		6.9
	.2720	I	
	.2756		7.0
	.2770	J	
	.2795		7.1
	.2810	K	
9/32	.2812		7.14
	.2835		7.2
	.2854		7.25
	.2874		7.3
	.2900	L	
	.2913		7.4
	.2950	M	
	.2953		7.5
19/64	.2969		7.54
	.2992		7.6
	.3020	N	
	.3031		7.7
	.3051		7.75
	.3071		7.8
	.3110		7.9
5/16	.3125		7.93
	.3150		8.0
	.3160	O	
	.3189		8.1
	.3228		8.2
	.3230	P	
	.3248		8.25
	.3268		8.3
21/64	.3281		8.33
	.3307		8.4
	.3320	Q	
	.3346		8.5
	.3386		8.6
	.3390	R	
	.3425		8.7
11/32	.3438		8.73
	.3445		8.75
	.3465		8.8
	.3480	S	
	.3504		8.9
	.3543		9.0
	.3580	T	
	.3583		9.1
23/64	.3594		9.12
	.3622		9.2
	.3642		9.25
	.3661		9.3
	.3680	U	
	.3701		9.4
	.3740		9.5
3/8	.3750		9.52
	.3770	V	
	.3780		9.6
	.3819		9.7
	.3839		9.75
	.3858		9.8
	.3860	W	
	.3898		9.9
25/64	.3906		9.92
	.3937		10.0
	.3970	X	
	.4040	Y	
13/32	.4062		10.31
	.4130	Z	
	.4134		10.5
27/64	.4219		10.71

Inch	Decimal	mm
	.4331	11.0
7/16	.4375	11.11
	.4528	11.5
29/64	.4531	11.51
15/32	.4688	11.90
	.4724	12.0
31/64	.4844	12.30
	.4921	12.5
1/2	.5000	12.70
	.5118	13.0
33/64	.5156	13.09
17/32	.5312	13.49
	.5315	13.5
35/64	.5469	13.89
	.5512	14.0
9/16	.5625	14.28
	.5709	14.5
37/64	.5781	14.68
	.5906	15.0
19/32	.5938	15.08
39/64	.6094	15.47
	.6102	15.5
5/8	.6250	15.87
	.6299	16.0
41/64	.6406	16.27
	.6496	16.5
21/32	.6562	16.66
	.6693	17.0
43/64	.6719	17.06
11/16	.6875	17.46
	.6890	17.5
45/64	.7031	17.85
	.7087	18.0
23/32	.7188	18.25
	.7283	18.5
47/64	.7344	18.65
	.7480	19.0
3/4	.7500	19.05
49/64	.7656	19.44
	.7677	19.5
25/32	.7812	19.84
	.7874	20.0
51/64	.7969	20.24
	.8071	20.5
13/16	.8125	20.63
	.8268	21.0
53/64	.8281	21.03
27/32	.8438	21.43
	.8465	21.5
55/64	.8594	21.82
	.8661	22.0
7/8	.8750	22.22
	.8858	22.5
57/64	.8906	22.62
	.9055	23.0
	.9062	23.01
29/32	.9219	23.41
59/64	.9252	23.5
15/16	.9375	23.81
	.9449	24.0
61/64	.9531	24.2
	.9646	24.5
31/32	.9688	24.6
	.9843	25.0
63/64	.9844	25.0
1	1.0000	25.4

GLOSSARY OF TERMS

AIR/FUEL RATIO: The ratio of air to gasoline by weight in the fuel mixture drawn into the engine.

AIR INJECTION: One method of reducing harmful exhaust emissions by injecting air into each of the exhaust ports of an engine. The fresh air entering the hot exhaust manifold causes any remaining fuel to be burned before it can exit the tailpipe.

ALTERNATOR: A device used for converting mechanical energy into electrical energy.

AMMETER: An instrument, calibrated in amperes, used to measure the flow of an electrical current in a circuit. Ammeters are always connected in series with the circuit being tested.

AMPERE: The rate of flow of electrical current present when one volt of electrical pressure is applied against one ohm of electrical resistance.

ANALOG COMPUTER: Any microprocessor that uses similar (analogous) electrical signals to make its calculations.

ARMATURE: A laminated, soft iron core wrapped by a wire that converts electrical energy to mechanical energy as in a motor or relay. When rotated in a magnetic field, it changes mechanical energy into electrical energy as in a generator.

ATMOSPHERIC PRESSURE: The pressure on the Earth's surface caused by the weight of the air in the atmosphere. At sea level, this pressure is 14.7 psi at 32°F (101 kPa at 0°C).

ATOMIZATION: The breaking down of a liquid into a fine mist that can be suspended in air.

AXIAL PLAY: Movement parallel to a shaft or bearing bore.

BACKFIRE: The sudden combustion of gases in the intake or exhaust system that results in a loud explosion.

BACKLASH: The clearance or play between two parts, such as meshed gears.

BACKPRESSURE: Restrictions in the exhaust system that slow the exit of exhaust gases from the combustion chamber.

BAKELITE: A heat resistant, plastic insulator material commonly used in printed circuit boards and transistorized components.

BALL BEARING: A bearing made up of hardened inner and outer races between which hardened steel ball roll.

BALLAST RESISTOR: A resistor in the primary ignition circuit that lowers voltage after the engine is started to reduce wear on ignition components.

BEARING: A friction reducing, supportive device usually located between a stationary part and a moving part.

BIMETAL TEMPERATURE SENSOR: Any sensor or switch made of two dissimilar types of metal that bend when heated or cooled due to the different expansion rates of the alloys. These types of sensors usually function as an on/off switch.

BLOWBY: Combustion gases, composed of water vapor and unburned fuel, that leak past the piston rings into the crankcase during normal engine operation. These gases are removed by the PCV system to prevent the build-up of harmful acids in the crankcase.

BRAKE PAD: A brake shoe and lining assembly used with disc brakes.

BRAKE SHOE: The backing for the brake lining. The term is, however, usually applied to the assembly of the brake backing and lining.

BUSHING: A liner, usually removable, for a bearing; an anti-friction liner used in place of a bearing.

BYPASS: System used to bypass ballast resistor during engine cranking to increase voltage supplied to the coil.

CALIPER: A hydraulically activated device in a disc brake system, which is mounted straddling the brake rotor (disc). The caliper contains at least one piston and two brake pads. Hydraulic pressure on the piston(s) forces the pads against the rotor.

CAMSHAFT: A shaft in the engine on which are the lobes (cams) which operate the valves. The camshaft is driven by the crankshaft, via a belt, chain or gears, at one half the crankshaft speed.

CAPACITOR: A device which stores an electrical charge.

CARBON MONOXIDE (CO): a colorless, odorless gas given off as a normal byproduct of combustion. It is poisonous and extremely dangerous in confined areas, building up slowly to toxic levels without warning if adequate ventilation is not available.

CARBURETOR: A device, usually mounted on the intake manifold of an engine, which mixes the air and fuel in the proper proportion to allow even combustion.

CATALYTIC CONVERTER: A device installed in the exhaust system, like a muffler, that converts harmful byproducts of combustion into carbon dioxide and water vapor by means of a heat-producing chemical reaction.

CENTRIFUGAL ADVANCE: A mechanical method of advancing the spark timing by using flyweights in the distributor that react to centrifugal force generated by the distributor shaft rotation.

CHECK VALVE: Any one-way valve installed to permit the flow of air, fuel or vacuum in one direction only.

CHOKE: A device, usually a moveable valve, placed in the intake path of a carburetor to restrict the flow of air.

CIRCUIT: Any unbroken path through which an electrical current can flow. Also used to describe fuel flow in some instances.

CIRCUIT BREAKER: A switch which protects an electrical circuit from overload by opening the circuit when the current flow exceeds a predetermined level. Some circuit breakers must be reset manually, while other reset automatically

COIL (IGNITION): A transformer in the ignition circuit which steps of the voltage provided to the spark plugs.

COMBINATION MANIFOLD: An assembly which includes both the intake and exhaust manifolds in one casting.

COMBINATION VALVE: A device used in some fuel systems that routes fuel vapors to a charcoal storage canister instead of venting them into the atmosphere. The valve relieves fuel tank pressure and allows fresh air into the tank as fuel level drops to prevent a vapor lock situation.

COMPRESSION RATIO: The comparison of the total volume of the cylinder and combustion chamber with the piston at BDC and the piston at TDC.

CONDENSER: 1. An electrical device which acts to store an electrical charge, preventing voltage surges.
2. A radiator-like device in the air conditioning system in which refrigerant gas condenses into a liquid, giving off heat.

CONDUCTOR: Any material through which an electrical current can be transmitted easily.

CONTINUITY: Continuous or complete circuit. Can be checked with an ohmmeter.

COUNTERSHAFT: An intermediate shaft which is rotated by a mainshaft and transmits, in turn, that rotation to a working part.

CRANKCASE: The lower part of an engine in which the crankshaft and related parts operate.

CRANKSHAFT: The main driving shaft of an engine which receives reciprocating motion from the pistons and converts it to rotary motion.

CYLINDER: In an engine, the round hole in the engine block in which the piston(s) ride.

CYLINDER BLOCK: The main structural member of an engine in which is found the cylinders, crankshaft and other principal parts.

CYLINDER HEAD: The detachable portion of the engine, fastened, usually, to the top of the cylinder block, containing all or most of the combustion chambers. On overhead valve engines, it contains the valves and their operating parts. On overhead cam engines, it contains the camshaft as well.

DEAD CENTER: The extreme top or bottom of the piston stroke.

DETONATION: An unwanted explosion of the air fuel mixture in the combustion chamber caused by excess heat and compression, advanced timing, or an overly lean mixture. Also referred to as "ping".

DIAPHRAGM: A thin, flexible wall separating two cavities, such as in a vacuum advance unit.

DIESELING: A condition in which hot spots in the combustion chamber cause the engine to run on after the key is turned off.

DIFFERENTIAL: A geared assembly which allows the transmission of motion between drive axles, giving one axle the ability to turn faster than the other.

DIODE: An electrical device that will allow current to flow in one direction only.

DISC BRAKE: A hydraulic braking assembly consisting of a brake disc, or rotor, mounted on an axle, and a caliper assembly containing, usually two brake pads which are activated by hydraulic pressure. The pads are forced against the sides of the disc, creating friction which slows the vehicle.

DISTRIBUTOR: A mechanically driven device on an engine which is responsible for electrically firing the spark plug at a predetermined point of the piston stroke.

DOWEL PIN: A pin, inserted in mating holes in two different parts allowing those parts to maintain a fixed relationship.

DRUM BRAKE: A braking system which consists of two brake shoes and one or two wheel cylinders, mounted on a fixed backing plate, and a brake drum, mounted on an axle, which revolves around the assembly. Hydraulic action applied to the wheel cylinders forces the shoes outward against the drum, creating friction and slowing the vehicle.

DWELL: The rate, measured in degrees of shaft rotation, at which an electrical circuit cycles on and off.

ELECTRONIC CONTROL UNIT (ECU): Ignition module, module, amplifier or igniter. See Module for definition.

ELECTRONIC IGNITION: A system in which the timing and firing of the spark plugs is controlled by an electronic control unit, usually called a module. These systems have not points or condenser.

ENDPLAY: The measured amount of axial movement in a shaft.

ENGINE: A device that converts heat into mechanical energy.

EXHAUST MANIFOLD: A set of cast passages or pipes which conduct exhaust gases from the engine.

FEELER GAUGE: A blade, usually metal, of precisely predetermined thickness, used to measure the clearance between two parts. These blades usually are available in sets of assorted thicknesses.

F-Head: An engine configuration in which the intake valves are in the cylinder head, while the camshaft and exhaust valves are located in the cylinder block. The camshaft operates the intake valves via lifters and pushrods, while it operates the exhaust valves directly.

FIRING ORDER: The order in which combustion occurs in the cylinders of an engine. Also the order in which spark is distributed to the plugs by the distributor.

FLATHEAD: An engine configuration in which the camshaft and all the valves are located in the cylinder block.

FLOODING: The presence of too much fuel in the intake manifold and combustion chamber which prevents the air/fuel mixture from firing, thereby causing a no-start situation.

FLYWHEEL: A disc shaped part bolted to the rear end of the crankshaft. Around the outer perimeter is affixed the ring gear. The starter drive engages the ring gear, turning the flywheel, which rotates the crankshaft, imparting the initial starting motion to the engine.

FOOT POUND (ft.lb. or sometimes, ft. lbs.): The amount of energy or work needed to raise an item weighing one pound, a distance of one foot.

FUSE: A protective device in a circuit which prevents circuit overload by breaking the circuit when a specific amperage is present. The device is constructed around a strip or wire of a lower amperage rating than the circuit it is designed to protect. When an amperage higher than that stamped on the fuse is present in the circuit, the strip or wire melts, opening the circuit.

GEAR RATIO: The ratio between the number of teeth on meshing gears.

GENERATOR: A device which converts mechanical energy into electrical energy.

HEAT RANGE: The measure of a spark plug's ability to dissipate heat from its firing end. The higher the heat range, the hotter the plug fires.

HUB: The center part of a wheel or gear.

HYDROCARBON (HC): Any chemical compound made up of hydrogen and carbon. A major pollutant formed by the engine as a byproduct of combustion.

HYDROMETER: An instrument used to measure the specific gravity of a solution.

INCH POUND (in.lb. or sometimes, in. lbs.): One twelfth of a foot pound.

INDUCTION: A means of transferring electrical energy in the form of a magnetic field. Principle used in the ignition coil to increase voltage.

INJECTION PUMP: A device, usually mechanically operated, which meters and delivers fuel under pressure to the fuel injector.

INJECTOR: A device which receives metered fuel under relatively low pressure and is activated to inject the fuel into the engine under relatively high pressure at a predetermined time.

INPUT SHAFT: The shaft to which torque is applied, usually carrying the driving gear or gears.

INTAKE MANIFOLD: A casting of passages or pipes used to conduct air or a fuel/air mixture to the cylinders.

JOURNAL: The bearing surface within which a shaft operates.

KEY: A small block usually fitted in a notch between a shaft and a hub to prevent slippage of the two parts.

MANIFOLD: A casting of passages or set of pipes which connect the cylinders to an inlet or outlet source.

MANIFOLD VACUUM: Low pressure in an engine intake manifold formed just below the throttle plates. Manifold vacuum is highest at idle and drops under acceleration.

MASTER CYLINDER: The primary fluid pressurizing device in a hydraulic system. In automotive use, it is found in brake and hydraulic clutch systems and is pedal activated, either directly or, in a power brake system, through the power booster.

MODULE: Electronic control unit, amplifier or igniter of solid state or integrated design which controls the current flow in the ignition primary circuit based on input from the pickup coil. When the module opens the primary circuit, the high secondary voltage is induced in the coil.

NEEDLE BEARING: A bearing which consists of a number (usually a large number) of long, thin rollers.

OHM: (Ω) The unit used to measure the resistance of conductor to electrical flow. One ohm is the amount of resistance that limits current flow to one ampere in a circuit with one volt of pressure.

OHMMETER: An instrument used for measuring the resistance, in ohms, in an electrical circuit.

OUTPUT SHAFT: The shaft which transmits torque from a device, such as a transmission.

OVERDRIVE: A gear assembly which produces more shaft revolutions than that transmitted to it.

OVERHEAD CAMSHAFT (OHC): An engine configuration in which the camshaft is mounted on top of the cylinder head and operates the valve either directly or by means of rocker arms.

OVERHEAD VALVE (OHV): An engine configuration in which all of the valves are located in the cylinder head and the camshaft is located in the cylinder block. The camshaft operates the valves via lifters and pushrods.

OXIDES OF NITROGEN (NOx): Chemical compounds of nitrogen produced as a byproduct of combustion. They combine with hydrocarbons to produce smog.

OXYGEN SENSOR: Used with the feedback system to sense the presence of oxygen in the exhaust gas and signal the computer which can reference the voltage signal to an air/fuel ratio.

PINION: The smaller of two meshing gears.

PISTON RING: An open ended ring which fits into a groove on the outer diameter of the piston. Its chief function is to form a seal between the piston and cylinder wall. Most automotive pistons have three rings: two for compression sealing; one for oil sealing.

PRELOAD: A predetermined load placed on a bearing during assembly or by adjustment.

PRIMARY CIRCUIT: Is the low voltage side of the ignition system which consists of the ignition switch, ballast resistor or resistance wire, bypass, coil, electronic control unit and pick-up coil as well as the connecting wires and harnesses.

PRESS FIT: The mating of two parts under pressure, due to the inner diameter of one being smaller than the outer diameter of the other, or vice versa; an interference fit.

RACE: The surface on the inner or outer ring of a bearing on which the balls, needles or rollers move.

REGULATOR: A device which maintains the amperage and/or voltage levels of a circuit at predetermined values.

RELAY: A switch which automatically opens and/or closes a circuit.

RESISTANCE: The opposition to the flow of current through a circuit or electrical device, and is measured in ohms. Resistance is equal to the voltage divided by the amperage.

RESISTOR: A device, usually made of wire, which offers a preset amount of resistance in an electrical circuit.

RING GEAR: The name given to a ring-shaped gear attached to a differential case, or affixed to a flywheel or as part a planetary gear set.

ROLLER BEARING: A bearing made up of hardened inner and outer races between which hardened steel rollers move.

ROTOR: 1. The disc-shaped part of a disc brake assembly, upon which the brake pads bear; also called, brake disc.
 2. The device mounted atop the distributor shaft, which passes current to the distributor cap tower contacts.

SECONDARY CIRCUIT: The high voltage side of the ignition system, usually above 20,000 volts. The secondary includes the ignition coil, coil wire, distributor cap and rotor, spark plug wires and spark plugs.

SENDING UNIT: A mechanical, electrical, hydraulic or electromagnetic device which transmits information to a gauge.

SENSOR: Any device designed to measure engine operating conditions or ambient pressures and temperatures. Usually electronic in nature and designed to send a voltage signal to an on-board computer, some sensors may operate as a simple on/off switch or they may provide a variable voltage signal (like a potentiometer) as conditions or measured parameters change.

SHIM: Spacers of precise, predetermined thickness used between parts to establish a proper working relationship.

SLAVE CYLINDER: In automotive use, a device in the hydraulic clutch system which is activated by hydraulic force, disengaging the clutch.

SOLENOID: A coil used to produce a magnetic field, the effect of which is produce work.

SPARK PLUG: A device screwed into the combustion chamber of a spark ignition engine. The basic construction is a conductive core inside of a ceramic insulator, mounted in an outer conductive base. An electrical charge from the spark plug wire travels along the conductive core and jumps a preset air gap to a grounding point or points at the end of the conductive base. The resultant spark ignites the fuel/air mixture in the combustion chamber.

SPLINES: Ridges machined or cast onto the outer diameter of a shaft or inner diameter of a bore to enable parts to mate without rotation.

TACHOMETER: A device used to measure the rotary speed of an engine, shaft, gear, etc., usually in rotations per minute.

THERMOSTAT: A valve, located in the cooling system of an engine, which is closed when cold and opens gradually in response to engine heating, controlling the temperature of the coolant and rate of coolant flow.

TOP DEAD CENTER (TDC): The point at which the piston reaches the top of its travel on the compression stroke.

TORQUE: The twisting force applied to an object.

TORQUE CONVERTER: A turbine used to transmit power from a driving member to a driven member via hydraulic action, providing changes in drive ratio and torque. In automotive use, it links the driveplate at the rear of the engine to the automatic transmission.

TRANSDUCER: A device used to change a force into an electrical signal.

TRANSISTOR: A semi-conductor component which can be actuated by a small voltage to perform an electrical switching function.

TUNE-UP: A regular maintenance function, usually associated with the replacement and adjustment of parts and components in the electrical and fuel systems of a vehicle for the purpose of attaining optimum performance.

TURBOCHARGER: An exhaust driven pump which compresses intake air and forces it into the combustion chambers at higher than atmospheric pressures. The increased air pressure allows more fuel to be burned and results in increased horsepower being produced.

VACUUM ADVANCE: A device which advances the ignition timing in response to increased engine vacuum.

VACUUM GAUGE: An instrument used to measure the presence of vacuum in a chamber.

VALVE: A device which control the pressure, direction of flow or rate of flow of a liquid or gas.

VALVE CLEARANCE: The measured gap between the end of the valve stem and the rocker arm, cam lobe or follower that activates the valve.

VISCOSITY: The rating of a liquid's internal resistance to flow.

VOLTMETER: An instrument used for measuring electrical force in units called volts. Voltmeters are always connected parallel with the circuit being tested.

WHEEL CYLINDER: Found in the automotive drum brake assembly, it is a device, actuated by hydraulic pressure, which, through internal pistons, pushes the brake shoes outward against the drums.

ABBREVIATIONS AND SYMBOLS

A: Ampere

AC: Alternating current

A/C: Air conditioning

A-h: Ampere hour

AT: Automatic transmission

ATDC: After top dead center

μA: Microampere

bbl: Barrel

BDC: Bottom dead center

bhp: Brake horsepower

BTDC: Before top dead center

BTU: British thermal unit

C: Celsius (Centigrade)

CCA: Cold cranking amps

cd: Candela

cm^2: Square centimeter

cm^3, cc: Cubic centimeter

CO: Carbon monoxide

CO_2: Carbon dioxide

cu.in., in^3: Cubic inch

CV: Constant velocity

Cyl.: Cylinder

DC: Direct current

ECM: Electronic control module

EFE: Early fuel evaporation

EFI: Electronic fuel injection

EGR: Exhaust gas recirculation

Exh.: Exhaust

F: Fahrenheit

F: Farad

pF: Picofarad

μF: Microfarad

FI: Fuel injection

ft.lb., ft. lb., ft. lbs.: foot pound(s)

gal: Gallon

g: Gram

HC: Hydrocarbon

HEI: High energy ignition

HO: High output

hp: Horsepower

Hyd.: Hydraulic

Hz: Hertz

ID: Inside diameter

in.lb.; in. lb.; in. lbs: inch pound(s)

Int.: Intake

K: Kelvin

kg: Kilogram

kHz: Kilohertz

km: Kilometer

km/h: Kilometers per hour

kΩ: Kilohm

kPa: Kilopascal

kV: Kilovolt

kW: Kilowatt

l: Liter

l/s: Liters per second

m: Meter

mA: Milliampere

mg: Milligram

mHz: Megahertz

mm: Millimeter

mm^2: Square millimeter

m^3: Cubic meter

MΩ: Megohm

m/s: Meters per second

MT: Manual transmission

mV: Millivolt

μm: Micrometer

N: Newton

N-m: Newton meter

NOx: Nitrous oxide

OD: Outside diameter

OHC: Over head camshaft

OHV: Over head valve

Ω: Ohm

PCV: Positive crankcase ventilation

psi: Pounds per square inch

pts: Pints

qts: Quarts

rpm: Rotations per minute

rps: Rotations per second

R-12: A refrigerant gas (Freon)

SAE: Society of Automotive Engineers

SO$_2$: Sulfur dioxide

T: Ton

t: Megagram

TBI: Throttle Body Injection

TPS: Throttle Position Sensor

V: 1. Volt; 2. Venturi

μV: Microvolt

W: Watt

$\propto$: Infinity

‹: Less than

›: Greater than

Index